Fundamental Algorithms for Computer Graphics

NATO ASI Series

Advanced Science Institutes Series

A series presenting the results of activities sponsored by the NATO Science Committee, which aims at the dissemination of advanced scientific and technological knowledge, with a view to strengthening links between scientific communities.

The Series is published by an international board of publishers in conjunction with the NATO Scientific Affairs Division

A **Life Sciences**	Plenum Publishing Corporation
B **Physics**	London and New York
C **Mathematical and Physical Sciences**	D. Reidel Publishing Company Dordrecht, Boston and Lancaster
D **Behavioural and Social Sciences** E **Applied Sciences**	Martinus Nijhoff Publishers Boston, The Hague, Dordrecht and Lancaster
F **Computer and Systems Sciences** G **Ecological Sciences**	Springer-Verlag Berlin Heidelberg New York Tokyo

Series F: Computer and Systems Sciences Vol. 17

Fundamental Algorithms for Computer Graphics

Directed by J.E. Bresenham, R.A. Earnshaw and M.L.V. Pitteway

Edited by

Rae A. Earnshaw

University of Leeds, United Kingdom

Co-sponsored by
Cambridge Interactive Systems Ltd.-UK
Hewlett Packard Laboratories Ltd.-UK
IBM UK Laboratories Ltd.
Systime Computers Ltd.-UK

Springer-Verlag Berlin Heidelberg New York Tokyo
Published in cooperation with NATO Scientific Affairs Division

Proceedings of the NATO Advanced Study Institute on Fundamental Algorithms for Computer Graphics held at Ilkley, Yorkshire, England, March 30 – April 12, 1985

ISBN 3-540-13920-6 Springer-Verlag Berlin Heidelberg New York Tokyo
ISBN 0-387-13920-6 Springer-Verlag New York Heidelberg Berlin Tokyo

Library of Congress Cataloging in Publication Data. Main entry under title: Fundamental algorithms for computer graphics. (NATO ASI series. Series F, Computer and system sciences ; vol. 17) "Published in cooperation with NATO Scientific Affairs Division" – T.p. verso. "Proceedings of the NATO Advanced Study Institute on Fundamental Algorithms for Computer Graphics held at Ilkley, Yorkshire, England, March 30 – April 12, 1985" – T.p. verso. 1. Electronic digital computers – Programming – Congresses. 2. Algorithms – Congresses. 3. Computer graphics – Congresses. I. Earnshaw, R. A. (Rae A.), 1944-. II. NATO Advanced Study Institute on Fundamental Algorithms for Computer Graphics (Ilkley, West Yorkshire) III. North Atlantic Treaty Organization. Scientific Affairs Division. IV. Series: NATO ASI series. Series F, Computer and systems sciences ; no. 17. QA76.6.F855 1985 006.6 85-22074 ISBN 0-387-13920-6 (U.S.)

Printing: Beltz Offsetdruck, Hemsbach; Bookbinding: J. Schäffer OHG, Grünstadt
2145/3140-543210

About the Directors

Dr Jack E. Bresenham

Dr Bresenham was born on 11 October 1937 in Clovis, New Mexico. He received a BSEE in 1959 from the University of New Mexico, and MS and PhD degrees in Industrial Engineering in 1960 and 1964 respectively from Stanford University. He joined IBM in 1960 at San Jose, California. Dr Bresenham currently is a Senior Technical Staff Member in CPD-HQ System Design Support at IBM's Development Laboratory in Research Triangle Park, North Carolina. His work has been recognised within IBM by receipt of a 1967 SDD Outstanding Contribution Award for management of three RPG compilers for System/360; a 1983 First Invention Plateau Award; a 1984 CPD Outstanding Contribution Award for "Bresenham's Algorithms"; and a 1985 Hursley Special Contribution Award for his Algorithmic and Microcode contribution to the IBM PC/GX Graphics Display. Pixel-level algorithms for use in raster graphics displays and programming support is his technical speciality. Dr Bresenham is a member of ACM, SIGGRAPH, Sigma Tau, Sigma Xi, and Phi Kappa Phi. He has worked as an engineer, manager, planner, programmer and administrator at IBM Laboratories in Hursley, Research Triangle Park, Milan, Mohansic and San Jose, and a Headquarter Operations in SCD – Harrison and World Trade – White Plains.

Dr Rae A. Earnshaw

Dr Earnshaw was born in York, England and educated at Roundhay School and the University of Leeds. He holds the BSc and PhD degrees and has been a faculty staff member for 15 years, and heads the graphics team responsible for campus-wide provision of computer graphics hardware and software in connection with the central computing facility. His PhD was the first in computer graphics to be awarded by the University. He is a Fellow of the British Computer Society and Chairman of the Displays Group. He has been a Visiting Professor at Illinois Institute of Technology, Chicago, and George Washington University, Washington DC. Dr Earnshaw has acted as a consultant to US companies and the College CAD/CAM Consortium and given seminars at a variety of UK and US institutions and research laboratories. More recently he has been a Visiting Professor in Xian, China, giving lectures on the current state of the art in computer graphics. His current interests are graphics algorithms, human-computer interface issues, integrated graphics and text, and display technology.

Professor Mike L. V. Pitteway

Born in 1934, Professor Pitteway was educated at Felsted School and Queens' College, Cambridge. With the assistance of the EDSAC computers he completed his PhD in 1956 for work in radio physics and then spent 2 years in the USA as a Harkness Fellow. After 3 years at the then Radio Research Station in Slough, he became Director of the Cripps Computing Centre at the University of Nottingham and was then appointed Professor and Head of the Computer Science Department at Brunel University. He is a Fellow of the British Computer Society, the Institute of Mathematics and its Applications, the Institute of Physics, and Associate Editor of Computer Graphics, Vision and Image Processing. Besides computer graphics, he still maintains a lively interest in radio physics and is a regular visitor to the United States to work at Los Alamos National Laboratories.

Acknowledgements

The Directors and Authors gratefully acknowledge the encouragement and assistance provided by the NATO Scientific Affairs Division, Brussels, Belgium, and also the following industrial sponsors who supported the venture: Cambridge Interactive Systems Ltd, Hewlett Packard Ltd, IBM UK Laboratories Ltd and Systime Computers Ltd. Without the generous financial and professional support provided by these organisations, this Advanced Study Institute on "Fundamental Algorithms on Computer Graphics" would not have been possible. We are very grateful to Dr Craig Sinclair, Director of the NATO ASI Programme, for his advice and guidance during the preparations for the Advanced Study Institute.

Thanks and appreciation are also due to the University of Leeds, Brunel University and IBM for their encouragement and moral support of the Directors. A special word of thanks is due to Mrs Frances Johnson and the Conference Office at the University of Leeds for handling all the administrative arrangements during the six month period leading up to the Institute and also during the two weeks of the Conference. Mrs Johnson and her staff successfully passed every provocation test with limitless patience, tolerance, and above all, a sense of perspective and good humour. The exceptionally good spirit at Ilkley was due in large measure to Mrs Johnson's personality and hospitality. We also thank the Craiglands Hotel for their support and cooperation in providing the venue and framework for the Conference.

The Invited and Contributing Lecturers spent many hours in preparing their lectures and also their written papers included in this volume, and in discussion at the Conference – we are very grateful to them for their contributions and support, without which there would have been no conference and no book. We thank the delegates who attended and contributed their ideas to the programme. We also thank all the secretaries who assisted us with the production of the many letters, documents, memos, programmes and schedules, and especially to Miss Susan Nemes who typed a number of papers for inclusion in this volume.

Finally, thanks are due to The George Washington University, Washington DC, with whom one of us (RAE) was on assignment during the first semester of 1985, for their full support and encouragement of the Advanced Study Institute.

Leeds, England   1 July 1985
Washington DC, USA   Jack E. Bresenham
Rae A. Earnshaw
Mike L. V. Pitteway

Preface

An Advanced Study Institute on the theme "Fundamental Algorithms for Computer Graphics" was held in Ilkley, England on March 30 – April 12, 1985 under the auspices of the Scientific Affairs Division of NATO. The Institute was organised by a Scientific Committee consisting of Dr J.E. Bresenham, IBM, Research Triangle Park, USA, Dr R.A. Earnshaw, University of Leeds, UK, and Professor M.L.V. Pitteway, Brunel University, UK. This book contains the majority of the formal presentations given at the Institute. In addition, the new book "Procedural Elements for Computer Graphics" by D.F. Rogers, McGraw-Hill, 1985, was used as the basis for the lectures given by Professor Rogers at the Institute. This material therefore does not appear in this volume since Professor Rogers' book is an up-to-date, self-contained presentation of this aspect of the subject.

Some 80 lecturers and delegates attended the Institute, representing 14 countries. These included Belgium, Czechoslovakia, Denmark, France, Iceland, India, Italy, Netherlands, Norway, Portugal, Turkey, United Kingdom, USA and Yugoslavia. Academia, industry, and government and research laboratories were represented in about equal proportions. This contributed greatly to the success of the Institute since it promoted effective interchange of information and experiences outside the formal sessions, and encouraged the generation of new ideas and perspectives.

The primary objectives of the Institute were to provide a comprehensive review of line, arc, conic, curve and character generation algorithms from the pioneering work of Bresenham in 1963 up to the present time. Thus the basic emphasis was on "fundamentals", i.e. the basic algorithms to enable picture elements to be formulated, described and displayed. This also included a review of encoding and compaction techniques. Upon this foundation higher-level functions and applications could be built, and some of these were examined in detail during the second half of the Institute. These included contouring, surface drawing, fractal geometries, picture representation, scene generation, animation, CAD and human factors. Program transformations and automatic algorithm generation were also studied in order to assess the tools currently available for the re-formulation, and hence the generation of new algorithms. Finally the topics of raster workstations, VLSI architectures, constructive solid geometry, and systolic array methodology were examined. All this material was covered principally by the Invited and Contributing Lecturers – each being a recognised authority in their particular area. In addition, the delegates were invited to submit papers on their own work relating to the themes of the Institute. Some sixteen delegate papers were accepted after review, and they also appear in this volume. The ordering of the material is divided into ten main sections, beginning with line and area algorithms, and then moving on through arcs, circles and conics to higher level functions and applications. It is envisaged that the tutorial and review nature of many of the Invited Lecturers' papers will be very useful in bringing together current and previous material together under one cover. The subject matter of this book is therefore suitable for a wide range of interests, ranging from the advanced student through to the graphics system designer and implementor. Portions of the book may be used as a standard text since the sections are fairly self-contained and self-explanatory.

The following Invited Lecturers contributed to the programme:

Dr J.E. Bresenham (IBM, Research Triangle Park, USA)
Ir R. Brons (Catholic University of Nijmegen, The Netherlands)

Professor J.H. Clark (Stanford University and Silicon Graphics Inc, USA)
Dr P. Coueignoux (Data Business Vision Inc, USA)
Dr P.M. Dew (University of Leeds, UK)
Dr R.A. Earnshaw (University of Leeds, UK)
Professor A.R. Forrest (University of East Anglia, UK)
Professor H. Fuchs (University of North Carolina at Chapel Hill, USA)
Dr R.A. Guedj (SiGRID s.a., France)
Mr R.J. Lansdown (System Simulation Ltd, UK)
Professor M.L.V. Pitteway (Brunel University, UK)
Professor D.F. Rogers (United States Naval Academy, USA)
Dr M.A. Sabin (Fegs Ltd, UK)
Dr R.F. Voss (Harvard University and IBM, Yorktown Heights, USA)

The following Contributing Lecturers each gave at least one presentation:

Dr K.W. Brodlie (University of Leicester, UK)
Mrs H. Brown (University of Kent, UK)
Mr C.J. Cartledge (University of Salford, UK)
Dr P.A. Dowd (University of Leeds, UK)
Mr D.J. Grover (British Technology Group, UK)
Dr A.C. Kilgour (University of Glasgow, UK)
Mr R.D. Parslow (Brunel University, UK)
Professor A. de Pennington (University of Leeds, UK)
Mr T. Sancha (Cambridge Interactive Systems Ltd, UK)
Dr C. Sinclair (NATO, Belgium)
Dr J.V. Tucker (University of Leeds, UK)

Tom Sancha, Managing Director of Cambridge Interactive Systems, keynoted the Institute with a presentation on "Unsolved Problems in Computer Graphics". With a unique blend of academic flair and industrial experience, the current progress towards solving Ivan Sutherland's "Ten Unsolved Problems in Computer Graphics" (1966) was reviewed. In view of the fact that some of these problems are not yet solved, even after 20 years, it is particularly relevant and timely to give serious attention to review, study, and appraisal of the fundamentals.

Dr Craig Sinclair, Director Advanced Study Institutes Programme (ASI), NATO, also gave a keynote address outlining the purpose and objectives of the NATO ASI Programme.

The Institute had a full programme of lectures and presentations. The Invited Lecturers' papers included in this volume contain the substance of these lectures. In some cases the original paper has been revised in the light of discussions at the Institute. Only the revised and up-to-date papers are included in this volume.

One of the objectives behind the series of Contributing Lectures was to explore topics in neighbouring disciplines and review their impact at the interface with computer graphics. If progress is to be made towards solving current problems in computer graphics, some degree of lateral thinking will be necessary. In particular, a study of inter-disciplinary aspects and the contributions they can make to a synthesis of current areas of interest is very valuable. In this connection, the following topics were covered: curve generation, typesetting, area-fill, geostatistical techniques for contouring, 3D interpolation, graphics algorithm protection, architectures for high-performance systems, 3D visualisation, and theoretical aspects of algorithm design.

The Directors wish to thank the NATO Scientific Affairs Division for their financial support of the original proposal, and also Dr Sinclair for his advice and guidance during the six month period leading up to Advanced Study Institute. We thank the Industrial Sponsors for providing financial support for Postgraduate Fellowship Awards. These included Cambridge Interactive Systems Ltd, Hewlett Packard Ltd, IBM UK Laboratories Ltd and Systime Computers Ltd. Thanks and appreciation are also due to the

University of Leeds for their encouragement and moral support; to Mrs Frances Johnson and the Conference Office at the University of Leeds for all their help and assistance with the administrative arrangements during the six month period leading up to the Institute and also during the two weeks of the conference; to the Craiglands Hotel, Ilkley, for their support and cooperation; to the Invited and Contributing Lecturers for giving of their time so freely (and also to their employers for allowing them to come); and to all the delegates who attended and contributed their ideas to the programme. Thanks are also due to The George Washington University – with whom the undersigned was on assignment during the first semester of 1985 – for their full support and encouragement of the Advanced Study Institute.

R.A. Earnshaw
1 July 1985

Table of Contents

Illustrations for "Antialiasing in Practice" by A.R. FORREST

Figure 1: Tonal Aliasing. **a** Full Colour Image, **b** Thresholding, 8 Colours, **c** 2 × 2 Dithering, 8 Colours, **d** 4 × 4 Recursive Dithering, 8 Colours, **e** 4 × 4 Magic Square Dithering, 8 Colours, **f** Floyd-Steinberg Dithering, 8 Colours

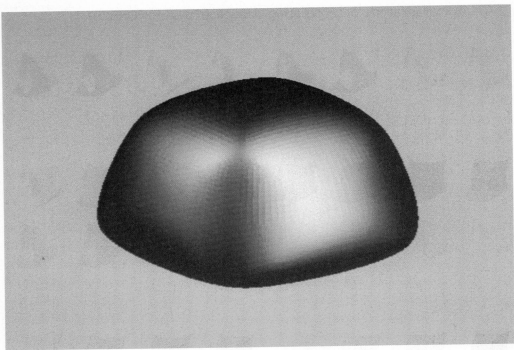

Figure 2: Geometric Aliasing and Mach Banding

Figure 3: Mach Banding

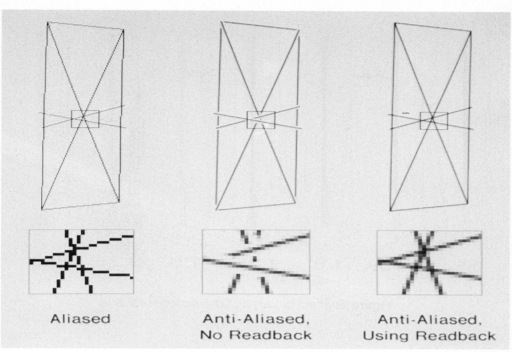

Figure 4: Approaches to Antialiasing

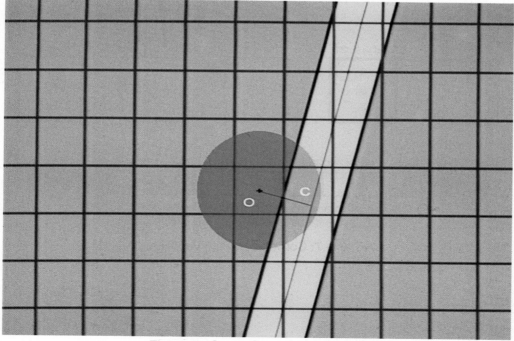

Figure 5: Gupta-Sproull Antialiasing

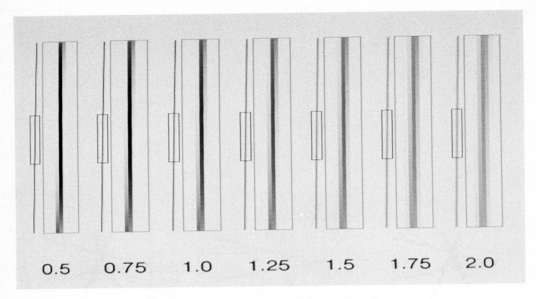

0.5   0.75   1.0   1.25   1.5   1.75   2.0

Figure 6: Effect of Varying Convolution Radius

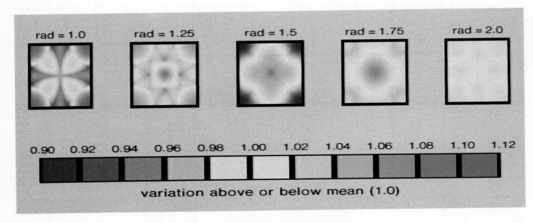

rad = 1.0   rad = 1.25   rad = 1.5   rad = 1.75   rad = 2.0

0.90 0.92 0.94 0.96 0.98 1.00 1.02 1.04 1.06 1.08 1.10 1.12

variation above or below mean (1.0)

Figure 7: Convolution Field Variation

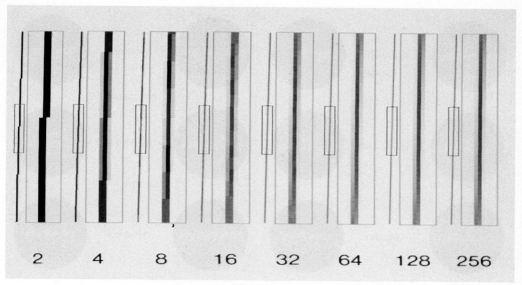

Figure 8: Varying Grey Levels

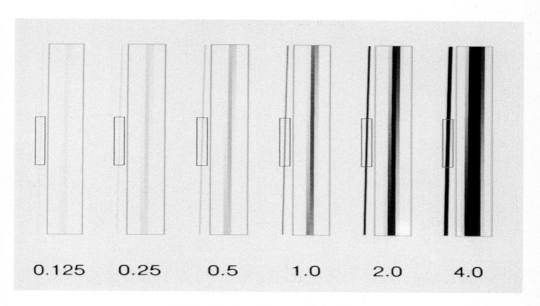

Figure 9: Varying Line Thickness

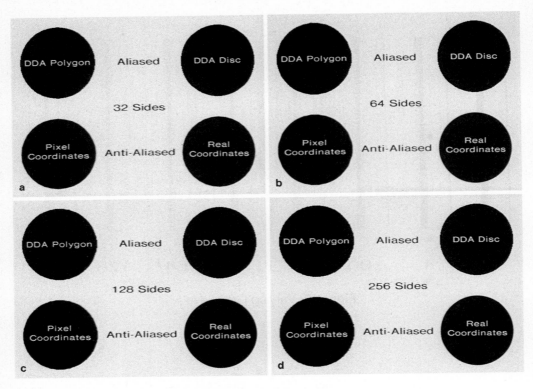

Figure 10: Geometric Aliasing

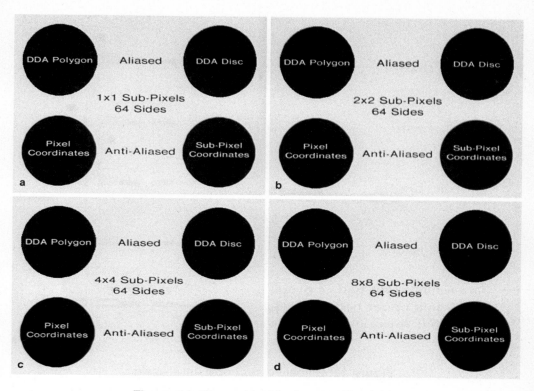

Figure 11: Geometric Aliasing and Precision

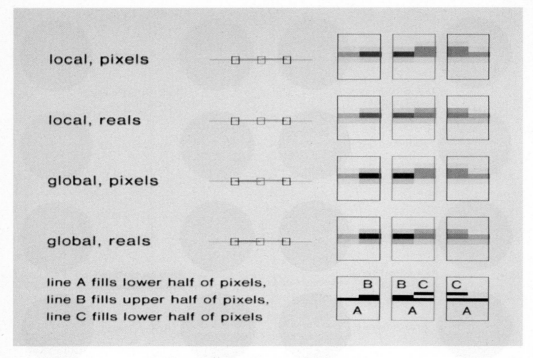

Figure 12: Global Versus Local Antialiasing

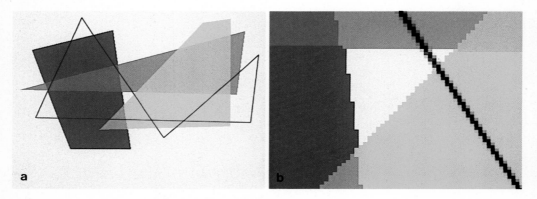

Figure 13: Test Image. Aliased

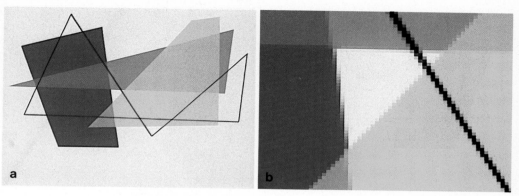

Figure 14: Antialiased Scan Conversion

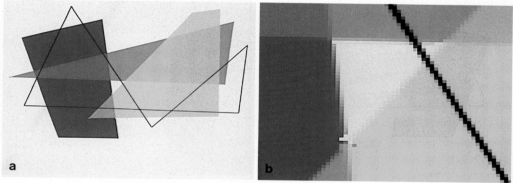

Figure 15: Edges Post-Antialiased. No Readback

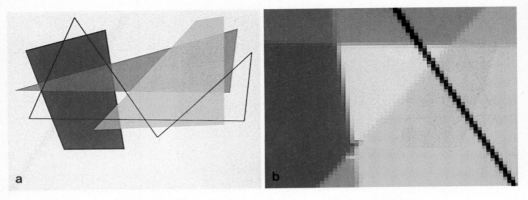

Figure 16: Edges Post-Antialiased. With Readback

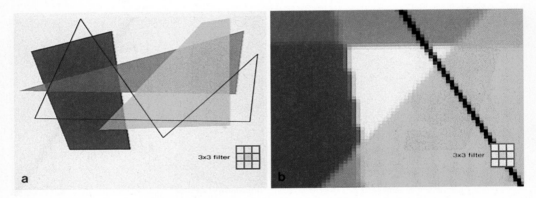

Figure 17: Post-Filtered. Gaussian Filter

Illustrations for "Systolic Array Architecture for high Performance CAD/CAM Workstations" by P. M. DEW, J. DODSWORTH and D. T. MORRIS
(Courtesy of IBM UK Scientific Centre LTD)

Figure 1: Primitive & Simple Composite CSG Solids

Figure 2: A Recursively Defined Solid Object (this object was defined in just a few lines of code)

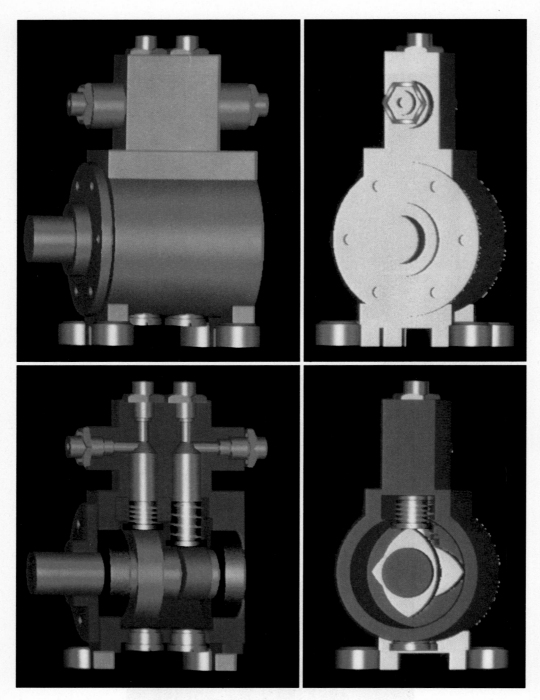

Figure 3: Camshaft Pump Using approximately 400 Primitives

Illustrations for "Random Fractal Forgeries" by R.F. VOSS

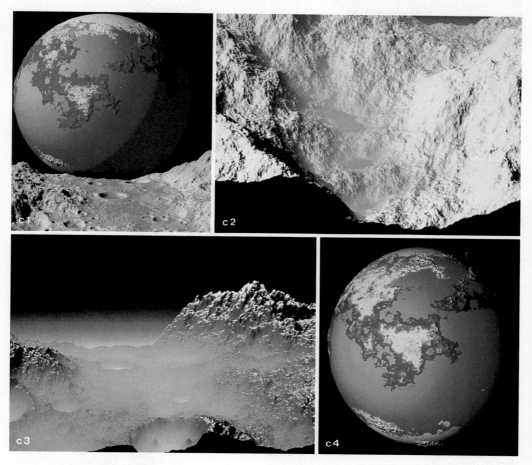

Figure C1. Fractal Planetrise. A variation of Brownian motion on a sphere (D=2.5) rising above a fractally cratered random Gaussian fractal surface (D=2.2)

Figure C2. A view into a typical fractal valley (with fog) for D=2.15

Figure C3. A fractal landscape (the same as Fig. 5(a)) with craters whose area distribution follow a fractal or power-law dependence with many more small craters than large ones.

Figure C4. The Brownian fractal planet (surface D=2.5) with an earth-like water level and polar caps.

Figure C7. The differing visual effect of changing the fractal dimension D for the same landscape. **a** D=2.15 **b** D=2.5 **c** D=2.8.   As D increases, the perceived surface roughness also increases. Also shown is fractal landscaping by scaling the surface height variations (relative to water level) by a power law.   **d** Height^3. **e** Height$^{1/3}$.

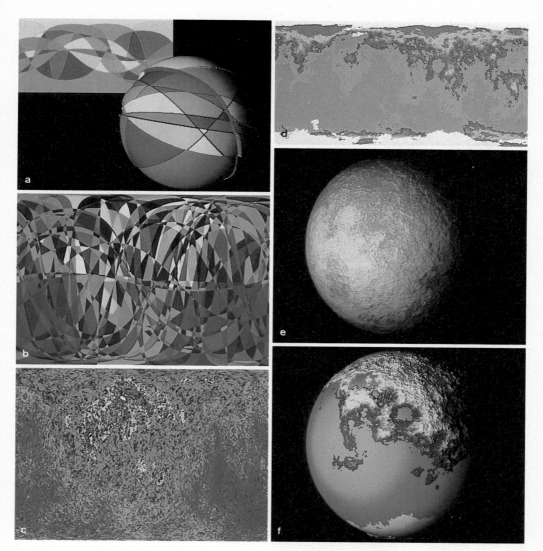

Figure C8. The stages of creating a fractal planet by adding random faults encircling the sphere. **a** The surface height variations (as indicated by color) after 10 faults shown both on the sphere and on a flat projection map. **b** The surface map after 60 faults where the colors indicate different land altitudes and ocean depths. **c** The surface map after 750 faults. **d** The surface after more than 10000 faults with added polar caps. **e** This Brownian fractal planet mapped back onto the sphere (surface D=2.5) with an earth-like water level and polar caps. This is a rotated version of Fig. C4. **f** The same planet without water.

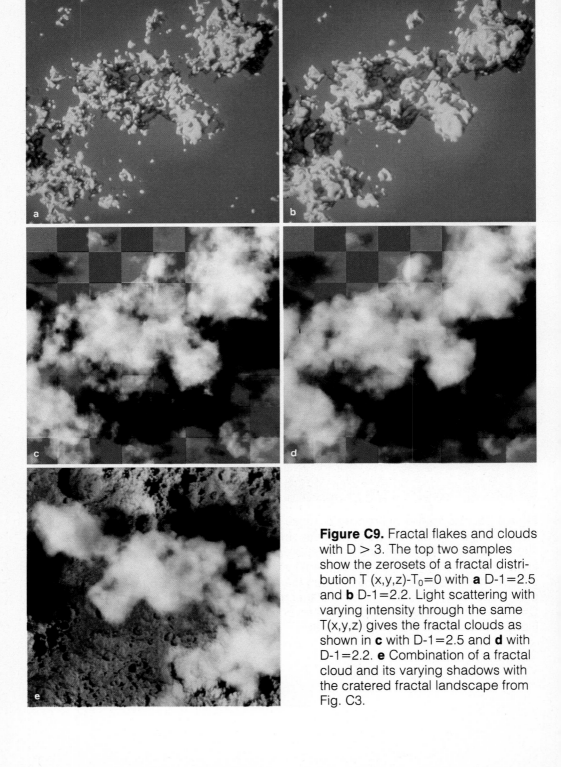

Figure C9. Fractal flakes and clouds with D > 3. The top two samples show the zerosets of a fractal distribution T (x,y,z)-T_0=0 with **a** D-1=2.5 and **b** D-1=2.2. Light scattering with varying intensity through the same T(x,y,z) gives the fractal clouds as shown in **c** with D-1=2.5 and **d** with D-1=2.2. **e** Combination of a fractal cloud and its varying shadows with the cratered fractal landscape from Fig. C3.

Section 1
Line and Area Algorithms

THEORETICAL AND LINGUISTIC METHODS FOR DESCRIBING STRAIGHT LINES.

Reyer Brons

Catholic University of Nijmegen

Department of Economic Affairs and Planning

6500 HC Nijmegen, The Netherlands

ABSTRACT

Two distinct approaches exist for the generation of a straight line in an arbitrary direction on a lattice, structural algorithms and conditional algorithms. A survey of these approaches is included in this paper.

Structural algorithms are of great theoretical value. From numbertheory the Farey-series can be used for directions on a lattice with a rational slope. With continued fractions it is also possible to approximate irrational numbers.
Knowing these properties it is possible to determine the set of all lines corresponding to a given chaincode for a segment of a line. This is useful for the estimation of properties of a line like length, slope and intercept. Research of this kind is related to pattern analysis and picture processing.
The structural algorithm can be presented by linguistic methods, for instance a context-free programmed grammar and a TOL-grammar, a variant of the Lindenmayer grammar with the important property that in each derivation each relevant symboltype in a string is rewritten at the same time by the same rule.

The principle of the conditional algorithm is more practical: given two points that determine the line, connected points on the lattice with minimal distance to the real line have to be selected. This method is very important for plotters and computer graphics displays.
The conditional algorithm can be presented by linguistic methods too, by using a programmed grammar with a tail. The tail has a bookkeeping function. Consequentially the grammar is context-sensitive.

Structural and conditional methods both generate lines satisfying the chord property, which is a conditional property. A structural property of a digitized straight line is spacing the least occurring type of chainelement as uniformly as possible. It is shown that this can be built into a conditional method. So an integration between both methods is achieved.

Finally some remarks on progress in the science of line drawing are made.

NATO ASI Series, Vol. F17
Fundamental Algorithms for Computer Graphics
Edited by R. A. Earnshaw
© Springer-Verlag Berlin Heidelberg 1985

1.   INTRODUCTION

As a student at the Delft Technical University in the Netherlands, I had the opportunity to explore the possibilities of linguistic methods for pattern recognition in addition to the statistical methods. After preparing a survey on this topic (in Dutch) I found for my masters thesis (1972) an application in the generation of straight lines on a lattice by linguistic methods. A publication in English followed in 1974 [4].

In [4] two different approaches for straight line generation are developed, a structural method and a conditional method. Both methods have been presented as algorithms and as linguistic methods. The essential difference is that on the one hand the structural method is based on theoretical reflections on the digitization of a straight line on a lattice, which leads to number theoretical conceptions like Farey series and continued fractions [13].
On the other hand the conditional method is very pragmatic. During the generation of a line from a certain point after each detection of a point on the lattice belonging to the digitized line, there is a test whether a condition has been fulfilled. The result of the test determines next point on the lattice. For a long time the leading conditional method was given by Bresenham in 1965 [2].
In chapter 2 of this paper chain coding and the concept of straightness are examined.
In chapter 3 a survey of the structural method and recent developments is given, and in chapter 4 the same for the conditional method.

After ten years it is very interesting to see that there was almost no communication between structural and conditional describers. Structural describers are mostly found in the world of picture processing and pattern recognition. Conditional describers are especially developing algorithms to drive plotters or graphic displays.

Reggiori [24] departed in 1972 from the conditional method and found some aspects of the structural approach by attempts to improve his method. Only very recently structural elements are explicitly introduced in conditional methods [3,10,23].
In chapter 5 this will be shown. In the same chapter some considerations about utility and efficiency will be given.

At the moment I have a job as head of the department of economic affairs and planning of a university in the Netherlands. One of the actual topics in our country is financing of research independent of educational costs ("conditional" financing). In the long run this will only be possible when there is some control on the direction of the development of knowledge and some evaluation of the results. In chapter 6 I reflect a while on this theme, given my recent experiences in the field of straight line generation.

2. CHAIN CODING AND STRAIGHTNESS.

2.1. Chain coding on a lattice.

For describing a line on a lattice, Freeman's chain coding scheme can be used [11]. Starting in (0,0), a chain element to (1,0) is coded by 0, to (1,1) by 1, to (0,1) by 2 etc. A digital arc S is a connected set of lattice points, all but two of which have exactly two 8-neighbours in S, while two exceptions (the endpoints) each have exactly one 8-neighbour in S [25].
The chaincode of a digital arc is represented by a string with elements 0, 1, 2, 3, ... 7.
This paper is restricted to straight lines with a direction from 0 $^{\circ}$ to 45 $^{\circ}$.
All other directions can be obtained by rotation and/or mirroring.

In papers from "structural authors" Freeman's coding scheme is usual. It is often mentioned the standard coding scheme. Conditional authors often use the symbol a for axial movement and d for diagonal movement (for instance [3,10]). In the first octant a corresponds to the Freeman 0 and d to the Freeman 1. I also found S (square) instead of a [23]. In technical reports one can find m1,m2....m7, where m1 corresponds to 0, m2 to 1, etc.
So a conditional standard doesn't exist. In this paper I hold to the structural standard, introduced by Freeman.

Finally a remark on the field with rows and columns where all this line drawing is occurring. In this paper I use the word "lattice". In other publications the words "grid" and "raster" can be found too.

2.2. Straightness of a digital arc.

In 1970 Freeman stated that strings representing straight lines must possess three specific properties:
1. At most two types of symbols can be present, and these can differ only by unity, modulo eight.
2. One of the two symbols always occurs singly.
3. Successive occurrences of the single symbol are as uniformly spaced as possible among codes of the other value.

In the last property "as uniformly spaced as possible" is a rather fuzzy statement.

In 1974 Rosenfeld [25] defined the "chord property" and he proved that a digital arc has the chord property if and only if it is the digitization of a straight line segment. To illustrate the chord property we define a real line L and a digital arc S.
We say that L lies near S if, for any point (x,y) on the real line L, there exists a lattice point (i,j) of S such

that MAX($|i - x|$, $|j - y|$) $<$ 1. S has the chord property if, for every point of S, the chord L lies near S. In terms of this paper the chord property is a conditional property and not structural like Freeman's three properties.

Using the chord property Rosenfeld investigates the first and the second specific properties mentioned by Freeman. He states that these properties can be extended to show that at most two types of substrings with the single occuring symbol can be present, and these substrings have only two lengths, which are consecutive integers, and so on. In this way the notion "as uniformly spaced as possible" is more operational.

In 1982 Wu [34] developed a strict presentation of the three properties mentioned by Freeman and he proved that in this presentation the three properties are sufficient and necessary conditions for the chaincode being the chaincode of a real line. So he proved that Freemans three properties and Rosenfelds chord property are equivalent. As Wu stated his presentation is too complicated to present in oral language.

In 1984 Hung and Kasvand [15] introduced the concept of unevenness. Two segments of a codestring of equal length are uneven when the sum of the values of the stringelements of these segments differ by more than 1. They proved that a digital arc has the chord property if there are not any uneven segments in its chaincode. The absence of uneven segments is one of the most fundamental structural properties of a digital straight line. It is simple to explain and simple to measure.

The state of the art is that there are three equivalent conditions for a digital arc to represent a straight line:
- Freemans three properties;
- Rosenfelds chord property;
- Hung and Kasvand's absence of unevenness.

The digital arc as mentioned before is the thinnest connected set of lattice points. Kim [18] is treating cellular arcs, which are not 8-connected like digital arcs but 4-connected. He proves for a cellular arc the theorem that it is a cellular straight line segment if and only if it has the chord property. In this case he is using a modified chord property not according to the real line, but to the chord between two endpoints of the cellular arc.

For practical reasons Tang and Huang [31] use a "straight strip" description, which can be much thicker than digital and cellular arcs.

Related to the straightness-item is the convexity-item. This will not be examined here. See for instance [17,18,19]

The concept of straightness is a very important general notion and though one of the properties is conditional, conditional authors hardly pay attention to this notion. On the other hand conditonal authors are interpreting real straight lines as simple geometric configurations to be handled by simple arithmetic operations. They approach circles and ellipses in the same way. I don't know any structural description of circles and ellipses.

3.   STRUCTURAL METHODS.

3.1. The structural algorithm for straight line generation.

In 1972 I developed an algorithm [4] to generate a line according to the third specific property of Freeman. To generate a line with slope p/q (a rational number when p and q are integers) one period (a string with lenght q since $p \leqslant q$ for directions from 0° to 45°) is enough. Other parts of the line are just repetitions of this period.

In case of just one specimen of the least occurring symbol,

there is no problem. We can place this symbol arbitrarily in the period, so we always choose the end of the period. When more specimens occur, we construct subperiods each containing one of the symbols which occur least frequently. There are two kinds of subperiods, one with n of the most frequent occurring symbols, the other with n + 1.

Next, we have to space these different subperiods as uniformly as possible. We now determine the number of the subperiods which are least frequent. If the number is one, we place it at the end of the string, otherwise we continue the process by constructing taller subperiods from the previous ones. We repeat this procedure until one subperiod appears singly.

To construct the period belonging to a slope p/q, we use a recursive algorithm with the following steps (the subscripts serve to count the number of times the algorithm is applied):

(1) Read p and q under the assumption
$$0 \leqslant p \leqslant q; \quad p \text{ and } q \text{ are integers.}$$

(2) Reduce p/q if possible, call the new values p_o and q_o.

(3) Calculate $r_o = q_o - p_o$. There are r_o symbols 0 and p_o symbols 1 in a period.

(4) Let $c_i = \text{MAX } (p_i, r_i)$; call symbols occuring c_i times C_i.

(5) Let $t_i = \text{MIN } (p_i, r_i)$; call symbols occurring t_i times D_i.

(6) If $t_i = 1$, generate the period $C_i^{c_i} D_i$ and stop the program.

(7) Calculate $n_i = \text{ENTIER } (c_i/t_i)$.

(8) Calculate $p_{i+1} = c_i - t_i n_i$.

(9) Calculate $r_{i+1} = t_i - p_{i+1}$.

(10) Generate r_{i+1} subperiods $C_i^{n_i} D_i$, call them B_{i+1}.

(11) Generate p_{i+1} subperiods $C_i^{n_i+1} D_i$, call them A_{i+1}.

(12) Go to step 4.

The condition $0 \leqslant p \leqslant q$ in step 1 is due to the restriction to slopes from 0 to 1.
The reduction in step 2 is necessary, because otherwise t_i will become 0, and then step 7 is not allowed.

Example.
In constructing the period for slope 14/39, we first see $p_o = 14$ and $q_o = 39$, so $r_o = 25$. A zeroeth approximation could be $0^{25} 1^{14}$. Bij applying the algorithm one time, we find 11 subperiods 001 and 3 subperiods 01. So a first approximation could be $(001)^{11} (01)^3$.

Applying the algorithm for the second time yields two subperiods $(001)^4 01$ and one subperiod $(001)^3 01$.

The third time one of the subperiods occurs singly, so we finish the construction. The string is $((001)^4 01)^2 (001)^3 01$, or

$$00100100100101001001001001010100100100101$$

When starting the real line in the lattice point (0,0) to the point (39,14) this algorithm generates a digitization of the line below the real line, except in the points (0,0) and (39,14). Of course, some correction is necessary for the generation of the best fitting digitization dependant of the intercept e $(- \frac{1}{2} \leqslant e \leqslant \frac{1}{2})$.

The best fit can be found by choosing another point in the period as starting point and translating the string. The above generated line is exactly corresponding to

$$y = (14/39)x - (19/39).$$

In 1978 Arcelli and Massarotti [1] developed a modified version of the structural algorithm which generates the best fitting line. They proved that the modified algorithm constructs lines possessing the chord property. Next they proved that every "nonregular digital arc with assigned slope" generated by the original structural algorithm can be enclosed between two parallel real straight lines bearing a mutual distance equal to that of a pair of parallel real straight lines enclosing a regular digital arc with the same slope.

Further they found, that the distance between the two parallel real straight lines is always smaller than 1. They conclude, that every digital arc generated by the structural algorithm possesses the chord property.

Finally in 1982 Wu [34] was capable to prove that [4] and [1] really correspond with [11] and [25].

Wu also showed the possibility to describe lines with irrational slopes.

In 1979 Cederberg [6] presented an algorithm similar to the structural algorithm. He also described a simple device to generate straight lines, mainly with counters and comparators. He presented a permutation method of centering the line to find the best approximation for a line through two given points. The method is rather complicated. Finally he shows that his method leads to the same code sequence as Bresenham's conditional method [2] .

Recently Dorst and Duin [7] thought about the accurancy of digitized straight lines and developed a "spirograph theory". They wrap the real points in the columns of a lattice around a circle. Their spirograph is defined by an edge and the number of columns one wishes to use. The spirograph theory includes the structural algorithm for rational and irrational slopes.

In [6] and [7] there isn't much attention for the case that the intercept $e \neq o$, but Dorst and Smeulders [8] define a phase shift s and they derive a rather complicated mathematical expression for the relation of s and e.

The whole procedure to generate a straight line with structural methods is consisting of three sequent steps:

1. Find the string for one period.

   Necessary input: p and q, maximal reduced.

   Method: a structural algorithm [4,6,28,34,7] .

2. Find a starting point.

   Necessary input: the string found in step 1 and e.

   Method: shifting [8] or centering [6] (only when e = o).

3. Generate the line incrementally.

   Necessary input: string found in step 1 and starting point found in step 2.

   Method: apply Freeman's chain code.

3.2. The structural algorithm and number theory.

Depending on the accepted distances between points on a lattice, certain slopes are possible. From number theory (see for instance Hardy and Wright [13]) Farey series can be obtained as a tool for the accuracy of a slope. For instance when accepting 4 as maximum distance possible slopes are indicated with a 4th order Farey serie:

$$F(4) = \left\{ \frac{0}{1}, \frac{1}{4}, \frac{1}{3}, \frac{1}{2}, \frac{2}{3}, \frac{3}{4}, \frac{1}{1} \right\}$$

with distance 6 we find:

$$F(6) = \left\{ \frac{0}{1}, \frac{1}{6}, \frac{1}{5}, \frac{1}{4}, \frac{1}{3}, \frac{2}{5}, \frac{1}{2}, \frac{3}{5}, \frac{2}{3}, \frac{3}{4}, \frac{4}{5}, \frac{5}{0}, \frac{1}{1} \right\}$$

Very interesting is that the slope between two slopes with the least distance can be found by adding the numerators and the denominators.

For instance

between $\frac{1}{3}$ and $\frac{1}{2}$ we find $\frac{2}{5}$ and between $\dfrac{4}{5}$ and $\dfrac{5}{6}$ we find $\dfrac{9}{11}$.

Number theory gives mighty tools for considerations about accuracy!

An interesting notion from number theory is the continued fraction. With this tool irrational slopes can be approximated by rational slopes.

For instance the slope 14/39 can be approximated by

$$\frac{14}{39} = \cfrac{1}{2+ \cfrac{11}{14}} = \cfrac{1}{2+ \cfrac{1}{1+ \cfrac{3}{11}}} = \cfrac{1}{2+ \cfrac{1}{1+ \cfrac{1}{3+ \cfrac{2}{3}}}} = \cfrac{1}{2+ \cfrac{1}{1+ \cfrac{1}{3+ \cfrac{1}{1+ \cfrac{1}{2}}}}} \quad .$$

Depending on the accuracy possible approximations are the slopes

$$\frac{1}{2}, \ \frac{1}{3}, \ \frac{4}{11}, \ \frac{5}{14}, \ \frac{14}{39}.$$

For the approximation of real numbers by fractions see the appendix of [7].

Another tool is Euclid's algorithm to calculate the highest common factor of two numbers. It is necessary for step 2 of the algorithm in section 3.1. In [4] the resemblance with the structural algorithm is shown.

3.3.   Grammars for the structural algorithm.

In [4] common grammars, programmed grammars, programmed grammars with a tail, stochastic programmed grammars, rule-labeled grammars and (table 0) Lindenmayer grammars are described. In this section only programmed grammars and Lindenmayer-grammars are examined. In section 4.2. programmed grammars with a tail and stochastic programmed grammars will be treated in relation to the conditional algorithm.

a. A programmed grammar is an interesting extension of a common grammar because of the addition of branches for the steering of the selection of production rules. Fu [12] illustrates the possibility to construct the language $0^n 2^n 4^n 6^n$, which could be interpreted as the language describing squares of a side lenght $n = 1,2,3,$ ...., with a context-free programmed grammar with 7 production rules. According to Fu [12] this is also possible with a context-sensitive common grammar of 19 production rules. Due to steering the production rules by the branches, easily some context-sensitive elements are introduced in a context-free grammar. This kind of extension is not difficult to handle by computer in contrast to a common context-sensitive grammar. In appendix 1 these grammars are illustrated. Further a context-sensitive common grammar with 6 production rules and a context free programmed grammar with 5 production rules are given.

The structural algorithm for the generation of a straight line can be expressed in the next programmed grammar:

$$PG = (V_N, V_T, S, J, P) \text{ with}$$
$$V_N = \{A, B, C, D, E, F, S\},$$
$$V_T = \{0, 1\},$$
$$J = \{1,2,3,4,5,6,7,8,9,10,11,12,13,14,15\},$$

$$P = \{$$

1.	S $\rightarrow$ F	S(2,3)	–	
2.	F $\rightarrow$ C	S(12,14)	–	
3.	F $\rightarrow$ CD	S(4,6,8,12,14)	–	
4.	D $\rightarrow$ E	S(4)	F(5)	
5.	E $\rightarrow$ CD	S(5)	F(4,6,8,12,14)	

6.	C $\longrightarrow$ A	S(6)	F(7)
7.	D $\longrightarrow$ B	S(7)	F(10)
8.	C $\longrightarrow$ B	S(8)	F(9)
9.	D $\longrightarrow$ A	S(9)	F(10)
10.	A $\longrightarrow$ CCD	S(10)	F(11)
11.	B $\longrightarrow$ CD	S(11)	F(4,6,8,12,14)
12.	C $\longrightarrow$ 0	S(12)	F(13)
13.	D $\longrightarrow$ 1	S(13)	–
14.	C $\longrightarrow$ 1	S(14)	F(15)
15.	D $\longrightarrow$ 0	S(15)	–

$\Big\}$.

The rules can be divided into four groups:

1,2,3 : the starting rules; they only are used once.

12,13,14,15 : the endrules. When arriving at these rules, the final result is determined.

6,7,8,9,10,11 : these rules complicate the period. The number of times that these rules are applied equals the number of applications of the structural algorithm in constructing the period.

4,5 : the number of times that this group is used before the group 6,7,8,9,10,11 determines the number of the most frequent occurring symbols or subperiods.

Example:

$$S \overset{1}{\Rightarrow} F \overset{3}{\Rightarrow} CD \overset{4,5}{\Rightarrow} CCD \overset{6,7}{\Rightarrow} AAB \overset{10,11}{\Rightarrow} (CCD)^2 CD \overset{4,5}{\Rightarrow} (C^4D)^2 C^3 D \overset{6,7}{\Rightarrow}$$

$$\Rightarrow (A^4B)^2 A^3 B \overset{10,11}{\Rightarrow} ((CCD)^4 CD)^2 (CCD)^3 CD \overset{12,13}{\Rightarrow} ((001)^4 01)^2 (001)^3 01$$

This example generates a period of a string representing a line with a slope of 14/39.

This programmed grammar is rather complicated, so I didn't try to find a context-sensitive grammar to obtain the same result.

b. The biologist Lindenmayer developed grammars to describe biological systems. Production rules rewrite each equal symbol at the same moment. So a linguistic concept totally different from the common grammars developed by Chomsky is created (see Herman and Rosenberg |14|).

In appendix 1 a very simple Lindenmayer grammar is given for the language $0^n 2^n 4^n 6^n$.

For the generation of a straight line a simple table 0 Lindenmayer grammar (TOLG) is existing:

$$
\begin{aligned}
\text{TOLG} &= (V,S,P) \text{ with} \\
V &= \{0,1\}, \\
S &= \{0\ \}, \\
P &= 1.\ \{1 \to 0,\quad 0 \to 1\} \\
&\quad\ 2.\ \{1 \to 1,\quad 0 \to 01\} \\
&\quad\ 3.\ \{1 \to 01,\quad 0 \to 0\}.
\end{aligned}
$$

The first group of production rules inverts the string. This group is not necessary in case we exclude a line with slope 1.

The second group has the same function as the rules 4 and 5 in the previous mentioned PG. The third group corresponds to the rules (6,7,8,9,10,11) in the PG.

Example:

$$
0 \overset{2}{\Rightarrow} 01 \overset{3}{\Rightarrow} 001 \overset{2}{\Rightarrow} (01)^2 1 \overset{3}{\Rightarrow} (001)^2 01 \overset{3}{\Rightarrow} (0^3 1)^2 0^2 1 \Rightarrow
$$

$$
\overset{3}{\Rightarrow} (0^4 1)^2 0^3 1 \overset{2}{\Rightarrow} ((01)^4 1)^2 (01)^3 1 \overset{3}{\Rightarrow} ((001)^4 01^2)(001)^3 01.
$$

Again slope 14/39 is represented.

This Lindenmayer grammar is more simple than the programmed grammar. This can be explained by the fact that it is essential for L-grammars that the rewriting of one symbol of a kind implies that all symbols are rewritten in the same way. An L-grammar is very convenient for this purpose due to the simultaneous application of the rules. In a programmed grammar it must be simulated, which costs additional rules.

In 1976 Rothstein and Weiman [28] gave a very interesting deduction from a continued fractions algorithm via Markov processes to the same TOL-grammar. They didn't need the first group of rules because of their restriction to slopes between 0 and 1.

The grammars in this section are producing every possible period. Which period is dependant of the number of times the production rules are used. Before generation this number must be determined with the aid of elements of the structural algorithm in 3.1.
The shifting or centering problem is not examined for structural grammars.

3.4. <u>Linguistic parsing.</u>

In [4] I wrote that parsing with grammars based on the structural methods is only possible when one finds a noiseless period. I stated that this would not be very interesting for practical purposes. What did happen after 1974?

Rosenfeld [25] states that his chord property theorem shows that the determination of all possible digitized line segments is a linear bounded problem. This corresponds with results earlier in this paper: every straight line can be generated by a context-free programmed grammar. When we know that every context-free programmed grammar can be translated in a context-sensitive common grammar (see chapter 2 of Fu [12]) and that every context sensitive common grammar can be recognized by a linear bounded automaton (an elementary theorem in automata theory, also treated in [12]), we conclude the same. Rothstein and Weiman [28] actually proved that the straight line generation algorithm they found (based on continued fraction, expressed in the previously mentioned TOLG) constitutes a context-sensitive language. Of theoretical interest is that Wu [34] developed the strict presentation of Freeman's three properties by constructing a recognition algorithm for straight lines, whether or not they have rational slopes (finite periods).

In 1982 Rosenfeld and Kim [26] gave some interesting mathematical elaborations of the recognition problem of digital straight lines.
The main thing a linear bounded automaton can learn us is whether the line is really straight. When the answer is no, we don't know whether this is due to "acceptable" noise or whether the line is not straight. Only in the case of a really straight line the automaton can produce output which is necessary to find the slope.
Schlien [29] made use of that fact to detect break points in a digital arc representing intersections of straight line segments with different slopes.
Lee and Fu [20] remarked that in real applications the ideal properties of digital straight lines are often missing. They developed a Fast Fourier-Transform algorithm to detect straight lines. It is interesting that by this way the gap between syntactical pattern recognition and statistical pattern recognition is bridged!
A very interesting attempt to recognize whether a line is straight or not has been given by Rothstein and Weiman [28].
When a TOL-grammar is able to produce parallel generation, there exists a poly automaton for parallel recognition (see also Butler [5]). They discuss the problem of the organisation of simple finite state automata (lattice cells getting information from their direct neighbours) organising themselves into an ad hoc linear bounded automaton to perform the recognition. An algebraic approach for parallel processing is given by Jelinek [16].

Though there is some progress in parsing, I still think it is very difficult to find an efficient way of looking bottom-up for more general structure. For a discussion on this general topic see for instance [12 (chapter 5), 27, 31].

3.5. Estimation of properties of line segments.

In pattern recognition and image processing it is important to be able to measure some properties of a line segment, such as length, slope and intercept. Recently it has been shown that the structural algorithm for straight line generation is useful for developing measuring instruments for this properties.

Vossepoel and Smeulders [33] developed a computational method for an unbiased estimate for the lenght of a straight line presented by a digital arc, a cellular arc and a cellular arc on a hexagonal lattice (6-connected). They use the structural properties mentioned in section 2.2. and derive a method with 3 parameters to estimate the length with greater accuracy than existing methods not using structural properties.

Building on this result Dorst and Smeulders [8] discussed more fundamentally the loss of information that occurs when a straight line is digitized on a regular lattice.

They proved that every straight chaincode string can be represented by a set of 4 unique integer parameters: (n,q,p,s). These parameters summarize basic properties of the straight string: n is its length, q is its smallest periodicity, p/q is the most simple slope, and s is a kind of phase shift. (The structural algorithm in section 3.1. is producing strings with $s = 0$). They give the exact definitions.

The formula to construct a chainelement c_i of the straight digital arc S is

$$c_i = \mathrm{ENTIER}\left(\frac{p}{q}(i-s)\right) - \mathrm{ENTIER}\left(\frac{p}{q}(i-s-1)\right) \quad \text{for } i=1,2,\ldots,n.$$

They presented a complicated mathematical expression for the set of all real line segments, which could have generated a given string. This set is called the domain of a chain code.

Their "domain theorem" has a close relation to Rosenfeld's

chord property.

Using this domain theorem in [9] best lineair unbiased estimators are developed for line length, angle, slope and intercept. They show that this BLUE-estimators give better results than estimators of other authors. Because of the complexity of the formula's for these estimators, these are not very attractive for application in practice. Their interest is theoretical: they form a basis for a performance analysis of other estimators. Of course they can also be used for an analysis of the relation between sample size and accuracy which is an important item in pattern analysis and image processing.

Dorst and Duin [7] introduced a spirograph theory, with a wink to a children's toy for drawing fancy curves. As indicated in previous sections this theory is related to number theory and it includes the structural generation algorithm. Dorst and Duin derive the positional accuracy in the worst case, and the average.

4.   CONDITIONAL METHODS.

4.1.   Conditional algorithms for straight line generation.

A straight line on a lattice can be generated by testing which lattice points are near the real line. The condition to be tested has been formulated by Rosenfeld [25] when he introduced the chord property (see section 2.2.). The most general conditional algorithm to generate a line with a given slope and a given starting point will be:
1. determine the real line on the lattice near the starting point;
2. determine for which of the neighbours (i,j) of the last found point of the digitized line a point (x,y) on the real line can be found such that
   $$\text{MAX} \left(|i - x|, |j - y| \right) < 1.$$

This point is the next point of the digitized line.
3. repeat step 2 as much as necessary to find the next point.

Rosenfelds chord property was published in 1974, but conditional algorithms can be found much earlier. Five examples of these algorithms:

a. The earliest dated algorithm I found in 1972 dates from 1968 (Morse [22]).
   He states that when a lattice point (i,j) is on the digitized line, the real line must be in the neighbourhood $(i\pm\frac{1}{2}, j)$ or $(i, j\pm\frac{1}{2})$ of (i, j).

   In the case of slopes form 0 to 1 the neighbourhood is determined by $(i, j\pm\frac{1}{2})$. It can easily be seen that Rosenfelds condition has also been satisfied.

   Knowing the neighbourhood of a point and assuming that the real line also goes through the point $(0,0)$, Morse determines a minimal and a maximal slope. In his generation algorithm for the decision which point can be part of the digitized line, he used the test whether the slope of the real line is between the earlier mentioned minimal and maximal slopes of the neighbourhood of that point.

   It is worth noticing that in the first octant when the real line goes through $(0,0)$ and a point (i,j) is on the digitized line, the minimal slope is $(j-\frac{1}{2})/i$ and the maximal slope $(j+\frac{1}{2})/i$. When we only know that $(0,0)$ is a point near the real line, there is less accuracy. Then the minimal slope is $(j-1)/i$ and the maximal slope $(j+1)/i$. The algorithm of Morse gives some indications for the accuracy of a measure of a slope of a digitized straight line (see section 3.5.).

b. In [4] I simplified the algorithm of Morse by changing a test on possible slopes in a test on the neighbourhood of the real line.

The equation for a straight line is

$$y = (p/q)x + e \text{ with } 0 \leqslant p/q \leqslant 1.$$

Each symbol 0 or 1 adds one step in the x-direction. The best point in the y-direction at the i-th is the one where $y_i - (p/q)i + e$ is minimal. We find this by rounding $(p/q)i + e$ to the nearest integer, or

$$y_i = \text{ENTIER}((p/q)i + e + \tfrac{1}{2}).$$

The Freeman symbol we find at the i-th step is

$$y_i - y_{i-1}.$$

By the rounding mechanism the lattice point is always chosen where the real line is in the neighbourhood as defined by Morse, so this conditional generation algorithm also generates lines with the chord property.

c. The leading conditional method was presented in 1963 by Bresenham on an ACM conference in Denver. It was published in 1965 [2] . The most simple derivation I know is given by Earnshaw[10]. When (i,j) is a correct digitized point of the real line $y = (p/q)x$, then next chain-element c_i will be 0 when the next point is (i+1, j) and 1 when the next point is (i+1, j+1).

The condition to test is

$$(p/q)(i+1) - j \geqslant j+1 - (p/q)(i + 1) \text{ or}$$
$$2(pi - qj) + 2p - q \geqslant 0$$

Let $d_i = 2(pi - qj) + 2p - q$

Easily can be seen that $d_o = 2p - q$ and that

if $d_i \geqslant o$, then $d_{i+1} = d_i + 2(p - q)$

$$c_{i+1} = 1 \qquad \text{(diagonal move)}$$

$$\text{else } d_{i+1} = d_i + 2p$$

$$c_{i+1} = 0 \qquad \text{(axial move)}$$

For further simplification subsitute $a = 2(q-p)$ and $b = 2p$. Bresenham's algorithm only requires a few very simple machine operations for each step.

d. A close related algorithm is given by Thompson [32].
   His testing algorithm can be written:
   if $|t_i + p| \geqslant |t_i + p - q|$ then $t_{i+1} = t_i + p - q$
   $$c_i = 1$$
   $$\text{else } t_{i+1} = t_i + p$$
   $$c_i = 0$$
   The starting value $t_o = 0$.
   Earnshaw [10] proved the equivalence of Thompson's and
   Bresenham's algorithm ($d_i = 2t_i + 2p - q$).
e. Earnshaw [10] presents a variant of b by testing whether
   $(p/q)i \geqslant j + 1/2$.

In [10] some other authors are mentioned, and considerations about more basic movements than only axial and diagonal are given.

In 1982 Sproull [30] presented an interesting relation between the above mentioned conditional algorithm b and Bresenham's algorithm c. See apendix 2.

Finally three remarks on Bresenham's algorithm:
1. Mostly the algorithm is presented, like above, with intercept e = 0. In other cases the starting value of d is
   changing:
   $$d_o = 2p - q + 2eq.$$
2. Because of the more simple handling by computer of integers, the algorithm is scaled by 2q. This will not be
   possible when p/q is irrational and not useful when p
   and q are very large. Without scaling the algorithm
   gives the same results. In that case we have to choose
   $$d_o = p/q + e - \tfrac{1}{2}$$
   $$a = 1 - p/q$$
   $$b = p/q .$$
3. The second step in the structural algorithm is to calculate $r_o = q_o - p_o$. In the following steps r_o and p_o are
   used.
   The Bresenham algorithm is steered by

$a = 2(q - p) = 2r_o$ and $b = 2p_o$. So there is a relationship!

4.2. Grammars for the conditional approach

In [4] a programmed grammar with a tail was given based on the conditional method. The tail has some bookkeeping function: in every cycle there is a test whether the tail exceeds length q.

Comparison with Thompson's algorithm learns that the grammaroperations are scaled up by q just like in Thompson's algorithm. The starting value is not 0 but q/2. Consequence is that the grammar can not be applied in case the line starts in (0,0) and q is odd.

In the next programmed grammar with a tail this problem is solved by scaling with 2q like in Bresenham's algorithm.

$PG = (V_N, V_T, S, J, P)$ with

$V_N = \{U, T, S\}$,

$V_T = \{0, 1\}$,

$J = \{1, 2, 3, 4, 5, 6\}$,

$P = \{$

1.	$S \rightarrow UT^m$	$S(4)$	—
2.	$UT^{2q} \rightarrow 1U$	$S(4)$	$F(3)$
3.	$U \rightarrow 0U$	$S(4)$	—
4.	$U \rightarrow UT^{2p}$	$S(2,5)$	—
5.	$UT^{2q} \rightarrow 1$	—	$F(6)$
6.	$U \rightarrow 0$	—	—	$\}$.

p and q again determine the slope p/q, m depends on e:

$$m = (2e + 1)q$$

This grammar is not context free. By the rules 2 and 5 is tested whether 2q symbols T occur. Then the next symbol to be generated is 1, else 0. As an example, we take $p/q = 2/5$ and $e = 3/10$, so $m = 8$. The successive productions for the first symbols are:

$$S \overset{1}{\Rightarrow} UT^8 \overset{4}{\Rightarrow} UT^{12} \overset{2}{\Rightarrow} 1UT^2 \overset{4}{\Rightarrow} 1UT^6 \overset{2,3}{\Rightarrow} 10UT^6 \overset{4}{\Rightarrow} 10UT^{10} \Rightarrow$$

$$\overset{2}{\Rightarrow} 101U \overset{4}{\Rightarrow} 101UT^4 \overset{2,3}{\Rightarrow} 101UT^4 \overset{4}{\Rightarrow} 1010UT^8 \overset{5,6}{\Rightarrow} 10100T^8.$$

The meaning of the tail T is not defined, so we can neglect these symbols. The generated chain is 10100.

The stright lines generated by the grammars above have discretization noise. Inspired by the stochastic programmed grammars as described by Fu in [12] a method is developed to add another kind of noise. We use an SPG and allow the Freeman symbols 2 and 7 besides 0 and 1. Depending on the number of T's in the tail, the probability for the production of a 2, 1, 0, or 7 is determined. The grammar is $SPG = (V_N, V_T, S, J, P, D)$ with:

$V_N = \{S, U, T, R\}$,
$V_T = \{2, 1, 0, 7\}$,
$J = \{1, 2, \ldots, 11\}$.

The labeled production rules P with the labels J and their probabilities D are:

1.	$S \rightarrow UT^{m+p}$	$S(2)$	(1)	–	–
2.	$T^{q+p} \rightarrow T^{q+p}$	$S(5,6,7,8)$	(c, a, a^2, a^3)	$F(3)$	(1)
3.	$T^q \rightarrow T^q$	$S(5,6,7,8)$	(a, d, a, a^2)	$F(4)$	(1)
4.	$T \rightarrow T$	$S(5,6,7,8)$	(a^2, a, d, a)	$F(5,6,7,8)$	(a^3, a^2, a, c)
5.	$U \rightarrow 2UR^{q+p}$	$S(10)$	(1)	–	–
6.	$U \rightarrow 1UR^{q-p}$	$S(10)$	(1)	–	–
7.	$U \rightarrow 0UT^p$	$S(9)$	(1)	–	–
8.	$U \rightarrow 7UT^{q+p}$	$S(9)$	(1)	–	–
9.	$TR \rightarrow e$	$S(9)$	(1)	$F(2,11)$	$(1 - b, b)$
10.	$RT \rightarrow e$	$S(10)$	(1)	$F(2,11)$	$(1 - b, b)$
11.	$U \rightarrow e$	–	–	–	–

$c = 1 - a - a^2 - a^3$, $\quad 0 < a < 1$, $\quad 0 < c < 1$,
$d = 1 - 2a - a^2$, $\quad 0 < b < 1$, $\quad 0 < d < 1$.
e is the empty word: $TR \rightarrow e$ means that both T and R vanish.

This grammar is only scaled by q and not by 2q, but that can easily be changed if necessary.

Opposite to the structural grammars of section 3.3., these conditional grammars are determined generating systems. After choosing m, p and q only one line can be generated, when we neglect the possible stochastic deviations.

4.3. Parsing and image processing with conditional methods.

Only in Morse [22] I found parsing or image processing methods based on the conditonal method. Actually he first developed his method with minimal and maximal slopes to test whether a line is straight or not. Next he constructed his generation method. In [4] I expressed my doubts on the practical utility of linguistic conditional methods for analytical purposes. The same doubts are relevant for conditional methods in general. Unless somebody shows the opposite, I believe conditional methods are only useful for the generation of lines and not for analysis.

5. STRUCTURAL AND CONDITIONAL METHODS COMPARED AND COMBINED.

5.1. Utility and theoretical interest of the structural and the conditional method.

In the previous chapter two different kinds of algorithms for straight line generation were shown.

The force of the structural approach is the relationship to a native part of mathematics: number theory. Many interesting theoretical considerations are available due to number theory. For a profound study of properties of lines and line segments the structural approach is of great value. In section 3.5 it has been shown that results can be derived being very useful for image processing and pattern recognition. I think this theoretical aspect of the structural method is the most important result of this approach. The use of the structural algorithm for straight line generation is rather complicated. The algorithm generates a string. Next some shifting or centering is necessary. Finally from the string the relevant lattice points must be derived. So the practical utility of the structural algorithm for straight line generation is limited until now. The same can be stated for the practical analysis of a given line with the structural algorithm. More classical measurement methods will be better suited, but the structural approach did contribute a lot to these methods.

The extension of the structural method to grammatical systems was an interesting topic in the early seventies. Reading the book of Fu [12] on syntactic pattern recognition of 1982 I am not very impressed by the rate progress in linguistic picture grammars since the early seventies. I think it is until now only a much promising excursion to a rather new part of mathematics: automata theory.

Perhaps an exception must be made for the Lindenmayer grammars. Parallel generation and maybe parallel processing with these rather simple developmental systems will give good results, provided that a good co-ordination between operations on lattice points at one side (generation or recognition), and top down operations at the other side can be assured. I think for pattern recognition and image processing this is still an interesting field of research.

The main value of the conditional algorithm is the rather simple generation method. It is developed for plotting routines and of course today it is useful for computer graphics. Of practical interest is the way to optimise the method by replacing additions and divisions with additions and signtests. The method is related to a middle-aged part of mathematics: numerical analysis.

For image processing purposes the conditional approach has little value. The excursion to linguistic systems based on the conditional method is less intriguing than the comparable excursion from the structural appraoch.

5.2. Efficiency of structural and conditional methods.

Looking for efficiency it is important to make a distinction between structure efficiency and generation efficiency. Structure efficiency is determined by the number of cycles of an algorithm before the structure and the position of a line is clear, and by the complexity of one cycle of the algorithm.

Generation efficiency is referring to the actual representation of the digitized line on the lattice. This is machine dependant. For instance it is complete different for a pen plotter and a graphics display.

The structure efficiency depends on the algorithm. I assume that generation efficiency is independent of the algorithm, so it can be omitted in considerations on overall efficiency. Of course many things can be done on generation efficiency (for instance parallel operations). About the structure efficiency of the derivation of a straight line with the structural algorithm presented in section 2.3 according to [4] can be said that after some reductions equations for t_{i+1} and c_{i+1} in relation to t_i, c_i, and n_i are

$$t_{i+1} = \text{MIN}(c_i - t_i \cdot n_i, t_i \cdot (1+n_i) - c_i),$$
$$c_{i+1} = \text{MAX}(c_i - t_i \cdot n_i, t_i \cdot (1+n_i) - c_i).$$

Considering that $t_{i+1} \quad \frac{1}{2} t_i$ the number of times the algorithm has to be applied is $\text{ENTIER}(^2\text{LOG}(\text{MIN}(p_o, r_o)))$. The case of slowest convergence is when every $n_i = 1$, and

$$t_{i+1} = c_i - t_i,$$
$$c_{i+1} = 2t_i + c_i$$

When we apply the algorithm in the opposite direction and start from the pair of numbers (t_{i+1}, c_{i+1}) with $(1,1)$, we find the following pairs:

$$(1,1), (2,3), (5,7), (12,17), (29,41), (70,99),..$$

In number theory [13] this is known to be a good approximation of $\frac{1}{2}\sqrt{2}$.

Restricting them to the half first octant with slopes in the interval (0, $\frac{1}{2}$) Arcelli and Masserotti [1] found that the number of cycles of the algorithm is of order $^2\log(p_o)$. Dorst and Duin [7] found that for their spirograph algorithm in the worst case the number of cycles is 2.08 $\ln(q_o)$ + 1.67 and on average 0.89 $\ln(q_o)$ + O(1), where O(1) means order 1.

I didn't find or invent anything about the efficiency of positioning methods (centering or shifting).

For the conditional algorithm it is essential that the algorithm is applied for every point, so the number of cycles is q_o. In general conditional algorithms are less complex than structural algorithms and they include the positioning!. Not being able to give an exact changing point, it is clear that for short periods or short line segments conditional methods are more efficient, while for long periods and long line segments the relative complexity of the algorithm will
be unimportant because the algorithm is only applied order $\log(p_o)$ times instead of q_o times or even more when the length of the line segment exceeds the period.
Cederberg [6] came to simular conclusions.

5.3. Bridging the gap between the structural and the conditional approach.

The conclusion of section 5.2. is not satisfying. There is a complete structural procedure (see the end of section 3.1.) but for many applications the overhead necessary for the structural approach is too much. Though there are variants in structural methods, there is no essential simplification. The structure and the position of the line must be derived before the real generation can start.
On the other hand many conditional authors were looking for optimisation of their procedures and sometimes they found

structural elements. Looking at their references I think often these structural elements are reinventions independent of earlier structural authors. Some examples:

a. Already in 1972 Reggiori [24] concluded that for slopes in (0, $\frac{1}{2}$) in the string to be generated the number of 0's before a 1 can only assume two value's, being consecutive integers. In fact he applied one cycle of the structural method. Next a conditional test was applied to select the best fitting substring.

   He compares the speed of this algorithm with Bresenham's algorithm and he concludes that his algorithm is faster. The conditional Bresenham algorithm needs q_o cycles and Reggiori is reducing this to p_o. Arcelli and Masserotti [1] show that the structure efficiency of the structural algorithm is better than by Reggiori. Of course that is only to be expected in case you use one step of an efficient algorithm and next a less efficient algorithm.

b. Recently Sproull [30], not refering to structural approaches, showed how to raise the generation efficiency by parallel processing of Bresenham's algorithm or by selecting precomputed strokes.

c. Earnshaw [10] described two compaction alternatives encoding either runlenghts, or repeated patterns. With the introduction of repeated patterns the structural notion of a period is shared in the conditional approach. He concludes that the information needed for graphs using only straight lines can be reduced with nearly 50%, and for overall purposes with 20% - 40%.

d. Bresenham [3] developed a procedure to incorporate both runlength and periodic patterns. He stated explicit not to treat substructure within the fundamental period. His algorithm is rather complex and only efficient for longer lines.

It is interesting that recently, with growing technical possibilities in hardware to raise the generation efficiency, there is a move to introduce structural elements in the algorithms to raise structure efficiency too. Unfortunately the result is increase of overhead and the consequence no improvement for short lines.

Analysing the essential difference between the structural and the conditional approach we see different sequences in the steps:
- in the structural approach first the structure is analysed, next the position is determined and finally each chain element is generated.
- in essence the conditional approach is only generating each chain element including the position. Structural elements can be included bij increasing the complexity of the algorithm.

The bridge over the gap between this approaches should be found in a conditional approach with increasing structural aspects so far as efficient. So the conditional approach should not only include the test of a condition regarding to Rosenfeld's chord property, but also a test whether structural information is easily available and implementable.

The last remark of section 4.1. mentions a relationship between the two steering factors of the structural algorithm and two of the three steering factors in Bresenham's algorithm: a $= 2r_o$ and $b = 2p_o$. (The third factor in Bresenham's algorithm d_o contains information necessary for the position and has no counter part in the structural algorithm.)

In essence the structural algorithm recursively constructs smaller r_i's en p_i's, combined with the substitution of simple chain strings by more complex strings. When $p_i < r_i$ wen can find $p_{i+1} = p_i - \text{ENTIER}(p_i/r_i)$ and the new chainelement is one time an old string and $\text{ENTIER}(p_i/r_i)$ times the other old string.

Pitteway and Green [23] presented an extinction of Bresenham's algorithm including this structure finding operations.

Describing the algorithm similar to the structural algorithm we obtain:

1. Read p, q and e, under the assumptions, $0 \leqslant p \leqslant q$ and $-\frac{1}{2} \leqslant e < \frac{1}{2}$.

2. Start with i = 0, string A = 0 and string B = 1. Calculate $d_o = 2p - q + 2eq$, $a_o = 2(q - p)$ and $b_o = 2p$.

3. If $d_i \geqslant 0$ generate string B and go to step 11, else generate string A.

4. If $b_i = 0$, continue generating string A.

5. Calculate $d_{i+1} = d_i + b_i$.

6. If $b_i < a_i$ then go to step 7. Else $b_{i+1} = b_i$ and $a_{i+1} = a_i$ and go to step 3.

7. Calculate $n_i = ENTIER(a_i/b_i)$.

8. If $n_i = a_i/b_i$ then $n_i := n_i - 1$.

9. Calculate $a_{i+1} = a_i - n_i b_i$ and $b_{i+1} = b_i$.

10. Substitute the old string B by BA^{n_i} and go to step 3.

11. Calculate $d_{i+1} = d_i - a_i$.

12. If $b_i < a_i$, then $b_{i+1} = b_i$, $a_{i+1} = a$, and go to step 3.

13. Calculate $n_i = ENTIER(b_i/a_i)$.

14. Calculate $b_{i+1} = b_i - n_i a_i$ and $a_{i+1} = a_i$.

15. Substitute the old string A by AB^{n_i} and go to step 3.

Rule 8 is necessary to avoid the situation that $a_i = 0$ before $b_i = 0$, in which case division by 0 is occurring in step 13. The algorithm isn't much more complex then the structural algorithm, especially when we consider that in a cycle only step 4-10 or 11-15 are used. Two advantages (besides the main purpose to include positional information) are that the algorithm is also usable for irrational slopes and that reducing (p/q) is not necessary.

In table 1 the working of the algorithm is illustrated for the same line as in section 3.1. The construction of the period is finished in the 9th cycle, the shift s = 24. Before the period is found, already 63 chain elements are produced.

Table 1. The bridge algorithm for $y = (14/39)x - (19/39)$.

cy-cle	string A	string B	d_i	a_i	b_i	n_i	output
0	0	1	-49	50	28	1	0
1	0	10	-21	22	28	-	0
2	0	10	7	22	28	1	10
3	010	10	-15	22	6	3	010
4	010	$10(010)^3$	-9	4	6	-	010
5	010	$10(010)^3$	-3	4	6	-	010
6	010	$10(010)^3$	3	4	6	1	$10(010)^3$
7	$(010)10(010)^3$	$10(010)^3$	-1	4	2	1	$(010)10(010)^3$
8	$(010)10(010)^3$	$10(010)^4 10(010)^3$	1	2	2	1	$10(010)^4 10(010)^3$
9	$(010)10(010)^3$	$10(010)^4 10(010)^3$	-1	2	0	-	final string A
	$10(010)^4 10(010)^3$		-	-	0	-	final string A
			-	-	0	-	final string A

In the scope of this paper after finding this integration between the structural and the conditional approach for generations purposes, still two questions are open:

1. Is a linguistic description of this algorithm possible? Of course the changing of the strings and producing the output is possible, but the problem is testing and calculating d_i, a_i and b_i to steer the production.
2. Is an inverse algorithm or procedure constructable for analysing and/or parsing?

6. A GLANCE AT PROGRESS IN KNOWLEDGE OF STRAIGHT LINES ON A LATTICE

It is interesting to look back at the development of the knowledge of straight line generation during the last 20 years, with the eyes of an advisor of the governing board of an university.

Some remarkable notes:

a. At the end of the sixties and at the beginning of the seventies there is much interest in theoretical consi- derations on straight lines on a lattice. About 10 years later you can see a second wave of interest. Much prag- matic interest was in the middle of the sixties and a second wave about 15 years later. I think for policy makers in government and industry it is almost impos- sible to make serious plans which have impact for more than three or four years. So a justified steering policy for the development of science based on citation indexes or other bibliometric data doesn't seem constructable for this field of research.

b. The research I did in 1972 was published in a journal in 1974. The first "serious" citation was published in 1978 [1] and a considerable number if citations has not been found before 1982. This time delay is so long that you can really ask what is wrong in communication between scientists. Of course a delay of 2 years is caused by first reporting in Dutch, but despite this fact I think there is a more fundamental problem. Is the publication duty for every scientist to survive so heavy that early communication is dangerous? Or is it the trouble that scientists can't write an interesting report in a short time? Or is the procedure for publishing in a journal to long?

c. Two schools of people have been busy with straight line generation, a "structural" school and a "conditional" school. In literature you find hardly communication between these schools. Only recently conditional authors refer to the earlier structural authors. It seems very strange for this practically oriented kind of knowledge where a big gap between theory and practice is almost intolerable. At the same time the question is whether raised or not computer science can already be considered as a consistent whole of knowledge.

d. Note a) is ending with the near impossibility of a jus- tified steering policy based on measurement techniques

usable for governing boards of university or a national
government, for this field of research. In a recent
paper Moed et al [21] give some results of a quantitative bibliometric study on 6.700 publications and 42.000
citations in a period of 10 years for two departments of
a Dutch university. They demonstrate there are existing
many objections to a straightforward interpretation of
bibliometric analysis, for instance the difference in
citation culture dependant of the discipline. An other
objection is the incompleteness of the science citation
index. For example: only half the number of citations of
[4] I saw are mentioned in the science citation index.
Moed et al only conclude that their kind of analysis is
giving a meaningful basis for discussion on the performance of research groups.

e. Notes b) and c) don't give much hope that judgement by
peers is a justified technique for finding indicators to
select directions in research to be stimulated or not.
(Possibly this pessimism doesn't uphold for every branch
in science.)

Perhaps these points can be somewhat mitigated when broader
themes are used like "picture processing" or "lattice operations".
But still I think, in essence giving money to a scientist
to do research is dispensing him from other kinds of labour, like in the fourteenth century. You can only hope the
scientist uses his time and money in a good way, one can
never be sure. So finally which scientist is getting the
money is an arbitrary policy decision which can hardly be
justified with criteria related to science.

APPENDIX 1: EXAMPLES OF GRAMMARS FOR SQUARES $0^n 2^n 4^n 6^n$.

Using the Freeman chaincodes 0,2,4 and 6 the language $0^n 2^n 4^n 6^n$ for n = 1,2,3.... is describing squares of sidelength 1,2,3... In Fu [12] a context sentive common grammar with 19 production rules is given to produce this language:

G_1 = (V_N, V_T, P, S) with
V_N = $\{ S, A, B, C, D, E, F, G \}$,
V_T = $\{ 0, 2, 4, 6 \}$,
P = $\{$ S $\rightarrow$ 0AB,   DB $\rightarrow$ FB,   6FB $\rightarrow$ 6F6,

     A $\rightarrow$ 0AC,   E6 $\rightarrow$ G6,   6F6 $\rightarrow$ F66,

     A $\rightarrow$ D,   4G $\rightarrow$ G4,   4F $\rightarrow$ F4 ,

     D4 $\rightarrow$ 4D,   6G $\rightarrow$ G6,   2F $\rightarrow$ 224,

     D6 $\rightarrow$ 6D,   0G $\rightarrow$ 024D, 0F $\rightarrow$ 02 ,

     DC $\rightarrow$ EC,   2G $\rightarrow$ 224D, 2B $\rightarrow$ 246,

     EC $\rightarrow$ E6 $\}$.

In [4] another context sentive common grammar with only 6 production rules us given:

G_2 = (V_N, V_T, S, P) is a grammar with
V_N = $\{ S, E, F \}$,
V_T = $\{ 0, 2, 4, 6 \}$,
P = $\{$ 1. S $\rightarrow$ ESF ,

     2. S $\rightarrow$ 0246 ,

     3. E0 $\rightarrow$ 0E ,

     4. E2 $\rightarrow$ 022 ,

     5. 6F $\rightarrow$ F6 ,

     6. 4F $\rightarrow$ 446 $\}$.

The numbers in P are for reference only. Suppose after n - 1 applications of rule 1, rule 2 is applied. Then we have the string E^{n-1} 0246 F^{n-1}. String and rules are symmetric. No exchange being possible between the left and the right half, we can restrict our attention to the left part and the rules 3 and 4. The nonterminal E can only move up to the right (rule 3) or vanish at the confrontation with 2 (rule 4), produ-

cing 02. The production stops when all E's have been elimi-
natied.

In [12] a context free programmed grammar with 7 labeled rules
is given:

$PG_1 = (V_N, V_T, P, S, J,)$ where
$V_N = \{S, A, B, C, D\}$,
$V_T = \{0, 2, 4, 6\}$,
$J = \{1, 2, 3, 4, 5, 6, 7\}$,
$P = \{$ 1. S $\rightarrow$ 2AB,   S(2,3)   –

2. A $\rightarrow$ 2AC,   S(2,3)   –

3. A $\rightarrow$ D,   S(4)   –

4. C $\rightarrow$ 6,   S(5)   F(6)   ,

5. D $\rightarrow$ 2D4,   S(4)   –

6. B $\rightarrow$ 6,   S(7)   –

7. D $\rightarrow$ 64,   –   – $\}$.

A grammar of this kind with only 5 rules can be found in [4]:
$PG_2 = (V_N, V_T, S, J, P)$ is a programmed grammar with
$V_N = \{S, E, F\}$,
$V_T = \{0, 2, 4, 6\}$,
$J = \{1, 2, 3, 4, 5\}$,
$P = \{$ 1. S $\rightarrow$ EF   S(2,4)   –

2. E $\rightarrow$ 0E2   S(3)   –

3. F $\rightarrow$ 4F6   S(2,4)   –

4. E $\rightarrow$ 02   S(5)   –

5. F $\rightarrow$ 46   –   – $\}$.

The failure branch of this PG is empty. Here n is determined
by the number of applications of rules 2 and 3.

Very spectacular is a 1-Lindenmayer grammar in [4] with only
one set of 2 rules:
$LG_1 = (V, P, S)$ where
$V = \{0, 2, 4, 6\}$,
$S = \{0246\}$,
$P = \{02 \rightarrow 0022, 46 \rightarrow 4466\}$.

There is also a 0-Lindenmayer grammar with the same set for V and S and one set of 4 rules:

$P = 0 \rightarrow 00, \ 2 \rightarrow 22, \ 4 \rightarrow 44, \ 6 \rightarrow 66$
but this grammar only generates squares with side length $1,2,4,8,16,\ldots$.

The examples show that a programmed grammar is more simple to handle than a common grammar, though the advantages are not very spectacular when you optimise the common grammars. A real improvement is the developmental Lindenmayer grammar which ought to be used more in picture generation.

APPENDIX 2: TRANSFORMATIONS OF CONDITIONAL ALGORITHMS.

Sproull [30] presents his algorithms in a PASCAL-like language. Every algorithm starts with declaration of the variables and the rule "for i = 0 to q do begin". Next some rules to determine j are following, a rule to display the point (i,j) and the rule "end". Omitting these general rules, his algorithms can be presented as below.

A1:
$y_i := (p/q)i$
$j := \text{ENTIER} \ (y_i + \tfrac{1}{2})$

This algorithm is the conditional algorithm of [4] in two steps for each point (i,j) on the digitized line.
You can observe that $y_{i+1} = y_i + p/q$. So it is possible to convert multiplication to incremental addition.

Starting with $y_o = 0$ a second algorithm is:

A2:
$j := \text{ENTIER} \ (y_i + \tfrac{1}{2})$
$y_{i+1} := y_i + p/q$

After a simple transformation $z_i = y_i + \frac{1}{2}$ and starting with $z_o = \frac{1}{2}$ we obtain:

<u>A3</u>:

$j := \text{ENTIER}(z_i)$

$z_{i+1} := z_i + p/q$

To reduce the number of operations we can break z_i in an integer part which is of couse j and a fractional part zf_i. So

$z_i = j + zf_i$; $0 \leqslant zf_i \leqslant 1$

We need to detect when in $z_{i+1} = z_i + p/q = j + zf_i + p/q$ $zf_i \geqslant 1$. The algorithm now is starting with $j = 0$ and $zf_o = \frac{1}{2}$.

<u>A4</u>:

if $zf_i + p/q \geqslant 1$, then $j := j+1$

$\qquad\qquad zf_{i+1} := zf_i + p/q - 1$

$\qquad$, else $zf_{i+1} := zf_i + p/q$.

Finally we find Bresenham's algorithm by replacing zf_i by d_i with next formula $d_i = 2p + 2(zf_i - 1)q$ or

$\qquad zf_i = (d_i - 2p)/2q + 1$.

The objectives of this transformation are to change the comparison $zf_i + p/q \geqslant 1$ in a sign check, and the elemination of division operations by scaling by 2q.

Since A4 started with $j = 0$ and $zf_i = \frac{1}{2}$, the Bresenham algorithm is starting with $j = 0$ and $d_o = 2p-q$.

<u>A5</u>:

$\qquad$ if $d_i \geqslant 0$, then $j := j + 1$;

$\qquad\qquad\qquad d_{i+1} := d_i - 2(p-q)$

$\qquad\qquad$ else $d_{i+1} := d_i + 2p$

This algorithm is steered by a very simple condition and it doesn't need complex machine operations like division, multiplication or floating-point approximations.

ACKNOWLEDGEMENT.

In preparing this paper I got a necessary reintroduction in the structural approach by L. Dorst from the Technical University Delft.
The contribution of Carla Wientjes and Yvonne Noordegraaf in preparing the manuscript is gratefully acknowledged.

REFERENCES

1.   C. Arcelli and A. Massarotti, On the parallel generation of straight digital lines, Comp. Grap. Image Process., 7, 1978, 67-83.
2.   J.E. Bresenham, Algorithm for computer control of a digital plotter, IBM Syst. J., 4, 1965, 25-30.
3.   J.E. Bresenham, Incremental line compaction, Computer Journal, 25, 1982, 116-120.
4.   R. Brons, Linguistic methods for the description of a straight line on a grid, Comp. Grap. Image Process., 3, 1974, 48-62.
5.   J.T. Butler, On the relationship between propagating contextdependent Lindenmayer systems and cellular automata systems, Information Sciences, 68, 1982, 63-67.
6.   R.L.T. Cederberg, A new method for vector generation, Comp.Grap. Image Process., 9, 1979, 183-195.
7.   L. Dorst and R.P.W. Duin, Spirograph Theory: a framework for calculations on digitized straight lines, IEEE Trans. Pattern Anal. Machine Intell., PAMI-6, 1984, 632-639.
8.   L. Dorst and A.W.M. Smeulders, Discrete representation of straight lines, IEEE Trans. Pattern Anal. Machine Intell., PAMI-6, 1984, 450-463.
9.   L. Dorst and A.W.M. Smeulders, Best linear unbiased estimators for properties of digitized straight lines, internal report Technical University Delft, the Netherlands, 1984.
10.   R.A. Earnshaw, Line tracking for incremental plotters, Computer Journal, 23, 1980, 46-52.
11.   H. Freeman, Boundary encoding and processing, in Picture processing and psychopictorics, B.S. Lipkin and A. Rosenfeld, Eds., New York, Academic, 1970, 241-266.
12.   K.S. Fu, Syntactic Pattern recognition and applications, Englewood Cliffs, N.J., Prentice Hall, 1982.
13.   G.H. Hardy and E.M. Wright, An introduction to the theory of numbers, 4th ed., London, Oxford at the Clarendon, 1960.
14.   G.T. Herman and G. Rozenberg, Development systems and languages, Amsterdam, North-Holland, 1975.
15.   S.H.Y. Hung and T. Kasvand, On the chord property and its equivalances, Proceedings 7th Int. Conf. on Pattern Recogn., Montreal, 1984, 116-119.
16.   J. Jelinek, An algebraic theory for parallel processor design, Computer Journal, 22, 1979, 363-375.

17.   C.E. Kim and A. Rosenfeld, Digital straight lines and
       convexity of digital regions, IEEE Trans. Pattern Anal.
       Machine Intell., PAMI-4, 1982, 149-153.
18.   C.E. Kim, On cellular straight line segments, Comp. Grap.
       Image Process., 18, 1982, 369-381.
19.   C.E. Kim, Digital convexity, straightness and convex
       polygons, IEEE Trans. Pattern Anal. Machine Intell., PAMI-
       4, 1982, 618-626.
20.   H.C. Lee and K.S. Fu, Using the FFT to determine digital
       straight line chain codes, Comp. Grap. Image Process., 18,
       1982, 359-368.
21.   H.F. Moed, W.J.M. Burger, J.G. Frankfort and A.F.J. van
       Raan, On the measurement of research performance, the use
       of bibliometric indicators, internal report Research policy
       unit OWZ/PISA, State University of Leiden, The Netherlands,
       1983. Presented at the 6th Forum of European AIR member's
       "Beyond retrenchment: planning for quality and efficiency",
       Brussels, august 1984. (Proceedings p.p. 23-32).
22.   S.P. Morse, Computer storage of contour-map data, Procee-
       dings 1968 ACM Nat. Conf., 1968, 45-51.
23.   M.L.V. Pitteway and A.J.R. Green, Bresemham's algorithm
       with run line coding shortcut, Computer Journal, 25, 1982,
       114-115.
24.   G.B. Reggiori, Digital computer transformations for irre-
       gular line drawings, Technical report 403-22, New York Uni-
       versity, 1972. Available from US Departement of Commerce as
       AD-745-015.
25.   A. Rosenfeld, Digital straight line segments, IEEE Trans.
       Comp., C-23, 1974, 1264-1269.
26.   A. Rosenfeld and C.E. Kim, How a digital computer can tell
       whether a line is straight, The Americal Mathematical
       Monthly, 89, 1982, 230-235.
27.   A. Rosenfeld, A.Y. Wu and T. Dubitzki, Fast Language
       acceptance by shrinking cellular automata, Information
       Sciences, 30, 1983, 47-53.
28.   J. Rothstein and C. Weiman, Parallel and sequential speci-
       fication of a context sensitive language for straight lines
       on grids, Comp. Grap. Image Process., 5, 1976, 106-124.
29.   S. Schlien, Segmentation of digital curves using linguistic
       techniques, Comp. Vis. Grap. Image Process., 22, 1983,
       277-286.
30.   R.F. Sproull, Using program transformations to derive
       line-drawing algorithms, ACM Trans. Graph., 1, 1982, 259-
       273.
31.   G.Y. Tang and T.S. Huang, A Syntactic-semantic approach to
       image understanding and creation, IEEE Trans. Pattern Anal.
       Machine Intell., PAMI-1, 1979, 135-144.
32.   J.R. Thompson, Straight lines and graph plotters, Computer
       Journal, 4, 1964, 227.
33.   A.M. Vossepoel and A.W.M. Smeulders, Vector code probabi-
       lity and metrication error in the representation of
       straight lines of finite length, Comp. Grap. Image Pro-
       cess., 20, 1982, 347- 364.
34.   L.D. Wu, On the chaincode of a line, IEEE Trans. Pattern
       Anal. Machine Intell., PAMI-4, 1982, 347-353.

RUN LENGTH SLICE ALGORITHM
FOR INCREMENTAL LINES

ABSTRACT

Lines displayed on devices such as incremental plotters, raster
CRT or plasma panel displays, and matrix printers must be approximated by sequences of discrete axial and diagonal unit steps in
which successive incremental movements are constrained to the
movement pattern of the king piece in a game of chess. Described
is a Freeman/Reggiori-like algorithm for generating directly the run
lengths of constant direction movement within the step sequence
in contrast to generating the sequence in its basic unit step
elements. The repetitive loop for generating lengths of alternating
runs of solely axial and solely diagonal steps requires only integer
addition/subtraction together with a sign test and will be executed
at most only half the number of times as the comparable loop used
to generate the single unit move sequence one step at a time. The
algorithm also can be used to examine repetitive patterns and
cycles which occur in rastered lines.

Jack E. Bresenham
IBM Communications Products Division
P.O. Box 12195
Department H91, Bldg 662
Research Triangle Park, North Carolina
USA   27709

NATO ASI Series, Vol. F17
Fundamental Algorithms for Computer Graphics

INTRODUCTION

For some incremental or raster display devices in which the unit movement pattern is that of a king piece in chess, it can be more convenient to deal with constant direction slices or multiple unit runs of either solely axial (i.e., horizontal or vertical) or solely diagonal moves than to deal individually with single incremental steps. The following describes a technique by which contiguous run lengths can be calculated directly rather than accumulated as a sum of unit steps. The description assumes the reader is familiar with properties of basic step generation algorithms for incremental or rastered line vectors.

Before proceeding with development of the direct slice algorithm, an example may clarify intent. The incremental line from (0, 0) to (45, 11) can be represented conventionally as a sequence of unit diagonal, d, and unit horizontal, h, steps:

$$\frac{hhd}{2} \quad \frac{hhhd}{3} \quad \frac{hhhd}{3} \quad \frac{hhhd}{3} \quad \frac{hhhd}{3} \quad \frac{hhhd}{3} \quad \frac{hhhd}{3} \quad \frac{hhhd}{3} \quad \frac{hhhd}{3} \quad \frac{hhhd}{3} \quad \frac{hhhd}{3} \quad \frac{hh}{2}$$

while its complementary image from (0,0) to (45,34) can be represented as:

$$\frac{ddh}{2} \quad \frac{dddh}{3} \quad \frac{dddh}{3} \quad \frac{dddh}{3} \quad \frac{dddh}{3} \quad \frac{dddh}{3} \quad \frac{dddh}{3} \quad \frac{dddh}{3} \quad \frac{dddh}{3} \quad \frac{dddh}{3} \quad \frac{dddh}{3} \quad \frac{dd}{2}$$

In a similar manner, the line from (0,0) to (45,6) can be
represented as:

$$\underline{hhh}d\ \underline{hhhhhhh}d\ \underline{hhhhhh}d\ \underline{hhhhhhh}d\ \underline{hhhhhh}d\ \underline{hhhhhhh}d\ \underline{hhh}$$
$$\ \ 3\ \ \ \ \ \ \ 7\ \ \ \ \ \ \ 6\ \ \ \ \ \ \ 7\ \ \ \ \ \ \ 6\ \ \ \ \ \ \ 7\ \ \ \ 3$$

and its complementary image from (0,0) to (45,39) as:

$$\underline{ddd}h\ \underline{ddddddd}h\ \underline{dddddd}h\ \underline{ddddddd}h\ \underline{dddddd}h\ \underline{ddddddd}h\ \underline{ddd}$$
$$\ \ 3\ \ \ \ \ \ \ 7\ \ \ \ \ \ \ 6\ \ \ \ \ \ \ 7\ \ \ \ \ \ \ 6\ \ \ \ \ \ \ 7\ \ \ \ 3$$

The algorithm to be described will calculate directly those run
lengths or slices of consecutive constant direction indicated by
underlining in the example representations.

As any line segment can be transformed and treated as a first octant situation, only the case of movement from the origin (0,0) to
an integer valued end point ($\Delta A, \Delta B$) in the first octant will be considered for analysis. A transformation scheme by which the normalizing octant transformation can be realized will be described as
part of the algorithm initialization procedure.

In raster line generating algorithms, an implied objective often is
to minimize complexity of the repetitive stepping loop and to constrain loop operations to simple sign testing and basic integer addi-
tion/subtraction. Although it requires a single integer divide with remainder operation for intialization, the run length slice algorithm retains these implied loop characteristics. The repetitive stepping loop
for run length slices is as compact and elementary as that used for
generating single unit steps. The slice stepping loop, however, will

be traversed only [minimum ΔB, (ΔA − ΔB)] times or at most only half the number of repetitions [ΔA] required for the single step loop.

The algorithm can be used with incremental digital plotters, or with CRT and plasma panel raster displays, or with an all points available printer such as wire matrix, laser, and ink jet devices. It offers the potential to use high speed slewing with mechanical plotters or efficient slice writing techniques with raster displays as well as being useful for formating printer graphics or compaction encoding of raster lines for storage or transmission.

NOTATION

Before analyzing the direct run length or constant direction slice approach to incremental vector generation, it is useful to establish notational conventions and highlight certain properties and identities. Iverson's notation [18] for representation of nearest integers and modulo residues will be used. The following definitions and notation will be used for analysis of the slice generating algorithm:

$\lceil z \rceil$ least integer greater than or equal to z, that is, the ceiling of z.

$\lfloor z \rfloor$ greatest integer less than or equal to z, that is, the floor of z.

$_W|^Z$ integer residue of integer Z modulo integer W. In many computer instruction sets, this residue is simply the remainder of a fixed point, integer divide with remainder operation such that:

$$_W|^Z = Z - W\lfloor Z \div W \rfloor$$

note that $\lfloor -z \rfloor = -\lceil z \rceil$.

and, for $0 < z \leq 1$, one has $\lfloor -z \rfloor = -1$
and, for $0 = z$, one has $\lfloor -z \rfloor = 0$
and, for any integer W, one has $\lfloor z \rfloor = W + \lfloor z - W \rfloor$
and, for any integers W and Z, one has $Z = {}_W|^Z + W(\lfloor Z \div W \rfloor)$
and, for any non-integer z, one has $\lceil z \rceil = \lfloor z \rfloor + 1 > z$
and, for any integer Z, one has $\lceil Z \rceil = \lfloor Z \rfloor = Z$

ΔA integer valued abscissa end point of a line beginning at the origin of a cartesian coordinate grid.

ΔB integer valued ordinate end point of a line beginning at the origin of a cartesian coordinate grid.

For analysis, values of ΔA and ΔB will be restricted to integers in the range $ΔA > ΔB \geq 1$. The actual statement of the algorithm will provide for integer values of ΔA and ΔB over the full first octant range $ΔA \geq ΔB \geq 0$. In the APL programming language [16] illustrations below, ΔA and ΔB will be referenced, respectively, as *ADEL* and *BDEL*.

$Q = \lfloor \Delta A \div \Delta B \rfloor$ in APL $Q \leftarrow \lfloor ADEL \div BDEL$

In many computer instruction sets, Q is simply the quotient of a fixed point, integer divide operation.

$1 \leq Q \leq \Delta A$

$R = \Delta B \big|^{\Delta A}$ in APL $R \leftarrow BDEL \mid ADEL$

In many computer instruction sets, R is simply the remainder of a fixed point, integer divide operation.

$0 \leq R \leq (\Delta B - 1)$

$M = \lfloor \Delta A \div 2\Delta B \rfloor$ in APL $M \leftarrow ADEL \div 2 \times BDEL$

M also can be calculated as $M = \lfloor Q \div 2 \rfloor$ which in binary amounts only to a truncated, one position right shift of Q.

in APL $M \leftarrow \lfloor Q \div 2$

$N = 2\Delta B \big|^{\Delta A}$ in APL $N \leftarrow (2 \times BDEL) \mid ADEL$

N also can be calculated as N = R if Q is even or as $N = R + \Delta B$ if Q is odd which in binary amounts only to a conditional addition based upon a test of the rightmost bit position of Q. For example, one easily can calculate both M and N by initially setting M←Q and N←R, then shifting M one bit in a truncated right shift and, if underflow is detected, forming the sum N←N+ΔB to conclude with appropriate values for M and N.

in APL $N \leftarrow R + BDEL \times 2 \mid Q$

$0 \leq N \leq (2\Delta B - 1)$

$$\lfloor -N \div 2\Delta B \rfloor = \begin{cases} 0 & \text{if } N = 0 \\ -1 & \text{if } N \neq 0 \end{cases}$$

$$T_i = {}_{2\Delta B} \left| \, {}^{(N + 2Ri)} \right. \qquad \text{in APL} \qquad T \leftarrow (2 \times BDEL) \mid N + 2 \times R \times I$$

where i is an integer $0 \leq i \leq (\Delta B - 1)$

$0 \leq T_i \leq (2\Delta B - 1)$ $\qquad 0 \leq T_i + 2R \leq 4\Delta B - 3$

$0 = \lfloor T_i \div 2\Delta B \rfloor$ $\qquad 0 \leq \lfloor (T_i + 2R) \div 2\Delta B \rfloor \leq 1$

$$\lfloor (T_i + 2R) \div 2\Delta B \rfloor = \begin{cases} 0 & \text{if } (T_i + 2R) < 2\Delta B \\ 1 & \text{if } (T_i + 2R) \geq 2\Delta B \end{cases}$$

$T_0 = N$

$$T_{i+1} = T_i + \begin{cases} 2R & \text{if } (T_i + 2R) < 2\Delta B \\ 2R - 2\Delta B & \text{if } (T_i + 2R) \geq 2\Delta B \end{cases}$$

$S_i = \lfloor (N + 2Ri) \div 2\Delta B \rfloor$ $\qquad$ in APL $\qquad S \leftarrow \lfloor (N + 2 \times R \times I) \div 2 \times BDEL$

where i is an integer $0 \leq i \leq (\Delta B - 1)$

$S_0 = 0$

$S_{i+1} = S_i + \lfloor (T_i + 2R) \div 2\Delta B \rfloor$

$$S_{i+1} = S_i + \begin{cases} 0 & \text{if } (T_i + 2R) < 2\Delta B \\ 1 & \text{if } (T_i + 2R) \geq 2\Delta B \end{cases}$$

For positive integers a, c, k, Δa, Δb, and I with:

Δa and Δb relatively prime

$\Delta a > \Delta b > 0$

$c\Delta a \geq a$

$c\Delta b - 1 \geq I \geq 0$

precise half points for the quantity

$$\left(\frac{c\Delta b}{c\Delta a}\right)a = I + \frac{1}{2}$$

require

Δa be even

Δb be odd

$$a = \left(\frac{1 + 2k}{2}\right)\Delta a \qquad k = 0, 1, \ldots, (c-1)$$

The sequence for a generates c instances of half points. One also can observe that

$$\left\lfloor \frac{c\Delta a}{c\Delta b} \right\rfloor = \left\lfloor \frac{\Delta a}{\Delta b} \right\rfloor$$

$$c\Delta b \left| \frac{c\Delta a}{c\Delta b} \right. = \left(\Delta b \left| \frac{\Delta a}{c} \right.\right)c$$

such that

$$\text{if } \left\lfloor \frac{c\Delta a}{c\Delta b} \right\rfloor = Q \quad \text{then} \quad \left\lfloor \frac{\Delta a}{\Delta b} \right\rfloor = Q$$

$$\text{and if } c\Delta b \left| \frac{c\Delta a}{c\Delta a} \right. = R \text{ then } \Delta b \left| \frac{\Delta a}{c} \right. = \left(\frac{1}{c}\right)R$$

where Q, R, and $\left(\frac{1}{c}\right)$ R are each integer.

Subsequent analysis makes use of the preceding relationships shown above. It is suggested that the analysis will be easier to follow if the reader is satisfied the noted ranges, recursions, and equalities are valid before proceeding. While the above quantities defined using ΔB apply to the standard first octant used for analysis, the actual run length slice algorithm itself will employ a standard first partial or arctan 0.5 octant in which the quantity $\nabla B = $ minimum $[\Delta B, (\Delta A - \Delta B)]$ is used in lieu of ΔB in calculating the above quantities Q, R, M, and N.

ANALYSIS

Consider a directed line segment starting at the origin (0,0) and terminating at an integer valued end point (ΔA, ΔB) which lies in the first octant of an overlaid rectangular coordinate grid mesh. The equation of this 'true' or 'continuous' line is:

$$b = (\Delta B \div \Delta A)\, a \qquad \text{where} \qquad \Delta A > \Delta B \geq 1$$
$$\text{with} \qquad \Delta A \text{ and } \Delta B \text{ both positive integers}$$

For an incremental or rastered representation of the line, it effectively can be shown that error, as measured along the normal distance from a grid mesh point to the true line, is minimized if one selects successive integer grid mesh point $(\ddot{A}, \ddot{B})$ as:

for each integer abscissa value $\qquad \ddot{A} = 0, 1, ..., \Delta A$

calculate a real ordinate value $\qquad \ddot{b} = (\Delta B \div \Delta A)\ddot{A}$

and select an associated integer valued ordinate $\ddot{B}$ as:

$$\text{either} \quad \ddot{B} = \lceil \ddot{b} \rceil \quad \text{if } \lceil \ddot{b} \rceil - \ddot{b} \leq 0.5$$

$$\text{(alternatively, if } \ddot{b} - \lfloor b \rfloor \geq 0.5)$$

$$\text{or} \quad \ddot{B} = \lfloor \ddot{b} \rfloor \quad \text{if } \lceil \ddot{b} \rceil - \ddot{b} \geq 0.5$$

$$\text{(alternatively, if } \ddot{b} - \lfloor \ddot{b} \rfloor \leq 0.5$$

where $\lceil \ddot{b} \rceil - \ddot{b} = 0.5 = \ddot{b} - \lfloor \ddot{b} \rfloor$ is an equal error or apparent 'don't care' case. The equal error condition initially will be defaulted here to $\ddot{B} = \lfloor \ddot{b} \rfloor$ which implies an axial step to resolve the mathematical ambiguity of rounding an exact half point.

The algorithm in [4,5], of course, does not use any multiplication or division to achieve the above effect. The algorithm to be described here will use a single division only in initialization; its repetitive loop will use only addition/subtraction and sign testing.

One can observe then that a diagonal move is required across those unit squares in which there lies an ordinate 'half point' value:

$$b = (1 + 2i) \div 2 \quad \text{where} \quad i = 0, 1, \ldots, (\Delta B - 1)$$

That is, whenever an ordinate half point lies in the unit square[1] having a lower left corner grid mesh point (A,B), a simultaneous

---

[1]When an ordinate half point falls on an integer abscissa, the unit square degenerates to a unit length vertical line whose midpoint is coincident with a point on the true line. The algorithm will provide for consistent processing of this equal error case. Our initial equal error default choice, as a consequence of the above lower left corner convention, specifies that the diagonal step will be taken across the unit square to the right of the unit length line thereby forcing an axial step to resolve the equal error ambiguity.

ordinate change from B to B + 1 in addition to the usual sequential abscissa change from A to A + 1 is required for the unit step. This suggests a means to calculate directly run lengths or constant direction slices and to use the smaller variable ΔB, rather than ΔA, as the stepping loop iteration count control.

Solving the alternate equation form of the line $a = (\Delta A \div \Delta B)b$ for those significant abscissa values a corresponding to half point ordinate values $b = (1 + 2i) \div 2$ yields:

$$a = [\Delta A(1 + 2i)] \div 2\Delta B \qquad i = 0, 1, \ldots, (\Delta B - 1)$$

such that the diagonal transition is across a unit square with lower left corner integer grid mesh point:

$$(\lfloor a \rfloor, \lfloor b \rfloor) = (A, B) = (A, i)$$

and, for consistency with an equal error (or $\lceil a \rceil = \lfloor a \rfloor = a$ case) default choice $B = \lfloor b \rfloor$, an upper right corner, not of simply ($\lceil a \rceil$, $\lceil b \rceil$), but of:

$$(\lfloor a \rfloor + 1, \lfloor b \rfloor + 1) = (A + 1, B + 1) = (A + 1, i + 1)$$

Intermediate abscissa or horizontal run lengths between these diagonal break points are thus from $(A_i + 1, i + 1)$ to $(A_{i+1}, i + 1)$ or a multiple unit, constant horizontal move of length

$$H_{i+1} = A_{i+1} - A_i - 1 \qquad \text{for } i = 0, 1, \ldots, (\Delta B - 2)$$

Ignoring initial and final horizontal runs for the moment, a look at the relation of successive abscissa break points leads to a simple algorithm for calculating intermediate run length slices. Using the notation defined earlier, the i-th lower left corner abscissa value A_i can be evaluated as:

$$A_i = \lfloor [\Delta A(1 + 2i)] \div 2\Delta B \rfloor = \lfloor (\Delta A \div 2\Delta B) + (i\Delta A \div \Delta B) \rfloor$$
$$A_i = \lfloor \{M + (N \div 2\Delta B)\} + \{iQ + (iR \div \Delta B)\} \rfloor$$
$$A_i = M + iQ + \lfloor (N + 2Ri) \div 2\Delta B \rfloor$$

The intermediate horizontal run lengths are then:

$$H_{i+1} = A_{i+1} - A_i - 1$$
$$H_{i+1} = \{M + (i + 1)Q + \lfloor [N + 2(i + 1)R] \div 2\Delta B \rfloor\} -$$
$$M + iQ + \lfloor (N + 2iR) \div 2\Delta B \rfloor\} - 1$$
$$H_{i+1} = Q + \lfloor [(N + 2iR) \div 2\Delta B] + 2R \div 2\Delta B \rfloor - \lfloor (N + 2iR) \div 2\Delta B \rfloor - 1$$
$$H_{i+1} = Q + \{S_i + \lfloor (T_i + 2R) \div 2\Delta B \rfloor\} - \{S_i + \lfloor T_i \div 2\Delta B \rfloor\} - 1$$
$$H_{i+1} = Q - 1 + \lfloor (T_i + 2R) \div 2\Delta B \rfloor$$

such that one arrives at the choice:

$$H_{i+1} = \begin{cases} Q & \text{if} \quad (T_i + 2R) \geq 2\Delta B \\ Q - 1 \,. & \text{if} \quad (T_i + 2R) < 2\Delta B \end{cases}$$

Letting $\nabla_{i+1} = T_i + 2R - 2\Delta B$, a decision scheme can be seen to be:

if $\nabla_i < 0$ use horizontal run length $H_i = Q - 1$ and update to
$$\nabla_{i+1} \leftarrow \nabla_i + 2R$$

or if $\nabla_i \geq 0$ use horizontal run length $H_i = Q$ and update to

$$\nabla_{i+1} \leftarrow \nabla_i + 2R - 2\Delta B$$

where the initial decision difference for intermediate runs is

$\nabla_1 = N + 2R - 2\Delta B$

Since movement starts from the origin (0,0), the initial horizontal run length is $H_0 = A_0$. Movement terminates not at the final diagonal transition but at $(\Delta A, \Delta B)$ hence the final horizontal run length is $H_{\Delta B} = \Delta A - A_{\Delta B - 1} - 1$. Diagonal runs of length two or more occur whenever one or more successive $H_i = 0$.

The initial horizontal run length is:

$$H_0 = A_0 = \lfloor \Delta A \div 2\Delta B \rfloor = \lfloor M + N \div 2\Delta B \rfloor = M + \lfloor N \div 2\Delta B \rfloor$$

$$H_0 = M$$

The terminal horizontal run length is calculated from:

$$A_{\Delta B - 1} = \lfloor [1 + 2(\Delta B - 1)]\Delta A \div 2\Delta B \rfloor = \lfloor \Delta A - (\Delta A \div 2\Delta B) \rfloor$$

$$A_{\Delta B - 1} = \lfloor \Delta A - [M + (N \div 2\Delta B)] \rfloor = (\Delta A - M) + \lfloor - (N \div 2\Delta B) \rfloor$$

such that

$$A_{\Delta B - 1} = \begin{cases} \Delta A - M & \text{if } N = 0 \\ \Delta A - M - 1 & \text{if } N \neq 0 \end{cases}$$

and since

$$H_{\Delta B} = \Delta A - A_{\Delta B - 1} - 1$$

one finds:

$$H_{\Delta B} = \begin{cases} M - 1 & \text{if } N = 0 \\ M & \text{if } N \neq 0 \end{cases}$$

Equal error default to an axial step is implicit in two aspects of the above first octant analysis:

1) Choosing to associate with $\nabla_i = 0$, an intermediate run length Q within the repetitive decision loop.

2) Choosing to associate with $N = 0$, a final run length $M - 1$ within the initialization.

EXTENDED ANALYSIS

Now for $N = 0$, one must have $\Delta A = 2M\Delta B$, where M is any positive integer. Therefore, if $N = 0$ one has $Q = 2M$, $R = 0$, and each $\nabla_i = -2\Delta B < 0$ so that the line is given by an initial run length pair $H_0 = M$, $D_0 = 1$ followed by $(\Delta B - 1)$ pairs of $H_i = 2M - 1$, $D_i = 1$ and terminated with the horizontal run $H_{\Delta B} = M - 1$.

The situation in which ΔA is an even multiple of ΔB is a special instance of the degenerate or equal error case in which some ordinate half points regularly fall precisely on an integer abscissa. If an equal error choice $B = \lceil b \rceil$ were used rather than the previous choice $B = \lfloor b \rfloor$, the initial and final horizontal runs would be interchanged such that $H_0 = M - 1$ and $H_{\Delta B} = M$ and the equal error default would be a diagonal step, rather than an axial step, in the first octant.

A choice therefore exists for coupling initial and terminal horizontal run lengths:

if $N = 0$ $\begin{cases} \text{either } H_0 = M - 1 & \text{and } H_{\Delta B} = M \\ \text{or} \quad H_0 = M & \text{and } H_{\Delta B} = M - 1 \end{cases}$

if $N \neq 0$ then $H_0 = M = H_{\Delta B}$

When ΔA is an odd multiple of ΔB, that is $\Delta A = (2M + 1)\Delta B$, one again has $R = 0$ hence the line can be shown to consist of an initial run length pair $H_0 = M$, $D_0 = 1$ followed by $(\Delta B - 1)$ pairs of $H_i = 2M$, $D_i = 1$ and a terminal single run $H_{\Delta B} = M$.

For $\Delta B < \Delta A < 2\Delta B$, the value of Q always is one, M is zero, and horizontal runs are constrained to lengths of one or zero. Since a zero length horizontal slice implies a diagonal run, output of the standard single diagonal move between horizontal slices could be deferred in this case to allow accumulation of diagonal run lengths until a horizontal run of length one is encountered. Step accumulation is contrary to our objective of direct calculation of runs so an alternate scheme is desirable. A complementary property between lines of $0°$ to arctan 0.5 inclination and lines of arctan 0.5 to $45°$ inclination provides the basis to calculate directly diagonal runs in the first octant. Only a trivial change to our previously developed approach will be needed if the equal error default is used to advantage as an apparent 'don't care' case.

In the first octant, a line from the origin to an end point $(\Delta A, \Delta B)$ has a complementary computational image in a counterpart line from the origin to a first octant end point $(\Delta A, \Delta A - \Delta B)$. For incremental vector generation, the approximation of the $(\Delta A, \Delta B)$ base line used successive integer values of $\ddot{A}$ to find

$$\ddot{b} = (\Delta B \div \Delta A)\ddot{A} \qquad \ddot{A} = 0, 1, \ldots, \Delta A$$

and applied the decision rule

$$\ddot{B} = \lceil \ddot{b} \rceil \quad \text{if} \quad \lceil \ddot{b} \rceil - \ddot{b} \leq 0.5 \qquad \text{or } \ddot{b} - \lfloor \ddot{b} \rfloor \geq 0.5$$

$$B = \lfloor b \rfloor \quad \text{if} \quad \lceil b \rceil - b \geq 0.5 \qquad \text{or } \ddot{b} - \lfloor \ddot{b} \rfloor \leq 0.5$$

For the $(\Delta A, \Delta A - \Delta B)$ complementary line, the same sequence of values of $\ddot{A}$ can be used to find:

$$\bar{b} = [(\Delta A - \Delta B) \div \Delta A]\ddot{A} = (1 - \Delta B \div \Delta A)\ddot{A} = \ddot{A} - \ddot{b}$$

Thus

$$\lceil \bar{b} \rceil = \lceil \ddot{A} - \ddot{b} \rceil = \ddot{A} - \lfloor \ddot{b} \rfloor$$

and one has

$$\lceil \bar{b} \rceil - \bar{b} = (\ddot{A} - \lfloor \ddot{b} \rfloor) - (\ddot{A} - \ddot{b}) = \ddot{b} - \lfloor \ddot{b} \rfloor$$

so that complementary ordinate $\bar{B}$ decisions can be made using base $\ddot{B}$ ordinate calculations and reversing the floor/ceiling choice as:

$$\bar{B} = \lceil \bar{b} \rceil \qquad \text{if} \qquad \ddot{B} = \lfloor \ddot{b} \rfloor$$

$$\bar{B} = \lfloor \bar{b} \rfloor \qquad \text{if} \qquad \ddot{B} = \lceil \ddot{b} \rceil$$

Base and complementary lines thus have a similar movement sequence. One only need reverse the role of diagonal and horizontal steps to obtain the complementary incremental step sequence from the base sequence calculations. Interchanging the role of diagonal and horizontal steps also interchanges the step choice for the equal error instance. Between 0 and arctan 0.5 degrees, the equal error default is an axial step; between arctan 0.5 degrees and 45 degrees, the equal error default is a diagonal step. That is, the equal error default is a step in the direction of the run length.

The algorithm statement will include a preliminary test to determine whether $\Delta A < 2\Delta B$. Whenever the test is true, the output sequence will be changed from H,D,...H, D, H to D, H,...D, H, D and the quantity $(\Delta A - \Delta B)$ will be used in lieu of ΔB for calculation. The same calculation scheme then provides direct determination of either diagonal or horizontal runs by normalizing calculations to a standard first partial octant. The algorithm statement therefore uses, in lieu of ΔB, the quantity $\nabla B = \text{minimum } [\Delta B, (\Delta A - \Delta B)]$.

While the above analysis provides a minimum error incremental line in the first octant, the real criteria applied to the ambiguity of the equal error case was that of convenience. For the general line, additional information can be applied to refine the arbitrary choice. As described by Boothroyd & Hamilton [3], one can use original half plane knowledge to bias the initial decision variable to generate re-traceable lines by:

$$\nabla_1 \longleftarrow \begin{cases} \nabla_1 & \text{if} \quad \Delta Y \geq 0 \\ \nabla_1 - 1 & \text{if} \quad \Delta Y < 0 \end{cases}$$

ALGORITHM

Given an integer starting point (x_s, y_s) and an integer terminating point (x_t, y_t), the following algorithm will calculate run lengths or slices of constant direction movement to increment a rastered line from (x_s, y_s) to (x_t, y_t) under the constraint that unit steps are restricted to those eight axial/diagonal moves in which the abscissa and/or ordinate positions change only by 1, 0, or -1 per step.

Half Octant Normalization

Normalize the directed line segment to a standard first partial octant, zero origin form.

1. $\Delta x \leftarrow x_t - x_s$ abscissa displacement

    $\Delta y \leftarrow y_t - y_s$ ordinate displacement

    $\Delta A \leftarrow \text{maximum} \quad \{|\Delta x|, |\Delta y|\}$ octant abscissa

$$\Delta B \leftarrow \text{minimum} \quad \{|\Delta x|, |\Delta y|\} \qquad \text{full octant ordinate}$$

$$\nabla B \leftarrow \text{minimum} \quad \{\Delta B, (\Delta A - \Delta B)\} \qquad \text{partial octant ordinate}$$

Determine true display incremental directions $(m_1 = m_{11}, m_{12})$ and $(m_2 = m_{21}, m_{22})$ which correspond to normalized full first octant diagonal and axial unit steps, then re-order as appropriate for pseudo-axial, pseudo-diagonal partial octant movement pairs $(s_1 = s_{11}, s_{12})$ and $(s_2 = s_{21}, s_{22})$.

2.

$$m_{21} \leftarrow \begin{cases} 1 & \text{if } \Delta x \geq 0 \\ -1 & \text{if } \Delta x < 0 \end{cases}$$

$$m_{22} \leftarrow \begin{cases} 1 & \text{if } \Delta y \geq 0 \\ -1 & \text{if } \Delta y < 0 \end{cases}$$

$$m_{11} \leftarrow \begin{cases} m_{21} & \text{if } |\Delta x| \geq |\Delta y| \\ 0 & \text{if } |\Delta x| < |\Delta y| \end{cases}$$

$$m_{12} \leftarrow \begin{cases} 0 & \text{if } |\Delta x| \geq |\Delta y| \\ m_{22} & \text{if } |\Delta x| < |\Delta y| \end{cases}$$

3.   If $\Delta A > 2\nabla B$; or if $\Delta A = 2\nabla B$ and $\Delta y \geq 0$ then partial octant directions for the alternating move sequence are

$$s_1 = (s_{11}, s_{12}) = (m_{11}, m_{12})$$
$$s_2 = (s_{21}, s_{22}) = (m_{21}, m_{22})$$

Otherwise if $\Delta A < 2\nabla B$; or if $\Delta A = 2\nabla B$ and $\Delta y < 0$, then half octant directions for the alternating move sequence are

$$s_1 = (s_{11}, s_{12}) = (m_{21}, m_{22})$$
$$s_2 = (s_{21}, s_{22}) = (m_{11}, m_{12})$$

where s_1 is the run length direction for pseudo-axial increments

s_2 is the single step direction for a pseudo-diagonal increment

Provisionally specify $H_{\tau B}$ to accommodate the degenerate cases of movement solely in an axial or diagonal direction.

4. $H_{\tau B} \longleftarrow \Delta A$

$$\text{Go To: } \begin{cases} \text{Termination } \#13 & \text{if } \nabla B = 0 \\ \text{Parameters } \#5 & \text{if } \nabla B \neq 0 \end{cases}$$

Parameters

Calculate parameters for repetitive run length generation loop.

5. $Q \leftarrow \lfloor \Delta A \div \nabla B \rfloor$ floor of $\Delta A \div \nabla B$ and intermediate run length when $\nabla \geq 0$

$R \leftarrow \nabla B \mid \Delta A$ residue of ΔA modulo ∇B

$$M \leftarrow \lfloor Q \div 2 \rfloor$$

floor of $\Delta A \div 2\nabla B$ and initial and terminal run length when ΔA is not an even multiple of ∇B

$$N \leftarrow \begin{cases} R & \text{if } Q \text{ even} \\ & \text{residue of } \Delta A \text{ modulo } 2\nabla B \\ R + \nabla B & \text{if } Q \text{ odd} \end{cases}$$

$$H_0 \leftarrow \begin{cases} M & \text{if } \Delta y \geq 0 \text{ or } N \neq 0 \\ M - 1 & \text{if } \Delta y < 0 \text{ and } N = 0 \end{cases}$$

$$H_{\nabla B} \leftarrow \begin{cases} M & \text{if } \Delta y < 0 \text{ or } N \neq 0 \\ M - 1 & \text{if } \Delta y \geq 0 \text{ and } N = 0 \end{cases}$$

$$\text{COUNT} \leftarrow \nabla B$$

As described by Boothroyd and Hamilton [3], bias the initial decision variable to generate retractable lines:

$$\nabla_1 \leftarrow \begin{cases} N + 2R - 2\nabla B & \text{if } \Delta y \geq 0 \\ N + 2R - 2\nabla B - 1 & \text{if } \Delta y < 0 \end{cases}$$

Initial Run Length

Output initial run length pair. First run of length H_0 is in direction given by $s_1 = (s_{11}, s_{12})$. The single step D of length one is in direction given by $s_2 = (s_{21}, s_{22})$.

6. Output $H \leftarrow H_0$ steps in direction s_1,
    $D \leftarrow 1$ step in direction s_2

Intermediate Run Length Loop

Select appropriate run and output successive intermediate run length pairs associated with movement directions given by s_1 and s_2.

7.   COUNT $\leftarrow$ COUNT $-$ 1

8.   Go To: $\begin{cases} \text{Termination \#13} & \text{if COUNT} \leq 0 \\ \text{Intermediate Run Length Loop \#9} \end{cases}$

                                                    if COUNT >0

9. $H_i \longleftarrow \begin{cases} Q - 1 & \text{if } \nabla_i < 0 \\ Q & \text{if } \nabla_i \geq 0 \end{cases}$

10.   Output H $\leftarrow$ H_i steps in direction s_1,
                D $\leftarrow$ 1 step in direction s_2

11. $\nabla_{i+1} \leftarrow \nabla_i + \begin{cases} 2R & \text{if } \nabla_i < 0 \\ 2R - 2\nabla B & \text{if } \nabla_i \geq 0 \end{cases}$

12.   Go To: Intermediate Run Length Loop #7

Termination

Output final single run length in direction s_1, $= (s_{11}, s_{12})$.

13.   Output H $\leftarrow$ $H_{\nabla B}$ in direction s_1

14.   Terminate

OBSERVATIONS

Though not used in the algorithm itself, some final observations may be worth noting. When ΔA is an integer multiple of either ΔB or $(\Delta A - \Delta B)$, that is $\Delta A = Q \nabla B$, the slice sequence is quite simple. If Q is even (i.e., $Q = 2M$, $R = 0$, $N = 0$) then the line consists of an initial run length pair

$$H_0 = M, D_0 = 1$$

followed by $(\nabla B - 1)$ pairs of

$$H_i = Q - 1, D_i = 1$$

and a terminal single run

$$H_{\Gamma B} = M - 1$$

where H_0 and $H_{\Gamma B}$ can be interchanged if desired. If Q is odd (i.e., $Q = 1 + 2M$, $R = 0$, $N \neq 0$) then the line consists of an initial run length pair

$$H_0 = M, D_0 = 1$$

followed by $(\nabla B - 1)$ pairs of

$$H_i = Q - 1, D_i = 1$$

and a terminal single run of
$$H_{\nabla B} = M$$

As can be demonstrated by solving $\nabla_1 = \nabla_{i+1}$ for i

i.e., $N = \dfrac{1}{2\nabla B}\,\Big|\ (N + 2iR)$

lines for which $R \neq 0$ also exhibit a repetitive cycling in their sequence

$$H_1 \ \ldots \ H_i \ \ldots \ H_{\nabla B - 1}$$

of intermediate run lengths. If $R \neq 0$, and c is the largest common factor of R and ∇B, and $\nabla b = \nabla B \div c$, then the intermediate sequence of $(\nabla B - 1)$ terms has the form

$(c - 1)$ cyclic repetitions of $\quad H_1 \ \ldots \ H_{\nabla b}$
followed by the partial cycle $H_1 \ \ldots \ H_{\nabla b - 1}$

Initial and terminal runs are $H_0 = M$ and $H_{\nabla B} = M$. As c is the largest common factor of ΔA and ∇B, it could be determined from these two larger quantities if more convenient.

Magnification or zooming by a positive integer scaling factor, say Z, amounts to little more than introducing the factor into both ΔA and ΔB. The basic slice parameters Q and M therefore are unchanged by such scaling. The 'scaled' initial and terminal slices, H_0 and $H_{Z\Delta B}$, will be the same as the 'unscaled' $\overline{H}_0$ and $\overline{H}_{\nabla B}$. The sequence of intermediate slices, H_i where $1 \leq i \leq Z\nabla B - 1$, can be formed easily from the original unscaled $\overline{H}_i$, where $1 \leq i \leq \nabla B - 1$, sequence when $\Delta A \neq 0$ or $\Delta B \neq 0$ or $\Delta A \neq \Delta B$. To generate the scaled intermediate sequence one need only append a rightmost term

$$\ddot{H}_{\overline{\nabla b}} = \begin{cases} Q & \text{if } R \neq 0 \text{ and } 0 = 2|Q \\ Q-1 & \text{if } R = 0 \text{ or } 1 = 2|Q \end{cases} = \overline{H}_0 + \overline{H}_{\nabla B}$$

and cyclically repeat the sequence

$$\overline{H}_1,\ldots,\overline{H}_i,\ldots,\overline{H}_{\nabla B-1},\ddot{H}_{\nabla b}$$

until $Z\nabla B - 1$ terms are generated. The scaled slice sequence is thus

$$\overline{H}_0, \quad \begin{cases} (Z-1) \text{ repetitions of } [\overline{H}_1...\ddot{H}_{\nabla b}] \\ \text{followed by the partial} \\ \text{cycle } [\overline{H}_1...\overline{H}_{\nabla B-1}] \end{cases} , H_{\nabla B}$$

First level patterns of repeated subsequences of Q or repeated subsequences of $(Q-1)$ within cycles can be observed by considering an approach something like:

Let $\delta_1 = (N + 2R - 2\nabla B) \div c$ and $r = R \div c$

If $\delta_j < 0$ and $J = \lceil -\delta_j \div 2r \rceil$

then there are J repetitions of the run length $(Q-1)$

and

$$\delta_{j+1} = 2rJ + \delta_j = (2r) \mid \{2r - [(2r) \mid (-\delta_j)]\}$$

If $\delta_j \geq 0$ and $J = 1 + \lfloor \delta_j \div 2(k-r) \rfloor$

then there are J repetitions of the run length Q

and

$$\delta_{j+1} = J(2r - 2k) + \delta_j = (2r - 2k) + [(2k - 2r) \mid \delta_j]$$

With appropriate terminal conditions, the above could be used iteratively to calculate patterns within the basic cycle period. While the indicated division by c is superfluous so far as subsequence determination is concerned, it is shown to reflect the fact that one always can use the values of ΔA and ∇B divided by their common factor to reduce the magnitude of variables processed.

Since run length selection amounts to a binary choice either of Q or $(Q - 1)$ for intermediate slices and of M or $(M - 1)$ for initial/terminal slices, one also could consider a line encoding using a sequence of 0's and 1's prefaced with a control packet specifying starting (x_s, y_s) coordinate, true S_1, S_2 direction codes, and basic run length determinant Q which could be shifted to obtain M. Additionally, the 'diagonal' D step could be implied rather than explicitly carried in the encoding.

Compaction algorithms are beyond the scope of this paper. Earnshaw [11,12] has published an interesting compaction study based upon encoding repeated code sequences of unit steps. His approach essentially folds the line into cycles around the first integer coordinate point pair through which the true line passes. Data from sample pictures indicate significant compression results can be realized from his technique. Compaction algorithms also are treated in [7].

Equal error anomalies are not the subject of this paper. The algorithm described defaults the equal error choice to a pseudo-axial or run length direction s_1 in the upper half plane and to a pseudo-diagonal or non-run length direction s_2 in the lower half plane. The effect is to produce retraceable lines.

RELATED TREATMENTS

Run length properties of incremental or "quantized" lines have been treated in a different fashion by authors with a picture pro-cessing orientation. To the best of the author's knowledge, H. Freeman [13,14] first published the observation that evenly spaced, run length slices must be present in any incremental line. He specified that only two directions (relative zero and forty-five degree steps in the first octant case) are required for a line, that appearances of one directional step would occur singly in the seg-ment's sequence and that these several singleton occurrences must be as uniformly spaced as possible among multiple unit runs of the remaining directional step. Reggiori [23], working with Freeman at

NYU, first published a run length algorithm, described a good encoded run length compaction scheme, and noted the effect of variable equal error choices[2] within a line.

As part of a paper concerning the chord length property of incremental lines, A. Rosenfeld [24] demonstrated that the multi-unit runs, exclusive of the beginning and end of a segment, would be constrained to two lengths which are consecutive integers, and in fact that the Freeman properties rigorously follow as a consequence of the chord length property.

---

[2]If an inconsistent equal error default choice is permitted within a line segment, one can create contrived anomalous chain encodings or incremental approximations of a straight line segment which strictly meet both the minimum error criteria and the chord length property, yet do not exhibit the consecutive integer run property. For example, a line from (0,0) to (16,4) has 16 possible distinct minimum error representations from which encodings could be chosen as:

	0100001001000100	'random default'
or	0100001001000010	'alternating default'

These two choices have run lengths of 2,3 and 4 or only 2 and 4 while a consistent rounding up or down for exact half points would encode with only a run length of 3 as:

	0100010001000100	'ceiling or diagonal default'
or	0010001000100010	'floor or axial default'

and hence be compatible with the Freeman conditions. The case, of course, relies upon extending the special 'single vertical rise', 'even horizontal displacement' line segment beyond its 'fundamental' period. Many analyses presuppose an irreducible slope, or single period, which here properly would require (0,0) to (4,1) to be the basic line segment and implicit consistency to be forced by the consequent limitation of exercise of the equal error default instance to a single opportunity.

Starting from the above three properties Freeman attributed to incremental lines, R. Brons [8] has published an iterative construction scheme for macro-determination of a movement string representing a straight line. His structural technique avoids the step by step conditional generation of an incremental line and successively refines the entire sequence for the line as a whole by dealing with nested periods of repeated subsequences within the chain encoding of a line. C. Arcelli and A. Massarotti [1] give a modification of the Brons algorithm and demonstrate that the Brons algorithm possesses the chord property addressed by Rosenfeld. These two picture processing approaches based upon the Freeman properties provide a structural chain encoding for a general line segment but do not treat explicitly a quantified error measure for closeness of fit such as specified in [4,5,19,20] for a specific line segment. The constructed chains or incremental movement sequences from the macro-structure approach can provide a least squares approximation if the sequence is rotated to account for the origin of a specific line segment having the identical irreducible rational fraction slope. Cederberg [9] describes run lengths from the macro-structure view and, as well, provides the rotation procedure to match a specific line. Cederberg also provides a good analysis and representation of the cyclic pattern nesting effect.

The Brons, Arcelli, and Massorotti structural construction, which is origin independent, gives the encoded chain (with 0 representing a zero degree step and 1 representing a forty-five degree step) for a line from (0,0) to (39,14) as:

00100100100101001001001001010010 0100101

while the minimum error distance incremental line for this integer end point line segment is:

0100101   00100100100101001001001001010010

where the blank spaces are inserted only for later reference purposes.

Beginning the above Brons sequence for a 14/39 slope line at the blank space and concatenating those elements originally to the left of the blank space of course will produce a match with the zero origin, minimum error instance. Conversely, beginning the latter at its indicated space and concatenating those elements originally to the left accommodates the begin/end segment split of a full run length (i.e. the sum of H_0 plus $H_{\nabla B}$ always is equal to either Q or Q − 1) and produces a match with the general structure of the Brons sequence which accounts only for slope and disregards specific origin. In his comments on properties of ambiguous chains, Reggiori notes that, $(H_0 + H_{\nabla B}) = $ either Q or (Q − 1). Cederberg includes the requisite concatenation adjustment for a specific line in his paper.

The essential point of either a picture processing or graphics approach is that the 'chain encoding' or 'digital arc' or 'lattice specification' or 'incremental approximation' of a straight line has a periodicity structure dependent only upon the true line's slope and that origin and consistent equal error default choice merely affect only the full period's specific concatenation. As a consequence, line translation on a superimposed grid can be seen to have no effect on the line's fundamental structure while rotation of the line alters its slope and hence can impact its underlying lattice approximation.

The various concatenations recognized by the picture processing structural approach provide for the finite number of discrete representations of the infinite number of parallel line segments having end points which needn't necessarily coincide with integer lattice points. Line segments longer or shorter than the fundamental full period of a fixed, irreducible rational fraction slope line will involve a truncated period from the appropriate concatenation selected for a given line segment origin relative to the superimposed lattice grid. For instance, the following line segments each have the same fundamental structure in a properly rastered representation:

start	end
(0, 0)	(39, 14)
(3.9, 1.4)	(7.8, 2.8)
(19.5, 7)	(117, 42)

One can note that incremental structure of the line segment from (3, 0.375) to (13, 1.625) is altered if start and end points are first rounded to integers, then displayed. If window boundary clipping or thickened line clipping is processed as intersection calculation followed by rounding to integer coordinates for subsequent display, such alterations will be commonplace.

Rosenfeld [24] also mentions in passing a point which should be considered by hardware and software implementors. "A digitized line segment need not be the digitization of the line segment between any two of its own points. Thus a digital picture can contain digitized line segments that are not digitizations of the line

segments joining any two points on the picture itself.'' For instance, a proper digital or rastered representation of the line segment from (1, 0.125) to (7, 0.875) will select points none of which
are on the underlying true line itself. If a raster display device provides automatic incremental line generation only for line segments
between its addressable lattice or grid points, then software support optionally may still need to generate lines as incremental
steps, rather than rely solely on the hardware line generator when
extreme accuracy or fidelity is desired. For some applications, the
error introduced by constraining line end points to integer lattice
points may be below the noise level with respect to that inherent in
the discreteness of the raster grid. In other instances though, a
user may wish to have the flexibility to maintain explicit control of
digitization inaccuracy and rely upon program generation of individual step sequences.

Raster display devices likely should accept both absolute end
points and relative specification (i.e. absolute lattice point addressing, relative integer displacement addressing, and relative string
encoded incremental or chain addressing) of lines while supporting
software should have provision to generate the alternatives. One
way to provide full flexibility would be to separate initialization
from the repetitive loop. That is, allow user preemption of algorithm
procedure steps 1-5 and provide user direct access to algorithm
procedure steps 6, 7 and 13 in addition to user direct access to
algorithm procedure step 1. For equal error control, one would provide a means for user preemption of algorithm procedure steps 2, 3
and 5.

Clip windows and subpixel coordinate specification are distinct but related topics. A full treatment is beyond the scope of this paper. A few artificially simple examples can illustrate an aspect of their relation to questions of picture fidelity. As operations such as BIT-BLIT implicitly encourage application focus on single pel accuracy, such questions likely may become of more than passing academic interest.

Consider the line $Y = 0.125X$ as a base case. Assume a 1:1 mapping of application or world coordinates to screen space and permit screen clip windows to provide multiple viewing windows for display of concurrent applications. Note that true point pairs on the line $Y = (1/8)X$ include:

      (0, 0)   to (32, 4)
      (3, 0.375) to (13, 1.625)
      (5, 0.625) to (32, 4)

Retraceability can be illustrated by drawing the unclipped line from (0, 0) to (32, 4) then EXOR (exclusive OR) the line from (32, 4) to (0, 0). The Boothroyd/Hamilton initial error bias can guarantee selection of identical pels drawing the line from either end as a starting point.

Now introduce a screen clip window bounded by $Y = 0$, $Y = 4$, $X = 0$, $X = 32$ inclusively. Potential perturbations from clipping can be illustrated on a clear screen by drawing the line from (0, 0) to (32, 4). Let a second application temporarily pre-empt and upon completion leave clear a screen partition bounded by $Y = 0$, $Y = 2$, $X = 0$, $X = 5$ inclusively. One view of efficient processing can be to restore the original application's full partition by then re-drawing only that portion of the original picture which was corrupted by the temporary, overlapping window. Clipping calculations should yield the line segment from (0, 0) to (5, 0.625). Assuming a line generator constrained to only integer end points, one draws the line from (0, 0) to (5, 1). Having now restored the original line in its full partition, EXOR the full line from (0, 0) to (32, 4). Do you have a few specious pels left in screen space rather than a completely empty space?

Now assume a clear screen and draw the line from (0, 0) to (32, 4). Let picture coordinates permit subpixel positioning but use a line generator constrained to only integer end points. In EXOR logic draw the portion of the line specified in subpixel coordinates from (3, 0.375) to (13, 1.625). Note that the drawn integer line from (3, 0) to (13, 2) does not match pel for pel the true line $Y = (1/8)X$. Is retraceability meant to include only the ability to draw pel for pel a line starting from either end point or, with subpixel input coordinates permitted, does retraceability include the ability to draw pel for pel intermediate segments of a longer line?

Another example can be seen by drawing the line from (0, 0) to (1023, 1). One would expect on a full 1024 by 1024 pel screen to see two horizontal runs:

from (0, 0) to (0, 511) and from (512, 1) to (1023, 1)

Now set a clip window bounded by $Y = 1$, $Y = 1023$, $X = 0$, $X = 1023$ inclusively, clip the line from (0, 0) to (1023, 1), and draw the result of your clipping. Did you draw the run from (512, 1) to (1023, 1) or did you draw only the single point at (1023, 1)?

If double width lines were to be drawn by, say, drawing the original line then, for first octant lines, decrementing the original line's Y.coordinate by one and redrawing the translated line, clipping without consideration of the line's run length slice structure could pose problems whenever the translated line has a portion outside the clip window. Try drawing a wide line from (0, 0) to (1023, 1) in a clip window which precludes negative coordinates. (The second line is from (0, −1) to (1023, 0); what does your clipping convention draw?) Could you contain such instances by clipping to half point boundary lines or by manipulating runs?

ACKNOWLEDGEMENTS

The contributions of Messrs. J. Pi, D. Grice and L. Zimmerman gratefully are acknowledged. Helpful as well were various discussions with Messrs. R. Bowater, M. Davis, R. Earnshaw, A.C. Gay, K. Hesse, M. Pitteway, Ms. N. Bull, and Ms. A. Castle.

REFERENCES

1. **C. Arcelli, and A. Massarotti,** On the parallel generation of straight digital lines. Computer Graphics and Image Processing **7** (No. 1), 67-83 (February 1978).

2. **K. Belser,** Comment on 'An improved algorithm for the generation of non-parametric curves'. IEEE Transactions Computers **C-25 1,** 103 (January 1976).

3. **J. Boothroyd and P. A. Hamilton,** Exactly reversible plotter paths. Australian Computer Journal **2** (No. 1), 20-21 (1970).

4. **J. E. Bresenham,** An incremental algorithm for digital plotting. ACM National Conference (August 1963).

5. **J. E. Bresenham,** Algorithm for computer control of a digital plotter. IBM Systems Journal **4** (No. 1), 25-30 (January 1965).

6. **J. E. Bresenham, D. G. Grice and S. C. Pi,** Run length slices for incremental lines. IBM Technical Disclosure Bulletin **22-8B,** 3744-3747 (January 1980).

7. **J. E. Bresenham,** Incremental Line Compaction: The Computer Journal **2** (No. 1) 116-120 (February 1982).

8. **R. Brons,** Linguistic methods for the description of a straight line on a grid. Computer Graphics and Image Processing **3** (No. 1), 48-62 (March 1974).

9. **Roger L. T. Cederberg,** A new method for vector generation: Computer Graphics and Image Processing **9** (No. 2), 183-195 (February 1979).

10. **Coueignoux and R. Guedj,** Computer generation of colored planer patterns on TV-like rasters. Proceedings of the IEEE **68** (No. 7) 909-922 (July 1980).

11. **R. A. Earnshaw,** Line tracking for incremental plotters. The Computer Journal **23** (No. 1), 46-52 (February 1980).

12. **R. A. Earnshaw,** Line generation for incremental and raster devices. Computer Graphics **11** (No. 2), 199-205 (Summer 1977 — SIGGRAPH '77 Proceedings).

13. **H. Freeman,** Boundary encoding and processing in Picture Processing and Psychopictorics, ed. by B. S. Lipkin and A. Rosenfeld, pp. 241-266. Academic Press, New York (1970).

14. **H. Freeman,** On the encoding of arbitrary geometric configurations. IRE Trans. EC-102, 260-268 (June 1961).

15. **M. D. Gibbs,** Angled vector generator program: IBM Technical Disclosure Bulletin **21** (No. 5), 2041-2044 (October 1978).

16. **L. Gilman and A. J. Rose,** APL An Interactive Approach. John Wiley and Sons, New York (1974).

17. **S. K. Hoo,** Accelerated Bresenham algorithm. IBM Technical Disclosure Bulletin **18** (No. 4), 1075-1077 (September 1975).

18. **K. E. Iverson,** A programming language, p. 12. John Wiley & Sons, Inc., New York (1962).

19. **B. W. Jordan, W. J. Lennon and B. C. Holm,** An improved algorithm for the generation of non-parametric curves: IEEE Transactions Computers **C-22** (No. 12), pp. 1052-1060 (December 1973).

20. **M. L. V. Pitteway,** Algorithm for drawing elipses or hyperbolae with a digital plotter. The Computer Journal **10** (No. 3), 282-289 (November 1967).

21. **M. L. V. Pitteway,** Bresenham's algorithm with run line coding shortcut. The Computer Journal **25** (No. 1) 113-115 (February 1982).

22. **J. Ramot,** Non-parametric curves. IEEE Transactions Computers **C-25** (No. 1), 103-104 (January 1976).

23. **G. B. Reggiori,** Digital computer transformations for irregular line drawings, pp. 46-61. Technical Report 403-22, New York University (April 1972). Available from US Department of Commerce as AD-745-015.

24. **A. Rosenfeld,** Digital straight line segments. IEEE Transactions Computers **C-23 12**, 1264-1269 (December 1974).

25. **F. Rubin,** Generation of non-parametric curves. IEEE Transactions Computers **C-25, 1,** 103 (January 1976).

26. **R. F. Sproull,** Using program transformations to Derive Line Drawing Algorithms: Transactions on Graphics **1** (No. 4) 259-273 (1982).

RUN LENGTH SLICE STRATEGY

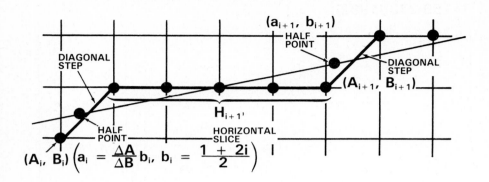

FIND 'HALF POINT' UNIT SQUARES — DIAGONAL TRANSITIONS —

BY SOLVING ALTERNATE EQUATION FORM

$$a_i = \frac{\Delta A}{\Delta B} b_i \qquad \text{where } b_i = \frac{1 + 2i}{2}$$

$$\text{and } i = 0, 1, ..., (\Delta B - 1)$$

DETERMINE LOWER LEFT CORNER COORDINATES

$$(\lfloor a_i \rfloor, \lfloor b_i \rfloor) = (A_i, i)$$

AND UPPER RIGHT CORNER COORDINATES

$$(\lfloor a_i \rfloor + 1, \lceil b_i \rceil) = (A_i + 1, i + 1)$$

HORIZONTAL RUN LENGTH BETWEEN TWO SUCCESSIVE 'HALF POINT' UNIT SQUARES

$$H_{i+1} = A_{i+1} - (A_i + 1) = A_{i+1} - A_i - 1$$

INTERMEDIATE HORIZONTAL RUNS ONLY TWO LENGTHS

$$Q = \left\lfloor \frac{\Delta A}{\Delta B} \right\rfloor$$

$$(Q - 1) = \left\lfloor \frac{\Delta A}{\Delta B} \right\rfloor - 1$$

'HALF POINT' RATIONALE

$$b_i = \frac{1 + 2i}{2} \qquad i = 0, 1, ..., (\Delta B - 1)$$

LIES WITHIN UNIT SQUARE

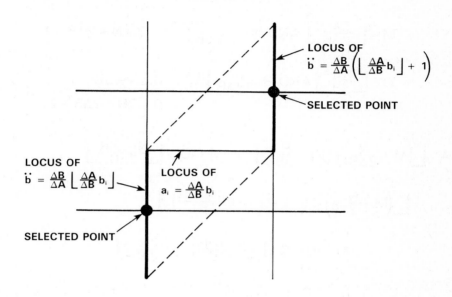

LOCUS OF
$$\ddot{b} = \frac{\Delta B}{\Delta A}\left(\left\lfloor \frac{\Delta A}{\Delta B} b_i \right\rfloor + 1\right)$$

SELECTED POINT

LOCUS OF
$$\ddot{b} = \frac{\Delta B}{\Delta A}\left\lfloor \frac{\Delta A}{\Delta B} b_i \right\rfloor$$

LOCUS OF
$$a_i = \frac{\Delta A}{\Delta B} b_i$$

SELECTED POINT

CONSIDER 'HALF POINT' UNIT SQUARE CONTAINING

$$b_i = \frac{1 + 2i}{2} \qquad i = 0, 1, ..., (\Delta B - 1)$$

SUCH THAT $a_i = \dfrac{\Delta A}{\Delta B} b_i = \dfrac{\Delta A}{\Delta B}\left(\dfrac{1 + 2i}{2}\right) \neq$ INTEGER

IN FIRST OCTANT CASE ONE MUST HAVE

$$\lfloor b_i \rfloor + 0.5 > \left[\frac{\Delta B}{\Delta A}\lfloor a_i \rfloor = \ddot{b}_j\right] > \lfloor b_i \rfloor - 0.5$$

HENCE $\hat{b}_j = \lfloor b_i \rfloor$

$$\lceil b_i \rceil + 0.5 > \left[\frac{\Delta B}{\Delta A}\lceil a_i \rceil = \ddot{b}_{j+1}\right] > \lceil b_i \rceil - 0.5$$

HENCE $\ddot{b}_{j+1} = \lceil b_i \rceil = (\lfloor b_i \rfloor + 1)$

TRANSITION FOR 'HALF POINT' UNIT SQUARE MUST BE A
DIAGONAL INCREMENT

DECOMPOSE 'HALF POINT' CORNERS

$$A_i = \left\lfloor \frac{\Delta A}{\Delta B} b_i \right\rfloor = \left\lfloor \frac{\Delta A}{\Delta B} \left(\frac{1 + 2i}{2} \right) \right\rfloor = \left\lfloor \frac{\Delta A}{2\Delta B} + i\frac{\Delta A}{\Delta B} \right\rfloor$$

LET $\quad M = \left\lfloor \frac{\Delta A}{2\Delta B} \right\rfloor$ AND $N = {}_{2\Delta B}\big|^{\Delta A} \quad 0 \le N \le 2\Delta B - 1$

$\qquad Q = \left\lfloor \frac{\Delta A}{\Delta B} \right\rfloor$ AND $R = {}_{\Delta B}\big|^{\Delta A} \quad 0 \le R \le \Delta B - 1$

$\qquad\qquad\qquad\qquad\qquad\qquad\qquad 0 \le 2R \le 2\Delta B - 2$

$$A_i = \left\lfloor \left(M + \frac{N}{2\Delta B} \right) + \left(iQ + \frac{iR}{\Delta B} \right) \right\rfloor = M + iQ + \left\lfloor \frac{N + 2iR}{2\Delta B} \right\rfloor$$

$$A_{i+1} = \left\lfloor \left(M + \frac{N}{2\Delta B} \right) + (i + 1) Q + \frac{(i + 1)R}{\Delta B} \right\rfloor =$$

$$M + iQ + Q + \left\lfloor \left(\frac{N + 2iR}{2\Delta B} \right) + \frac{2R}{2\Delta B} \right\rfloor$$

LET $\quad S_i = \left\lfloor \frac{N + 2iR}{2\Delta B} \right\rfloor$ AND $T_i = {}_{2\Delta B}\big|^{(N + 2iR)} \; 0 \le T_i \le 2\Delta B - 1$

$\qquad$ SUCH THAT $\quad 0 \le T_i + 2R \le 4\Delta B - 3$ AND $0 \le \left\lfloor \frac{T_i + 2R}{2\Delta B} \right\rfloor \le 1$

$\qquad\qquad$ AND NOTE $\quad T_{i+1} = \begin{cases} T_i + 2R & \text{IF } T_i \; 2R < 2\Delta B \\ T_i + 2R - 2\Delta B & \text{IF } T_i + 2R \ge 2\Delta B \end{cases}$

$$A_i = M + iQ + S_i + \left\lfloor \frac{T_i}{2\Delta B} \right\rfloor = M + iQ + S_i$$

$$A_{i+1} = M + iQ + Q + S_i + \left\lfloor \frac{T_i + 2R}{2\Delta B} \right\rfloor = M + iQ + S_i + Q + \begin{cases} 0 \\ 1 \end{cases}$$

$$H_{i+1} = A_{i+1} - A_i - 1 = \begin{cases} Q - 1 & \text{IF } T_i + 2R < 2\Delta B \\ Q & \text{IF } T_i + 2R \ge 2\Delta B \end{cases}$$

SINGLE STEP ALGORITHM

START FROM P_0 (0,0)

HENCE $a_0 = 0$ $\hat{b}_0 = 0$
  $\nabla_1 = (2\Delta B)\, a_0 - (2\Delta A)\, \hat{b}_0 + (2\Delta B - \Delta A)$
  $\nabla_1 = 2\Delta B - \Delta A$
  COUNT $= \Delta A$
  move M1 $= (1,0)$ axial
  move M2 $= (1,1)$ diagonal

① **IF COUNT ≤ 0 : TERMINATE**

② **IF $\nabla_i \geq 0$: DIAGONAL STEP**
        & $\nabla_{i+1} \leftarrow \nabla_i + (2\Delta B - 2\Delta A)$
  IF $\nabla_i \leq 0$: HORIZONTAL STEP
        & $\nabla_{i+1} \leftarrow \nabla_i + 2\Delta B$

③ **COUNT $\leftarrow$ COUNT -1**
        & RETURN TO ①

NOTE $(2\Delta B - 2\Delta A)$ & $2\Delta B$ ARE SIMPLY
    CONSTANTS WHICH CAN BE SET
    OUTSIDE OF LOOP

SLICE ALGORITHM

— INITIALIZATION —

DETERMINE ΔA, ΔB, 'H', 'D' AS IN SINGLE STEP

SELECT $\nabla B \leftarrow$ MINIMUM $\{ \Delta B, (\Delta A - \Delta B) \}$

ESTABLISH ALTERNATING MOVE SEQUENCE

$$S = \begin{cases} s_1\text{: axial } s_2\text{: diagonal} & \text{if } \nabla B = \Delta B \\ s_1\text{: diagonal } s_2\text{: axial} & \text{otherwise} \end{cases}$$

TEMPORARILY PROVIDE SPECIAL CASE ESCAPE

$H_{\nabla B} \leftarrow \Delta A$

IF $\nabla B = 0$: GO TO FINAL OUTPUT

SLICE ALGORITHM

— PARAMETER —

CALCULATE REGULAR CASE PARAMETERS

$$Q \leftarrow \left\lfloor \frac{\Delta A}{\nabla B} \right\rfloor \quad R \leftarrow {}_{\nabla B}\big|^{\Delta A}$$

INTEGER ÷ WITH REMAINDER BINARY, TRUNCATED RIGHT SHIFT

$$H_0 \leftarrow M \leftarrow \lfloor Q \div 2 \rfloor$$

$$N \leftarrow \begin{cases} R & \text{IF Q EVEN NO UNDERFLOW:} \\ & \text{RIGHT SHIFT} \\ R + \nabla B & \text{IF Q ODD UNDERFLOW:} \\ & \text{RIGHT SHIFT} \end{cases}$$

$$H_{\nabla B} \leftarrow \begin{cases} M - 1 & \text{IF } N = 0 \\ M & \text{IF } N \neq 0 \end{cases}$$

$$\nabla_1 \leftarrow N + 2R - 2\nabla B$$

$$\text{COUNT} \leftarrow \nabla B$$

SLICE ALGORITHM

— OUTPUT —

INITIAL OUTPUT
H_0 LENGTH SLICE IN DIRECTION S_1
1 UNIT IN DIRECTION S_2

INTERMEDIATE OUTPUT LOOP

① COUNT $\leftarrow$ COUNT $-$ 1

② IF COUNT $\leq$ 0 : GO TO FINAL OUTPUT

③ IF $\nabla_i <$ 0 THEN $H_i \leftarrow Q-1$ & $\nabla_{i+1} \leftarrow \nabla_i + 2R$

IF $\nabla_i \geq$ 0 THEN $H_i \leftarrow Q$ & $\nabla_{i+1} \leftarrow \nabla_i + (2R - 2\nabla B)$

④ OUTPUT H_i LENGTH SLICE IN DIRECTION S_1
1 UNIT IN DIRECTION S_2

⑤ GO TO ①

FINAL OUTPUT
$H_{\nabla B}$ LENGTH SLICE IN DIRECTION S_1
TERMINATE

THE RELATIONSHIP BETWEEN EUCLID'S ALGORITHMS AND
RUN-LENGTH ENCODING

M.L.V. Pitteway

The sequence of plotter moves generated by Bresenham's
algorithm for a single straight line can be expressed recursively
as a sequence of repeated patterns. A similar pattern can
be seen in the flow of Euclid's algorithm if it is applied
to find the highest common factor of the two integer parameters
defining the gradient and end point of the given line. The
analysis suggests a simple extension of Bresenham's algorithm
which provides an automatic shortcut (Computer Journal $\underline{25}$,
114).

1   INTRODUCTION

In a classic work, Bresenham (1963) published an "algorithm
for computer control of a digital plotter", which shows how
a sequence of incremental pen movements can be generated which
"best fits", in a defined sense, a straight line of arbitrary
gradient. The technique is directly applicable to simple,
point-to-point graphic displays, and can be easily extended
to cater for plotters and displays offering a more elaborate
repertoire of basic moves.

In its simplest form, Bresenham's algorithm provides a
sequence of square and diagonal moves, a total of u moves,
of which v are diagonal and (u-v) are square, to represent
a straight line drawn from a point denoted as origin, (0,0),
to the point (u,v), where $0 < v < u$, i.e. the first octant; other
octants are dealt with similarly. (The cases where v=0 or
v=u are trivial, one move repeated u times, and need not concern
us here).

As has been stated elsewhere (e.g. Earnshaw 1980, Bresenham
1982), however, for long lines the moves are repeated many
times in cyclic patterns, which can be used to compress the

NATO ASI Series, Vol. F17
Fundamental Algorithms for Computer Graphics
Edited by R. A. Earnshaw
© Springer-Verlag Berlin Heidelberg 1985

the data for storage purposes. Moreover, the technique
can be used to accelerate the performance of the basic
algorithm (Pitteway and Green, 1982). The pattern recognition
process involved is closely related to the running of Euclid's
algorithm, as applied to find the highest common factor of
the input parameters, u and v, or their equivalent, as is
illustrated in this paper through simple examples.

2   A SIMPLE EXAMPLE

Suppose Bresenham's algorithm is applied to draw a straight
line from (0,0) to (131,16), thus 115 x-steps, or square moves,
"S", and 16 diagonal steps, "D", - 131 steps in all. Using
a convenient shorthand notation thus, S^4 to represent the 4
consecutive square moves SSSS, and parentheses for repeated
groupings, e.g. $(DS^7)^4$ represents the sequence $D.S^7$ repeated
4 times, Bresenham's algorithm generates the 131 steps in the
sequence:

$$S^4 \ (DS^7)^4 \ DS^8 \ (DS^7)^5 \ DS^8 (DS^7)^4 \ DS^4 \tag{1}$$

The notation appears slightly clumsy, in that it masks a rather
pleasing palindromic symmetry. (1) could equally well be
written:

$$S^4 D.(S^7 D)^4 \ S^8 \ D(S^7 D)^5 \ S^8 D(S^7 D)^4 \ S^4.$$

It appears, however, that this symmetry is not particularly
useful in the notation, and in any case it is not always
present: The example given here was chosen carefully to avoid
the awkward case when the intended line passes through a mesh
midpoint, where the sequences SD or DS are equal alternatives,
and the symmetry is destroyed. So it is, too, if we allow
for a small displacement of the line, up to half an increment
in the y direction (but no more, for otherwise we should be
starting from a different place).

If, now, the straight line from (0,0) is continued through,
instead of stopping at, (131,16), the pattern (1) is repeated

cyclicly, so the initial S^4 combines with the terminating DS^4 to form a third (DS^8) grouping. The repeated cycle (and note that with a small initial displacement, as mentioned in the previous paragraph, the cyclic pattern is unchanged, though the starting point in the cycle is moved) consists entirely of DS^7 and DS^8 groupings.

From an inspection of this output string, this fact alone is enough to require that the gradient of the line is between $\frac{1}{8}$ and $\frac{1}{9}$, even if the input parameters are unknown. Note that $16/131 = 1/8.1875$, between $1/8$ and $1/9$ as expected. A sequence in which 2 diagonal moves are separated by 9, or only 6 square moves is never permitted, for this would imply that the mix of square and diagonal moves was out of balance, implying curvature.

Next, we note that the repeated cyclic sequence (1) consists of the combined groupings (DS^8) (DS^7)^4 and (DS^8) (DS^7)^5, implying a gradient between 5/141, which is equal to $1/(8+1/5)$, and 6/49, which is equal to $1(8+1/6)$. $16/131=1/(8+1/(5+1/3))$, which can be written more conveniently in the notation of continued fractions as $1/8+ 1/5+ 1/3$. Clearly, in our cyclic string, the 3 represents the occurrence of the extra (DS^7) one time in three.

Now suppose we were to apply Euclid's algorithm, in the usual way, to find the highest common factor of 131 and 16, – or some multiple therefore, 524 and 64, for example, if we have 4 repeated cycles in our line. The first step involves dividing 524 by 64, giving 8 with a remainder of 12. Then 64 divided by 12 gives 5, with remainder 4, and finally 12 divided by 4 gives 3 exactly. The successive quotients, 8, 5 and 3, clearly reveal the pattern to be observed in the repeated cyclic string (1). A similar principle applies even if the pattern is never repeated as, for example, if we apply Bresenham's algorithm to generate an incremental representation of a straight line with gradient $1/\pi$, starting from the origin thus:

$$S(DS^2)^4 \ (S(DS^2)^7)^{16} \ (DS^2(S(DS^2)^7)^{15}) \ \dots$$
$$\dots (S(DS^2)^8 \ (S(DS^2)^7)^{15})^{146}$$
$$\dots (DS^2(S(DS^2)^7)^{15} \ (S(DS^2)^8 \ (S(DS^2)^7)^{15})^{293}) \ \dots$$

In this case, of course, the irrationality of π also implies
that the awkward half mesh point case can never occur, (except
that any actual computer implementation of the algorithm
implies that π should be approximated as a floating-point
"real"). The pattern from the continued fraction expansion
of $1/\pi$ = $1/3 + 1/7 + 1/16 - 1/294+$ is easily seen.

3   RECOGNITION OF A STRAIGHT LINE

The technique illustrated above is useful if, for example,
we need to rescale a plotter output file. It is easy engough
to increase the size of a drawing by outputting each incremental move twice, three times or whatever, but this would
be very rough, exaggerating the "jaggies" unnecessarily, and
is inappropriate in any case for a reduced size, or a magnification by other than integar factors. It might be possible
to rerun the code which provided the file, of course, but if
this is inconvenient we would seek to recognise, as far as
possible, straight lines which can be subsequently scaled and
regenerated by Bresenham's algorithm, and to fit circles or
other curves with short, straight line segments.

If S, for example, is the more frequent symbol of the
two, then we look for an integer n, possibly 1, such that the
string is represented by the combinations DS^n and DS^{n+1} only.
(Note that, for a given n, DS^{n-1} or DS^{n+2} can never occur in
a single straight line segment). We then apply a similar
recognition technique to the string of DS^n and DS^{n+1}, and so
on recursively. Each step gives the next term in the continued
fraction expansion of the originating gradient, (though in
a practical implementation, there are problems with end effects).

4   RUN-LENGTH ENCODING SHORTCUT

The algorithms of Pitteway and Green (1982), which uses
the groupings to shortcut the running of Bresenham's algorithm,
is reproduced in figure 1. The basic idea is very simple,
though alternatives are easily derived, and may well prove
to more efficient in some cases, though not in others. The
top part of the flow chart is Bresenham's algorithm, though
with the initial conditions omitted. For a line to be drawn
from $(0,0)$ to (u,v), when $0 < v < u$, the initial conditions
are: $2v \to b$, $2u - v \to a$, $b - u \to d$; for the line $y = mx + c$,
when $0 < m < 1$ and $|c| < \frac{1}{2}$, $m \to b$, $1 - m \to a$ and $m + c - \frac{1}{2} \to d$.
"Move 1" is to be set to output the single, square move x-step
character "S" at the start, and "move 2" to the diagonal step
"D", though these are to be extended into output strings of
ever increasing length as the run proceeds. In the lower part,
the figure represents Euclid's algorithm, and provides the
short cut operations which work as follows: suppose we are
passing down the left-hand, $d \geq 0$, branch of Bresenham's
algorithm without the short cuts, and it happens that $a > b$,
it follows inevitably that any time a "move 2" is subsequently
called for, the operation "$d - a \to d$" must make d negative,
so "move 1" must follow next. Accordingly, we incorporate
this with the "move 2" instruction, outputting the two moves
at the one call, with the necessary adjustment to the stored
parameter 'a' in order to move d to its new value. Similarly
from the $d \geq 0$ branch if b is larger than a. The tests in the
figure have been carefully contrived so that once we reach
the condition $b = a$, b is set to 0 on the passage down the
$d \geq 0$ branch, and thereafter is trapped as a repeated output
string at "move 1". This trap can be omitted if the right-
hand "$b < a$" test is amended to read "is $b \leq a$?", but although
this perhaps looks more elegant we miss the last step of the
short cut, passing through the left- and right-handed branches
alternately in generating a repeated output sequence.

As mentioned above, other variants are possible. After
the first short cut operation on either side of the loop, for

example, we can return to "is d< 0?", so that output increments
are initially generated more quickly, though the running down
of a and b is delayed, losing time later for the longer lines,
a trade-off perhaps worthy of further study. Moreover, in
hand runs of the algorithm, it is very noticeable that, if
a $\gg$ b (as occurs with the 294 in the continued fraction
expansion of the 1/π example), we spend much time in the left-
hand branch firstly on the division-by-repeated-subtraction
a - b a, and then a corresponding number of d + b operations
(and similarly for the right-hand branch if b $\gg$ a). It
should be possible to combine the two, and perhaps to allow
each side of the branch to produce a short cut for itself,
instead of only for the other branch.

Finally, it might even be possible to eliminate the basic
skeleton of Bresenham's algorithm altogether, running the
Euclid portion until the output is accumulated as a single
string, to be output in one fell swoop. Implicit in the study
might also be a solution of the vexing question of the algorithms
termination, the version of figure 1 requiring some additional
test on output to avoid overshooting. The attempts of the
present author to achieve this have so far proved unsuccessful,
however - and it isn't for want of trying.

111

REFERENCES

Bresenham J.E.   'Algorithm for Computer Control of a Digital
                               Plotter' IBM Systems Journal, Vol.4., No.1.,
                               pp 25 - 30, 1965.

Bresenham J.E.   'Incremental Line Compaction'
                               Computer Journal, Vol.25, No.1, pp 116-120, 1982.

R.A.Earnshaw   'Line Tracking for Incremental Plotters'
                               Computer Journal, Vol. 23, No.1.
                               pp 46-52, 1980.

Pitteway ML.V. and   'Bresenham's Algorithm with Run-line Coding
Green A.J.R.   Shortcut'
                               Computer Journal, Vol.25, No.1, pp 114-115, 1982.

LEGEND

Figure 1   Euclid's algorithm, to calculate the highest common
                               factor of the controlling parameters b and a, can be
                               used within Bresenham's algorithm to speed the working
                               when drawing lines on an incremental plotter or an
                               equivalent graphic display device.

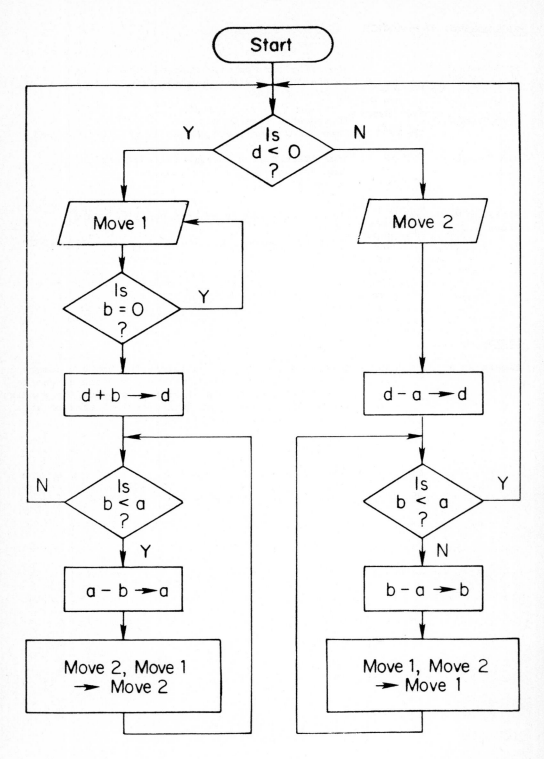

ANTIALIASING IN PRACTICE

A. R. Forrest
University of East Anglia
Computational Geometry Project
School of Information Systems
Norwich, NR4 7TJ, U. K.

Abstract

Aliasing, that is to say the artefacts which arise from under-sampling when rendering geometric objects, is a pervasive problem in computer graphics. The paper discusses aliasing first in the broadest terms by including problems of colour reproduction due to under-sampling in colour space and geometric aliasing due to under-sampling of the object to be rendered in geometric terms as well as the more conventional application of the term to spatial and temporal problems of raster graphics rendering. The paper then concentrates on spatial antialiasing with an emphasis on practical aspects. The importance of adequate precision in geometric computations is emphasised. Trade-offs between speed and quality of image generation are discussed and it is suggested that the graphics environment should offer the user a choice of quality levels for image generation rather than a single method of rendering.

1. Introduction

From our own experiences of visual perception of the real world, we tend to think of images as being continuous rather than discrete in terms of space, colour and tone, and time. Most practical computer peripherals, and indeed many practical image reproduction devices, are of finite resolution in terms of space, tone and colour, and time.. It is not surprising, therefore, that there are problems when we attempt to approximate continuous reality on a discrete device. Straightforward computer graphics generates images based on a fixed integer grid,

NATO ASI Series, Vol. F17
Fundamental Algorithms for Computer Graphics
Edited by R. A. Earnshaw
© Springer-Verlag Berlin Heidelberg 1985

using a fixed number of colours or intensities, and computing frames or plots at discrete time intervals. The results are well known: images exhibit steps or *jaggies*, there is banding in what should be continuous tone images, and moving sequences tend to jerk or otherwise have an unnatural appearance. These artefacts, *aliasing*, are all due to *sampling* a continuous model (if the image is synthetically generated) or image (if the image is digitised) at discrete intervals, and the practice of *antialiasing* is the art of removing such artefacts.

We know from personal experience of television, printing, and films that it is possible to convey the *illusion* of continuity using discrete devices. For example, on a domestic television receiver, which is hardly of the highest quality, it is possible to identify a single misplaced hair on the newsreader's head. A back of the envelope calculation indicates this substantially exceeds the expected spatial resolution along the television scanline, yet the hair is perfectly visible. In effect, what is rendered on the television set is a blurred and filtered version of the hair, and the human eye-brain system, with its built in edge detection hardware, refocuses the image. Similarly, we are all familiar with the reproduction by printing of grayscale and full colour images using binary methods. Close inspection reveals the characteristic half-tone patterns employed in printing, but from a suitable viewing or reading distance, the dots cannot be differentiated and the eye-brain system successfully integrates the image to give the illusion of tonal continuity. Movies similarly capitalise on the eye-brain combination, reconstructing from a sequence of blurred images the illusion of continuous movement of objects in perfect focus.

In computer graphics, it is common to talk of *spatial aliasing* and *temporal aliasing*. Spatial aliasing gives rise to the staircase effect and temporal aliasing to the jerky motion of objects. The term temporal aliasing is sometimes used incorrectly for what is also called twinkling: small objects, usually of sub-pixel size, tend to pop in and out of view unless properly treated. This is not really a problem of time but one of location since items covering sub-pixel regions may be rendered visible in one particular position but may not be visible when rendered elsewhere. If the spatial aliasing problem is handled correctly then this apparently temporal-related twinkling phenomenon no longer arises.

The problems of colour and tone reproduction are seldom thought of as being caused by aliasing although from a broader viewpoint they are. We might call these problems, for a lack of a better term, *tonal aliasing*.

One particular form of aliasing, which we will term *geometric aliasing*, is particularly prevalent in computer graphics: it arises in the rendering of geometric objects. In rendering curves and surfaces it is common practice to employ polygonal and polyhedral approximations, a form of *geometric* undersampling. The aliasing we get here gives rise to facets, edges, and vertices where none exist or should exist in the model. To overcome the problem, we can simply sample at higher geometric frequencies using tolerances based on geometric measures. In many practical cases, geometric sampling can be increased, at cost of increased computation, with satisfactory results. It is worth pointing out that Gouraud and Phong shading *[FovD82, NeSp79]*, which attempt visually to remove geometric aliases, have similarities with area sampling and other filtering techniques for spatial antialiasing, but cannot conceal geometric aliasing along boundaries and silhouettes. Another example of geoemtric aliasing is the ploughed field effect where curved surfaces are cut by numerically controlled machine tools. In such cases the aliasing is normally removed by hand finishing.

Aliasing, in all of its manifestations in computer graphics, is due fundamentally to *undersampling* the model to be rendered [Cro77]. The Sampling Theorem states that in order to reproduce phenomena of frequency *f*, the model or image must be sampled at twice that frequency. Thus a raster device with 512 pixels per scan line can reproduce 256 distinct vertical lines, but phenomena of higher frequency will not be reproduced accurately or faithfully. In the broadest sense, many of the problems discussed by other authors in this book can be regarded as due to the finite samples forced on us by the use of computers, whether working with integers or floating point numbers.

Given the clear indication of what *can* be done in terms of television, printing and films, we seek to exploit to the maximum the powerful image processing facilities of the human eye-brain combination and to match our techniques as far as possible both to the technology of the graphics devices and to the capabilities of the eye-brain system.

In this paper we shall concentrate mainly on the problems of spatial antialiasing and approach them from a practical viewpoint. Before doing so, we give some examples of other forms of aliasing. Figure 1 shows of the problems of tonal aliasing and approaches which have been taken to reproduce full colour images on low colour resolution devices [FovD82, Rog85]. Figure 2 (courtesy A. Nasri, [Nas84]) is an example of geometric aliasing where the object appears to have scalloped facets. This facetting is visually exaggerated by a phenomenon known as Mach banding where the eye-brain enhances edges between regions of constant tone. This edge enhancement is also observable in nature, and in Figure 3 we approximate the effect of receding mountain ranges which, given the right atmospheric conditions, illustrate Mach banding quite dramatically. In Figure 4 we demonstrate the common phenomenon of jaggies or staircasing in line drawings on raster devices, and give two examples of where this phenomenon is removed. Examples of temporal antialiasing are of course impossible to illustrate in a book.

2. Spatial Antialiasing

In spatial antialiasing, the usual solution is either to filter out frequencies higher than the absolute sampling frequency dictated by the output device, thus removing detail, or to convolve the image in such a way that the high frequency signals are spread out and folded back into lower frequency signals. The effect in this case is to blur the image, with the eye-brain refocusing and presenting an apparently sharp image to the observer.

Perhaps the simplest form of antialiasing for lines and edges is area sampling [Cro77, Cro81, NeSp79, FovD82] in which each pixel is coloured according to the fraction of that pixel overlaid by the line or edge in question. In filtering terms this is equivalent to convolving the image with a simple box filter which is of height 1 and covers a single pixel. This approach is easy to implement and can be incorporated with little difficulty in a Bresenham style line drawing algorithm. However, in the raster graphics environment we implemented at the University of East Anglia, we chose to adopt a more complex solution, that suggested by Gupta and Sproull [GuSp81]. Here the line or edge is convolved with a conical filter. The cone is centred at the centre of a pixel and is of volume one (in "pixel unit" terms). The antialiasing fraction is derived by intersecting the cone with the line or edge and evaluating the fraction of total volume of the cone cut off by the line or edge, Figure 5. This fraction is then used in deciding what colour to paint the pixel at the centre of the cone. Gupta and Sproull have given a modification of the Bresenham line drawing algorithm [Bre65] which incorporates this type of filtering. Because the filter is circularly symmetric, it is possible to create, *a priori*, a look-up table for lines at all angles. In our implementation the basic table is based on edges, and once the radius of the cone, that is to say the radius of the convolution filter, is decided, a table for convolution of an edge can be computed. This table can be indexed in terms of the perpendicular distance between the centre of the cone and the edge being antialiased. In line drawing, Gupta and Sproull adopt a similar approach in that the line look-up table is indexed in terms of the perpendicular distance between the cone centre and the centre of the line being drawn. Since antialiasing offers the opportunity of drawing lines of any thickness, it is necessary to construct a new line table for each line thickness. Fortunately this is a simple matter involving differencing between entries in the edge table. That is to say we construct a line table simply by taking the difference between two sets of entries in the edge table, these entries being spaced by a step which is a function of line thickness. It is thus a relatively trivial process to create a line table, although computation of the edge table is rather more expensive in terms of arithmetic. This however is not a serious consideration since the edge table is computed once-and-for-all for a particular device.

The reason for choosing Gupta Sproull antialiasing in our case was that we believed it approximated more closely to the *physics* of image production on the cathode ray tube. The distribution of antialiasing fraction obtained by convolving an edge with a cone is approximately Gaussian and this is believed to approximate the actual distribution of light emitted by a spot on a CRT. The radius of the filter is chosen experimentally to give the best results on a particular CRT, and in the case of the monitor we normally use, that radius is approximately 1.25 pixels for normal viewing distances. The effect of varying the convolution radius can be seen in Figure 6. If the radius is small then aliasing artefacts are still visible in the form of apparently varying thickness of the lines drawn. If the radius is large then the line becomes rather too blurred for viewing at a normal distance. In passing we emphasise the importance of sitting at an appropriate distance from a monitor when antialiasing. Viewed too close, an antialiased image is revealed as being blurred, whilst at a reasonable viewing distance, say three or four feet or more, the picture can appear perfectly sharp. There is a tendency to sit far too close to the screen and hence to defeat the purpose of the exercise. In our laboratory, colour monitors are, where possible, mounted more than arms distance from the viewer.

Some authors [PiWa80, Pit81] have reported that Gupta-Sproull antialiasing gives lines which appear to be banded or of variable thickness. We too have observed this effect but attribute it to four separate causes, three of which can be minimised. Firstly, as mentioned above, choice of the correct convolution filter for the output device is vital. Secondly, it is essential that gamma correction be applied [FovD82] and too often this is ignored. It is very convenient from a practical point of view in antialiasing to be able to treat the repsonse on the screen as being linear. If possible gamma correction should be done behind the user's back, so that once calibrated, the system appears to behave linearly. The images reproduced in this book have *not* been gamma corrected because two separate gammas are involved: that of the monochrome CRT hardcopy device and that of photographic emulsion. Reproduction by printing adds yet another non-linear imponderable and in practice it would be extremely expensive, not to say tedious, to attempt to supply all the necessary corrections to reproduce apparently linear response on the printed page.

The third cause of poor quality is a fundamental problem with the Gupta-Sproull approach. Consider a cone positioned at the centre of every pixel on the screen and look at the field formed by summing all these cones. Since the volume of each cone is unity, the *average* value of the field is unity, but it has bumps and hollows, as illustrated in Figure 7. In a perfect device, the result of painting the entire image with a uniform intensity as far as the frame store is concerned should be a perfectly uniform intensity image, that is to say a totally flat field in energy terms. Since, however, the screen is scanned left to right, and the beam energy is distributed in a Gaussian manner, one might assume that the appropriate surface would be something resembling a horizontally-oriented ploughed field, although the difference of magnitude between the peaks and hollows of that surface would be relatively small. The Gupta-Sproull filter is far from ideal in this respect and contributes considerably to the observed banding. It would be possible to construct other convolution filters which would give a flat field, but we would lose out in terms of speed of computation because these filters would no longer be circularly symmetric. We would not then be able to construct a look-up table to use for all lines since the look-up table would have to vary with the angle of the line to be drawn. As the radius of the filter increases, the variations in the field are smoothed out but the image becomes more blurred, and the choice of correct filter size is therefore a compromise.

The fourth source of apparent banding of lines is attributable to the geometry of the pixels themselves. Lines can appear to be of different widths when drawn at different angles due to the pixels being square or, in our case, rectangular. It is possible, but slightly expensive, to modify the line or edge drawing routines to compensate for the geometry of the pixel, but again this depends on the orientation of the line or edge. Although pixel geometry does affect the line drawing in the sense of variation in width along a line, the effect is marginal, but the effect on apparent line width for different line angles *is* noticeable and perhaps ought to be compensated for. For aliased lines, the effective width of a line varies, for square pixels, from 1.0 for horizontal or vertical lines to 0.707 for lines at 45°. For correct results, we require the colour contribution of a line segment to match the colour contribution of the ideal line segment, i.e., if f_{ij} denotes the fraction of pixel(i,j) painted by a line segment, then:

$$\Sigma \, f_{ij} = \text{area of line segment (in pixel units)}$$

At the University of East Anglia, although we have a frame buffer with 24 bits per pixel, that is to say a full colour frame buffer, our software is written so that we may vary the number of bits of gray level available. It is interesting then to vary the number of bits available and to observe the effects of antialiasing, Figure 8. On the monitor, with a discerning viewer, the aliasing artefacts finally disappear with 8 bits per pixel, but the marginal improvement between 7 and 8 bits is very slight. However, there is a dramatic improvement in quality between 1 bit and 2 bits and thereafter diminishing returns for adding extra bits of intensity. It is well known and has been established many times [Lei80] that 8 bits of intensity are sufficient for correct antialiasing. What is not so widely publicised is that dramatic improvements in quality can be achieved by going from 1 bit to 2 bits. The Cadlinc workstation offers 2 bit intensity antialiasing for coloured lines on a 1000 line monitor and the improvement in image quality between 1 bit and 2 bits is much higher than one might expect. With rather fewer than 8 bits for intensity, the Gupta-Sproull approach is hardly appropriate and area sampling methods are indicated. One suggestion is to work, in the case of 2 bits per pixel, with 2x2 subpixels (i.e. post-filtering), and it is possible to achieve antialiased line drawing by running Bresenham algorithms in parallel based on 2x2 subpixel end positionings. Cadlinc employ a method due to Turkowski [Tur82] in their workstations.

One of the motivations for antialiasing is of course the ability to display geometric objects of less than pixel dimension. Figure 9 shows a variety of line thicknesses, and demonstrates as has been clearly shown by others, that given 8 bits per pixel, lines of 1/8 pixel width can readily be drawn and viewed. In practice we have managed to display lines of even smaller thickness. A rough rule of thumb appears to be that given n bits per pixel, it is possible to improve the apparent spatial resolution by a factor of n in both x and y dimensions. Thus a doubling of the number of bits per pixel can produce an image quality akin to that of quadrupling the number of pixels in the image store. Of course it is not possible to resolve closely spaced lines where that spacing is a pixel or less, but for isolated lines, sub-pixel resolution can be achieved.

The apparent improvement in resolution which can be achieved by antialiasing has an important but often ignored consequence for raster graphics software. Consider, for example, the experiment demonstrated in Figure 10, where we attempt to draw circular discs. In each image we draw the disc four times, the top two exhibiting aliasing artefacts and the bottom two being antialiased. In each image the top right disc is drawn by a simple DDA algorithm, whilst the other three discs are drawn as polygonal approximations. We would expect to see some geometric aliasing, as mentioned earlier, due to that polygonal approximation, and it is interesting to determine at what stage the geometric aliasing disappears. We thus show a series of images in which the number of sides in the approximating polygon is increased by powers of two from 32 to 256. The top left image in each case is drawn using hardware edge drawing and has aliased edges as a consequence. The bottom two images are drawn with the edges antialiased. The difference between bottom left and the bottom right images is that in the bottom left the vertices of the polygon are rounded to the nearest pixel centres, that is to say they are computed in terms of *pixel co-ordinates*, whilst in the right hand image we use the full floating point accuracy. For 32 sides, all three polygons appear polygonal, whilst when we reach 64 sides the polygon whose vertices are computed in terms of floating point *looks* circular. We can still see the vertices, however, in both the aliased and antialiased pixel co-ordinate polygons. Naively we decide to increase the number of sides to 128. The real disc still appears circular but the pixel co-ordinate disc is still polygonal. Going to 256 sides, the real disc remains circular but the pixel co-ordinate disc appears aliased! On reflection this is hardly surprising since by the time we reach 256 sides and are rounding all the vertices to the nearest pixel centres, all the edges are relatively short and usually horizontal, vertical or at 45°, joining adjacent pixels. There is little point in antialiasing such a polygon! What we learn from this is that it is impossible to draw a satisfactory antialiased polygonal approximation to a circle simply by computing and rounding all the geometry to the nearest pixel centres. However, if we work in terms of real co-ordinates throughout, a perfectly acceptable circular disc can be achieved.

What precision is necessary to achieve the correct results? In Figure 11 we show a series of four images similar to the preceding set, but in this case the bottom right hand disc is computed with vertices rounded to the nearest sub-pixel centre and we increase the sub-pixel resolution from 1x1 to 2x2 to 4x4 to 8x8. By the time we reach 8x8 sub-pixels, on the monitor we use, the polygonal nature of the disc has disappeared. In a sense this confirms the apparent increase in visual resolution. The corollary to that increase in resolution is that in order to exploit it we must compute *all* our geometry to *at* least that precision. In practice, we work with monitors capable of displaying at most 2500 scan lines, necessitating 11 bits for pixel addressing, and with up to 256 intensity levels, effectively requiring 3 bits for sub-pixel positioning. It would would seem sensible to compute all geometry, if, for the sake of efficiency, the arithmetic is to be done in terms of integers, to 15 bits precision plus sign and to truncate or round where necessary for output. We then stand a chance of overcoming the geometric aliasing problem and employing antialiasing correctly.

One of the great benefits of device-independent calligraphic software is the ability to describe drawings without reference to the actual co-ordinate systems and units used by the output device. The practice in raster graphics has been rather different, with the user being expected to work in terms of pixels. Whilst this is appropriate for some applications, such as image processing and image painting, there are many other applications, particularly the rendering of geometric objects, where working in terms of pixels is *positively harmful*. We have just given one particular example. In practice, to achieve some of the effects possible with raster graphics, the user *does indeed* need to deal with pixels and to know about their properties, but in most cases pixels are to be avoided as an unnecessary complication, an irrelevance, and a barrier to correct rendering.

3. *Quality Levels for Antialiasing*

Confining our attention to output on cathode ray tube raster displays, any device capable of drawing antialiased lines can be used with equal facility to draw *aliased* lines by software. In general, because fewer pixels are written, aliased lines can be drawn rather faster and most devices do of course provide hardware aliased line drawing. Some devices offer hardware antialiasing for lines, generally permitting the lines of nominal single pixel width to be drawn using a modified version of the Bresenham line drawing algorithm combined with specially constructed colour maps. Other approaches are sometimes employed with displays used purely to draw lines rather than regions on a raster device. Line generation speed is in both of these cases rapid, but there are limitations as to what can be achieved. Basically the colour maps are set to contain blends between a given background colour and a given line colour, and the line drawing process involves only writing. Problems arise where lines cross or overlap. Better results can achieved by blending the desired line colour with the background colour, but this involves readback from the frame store in order to determine the eventual colour for each pixel. Inevitably this read—modify—write cycle takes rather longer than a straight write cycle to the frame store. Not all raster devices of course allow the user the facility to read back from the frame store, but where such readback is permitted we now see that there are three possible ways of drawing lines: aliased, antialiased with no readback, and antialiased with readback.

Antialiased lines are drawn as strips of pixels, the trend of the strips being aligned with the direction of the line. Unfortunately, unless the lines are horizontal or vertical, it is inconvenient to retrieve by a single block readback all those pixels which have to be modified in order to draw any given line. Frame buffer memory architecture generally permits rapid access of paraxially aligned rectangular regions but not of diagonally aligned regions. Since lines drawn using the Bresenham algorithm consist of repeated sequence of horizontal or vertical runs, conceivably this could be exploited by reading back the paraxially aligned rectangles corresponding to the runs, but the complexity of the resulting algorithm would almost certainly outweigh the potential speed gained in the readback process.

The raster graphics software environment developed within the Computational Geometry Project at the University of East Anglia recognises that there are a variety of options when rendering many geometric objects using raster graphics and encapsulates these options by means of the concept of *quality levels*. The user is given a choice, permitting him to trade speed for precision and quality, and with the facility to opt for differing quality levels for different items such as lines, regions, text, etc.

With lines, we recognise five quality levels. Quality level 0 represents whatever the hardware can perform quickly, and, in our case, consists of aliased Bresenham line drawing. At quality level 1, we permit the user to specify a background colour and a line colour, and lines are then drawn antialiased without using readback. At quality level 2, lines are antialiased with readback. Figure 4 shows these three quality levels for the same image, the quality increasing from 0 on the left to 2 on the right. Note that at quality level 1, intersecting lines have tracks ploughed through them depending on the order in which they were drawn. These tracks are more noticeable if there is high contrast between the line colour and the background colour and the convolution radius is large. If we employ area sampling for our antialiasing, the tracks are less noticeable (due to the lack of overlap between convolution filters), but the antialiasing would be less effective than with conical filtering, as mentioned previously.

Although antialiasing for lines and edges can be achieved relatively simply, there still remains a problem when dealing with vertices. All published algorithms for antialiasing vertices, or indeed line ends, involve considerably more work for a relatively small region of an image than is required for processing edges [FeLe80, GuSp81, Tur82]. We have not yet found a method which seems to us entirely satisfactory. However, once again it seems that nature can help us in this regard. Whilst we have built in edge detection, we appear to view vertices rather less critically. Warnock [War80] has shown that it is possible to produce perfectly adequate antialiased characters using only 16 gray levels. Since in characters vertices tend to dominate over edges, or at least are of rather more frequent occurence than in other graphics, there is reason to believe that although 256 gray levels are necessary for antialiasing edges, we can produce adequate vertex antialiasing using only 16 levels. If we were to adopt a look-up table approach to vertex antialiasing, then it is clear that that table has to be two-dimensional rather than one-dimensional, and obviously a table of the order of 256^2 is still unacceptably large for modern day devices. A table of size 16^2 fits rather neatly with a table of size 256 for edges. Notionally, in our quality hierarchy, quality level

3 for lines solves the line end problem, permitting squared line ends and mitred vertices, or rounded line ends and vertices, but at increased cost of computation.

As mentioned earlier, in order to produce a correct image it is necessary to know for each pixel what geometric objects affect the colour in that pixel. Antialiasing on a per line basis using readback is only an approximate solution since the geometry contributing to the previous colour of a pixel is not available at the time of readback. We can only make a guess at the geometric configuration to be used in blending. Figure 12 shows four versions of rendering adjacent and neighbouring half-pixel wide lines. The true geometric configuration is indicated, and this is rendered by rounding to pixel coordinates and by using real coordinates, on a line-by-line basis and by simultaneous rendering of both lines. Note that in the line-by line cases, the difference between pixel coordinates and real coordinates is not straightforward, and the 'best' result appears to depend on the precise geometry. In the global case, however, real precision is superior. Essentially what we are saying is that the only proper way to produce the highest quality antialiasing is to perform a *global scan conversion* of the entire image to be rendered, as pointed out by Fuchs and Barros *[FuBa79]* and more recently by Catmull *[Cat84]*. Inevitably this involves some sorting and prioritising of the image, and it is not possible simply to perform a linear scan through the user's data structure in order to render the image. Quality level 4 in our hierarchy therefore performs a global scan conversion in which *all* the geometry within a pixel is treated *in parallel*. Obviously, this may take some considerable time.

One way in which the notion of quality hierarchies might conveniently be exploited is in the context of personal workstations. Since these workstations *are* personal, there will necessarily be spare CPU cycles available when the user is thinking or otherwise engaged. If one conceives of a system in which an image is rendered firstly as rapidly as possible at quality level 0 but if the user takes no immediate action, then the quality level is immediately raised and a rather better image appears, then the longer the user remains inactive the better the image appears until quality level 4 is reached. However, if the user changes the object to be rendered or changes its position, etc. then the image is recomputed at quality level 0, and so on. Thus during periods of rapid interaction, the image is not generated with high quality, but where more reflective interaction is taking place or closer inspection is occurring, the image will be of better quality and better visual resolution.

Given this idea of progressive improvement of image quality, we have carried out experiments as to how this might be achieved with minimum additional effort. In the case of lines, there appear to be no short cuts. However, with areas, inexpensive improvements are possible. Many devices now offer high speed area fill to boundaries which are aliased. What we need to do is to antialias the edges of these regions to improve their visual quality. In Figure 13 we show a test image involving polygonal regions drawn with aliased edges. The *lines* on the test image have, however, been antialiased. In Figure 14 we show the same image generated with antialiased scan conversion of the regions. In Figure 15 we have post antialiased the edges, given knowledge of the colours on either side of each edge. That is to say, we assume that we can retrieve, from the user's data structure, information as to the adjacency of polygons and background and can decompose edges into lengths whose left and right colours are known. Edges can then be antialiased without readback and the process is rapid. Note, however, that where edges meet at a vertex, the results are less than satisfactory due to the problem we encountered with quality level 1 lines, i.e. tracks. In Figure 16 we have again post-processed the edges and antialiased them, but in this case using readback. Since the antialiasing involves reading back strips across the edge, we assume as the relevant colours to be used in the antialiasing process those colours which are found at the exremities of the strips. In some cases the results will not be quite what can be achieved by antialiased scan conversion (Figure 14) but the results are generally good and it will be noted that the vertex problem, whilst not completely solved, is rather better than in the case with no readback, Figure 15.

Finally, since antialiasing is a form of image blurring, we demonstrate in Figure 17 the effect of post-filtering the entire image using a 3x3 filter which approximates a Gaussian filter. The filter icon indicates the filter weightings by shading from white (low) to red (high). Clearly, all that is achieved is an overall blurring of the aliased image rather than antialiasing! If it were not already apparent, this simply shows that antialiasing must take into account the items being drawn and work in geometric object space rather than in an image space devoid of knowledge of the objects being rendered.

With shaded images, antialiasing is only important where sub-pixel detail is important, e.g. for texturing, at region edges, or in the case of rendering of three-dimensional objects, silhouette edges. Rendering *smooth shaded* areas first without antialiasing, followed by post-processing of edges to antialiase them seems a perfectly acceptable procedure. Post-processing of aliased lines to produce antialiased lines is not so attractive since it is only really feasible where the line widths are multiples of a pixel.

4. Conclusions

Although we have concentrated on practical aspects of spatial anitaliasing, we have broadened the generally accepted use of the term aliasing in graphics to encompass geometric and colour/tone reproduction issues. The importance of adequate geometric sampling and adequate geometric precision have been stressed. Techniques adopted should be matched to the physics of the output device, and users should be given a choice of quality levels to enable them to trade between speed and accuracy of image generation.

Some of the results and opinions in this chapter arise from a conviction that whereas the time is certainly ripe for the adoption of calligraphic graphics standards [HoDu83], sufficiently little experience has been gained in terms of *device independent raster graphics* for standards to be established. Raster graphics systems ought to be based on edges, vertices, and regions, not on points and lines. Certainly, for spatial antialiasing, the fundamental operators are based on edges and vertices, and accommodating raster graphics simply by providing pixel or pixel-like arrays is a recipe for low quality, as we have demonstrated. Furthermore, the notion of quality hierarchies and tradeoffs fits inadequately with current standards.

Perhaps the most fundamental argument against using the current standard proposals for raster graphics is that these standards assume the classic graphics pipeline where geometry is passed item by item to the graphics system for rendering. In other words, for each geometric object to be rendered, we seek to identify those pixels which have to be modified. But, as Catmull indicates [Cat84] and our quality hierarchy implies, for the highest quality we seek to identify, for

.each pixel, those geometric objects which affect that pixel, involving a global two-dimensional sorting process which is completely counter to the pipeline model.

Finally, we observe that just as the solution of integer programming problems is fundamentally harder than the solution of linear programming problems, so the optimal rendering of geometric objects on an integer device is fundamentally harder than the optimal rendering on a calligraphic device.

5. Acknowledgements

This work was funded by the U.K. Science and Engineering Research Council with additional support from I.B.M (U.K.) Laboratories. Chris Weikart, Ahmad Nasri, and Gillian Hall contributed both software and helpful suggestions.

6. References

[Blo83]   Bloomenthal, J.
Edge Inference with Applications to Antialiasing. *Computer Graphics*, Volume 17, Number 3, July 1983 (Proceedings of SIGGRAPH '83).
[Bre65]   Bresenham, J. E.
Algorithm for Computer Control of a Digital Plotter. *I. B. M. Systems Journal*, Volume 4, Number 1, 1965.
[Car84]   Carpenter, L.
The A-Buffer, An Antialiased Hidden Surface Method. *Computer Graphics*, Volume 18, Number 3, July 1984 (Proceedings of SIGGRAPH '84).
[Cat84]   Catmull, E.
An Analytic Visible Surface Algorithm for Independent Pixel Processing. *Computer Graphics*, Volume 18, Number 3, July 1984 (Proceedings of SIGGRAPH '84).
[Cro77]   Crow, F. C.
The Aliasing Problem in Computer-Generated Shaded Images. *Communications of the ACM, Volume 20, Number 4, November 1977.*
[Cro78]   Crow, F. C.
The Use of Grayscale for Improved Raster Display of Vectors and Characters. *Computer Graphics*, Volume 12, Number 2, 1978 (Proceedings of SIGGRAPH '78).

[Cro81]   Crow, F.C.
A Comparison of Antialiasing Techniques. *IEEE Conmputer Graphics and Applications*, Volume 1, Number 1, January 1981.

[FeLe80]   Feibush, E.A., Levoy, M. & Cook, R.L.
Synthetic Texturing Using Digital Filters. *Computer Graphics*, Volume 14, Number 3, July 1980 (Proceedings of SIGGRAPH '80).

[FlSt75]   Floyd, R. & Steinberg, L.
An Adaptive ALgorithm for Spatial Gray Scale. *Society for Information Display*, International Symposium on Digital Technology Papers, 1975, page 36.

[FovD82]   Foley, J.D. & van Dam, A.
Fundamentals of Interactive Computer Graphics. Addison-Wesley, 1982.

[For79]   Forrest, A.R.
On the Rendering of Surfaces. *Computer Graphics*, Volume 13, Number 2, August 1979 (Proceedings of SIGGRAPH '79).

[For82]   Forrest, A.R.
A Pragmatic Approach to Interaction. *Computers in Industry*, Volume 3, Numbers 1/2, March/June 1982.

[FuBa79]   Fuchs, H. & Barros, J.
Efficient Generation of Smooth Line Drawings on Video Displays. *Computer Graphics*, Volume 13, Number 2, August 1979 (Proceedings of SIGGRAPH '79).

[Fulw83]   Fujimoto, A. & Iwata, K.
Jag-Free Images on Raster Displays. *IEEE Computer Graphics and Applications*, Volume 3, Number 9, December 1983.

[FuPeIw84]   Fujimoto, A., Perrot, C.G. & Iwata, K.
A 3-D Graphics Display System with Depth Buffer and Pipeline Processor. *IEEE Computer Graphics and Applications*, Volume 4, Number 6, June 1984.

[GuSp81]   Gupta, S. & Sproull, R.F.
Filtering Edges for Gray-Scale Displays. *Computer Graphics*, Volume 15, Number 3, August 1981 (Proceedings of SIGGRAPH '81).

[HoDu83]   Hopgood, F.R.A., Duce, D.A., Gallop, J.R. & Sutcliffe, D.C.
Introduction to the Graphical Kernel System G.K.S. Academic Press, 1983.

[Hec82]   Heckbert, P.
Color Image Quantization for Frame Buffer Display. *Computer Graphics*, Volume 16, Number 3, July 1982 (Proceedings of SIGGRAPH '82).

[Kub84]   Kubo, S.
Continuous Color Presentation Using a Low-Cost Ink Jet Printer. *Proc. Computer Graphics Tokyo '84.*

[Lel80]   Leler, W.J.
Human Vision, Anti-aliasing, and the Cheap 4000 Line Display. *Computer Graphics*, Volume 14, Number 3, July 1980 (Proceedings of SIGGRAPH '80).

[NeSp79]   Newman, W.M. & Sproull, R.F.
Principles of Interactive Computer Graphics. 2nd Ed., McGraw-Hill, 1979.

[Pho75]   Phong, Bui-Tong
Illumination for Computer-Generated Pictures. *Communications of the ACM*, Volume 18, Number 6, June 1975.

[Pit81]   Pitteway, M.L.V.
On Filtering Edges for Grey-Scale Displays. *Computer Graphics*, Volume 15 Number 4, December 1981 (Proceedings of SIGGRAPH '81).

[PiGr82]   Pitteway, M. L. V. & Green, A. J. R.
    Bresenham's Algorithm with Run Line Coding Shortcut. *Computer Journal*,
    Volume 25, Number 1, 1982.
[PiWa80]   Pitteway, M. L. V. & Watkinson, D.
    Bresenham's Algorithm with Grey Scale. *Communications of the ACM Volume
    23, Number 11*, November 1980.
[Rog85]   Rogers, D. F.
    Procedural Elements for Computer Graphics. McGraw-Hill, 1985
[Tur82]   Turkowski, K.
    Anti-Aliasing through the Use of Coordinate Transformations. *ACM Transactions
    on Graphics*, Volume 1, Number 3, July 1982.
[War80]   Warnock, J. E.
    The Display of Characters Using Gray Level Sample Arrays. *Computer
    Graphics*, Volume 14, Number 3, July 1980 (Proceedings of SIGGRAPH '80).

AN APPLICATION OF EUCLID'S ALGORITHM TO DRAWING STRAIGHT LINES

by C.M.A.Castle & M.L.V.Pitteway

ABSTRACT

An algorithm is proposed which uses Euclid's Algorithm to control two production rules which can construct the "best-fit" incremental line. The advantages of its implementation are discussed.

Introduction

The increasing use of non-vector graphics output peripherals, (such as raster scan devices and incremental plotters) has accelerated the search for efficient algorithms to produce "best-fit" straight lines. Effectively, on a raster scan device, each straight line must be "approximated" by a quantised sequence of diagonal and/or square movements, and the "best-fit" is obtained by applying the constraint that after each incremental step, the pixel nearest to the "real" line is the one selected for illumination.

Using this criterion, it is possible to select the appropriate pixel by using either a floating-point differential analyser (Newman & Sproull), or a form of Bresenham's integer based algorithm (Stockton 1963, Bresenham 1965). Sproull has shown that the Bresenham algorithm can be derived from the differential analyser, thus establishing that both generate identical output strings.

A significant property of both of these algorithms is that, in general, they both require one test per output move.

The Output of the Algorithm

Even a cursory glance at the output of a "best-fit" algorithm reveals a profound symmetry which is at first sight most surprising.

If,for example, a line is drawn from (0,0) to any pair of prime co-ordinates (u,v) with u>v>0, the output is a palindrome, symmetrical about the central element.

eg from (0,0) to (23,7) produces:

S D SS D SSS D SS D SS D SSS D SS D S

(Spaces added to improve readability)

CONTROLLING THE PRODUCTION RULES WITH EUCLID'S ALGORITHM

Analysis of the output of a "best-fit" algorithm suggests that it is a regular language. Furthermore, it is a language which when u and v are prime, is of the form:

$$L = L^{-1} \quad \text{(ie a palindrome)}$$

This strongly suggests that any move concatenation technique controlled by Euclid's algorithm , would require production rules of the form:

$$R := T.R^{-1}$$

(Where A.B represents string A contatenated with string B)

Fig (1) shows the algorithm which employs Euclid's algorithm as a discriminator between two symmetric production rules. If a "best-fit" line is to be drawn from (0,0) to (u,v) (with u>v>0 to keep within the first octant), then the initial selection for a and b would be:

$$b := v \quad \text{(the number of diagonal moves to be made)}$$
$$a := u-v \quad \text{(the number of square moves)}$$

Move 1 has an initial value of S, move 2 has an initial value D

Eg   The following table represents the output of the algorithm in constructing the line (0,0) to (51,11)

a	b	Move 1	Move 2
40	11	S	SD
29	11	S	SDS
18	11	S	SSDS
7	11	SSDSS	SSDS
7	4	SSDSS	SSDSSSDSS
3	4	SSDSSSDSSSSDSS	SSDSSSDSS
3	1	SSDSSSDSSSSDSS	SSDSSSDSSSSDSSSSDSSSSDSSSDSS
2	1	SSDSSSDSSSSDSS	SSDSSSDSSSSDSSSSDSSSDSSSSDSSSSDSSSDSS
1	1		

OUTPUT move2(move1)$^{-1}$ repeated a times, giving:

SS D SSS D SSSS D SSSS D SSS D SSSS D SSSS D SSS D SSSS D SSSS D SSS D SS

In this example, the complete 51 move "best-fit" output stream was determined in just 8 tests. If the selected values of u and v share a common factor, then the algorithm will generate the "best-fit" output up to the point where the "real" line passes through a pixel. This pattern is then to be repeated the highest common factor number of times.

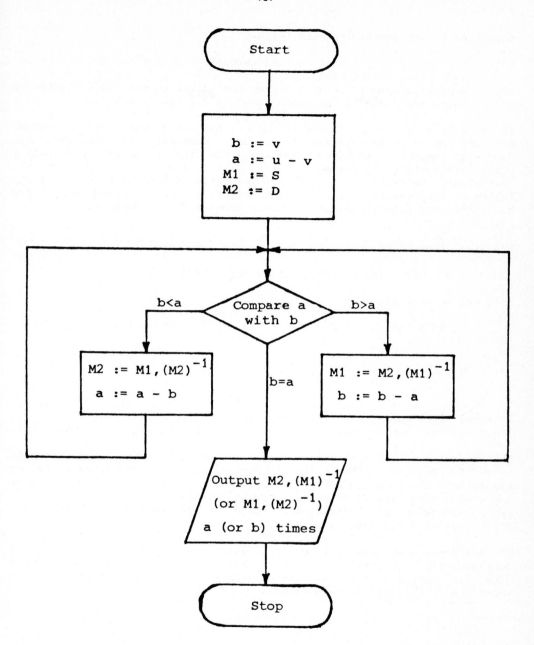

Fig (1)   The algorithm for generating "best-fit" output, with Euclid's
algorithm acting as a discriminator between two production rules.
(u > v > 0, the output in other octants being produced by
symmetry).

(A comma denotes the concatenation of two ouput strings, and $(Mx)^{-1}$
denotes the reversal of the string Mx.)

This type of pattern is produced because:

(1)   The "real" line only passes through "best-fit" pixels at its two ends (and nowhere else).

(2)   Appeal to symmetry requires that the output associated with drawing from either end to the centre must be indistinguishable.

If u and v are not themselves prime, but can be expressed as a prime multiple of a common factor, it is only necessary to construct the "best-fit" output up to the point where the "real" line passes through a pixel; thereafter the same pattern will be regenerated, and the regenerated pattern will itself show reflected symmetry. More generally, following the removal of any common factor, if the remaining numbers are not themselves prime, reflection may be about a double element.

The line from (0,0) to (28,6), for example, produces:

SS D SSS D SSSS D SSSS D SSS D SSSS D SS

This can be re-written as:

B is the place where the "real" line passes through pixel (14,3)
A & C are the double element about which the sub-strings are symmetrical.

The importance of any common factor to the form of the output has been noted by Earnshaw (1978). In 1982, Pitteway & Green presented an algorithm which employed Euclid's algorithm to trap the common factors. These were then used to drive appropriate move concatenation techniques which improved the operational speed of Bresenham's Algorithm, while still retaining its basic stucture.

In this paper , we show that Euclid's algorithm ALONE can be used to control the appropriate output sequence for an integer based "best-fit" generator. This effects a further saving in arithmetic from the algorithm of Pitteway & Green (1982).

Implementation

Any hardware which is capable of Left or Right rotation of one register into another, can perform the move transposition operation in just one machine cycle. (fig 2) This would help to make implementation of this algorithm very efficient.

Regiister 1   S S S S D S S S S D S S S

Register 2   S S S D S S S S D S S S S

Fig (2). Register 1 contains the current state of movel. Register 2 contains the result of performing $(movel)^{-1}$

References

(1) EUCLID, Elements (Book 7) Proc. Platonic Acad. c.350BC Vol 4009

(2) STOCKTON, F.G. (1963) Algorithm 162   CACM, Vol 6, No. 4

(3) BRESENHAM, J.E. (1965) Algorithm for computer control of a digital plotter.   IBM Systems Journal, Vol 4, No 1, pp 25-30

(4) PITTEWAY, M.L.V. & GREEN, A.Bresenham's Algorithm with run line coding shortcut. The Computer Journal, Vol 25, No 10

(5) EARNSHAW, R.A. Line tracking with incremental plotters. The Computer Journal Vol 23, No 1

(6) NEWMAN, W.M. & SPROULL,R.F. Principles of interactive computer graphics 1981 McGraw Hill pp 23-28

THE ACCURACY OF THE DIGITAL REPRESENTATION OF A STRAIGHT LINE

Leo Dorst

Pattern Recognition Group

Department of Applied Physics

Delft University of Technology

DELFT

The Netherlands

1 Introduction

Both in Image Processing and in Computer Graphics digital straight line segments play a role as the simplest way to connect pixels. But while in Computer Graphics the emphasis is on the generation of these lines, given the parameters intercept and slope, the focus in Image Processing is on measuring the parameters, given the lines. Aspects of this analysis are the so-called linearity conditions (specifying the necessary and sufficient conditions for a set of points to be a digitized straight line segment) and the accuracy of the representation (specifying how accurately a given digitized straight line segment describes the underlying continuous reality). Both aspects have been investigated in depth [1]-[9]. The question of accuracy has recently been solved completely, when mathematical expressions were given for the set of all continuous line segments that could have generated a given digital straight line segment [8]. These expressions are in fact the formulas for the inversion of the digitization process. As such, they are also interesting for Computer Graphics.

2 Digitization

In image processing, digitized straight lines commonly occur when an object with a straight boundary is digitized on a regular grid of digitizing points.

NATO ASI Series, Vol. F17
Fundamental Algorithms for Computer Graphics
Edited by R. A. Earnshaw
© Springer-Verlag Berlin Heidelberg 1985

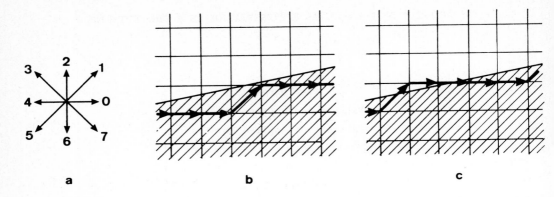

a b c

Fig. 1 a) the Freeman chaincode scheme; b) Object Boundary Quantization;
c) Grid Intersect Quantization

There are two ways of representing this set of digitized boundary points by a
string of chain codes (figure 1).

- OBQ (object boundary quantization), where the outermost points still
  belonging to the object are connected by a chaincode string
- GIQ (grid interset quantization), where grid points closest to the
  continuous object boundary are connected by a chaincode string

In this paper, we will restrict ourselves to OBQ, since it makes the formulas
slightly simpler. For GIQ, the story is essentially the same (see [7],[8]).

We take the digitizing grid to be a square grid, and the chaincode strings to
be made up of 8-connected chaincodes. It has been shown that this case can be
generalized to other regular grids (e.g. the hexagonal grid) or other connec-
tivities by straightforward computations [7].
For convenience in the mathematics, we will only consider strings consisting
of chaincodes 0 and/or 1. This is no restriction: since the straight strings
satisfy the linearity conditions, they consist of at most two different
chaincode elements, differing 1 (mod 8). By a suitable choice of coordinate
axes, one can therefore write a straight string as a string consisting only of
the chaincode elements 0 and/or 1, corresponding to the directions $\binom{1}{0}$ and
$\binom{1}{1}$.

Consider a line in the first octant of a Cartesian coordinate system, given by $y(x) = \alpha x + e$. The OBQ-digitization of this line is, in the first $n+1$ columns, given by:

$$\lfloor y(i) \rfloor = \lfloor \alpha i + e \rfloor \qquad i = 0,1,2,\ldots,n \qquad (1)$$

In this paper, $\lfloor x \rfloor$ denotes the floor function, defined as the largest integer not exceeding x. We will also need the ceiling-function, $\lceil x \rceil$, defined as the smallest integer not smaller than x.

We will denote a chaincode string by its symbol, followed by a description of the i-th element c_i. The chaincode string C corresponding to (1) is:

$$C : c_i = \lfloor y(i) \rfloor - \lfloor y(i-1) \rfloor \qquad i = 1,2,\ldots,n \qquad (2)$$

The natural question: "Given a string C, what is the set of lines $y = \alpha x + e$ that could have generated it?" will be answered in this paper.

3 The Domain of a Chaincode String

Many continuous line segments produce, when digitized, the same digital line segment. So, conversely, given a digital line segment (represented as straight chaincode string), there is not just one, but there are many continuous lines that could have been the original. The digitization process is irreversible, and this leads to a basic inaccuracy in the chaincode string representation. The problem is to determine just how large this inaccuracy is.

(The problem is solved mathematically in [8]; here we will outline the reasoning and present the result in a less precise but presumably better readable form.)

A continuous line segment, extending over n columns of a grid, is given by the familiar equation

$$y = \alpha x + e \qquad\qquad ; \; 0 < x \leqslant n \qquad (3)$$

That is, there are two parameters e (intercept) and α (slope) determining the line, and a parameter n (number of columns) determining the extent of the segment.

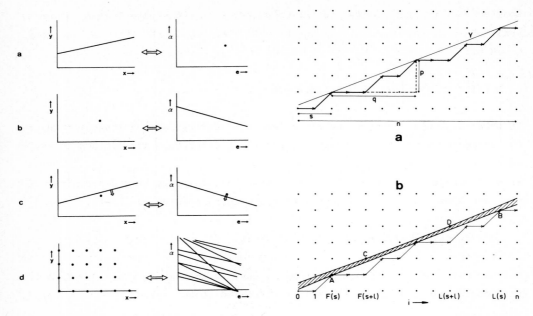

Fig.2. The relation between (x,y)-plane and the (e,α)-plane (see text).

Fig.3. a) a digitized straight line segment and the quadruple (n,q,p,s)
b) the domain in the (x,y)-plane

Thus, if we want information about all chaincode changes that may occur, we just have to transform all grid points in (x,y)-space using formula (6). This partitions (e,α)-space in cells bounded by straight lines (figure 2d). Within each cell are points (e',α') representing lines y= α'x + e' with an identical chaincode string. As soon as the boundary of a cell is traversed this corresponds to a line traversing a point in (x,y)-space, and thus to a change in the chaincode string. In this way a chaincode string directly corresponds to a cell in (e,α)-space, called the 'domain' of the string. If we can determine these domains and relate them to the string, then the basic question is answered: the e's and α's of the points within the domain specify the set of all lines that generate the same string.

4 The Structure of a Straight String

The way to solve our problem is to study the structure of a straight string first. An important theorem is the following (Theorem 4 from [8], reproduced here with the instructive proof)

Theorem. Any straight string C can be written in the form

$$C: \quad c_i = \left\lfloor \frac{P}{Q}(i-S) \right\rfloor - \left\lfloor \frac{P}{Q}(i-S-1) \right\rfloor ; \qquad i = 1,2,\ldots,N \qquad (9)$$

where P, Q, S and N are integers, P/Q is an irreducible fraction, and $0 \leqslant S < Q$.

Proof Let the line to be digitized be given by $y = \alpha x + e$ and consider its digitization in N+1 columns of the grid, leading to a string of N elements.

We chose two integers P and Q satisfying two constraints:

1) P/Q is an irreducible fraction.

2) In the N+1 columns considered, the digitization of the line $y = \alpha x + e$ is identical to the digitization of $y = \frac{P}{Q}x + e$.

(These conditions mean that $\frac{P}{Q}$ is a "very good" rational approximation of α. Since the set of rationals is dense in the set of reals, pairs of P and Q exist; in fact, one can always find an infinity of values satisfying the constraints [9].)

For the intercept $\lfloor y(i) \rfloor$ of the column $x = i$ by the digitized line we thus have:

$$\lfloor y(i) \rfloor = \lfloor \alpha i + e \rfloor = \left\lfloor \frac{P}{Q}i + e \right\rfloor$$

$$= \left\lfloor \frac{Pi + \lfloor eQ \rfloor}{Q} + \frac{eQ - \lfloor eQ \rfloor}{Q} \right\rfloor \qquad (10)$$

$$= \left\lfloor \frac{Pi + \lfloor eQ \rfloor}{Q} \right\rfloor$$

where the last transition is allowed since the first term between the brackets in (10) is a fraction with integer numerator and denominator Q, and for the second term we have: $0 \leqslant (eQ - \lfloor eQ \rfloor)/Q < 1/Q$.

This equation can be rewritten:

$$\lfloor y(i) \rfloor = \left\lfloor \frac{Pi + \lfloor eQ \rfloor}{Q} \right\rfloor = \left\lfloor \frac{P}{Q}(i - \lfloor eQ \rfloor \ell') + \lfloor eQ \rfloor \frac{\ell'P+1}{Q} \right\rfloor$$

for any value of ℓ'. In particular, we can take ℓ' to be an integer L in the range $0 \leqslant L < Q$ such that $LP = Q - 1 \pmod{Q}$. A basic result from Number Theory (Theorem 1 in [8]) guarantees the existence and uniqueness of L, given P and Q. It follows that $LP+1 = 0 \pmod{Q}$, so $(LP+1)/Q$ is an integer, and we have

$$\lfloor y(i) \rfloor = \left\lfloor \frac{P}{Q} \left(i - \lfloor eQ \rfloor L \right) \right\rfloor + \lfloor eQ \rfloor \frac{LP+1}{Q}$$

so, using formula (2):

$$c_i = \left\lfloor \frac{P}{Q}(i - \lfloor eQ \rfloor L) \right\rfloor - \left\lfloor \frac{P}{Q}(i - \lfloor eQ \rfloor L - 1) \right\rfloor, \qquad i = 1,2,\ldots,N$$

which can be rewritten as:

$$c_i = \left\lfloor \frac{P}{Q} (i - S) \right\rfloor - \left\lfloor \frac{P}{Q} (i - S - 1) \right\rfloor, \qquad i = 1,2,\ldots,N \qquad (11)$$

where $S = \lfloor eQ \rfloor L +$ (any multiple of Q). We will choose
$S = \lfloor eQ \rfloor L - \left\lfloor \frac{\lfloor eQ \rfloor L}{Q} \right\rfloor Q$, implying that $0 \leqslant S < Q$.

QED

This theorem states that any straight string can be characterized by 4 integer parameters N,P,Q,S. It can be shown that one can find from these a quadruple of unique parameters (n,q,p,s) characterizing an arbitrary string C. Here n is the number of elements, q the periodicity of the simplest periodic string of which s can be thought to be a part, p the number of codes 1 in a period q, and s a phase shift. Since there is a one-to-one correspondence between these parameters and the string from which they were derived, we may use the quadruple (n,q,p,s) instead of the string C. From these parameters the string can be reconstructed easily as

$$c_i = \left\lfloor \frac{p}{q} (i-s) \right\rfloor - \left\lfloor \frac{p}{q} (i-s-1) \right\rfloor \quad ; \ i=1,\ldots,n$$

which is the digitization of (among others) the line

$$Y : y = \frac{p}{q} x + \left\lceil \frac{sp}{q} \right\rceil - \frac{sp}{q} \qquad (12)$$

in n columns. This line is drawn in figure 3a. The domain string C is determined by some crucial points in the digitization, and these turn out to be directly related to the quadruple (n,q,p,s).

The line Y passes through a grid point in the columns

$$x = s, \ s+q, \ s+2q, \ \ldots$$

Let the last column in which it passes through a grid point be L(s). (We will explain this notation in the next section.) Shifting this line vertically, parallel to itself, we encounter other grid points, lying some distance above the line Y. The lowest grid points above the line lie at a vertical distance $\frac{1}{q}$. If the one with the smallest x-coordinate lies in the column F(s+ℓ), then the other points of this kind lie in the columns

$$x = F(s+\ell), \ F(s+\ell) + q, \ F(s+\ell) + 2q, \ \ldots$$

Let the last column of this kind be the column L(s+ℓ). It can be shown that the 4 points indicated in the columns s, L(s), F(s+ℓ) and L(s+ℓ) determine the domain of C completely. More precisely, all lines passing through the shaded area in figure 3b have as their chaincode string the string C, while lines not passing entirely through the shaded area have a different chaincode string. Therefore, the shaded area determines the domain of C.

For some strings the columns s and L(s), or F(s+ℓ) and L(s+ℓ) may coincide. In that case the domain is determined by three points, and its representation in the (e,α)-plane will be triangular.

5. Expression for the Domain

The exact expression for a domain of a string characterized by (n,q,p,s) has been derived in [8]. Introducing two functions L(x) ("last x") and F(x) ("first x") by

$$L(x) = x + \left\lfloor \frac{n-x}{q} \right\rfloor q$$

and

$$F(x) = x - \left\lfloor \frac{x}{q} \right\rfloor q$$

and an integer ℓ by the implicit definition

$$0 \leqslant \ell < q \qquad \text{and} \qquad 1 + \left\lceil \frac{\ell p}{q} \right\rceil - \frac{\ell p}{q} = \frac{1}{q}$$

the domain is described by the domain theorem in [8]:

Domain Theorem

The domain of a chaincodestring

$$c_i = \left\lfloor \frac{p}{q}(i-s) \right\rfloor - \left\lfloor \frac{p}{q}(i-s-1) \right\rfloor \qquad i = 1,\ldots,n$$

characterized by the quadruple (n,q,p,s) consists of the lines $y = \alpha x + e$, with e and α satisfying one of the following conditions:

1) $\quad \dfrac{p}{q} \leqslant \alpha < \dfrac{p}{q} + \dfrac{1}{q\{L(s+\ell)-F(s)\}}$ and

$$\left\lceil F(s) \frac{p}{q} \right\rceil - \alpha F(s) \leqslant e < 1 + \left\lfloor L(s+\ell) \frac{p}{q} \right\rfloor - \alpha L(s+\ell)$$

OR

2) $\quad \dfrac{p}{q} - \dfrac{1}{q\{L(s)-F(s+\ell)\}} < \alpha \leqslant \dfrac{p}{q}$ and

$$\left\lceil L(s) \frac{p}{q} \right\rceil - \alpha L(s) \leqslant e < 1 + \left\lfloor F(s+\ell) \frac{p}{q} \right\rfloor - \alpha F(s+\ell)$$

This solves the problem.

6. Plots of the Domains

The domains and the corresponding chaincode strings are plotted in figure 4, for all strings consisting of 6 elements. Several remarks can be made about these pictures.

Firstly, we can see that indeed each domain is bounded by 4 or 3 straight lines, as expected from section 4.

Secondly, it is seen that not all domains are of the same size: some chaincodestrings apparently determine the corresponding lines more accurately than others. Especially the 'simple' slopes $\frac{0}{1}$, $\frac{1}{1}$, $\frac{1}{2}$, $\frac{1}{3}$, $\frac{2}{3}$ and so on are generally less strictly bounded than others, and thus have larger domains.

Thirdly, the domain of a string characterized by (n,q,p,s) is centered around $\alpha = \frac{p}{q}$. In some sense, a line with slope $\frac{p}{q}$ is the 'best' line corresponding to the string (see [10]).

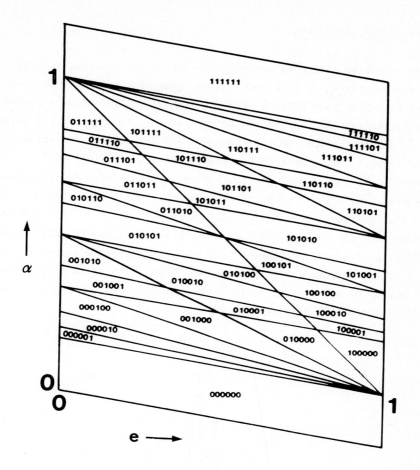

Fig.4. The (e,α)-plane with all domains of strings of 6 elements (n=6).

Fourthly, one can use the domains to estimate properties of the lines, such as linelength or slope, from the chaincode strings in an optimal way. The estimators that result from a weighted averaging of the properties over all lines in a domain are so-called BLUE: Best (in the sense of minimizing the means quare error), Linear, and Unbiased. The results will be published in a future paper [10]. A comparison to other estimators can be found in [11].

7. Accuracy of Representation

To show the potential of the information present in the domains, we will discuss a simple problem dealing with the accuracy of representation. The question to be solved is: "Given a straight line of a fixed slope α , what vertical shift (along the y-axis) can be applied to this line without being detected? ". In other words, what is the accuracy in vertical direction, as a function of slope α ? This problem is readily solved. All lines with a slope α' are on one line $\alpha = \alpha'$ in the (e,α)-plane. This line passes through several domains, say a total of D. The line is thus cut by the domain boundaries in D parts, of lengths d_i (in total i = 1,...,D). Within a domain the chaincode does not change, and thus any change in (e,α') is undetectable from the digitization data. In domain i we can thus perform a change in the intercept e of d_i, without it being detected. Thus, for a fixed α, the maximum shift that cannot be detected is $\max\{d_i\}$. This function is plotted in figure 5a (from [9]). The figure presents the worst case.

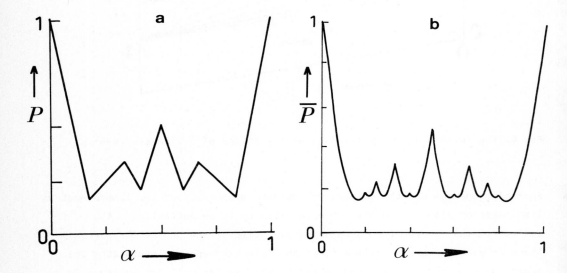

Fig. 5 a)The positional accuracy as a function of the slope α, for n=6.
b)The average positional accuracy as a function of α, for n=6.

If the lines with slope α are uniformly distributed in e (this corresponds to a uniform distribution in the so-called polar parameters, see [9]), the probability of occurrence of an undetectable shift d_i is the probability that a line is in domain i. This probability of occurrence is d_i. Thus on average, the undetectable shift that may be applied to a line of slope α is $\sum_{i=1}^{D} d_i^2$. This function is plotted in figure 5b (also from [9]).

Both figure 5 and figure 6 show that lines with simple slopes $\frac{0}{1}$, $\frac{1}{1}$, $\frac{1}{2}$ etc. are relatively less accurately determined than other slopes. Formulas for the curves, and some interesting properties, are discussed in [9]. Here, we have used it as an illustration how a powerful and interesting result follows immediately from the exact knowledge of the domains in (e,α)-space.

8. Resumé

The domains of chaincode strings, specified in the domain theorem and plotted in figure 4, provide an "inversion of the digitization process", in that the domain of a string specifies the set of all lines that could have been its pre-image before digitization. As such, they contain all information about the digitization process of straight lines in a concise and useful form.

In the course of the derivation of this result, 4 parameters were found characterizing an arbitrary chaincode string in a unique way. Though this quadruple (n,q,p,s) was just used as an intermediate result, they may be useful in image coding.

It should be noted that the results derived are mainly interesting in the field of image processing and measurement, and less so in the field of computer graphics. The digital lines are not artificially generated, but found in an image that is derived from the real, continuous world. For straight lines, the question how accurately one can reconstruct reality from this digital image has been answered completely by the research reported in this paper.

References

[1] H. Freeman, "Boundary encoding and processing", in *Picture Processing and Psychopictorics*, B.S. Lipkin and A. Rosenfeld, Eds. New York: Academic, 1970, pp. 241-266.

[2] A. Rosenfeld, "Digital straight line segments", *IEEE Trans. Comput.*, vol. C-23, pp. 1264-1269, 1974.

[3] R. Brons, "Linguistic Methods for the Description of a straight Line on a Grid", *Comp. Graph. Image Proc.*, vol. 3, 1974, pp. 48-62.

[4] C. Arcelli and A. Massarotti, "On the Parallel Generation of Straight Digital Lines", *Comp. Graph. Image Proc.*, vol. 7, 1978, pp. 67-63.

[5] L.D. Wu, "On the Chain Code of a Line", *IEEE Trans. Pattern Anal. Machine Intell*, vol. PAMI-4, 1982, pp. 347-353.

[6] F.C.A. Groen and P.W. Verbeek, "Freeman-code probabilities of object boundary quantized contours", *Comput. Graphics Image Processing*, vol. 7, pp. 391-402, 1978.

[7] A.M. Vossepoel and A.W.M. Smeulders, "Vector code probability and metrication error in the representation of straight lines of finite length", *Comput. Graphics Image Processing*, vol. 20, pp. 347-364, 1982.

[8] L. Dorst and A.W.M. Smeulders, "Discrete Representation of Straight Lines", *Pattern Anal. Machine Intell*, vol. PAMI-6, no. 4, 1984, 450-463.

[9] L. Dorst and R.P.W. Duin, "Spirograph Theory, a Framework for Calculations on Digital Straight Lines", *Pattern Anal. Machine Intell.*, vol. PAMI-6, no. 5, 1984, 632-639.

[10] L. Dorst and A.W.M. Smeulders, "Best Linear Unbiased Estimators for Properties of Digitized Line Segments", *internal report*, Technical University Delft, Delft, The Netherlands, 1985

[11] L. Dorst, "Length Estimators Compared", *4th Scandinavian Conference on Image Analysis*, Trondheim, Norway, June 17-20, 1985

EXPERIENCE IN PRACTICAL IMPLEMENTATION
OF BOUNDARY-DEFINED AREA FILL

A.C. Gay
Graphics Advanced Development
IBM (UK) Laboratories Ltd
Hurslry Park
Winchester
Hampshire

ABSTRACT

This short paper describes a practical implementation of
a boundary-defined area filling algorithm for a raster display
device. The actual algorithm selected is explained in a terse
'how-to-do-it' style and selection tradeoffs with other algorithms are explained, hopefully justifying the choice.

INTRODUCTION

This paper describes a practical implementation of a
boundary-defined area filling algorithm for a raster display
device.

Other 'region' or 'area' filling algorithms for raster
displays are well described in the references.

BOUNDARY SPECIFICATION REQUIREMENTS

In our particular application, the Area Boundary Definition has a number of requirements:
- Capable of handling complex non-convex areas with boundary segments defined by lines and curves.
- Boundary segments specified in any temporal order.
- An infinite number of boundary segments must be handled
  but the boundary definition must only be processed once
  so that no additional storage is required.
- Boundary definition can specify multiple closed 'figures'

NATO ASI Series, Vol. F17
Fundamental Algorithms for Computer Graphics
Edited by R. A. Earnshaw
© Springer-Verlag Berlin Heidelberg 1985

i.e. multiple separate, intersecting or enclosed shapes
(Figure 1).

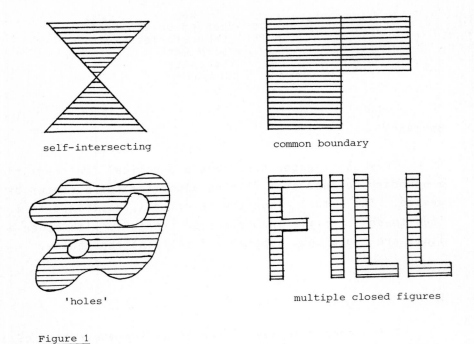

self-intersecting   common boundary

'holes'   multiple closed figures

Figure 1

. Abutting areas must not overlap, especially when filled
  with a pattern.
. Boundary segments will define a closed area.

BASIC PBP ALGORITHM

The basic PBP algorithm is described in (1). The algorithm requires a 1 bit/pel store corresponding to the display
screen. This could be a real bit plane or a piece of processor
memory, logically organised in the same layout as the screen,
and will be called a 'Pseudo Bit Plane' (PBP). Each boundary
segment is processed as received. The line or curve is drawn
into the PBP, as if rastering a normal line or curve, so that
after the last segment has been processed, the PBP contains a
closed, 1 bit/pel outline of the area to be filled.

The PBP is then scanned, one scan line at a time, from left to right (or right to left, if you like), looking for bits representing the outline. Scanning starts 'outside' the area. When an outline bit is found, the corresponding screen X ordinate is saved and scanning continues 'inside'. When the next outline bit is found, the scan line segment between the saved and the current X ordinate is filled and scanning reverts to 'outside'. The process continues in this fashion until the right edge of the screen is reached. All scan line segments will then have been filled on the current line (unless you have a bug). Of course, in some implementations, when 'inside', filling could proceed in parallel with searching for the next outline bit.

If the boundary of the area is drawn in the PBP using 'normal' line/curve drawing, problems occur during the edge scanning process (Figure 2):

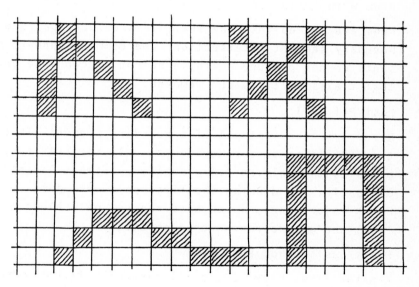

Figure 2

- Y-axis vertices result in a single pel defining the scan line segment to be filled instead of the required pair.
- Boundary self-intersections and common segments also result in a single pel.

. X-major lines/curves generate runs of pels along a scan
line. This would cause the edge-scanner to switch between
inside/outside along the scan line and would result in
inside/outside inversion, depending upon run length.

'DRAWING' RULES

The following simple-to-implement rules, used in combination, solve these problems.

1. Force Drawing Direction

Always draw boundary segments in a fixed Y direction, say,
from the endpoint with highest Y ordinate to the endpoint
with the lowest Y ordinate (swapping endpoints as necessary).

2. Draw with Exclusive-Or (XOR)

Pens are XOR-ed into the PBP. This ensures pairs of
boundary segment intersections and common boundary segments do not produce a single pel on a scan line and
that Y-axis vertices are removed.

3. Last Pel Null

Never draw the last pel of a boundary segment. This stops
the XOR-ing process removing not only the Y-axis vertices,
but also the pels at every boundary segment 'joint'.
Obviously, not drawing the first pel works just as well.
For X-major lines, which have runs of pels along a scan
line, the entire run must be omitted.

4. First/Last Pel of Run

X-major lines have horizontal runs of pels. Only the
first pel of a run for octants 1 and 5, and only the
last pel is drawn for octants 4 and 8. This ensures the
required pair of pairs per scan line segment to be filled,
and that areas abut symmetrically.

5. Reject

Single pels and horizontal segments are ignored as their
endpoints are shared with neighbouring boundary segments.

It should be noted that if Rule 1 is changed to 'draw bottom-to-top' then by symmetry, Rule 3 should change to 'First Pel Null'.

NO SPARE BIT PLANE!

Some implementers are lucky, in that they either have, or their customers can pay for, a physical spare bit plane, the same size as the displayable screen. Some don't. However, any piece of storage will do. In fact this algorithm has been implemented for a 1024X1024 raster device using a 16K-byte work area i.e. one-eighth of the physical screen, by performing multiple passes in a 'swathing' fashion; although in this particular case, additional storage (in the application program) was obviously needed to retain the description of the boundary.

HARDWARE IMPLEMENTATION

Most raster display devices already have hardware line generators and the ability to write into the image planes using XOR. 'Last pel null' is simply a case of reducing the loop count by one before drawing. A simple modification of the standard line drawing algorithm gives 'one pel per scan line' for X-major lines and single pels and horizontals can be rejected by software.

Once the outline is drawn, either software can read the image plane and scan for edges or specialised hardware can easily be provided which can scan thePBP and fill at the same time.

OPTIMISATION

A number of obvious optimisations can be made to improve performance:
- In a software implementation, optimised code loops should be written for Y-major, X-major, 45 degree and vertical

segments. Also, if a fast divide operation is available, Bresenham's Run Length Line Generation algorithm could be used for X-major lines simplifying the one pel per horizontal run operation.

. As the boundary segments are processed, the 'bounding box' should be recorded i.e. the minimum and maximum X and Y coordinates. These are used to restrict the edge scanner to the region of the PBP containing the area outline.

. Although the algorithm is intentionally general, convex areas, especially rectangles, should be detected and can then be processed in a pairwise fashion eliminating the need to actually draw the outline in the PBP and scan for edges.

. Multipass versions can be optimised by determining the swathe(s) in which the area starts and ends, processing these swathes only and only edge scanning when something is drawn in the current swathe.

COMPARISON WITH OTHER ALGORITHMS

Any form of interior-fill algorithm was out of the question for our implementation, simply because although the outline could easily be drawn into the real image planes, and a point inside the area could be found, part of the overall picture would be there already and would 'interfere' with the flood fill.

Parity-Fill algorithms which use the image planes as working storage i.e. no additional storage required, take up to twice as many bit plane accesses as the PBP algorithm and the algorithm requires the data to be XOR-ed into the existing picture. It also makes the handling of pattern fill difficult. One might also object to the flashing effects on the screen as the boundary is traversed.

Using a Parity-Fill algorithm to generate a representation of the area to be filled in a spare bit plane solves the XOR and pattern problems, but takes up to three times the bit plane accesses.

The other practical choice for a GENERAL boundary-defined area fill algorithm is the 'Active Edge List' (AEL) method described in (3). In fact, the choice is not an obvious one, so both the PBP and AEL algorithms were implemented and compared for a 1024x1024 screen. The PBP implementation was actually a four-pass 32K-byte version.

From a drawing performance point of view, both algorithms were used on a number of test areas. ThePBP algorithm performance is proportional to the 'bounding box' of the area definition, whilst the AEL algorithm is proportional to the number of active edges. The AEL algorithm only outperforms the PBP algorithm for areas with few edges and large physical area.

Another disadvantage of the AEL algorithm for our application was that we use (for speed) a cording type of curve generation algorithm i.e. straight line approximation. Thus for each curve segment of the area boundary definition, many straight line segments are generated, requiring much additional storage in the edge lists and slightly increasing the sort time. The PBP algorithm, of course, draws each straight line segment as generated and requires no additional storage.

Also, AEL algorithm would be more difficult and expensive to implement in hardware and thus cannot compete with the PBP algorithm on that basis.

Finally, triangulation of the general non-convex outline into easily processable (convex) triangles was considered, but the performance improvement gained by this is soon lost on complex outlines, such as in cartography, and by outlines consisting of curves, as one ends up with a large number (at worst, one per scan line covered by the area) of long thin triangles.

REFERENCES

1. Ackland, B.D. and Weste, N.H., "The Edge Flag Algorithm - A Fill Method for Raster Scan Displays, IEEE Trans. Comput., C-30, 1, January 1981, p41.

2. Dunlavey, M.R., "Efficient Polygon-Filling Algorithms for

Raster Displays", ACM Transactions on Graphics, Vol. 2, No. 4, October 1983, p264.

3. Foley, J.D. and Van Dam, A., "Fundamentals of Interactive Computer Graphics", Addison-Wesley, 1982, p456.

4. Pavlidis, T., "Filling Algorithms in Raster Graphics", Computer Graphics and Image Processing, Vol. 10, No. 2, June 1979, p126.

5. Pavlidis, T., "Contour Filling in Raster Graphics", Computer Graphics, Vol. 15, No. 3, August 1979, p29.

6. Quarendon, P., "Area Rendering Algorithm for Cell Graphics", IBM Technical Disclosure Bulletin, Vol. 22, No. 3, August 1979, p1208.

Abstract

The implementation of fill area for GKS

The paper describes the generation of a GKS fill area by a series of
hatch lines. The complexity of the problem and the effect of sorting
is discussed. Two methods of sorting both of which generate lists are
described, code is presented and performance is discussed. Two
methods of handling corners are described and Fortran 77 code is
presented for the complete algorithm using one method.

C J Cartledge & G H Weeks

Computing Sevices Section
University of Salford
Salford M5 4WT
England

NATO ASI Series, Vol. F17
Fundamental Algorithms for Computer Graphics
Edited by R. A. Earnshaw
© Springer-Verlag Berlin Heidelberg 1985

Implementation of Area Fill for GKS

1   Introduction

The adoption of GKS as a Standard in the UK (BS6390 whose text is identical to [2]), and its impending adoption both as an International Standard [1] and as an ANSI Standard, means that those algorithms required by GKS should be thoroughly investigated with a view to optimising their implementation. In the past a number of methods have been used to define the area enclosed by a boundary. There is now the requirement to focus on the single method prescribed by GKS.

Many devices currently do not support the algorithms required by GKS. For such devices, implementations must simulate complex primitives by a series of more simple ones.

In particular this paper discusses the filling of areas by a succession of horizontal lines, scan line conversion [5], [6]. On real devices, lines have non-zero thickness so a finite number of lines will fill an area.

With an increasing number of devices having GKS capabilities the code will move into those devices but this will not remove the need for the code to be implemented efficiently. Indeed for one class of device, the workstation with a memory mapped display, fast graphics depends either on the efficient implementation of graphics algorithms or on the provision of special hardware. Even such special hardware should contain adroit implementations of efficient algorithms.

Thanks are due to Kelvyn Hipperson who implemented the first version of the Fortran fill area code as part of a third year undergraduate project.

2   GKS

2.1 Polygon definition

GKS [1] addresses a physical device through an interface called a workstation. Although an output graphical device may only have, for example, the ability to mark specified points on a display surface and to clear that surface, a GKS workstation has defined capabilities. One of the capabilities that must be provided by a GKS output workstation is the ability to represent a fill area.

The GKS fill area output primitive is a polygon specified by three or more points, N say. These points define N lines

$$P_i \text{ to } P_{i+1} \qquad\qquad 0 < i < N$$

$$P_N \text{ to } P_1$$

which are the edges of the polygon so the points are the successive vertices of the polygon.

2.2 Polygon interior

GKS defines the interior of the polygon as follows (note that there
has been a significant change in the definition from GKS 7.2 [2] to
GKS 7.4 [1]).

> For a given point, create a straight line starting at that point
> and going to infinity. If the number of intersections between
> the straight line and the polygon is odd, the point is inside
> the polygon; otherwise it is outside. If the straight line
> passes a polygon vertex tangentially, the intersection count is
> not affected. If a point is within the polygon, it is included
> in the area to be filled, subject to the rule for boundaries.
>
> If, after the workstation transformation, all points coincide,
> no error is generated and whether anything is drawn is
> workstation dependent. If, after the workstation
> transformation, some or all of the lines in a bounding polygon
> have a line segment in common, no error is generated. Whether
> the resulting line is regarded as part of the boundary to be
> drawn or not is workstation dependent.

Though this definition has driven the implementation of area fill
described in the paper and will be referred to in subsequent sections,
it provides an inadequate definition of the interior. The case where
the straight line is tangential to the boundary is described, but the
other special case where the line passes through a vertex is not.

The polygon may be transformed and it must be clipped within GKS, but
these operations are not discussed in this paper.

2.3 Fortran binding

The Fortran 77 [10] GKS binding [3] specifies the following form for a
point array.

> POINT ARRAY   INTEGER giving length of the POINT ARRAY, REAL
>   array1(length) containing the X-values, REAL
>   array2(length) containing the Y-values. Note that
>   the implementation may trap length >1 by using * to
>   dimension the formal arguments. (sic)

The output function fill area is, in the Fortran binding, a subroutine
called GFA, so the following program fragment:

```
      PROGRAM FILL
      REAL X(3), Y(3)
      DATA X / 0.1, 0.9, 0.5 /
      DATA Y / 0.3, 0.2, 0.8 /
*
* Open GKS.
      . . .
* Output an area
      CALL GFA(3,X,Y)
      . . .
```

outputs the triangle with edges (0.1,0.3),(0.9,0.2);
(0.9,0.2),(0.5,0.8); (0.5,0.8),(0.1,0.3) subject to the current fill
area attributes.

It is worth noting that the Fortran binding does not follow the spirit
of the Functional Description. Though it may seem natural in the
context of a Fortran program to represent an array of points as two
one-dimensional arrays, one containing X-values and the other
containing Y-values, it does not seem natural in any other context.
Other language bindings are not using a similar representation to
Fortran and are following the Standard more closely.

There is an advantage in the Fortran approach for an implementor,
though. The lack of structured data means that, for example, a
standard sort may be used to sort coordinates without the sort knowing
that the values being sorted are in any way related to points.

3 Fill area styles

3.1 Definitions

GKS [1] specifies that four forms of fill area style may be available,
though an impoverished workstation in an impoverished implementation
need not provide any other than HOLLOW.

l   a) HOLLOW: No filling, but draw the bounding polyline, using the
fill area colour index currently selected.

    b) SOLID: Fill the interior of the polygon using the fill area
colour index currently selected.

    c) PATTERN: Fill the interior of the polygon using the fill area
style index currently selected as an index into the
pattern table.

    d) HATCH: Fill the interior of the polygon using the the fill
area style index currently selected. The fill area
style index is taken as a pointer into the list of
hatch styles, in which case it is sometimes referred as
the hatch index.

3.2 HOLLOW

As the definition indicated this does not cause the area to be filled
and so is discussed no further in this paper.

3.3 SOLID

SOLID fill may be achieved by drawing a set of lines of finite width
parallel to one another and one line width apart in the appropriate
colour. It is usual to draw the lines horizontally on the device and
this is most conveniently done in device coordinates, after
transformations. Drawing the lines at any angle other than horizontal
or vertical will, almost inevitably, result in gaps on raster devices
due to the sampling effect of rasterisation on the lines.

Some devices have hardware to fill polygons that satisfy certain restrictions, and other devices have used a different definition of the interior of a polygon from GKS. It is possible to make limited use of such hardware capabilities, usually for solid fill only.

(a) If the device has an archaic definition for the interior of the polygon then the definition will almost certainly hold good for convex polygons. It is simple to check for a convex polygon by testing to see if the cross-product of successive polygon edges all have the same sign.

(b) If the device is capable of filling triangles then any convex polygon may be filled by a succession of triangles where one point is fixed at a vertex of the polygon and the other two points are ends of each of the other sides of the polygon in turn.

(c) If the device is capable of filling rectangles parallel to the major axes, it is worth making use of the feature, since such shapes are used in many applications.

3.4 PATTERN

PATTERN fill may be achieved in two ways, either by filling with set of lines each having a style corresponding to the correct slice from the pattern or by taking each rectangle of the pattern, clipping the polygon against that rectangle and filling the resultant shape in style SOLID in the correct colour. The latter technique would only be appropriate for large pattern sizes. The former method can be split into two phases, the first being the generation of horizontal lines as for solid fill above, then instead of drawing each line in a single colour as it is generated, it is drawn in a pattern that matches a horizontal slice from the specified fill area pattern.

On devices with 'rasterop' capabilities there is a means of speeding up the process. Before filling a area, the complete pattern selected by the pattern index, shifted to the pattern origin and distorted by transformations, is replicated across the width of the picture using rasterop in an area of memory that is off-screen. Then, as each line is generated, an appropriate section of the pattern may copied to the screen again using rasterop.

Patterns may or may not be affected by tranformations, though the Standard implies that it is preferable that they be transformable. For the same reason as for solid fill, the raster lines should be drawn horizontally in device coordinates which means that the patterns rather than the scan lines should be taken through transformations.

Patterns are user definable and are potentially very powerful. A pattern definition may be obtained by reading back any combination of output primitives from a device supporting the inquire pixel array function. This pattern definition, which might be a piece of text for example, may then be replicated across an area on any other active workstation. There are problems though, the pattern will only be of the resolution of the device supporting inquire pixel array. In addition some implementors may decide to limit the complexity of definable patterns, though the GKS Standard provides no error for exceeding such a limit. A friendly GKS implementor might provide a workstation with pixel read-back and high resolution which has no physical display surface (like the metafile output workstation) but which supports read pixel array. Patterns would then not have to be physically displayed before being used.

Patterns are specified in a raster manner and so are unsuited to vector devices. The example given above of a piece of text being used as a pattern would give degraded output on a vector device, the text having been scan converted. It would also take an age to draw on a pen plotter so implementors may reasonably take the decision not to support patterns on vector devices.

3.5 HATCH

HATCH styles are not user specifiable so it is up to the implementor what he provides on any particular workstation. HATCH need not be provided on a workstation but if it is, at least three different styles must be provided. It is up to the implementor whether hatching is or is not affected by transformations. Hatching will typically be provided on vector displays where solid and pattern styles may not be supported.

The requirements of hatching in current applications require that a good implementation provides:

  (a) hatching with lines at different angles;

  (b) hatching at different densities;

  (c) cross hatching;

  (d) hatching with different line styles;

  (e) hatching with symbols, fir trees for forests, etc.

It is possible to hatch at an angle by transforming the points before entry to a hatch routine and by inversely transforming the lines generated. Cross hatching may be performed by making multiple entries to a routine that does single hatching.

Hatching with different line styles may be achieved by imposing a line style on the lines output by a hatching routine, but some consideration must be given to maintaining coherence of the patterns.

Hatching with symbols is best tackled differently, by clipping the lines of each symbol against the polygon defining the area. Code for such a process is given in [4].

The lack of specification of hatching in GKS is a nightmare for the user. For example, to achieve the simple requirement of hatching at different densities on different workstations (even in the same implementation) an application may:

(a) where hatching is affected by tranformations (including segment
transformations), have to scale the data and alter the limits
of world coordinates;

(b) select an appropriate hatch index specific to the workstation;

(c) not be able to do it!

It would seem to me that anyone seriously wishing to use hatching on a
GKS implementation and wishing to maintain portability should only
call both hatch style selection and the fill area routine from within
a interface layer which could be expected to need rewriting for each
GKS implementation used or even for each workstation on a single
implementation.

3.6 Using the facilities

With the weak definition of hatch style, it is probably best avoided
where possible by writers of applications. It is possible to discover
which fill styles are available using the inquire fill area facilities
function. Although it is possible for the application to inquire what
facilities are available, it is not possible to inquire as to their
cost, so the enthusiastic implementor who provides all fill area
styles for all workstations, whatever the cost (pattern and solid are
potentially very expensive on pen plotters), is doing the user no
favours. One can only reach the conclusion that many applications
will have to provide their own hatching routines due to the inadequate
control provided by GKS.

4 Fill area support

4.1 Requirements

It may be seen that by the transformation of points before entry to a
fill area support routine and the manipulation of the lines generated
that the basic requirement is for scan conversion of a polygon by
horizontal lines with a specifiable gap between successive scan lines.

The algorithm should be efficient, in some sense, and the algorithm
presented here uses sorting to reduce the work required in typical
cases.

4.2 The basic algorithm

The naive approach to the problem is to:

(a) initialise a scan line Y-value generator;

(b) generate the next scan line value;

   (c) initialise a polygon edge index;

      (d) intersect the scan line with the next polygon edge,
          saving the intersection value;

   (e) repeat (d) until no more polygon edge;

(f) each point on the scan line between the left-most
intersection and next left-most has an odd number of
intersections with the polygon between it and infinity,
so from the definition (2.2) is inside the area, so draw
a line from the left-most to next left-most and discard
the two points;

(g) repeat (f) until no more points remain;

(h) repeat (b) onwards until no more scan lines remain to be
generated.

If there are N points in the polygon and M scan lines then it may be
seen that (d) is performed N*M times and that (f) is performed at most
N*M times. The complexity of the algorithm is potentially N*M. The
example below shows that this may be achieved in practice with a very
simple case so there is no prospect of improving the worst case.

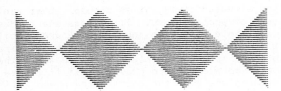

In the example above, every scan line has an intersection with every
polygon edge making the complexity of scan line generation N*M. It is
possible to improve the typical case in a number of ways.

4.3 Vertices

4.3.1

The algorithm as described above breaks down at vertices. Where a
scan line is coincident with a vertex, two or zero intersections may
result where for correctness exactly one must be found, unless the
point is a local minimum or maximum in Y-value. A robust algorithm
must cope with this reliably.

4.3.2 Exact test

One technique is to use an exact test to make one end of the line an
open interval and the other end a closed interval in a consistent way.
Only those polygon edges with the following relationship to the scan
line are considered

$l \quad P_i, \ P_j$ i,j having the relationship in 2.1

where

$P_{i_Y} \leq$ Scan line Y $< P_{j_Y}$ P_{i_Y} being the Y-coordinate of P_i

Where a scan line coincides with a vertex one intersection will
result, except for local minima where two intersections will result
and local maxima where zero intersections will result. Horizontal

lines will be ignored which is consistent with the definition of the interior of a polygon in section 2.2.

This technique is used in the Fortran that appears later but it is worth noting that although no explicit exact comparison is made of the scan line Y-value and the Y-value of points, the correct operation of the algorithm depends on exactly one of A $\leq$ B and A > B being consistently true at more than one instance in the program. This will not, in general be the case with an optimising compiler (Cody [8]), where floating point representation is being used.

The code as presented is vunerable to such errors since the value of the scan line Y-value (YSCAN) could be calculated into an over-length register, used, put into store and then brought back into a register for use later in the calculation where it would have a different value, giving rise to inconsistent answers.

The points, being in arrays will not suffer such damage. This technique is only unsafe using floating point numbers, fixed point numbers do not usually suffer the problem. It is worth noting that it is very easy to implicitly test two floating point numbers for equality without doing it explicitly.

4.3.3 Moving the scan line

Another technique is to move the scan line up by a small amount if it coincides with a vertex. A suitable value for the small amount is

$$(1.0+EPS)*MAX(ABS(P_{i_Y}))*EPS \qquad \text{for all } i, 1 \leq i \leq N$$

where EPS is the smallest number such that 1.0+EPS > 1.0 on the machine on which the implementation is being performed.

For consistency, when the scan line is moved, all intersections with the given scan line previously generated must be discarded and recalculated to prevent inconsistent intersections being found. The movement need not be reflected in the output Y-value.

4.3.4 Moving the vertex

A third option is to move the vertex by a small amount, but this means that the input polygon must be written to. Similar considerations as in 4.3.3 apply.

4.4 Sorting on Y

In step 4.2(d), the work would be reduced if only those polygon edges that span the scan line are considered. There is no improvement in the worst case shown in 4.2 since there, all scan lines cross all polygon edges.

It is not immediately clear how to sort lines but what one can do is sort the points. The form in which the polygon is defined is compact, since each point only appears once even though it is an end point of two edges. Each point is connected to its two neighbours tomake polygon edges (taking points 1 and N to be neighbours). If the points were physically moved during a sort then this information about neighbours would be lost.

A sort should be used that retains the position of the points and either an index array or a chained list (Knuth [7]) could be used to reference the points in their sorted order. For the purposes of this algorithm we wish to discard lines and not consider them further once the scan line has passed them by. The advantage of a chained list is that elements may be trivially dropped, making it appropriate in this application. The points are sorted using their Y-value as a key.

It is important to make best use of the sort information, with as many as possible of those polygon edges that do not span the infinite scan line being ignored as possible. The following approach is taken:

(a) from a given point

$$P_i$$

the edges to both adjacent points

$$P_{i-1} \text{ and } P_{i+1}$$

(including wrap round between N and 1), are considered;

(b) lines not increasing in Y are rejected, so lines where

$$P_{i\pm1_Y} \leq P_{i_Y}$$

are not considered.

This results in horizontal lines being rejected, consistent with the definition is section 2.2 and other lines being considered exactly once. Effectively, without altering the way points are stored, the polygon edges have been sorted on their smallest Y-value. The vertices are considered exactly once, using the technique descibed in 4.3.2.

Points where both

$$P_{i+1_Y} \leq P_{i_Y} \qquad \text{(wrapping round between 1 and N as before)}$$

and

$$P_{i-1_Y} \leq P_{i_Y}$$

are true can be dropped from the list. In addition points which the scan line has passed by, where both

$$P_{i+1_Y} \leq \text{ scan line Y-value}$$

and

$$P_{i-1_Y} \leq \text{ scan line Y-value}$$

are true can be dropped. The other advantage of this approach that
the loop over polygon edges for a given scan line can be terminated as
soon as the first point where

$$P_{i_Y} > \text{scan line Y-value.}$$

is reached since the points are sorted and we only consider lines
which increase in Y-value. The code for this is in the lines of code
sequenced 0880 to 1400.

4.5 The butterfly sort

The particular sort chosen, the butterfly sort, is due to Hart [8].
It is a list merge sort. The routine has been translated from BASIC
and the termination condition for a list, the null pointer, has been
changed from pointing to itself to pointing to zero. This enables the
last item of a list to be removed without that being a special case.
In Fortran 77, there being no pointer type, integers have been used as
pointers. The case of N being two has been treated as a special case.
The butterfly sort is particularly low in its workspace requirement,

$$N + INT(\ LOG_2 N\ ) + 2$$

pointers being the space required, except for a small number of
temporaries. These have to be in a single array as programmed in
Fortran, but in languages with genuine pointers all but N values could
conveniently be of fixed allocation.

The sort is one that minimises the number of comparisons, though with
the comparison of numbers cheap, this is not very relevent in this
application. The sort as programmed is not stable (equal values may
not be output in the in the same order as they were input), although
it the original Hart code and the alternative code presented are
stable, but again this is not relevent in this application.

The following program

```
      REAL X(3)
      INTEGER IP(6)
      DATA X / 10, 5, 8 /
      CALL GKSORT(X, 3, IP, 6)
      PRINT *, IP(1), IP(2), IP(3), IP(4)
      END
```

illustrates the chains generated, outputting

        0   3   1   2

The output is interpreted as follows:

   IP(4) - IP(N+1), the root of the chain points to (has the value) 2
        which is the smallest element of X;

   IP(2) points to 3 which is the next smallest element of X;

IP(3) points to 1 which is largest element of X and

IP(1) points to 0 indicating it is the end of the chain.

The sort has a run time that is almost independent of the data values presented. Its run time, assymtotically, is proportional to N*LOG(N) for all input data. As presented here a number of small changes could be made to improve run times.

(a) The divisions by 2 (lines sequenced 2690, 2820 and 2860) are of positive integers and so could be replaced by shift operations (not in standard Fortran 77!).

(b) The merge machine, which occupies the bulk of the run time contains redundant operations. Four different codings were tried (including the one in Hart's paper) and the following longer and more obscure Fortran code replacing lines sequenced 3250 to 3370 minimises number of instructions executed for a merge on a Prime using the Salford Fortran compiler [9] and also stabilises the sort.

```
     5         IF(X(L1).GT.X(L2))THEN
               SX(LO)=L2
               LO=L2
               L2=SX(LO)
               IF(L2.NE.0)GOTO 1040
               SX(LO)=L1
               GOTO 1050
               ELSE
               LO=L1
               L1=SX(LO)
               IF(L1.NE.0)GOTO 5
               SX(LO)=L2
               GOTO 1050
               ENDIF
     1040      IF(X(L1).GT.X(L2))THEN
               LO=L2
               L2=SX(LO)
               IF(L2.NE.0)GOTO 1040
               SX(LO)=L1
               ELSE
               SX(LO)=L1
               LO=L1
               L1=SX(LO)
               IF(L1.NE.0)GOTO 5
               SX(LO)=L2
               ENDIF
     1050      CONTINUE
```

The improvements resulting from recoding are small, and significant improvements could only be made by coding in machine code.

4.6 An alternative sort

The above sort, using comparisons is much slower assymtotically, than
a bucket or category sort where values are allocated to a position in
the list algorithmically. In the case we are considering, we do not
care about the exact Y order of points, but between which two scan
lines they appear. Such sorts are called category, radix or bucket
sorts. They require no comparisons and run in time directly
proportional to N, but with a overhead dependent on the number of
buckets M. A bucket sort is particularly appropriate for hatching on
a device of low resolution. The sort time is totally independent of
the data presented. Workspace of size N+M is required. Suitable code
to replace GKSORT follows.

```
          SUBROUTINE RL256(X, N, L, M)
C
C Alternative to butterfly sort - a radix list sort
C
          REAL
     +    A,
     +    X(N)
          INTEGER
     +    I, ICAT,
     +    J,
     +    L(M),
     +    MAXCAT, MINCAT,
     +    N
* Currently have MAXCAT and MINCAT as parameters.
          PARAMETER (MAXCAT = 256, MINCAT = 0)
* Statement function ICAT.
          ICAT(A) = A*256
*
* Zero all the category lists. Store the category lists in elements N+2
* onwards of L.
          DO 10 I = MINCAT, MAXCAT
            L(N+2+I-MINCAT) = 0
10        CONTINUE
* Scan the points, from the last to the first to make the sort stable,
* and put each on the front of its category list, generating
* MAXCAT-MINCAT+1 lists.
          DO 20 J = N, 1, -1
            I = ICAT(X(J))
            L(J) = L(N+2+I-MINCAT)
            L(N+2+I-MINCAT) = J
20        CONTINUE
* The list root is in L(N+1).
          J = N+1
* Concatenate the MAXCAT-MINCAT+1 lists into one.
          DO 40 I = MINCAT, MAXCAT
* Skip null lists.
            IF(L(N+2+I-MINCAT).NE.0)THEN
* Chain the next list on.
              L(J) = L(N+2+I-MINCAT)
* Follow the list to its end.
30            J = L(J)
              IF(L(J).NE.0)GOTO 30
            ENDIF
40        CONTINUE
          END
```

As presented the routine assumes that the points lie in the range zero to one and exactly 256 buckets are required. To replace GKSORT in a practical enviroment, additional information would be required as arguments to remove these assumptions. The relative performance the butterfly sort and two category sorts appears below. Features to note are:

(a) the large overhead of the category sorts which is proportional to M;

(b) the precise straight line of low angle of the category sorts showing that their timings are truely proportion to N with a low factor;

(c) the much steeper angled line for the butterfly due its code being more complicated than that of the category sorts;

(d) the butterfly sort line curves slightly upwards showing N*LOG(N) cost of a true sort based upon comparisons.

Sort times for the butterfly sort (BFSORT) and bucket sort with 256 bins (RS256) and 1024 bins (RS1024)

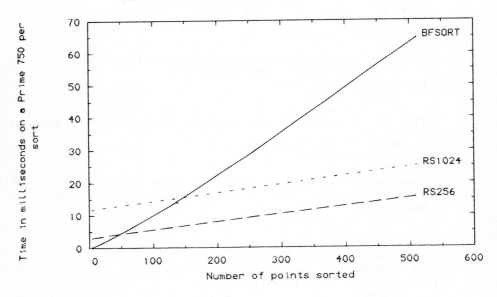

4.7 Sorting on X

The simplest way of finding the left-most intersection, step 4.2(f) is to sort the intersections on their X-value. It seems sensible to use the same sort as for Y. In the case of intersections, there will usually be only two values which was the reason for making this a special case in the sort routine, GKSORT (lines sequence 2430 to 2510).

4.8 Removing redundant points

From the definition of the interior of a polygon in 2.2 it can be seen that pairs of coincident points may be eliminated, whether forming a bridge or a cut of the polygon. The code presented eliminates redundant points using an exact test (line sequenced 1560) for equality which, in a floating point enviroment will almost never happen, though the test would be satisfactory is a fixed point enviroment. The equality test should be replaced by a test with a tolerance, but the tolerance used will depend on whether the hatching is being done in world coordinates or device coodinates. In world coordinates it should be tight, probably

$$(1.0+EPS)*MAX(ABS(P_{i_X}))*EPS \qquad \text{for all } i, 1 \leq i \leq N$$

In device coordinates the tolerance can be half the resolution of the device.

4.9 Optimising the pen path

For pen plotters and devices limited in speed by a slow line between the device and machine it is worthwhile optimising the pen path. The code contains two forms of path optimisation. The first is that successive scan lines are drawn in opposite directions. The second is more subtle and affects the classification of the algorithm [6]. Multiple passes of the data are made (up to the limit specified by the parameter MXPASS) with only one pair of intersections being taken each time, eliminating multiple long moves where the pen is drawing nothing. MXPASS simply limits the number of passes over the data. As programmed, the Y-sort is performed for once each pass, but the need for more than one sort may be removed by supplying additional workspace to keep two copies of the Y-sort list. This optimisation decreases the locality of algorithm for a bit mapped display and may be disabled by setting MXPASS to zero. MXPASS could be made an argument to the routine.

The combined effect of the two optimisations is to reduce the data transmitted down a line by about 30% to a device using Tektronix 4010 protocol.

4.10 Other considerations

The routine has been made device independent by making the output routine an argument. In the example program supplied GPL, the GKS polyline routine has been used, but in a practical environment this would be a device specific routine.

Care has been taken to ensure that overflow can never occur and the statement function XVALUE (lines sequenced 0460 and 0470) has brackets placed to prevent this. An optimising compiler might reorder the expression, overiding the brackets and making the code less safe. Underflow can occur in the statement function, but the normal action on underflow of truncation to zero is correct.

5 Conclusions

A Fortran 77 routine is described and presented that does line scan conversion for the GKS fill area primitive. Although the code is portable, a few features of the code are identified which may cause problems with optimising compilers on some processors. The code has been tested on a large number of cases in a Fortran 77 system that makes extensive checks for conformance with the Standard, both statically and at run time. Reasonable efforts have been made to make the algorithm efficient and alternative techniques have been suggested for specific environments.

6 Fortran 77 fill area scan conversion code

```
      SUBROUTINE GKWFA ( NPT , XPT , YPT , YDIFF , NSY , SY , NXI , XI, 0010
     *                    NSXI , SXI , GKNWPL )                         0020
*****************************************************************************0030
*                                                                       *0040
* SYN GKWFA system routine to output fill area primitive               *0050
* This routine performs the interior style hatching for the fill       *0060
* area primitive.                                                       *0070
* INPUT-OUTPUT                                                          *0080
* INPUT NPT, Number of points  (INTEGER).                              *0090
* INPUT XPT,  X coordinates  (REAL).                                   *0100
* INPUT YPT,  Y coordinates  (REAL).                                   *0110
* INPUT YDIFF, gap between successive scan lines  (REAL).              *0120
* INPUT NSY, Dimension of workspace  SY  (INTEGER).                    *0130
* OUTPUT SY, Workspace to hold chain for coordinates  (INTEGER).       *0140
* INPUT NXI, Dimension of workspace  XI  (INTEGER).                    *0150
* OUTPUT XI, Workspace to hold  X intersections for scan line  (REAL). *0160
* INPUT NSXI, Dimension of workspace  SXI  (INTEGER).                  *0170
* OUTPUT SXI, Workspace to hold chain for X intersections  (INTEGER).  *0180
* INPUT GKNWPL, Routine to output polylines  (EXTERNAL).               *0190
* DATE   9/07/84, GHW.                                                  *0200
*        18/03/85, CJC Removal of INCLUDEs.                            *0210
*                                                                       *0220
*****************************************************************************0230
      INTEGER                                                           0240
     *          I,IINT,IPASS,                                           0250
     *          K0,K1,K2,K3,                                            0260
     *          MAXINT,MXPASS,                                          0270
     *          NPASS,NPT,NSXI,NSY,NXI,                                 0280
     *          SIINT,SXI(NSXI),SY(NSY)                                 0290
      REAL                                                              0300
     *          X(2),XI(NXI),XPT(NPT),XVALUE,                           0310
     *          Y(2),YDIFF,YMAX,YMIN,YPT(NPT),YSCAN                     0320
      LOGICAL                                                           0330
     *          DUP,                                                    0340
     *          EVEN                                                    0350
      INTRINSIC                                                         0360
     *          AINT,                                                   0370
     *          INT,                                                    0380
     *          MAX                                                     0390
      EXTERNAL                                                          0400
     *          GKNWPL,GKSORT                                           0410
      PARAMETER ( MXPASS = 4 )                                          0420
C                                                                       0430
C DEFINE STATEMENT FUNCTION                                             0440
C                                                                       0450
      XVALUE(I)=XPT(K1)+(XPT(I)-XPT(K1))*((YSCAN-YPT(K1))/              0460
     +           (YPT(I)-YPT(K1)))                                      0470
C                                                                       0480
C INITIALIZATION                                                        0490
C                                                                       0500
      MAXINT=0                                                          0510
      NPASS=0                                                           0520
  1   EVEN=.TRUE.                                                       0530
      NPASS=NPASS+1                                                     0540
C                                                                       0550
C SORT MASK INTO INCREASING Y                                           0560
C                                                                       0570
```

```
      CALL GKSORT(YPT,NPT,SY,NSY)                               0580
C                                                               0590
C FIND MAX (YMAX) AND MIN (YMIN) VALUES OF Y                    0600
C                                                               0610
      K1=NPT+1                                                  0620
C                                                               0630
C ENSURE HATCHING IS COHERENT, I.E. ONE HATCH LINE WOULD GO THROUGH  0640
C THE ORIGIN                                                    0650
C                                                               0660
      YMIN=AINT(YPT(SY(K1))/YDIFF-0.5)*YDIFF                    0670
      DO 2 I=1,NPT                                              0680
        K1=SY(K1)                                               0690
   2    CONTINUE                                                0700
      YMAX=YPT(K1)+(0.5*YDIFF)                                  0710
C                                                               0720
C SCAN ALL Y VALUES                                             0730
C                                                               0740
      DO 3 YSCAN=YMIN,YMAX,YDIFF                                0750
        EVEN=.NOT. EVEN                                         0760
C                                                               0770
C NO INTERSECTIONS YET                                          0780
C                                                               0790
        IINT=0                                                  0800
C                                                               0810
C START OF SORTED LIST IS AT NPT+1                              0820
C                                                               0830
        K0=NPT+1                                                0840
C                                                               0850
C LOOP FOR CONSIDERING BOUNDARY LINES AT THIS Y                 0860
C                                                               0870
  4     K1=SY(K0)                                               0880
C                                                               0890
C ARE WE FURTHER UP THE MASK THAN CURRENT Y OR AT END OF MASK   0900
C                                                               0910
        IF (K1 .NE. 0) THEN                                     0920
          IF (YPT(K1) .LE. YSCAN) THEN                          0930
C                                                               0940
C NO - GET ADJACENT POINTS IN MASK WRAPPING ROUND ENDS          0950
C                                                               0960
            K2=K1+1                                             0970
            IF (K2 .GT. NPT) K2=1                               0980
            K3=K1-1                                             0990
            IF (K3 .LE. 0) K3=NPT                               1000
C                                                               1010
C CAN WE ELIMINATE THIS POINT FROM THE LIST                     1020
C                                                               1030
            IF (((YPT(K1) .GE. YPT(K2)) .AND.                   1040
     +           (YPT(K1) .GE. YPT(K3))) .OR.                   1050
     +          ((YSCAN .GE. YPT(K2)) .AND.                     1060
     +           (YSCAN. GE. YPT(K3)))) THEN                    1070
C                                                               1080
C ELIMINATE POINT FROM LIST BY MISSING IT OUT                   1090
C                                                               1100
              SY(K0)=SY(K1)                                     1110
            ELSE                                                1120
C                                                               1130
C CONSIDER THE MASK LINE FROM K1 TO K2                          1140
C                                                               1150
              IF (YPT(K2) .GT. YSCAN) THEN                      1160
```

```
C                                                                1170
C THERE IS AN INTERSECTION - RECORD IT                          1180
C                                                                1190
                  IINT=IINT+1                                    1200
                  XI(IINT)=XVALUE(K2)                            1210
                ENDIF                                            1220
C                                                                1230
C AND THE MASK LINE FROM K1 TO K3                               1240
C                                                                1250
                IF (YPT(K3) .GT. YSCAN) THEN                    1260
C                                                                1270
C THERE IS AN INTERSECTION - RECORD IT                          1280
C                                                                1290
                  IINT=IINT+1                                    1300
                  XI(IINT)=XVALUE(K3)                            1310
                ENDIF                                            1320
              ENDIF                                              1330
C                                                                1340
C GET NEXT POINT                                                1350
C                                                                1360
            KO=K1                                                1370
            GOTO 4                                               1380
          ENDIF                                                  1390
        ENDIF                                                    1400
C                                                                1410
C WE HAVE ALL THE INTERSECTIONS - SORT THEM ZERO CASE TO BE COPED WITH 1420
C                                                                1430
      IF(IINT.LE.0) GOTO 3                                       1440
      CALL GKSORT(XI,IINT,SXI,NSXI)                              1450
C                                                                1460
C SCAN ALL THE X VALUES, REMOVING ALL CUT LINES AND DUPLICATE POINTS 1470
C                                                                1480
      SIINT=0                                                    1490
 5    DUP=.FALSE.                                                1500
      KO=IINT+1                                                  1510
      K1=SXI(KO)                                                 1520
 6    IF (K1 .NE. 0) THEN                                        1530
        K2=SXI(K1)                                               1540
        IF (K2 .NE. 0) THEN                                      1550
          IF (XI(K1) .EQ. XI(K2)) THEN                           1560
            K1=SXI(K2)                                           1570
            SXI(KO)=K1                                           1580
            SIINT=SIINT+2                                        1590
            DUP=.TRUE.                                           1600
          ELSE                                                   1610
            KO=K1                                                1620
            K1=K2                                                1630
          ENDIF                                                  1640
          GOTO 6                                                 1650
        ENDIF                                                    1660
      ENDIF                                                      1670
      IF (DUP) GOTO 5                                            1680
      K1=IINT+1                                                  1690
      IINT=IINT-SIINT                                            1700
      IF (IINT .GT. 0) THEN                                      1710
        MAXINT=MAX(MAXINT,IINT)                                  1720
        IPASS=NPASS*2                                            1730
C                                                                1740
C NULL LOOP TO FIND HEAD OF CURRENT LIST                        1750
```

```
C                                                              1760
         DO 7 I=1,IPASS-2                                      1770
           K1=SXI(K1)                                          1780
           IF (SXI(K1) .EQ. 0) GOTO 3                          1790
7        CONTINUE                                              1800
         IF (NPASS .GT. MXPASS) IPASS=IINT                     1810
         DO 8 I=NPASS*2-1,IPASS,2                              1820
           K0=SXI(K1)                                          1830
           K1=SXI(K0)                                          1840
           IF (EVEN .AND. (NPASS .LE. MXPASS)) THEN            1850
             X(1)=XI(K1)                                       1860
             X(2)=XI(K0)                                       1870
           ELSE                                                1880
             X(1)=XI(K0)                                       1890
             X(2)=XI(K1)                                       1900
           ENDIF                                               1910
           Y(2)=YSCAN                                          1920
           Y(1)=YSCAN                                          1930
           CALL GKNWPL ( 2 , X , Y )                           1940
8        CONTINUE                                              1950
      ENDIF                                                    1960
3     CONTINUE                                                 1970
      IF (MAXINT .GT. IPASS) GOTO 1                            1980
      END                                                      1990
```

```
      SUBROUTINE GKSORT ( X , NX , SX , NSX )                        2000
************************************************************************2010
*                                                                    *2020
* SYN GKSORT system routine to sort an array returning a chain       *2030
* The routine sorts the  NX elements of  X. No exchanges are done,   *2040
* instead the routine produces a chain in  SX which is dimensioned   *2050
* NSX.  SX(NX+1) points to first element. The last element points    *2060
* to zero.  NSX must be greater than or equal to INT(NX+LOG2(NX)+2). *2070
* The special cases  NX.EQ.1 and  NX.EQ.2 have been specially coded, *2080
* and the only 2 lines contain a comparison for sorting are marked.  *2090
* DESCRIPTION                                                        *2100
* The algorithm has been taken from  R. HART, SOFTWARE  PRACTICE     *2110
* and  EXPERIENCE, vol 10, no 5 (1980), pages 405-417.               *2120
* INPUT-OUTPUT                                                       *2130
* INPUT X, Array of elements to be sorted  (REAL).                   *2140
* INPUT NX, Number of elements to be sorted  (INTEGER).             *2150
* OUTPUT SX, Chain for sorted elements  (INTEGER).                   *2160
* INPUT NSX, Dimension of array  SX  (INTEGER).                      *2170
* DATE 11/07/84, GW.                                                 *2180
*      18/03/85, CJC, single exit and INTEGER SX.                    *2190
*                                                                    *2200
************************************************************************2210
      INTEGER                                                         2220
     *        B1,B2,                                                  2230
     *        I,                                                      2240
     *        J,                                                      2250
     *        K1,K2,                                                  2260
     *        L0,L1,L2,                                               2270
     *        M1,                                                     2280
     *        NX,NSX,                                                 2290
     *        S0,S1,SX(NSX),                                          2300
     *        T0,T1,T2,T3,T4                                          2310
      REAL                                                            2320
     *        X(NX)                                                   2330
C                                                                     2340
      IF (NX .LE. 1) THEN                                             2350
         SX(1)=0                                                      2360
         SX(2)=1                                                      2370
         RETURN                                                       2380
      ELSEIF (NX .EQ. 2) THEN                                         2390
C                                                                     2400
C ** COMPARISON **                                                    2410
C                                                                     2420
         IF (X(1) .GT. X(2)) THEN                                     2430
            SX(3)=2                                                   2440
            SX(2)=1                                                   2450
            SX(1)=0                                                   2460
         ELSE                                                         2470
            SX(3)=1                                                   2480
            SX(1)=2                                                   2490
            SX(2)=0                                                   2500
         ENDIF                                                        2510
         GOTO 6                                                       2520
      ENDIF                                                           2530
      J=NX+1                                                          2540
      SX(1)=0                                                         2550
      SX(J)=1                                                         2560
      K2=1                                                            2570
      K1=0                                                            2580
```

```
          B2=0                                          2590
          I=0                                           2600
          M1=0                                          2610
          T2=0                                          2620
          T4=0                                          2630
          S1=NX                                         2640
    1     IF (S1 .GE. 4) THEN                           2650
             B2=K2                                      2660
             K2=K2*2                                    2670
             S0=S1                                      2680
             S1=S1/2                                    2690
             T4=T4+(S0-S1*2)*B2                         2700
             GOTO 1                                     2710
          ENDIF                                         2720
          T4=K2-T4                                      2730
    C                                                   2740
    2     IF (K1 .NE. K2) THEN                          2750
             K1=K1+1                                    2760
             T1=K1                                      2770
             B1=B2                                      2780
             T3=T2                                      2790
    C                                                   2800
    3        T0=T1                                      2810
             T1=T1/2                                    2820
             IF (T1*2 .EQ. T0) THEN                     2830
                M1=M1+1                                 2840
                T2=T2-B1                                2850
                B1=B1/2                                 2860
                GOTO 3                                  2870
             ENDIF                                      2880
             T2=T2+B1                                   2890
    C                                                   2900
             IF ((S1.EQ.2) .EQV. (T3.GE.T4)) THEN       2910
    C                                                   2920
    C 3 GROUP                                           2930
    C                                                   2940
                I=I+1                                   2950
                SX(I)=0                                 2960
                SX(J)=I                                 2970
                J=J+1                                   2980
                M1=M1+2                                 2990
             ELSEIF (S1 .EQ. 2) THEN                    3000
    C                                                   3010
    C 2 GROUP                                           3020
    C                                                   3030
                M1=M1+1                                 3040
             ELSE                                       3050
    C                                                   3060
    C 4 GROUP                                           3070
    C                                                   3080
                M1=-M1                                  3090
             ENDIF                                      3100
    C                                                   3110
    4        I=I+1                                      3120
             L1=I                                       3130
             SX(I)=0                                    3140
             SX(J)=I                                    3150
             L0=J                                       3160
             J=J+1                                      3170
```

```
        I=I+1
        L2=I                                                      3180
        SX(I)=0                                                   3190
        SX(J)=I                                                   3200
C                                                                 3210
C ** COMPARISON **                                                3220
C                                                                 3230
  5     IF (X(L1) .GT. X(L2)) THEN                                3240
                                                                  3250
          SX(LO)=L2                                               3260
          LO=L2                                                   3270
          L2=SX(LO)                                               3280
          IF (L2 .NE. 0) GOTO 5                                   3290
          SX(LO)=L1                                               3300
        ELSE                                                      3310
          SX(LO)=L1                                               3320
          LO=L1                                                   3330
          L1=SX(LO)                                               3340
          IF (L1 .NE. 0) GOTO 5                                   3350
          SX(LO)=L2                                               3360
        ENDIF                                                     3370
C                                                                 3380
        M1=M1-1                                                   3390
        IF (M1 .GT. 0) THEN                                       3400
          J=J-1                                                   3410
          LO=J-1                                                  3420
          L1=SX(LO)                                               3430
          L2=SX(J)                                                3440
          GOTO 5                                                  3450
        ELSEIF (M1 .LT. 0) THEN                                   3460
          M1=1-M1                                                 3470
          GOTO 4                                                  3480
        ELSE                                                      3490
          GOTO 2                                                  3500
        ENDIF                                                     3510
      ENDIF                                                       3520
  6   END                                                         3530
```

7   An example program

```
      PROGRAM DEMO                                                     0010
*                                                                      0020
* Simple program to show the operation of GKWFA.                       0030
*                                                                      0040
      EXTERNAL GPL                                                     0050
      REAL XVERTS(5),YVERTS(5),XI(5)                                  0060
      INTEGER LUER,LUWK,TYPEWK,SY(9),SXI(9)                           0070
      PARAMETER (LUER=1, LUWK=1, TYPEWK=4010, IDWK=1)                 0080
      DATA XVERTS / 0.2,0.5,0.8,0.1,0.9 /                             0090
      DATA YVERTS / 0.1,0.9,0.1,0.6,0.6 /                             0100
*                                                                      0110
      CALL GOPKS(LUER)                                                0120
      CALL GOPWK(IDWK, LUWK, TYPEWK)                                  0130
      CALL GACWK(IDWK)                                                0140
*                                                                      0150
      CALL GKWFA(5, XVERTS, YVERTS, 0.01, 9, SY, 5, XI, 9, SXI, GPL)  0160
      CALL GUWK(IDWK, 0)                                              0170
*                                                                      0180
      CALL GDAWK(IDWK)                                                0190
      CALL GCLWK(IDWK)                                                0200
      CALL GCLKS                                                      0210
      END                                                            0220
```

Output from the example program

References

[1]   GKS 7.4: ISO TC97/SC5/WG2 N262, International Standard ISO 7942 (draft),
      Information Processing Systems - Computer Graphics - Graphical Kernel
      System (GKS) Functional Description, 1984.

[2]   GKS 7.2: Draft International Standard ISO/DIS 7942,
      Information Processing Systems - Computer Graphics - Graphical Kernel
      System (GKS) Functional Description, 1983.

[3]   GKS Fortran binding: ISO/TC97/SC5/WG2 N316,
      Information Processing Systems - Computer Graphics - Graphical Kernel
      System (GKS) Language Bindings, Part 1: FORTRAN, 1984.

[4]   A J Matthew, Polygonal Clipping of Polylines, to be published
      in Computer Graphics Forum.

[5]   J D Foley, A Van Dam, Fundementals of interactive computer graphics,
      Adison-Wesley Systems Programming Series, 1983, ISBN 0-201-14468-9.

[6]   W M Newman, R F Sproull, Principles of interactive computer graphics,
      McGraw-Hill computer science series, 1979, ISBN 0-07-046338-7.

[7]   D E Knuth, The Art of Computer Programming, Volume 3, Sorting and
      Searching, Addison-Wesley series in Computer Science and Information
      Processing, 1973, ISBM 0-201-03803-X.

[8]   W J Cody, Basic Concepts for Computational Software, Argonne National
      Laboratory, Technical Memorandum No. 360, 1980.

[9]   D Bailey, D M Vallance, N D H Ross, The University of Salford FNT77
      Reference Manual, University of Salford, 1983.

[10] Fortran 77, ISO 1539 Programming Languages - FORTRAN.

A SIMPLE ALGORITHM FOR DETERMINING WHETHER A POINT RESIDES WITHIN AN ARBITRARILY SHAPED POLYGON

Andrew P. Surany, RCA Government Communications Systems (GCS)

Abstract

This algorithm is especially useful for locating points that reside within a region bounded by a polygon. It can also be used for locating an arbitrary point for use with those graphics systems that require a seed for video "fill". The algorithm will be presented for left-handed polygons, and will include a simple polygon validation technique. Adaptability to right-handed polygons will be also be touched upon.

Introduction

The process of validating a test point consists of constructing a vertical line which passes through the test point. An equation of intersection is then generated between this vertical trace and the equation of the closed surface. Since the closed area is a polygon, then each side is compared with the vertices of the side in question for validation. The relative positions of the points of intersection and that of the test point are compared and evaluated to determine whether or not the test point resides within the closed area.

Formulation

When discussing a polygon, a clear definition is necessary. For purposes of this discussion, a polygon is defined as a closed figure intersecting only at the vertices of each segment. Given any set of points defining the polygon where the quality of data is in question (it is uncertain whether or not the polygon meets the specified definition), a validation technique must be applied.

Validation consists of developing the line equations of each side of the polygon, and combining pairs of equations to find points of intersection. Any point of intersection found that is not a vertex invalidates the figure.

Once it is determined that the polygon is valid, it is necessary to make a determination on the type of polygon, right or left. A right polygon is one that follows a "right handed rule", or:

$$|v| = |a| \, |b| \, \sin \theta \tag{1}$$

Similarly, a "left polygon" is expressed as:

$$|v| = -|a| \, |b| \, \sin \theta \tag{2}$$

where $|a|$ and $|b|$ are the lengths of adjacent polygon sides.

See Figure 1.

NATO ASI Series, Vol. F17
Fundamental Algorithms for Computer Graphics
Edited by R. A. Earnshaw
© Springer-Verlag Berlin Heidelberg 1985

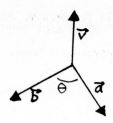

Figure 1.

To avoid having to perform this cross product on all the sides of the polygon, a single test may be made.

Let A be the set of N points comprising the vertices of the polygon. Each member of A contains two components, an X-axis and Y-axis coordinate, such that:

$$A = [(X_i, Y_i) \mid 1 \leq i \leq N] \tag{3}$$

Where (X_i, Y_i) is connected to (X_{i+1}, Y_{i+1}), and (X_N, Y_N) is connected to (X_1, Y_1). The maximum X-axis coordinate can be defined as follows:

Let:

$$X_m = [X_i \mid X_i \geq X_j \; \forall j] \tag{4}$$

$$f_x (X_i, Y_i) = X_i, \text{ is the projection of the point on the X-axis} \tag{5}$$

$$f_y (X_i, Y_i) = Y_i, \text{ is the projection of the point on the Y-axis} \tag{6}$$

then the following exists:

$$f_x (X_m, Y_m) \geq f_x (X_{m+1}, Y_{m+1}), \text{ where m+1 = 1 if m=N} \tag{7}$$

$$f_x (X_m, Y_m) \geq f_x (X_{m-1}, Y_{m-1}), \text{ where m-1 = N if m=1} \tag{8}$$

Let:

$$a1 = f_x (X_m, Y_m) - f_x (X_{m+1}, Y_{m+1}) \tag{9}$$

$$a2 = f_y (X_m, Y_m) - f_y (X_{m+1}, Y_{m+1}) \tag{10}$$

$$b1 = f_x (X_m, Y_m) - f_x (X_{m-1}, Y_{m-1}) \qquad (11)$$

$$b2 = f_y (X_m, Y_m) - f_y (X_{m-1}, Y_{m-1}) \qquad (12)$$

then:

$$|a| = SQRT [a1^2 + a2^2] \qquad (13)$$

$$|b| = SQRT [b1^2 + b2^2] \qquad (14)$$

Substituting (13) and (14) into (1), and taking θ as the angle between $|a|$ and $|b|$, if the direction of $\vec{v}$ is positive then the polygon is a right polygon; otherwise it is a left polygon. For the duration of this discussion, only a left polygon will be considered.

Let B be the set of M points residing within the polygon, each member of B having a pixel representation, making M finite. Each member of B contains two components, an X-axis and Y-axis coordinate, such that:

$$B = [(X_b, Y_b) | 1 \leq b \leq M] \qquad (15)$$

We must now consider each point of B to determine whether the point resides within the polygon. Consider the point (X_{b1}, Y_{b1}). A vertical line passing through the point has the equation:

$$X = X_{b1} \qquad (16)$$

See Figure 2.

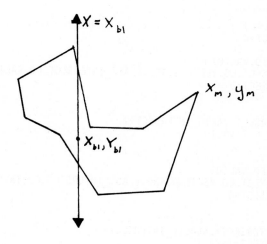

Figure 2.

Equation (16) is solved simultaneously with the equation of each polygon side for intersections. If the intersection (X_{ib}, Y_{ib}) is valid, such that:

$$[\quad f_x (X_{i+1}, Y_{i+1}) \leq X_{ib} \leq f_x (X_i, Y_i) \mid \begin{array}{l} f_x(X_{i+1}, Y_{i+1}) \leq f_x(X_i, Y_i), \\ f_y(X_{i+1}, Y_{i+1}) > f_y(X_i, Y_i) \end{array}] \quad (17)$$

$$Y_{bl} \geq Y_{ib} \tag{18}$$

then it is logged as such. Otherwise, it is logged as an invalid intersection as follows:

$$\text{Valid Intersect} = \text{Valid Intersect} + 1$$

or

$$\text{Invalid Intersect} = \text{Invalid Intersect} + 1$$

If the slope M of the polygon side under test is equal to zero, then test (18) is replaced with (19):

$$Y_{bl} \geq f_y(X_i, Y_i) \tag{19}$$

The previous analysis is dependent upon the actual values obtained for the polygon vertices. If:

$$[\quad f_x(X_{i+1}, Y_{i+1}) > f_x(X_i, Y_i) \quad]$$

$$[\quad f_y(X_{i+1}, Y_{i+1}) < f_y(X_i, Y_i) \quad]$$

then the equalities must be adjusted accordingly.

When a point and vertex reside along the line of intersection, the test may have to be modified as follows:

```
CONDITIONAL
  (SIDE.EQ.VERTICAL)
    LAST_INTERSECT=0
    FIN
  (INTERSECTION.EQ.VALID)
    WHEN ((INTERSECT.EQ.VERTEX).AND.(LAST_INTERSECT.EQ.VALID))
      LAST_INTERSECT=0
      FIN
    ELSE
      VALID_INTERSECT=VALID_INTERSECT+1
      LAST_INTERSECT=VALID
      FIN
    FIN
  (INTERSECTION.EQ.VALID)
    WHEN ((INTERSECT.EQ.VERTEX).AND.(LAST_INTERSECT.EQ.INVALID))
      LAST_INTERSECT=0
      FIN
    ELSE
      INVALID_INTERSECT=INVALID_INTERSECT+1
      LAST_INTERSECT=INVALID
      FIN
    FIN
  FIN
```

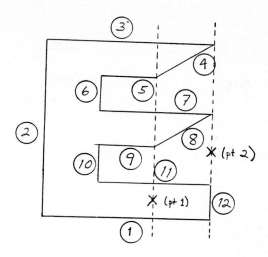

Figure 3.

An example follows:

Given the polygon shown in Figure 3, each side is classified as follows for point 1:

SIDE	VALID	INVALID	SPECIAL
1	X		
2			N/A
3	X		
4		X	VERTEX
5		X	
6			N/A
7	X		
8		X	VERTEX
9		X	
10			N/A
11	X		
12			N/A

Side 5 and 9, however, follow a vertex intersection and have the same validity as the previous side. The total intersections are classified as follows:

    TOTAL VALID = 4
    TOTAL INVALID = 2

Therefore, point 1 is in the polygon.

For point 2,

SIDE	VALID	INVALID	SPECIAL
1	X		
2			N/A
3	X		VERTEX
4		X	
5		X	
6			N/A
7	X		VERTEX
8		X	
9		X	
10			N/A
11		X	
12			N/A

TOTAL VALID = 3
TOTAL INVALID = 5

Therefore, point 2 is not in the polygon.

All sides of the polygon are tested in this method summing up the total valid intersections and invalid intersections per test point. The final test involves comparing the number of valid intersections to the number of invalid intersections.

If both:

$$\text{Valid Intersect} \geq 2 \tag{20}$$

$$\text{Valid Intersect} > \text{Invalid Intersect} \tag{21}$$

then the point lies with the polygon.

Conclusions

In establishing a reference point for "video" fill, a vertical trace intersecting the specific polygon is defined, as in (16), and after establishing the first insection point, processing points occuring on the line after the point of intersection.

Nomenclature

$| =$ such that
$\forall =$ for all

Acknowledgements

The author acknowledges the assistance of Mr. Richard L. Grossman and Mr. Dennis J. Hearn in test of this algorithm; and Mr. Allen L. Starr for his assistance in evaluation of this algorithm.

References

1. Riddle, D.F.: "Analytic Geometry with Vectors", 1972, Wadsworth, Belmont, California.

2. Ferguson, et al: "Point in Polygon Algorithms", 1973, National Science Foundation Report No. UDC-NSF-7341

Section 2
Arcs, Circles and Conics

ALGORITHMS
for
CIRCULAR ARC GENERATION

ABSTRACT

By much the same methodology as is employed in algorithms
which generate a quantized representation of a straight line,
incremental algorithms using only addition/subtraction and
sign testing can generate a close approximation of a circular
arc. Several mathematical measures of 'closeness' to the true
circle can be defined. Discussed will be closeness measures
of function residue or squared error, normal deviation or radial
error, and rounded or axial intercept error as they apply to
both a tri-directional and a bi-directional algorithm for pel by
pel generation of a quantized circular arc.

The original paper on which this discussion is based is: A
Linear Algorithm for Incremental Digital Display of Circular
Arcs. Jack Bresenham. Communications of the ACM 20 (No. 2)
p100-106 (February, 1977)

Jack E. Bresenham
IBM Communications Products Division
P.O. Box 12195
Department H91, Bldg 662
Research Triangle Park, North Carolina
USA   27709

NATO ASI Series, Vol. F17
Fundamental Algorithms for Computer Graphics
Edited by R. A. Earnshaw
© Springer-Verlag Berlin Heidelberg 1985

CIRCULAR ARC ERROR CRITERIA

Let circle be given by $X^2 + Y^2 = R^2$

Illustrate in 2nd octant from 90 degrees to 45 degrees

$X^2 + Y_i^2 = R^2$

Y_c = ceiling Y_i

Y_f = floor Y_i

X an integer

Y_i non-integer

Enlarged circle if select X, Y_c $X^2 + Y_c^2 = R_2^2$

Reduced circle if select X, Y_f $X^2 + Y_f^2 = R_1^2$

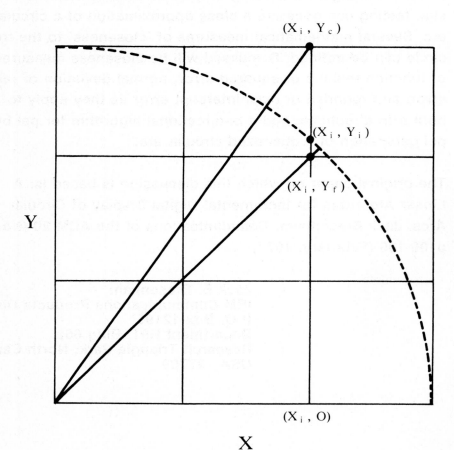

(X_i, Y_c)

(X_i, Y_i)

(X_i, Y_f)

Y

(X_i, O)

X

CIRCULAR ARC ERROR MEASURES
2ND OCTANT ILLUSTRATION

- RESIDUE OR SQUARED
- NORMAL DEVIATION OR RADIAL
- ROUNDED OR VERTICAL OR AXIAL

True circle $X_i^2 + Y_i^2 = R^2$

With integer X_i, set Y_c = ceiling $\quad Y_i = 1 + \lfloor Y_i \rfloor$
$\qquad\qquad\qquad Y_f$ = floor $\qquad Y_i = \lfloor Y_i \rfloor$

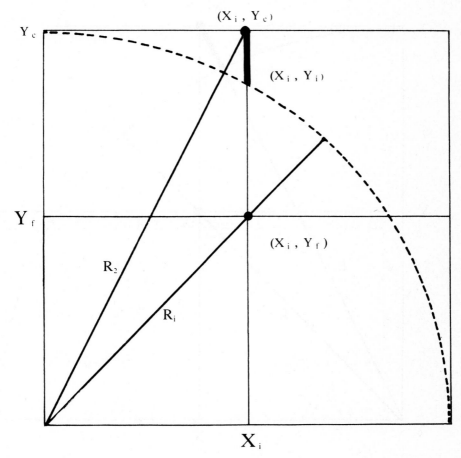

AXIAL ERROR

Select point (X, Y_f) if $|Y_f - Y_i| < |Y_c - Y_i|$

Alternatively: $\qquad$ if $(Y_c - Y_i) - (Y_i - Y_f) > 0$

CIRCULAR ARC ERROR MEASURES
2ND OCTANT ILLUSTRATION

- RESIDUE OR SQUARED
- NORMAL DEVIATION OR RADIAL
- ROUNDED OR VERTICAL OR AXIAL

True circle $X_i^2 + Y_i^2 = R^2$

With integer X_i, set Y_c = ceiling $\quad Y_i = 1 + \lfloor Y_i \rfloor$

$\qquad\qquad\qquad\quad Y_f$ = floor $\qquad Y_i = \lfloor Y_i \rfloor$

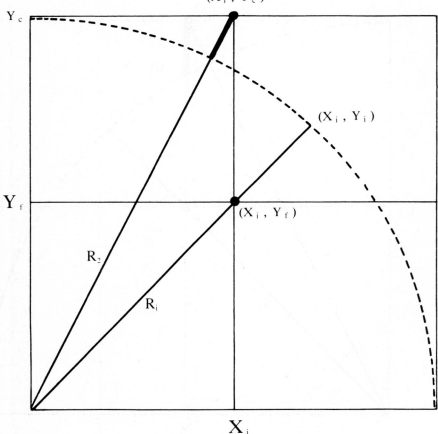

(X_i, Y_c)

Y_c

(X_i, Y_i)

Y_f

(X_i, Y_f)

R_2

R_i

X_i

RADIAL ERROR

Select point (X, Y_f) if $|R_i - R| < |R_2 - R|$

Alternatively: $\qquad$ if $(R_2 - R) - (R - R_i) > 0$

CIRCULAR ARC ERROR MEASURES
2ND OCTANT ILLUSTRATION

- RESIDUE OR SQUARED
- NORMAL DEVIATION OR RADIAL
- ROUNDED OR VERTICAL OR AXIAL

True circle $X_i^2 + Y_i^2 = R^2$

With integer X_i, set Y_c = ceiling $\quad Y_i = 1 + \llcorner Y_i \lrcorner$

$\qquad\qquad\qquad\quad Y_f$ = floor $\qquad Y_i = \llcorner Y_i \lrcorner$

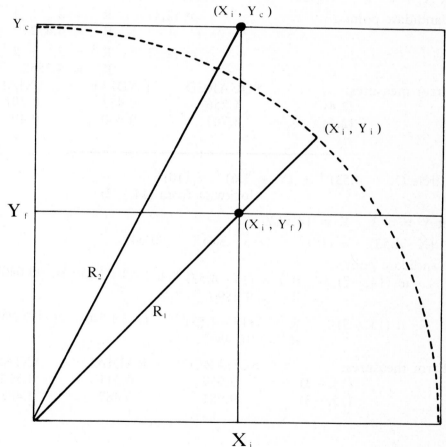

SQUARED ERROR

Select point (X, Y_f) if $|R_i^2 - R^2| < |R_2^2 - R^2|$

Alternatively: $\qquad$ if $(R_2^2 - R^2) - (R^2 - R_i^2) > 0$

$\qquad\qquad\quad$ or $R_i^2 + R_i^2 - 2R^2 > 0$

NON-INTEGER CIRCLES
DIFFERENT ERROR MEASURES
YIELD DIFFERENT STEPS

EXAMPLES

Circle $X^2 + Y^2 = (4.925)^2$ clockwise from $(1,5)$

at $X = 2$ $Y = 4.5006$ $Y^2 = (4.925)^2 - 2^2 = 20.255625$

Candidate points: at $(2,4)$ $R^2 = 2^2 + 4^2 = 20$
                                        $R = 4.4721$

                           at $(2,5)$ $R^2 = 2^2 + 5^2 = 29$
                                        $R = 5.3852$

Error measures:	SQUARED	RADIAL	AXIAL
$(2,4)$	4.256	0.453	0.501
$(2,5)$	4.744	0.460	0.499

Circle $(X - 4.53)^2 + (Y + 3.6)^2 = (10)^2$
             clockwise from $(14, -2)$

at $Y = -3$ $X = 14.5120$

$(X - 4.53)^2 = (10)^2 - (-3 + 3.6)^2 = 99.64$

Candidate points:

at $(14, -3)$ $R^2 = (14 - 4.53)^2 + (-3 + 3.6)^2 = 90.0409$
                $R = 9.4890$

at $(15, -3)$ $R^2 = (15 - 4.53)^2 + (-3 + 3.6)^2 = 109.9809$
                $R = 10.4872$

Error measures:	SQUARED	RADIAL	AXIAL
$(14, -3)$	9.959	0.511	0.512
$(15, -3)$	9.981	0.487	0.488

CIRCULAR ARC ERROR CRITERIA

Let circle be given by $X^2 + Y^2 = R^2$

Illustrate in 2nd octant from 90 degrees to 45 degrees

$X^2 + Y_i^2 = R^2$

$Y_c = $ ceiling Y_i

$Y_f = $ floor Y_i

X an integer

Y_i non-integer

Enlarged circle if select X, Y_c $\qquad X^2 + Y_c^2 = R_2^2$

Reduced circle if select X, Y_f $\qquad X^2 + Y_f^2 = R_i^2$

COMMONLY USED MEASURES OF CLOSENESS

- **FUNCTION RESIDUE OR SQUARED ERROR**

  Select point (X, Y_f) if $|R_i^2 - R^2| < |R_2^2 - R^2|$

  Alternatively, if $(R - R_i) < (R_2 - R)$

- **RADIAL ERROR**

  Select point (X, Y_f) if $|R_i - R| < |R_2 - R|$

  Alternatively, if $(R - R_i) < (R_2 - R)$

- **ROUND CIRCUMFERENCE INTERSECTION OR AXIAL ERROR (VERTICAL ERROR)**

  Select point (X, Y_f) if $|Y_f - Y_i| < |Y_c - Y_i|$

  Alternatively, if $(Y_i - Y_f) < (Y_c - Y_i)$

QUADRANT CIRCLES

Clockwise first quadrant movement from (O,R) at (X, Y) consider step to either (X, Y − 1) or (X + 1, Y − 1) or (X + 1, Y)

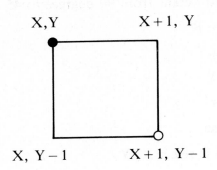

X,Y   X + 1, Y

X, Y − 1   X + 1, Y − 1

Residue at diagonally adjacent pel

$$D = [(X + 1)^2 + (Y − 1)^2] − R^2$$

D = 0   then (X + 1, Y − 1) on circle

D < 0   then (X + 1, Y − 1) 'inside' circle
circle crosses line x = X + 1 above Y − 1
choice (X + 1, Y) or (X + 1, Y − 1)

D > 0   then (X + 1, Y − 1) 'outside' circle
circle crosses line y = Y − 1 left of X + 1
choice (X, Y − 1) or (X + 1, Y − 1)

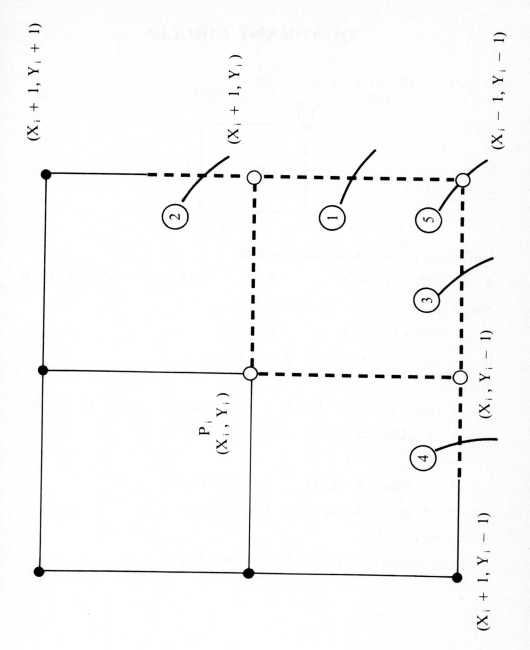

QUADRANT CIRCLES

$D < 0$ $(X+1, Y-1)$ inside circle

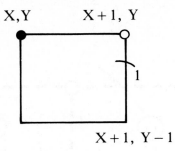

X,Y   X+1, Y

1

X+1, Y-1

Difference in candidate point residues

$$d = |[(X+1)^2 + Y^2] - R^2| - |[(X+1)^2 + (Y-1)^2]| - R^2$$

Note case 1:

$$[(X+1)^2 + Y^2] - R^2 \geq 0$$

$$D = [(X+1)^2 + (Y-1)^2] - R^2 < 0$$

So:

$$d = \{[(X+1)^2 + Y^2] - R^2\} + \{[(X+1)^2 + (Y-1)^2] - R^2\}$$

$$= 2\{[(X+1)^2 + (Y-1)^2] - R^2\} + 2Y - 1$$

$$= 2D + 2Y - 1$$

$d \leq 0$ select $(X+1, Y)$ horizontal step

$d > 0$ select $(X+1, Y-1)$ diagonal step

Note case 2:

Can be shown $d < 0$ so still select $(X+1, Y)$

QUADRANT CIRCLES

In like manner, analyze diagonal outside
find in summary

D < 0   form $\mathbf{d} = \mathbf{2D} + \mathbf{2Y} - \mathbf{1}$

$\quad\quad\quad\quad$ d ≤ 0   horizontal to (X + 1, Y)

$\quad\quad\quad\quad$ d > 0   diagonal to (X + 1, Y − 1)

D > 0   form $\mathbf{d}' = \mathbf{2D} - \mathbf{2X} - \mathbf{1}$

$\quad\quad\quad\quad$ d′ ≤ 0   diagonal to (X + 1, Y − 1)

$\quad\quad\quad\quad$ d′ > 0   vertical to (X, Y − 1)

D = 0   diagonal to (X + 1, Y − 1)

$\quad\quad\quad\quad$ will find also could form d or d′

$\quad\quad\quad\quad$ with $\mathbf{d} > \mathbf{0}$ and $\mathbf{d}' < \mathbf{0}$

$\quad\quad\quad\quad$ so even here, second difference

$\quad\quad\quad\quad$ will select proper diagonal step

QUADRANT CIRCLES

If **Horizontal** step, select $(X+1, Y)$

$X_i \leftarrow X+1$

$Y_i \leftarrow Y$

$$D_i = (X+1+1)^2 + (Y-1)^2 - R^2$$

$$= (X+1)^2 + 2(X+1)^2 + 1 + (Y-1)^2 - R^2$$

$$= (X+1)^2 + (Y-1)^2 - R^2 + 2X_i + 1$$

$$D_i = D + 2X_i + 1$$

Similarly:

If **Diagonal** step, select $(X+1, Y-1)$

$X_i \leftarrow X+1$

$Y_i \leftarrow Y-1$

$D_i \leftarrow D + 2X_i - 2Y_i + 2$

If **Vertical** step, select $(X, Y-1)$

$X_i \leftarrow X$

$Y_i \leftarrow Y-1$

$D_i \leftarrow D - 2Y_i + 1$

QUADRANT CIRCLES

Start at $(0, P_i)$

then
$$X_0 = 0$$
$$Y_0 = R$$
$$D_0 = (X+1)^2 + (Y-1)^2 - R^2$$
$$= (0+1)^2 + (R-1)^2 - R^2$$
$$= 1 + R^2 - 2R + 1 - R^2$$
$$D_0 = 2 - 2R$$

easy starting conditions: linear terms
easy stepping with sign testing and additions
employ variables $X' = 2X + 1$ $Y' = 2Y - 1$
easy stop when reach $Y = 0$
  alternatively when $Y \leq 0.5$
          or $Y' \leq 0$

separate display coordinates from algorithm
set display (X,Y) then steps add
          horizontal $(1,0)$
          diagonal $(1,-1)$
          vertical $(0,-1)$

Initial conditions

$X_0' = 1$ $Y_0' = 2R - 1$ $D_0 = 2 - 2R = 1 - Y_0'$

$M_1 = (1,0)$ $M_2 = (1,-1)$ $M_3 = (0,-1)$

Quadrant Crossings: reinitialize X', Y', D
          modify M_1, M_2, M_3

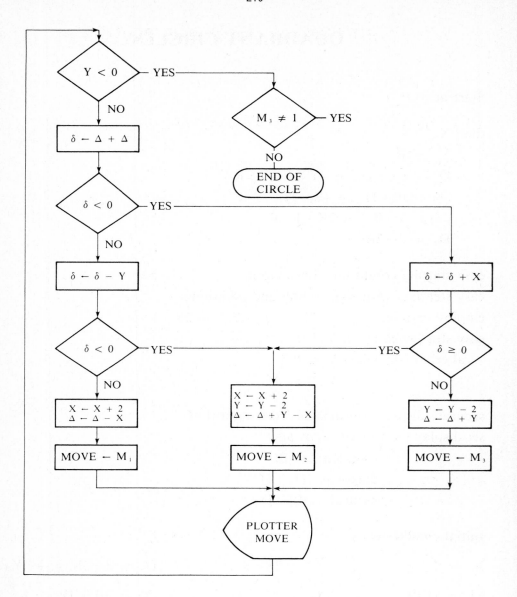

ARBITRARY STARTING POINTS
FOR
INTEGER CIRCULAR ARCS

FIRST QUADRANT: Circumference Point (x,y)

STRATEGY:
   Find nearby integer point
   Which full circle would select
   When incrementing step by step

TECHNIQUE:
   Consider unit square
   In which starting point falls
   Find 'closest' corner
   Calculate appropriate X,Y,D

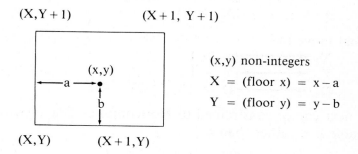

$(X, Y+1)$ $(X+1, Y+1)$

(x,y)

—a— •

b

(X,Y) $(X+1,Y)$

(x,y) non-integers

$X = (\text{floor } x) = x - a$

$Y = (\text{floor } y) = y - b$

CALCULATE:
   Residue magnitude at each corner
   Choose corner with minimum residual
   $R_{00} = (X^2 + Y^2) - (x^2 + y^2) = X^2 + Y^2 - R^2$
   $R_{10} = R_{00} + 2X + 1$
   $R_{11} = R_{01} + 2Y + 1$
   $R_{01} = R_{11} - 2X - 1$

SELECT:
   (X_0, Y_0) and set $D_0 = R_{(X_0, Y_0)} + 2(X_0 - Y_0 + 1)$

OCTANT CIRCLES

In 2nd octant, steps turn out to be only Horizontal or Diagonal

Effect of using this can be modeled as follows

Horizontal move has

$$X_i \longleftarrow X + 1$$
$$Y_i \longleftarrow Y_i$$
$$D_i \longleftarrow D + 2X_i + 1$$

For next choice constrained to Horizontal or Diagonal final decision variable is d rather than d ′

$$
\begin{aligned}
d_i &= 2D_i + 2Y_i - 1 \\
&= 2D_i + 2Y - 1 \\
&= 2D + 4X_i + 2 + 2Y - 1 \\
&= (2D + 2Y - 1) + 4X_i + 2 \\
d_i &= d + 2(2X_i + 1)
\end{aligned}
$$

Diagonal move has

$$X_i \longleftarrow X + 1$$
$$Y_i \longleftarrow Y - 1$$
$$D_i \longleftarrow D + 2X_i - 2Y_i + 2$$

For next choice constrained to Horizontal or Diagonal final decision variable is d rather than d ′

$$
\begin{aligned}
d_i &= 2D_i + 2Y_i - 1 \\
&= 2D_i + 2Y - 2 - 1 \\
&= 2D + 4X_i - 4Y_i + 4 + 2Y - 2 - 1 \\
&= (2D + 2Y - 1) + 4X_i - 4Y_i + 2 \\
d_i &= d + 2(2X_i - 2Y_i + 1)
\end{aligned}
$$

Conclusion

Can skip intermediate calculation of D
 run stepping recursion directly with d
 use algorithm variables

$$U = 2X + 1$$
$$V = 2X - 2Y + 1$$

OCTANT CIRCLES

Let $E = (0.5)d$ $U = 2X + 1$ $V = 2X - 2Y + 1$
     $U_0 = 1$ $V_0 = 1 - 2R$ $\mathbf{E = 1.5 - R}$
set display to $(0,R)$

if $E \leq 0$ horizontal step
            increment display coordinates by $(1,0)$
            update algorithm variables
            $U_i \longleftarrow U + 2$
            $V_i \longleftarrow V + 2$
            $E_i \longleftarrow E + U_i$

if $E > 0$ diagonal step
            increment display coordinates by $(1, -1)$
            update algorithm variables
            $U_i \longleftarrow U + 2$
            $V_i \longleftarrow V + 4$
            $E_i \longleftarrow E + V_i$

continue until $X = Y$
alternatively until $X - Y + 0.5 > 0$
but $V = 2X - 2Y + 1$
so stop when $V_i > 0$

Notice E changes only by **integer** amounts and $E \neq 0$

    thus if $E \leq 0$ then $E' = E - 0.5 \leq 0$
       if $E > 0$ then $E' = E - 0.5 > 0$

So apply same decision rules with

    $E' = E - 0.5$ where E' is integer and $\mathbf{E_0' = 1 - R}$

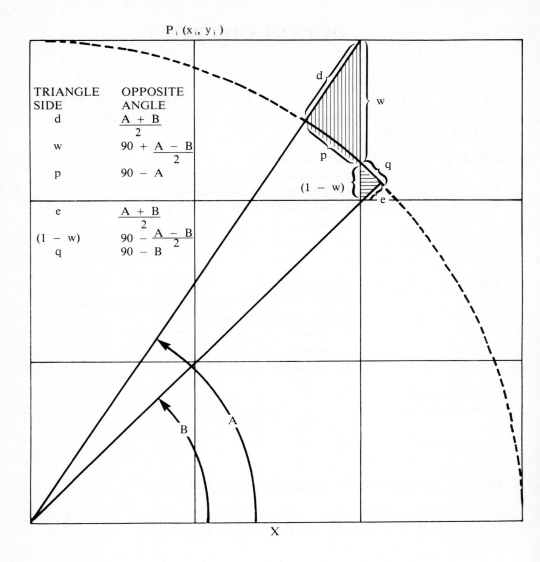

P_i (x_i, y_i)

TRIANGLE SIDE	OPPOSITE ANGLE
d	$\dfrac{A + B}{2}$
w	$90 + \dfrac{A - B}{2}$
p	$90 - A$
e	$\dfrac{A + B}{2}$
(1 − w)	$90 - \dfrac{A - B}{2}$
q	$90 - B$

X

CIRCULAR ARCS

COMMENTS

Can be shown

For integer radius, integer center point
   always have same step selection for
   squared error, radial error, axial error
   and maximum radial error < 0.5.

For stepping past octant or quadrant boundaries
   simple re-initialization of algorithm variables
   from just current values at crossing and can
   modify stepping increments easily
   ie., by Quadrants clockwise

Cross when $Y_i < \frac{1}{2}$ or $T = (2Y - 1) < 0$

then $X_0 \longleftarrow Y_i$

$\quad\; Y_0 \longleftarrow X_i$

$\quad\; D_0 \longleftarrow D_i - 4X_i$ eg. 1st to 4th transition

$\quad\; M1_0 \longleftarrow M3$ $M1_0 \longleftarrow (0, -1)$

$\quad\; M2_0 \longleftarrow M2_2, - M2_1$ $M2_0 \longleftarrow (-1, -1)$

$\quad\; M3_0 \longleftarrow M3_2, - M3_1$ $M3_0 \longleftarrow (-1, 0)$

For counter clockwise stepping, comparable method
   just alter initial step increments and transition

For non-integer radius and/or centerpoint
   effect initialization, comparable method
   maximum radial error less than $0.5 (1 + \frac{1}{2R})$

CIRCULAR ARCS

COMMENTS

PITTEWAY (BRUNEL UNIVERSITY, ENGLAND) has shown tie between 'squared' and 'axial' error.

Refactor decision variable

Squared: • 2nd Octant •

$$e_s = (X+1)^2 - (Y-\tfrac{1}{2})^2 - (R^2 - \tfrac{1}{4})$$

Axial: • 2nd Octant •

$$e_A = (X+1)^2 + (Y-\tfrac{1}{2})^2 - R^2$$

In essence, both evaluate residue of

Function: $F_{(W,Z)}$ $= \dfrac{\mathbf{W}^2 + \mathbf{Z}^2 - \mathbf{P}^2}{}$

at $W = (X+1)$ $Z = (Y - \tfrac{1}{2})$

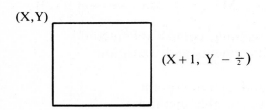

(X,Y)

$(X+1, Y - \tfrac{1}{2})$

with 'squared'   'axial'

$$P = R \sqrt{1 - \tfrac{1}{4R^2}}$$ $$P = R$$

OTHER CONSIDERATIONS

3-D

PERSPECTIVE

DOT/DASH LINE STYLES

WIDE LINE TYPES: RING

RETRACEABILITY

RUN LENGTHS

AREA FILL: DISKS

CLIPPING

POLYGON CHORD ALTERNATIVE

ALGORITHMS OF CONIC GENERATION

M.L.V. Pitteway

The published algorithm (Computer Journal $\underline{10}$, 282) behaves badly if the gradient of the curve being plotted changes too sharply, so that two or more changes of octant are called for in the space of a single plotter increment or display pixel. It seems that the problem can be solved for circles, and for other conic sections if diagonal moves are forbidden, by elaborating the tests which determine when a change of octqant (or quadrant, with no diagonal moves) is required and re-entering the inner loop at the test which decides the next move for output; but the general problem has yet to be solved.

1. Introduction

Bresenham's algorithm (1965) is now well established as standard for generating straight lines of arbitrary gradient with an incremental plotter or graphic display. The representation is a "best" **fit**, in the sense that, with a plotter, the pen is left as near as possible to the intended line after each incremental step. If, instead of a straight line, we wish to represent a circular arc, ellipse, or some other curve, a natural mathematical approach is to seek adequate representation of the intended curve as a sequence of short, straight line segments (e.g. Cohen 1970, Smith 1971), and indeed this is required in any case to exploit vector systems which are capable of generating these straight line segments automatically (often by an implementation of Bresenham's algorithm, or its equivalent, in the hardware itself).

When we are not committed to vector generating hardware, however, it seems more sensible to specify the curve generation in the basic algorithm itself, rather than through an overlying procedure or routine calling Bresenham for the short, straight line segments, and it is with such an analysis, for the incremental representation of the conic sections, that this paper is concerned. The special case of circles and circular arcs has been dealt with extensively elsewhere (e.g. Bresenham 1977, McIlroy 1983), but this paper is concerned with problems arising in the more general case.

NATO ASI Series, Vol. F17
Fundamental Algorithms for Computer Graphics
Edited by R. A. Earnshaw
© Springer-Verlag Berlin Heidelberg 1985

The analysis is presented here in terms of "real" variables, or their floating point representation in a digital computer. It is possible to restrict the parameters for integer working, but in the general case we meet a problem not experienced with straight lines, or with circles or circular arcs of integer radius, in that the user would have to choose from a strangely limited subset of possibilities. For the usual run of sensible curves, in which the gradient changes only slowly compared with the mesh size of the plotter or display, the curvature parameters, denoted K1, K2 and K3 in the algorithm of figure 2 are much smaller in magnitude than the working variables denoted b,a and d, and so there are fewer sensible values to chose from in integer working. It turns out that a good repetoire of fat almost circular ellipses can be made available, but the range of thin ellipses is much more severely restricted, jumping from a straight line to a comparatively tubby curve even for unit values of K1, K2 or K3. Indeed, this awkward nuisance has limited the development of the algorithm severely in hardware implementations, and is not yet fully analysed.

This paper is mainly concerned with current, "state of the art" research on another problem, however, dealing with the comparatively sharp corners which can occur with conic sections, when the intended curve happens to change direction significantly (by more than about 45°) in a distance comparable with, or even less than, the incremental mesh size of the plotter or display in use. In my basic mathematical analysis (1967), which is reproduced in a simplified form in the next section of this paper, the problem was avoided by requiring that at least one incremental output move be generated between any two consecutive changes of "octant" so the undesirable possibility of an infinite loop, with continual repeated octant changes in lieu of any output, is prohibited from the outset.

There seems to be two alternative but complementary approaches to an analysis of this problem, presented in sections 3 and 4 of this paper respectively. Firstly, and as detailed in section 3, we could seek to establish an appropriate "best fit" criterion which defines the incremental represent- ation for any given conic section curve, just as Bresenham defines a best fit for a straight line as choosing whether the appropriate square move or diagonal move leaves the pen nearest to the intended line. Simple Euclidean geometry reduces this to asking whether the intended line passes above or below a point mid-way between the two possible ending positions for the pen. Alternative criterions are possible for the circle, including the smallest "radial" error in which the pen is left at a distance from the circle's origin approximating, as nearly as possible, the intended radius, or alternatively leaving the squared residue $R^2 - (i-x_c)^2 - (j-y_c)^2$ as small as possible, where R is the radius of the circle centred at x_c, y_c, and i,j denotes a possible candidate for the next pen position. These both reduce to Bresenham's criterion if the radius of the circle is allowed to increase indefinitely, and, for the case of a circle of integer radius R centred at an integer mesh point x_c, y_c, it can be shown that the two alternatives always generate the same circle. Moreover, a third possibility, as used in the next section of this paper for the general conic, and which involves simply choosing between two moves according to whether the intended curve passes above or below the mid-point between the alternative pen ending position, is, in the case of a circle, identically equivalent to the squared residue criterion, except that the radius is changed from R to $\sqrt{R^2 + \frac{1}{4}}$. This, too, reduces to Bresenham's criterion if the radius of the circle increases to infinity, and in general it might seem a useful clue, in our search for an "ideal" criterion for the incremental representation of a general conic, that it should correspond to Bresenham's criterion in the special case of a straight line.

Unfortunately, it turns out that this simple "sign-of-the-residue-at-the-midpoint" criterion doesn not give a sensibly behaving algorithm for a conic section with a sharp corner, for reasons explained in the next section. Other alternatives are considered and dismissed, as seemingly too complicated for a sensible mathematical analysis which might lead to an "elegant" (ie. efficient and easily understood) algorithm, either by conventional mathematics or possibly by program transformation (following Sproull 1982) from an "obviously correct" version.

Alternatively, as suggested in section 4, if we could discover a version of the conic drawing algorithm, with its octant change tests and related arithmetic operations, which behaved sensibly in all cases tested, we could no doubt establish, by an analysis of our magic algorithm, some appropriate mathematical "best fit" criterion as represented by its behaviour. Some progress has been made with this particular line of attack, in that the algorithm of figure 6 seems to behave sensibly in all cases, though for a more restricted problem in which diagonal moves are banned, so that the plotter is supposed to be capable of incrementing in the cardinal x-step, or y-step, square move directions only. But an appropriate mathematical analysis of even this restricted algorithm is beyond the scope of this paper, as is also the establishment of a sensible and seemingly unbreakable algorithm to include diagonal moves.

2. Mathematical Development.

Following the Cartesian axial system laid out in figure 1, the equation of an ellipse, hyperbola or other conic section can be expressed by equating the quantity d(x,y) to zero, where the quadratic form d(x,y) is defined by :

$$d(x,y) \equiv 2 v x - 2 u y + c - \alpha y^2 - \beta x^2 - 2\gamma xy \qquad (1)$$

The incremental mesh or pixel scale in x and y is taken as the unit of length, and c is supposed to be small, or zero, so that the curve d = 0 passes near to, or through, the origin, which is thus supposed to be a sensible starting point for the incremental algorithm. α, β and γ (the factor of 2 is introduced with γ for mathematical simplicity) are supposed to be small, causing the gradient, initially v/u (following Bresenham's notion of a line drawn from the origin to some point u,v) to vary slowly, and in fact to decrease for positive α, β and γ). For convenience the analysis assumes that the starting direction of the curve lies in the first octant, so that $0 < v < u$, i.e. $0 < dy/dx < 1$, but the other octants can be treated similarly, and are in fact all involved, through the octant change arithmetic described later in this section, in completing a full ellipse for example.

The conic drawing algorithm outlined in figure 2 operates by simple differencing: from each pen position reached in the loop, denoted i,j, d is evaluated at the point i+1, j+½, mid-way between the next possible pen movement positions, to i+1,j (x-step or square move), or to a i+1,j+1 (diagonal move). If d < 0 at this point the curve passes below, and an x-step is called for;   otherwise (the case when d = 0 being a nuisance, when either move is equally bad) a diagonal move is the better.

In order to avoid multiplications in the loop, d is computed by simple differencing.

First note that along the curve:

$$\frac{dy}{dx} = \frac{v - \beta x - \gamma y}{u + \gamma x + \alpha y} \qquad (2),$$

and we equate the algorithmic variable b with the quantity $2(v - \beta x - \gamma y)$, and a+b with $2(u + \gamma x + \alpha y)$, again following Bresenham's algorithmic framework for the straight line case when $\alpha = \beta = \gamma = 0$. Then we simply set up the appropriate initial conditions:

$$K1 = 2\beta$$
$$K2 = 2\gamma + K1$$
$$K3 = 2\alpha + 2\gamma + K2$$
$$b = 2v - \beta - \gamma \qquad (3)$$
$$a = 2u - b$$
$$d = b - u - \tfrac{1}{4}\alpha + k$$

The variables b and a are stepped incrementally following the plotter moves, and are subsequently used to provide the appropriate second order differences for d, starting from its initial value calculated at $x = 1$, $y = \tfrac{1}{2}$ as required to choose the very first move. With the ordering of the instructions shown in figure 2, the variables b and a are stepped before d, so that b is initially set to $d(1,\tfrac{1}{2}) - d(0,\tfrac{1}{2})$, and a to $d(0,-\tfrac{1}{2}) - d(1,\tfrac{1}{2})$, the signs being chosen to work with b and a positive throughout, but this ordering could be reversed (with an appropriate change in the initial values) if this proved convenient for other purposes, notably the location of the octant change test conditions described below.

With the signs as shown, α, β and γ, and thus K1, K2 and K3, all positive, the gradient dy/dx, defined through the parameters b and a as b/(a+b), will reduce as the algorithm runs, until eventually b, and thus the gradient, becomes negative. At this point, marked in figure 1, remedial action is called for, otherwise an endless succession of square moves will be output, with d remaining permanently negative, and the algorithm locked on the lefthand side of figure 2. Similarly, if a decreases it, too, can become negative, causing a similar failure with the gradient of the intended curve exceeding one, locking onto the righthand side of figure 2, **and** an endless sequence of diagonal moves

A possible location for traps on these conditions is suggested in figure 2, it being understood that, for reasonable slowly varying curves, the normal flow will continue down through the usual positive value for b and a as shown. Note that the location indicated has been carefully chosen so that it is possible for a square octant change to occur, for example, between two diagonal moves, as well as between square moves. After one diagonal move, in the first octant from i,j to i+j,j+1 as shown in figure 1, control continues down the righthand side of the algorithm of figure 2, returning eventually to the main branch "is d < 0?" test. At this point, if in fact a diagonal move in the eighth octant is really the next move needed, the test on d will at least push control down the left-hand side of figure 2 towards the x-step or square move, which is certainly preferable in any case to a further diagonal move up and to the right, but then the test "is b < 0?" can operate to trigger appropriate remedial action before any harm is done by the unwanted square-move output instruction. It is for this reason that it is not necessary to incorporate both octant change tests, "is b < 0?" and "is a < 0?", into both branches of the algorithm of figure 2.

The arithmetic required for an octant change can be established by convential mathematics, or more conveniently by manipulation of the basic algorithm itself, as described in a companion paper on "The algebra of algorithms". Either way, of course, it is extremely useful to reset the variables b, and and d, and the constants (as far as the inner loop is concerned) K1, K2 and K3 by calculations from their current values, rather than starting again from the conic parameters u,v, c, α, β and γ, partly to simplify the computational arithmetic, but also to ensure that the transformations, once established for one square or diagonal octant change, may be applied for subsequent changes through all eight octants to complete any given ellipse or other conic that may be required.

With the ordering carefully chosen to avoid overwriting parameters, so that the transformations appear the same in both algebraic and algorithmic expression, the octant transformations may be written:

For the square octant change:

$$-d - a - b - K2 + K1 \rightarrow d$$
$$a + 2b + K2 - K1 \rightarrow a$$
$$- b - K2 + K1 \rightarrow b \qquad\qquad (4)$$
$$4K2 - 4K1 - K3 \rightarrow K3$$
$$K2 - 2K1 \rightarrow K2$$
$$- K1 \rightarrow K1$$

(and change the diagonal move for the adjacent octant, e.g. to ↘ from ↗ if moving from the first to the eighth octant).

For the diagonal octant change:

$$- d + b + \tfrac{1}{2} a - \tfrac{1}{2} K2 + \tfrac{3}{8} K3 \rightarrow d$$
$$b + a - \tfrac{1}{2} K2 + \tfrac{1}{2} K3 \rightarrow b$$
$$- a + K2 - \tfrac{1}{2} K3 \rightarrow a$$
$$2K2 - K3 - K1 \rightarrow K1 \qquad\qquad (5)$$
$$K2 - K3 \rightarrow K2$$
$$- K3 \rightarrow K3$$

(and change the square move for the next adjacent octant, e.g. from an x-step to a y-step if changing from the first to the second octant).

Note that this arithmetic assumes, in both cases, that we plan to return control to the same place, or its equivalent, in the flow chart of figure 2, i.e. to one of the three test locactions, "is d < 0?", "is b < 0?" or "is a < 0?" ahead of the output commands or subsequent arithmetic. (In the version restricted to square moves only, figure 6, part of the inner loop arithmetic is picked up to simplify the octant change code). However, as mentioned in the introduction, this simple version of the algorithm is not satisfactory. It, after an octant change, control is is returned to "is d < 0?", a loop of continually repeated octant changes can occur, even for a seemingly innocuous, gently curving ellipse. This can be suppressed by returning from the square octant change to the square move output, and similarly from the diagonal octant change to the diagonal move output, thus forcing at least one move between adjacent octant changes, but then the d < 0 condition is not achieved if, as mentioned above the square change from octant 1 to 8 really requires an output sequence like → → ↗ ↘ → →, or similarly if the diagonal change from octant 1 to 2 needs → ↑, while the possibility of sharp corners, or catering for very small circles for example, is lost.   This problem is discussed in more detail in the next two sections of this paper.

3. Possible "best fit" criteria.

In order to design an algorithm for drawing conic sections which behaves sensibly at all changes of octant, conventional analysis would suggest that we should first define precisely just what it is the computer is supposed to do. In particular, in this section, we consider various alternative best fit definitions that might be considered, though it seems to result in little progress beyond the basic algorithm of figure 2.

Firstly, and following Bresenham's orginal suggestion, an algorithm might be developed to choose, at each incremental step, the next move which leaves the plotter pen (or graphic equivalent) as close as possible to the intended curve, but this involves dropping perpendiculars from (i,j) and $(i+1,j)$ to the curve, and the resulting algebra seems horrendous. Accordingly, it seems sensible to move on to the simpler concept used in the previous section, of using the midpoint residual to choose each move, even though this does not have the geometric equivalence to the nearest pen position established by Bresenham for the case of a straight line. Thus, for an ellipse, the plotter would be required to outline a perimeter enclosing all negative mesh point values for d (and note that this involves the sign for d following the diagonal octant changes at points like $(i \pm \frac{1}{2}, j)$ as well as $(i, j \pm \frac{1}{2})$, while excluding the mesh points where d is positive.

That this is not in itself enough, however, can be seen by considering thin ellipses like those sketched in figure 3; the presence of such ellipses cannot be detected by a test on d values for the midpoints involved in the algorithm (though the values of b and a could afford some aid). Also a version choosing the smallest residual at the pen positions is not ruled out, though I have made no progress with it. It seems fairly obvious that a plotter should simply move to and fro to represent the shapes of figure 3, but this requires a more sophisticated definition of **"best fit" than than** used in section 2. A **criter**ion suggested

by Freeman and Glass (1969) is shown diagramatically in figure 4a.
Imagine that the ellipse (or other curve) is gradually traversed as some
parameter is varied then, each time the curve crosses a square grid drawn
through the integer x y values, as indicated in figure 3, the plotter pen
responds by moving to the nearest integer point.   In effect the pen is
"captured" by the point whenever the intended curve touches one of the four
catchment lines extending half a step in the horizontal and vertical
directions.   This handles the case of the long thin horizontal ellipses
shown in figure 3, but seems too insensitive in the case of the short
diagonal ellipse, where we might reasonably expect the plotter to move to
and fro along the diagonal move as the ellipse is traversed.

In figure 4b the catchment lines have been extended into the largest possible
"catchment areas" still consistent with Bresenham's algorithm.   The pen moves
to the appropriate point when the intended curve enters its associated area.
In this case, the catchment areas are possibly too large or sensitive.   For
example, suppose the intended curve happens to follow the trajectory shown
in the figure by a dotted line, the pen will first move diagonally downwards,
then vertically up;   if the curve were traversed in the opposite direction
the pen simply moves back horizontally, which seems illogical.   The
reduced catchment areas of figure 4c, the, seem more sensible in that they
are the most sensitive, consistent with both Bresenham and reversability.

Unfortunately, however, even the algebra involved in deciding whether some
given ellipse reaches, or just fails to reach, a line drawn vertically
through the next possible x coordinate value seems to be horrendous, and
unlikely to lead to an elegant algorithm.

Finally, and to complete this section, it is of interest to consider
another mathematical aspect which might provide a clue: It is well known,
of course, that two intersecting straight lines are a special case of conic
sections, and that, as the conic parameters are varied, the crossing
lines can split into alternate hyperbola, as shown in figure 5a.   Thus
a very small change in c, for example, can effectively decide which of
three branches is to be followed from the crossing point. Clearly there
ought to be some corresponding feature in the octant change tests which
describes this precise behaviour? Note, too that there is a related
problem even for straight lines if we generalise Bresenham's algorithm

so that the integer mesh points are not specified for the start and finish of a straight line. Suppose, for example, that we want to represent a line starting from the origin with gradient $\frac{1}{3}$, thus $y = x/3$, and continue until it crosses another line, $y = 3 - x/3$; then we wish to follow the second line back until it crosses the y axis at $y = 3$. These two lines cross at the point $x = 4\frac{1}{2}$, $y = 1\frac{1}{2}$, which, of course, is not available as a pen position.   The sensible behaviour suggested in figure 5b involves a single y step at $x = 4$ from $y = 1$ to $y = 2$, but this y step is not involved in the Bresenham representation of either constituent line, and so cannot be achieved by a simple adaption of the end condition for the straight line algorithm.

We now go on to consider the problem from an algorithmic standpoint.

4. Algorithmic Approach

In the previous section of this paper, it is suggested that a mathematical approach to the problem of handling conic sections with sharp corners is somewhat sterile. In this section, we follow an alternative approach: Is it possible to establish an algorithm which behaves reasonably and sensibly in all cases, which can be adopted as a pragmatic solution, and submitted for a detailed mathematical analysis in order to establish the physical understanding that, once it is established, should no doubt have been obvious all along, (though it never is)?.

From an algorithmic standpoint, then, the problem with the algorithm of figure 2 is simply stated: If we return control from the octant changes to the output move instructions following the test which triggered the octant change call, we limit the algorithm to only one octant change per move, thus ruling out very sharp corners.   But if, as suggested in the text of section 2, we return control back to the is "d < 0?" branch test we open up the possiblity of an infinite loop, even with perfectly innocuous seeming ellipses, with octant changes to and fro, or cycling round the octants, with no output at all.   (But note that, from an algorithmic viewpoint, cycling round all eight octants might still be a perfectly reasonable behaviour if, for example, we call for the completion of a full circle with radius less than about half an increment, or an equally tiny ellipse).

Firstly, let us consider the looping which can occur if we satisfy the square octant change condition "is b < 0?", and it turns out that, because of non-zero values for the curvature parameters K1 and K2, b is still negative after completing the octant change arithmetic which is supposed to reset it to a positive value for a sensible continuation of the inner loop, i.e. the quantity $-b-K2 + K1$, is also negative. This suggests, however, that we can avoid the looping if, instead of testing for the exception condition that b has become negative, we ask instead whether making a square octant change would make b less negative, i.e. "is $-b - K2 + K1 > b$?", which is, of course, algorithmically equivalent to asking "is $b < \frac{1}{2}(K1-K2)$?". Similarly, we can avoid the continual, to-and-fro looping that can occur for a diagonal octant change by asking not whether a is negative, but rather whether the diagonal octant change arithmetic "$-a + K2 - \frac{1}{2}K3 \to a$" improves matters, in that $- a + K2 - \frac{1}{2}K3 > a$, so that the test "is a < 0?" becomes instead "is $a < \frac{1}{2}K2 - \frac{1}{4}K3$?".

Unfortunately, this remedial correction still leaves open the possibility of looping around the eight octants in a clockwise or anticlockwise direction, by way of the "is d < 0?" branch, again even for innocuous seeming ellipses that one would not expect to cause such trouble. More-over, even if this does not occur, it can happen that the square octant change condition, for example, can be triggered too late, so that a mesh mid-point can be excluded from the ellipse that should, at least according to the sign of d, have been included, or a point that should have been excluded becomes included, and similarly for the diagonal octant change. Again, we can design the square octant change test deliberately to pick this up: Having taken the lefthand branch of figure 2, from the test "is d < 0?", on the grounds that d is indeed negative, so the square move is preferable to the diagonal, we can then ask "would the sign of d after making the square change still indicate a point above the curve?" (albeit positive now, because of the sign reversal associated with the octant change). Thus we need a square change of octant, followed immediately by a (downwards) diagonal move if, besides d < 0, we also satisfy the condition $d + a + b + K2 - K1 < 0$, and similarly for the diagonal octant change, the test for which becomes rewritten "is $d - b - \frac{1}{2} a + \frac{1}{2}K2 - \frac{3}{8}K3 < 0$?" But this seems to be very heavy handed and inelegant, not at all the sort of thing we are looking for.

So, noting that the thinking above leads to the suggestion that d might
be incorporated, along with the parameters b and a, in the octant test
conditions, another thought occurs: We need the octant change to trap
b < 0, or a < 0, because clearly the basic inner loop, representing as it
does a slowly varying gradient version of Bresenham's algorithm, will
fail otherwise. But equally in its normal operation, Bresenham's algorithm
for a straight line requires that d be maintained in the working range
-a $\leqslant$ d < b. So we look for trouble, calling for remedial octant change
application, if d moves outside this range, i.e. "is b $\leqslant$ d?" to call for
a square octant change, and similarly "is a < - d?" to call for a diagonal
octant change.   But again, unfortunately, it doesn't seem to work
sensibly in all cases.

Finally, in an attempt to simplify the problem, a version has   been
developed, and is presented in figure 6, for a plotter or pixel display in
which diagonal moves are supposed to be inhibited, so we are dealing with
just the four quadrants, rather than eight octants, starting in the first
quadrant with a choice between an x-step (as before) or a y-step (in place
of the previous diagonal) at each stage.   The intial conditions are now:

$$
\begin{aligned}
2\beta &\rightarrow K1 \\
2\gamma &\rightarrow K2 \\
2\alpha &\rightarrow K3 \\
2v- \gamma &\rightarrow b \\
2u+ \gamma &\rightarrow a \\
v-u+c-\tfrac{1}{4}\alpha-\tfrac{1}{4}\beta-\tfrac{1}{2}\gamma &\rightarrow d
\end{aligned}
\qquad (6)
$$

(d being evaluated now at the midpoints $i+\tfrac{1}{2},j+\tfrac{1}{2}$, so initially $d(\tfrac{1}{2},\tfrac{1}{2})$).
The quadrant change arithmetic is so simple that it is written into the
figure itself, though using some of the code from the inner loop by
careful choice of the rejoining back to the "is d < 0?" branch test. (That
this is possible provides in itself a tantalizing clue in the search for
an elegant algorithm).

Note that in this version of the algorithm, the curvature constant K2, 2γ from the basic equation of the conic in (1), is invariant to a change of quadrant, so the tests for quadrant change, modified to prevent the simple to-and-fro infinite loop, can be expressed conveniently in terms of , rather than the $\frac{1}{2}$K2 which would otherwise have been required. Furthermore, infinite looping in a clockwise or anticlockwise direction around the quadrants is impossible without a move, as $b + \gamma$ and $a - \gamma$ must both be positive in one of the quadrants.

This algorithm has been tested in a number of difficult looking cases, some of which are exhibited in figure 7, and the results seem quite promising. Certainly it seems more successful than any of the versions with diagonal moves and eight octants permitted. It is also worth noting, in passing, that a version of figure 6 which chooses, at each step, the move which results in a minimum value for $|d|$ has been developed, and shows very little change, just as in the case of a circle. The initial value for d is $v - u + c - \frac{1}{2}\alpha - \frac{1}{2}\beta$, and d becomes $\gamma - d$ for both quadrant changes shown in the flow chart of figure 6.

Conclusion.

The handling of conics with sharp corners is a topic deserving further research in both integer and floating point working.

References.

J.E. Bresenham 1977, "A linear algorithm for incremental digital display of circular arcs", ACM Communications 20, 100 - 106.

M.D.McIlroy 1983, "Best approximate circles on integer grids", ACM Transactions on Graphics" 2, 237 - 263.

M.L.V.Pitteway 1967, "Algorithm for drawing ellipses or hyperbolae with a digital plotter", Computer Journal 10, 282 - 289.

J.E.Bresenham 1965, "Algorithm for computer control of a digital plotter", IBM Systems Journal, 4, 25 - 30.

Herbert Freeman and Jeremy M. Glass 1969, "On the quantization of line-drawing data", IEEE Transactions on Systems Science and Cybernetics 5, 70 - 79

Dan Cohen 1970, "On linear differences curves", from "Advanced Computer Graphics, Economics, Techniques and Applications" Plenum Press (London and New York 1971), (Edited by R.D.Parslow and R.Elliot Green) 1143 - 1177.

L.B.Smith 1971, "Drawing ellipses, hyperbolas with a fixed number of points and maximum inscribed area", Computer Journal 14, 81 - 85.

Robert F. Sproull 1982, "Using program transformation to derive line-drawing algorithms", ACM Transactions on Graphics 1, 259 - 273.

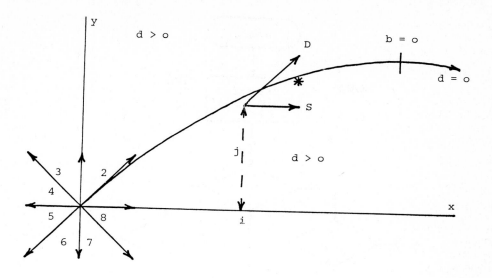

figure 1.

Geometry for a curve plotted in the first octant, starting with gradient dy/dx = v/u, where 0 < v < u. From each point i,j, we choose a square move (to i + 1,j) if the quadratic residue d, evaluated at the midpoint (marked **x**) at i + 1,j + ½) is negative, and a diagonal move (to i + 1,j + 1) otherwise. The curve as drawn meets the condition b < 0 at the point shown, where a "square" octant change is called for, so that the diagonal move is subsequently looking for a move to i + 1,j - 1.

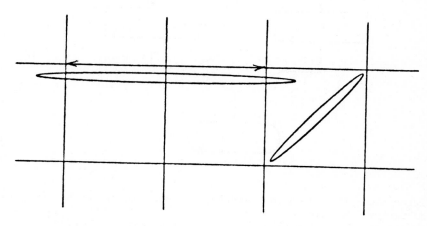

figure 3.

The thin, horizontal ellipse cannot be drawn by an algorithm which relies only on the sign of the quadratic residue d evaluated at the mesh points (marked with a *) to detect its presence; all the points marked are situate outside the ellipse, so d is positive wherever it is evaluated. Yet clearly the plotter should respond by drawing the appropriate horizontal line marked ↔. The criterion suggested by Freeman and Glass (1969) deals with this case, but is not sensitive enough to handle the short diagonal ellipse, which obviously can be sensibly represented by a diagonal move (and return).

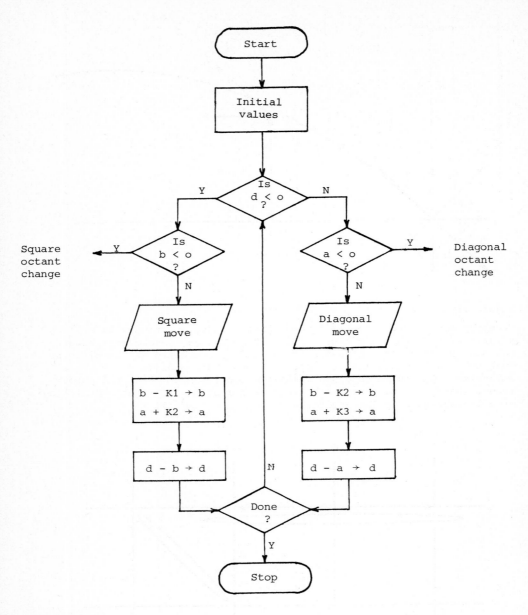

figure 2.

Conic drawing algorithm based on Bresenham's algorithm but with curvature
introduced through the parameters K1, K2 and K3, which causes b and a,
and thus the gradient b/(a + b), to vary. Special action is required to
trap the exception octant change conditions, if either b or a becomes
negative.

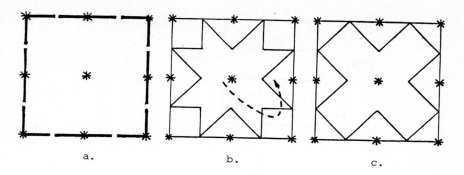

figure 4.

      Catchment areas/

      (a)   Freeman and Glass.
      (b)   Most sensitive compatable with Bresenham for a straight line.
      (c)   Reversible.

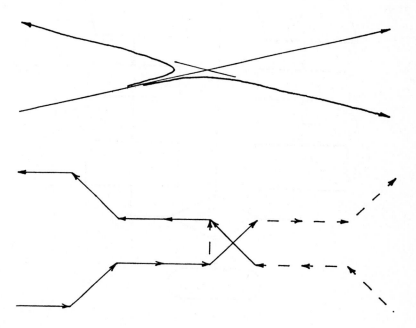

figure 5.

Two crossing straight lines as a degenerate case of the conic sections,
(a), showing that the correct branch to be followed can be very
sensitive to a small change in the controlling parameters. Note that
a sensible plotter representation joining the two straight lines,
(b), may require a plotter increment, a y-step in this case, which is not
involved in the Bresenham sequence of either of the two lines.

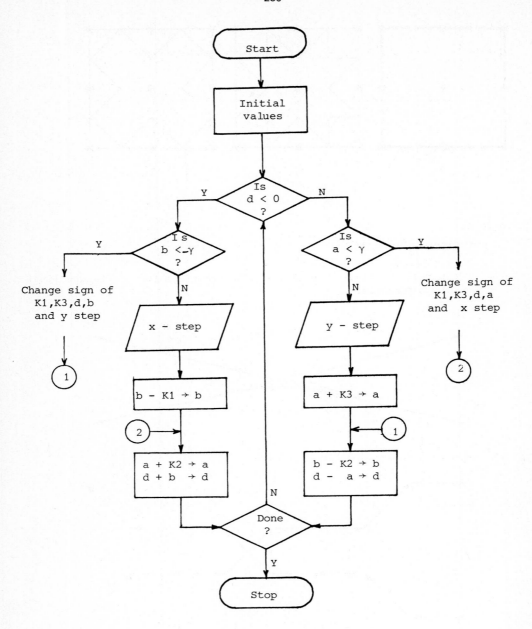

figure 6.

Conic drawing algorithm for a plotter which permits only square moves.

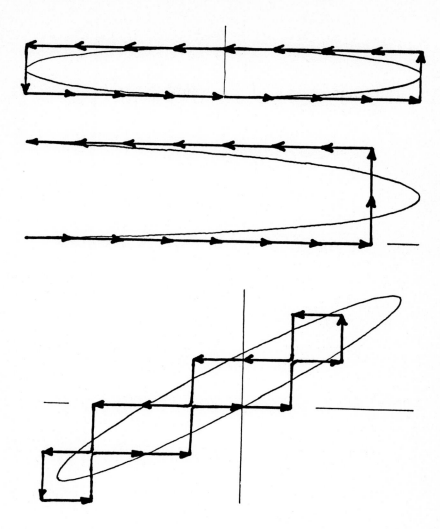

figure 7.

Three examples showing the behaviour of the algorithm of figure 6 at sharp corners:

(a) $x^2 + 64y\,(y-1) = 0$

(b) $x^2 + 100y\,(y-2) = 0$ (shown for x - values $\geqslant$ 2 only)

(c) $67x^2 + 193y^2 - 218xy + 128x - 222y = 0$

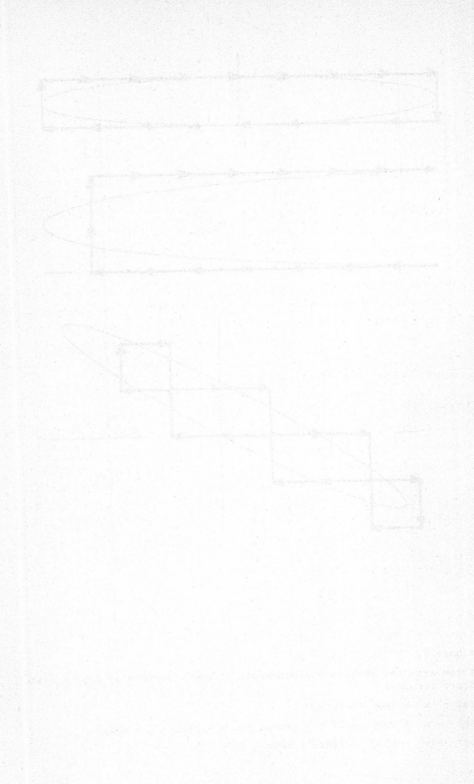

A High Precision Digital Differential Analyzer for Circle Generation*

Hong Tao**

Abstract

In most applications of computer graphics, circles and circular arcs are frequently displayed. It is possible to contruct a DDA that draws a true circle; however, the logic needed for multiplications and trigonometric functions makes it less suited to hardware implementation, and the computations are performed too slowly by software on a computer to be acceptable. Other incremental methods perform computations without multiplications and trigonometric functions, but the common weakness of these methods is lower accuracy.

In this paper the author presents a new incremental algorithm for circle-generating DDA. The accuracy of this algorithm is much higher than that of others, and almost the same as that of the equation for the true circle. The logic of this method is as simple as the other incremental algorithms. Furthermore, where line-generating hardware exists, if we decrease the accuracy of this algorithm by one order of magnitude, the speed of drawing the circle may be raised considerably. Because of its simplicity and use only of elementary addition, subtraction, shift and sign testing, this method is also appropriate for use in numerical control, drafting machines or raster display, where closeness of fit is necessary.

---

* Chinese original published in Journal of North-western Polytechnical University, Vol. 2, No. 1, Jan. 1984

** Associate Professor

1. Introduction

The fact that circles and circular arcs occur with considerable frequency in most applications of computer graphics presents a problem, because the majority of graphics displays have hardware only for line generation, not circle drawing. A number of incremental methods have been invented to plot circles and arcs [1, 2, 3]. In addition, D. Cohen has presented two kinds of Digital Differential Analyzer, which generate a sequence of regularly spaced points on a circle [4, 1]. It is possible to construct a DDA that draws an exact circle; however, the need for multiplications and trigonometric functions makes it less suited to hardware implementation, and the slowness of the computations performed by software on a computer is unacceptable. Almost all incremental methods for circle generation involve computations without multiplications and trigonometric functions, and some of them adopt the integer coordinates in order to further simplify the logic. But the common weakness of these methods is lower accuracy.

In this paper the author proposes a new incremental algorithm for circle-generating DDA (MPC-DDA). The accuracy of this algorithm is far higher than that of all of the others, and almost the same as that of the equation for the true circle. The logic of this method is as simple as the other incremental algorithms. It is entirely possible to increase its speed of calculation and display. Its simplicity and use of only elementary addition, subtraction, shift and sign testing also makes it appropriate for use in drafting machines, raster displays or numerical control.

2. Several Incremental Algorithms
for Circle Generation

Bresenham [1] has developed an incremental algorithm for circle generation based on mesh point selection. When a circle's center and radius are integers, only integer calculations are required. For simplicity, suppose the circular function is given by $x^2 + y^2 = R^2$. In the first quadrant arc of circle from (0, R) to (R, 0), y is a monotonically decreasing function of x. Clockwise movement in this quadrant can therefore be accomplished by a sequence of moves involving only m_1, m_2, and m_3, as shown in Fig. 1.

Choosing one of these three possible movements, we must make certain that out of the **three absolute differences** between R^2 and the squares of the constraint radii of the three possible points, the least absolute difference should be selected. Take Δ_i as follows:

$$\Delta_i = \{[(x_i + 1)^2 + (y_i - 1)^2] - R^2\} = 2(x_i - y_i + 1)$$

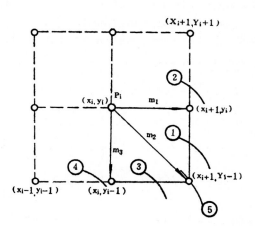

Fig. 1 Determination of points for Bresenham's
circle generator

(a) If $\Delta_i < 0$, then point $(x_i + 1, y_i - 1)$ is in the interior of the true circle, i.e. case ① or ② in Figure 1. In case ① the closer of the two points can be found by observing the sign of the following difference δ :

$$\delta = \{[(x_i+1)^2+y_i^2]-R^2\} + \{[(x_i+1)^2+(y_i-1)^2]-R^2\}$$
$$= 2\triangle_i + 2y_i - 1$$

where for $\delta \leqslant 0$ move m_1 is chosen, and for $\delta > 0$ move m_2 is chosen.

(b) If $\triangle_i > 0$, then (x_1+1, y_1-1) is outside the true circle, i.e. cases ③ and ④ in Figure 1. In like manner, another difference δ' can be found:

$$\delta' = 2\triangle i - 2 x i - 1$$

where for $\delta' \leqslant 0$ move m_2 is chosen and for $\delta' > 0$ move m_3 is chosen.

(c) If $\triangle i = 0$ then (x_1+1, y_1-1) is on the true circle, i.e. case ⑤ , and the move m_2 should be chosen.

The radial errors of this method for the circle with a radius of 10 are approximately 0.511 and 0.487, according to own calculations.

Danielsson [2] discovered that using the classical DDA for parametric function may result in degradation of curve, thus producing a curve far away from the actual curve. He proposed an interpolation algorithm using a nonparametric function. Consider a two-dimensional curve described by $f(x, y) = 0$. From Taylor's expansion we can easily derive the following four formulas:

$$f(x+1,y) = f(x,y) + \frac{\partial f}{\partial x} + \frac{1}{2}\frac{\partial^2 f}{\partial x^2} + \cdots\cdots$$

$$f(x-1,y) = f(x,y) - \frac{\partial f}{\partial x} + \frac{1}{2}\frac{\partial^2 f}{\partial x^2} - \cdots\cdots$$

$$f(x,y+1) = f(x,y) + \frac{\partial f}{\partial y} + \frac{1}{2}\frac{\partial^2 f}{\partial y^2} + \cdots\cdots$$

$$f(x,y-1) = f(x,y) - \frac{\partial f}{\partial y} + \frac{1}{2}\frac{\partial^2 f}{\partial y^2} - \cdots\cdots$$

Danielsson assumed that every step was along either abscissa axis or ordinate axis only. Therefore there are four possible directions from which to choose. Judging from the signs of $f(x, y)$, $\frac{\partial f}{\partial x}$ and $\frac{\partial f}{\partial y}$ in the above four formulas, we can narrow the four directions down to two. Then he introduced direction v of travel along the curve in order to determine whether the x-axis or y-axis should be selected. The peak error of this method is about one unit.

Jordan, Lennon and Holm improved Danielsson's nonparametric representation of curve [3]. Danielsson limited the
possible choices to (x+ Δ x, y) or (x, y+Δ y), but they increased the possible choices to include (x+Δ x, y+Δ y) which
is move m_2 shown in Fig. 1, where Δ x, Δ y= $\pm$ 1. Out of four
possible combinations of Δ x and Δ y the proper combination
is selected by considering the direction of travel and the
values of errors. Then it is only necessary to compare the
absolute function values $|f(x+\Delta x, y)|$, $|f(x, y+\Delta y)|$ and
$|f(x+\Delta x, y+\Delta y)|$ to decide which point (x+Δ x, y), (x, y+Δ y)
or (x+Δ x, y+Δ y) to choose. This was called an eight-point
algorithm for the generation of a circle. If the incremental
steps are limited to either a step in x or a step in y as in
Danielsson's algorithm, it is called a four-point algorithm.
The peak error of the eight-point algorithm is about 0.5 units,
and the peak error of the four-point algorithm is about 0.7
units.

Cohen presented two approximate algorithms of DDA, which
are abbreviated to SC-DDA and E-DDA in this paper. The iterative computing method of SC-DDA can be written in matrix
form as

$$[x_{i+1} \ y_{i+1}] = [x_i \ y_i] \begin{bmatrix} 1 & -\varepsilon \\ \varepsilon & 1 \end{bmatrix}$$

where $\varepsilon = 2^{-n}$ and $2^{n-1} \leq R < 2^n$. Unfortunately the method just
described plots a spiral, not an exact circular arc. When
R= 10 and R= 125, the peak errors of circular arc δ_R= 0.397
and δ_R= 0.715 respectively. The second Cohen's method reduced the margin of error, generating a closed curve. Actually it approximates an ellipse, and its iterative function
can be written as follows:

$$[x_{i+1} \ y_{i+1}] = [x_i \ y_i] \begin{bmatrix} 1 & -\varepsilon \\ \varepsilon & 1-\varepsilon^2 \end{bmatrix}$$

When the starting point is on the ordinate axis, the peak error
occurs at the point lying at a distance of $\pi R/4$ from the
starting point. For example, when R= 10, δ_R =-0.154, and for
R= 125, δ_R = -0.243.

3. The High Precision Circle-Generating DDA

The author has proposed an algorithm of High Precision Circle—Generating DDA, which is abbreviated to MPC—DDA in this paper. We assume that the coordinates of a circle are center (x_c, y_c), and suppose $\varepsilon = 2^{-n} < R^{-1} \leq 2^{-n+1}$, where R is the radius of the circle. Then using the exact recurrence formula of the circle, we may obtain the following approximate formulas, i.e.

$$[x_{i+1} - x_c \quad y_{i+1} - y_c] = [x_i - x_c \quad y_i - y_c]\begin{bmatrix} \cos\theta & -\sin\theta \\ \sin\theta & \cos\theta \end{bmatrix}$$

if $\qquad \sin\theta = \varepsilon$

we may obtain the series:

$$\cos\theta = 1 - \frac{1}{2}\varepsilon^2 - \frac{1}{8}\varepsilon^4 - \frac{1}{16}\varepsilon^6 - \frac{5}{128}\varepsilon^8 - \cdots\cdots$$

$$\doteq 1 - \frac{1}{2}\varepsilon^2$$

then

$$[x_{i+1} - x_c \quad y_{i+1} - y_c] = [x_i - x_c \quad y_i - y_c]\begin{bmatrix} 1 - \frac{1}{2}\varepsilon^2 & -\varepsilon \\ \varepsilon & 1 - \frac{1}{2}\varepsilon^2 \end{bmatrix}$$

$$= [x_i - x_c \quad y_i - y_c]\begin{bmatrix} 1 - 2^{-2n-1} & -2^{-n} \\ 2^{-n} & 1 - 2^{-2n-1} \end{bmatrix}$$

This method is almost as simple as the above—mentioned methods. There is no need for multiplications and division, only for addition, subtraction, shift and sign testing. We can easily calculate the interpolated points of the circle. The accuracy of this method is much higher than almost all the other methods, furthermore, the greater the radius of the circle, the less the peak error of the circle. For example, when R= 10, then δ_R=0.000456, and when R= 125, then δ_R = 0.0000153; when R= 1000, then δ_R approaches zero. On the other hand, the existing methods described above cannot guarantee that the generated curve will pass through an arbitrarily given endpoint.

The flow chart of MPC—DDA for the generation of arbitrary circular arc is shown in Fig. 2, where (x_0, y_0) and (x_e, y_e) are the starting and stopping points of the circular arc, respectively.

There are several methods for determining the criterion for terminating the drawn arc. For example, one criterion for termination is based on arc length. A stopping criterion for analog circuits is to stop after a given time has elapsed. This is equivalent to stopping after a given arc length has been traversed. But since the velocity along the curve is not quite constant, arc length is not a linear function of the number of steps taken, and this nonlinearity must be accounted for to prevent errors in the termination point. On the other hand some methods use the total steps traversed to control drawing arcs. For the four-point and

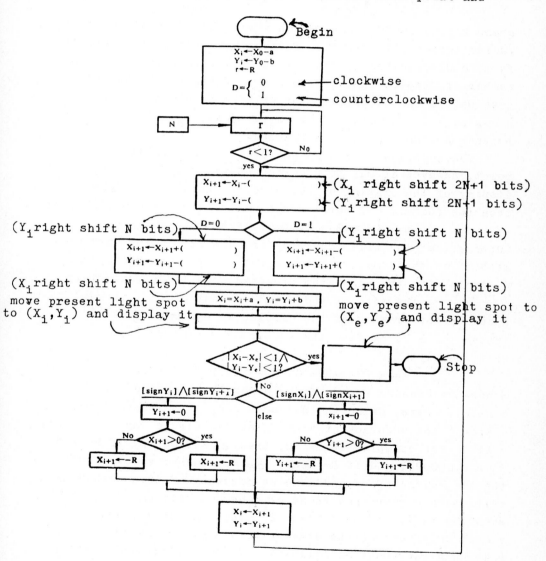

Fig. 2 Flow chart of MPC-DDA

Danielssons algorithm, the total steps traveled per quadrant ($\pi R/2$ arc) are equal to 2R, and approximately $4(\sqrt{2}-1)R = 1.656R$ for the eight-point and Bresenhams algorithm.

The total steps of the method proposed in this paper are a little more than those of SC-DDA, and equal to those of E-DDA. Let m be the number of steps taken per quadrant, then

$$m = k \cdot 2^n$$

where k is a coefficient, which varies by steps with the radius between $1.5 \sim 1.571$. Because k is not a constant, it is more complicated to control the stepping point with the number of steps. In the flow chart of Figure 2, the point just before the stopping point will be determined in accordance with the condition $|x_i - x_e| < 1 \wedge |y_i - y_e| < 1$. One step further on the stopping is reached.

The number of steps is not used for controlling the endpoint, however it may be used to analyze roughly the speed of display of the drawing of the circle. Because $2^{n-1} \le R < 2^n$, then the formula for total steps can be rewritten as follows:

$$m = k(R \sim 2R) = 1.5R \sim 3.142R$$

Suppose that the time required for each step using various methods is the same, then the speed of drawing or displaying a circle with the algorithm proposed here is approximately the same as the speed of most of the others. To speed up the drawing of the circle, we can make $\varepsilon = 2^{-n+1}$ instead of 2^{-n}, so that the number of cycles is reduced to half, namely

$$m = k(R/2 \sim R) = 0.75R \sim 1.571R$$

Hence the drawing speed of the algorithm proposed here can be doubled. Here, owing to increased step (increased length of a step), the accuracy of drawing of the circle may be lowered a bit. For example, if R= 10, then $\delta_R = 0.00366$, if R= 125, $\delta_R = 0.000093$, and if R= 1000, δ_R approaches zero. Thus, the displaying speed and drawing accuracy of this method are still both higher than those of other algorithms. Especially when the radius is more than 2^5, the increased speed has almost no effect on the drawing accuracy. Therefore we can make an arrangement as follows: if $R \le 32$, still $\varepsilon = 2^{-n}$, and if $R > 32$, instead $\varepsilon = 2^{-n+1}$. The reason is that in the case of small radius the number of steps is not very large, and the drawing speed is not very important, but the improvement in accuracy is very significant. When displaying a large circle, where the number of steps is much greater, it is necessary to pay attention to the drawing speed. Both the displaying speed and the drawing accuracy need to be considered. If the requirement of the drawing speed is high, we can enlarge the step, e.g. if R= 500, we make ε equal to 2^{-9}, then δ_R approaches zero, or we make ε equal to 2^{-5}, then $\delta_R = 0.00298$. Drawing speed is thereby raised by $2^4 = 16$ times! But if we enlarge the step we must consider the secondary fitting error Δ, and sometimes Δ may be greater than the calculation error δ_R of interpolation. When $\Delta_{R=500, m=50} = 0.06168$, then $\delta_\Sigma = \Delta_R - \delta_R = 0.0587$. Yet, even when we consider the secondary fitting error and raise the drawing speed by 16 times, the accuracy of the large circle is still higher than that of all other algorithms.

4. Accuracy Analysis

In accuracy analysis we assume that there is no error at the starting point (x_0, y_0), and $\delta_{R,j}$ denotes the radial deviation of the interpolation point from the starting point through j steps. Then the error formula of interpolation in the MPC—DDA algorithm is as follows:

$$\delta_{R,j} = R\left[\left(1 + \frac{\varepsilon^4}{4}\right)^{j/2} - 1\right] = R[(1 + 2^{-4n-2})^{j/2} - 1]$$

From the flow chart in Fig. 2, we can see that the maximum error occurs after m steps or after passing through a quadrant:

$$\delta_{R,max} = R[(1 + 2^{-4n-2})^{m/2} - 1]$$

It seems as if the greater the radius, the bigger is the error, but this is not true. When the radius increases the value ε dwindles, and the limit of the expression in brackets approaches zero.

When we analyze the radial peak error of some equipment, except the calculating error of the interpolation point, we must deal with the secondary fitting error. Because a straight line is connected to two calculated interpolating points, the height Δ_R between the chord and the arc, i.e. the segment of the circle shown in Fig. 3, equals

$$\Delta_R \doteq R\left[1 - \cos\left(\frac{\pi}{4m}\right)\right]$$

The approximating circle is smaller than the exact circle, thus the formula of the total radial peak error is

$$\delta_{R,\Sigma} = \Delta_R - \delta_{R,\max}$$

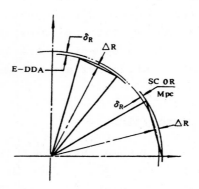

Fig. 3   The secondary fitting error

When R= 10, Δ_R = 0.00535 and $\delta_{R,\Sigma}$ = 0.00489, and when R= 125, then Δ_R = 0.000964 and $\delta_{R,\Sigma}$ = 0.000949.

Similarly, we can also deduce the formula of the errors of ordinates, it being very useful to analyze errors of drawn arcs. Suppose that there are no errors on the abscissas, then the error of the ordinate is represented by $\delta_{y,j}$. If $\bar{y}_1$ denotes the true value of the ordinate, then $\delta_{y,j}$ and $\delta_{y,\max}$ are as follows:

$$\delta_{y,j} = Y_j - \bar{y}_j = \sqrt{\bar{y}_j^2 + R^2\left[\left(1 + \frac{e^4}{4}\right)^j - 1\right]} - \bar{y}_j$$

$$\delta_{y,\max} = \sqrt{\bar{y}_j^2 + R^2[(1 + 2^{-4n-2})^m - 1]} - \bar{y}_j$$

The calculated results on a computer are that when R= 10, $\delta_{y,\max}$= 0.00659, and that when R=125, $\delta_{y,\max}$=0.00141. Both $\delta_{y,\max}$ and $\delta_{R,\max}$ are very small decimals, hence the stop-

ping conditions for arc drawing in the flow chart in Fig. 2
—— $|x_i - x_e| < 1$ and $|y_i - y_e| < 1$ —— may be satisfied
simultaneously.

Now we make a comparison between this algorithm and other
algorithms. In the SC-DDA algorithm, $\delta_{R,j}$ —— the radial
error of the interpolation point after j steps —— and
$\delta_{R,max}$ —— the maximum radial error —— are respectively

$$\delta_{R,j} = R[(1 + \varepsilon^2)^{j/2} - 1]$$
$$= R[(1 + 2^{-2n})^{j/2} - 1]$$
$$\delta_{R,max} = R[(1 + 2^{-2n})^{m/2} - 1]$$

The secondary fitting error Δ_R and the total radial peak error
$\delta_{R,\Sigma}$ are still respectively

$$\Delta_R \doteq R\left[1 - \cos\left(\frac{\pi}{4m}\right)\right]$$
$$\delta_{R,\Sigma} = \Delta_R - \delta_{R,max}$$

The errors of the ordinates are as follows:

$$\delta_{y,j} = \sqrt{\bar{y}_j^2 + R^2[(1 + \varepsilon^2)^j - 1]} - \bar{y}_j$$
$$= \sqrt{\bar{y}_j^2 + R^2[(1 + 2^{-2n})^j - 1]} - \bar{y}_j$$
$$\delta_{y,max} = \sqrt{\bar{y}_j^2 + R^2[(1 + 2^{-2n})^m - 1]} - \bar{y}_j$$

When R= 10 the peak error of ordinate $\delta_{y,max}$ = 1.63777; R=125,
$\delta_{y,max}$ = 10.51197; and R= 500, $\delta_{y,max}$ = 22.99169. Although
sometimes the radial peak error $\delta_{R,max}$ of the SC-DDA algorithm is acceptable, the maximum error of ordinate $\delta_{y,max}$
is so large that it leads to the error of arc length of the
same order of magnitude, and this is not desirable.

In the algorithm of E-DDA, the radius error after j steps
is

$$\delta_{R,j} = \sqrt{R^2 + \varepsilon^2\left[\sum_{k=1}^{j-1}(X_k^2 - Y_k^2)\right] + \varepsilon^2[X_j^2 - Y_0^2]} - R$$

If the starting point is on either coordinate axis, the
radial peak error does not occur in the case of $\pi R/2$ arcs,
but occurs in the case of $\pi R/4$ arcs and when j= m/2. If
the starting point is not on either coordinate axis, the peak
errors always occur on points at a distance $\pi R/4$ from either
axis regardless of where the starting point is, then

$$\delta_{R,\max} = \sqrt{R^2 + \varepsilon^2 \left[\sum_{k=1}^{\frac{m}{2}-1} (X_k^2 - Y_k^2) \right] + \varepsilon^2 (X_{\frac{m}{2}}^2 - Y_0^2)} - R$$

Because the fitting circle is smaller than the exact circle, the total peak error of radius is as follows:

$$\delta_{R,\Sigma} = \varDelta_R + \delta_{R,\max}$$

The error of the ordinate after j steps is

$$\delta_{y,j} = \sqrt{\bar{y}_j^2 + \varepsilon^2 \left[\sum_{k=1}^{j-1} (X_k^2 - Y_k^2) + (X_j^2 - Y_0^2) \right]} - \bar{y}_j$$

From the calculated results on a computer, when R= 10, $\delta_{y,\max}$ = -0.23913; and when R=125 $\delta_{y,\max}$ = -0.47963.

Observing three types of formulas of radial error, we find that $\delta_{R,\max}$ of the SC-DDA and E-DDA algorithms are function of ε^2, and $\delta_{R,\max}$ of the MPC-DDA algorithm is a function of $\varepsilon^4/4$. Because ε is a decimal, the radial peak errors of the latter are certainly much less than those of the former two algorithms. In Fig. 4 the total peak errors of various radii obtained by the above mentioned algorithms are drawn together in one diagram for comparison. The values of errors of Danielsson's algorithm, the four-point algorithm and the eight-point algorithm are found in [3]. The values

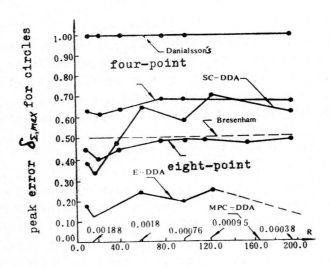

Fig. 4 Peak errors for circles of
various radii

of errors of Bresenham's algorithm are taken from his paper
[1]. Moreover, the values of errors of SC-DDA, E-DDA and
MPC-DDA are results from the author's calculations on a computer.

5. Results

According to these three type of DDA algorithms, the
coordinates and the errors at R= 5, 7, 10, 12.5, 16, 60, 100,
125, 500, have been calculated on a DJS-6 computer. The values
of errors associated with the three type of DDA algorithms are
completely consistant with the results of theoretical formulas.
That is to say, accumlated rounding errors are not significant.
To save space in this paper, only the characteritic data of
R= 7.0 and R= 100.0 obtained by the three types of DDA algorithms are selected in table 1 and 2. It is shown that, for
the MPC-DDA algorithm in all integers of R≥4.0 the errors of
R= 7.0 are the largest. But its radial errors are still less
than the errors of the other algorithms by two orders of magnitude. When R≥100.0 its radial errors reflect only the
effect of rounding errors, and the errors of this algorithm
approaches zero.

Fig. 5, Fig. 6 and Fig. 7 are photos of these figures
obtained by the three types of algorithms. In the figures the
dotted-dash lines represent the center lines, the dotted line
is the contour of the exact circle, and the solid lines denote
the contours obtained by the DDA algorithms. These figures
displayed on the graphics screen were drawn on a drafting
machine connected with a computer. Because the original graphs take
up too much space, we omit them when this paper is published.

Table 1

R = 7.0

method	I	X_j	Y_j	$\bar{y}_j$	$\delta_{v,j}$	real δ	theoretical
SC-DDA	1	0.00000	7.00000	7.00000	0.0	0.0	0.0
	2	0.87500	7.00000	6.94510	0.05490	0.05448	0.05448
	3	1.75000	6.89062	6.77772	0.11290	0.10937	0.10938
	5	3.44531	6.34546	6.09342	0.25204	0.22046	0.22046
	6	4.23849	5.91479	5.57092	0.34387	0.27664	0.27665
	8	5.65097	4.76275	4.13117	0.63158	0.39035	0.39035
	9	6.24631	4.05638	3.15968	0.89670	0.44786	0.44786
	10	6.75336	3.27559	1.84178	**1.43381**	0.50582	0.50582
E-DDA	1	0.00000	7.00000	7.00000	0.0	0.0	0.0
	2	0.87500	6.89062	6.94510	−0.05448	−0.05404	−0.05404
	3	1.73633	6.67358	6.78124	−0.10766	−0.10424	−0.10424
	7	4.78333	4.82053	5.11075	−0.29022	**−0.20899**	−0.20900
	8	5.38589	4.14729	4.47126	−0.32397	−0.20237	−0.20236
	11	6.65771	1.78573	2.16216	**−0.37643**	−0.10696	−0.10697
	12	6.88092	0.92562	1.28565	−0.36003	−0.05710	−0.05710
	13	6.99662	0.05104	0.21736	−0.16632	−0.00319	−0.00319
MPC-DDA	1	0.00000	7.00000	7.00000	0.0	0.0	0.0
	2	0.87500	6.94531	6.94510	0.00021	0.00021	0.00021
	3	1.73633	6.78168	6.78124	0.00044	0.00043	0.00043
	7	4.78229	5.11347	5.11172	0.00175	0.00128	0.00128
	8	5.38412	4.47574	4.47340	0.00234	0.00150	0.00150
	11	6.65204	2.18639	2.17954	0.00685	0.00214	0.00214
	12	6.87337	1.33780	1.32545	0.01235	0.00235	0.00235
	13	6.98690	0.46818	0.42813	**0.04005**	**0.00257**	0.00256

note: 1. Boldface type in the Table denotes the maximum
errors
2. j= I−1

Table 2   **R = 100.0**

method	I	X_j	Y_j	$\bar{y}_j$	$\delta_{y,j}$	$\delta_{m,j}$ real	$\delta_{m,j}$ theoretical
SC-DDA	1	0.00000	100.00000	100.00000	0.0	0.0	0.0
	2	0.78125	100.00000	99.99695	0.00305	0.00305	0.00305
	3	1.56250	99.99390	99.98779	0.00611	0.00610	0.00610
	100	70.07014	71.76894	71.34546	0.42348	0.30257	0.30257
	101	70.63084	71.22152	70.79042	0.43110	0.30564	0.30563
	186	99.77506	12.58927	6.70359	5.88568	0.56616	0.56615
	187	99.87341	11.80975	5.03011	6.77967	0.56922	0.56922
	188	99.96567	11.02951	2.61994	**8.40957**	**0.57229**	0.57229
E-DDA	1	0.00000	100.00000	100.00000	0.0	0.0	0.0
	2	0.78125	99.99390	99.99695	−0.00305	−0.00305	−0.00305
	3	1.56245	99.98169	99.98779	−0.00610	−0.00610	−0.00610
	100	69.86057	71.27832	71.55068	−0.27236	−0.19470	−0.19476
	101	70.41743	70.72818	71.00271	−0.27453	**−0.19474**	−0.19475
	199	99.97216	2.00100	2.35940	−0.35840	−0.00782	—
	200	99.98779	1.21984	1.56232	−0.34248	−0.00477	—
	201	99.99732	0.43861	0.73145	−0.29284	−0.00172	—
MPC-DDA	1	0.00000	100.00000	100.00000	0.0	0.0	0.0
	2	0.78125	99.99695	99.99695	0.0	0.00000	0.00000
	3	1.56245	99.98779	99.98779	0.0	0.00000	0.00000
	100	69.86046	71.55080	71.55079	0.00001	0.00000	0.00000
	101	70.41732	71.00283	71.00282	0.00001	0.00000	0.00000
	199	99.97144	2.39033	2.38994	0.00039	0.00001	0.00001
	200	99.98706	1.60923	1.60866	0.00057	0.00001	0.00001
	201	99.99658	0.82803	0.82691	**0.00112**	**0.00001**	0.00001

note: 1. Boldface type in Table denotes the maximum errors
2. $j = I - 1$

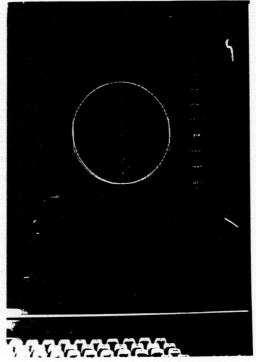

Fig. 5 Displaying circle by SC-DDA algorithm

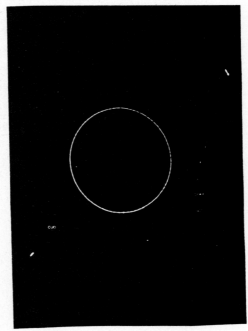

Fig. 6 Displaying circle by E-DDA algorithm

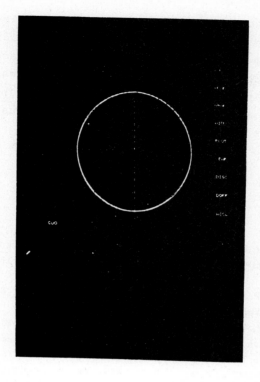

Fig. 7   Displaying circle by MPC-DDA algorithm

In conclusion, when the first draft of this paper was finished this algorithm was grafted onto the micro computer-plotting system MC-6800^0 by NPU Associate Professor Chen (D. Y. Chen) and Mr. Shi Yao-yao (Y. Y. Shi), and it was proved that the interpolating accuracy of the algorithm proposed here is higher than those of all the other algorithms used in comparison in this paper.

References

[1] Bresenham, J. E., 《A Linear Algorithm for Incremental Digital Display of Circular Arcs》, Communications of ACM, Vol. 20, No. 2, Feb. 1977, pp. 100 -106.

[2] Danielsson, P. E., 《Incremental Curve Generation》, IEEE Transactions on Computers, Vol. C-19, No. 9, Sept. 1970, pp. 783-793.

[3] Jordan, B. W., Lennon, W. J., and Holm, B. C. 《An Improved Algorithm for the Generation of Nonparametric Curves》, IEEE Tansactions on Computers, Vol C-22, No. 12, Dec. 1973, pp. 1052-1060.

[4] Newman, W. M. and Sproul, R. F., 《Principles of Interactive Computer Graphics》, Second Edition, McGraw-Hill, 1979. pp. 27-28.

AN ELLIPSE-DRAWING ALGORITHM FOR RASTER DISPLAYS

Michael R. Kappel

The George Washington University

School of Engineering and Applied Sciences

Washington, D. C. 20052

Abstract

An original algorithm is presented for generating discrete approximations to ellipses for display on raster devices. The approach is not new, but it is original in the sense that existing ideas have been combined to render a better algorithm. The new algorithm is evaluated from the benchmarks of efficiency, accuracy and elegance.

NATO ASI Series, Vol. F17
Fundamental Algorithms for Computer Graphics
Edited by R. A. Earnshaw
© Springer-Verlag Berlin Heidelberg 1985

1. INTRODUCTION

The fundamental problem is the choice of a set of discrete pixels on a raster graphics display that approximates a continuous curve. The situation is depicted in Figure 1. The center of each pixel lies at an integer grid point. The distance between vertically or horizontally adjacent grid points is one. When the curve passes between two adjacent grid points, the "closer" grid point is selected based upon the underlying definition of absolute error. The discrete approximation must visually represent the curve and the generating algorithm must execute efficiently.

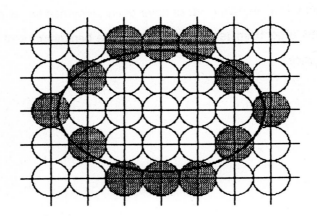

FIGURE 1 Discrete Approximation

2. MIDPOINT APPROACH

B. K. P. Horn [HORN76] employed a midpoint strategy to generate discrete approximations to circles. His algorithm is reprinted in Figure 2. Horn defines absolute error to be the distance from a grid point to the circle, measured horizontally in the first octant and vertically in the second octant (Figure 3). The position of the midpoint between two adjacent grid points relative to the circle determines which grid point is closer to the circle. If the midpoint is inside the circle, the exterior grid point is closer than the interior one to the circle, and vice versa.

For a circle defined by the equation $f(x,y) = x^2 + y^2 - r^2 = 0$, the functional values are:

> 0 for points outside the circle,

< 0 for points inside the circle, and

= 0 for points on the circle.

```
circle (x₀, y₀, r):    do for negate_x = f, t
                         do for negate_y = f, t
                          do for swap_xy = f, t
                           sector (r)
                          end
                         end
                        end
 end
 sector (r):           x ← r; y ← 0; s ← −r
                        do until y > x
                         plot (x, y); s ← s + 2y + 1; y ← y + 1
                         if s > 0, then s ← s − 2x + 2; x ← x − 1
                        end
 end
 plot (x, y):          if swap_xy, then x ↔ y
                        if negate_y, then y ← −y
                        if negate_x, then x ← −x
                        point (x + x₀, y + y₀)
 end.
```

FIGURE 2 Horn's Circle-Drawing Algorithm

Reprinted from HORN76

Thus if the functional value at the midpoint is:

> 0 the interior grid point is selected,

< 0 the exterior grid point is selected, or

= 0 either grid point is selected by some convention.

The nearest grid point is then at most one-half of a grid unit distant from the curve. In other words, the absolute error is bounded by one-half.

In his article, Horn goes on to say:

> The method also can be generalized to curves defined by arbitrary polynomials in x and y, including conic sections. Conic sections can be generated much in the same way as circles, but higher-order curves require multiplications for the incremental calculation ..., as well as dynamic decisions about what octant the curve falls in ...

The generalization to conic sections is not as trivial as the phrase "much in the same way" suggests. Dynamic decisions for octant changes are required for conic sections, but ways have been found to reduce their computational impact as seen in the following section.

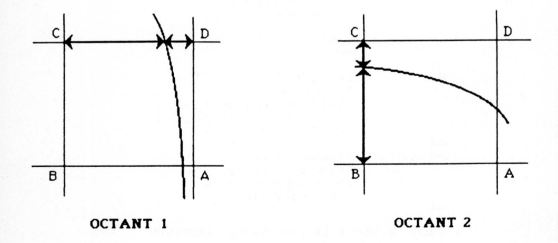

OCTANT 1   OCTANT 2

FIGURE 3   Absolute Error

3. CONIC SECTIONS

The generalization to conic sections is accomplished by M. L. V. Pitteway [PITT77]. Pitteway's algorithm (reprinted in Figure 4) is general in the sense that discrete approximations to arbitrary conic sections can be generated. His synthesis is based upon Bresenham's difference formulas [BRES65] rather than a midpoint strategy. "Multiplications for the incremental calculations" are avoided; only a few additions in the main loop are performed.

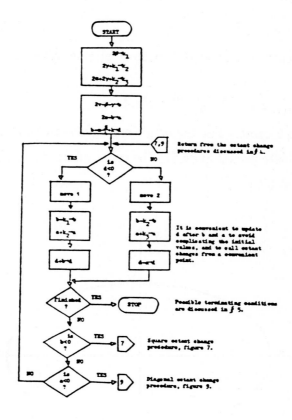

FIGURE 4 Pitteway's Algorithm

Reprinted from PITT77

"Dynamic decisions about what octant the curve falls in" are handled by an approximation to the slope of the curve. Three decision variables – d , a and b – are employed. d determines the nearest pixel on the next step; a detects a diagonal octant change; and b detects a square octant change. The values of a and b, which approximate components of the slope, are already computed in the main loop to modify the value of d.   Thus additional calculations for dynamic octant changes are avoided.

4. ELLIPSES

Van Aken addresses a specific class of ellipses given by the nonparametric equation:

$$f(x,y) = b^2 x^2 + a^2 y^2 - a^2 b^2 = 0 \qquad\qquad (1).$$

Such ellipses are centered at the origin and have major and minor axes aligned with the coordinate axes (Figure 5). The curve intersects the x-axis at a and –a and the y-axis at b and –b.

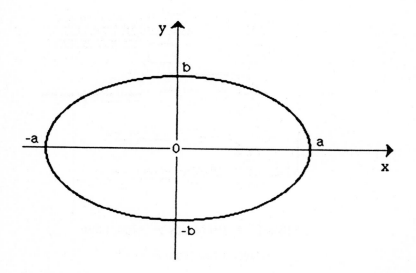

FIGURE 5 Sample Ellipse

Van Aken's midpoint algorithm for ellipses (reprinted in Figure 6) employs the midpoint strategy of Horn. Discrete approximations to ellipses given by Equation 1 are generated in the first quadrant. Through vertical and horizontal symmetry, the points in the other three quadrants can be obtained easily. A simple translation can be performed for ellipses not centered at the origin.

```
x := trunc(a + 1/2) ;   y := 0 ;
t1 := a * a ;    t2 := 2 * t1 ;    t3 := 2 * t2 ;
t4 := b * b ;    t5 := 2 * t4 ;    t6 := 2 * t5 ;
t7 := a * t5 ;   t8 := 2 * t7 ;    t9 := 0 ;
d1:= t2 - t7 + t4 / 2 ;   d2 := t1 / 2 - t8 + t5 ;
while d2 < 0 do                 (* region 1 of ellipse *)
  begin
    setpixel(x,y) ;             (* turn on pixel at (x,y) *)
    y := y + 1 ;                (* increment y regardless *)
    t9 := t9 + t3 ;
    if d1 < 0 then              (* step to pixel D *)
      begin
        d1 := d1 + t9 + t2 ;
        d2 := d2 + t9
      end
    else                        (* step to pixel C *)
      begin
        x := x - 1 ;
        t8 := t8 - t6 ;
        d1 := d1 - t8 + t9 + t2 ;
        d2 := d2 - t8 + t5 + t9
      end
  end ;
repeat                          (* region 2 of ellipse *)
  setpixel(x,y) ;               (* turn on pixel at (x,y) *)
  x := x - 1 ;                  (* decrement x regardless *)
  t8 := t8 - t6 ;
  if d2 < 0 then                (* step to pixel C *)
    begin
      y := y + 1 ;
      t9 := t9 + t3 ;
      d2 := d2 - t8 + t5 + t9
    end
  else                          (* step to pixel B *)
    d2 := d2 - t8 + t5
until x < 0
```

FIGURE 6 Van Aken's Midpoint Algorithm

Reprinted from VANA84

Due to the simple nature of this elliptical class, only one diagonal change from the first to second octant is required. Two decision variables – d1 and d2 – are employed. d1 is twice the functional value at the midpoint between pixels C and D (Figure 3). The sign of d1 determines the next incremental step to pixel C or D in the first octant. The second decision variable, d2, is twice the functional value at the midpoint between pixels B and C. The sign of the d2 determines the next step to pixel B or C in the second octant.

The second decision variable is monitored in the octant 1 to detect a transition to octant 2. Additional calculations are required for d2 in the first octant. Thus the detection of an octant change incurs computational costs in Van Aken's algorithm. Pitteway's algorithm is superior in this regard.

5. NEW ALGORITHM

Pitteway's strategy for detecting a diagonal octant change suggests an enhancement to Van Aken's midpoint algorithm for ellipses. The slope of a curve defined by Equation 1 is given by:

$$\frac{dy}{dx} = \frac{-f_x}{f_y} = \frac{-2b^2x}{2a^2y}$$

where f_x and f_y are the partial derivatives of the function with respect to x and y. An octant change occurs when the slope becomes greater than -1:

$$\frac{-2b^2x}{2a^2y} > -1$$

or $\qquad 2b^2x < 2a^2y.$

Notice that these two quantities are already calculated at each step to modify the values of the decision variables in the midpoint algorithm (Figure

6). Thus the calculation of d2 in the main loop for the first octant can be discarded. The removal of the three repetitive additions reduces computational costs. The new algorithm, which employs the slope components to detect an octant change in lieu of d2, is shown in Figure 7.

When an octant change occurs, the choice of pixels shifts from C and D to B and C (Figure 3). Instead of using the functional value at $(x_i-1/2, y_i+1)$ as the decision variable, a new value of fmid is required at $(x_i-1, y_i+1/2)$. The old value of fmid is given by:

$$f(x_i-1/2, y_i+1) = b^2 (x_i-1/2)^2 + a^2 (y_i+1)^2 - a^2 b^2$$
$$= b^2 (x_i^2 - x_i + 1/4) + a^2 (y_i^2 + 2y_i + 1) - a^2 b^2.$$

The new value of fmid is given by:

$$f(x_i-1, y_i+1/2) = b^2 (x_i-1)^2 + a^2 (y_i+1/2)^2 - a^2 b^2$$
$$= b^2 (x_i^2 - 2x_i + 1) + a^2 (y_i^2 + y_i + 1/4) - a^2 b^2.$$

The difference between the new and old values of fmid is:

$$b^2 (-x_i + 3/4) + a^2 (-y_i - 3/4).$$

In terms of the algorithm's variables, this reduces to:

$$-.5 * (xslope + yslope) + .75 * (bsquare - asquare).$$

This difference is added to the last functional value calculated in octant 1, once upon octant change, to initialize the decision variable for octant 2.

6. FURTHER ENHANCEMENTS

A critical review of Van Aken's midpoint algorithm for ellipses suggests further enhancements to the new algorithm.

```
x = a                              (* initialize loop variables *)
y = 0
asquare = a * a
bsquare = b * b
a22 = asquare + asquare
b22 = bsquare + bsquare
xslope = b22 * a
yslope = 0
fmid = bsquare * (.25 - a) + asquare
while xslope > yslope do           (* begin loop for octant 1 *)
   setpixel (x,y)
   y = y + 1
   yslope = yslope + a22
   if fmid < 0 then                (* vertical step *)
      fmid = fmid + yslope + asquare
   else                           (* diagonal step *)
      x = x - 1
      xslope = xslope - b22
      fmid = fmid - xslope + yslope + asquare
   endif
endwhile
fmid = fmid - (yslope + xslope) / 2 + .75 * (b2 - a2)
repeat                             (* begin loop for octant 2 *)
   setpixel (x,y)
   x = x - 1
   xslope = xslope - b22
   if fmid > 0 then                (* horizontal step *)
      fmid = fmid - xslope + bsquare
   else                           (* diagonal step *)
      y = y + 1
      yslope = yslope + a22
      fmid = fmid - xslope + yslope + bsquare
   endif
until x < 0
```

FIGURE 7   The New Algorithm (Integer Form)

6.1 Real Form

In his paper, Van Aken assumes that the coefficients a and b are restricted to integers. This assumption simplifies the calculation of the initial values of the decision variables and restricts the inner loop computations to integer arithmetic. However, in the specification of the midpoint algorithm (Figure 6), he initializes the value of x to trunc (a + 1/2). Obviously, if a is an integer, the rounding to the nearest integer is superfluous.

The general form of the new algorithm to support real-valued coefficients is very similar to the integer version. The only difference resides in the initial values:

$$x_0 = \text{trunc} (a + 1/2)$$

$$fmid = b^2 (x_0^2 - x_0 + 1/4) + a^2 - a^2 b^2.$$

Other than x and y, all variables are of real type. The general real-valued algorithm is presented in Figure 8.

6.2 Factor of Two

Van Aken defines the decision variables to be equal to twice the functional values at the midpoints. Perhaps the factor of two was employed to manifest the similarity between the midpoint and two-point algorithms (Section 11). The inclusion of the factor, however, serves only to complicate the mathematical formulation of the algorithm and reduce its efficiency. Specifically, three extra multiplications are introduced to compute the values of the temporary variables t3, t6 and t8 (which are just twice the values of t2, t5 and t7, respectively). This factor of two is eliminated in the formulation of the new algorithm.

```
x = trunc (a + 1/2)                    (* initialize loop variables *)
y = 0
asquare = a * a
bsquare = b * b
a22 = asquare + asquare
b22 = bsquare + bsquare
xslope = b22 * a
yslope = 0
fmid = bsquare * (x * x - x + .25) + asquare - asquare * bsquare
while xslope > yslope do               (* begin loop for octant 1 *)
    setpixel (x,y)
    y = y + 1
    yslope = yslope + a22
    if fmid < 0 then                   (* vertical step *)
        fmid = fmid + yslope + asquare
    else                               (* diagonal step *)
        x = x - 1
        xslope = xslope - b22
        fmid = fmid - xslope + yslope + asquare
    endif
endwhile
fmid = fmid - (yslope + xslope) / 2 + .75 * (b2 - a2)
repeat                                 (* begin loop for octant 2 *)
    setpixel (x,y)
    x = x - 1
    xslope = xslope - b22
    if fmid > 0 then                   (* horizontal step *)
        fmid = fmid - xslope + bsquare
    else                               (* diagonal step *)
        y = y + 1
        yslope = yslope + a22
        fmid = fmid - xslope + yslope + bsquare
    endif
until x < 0
```

FIGURE 8   The New Algorithm (Real Form)

6.3 Addition Preferred

Van Aken utilizes several temporary variables in his midpoint algorithm. Variables t2, t3, t5, t6 and t8 are twice their predecessor. He uses Pascal assignment statements of the form:

t2 := 2 * t1.

A more efficient way to perform this computation is:

t2 := t1 + t1.

Such additions are incorporated into the formulation of the new algorithm. Even better, a shift function may be available to perform a binary left shift of one.

7. SLOPE APPROXIMATION

The decision to switch octants in the new algorithm is based upon the values of xslope and yslope. Since the value of xslope is computed at the nearest grid point, it only approximates the actual value of the partial derivative of the ellipse equation with respect to x at the y-crossing. This approximation is a convenient working choice, but does not handle exceptional cases properly.

If the nearest grid point lies outside the ellipse, the approximation given by xslope is greater than the actual partial derivative since $x_{nearest} > x_{actual}$ for a given integer y value. This has the potential of delaying entry into octant 2. Suppose the approximate slope is slightly greater than -1 while the actual slope is less than -1 (Figure 9). Using the approximation, an octant 1 choice is made between pixels C and D. The actual choice should however be between pixels B and C in octant 2. The same pixel (C) is chosen in either case except if

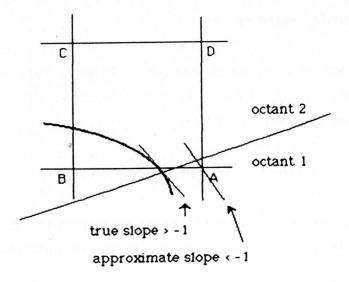

FIGURE 9 Slope Approximation (Case 1)

the slope of the ellipse changes drastically. Since the slope is given by $dy/dx = -bx/ay$, the rate of change in the slope is:

$$\frac{d^2y}{dx^2} = \frac{b(1 - \frac{bx^2}{ay^2})}{ay}$$

This value is large when y is small and b >> a. These conditions describe a highly eccentric ellipse as drawn in Figure 10. Therefore, this potential discrepancy of one pixel can arise in only a small class of ellipses. The maintenance of the second decision variable in octant 1 by Van Aken's midpoint algorithm avoids this problem.

Now suppose that the nearest grid point lies inside the ellipse. The approximation given by xslope is less than the actual partial derivative. The second octant may be entered prematurely (Figure 11). Using the approximation, an octant 2 choice is made between pixels B and C. The actual choice should however be between pixels C and D in octant 1. It is sufficient to show that pixel C is closer than D to the ellipse.

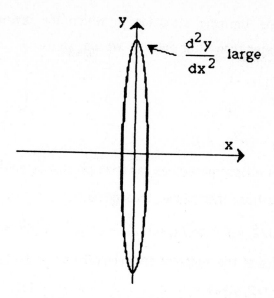

FIGURE 10   Exceptional Case

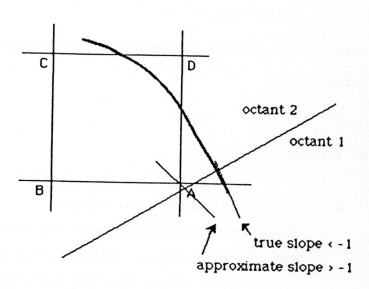

FIGURE 11   Slope Approximation (Case 2)

Consider the limiting situation in which the approximate slope is infinitesmally greater than -1 at pixel A. We may write:

$$\frac{-2b^2 x_i}{2a^2 y_i} = -1$$

or
$$2a^2 y_i - 2b^2 x_i = 0 \tag{2}$$

Suppose the actual ellipse passes as far from pixel A as possible with pixel A still chosen. The ellipse then passes through point $(x_i + 1/2, y_i)$. Hence,

$$f(x_i + 1/2, y_i) = b^2 (x_i + 1/2)^2 + a^2 y_i^2 - a^2 b^2 = 0 \tag{3}$$

The functional value at the midpoint between pixels C and D is:

$$f(x_i - 1/2, y_i + 1) = b^2 (x_i - 1/2)^2 + a^2 (y_i + 1)^2 - a^2 b^2$$

Subtracting Equation 3, we obtain:

$$f(x_i - 1/2, y_i + 1) = -2 b^2 x_i + 2 a^2 y_i + a^2$$

Subtracting Equation 2, we obtain:

$$f(x_i - 1/2, y_i + 1) = a^2$$

Since $f(x_i - 1/2, y_i + 1) > 0$, the midpoint lies outside the ellipse so that pixel C is closer than D.

8. ACCURACY

Absolute error can be defined in several ways.

> Absolute error is defined to be the distance from the grid
> point to the ellipse, measured in a direction parallel to the
> x axis in octant 1 and parallel to the y axis in octant 2   (Def 1).

Since the new and midpoint algorithms are designed to minimize this error, both algorithms are optimal in these terms. Pitteway's algorithm also exhibits this optimality.

Consider a second definition of absolute error:

Absolute error is defined to be the distance from the grid

point to the nearest point on the ellipse   (Def 2).

This distance lies along the normal to the curve that passes through the grid point (Figure 12). In these terms, the errors in the new, midpoint, and Pitteway algorithms are bounded by 1/2, but are no longer optimal. As seen in Figure 12, pixel A would be chosen over pixel B since the midpoint lies inside the ellipse. However, due to the curvature of the ellipse, pixel B is in fact closer than A using the second definition of absolute error.

The determination of the distance from a given grid point to the nearest point on the ellipse is computationally expensive. For this reason, all of the incremental algorithms do not choose pixels to minimize this error. Although

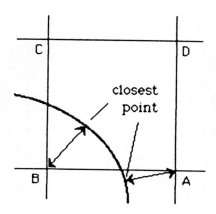

FIGURE 12   Absolute Error (Alternate Definition)

the new, midpoint, and Pitteway algorithms are not optimal in this sense, the following argument shows that their simpler definition of absolute error is more than just a convenient working choice.

Consider the section of an ellipse passing through the grid points in Figure 13. The path of the ellipse is such that pixels D and E are closer than C using error definition 1, while pixel C is closer using definition 2. Hence pixels A, D, E and F are chosen in the first case, while A, C and F are chosen in the second case. The human eye forms an image of a continuous curve from discrete pixels. Thus it is reasonable to consider the line between pixels D and E as representing the path of the ellipse. Due to the curvature of the ellipse, the diagonal line is closer to the ellipse than pixel C. Therefore, the discrete approximation generated with the simpler error definition is visually more representative.

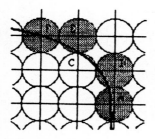

Using Error Definition 1

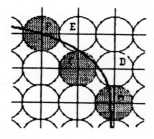

Using Error Definition 2

FIGURE 13   Comparison of Error Definitions

9. MIDPOINT / TWO-POINT COMPARISON

Van Aken devotes a large portion of his article to a comparison of his midpoint algorithm (Figure 6) with an extension of Bresenham's circle-drawing algorithm, which Van Aken refers to as the two-point algorithm (Figure 14). The strategy of the two-point algorithm is to compare the magnitudes of the functional values at two adjacent grid points. The grid point with the smaller value is deemed "closer".

```
x := trunc(a + 1/2) ;   y := 0 ;
t1 := a * a ;    t2 := 2 * t1 ;    t3 := 2 * t2 ;
t4 := b * b ;    t5 := 2 * t4 ;    t6 := 2 * t5 ;
t7 := a * t5 ;   t8 := 2 * t7 ;    t9 := 0 ;
d1 := t2 - t7 + t4 ;    d2 := t1 - t8 + t5 ;
while d2 < 0 do                 (* region 1 of ellipse *)
  begin
    setpixel(x,y) ;             (* turn on pixel at (x,y) *)
    y := y + 1 ;                (* increment y regardless *)
    t9 := t9 + t3 ;
    if d1 < 0 then              (* step to pixel D *)
      begin
        d1 := d1 + t9 + t2 ;
        d2 := d2 + t9
      end
    else                        (* step to pixel C *)
      begin
        x := x - 1 ;
        t8 := t8 - t6 ;
        d1 := d1 - t8 + t9 + t2 ;
        d2 := d2 - t8 + t5 + t9
      end
  end ;
repeat                          (* region 2 of ellipse *)
  setpixel(x,y) ;               (* turn on pixel at (x,y) *)
  x := x - 1 ;                  (* decrement x regardless *)
  t8 := t8 - t6 ;
  if d2 < 0 then                (* step to pixel C *)
    begin
      y := y + 1 ;
      t9 := t9 + t3 ;
      d2 := d2 - t8 + t5 + t9
    end
  else                          (* step to pixel B *)
    d2 := d2 - t8 + t5
until x < 0
```

FIGURE 14 Two-Point Algorithm

Reprinted from VANA84

Bresenham [BRES77] gives a rigorous geometric proof of the optimality of the circle-drawing algorithm with respect to radial error. However, the same proof of optimality does not hold for ellipses due to their different geometry. Functional values increase more rapidly outside the ellipse than they decrease inside. It is possible, in a situation where the ellipse passes just outside the midpoint, that the interior grid point is selected over the closer exterior one. The absolute error (definition 1) then exceeds one-half. Thus Van Aken is basing the merit of his midpoint algorithm on a comparison with a non-optimal counterpart.

When comparing the absolute errors (definition 2) for ellipses generated by the midpoint and two-point algorithms, Van Aken states:

> In general, the error produced by the two-point algorithm can be expected to increase [exceeding 1/2] as the ratio a/b increases.

Due to the symmetry between the roles of x and y in the first and second quadrants, a similar statement should hold for "as the ratio b/a increases". The only difference between the two algorithms resides in the initial values of the decision variables. For the midpoint algorithm,

$$d1_0 = 2 a^2 - 2 a b^2 + b^2 / 2$$

$$d2_0 = a^2 / 2 - 4 a b^2 + 2 b^2$$

and for the two-point algorithm,

$$d1_0 = 2 a^2 - 2 a b^2 + b^2$$

$$d2_0 = a^2 - 4 a b^2 + 2 b^2.$$

The initial values for d1 differ by $b^2/2$ and those for d2 differ by $a^2/2$. These differences are more pronounced when b >> a or a >> b, respectively. Thus Van Aken's statement about the error produced by the two-point algorithm should be extended to include the symmetric case of b >> a.

Van Aken states:

> For the special case of circles, the two-point and midpoint
> algorithms are seen to perform equally well in terms of linear
> accuracy [error definition 2].   This is consistent with
> Bresenham's proof of the accuracy of the two-point
> circle-drawing algorithm.

Van Aken implies that the midpoint algorithm is optimal in terms of error definition 2. This is not true as evidenced in the following argument.

Consider the situation depicted in Figure 15 in which pixel D is selected by the midpoint algorithm while pixel C is selected by the two-point algorithm. For circles, radial error and absolute error (definition 2) are equivalent. The two-point algorithm minimizes this error in its choice of pixel C. The midpoint algorithm is therefore non-optimal in this sense in its choice of pixel D.

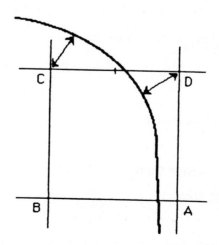

FIGURE 15   Midpoint / Two-Point Comparison

10. SYMMETRY

The exploitation of the symmetry between the first and second octants with respect to the roles of x and y renders an elegant algorithm. The midpoint algorithm maintains two decision variables in octant 1 and one decision variable in octant 2. The symmetry between the octants is thereby lost.

The new algorithm treats both octants equally. The logic is similar except for the roles of x and y. Therefore, it is possible to collapse the new algorithm given in Figure 7 or 8 (as Horn [HORN76] and Pitteway [PITT77] do) into one loop with the appropriate transformations occurring upon octant change.

Furthermore, the specification of the midpoint algorithm does not exhibit the symmetry that it still posseses. The inner loop for octant 1 should be similar to the inner loop for octant 2 except for the second decision variable and the roles of x and y. However, the form of the octant 1 loop is:

> **if** midpoint inside **then**
> > vertical step
>
> **else**
> > diagonal step
>
> **endif**

while the form of the octant 2 loop is:

> **if** midpoint inside **then**
> > diagonal step
>
> **else**
> > horizontal step
>
> **endif** .

The symmetry is more apparent if the logic of the octant 2 loop is not inverted as formulated in the new algorithm:

```
if midpoint outside then
    horizontal step
else
    diagonal step
endif.
```

11. CONCLUSIONS

An original algorithm for generating discrete approximations to ellipses has been presented. It embodies the midpoint scheme of Horn, the octant change criteria of Pitteway, and the algorithmic framework of Van Aken. The combination of ideas results in a new algorithm that has been shown to be more efficient than its predecessors. The accuracy of the new algorithm which employs a convenient working definition of absolute error has been argued to be superior to a more costly definition of error. Furthermore, the algorithm manifests the inherent symmetry between the first and second octants. The strengths and weaknesses of the various algorithms referenced in this paper are compared in Figure 16.

12. REFERENCES

BRES65 J. E. Bresenham, "Algorithm for Computer Control of a Digital Plotter",
    IBM Systems Journal, Vol. 4, No. 1, 1965, pp. 25-30.
BRES77 J. E. Bresenham, "A Linear Algorithm for Incremental Digital Display of

Circular Arcs", _Communications of the ACM_, Vol. 20, No. 2, February 1977, pp. 100-106.

HORN76 B. K. P. Horn, "Circle Generators for Display Devices", _Computer Graphics and Image Processing_, Vol. 5, 1976, pp. 280-288.

PITT77 M. L. V. Pitteway, "Algorithm for Drawing Ellipses or Hyperbolae with a Digital Plotter", _Computer Journal_, Vol. 10, No. 3, November 1967, pp. 282-289.

VANA84 J. R. Van Aken, "An Efficient Ellipse-Drawing Algorithm", _Computer Graphics and Applications_, September 1984, pp. 24-35.

ALGORITHM	CURVE	EFFICIENCY	ACCURACY	ELEGANCE
Horn	Circle	Incremental	Error bounded by 1/2	Symmetric
Bresenham	Circle	Incremental	Radial error minimized	Symmetric
Van Aken	Ellipse	Additional comp. for octant change	Error bounded by 1/2	Not symmetric
Two-point	Ellipse	Additional comp. for octant change	Error not bounded by 1/2	Not symmetric
New	Ellipse	Incremental	Error bounded by 1/2	Symmetric
Pitteway	Conic Section	Generality incurs comp. costs	Error bounded by 1/2	Symmetric

FIGURE 16   Comparison of Algorithms

AN ALGORITHM FOR DETERMINING THE DRAW START POINT OF A
HYPERBOLA GIVEN THE SYSTEM DIRECTION OF DRAW AND THE COORDINATES
OF THE VIDEO WINDOW

Andrew P. Surany, RCA Government Communications Systems (GCS)

Abstract

This algorithm was developed to offload conic generation from the graphics processor cpu onto the host cpu such that the conic generation time is substantially decreased. This algorithm is used to draw limited sections of a
particular hyperbola whose equation is of the form:

$$A * X**2 + B * y**2 + C*X*Y + D*X + E*Y + F = 0$$

Introduction

Since the intersection of the equation of any of the video window sides and that
of the hyperbola will yield two solutions (assuming that the video window side
is not parallel to either asymptote of the hyperbola), the correct solution
must be obtained according to the system direction of draw. The correct solution is chosen by correlating the angle of rotation of the hyperbola to that of
the slope of both asymptotes. For any hyperbola, the final solution of intersection is a function of the window coordinates, the slope of the hyperbolic
asymptotes, and the rotation of the conic.

Formulation

Given any hyperbola of arbitrary rotation θ semimajor axis length "a" and
semiminor axis length "b", displaced from the cartesian origin by (h, k), the
equations of its asymptotes can be represented by:

$$Y = [Tan[Arctan (a/b) + \theta]] \tag{1}$$

$$Y = [Tan[Arctan (-a/b) + pi/2 + \theta]] \tag{2}$$

Let θ, the angle of rotation of the hyperbola from the X-axis, vary through the
spectrum:

$$0 \leq \theta < 2*pi \tag{3}$$

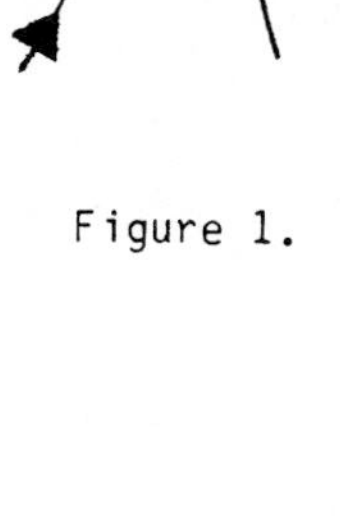

Figure 1.

NATO ASI Series, Vol. F17
Fundamental Algorithms for Computer Graphics
Edited by R. A. Earnshaw
© Springer-Verlag Berlin Heidelberg 1985

For purposes of this discussion, we will define the system direction of draw as in Figure 1, and deal only with one half of the hyperbola such that:

$$a > 0 \qquad (4)$$

where a is the length of the semimajor axis. The other half of the hyperbola can be analyzed by examining the hyperbola at:

$$\theta = \theta + pi \qquad (5)$$

When the window side is parallel to the asymptote, then only one point of intersection exists for that side.

All other rotations yield two intersections for each window side. Let us first consider a subset of (3), range θ' to θ'',

$$Z = Arctan\ (b/a) \qquad (6)$$

$$\theta' > Z \qquad (7)$$

$$\theta'' < pi - Z \qquad (8)$$

then the solutions of intersection for each side can be defined as having a maximum and minimum value along the side in question. Table 1 gives the valid solution of intersection for the defined subset according to (4).

SIDE	FIGURE REFERENCE	VALID INTERSECTION COORDINATES
Top	Figure 2.1	X = Minimum, Y = Top
Left	Figure 2.2	X = Left, Y = Maximum
Bottom	Figure 2.3	X = Maximum, Y = Bottom
Right	Figure 2.4	None

Table 1.

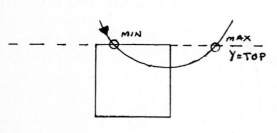

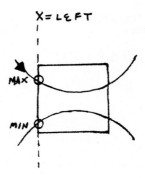

Figure 2.1

Figure 2.2

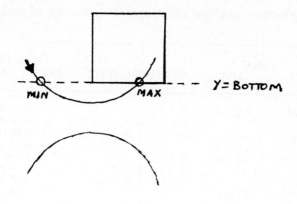

Figure 2.3

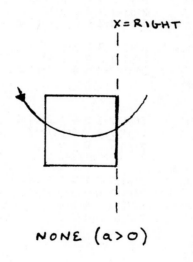

NONE (a > 0)

Figure 2.4

The validity of intersections for all θ according to (4) is defined in Table 2.

RANGE θ' -> θ''	SIDE	ADDITIONAL RESTRICITONS	VALID INTERSECTION COORDINATES
pi/2+Z > θ > pi/2-Z	Top	θ < Z	X = Maximum, Y = Top
		pi-Z > θ > pi-Z	X = Minimum, Y = Top
		pi/2+Z > θ > pi-Z	None
	Left		X = Left, Y = Maximum
	Bottom	θ < Z	None
		pi-Z > θ > Z	X = Maximum, Y = Bottom
		pi/2+Z > θ > pi-Z	X = Minimum, Y = Bottom
	Right		None
pi+Z > θ > pi-Z	Top		None
	Left	pi/2+Z > θ > pi-Z	X = Left, Y = Maximum
		3*pi/2-Z > θ > pi/2+Z	X = Left, Y = Minimum
		pi+Z > θ > 3*pi/2-Z	None
	Bottom		X = Maximum, Y = Bottom
	Right	pi/2+Z > θ > pi-Z	None
		3*pi/2-Z > θ > pi/2+Z	X = Right, Y = Maximum
		pi+Z > θ > 3*pi/2-Z	X = Right, Y = Minimum
3*pi/2+Z > θ > 3*pi/2-Z	Top	pi+Z > θ > 3*pi/2-Z	None
		2*pi-Z > θ > pi+Z	X = Minimum, Y = Top
		3*pi/2+Z > θ > 2*pi-Z	X = Maximum, Y = Top
	Left		None
	Bottom	pi+Z > θ > 3*pi/2-Z	X = Minimum, Y = Bottom
		2*pi-Z > θ > pi+Z	X = Maximum, Y = Bottom
		3*pi/2+Z > θ > 2*pi-Z	None
	Right		X = Right, Y = Minimum
2*pi > θ ≥ 2*pi-Z or Z > θ ≥ 0	Top		X = Maximum, Y = Top
	Left	3*pi/2+Z > θ > 2*pi-Z	None
		2*pi > θ > 3*pi/2+Z	X = Left, Y = Minimum
		pi/2-Z > θ > 0	X = Left, Y = Minimum
		Z > θ > pi/2-Z	X = Left, Y = Maximum
	Bottom		None
	Right	3*pi/2+Z > θ > 2*pi-Z	X = Right, Y = Minimum
		2*pi > θ > 3*pi/2+Z	X = Right, Y = Maximum
		pi/2-Z > θ > 0	X = Right, Y = Maximum
		Z > θ > pi/2-Z	None
Other	Top		X = Minimum, Y = Top
	Left		X = Left, Y = Minimum
	Bottom		X = Maximum, Y = Bottom
	Right		X = Right, Y = Maximum

Table 2.

The values of h and k must be compared with the coordinates of the video window as the specified vertex of the hyperbola may be displaced outside the window thereby invalidating the algorithm.

Conclusions

This algorithm is very easy to implement as it can be programmed as a conditional or case based upon the angle of rotation. A check for the validity of the solutions of intersection, real or complex, must be made for cases where the angle of rotation is such that the slope of the hyperbolic asymptotes is either exactly zero or undefined. In such cases the real solution is always the correct solution.

Acknowledgements

The author acknowledges the assistance of Mr. Richard L. Grossman and Mr. Dennis J. Hearn in test of this algorithm; Mr. Allen L. Starr for his assistance in evaluation of this algorithm; and to Dr. Steven Minsker, Department of Computer Science, Rutgers University for his assistance in sorting some of the theory involved.

References

1. Riddle, D. F.: "Analytic Geometry with Vectors", 1972, Wadsworth, Belmont, California.

2. Ramtek Corporation: RM9460 Graphic Display System, Software Reference Manual, 1983.

Section 3
Curves and Curve Drawing

A REVIEW OF CURVE DRAWING ALGORITHMS

R.A. Earnshaw
University of Leeds, UK
George Washington University, USA

ABSTRACT

A variety of curve drawing methods have now been devised for computer graphics and CAD. These range from simple, piece-wise interpolating curves through a set of points in a plane, to complex, smoothing curves for CAD, and approximation curves which allow error bounds on individual points to be specified and in-corporated in the curve definition.

Such curves can be classified according to a number of characteristics as follows (an individual curve may fall into more than one of these categories) -
  (i)   Single-valued or multi-valued in either coordinate
  (ii) Shape and axis-independence on transformation (e.g. rotational invariance)
  (iii) Smoothness and fairness - mathematical, aesthetic, or model-based
  (iv) Global and local control of shape
  (v)   Approximation functions

The importance of a particular characteristic is often related to the requirements of the application area under con-sideration, so it is possible to select an approach which satis-fies the prime requirement. However, there are advantages and disadvantages to the different methods.

The interface between curve generation and curve display necessitates a consideration of how best to translate curve specifications into drawn curves (e.g. by some optimal vector sequence) and also what primitive functions it is desirable for graphical output devices to accommodate or emulate, in order to facilitate specification of this interface at a high level.

The development of curve drawing algorithms from the early ad hoc approaches in the 1960's to the sophisticated poly-

NATO ASI Series, Vol. F17
Fundamental Algorithms for Computer Graphics
Edited by R. A. Earnshaw
© Springer-Verlag Berlin Heidelberg 1985

nomials of the 1980's will be reviewed, concentrating on those
methods and algorithms which are believed to be fundamental, and
the basis for future development.

1   HISTORICAL REVIEW

1.1   PIECEWISE POLYNOMIALS

Given an ordered set of points in the plane, one of the
earliest requirements was to obtain a smooth curve (multi-valued
where appropriate) through the points. The simplest criteria
were:
  (i)   The curve must pass through the points in the order spec-
        ified by the user (i.e. analogous to the user drawing the
        curve manually freehand or using a 'flexi-curve')
  (ii) The slope of the curve must be continuous at the points
        (i.e. there must be no irregularities in the curve as we
        pass from point to point or interval to interval).

Initially there was much less interest in the 'type' of
such curves and their associated coefficients, compared to their
ability to represent points in a smooth fashion. The emphasis
was therefore upon the graphical presentation and appearance of
the curve, rather than being able to utilise it for mathematical
interpolation. This was the converse of the approach usually
taken by mathematicians and numerical analysts!

To satisfy the above simple criteria, Van Berckel and
Mailloux (1965) (Reference 1) began with a discrete quadratic
polynomial for each interval between the points. The complete
curve could therefore be regarded as a set of different quadratics all connected together and with the above constraint conditions in common (i.e. joined at their ends, and gradients
matched at the ends). Use of discrete quadratics was known to
allow the shape in particular interval to be adequately represented since only the local defining points are used in obtaining the coefficients of the quadratic. This lent itself to
easy implementation since the defining points could be taken
an interval at a time and the appropriate discrete polynomial
obtained. However, it was soon noticed that the shape of the

curve in a given interval was not always completely insulated from the behaviour of the quadratics in adjacent intervals. In particular, intervals which contained sharp changes in gradient tended to generate instabilities and oscillations in the curves defining subsequent intervals. The use of cubic polynomials overcame this difficulty, and the overall resultant curve was fairly independent of past and future points.

The defining cubic polynomial for a given interval was obtained by using the two end points of the interval, the next point in sequence, and the slope of the curve at the end-point of the previous interval (the starting point of the current interval). This yielded the coefficients uniquely. The first and last intervals were treated as special cases, except where last point was the same as the first point (i.e. the 'curve' was closed). In order to cater for a multi-valued curve, a decision was made at the beginning of each interval to choose either x or y to be the independent variable for the interval. Such a change from one interval to the next necessitated the use of the reciprocal of the slope rather than the slope itself. A typical test for the choice of independent variable in the interval was as follows:-

$$\max(|y'_i|, |y'_{i+1}| \leq (|1/y'_i|, |1/y'_{i+1}|)$$

If the above condition were true, the choice of independent variable in the previous interval was accepted for the current one, otherwise the values of x and y were interchanged.

This approach gave a satisfactory smooth curve through a set of data points, especially in those cases where the number of data points was adequate rather than sparse, and the change of gradient across the interval between the points was small rather than large.

Practical implementations of this algorithm also had to take into account the following:-

(i) Three or more successive points in line, whether at the beginning, the end, or any section along the curve, and either horizontally or vertically.

(ii) The calculated value of the gradient being either zero or infinity in a given interval.

(iii) Coincident data points (i.e. points closer than the spac-
       ing of the raster being used to display the curve, and
       therefore the basis for the calculation of coordinate
       values).

(iv) Facility for annotating the points with a symbol as the
      curve is being generated.

The first was catered for by using straight lines for
slope calculation, but cubic polynomials were still used for
the intervals. Only if four points are in line is it certain
that the middle interval is best represented by a straight line.
The second was accomplished by assigning an arbitrarily low or
high value to the slope. The third was handled by ignoring
points which were effectively coincident. The fourth was accomplished by providing access to a table of symbols as the curve
is being generated and drawn.

Once the sequence of polynomials were generated, they
have to be converted into the appropriate vector or raster movements for the particular graphics device being used. This
usually involves interpolation of the functions for successive
values of x or y, and is done by the calculation of successive
differences. This incremental calculation of function values
saves on computation time, which is important when the raster
size is small (e.g. for an incremental plotter).

The advantages of treating curve generation in this way
may be summarised as follows:-

(i) There was no restriction on the number of points that
     can be handled; for a given interval only three pairs of
     coordinates were held at any one time, and these 'nested
     down' (the first being lost) when the next interval is
     to be considered.

(ii) In the majority of cases a smooth curve was obtained,
      except in those circumstances where there was sharp
      change in gradient across a given interval when, in order
      to yield a smooth curve, more points within the interval
      had to be specified. This corresponded to 'smoothing
      out' the change in gradient across the interval.

1.2   PIECEWISE PARAMETRIC POLYNOMIALS

The approximation that between any two consecutive points a curve may be described by $y = f(x)$ or $x = g(y)$ can be quite drastic when only a few points are available. The method was therefore extended by parametric definition as follows:-

$$y = f(t)$$
$$x = g(t)$$

where $f(t)$ and $g(t)$ are cubic polynomials in t (the parameter) which represent the curve between any two points. Heap (1974) (Reference 2) used the cumulative chord length between the points as the parameter t. To obtain the coefficients of $f(t)$ and $g(t)$ for each interval, the first derivatives with respect to t at the beginning and end of each interval must be known. These were approximated to by considering the quadratic passing through the point and its two subsequent neighbours.

The piecewise parametric cubic gives a good representation of the curve, especially when there is a sharp change in gradient across a given interval. It is also rotationally invariant. However, there was 60% more computation than the normal cubic method.

Further papers include Hayes (1974, Reference 3), Akima (1970, Refernece 4), McConalogue (1970, Reference 5).

1.3   CUBIC SPLINES

The smoothness criteria may be improved by imposing the further condition that the second derivative be continuous across interval boundaries. This corresponds to a spline, and must in some sense be the optimum smooth curve that can be obtained since it can be shown that in physical terms the energy density in the curve is a minimum (and this corresponds to the draftsman's original use of this form of curve). However, to calculate the coefficients of the polynomials necessitates taking all the points together and solving the set of linear simultaneous equations. This means that all points need to be in memory at the same time (unlike the previous approaches).

Such a spline has its defining knots coincident with the points, but it is possible to define splines where the controlling knots define a convex polygon within which the curve will be drawn. Changing the position of a point produces a local change in the shape of the curve near to it and acts as a kind of 'handle' by which the shape of portions of the curve may be varied. This is often used in CAD applications where such local control is important (Lang, 1974, Reference 6).

Reference texts include 'The Theory of Splines and their Applications' by Ahlberg, Nilson and Walsh (1967, Reference 7) and 'Theory and Application of Spline Functions' by Greville (1969, Reference 8). Further papers include Forrest (1972), Reference 9), Ahuja (1968, Reference 10).

1.4   SMOOTHING SPLINES

So far we have considered points to be precisely defined in the plane. Often this is not the case since data which represents experimental measurements may have errors in either or both coordinates. It therefore becomes important to consider the curve generation operation as a data fitting procedure rather than simple interpolation. Such procedures have been the domain of numerical analysts for a long time and a considerable body of literature has been built up. This has been summarised (in theory and practice) in the Curve and Surface Fitting section of the NAG Manual (Reference 11). More recently, the addition of the NAG Graphics chapter to the earlier numerical routines enables the mathematical curve (obtained as a result of a fitting operation) to be output directly in a graphical form on some appropriate device.

One of the earliest references to the use of splines for smoothing data is to be found in Reinsch (1967, Reference 12) who applied a weighting function to the data values. This allowed the user to essentially assign error bounds to each point. The calculated spline function thus takes these constraints into account. The author implemented a version of this algorithm and it gave good results. However, the majority of scientists with data points containing errors showed no inclination to use the implementation; use of a simple interpolation assuming the errors do not exist, is the preferred approach!

1.5   CONVERSION OF CURVES TO COORDINATES

As indicated in 1.1 once the sequence of polynomials has been generated they have to be converted into the appropriate vector or raster movements for the particular graphics device being used. An early approach was outlined by Stone (1961, Reference 13). More recently interpolation of the polynomials is done by successive differences since this saves on computation time. It can be shown that for the polynomial $f(x) = ax^3 + bx^2 + cx$, the following differences can be obtained:

$$f(x + h) = f(x) + \Delta f(x)$$
$$\Delta^2 f(x) = 6ah^2(x + h) + 2bh^2$$
$$\Delta^3 f(x) = 6ah^3$$
$$\text{Thus } \Delta^2 f(x - h) = \Delta^2(x - 2h) + \Delta^3 f(x)$$
$$\Delta f(x) = \Delta f(x-h) + \Delta^2 f(x-h)$$
$$f(x + h) = f(x) + \Delta f(x)$$

Hence we obtain $f(x + h)$ and the values of Δf and $\Delta^2 f$ required for the next step.

1.6   RECURSIVE CURVE GENERATION

As early algorithm by Le Riche (1969, Reference 14) was a procedure for defining a vector representation of a function by recursive subdivision. A particular curve length is divided into two and the two chords drawn. These two chords are in turn divided into two, and the process repeated. This subdivision continues until the chords in adjacent subdivisions differ in direction by less than a certain angle, or the chord lengths are shorter than a certain length. These quantities are pre-defined and obviously govern the extent of the recursive sub-division and the precision of the result. The maximum chord length satisfying these conditions is found at all points and drawn - this is the representation of the curve. The interesting feature of this appraoch is that it enables rapid changes of gradient in certain intervals of the curve to be handled correctly and appropriately: the algorithm automatically recurses more in these areas of high curvature, but leaves the other areas unchanged. In addition, finite discontinuities of the function and its derivatives will be drawn correctly.

1.7   OPTIMAL CURVE SEGMENTATION

An alternative approach to the conversion of curves to vectors is to use a method devised by Reumann and Witkam (1973, Reference 15). A formula is used to derive the optimum vector sequence to represent the curve; this sequence is optimum in the sense that it allows display of the curve with no loss of information (for a device of a given resolution) and also minimises the memory required for holding the coordinate information.

2.   CURRENT DEVELOPMENTS AND ADVANCES

Current work has been summarised in Foley and Van Dam (1982, Reference 16), and also in more recent papers by Barsky, Beatty and Greenberg (e.g. References 17-21).

Although one needs to exercise caution in assuming 2D curves may be naturally extended to cater for 3D surfaces (Forrest, 1982, Reference 22), it is convenient to adopt this approach for purposes of simpliciation. Out of the many possible ways of describing curves, three are chosen for purposes of comparison. These are Hermite, Bezier and B-spline.

The basic cubic polynomial could be defined as follows:-

$$x = x$$
$$y = f(x)$$
$$z = g(x)$$

but this leads to a number of problems. In particular, the representation of an infinite slope at any point on the curve is difficult. Following the approach outlined above, we may represent the polynomial parametrically:-

$$x = f(t)$$
$$y = g(t)$$
$$z = h(t)$$

where $0 < t < 1$. This allows closed and multiple-valued functions to be represented, and replaces slopes with tangent vectors.
The parametric cubic with its four coefficients is the lowest
order parametric curve that can meet the four conditions (position and slope at each end of the interval). Higher-order curves
can be used, but tend to manifest undesirable oscillations in
some cases. The cubic is the lowest-order parametric which can
describe a non-planar curve. This is therefore essential for
3D surfaces.

The Hermite form of the parametric cubic is determined
from the end points and the end point tangents. The Bezier
form defines the positions of the curve's endpoints and uses
two other points (not necessarily on the curve) to define the
tangents at the curve's end points. The B-spline approximates
the end points rather than matching them, but allows both the
first and second and derivatives to be continuous at the interval's end points. Thus as outlined earlier, the B-spline is in
general terms the 'smoother' curve. Both the Bezier and B-
spline forms are suitable for interactive curve definition.
Since the Bezier curve has four control points (which define a
convex polygon called the convex hull) these four points may be
moved by a locator device to enable the user to mould the curve
to the exact shape required. This finds natural use in design
applications. In addition, the convex polygon provides advance
information for clipping a curve against a window or view
volume. The convex hull property also holds for B-spline curves:
in this case the four control points are the two for the interval and the previous and next points.

Such cubic curves may be extended to cater for surfaces
by bicubic specification as follows:-

$$x = f(s,t)$$
$$y = g(s,t)$$
$$z = h(s,t)$$

where varying s and t from 0 to 1 defines all the points on
the surface patch. If one parameter is assigned a constant

value and the other is varied, the result is a cubic curve as previously described.

Surfaces may be represented in the Hermite form, the Bezier form, or the B-spline form, by extending the treatment previously outlined. In general, the same characteristics and properties hold for surfaces as applied to curves. In particular, the Hermite form of the bicubic surface patch is one form of the Coons' patch. In the Bezier form, continuity across patch edges is obtained by making the four control points on the edges equal. Continuity of slope is obtained by making the two sets of four control points on either side of the edge collinear with the points on the edge.

One of the advantages of the points definition of surfaces is that to transform (i.e. scale, rotate, translate etc) a curve or surface all we have to do is to transform the set of underlying curve definition points and then redraw the curve. We do not need to transform every point on the original surface.

Calculation of the points on the surface for purposes of drawing it out on a graphics device is a time-consuming process if we iteratively vary s and t over the surface to generate x, y and z values. It is much more efficient to use difference formulae analogous to those already described for the 2D case.

More recently, a generalisation of the B-spline has been developed by Barsky which allows the constraining conditions of slope and curvature continuity to be relaxed. These are replaced by continuity of unit slope and curvature vectors (geometric continuity) whilst providing the additional controls of bias and tension to the curve. Since the constraining equations are more relaxed, new design freedom is gained without resorting to a higher order polynomial. For appropriate values of bias and tension, the Beta-spline reduces to a uniform cubic B-spline.

3.   FURTHER DEVELOPMENTS

Solid modelling systems are becoming of increasing importance, due to their facilities in the areas of mass properties, machining and material strength, in addition to the usual design capabilities. These systems include boundary representation, constructive solid geometry, cuberille (or voxel) spaces, and octree encodings. Curved surface patch systems are used both for their smooth surface design capabilities, and also for creating more natural compound shapes.

One result of solid modellers based on boundary representations (such as polyhedral networks) is the availability of fast graphics devices capable of accepting polygons directly and producing a visible surface rendering (usually by the z-buffer method). Examples of such systems are Lexidata Solid-view, Raster Technologies 1/25S, and the Weitek Tiling Engine.

Curved surface systems are being used in medical applications, as well as the traditional aircraft, car, and mechanical component design areas. Mathematical properties of curve types are being further investigated, and using splines for modelling is being studied (Plass and Stone, 1983, Reference 23). Research at the University of Utah is seeking to define and implement set operations on B-spline patches (Cohen, 1983, Reference 24).

A further interesting development is the use of deformable superquadric solids for modelling. These are based on a simple mathematical surface which can be used to produce a wide range of shapes such as prisms, spheres, cylinders, disks and plates, by varying a parameter. In addition, deformation transformations can be used to create twisted surfaces, spirals, cones, and tubes (Barr, 1981, Reference 25). Other work has used algebraic surfaces (Blinn, 1982, 1984, References 26 and 27).

4. REFERENCES

1. 'Some Algol Plotting Procedures', J.A.Th.M. Van Berckel and B.J. Mailloux, MR73, Mathematisch Centrum, Amsterdam, 1965.

2. 'Methods for Curve Drawing', B.R. Heap, National Physical Laboratory, 1970.

3. 'Numerical Methods for Curve and Surface Fitting', J.G. Hayes, Bulletin of the Institute of Mathematics and its Applications, Vol 10, No 5/6. 1974, pp 144-152.

4. 'A New Method of Interpolation and Smooth Curve Fitting based on Local Procedures', H. Akima, JACM, Vol 17, No. 4, 1970, pp 589-602.

5. 'A Quasi-Intrinsic Scheme for passing a Smooth Curve through a Discrete Set of Points', D.J. McConalogue, Computer Journal, Vol 13, No. 4, 1970, pp 392-396.

6. 'Achievements in Computer-Aided Design', C.A. Lang, IFIP Proceedings, 1974.

7. 'The Theory of Splines and their Applications', J.H. Ahlberg, E.N. Nilson, J.L. Walsh, New York: Academic Press, 1967.

8. 'Theory and Application of Spline Functions', T.N.E. Greville (Ed), Academic Press, 1969.

9. 'Mathematical Principles for Curve and Surface Representation', A.R. Forrest, IPC Science and Technology Press, Proceedings of the Conference 'Curved Surfaces in Engineering', Churchill College Cambridge, 1972, pp 5-13.

10. 'An Algorithm for generating Spline-Like Curves', D.V. Ahuja, IBM Systems Journal, Nos 3,4, 1968, pp 206-217.

11. 'Numerical Algorithms Group Library', NAG Ltd, Oxford, 1976.

12. 'Smoothing by Spline Functions', C.H. Reinsch, Numerische Mathematik, Vol 10, 1967, pp 177-183.

13. 'Approximation of Curves by Line Segments', H. Stone, Mathematics of Computation, Vol 15, 1961, pp 40-47.

14. 'Procedure Curve', P.J. Le Riche, Computer Journal, 1969, p 291.

15. 'Optimizing Curve Segmentation in Computer Graphics', K. Reumann and A.P.M. Witkam, Proceedings of the International Computing Symposium 1973, A . Gunther et al. (Eds), North Holland, 1974, pp 467-472.

16. 'Principles of Interactive Computer Graohicsp, J.D. Foley and A. van Dam, Addison Wesley, 1982, pp 514-536.

17. 'An Introduction to the Use of Splines in Computer Graphics', R.H. Bartels, J.C. Beatty, and B.A. Barsky, University of Waterloo TR CS-83-09, UC Berkeley, TR UCB/CSD 83-136, Revised May 1984.

18. 'Computer-Aided Geometric Design', B.A. Barsky, IEEE CG & A, July 1981, pp 67-109.

19. 'A Description and Evaluation of Various 3-D Models', B.A. Barsky, IEEE CG & A, January 1984, pp 38-52.

20. 'Local Control of Bias and Tension in Beta-Splines', B.A. Barsky and J.C. Beatty, ACM Transactions on Graphics, Vol. 2, No. 2, 1983, pp 109-134.

21. 'Algorithms for the Evaluation and Perturbation of Beta-Splines', B.A. Barsky, IEEE CG & A, 1984.

22. 'User Interfaces for Free-Form Surface Design', A.R. Forrest, University of East Anglia, CGP 82/4, 1982.

23. 'Curve-fitting with Piecewise Parametric Cubics', M. Plass and M. Stone, Computer Graphics Vol. 17, No 3, 1983, pp 229-239.

24. 'Some Mathematical Tools for a Modeller's Workbench', E. Cohen, IEEE CG & A, Vol 3, No 7, 1983, pp 63-66.

25. 'Superquadrics and Angle-Preserving Transformations', A.H. Barr, IEEE CG & A, Vol 1, No 1, 1981, pp 11-23.

26. 'A Generalization of Algebraic Surface Drawing', J.F. Blinn, ACM Transactions on Graphics, Vol 1, No 3, 1982, pp 235-256.

27. 'The Algebraic Properties of Homogeneous Second Order Surfaces', J.F. Blinn, SIGGRAPH 84 Tutorial Notes 15 'The Mathematics of Computer Graphics'.

METHODS FOR DRAWING CURVES

K.W. Brodlie
Computer Laboratory
University of Leicester
Leicester, UK.

1. INTRODUCTION

Curve drawing is a fundamental aspect of computer graphics. It occurs in a great variety of different applications. The scientist or engineer, having observed or calculated a sequence of data values, will frequently wish to display an estimate of the function underlying these values by drawing a curve through the data points. If the data points are known to be subject to error, the problem changes to one of drawing a smooth curve which best approximates the data. The cartographer may use curve drawing to depict the boundary of a region, given only a discrete set of boundary points. The designer of a ship or motor car, starting from some initial trial curve will wish to transform it interactively into some desired shape. The animator too will make use of curve drawing in the production of cartoons – not only for pictures on individual frames, but also to construct automatically 'in-between' frames, where corresponding points on successive 'key' frames are interpolated by a curve to give a smooth transition.

In all these applications the problem of curve drawing has two quite distinct aspects. First a mathematical_representation of the desired curve must be constructed; then a means is needed of displaying that mathematical representation as a smooth-looking curve on a graphical display surface.

It is perhaps best to begin, therefore, by formulating in mathematical terms the various curve drawing problems described above.

NATO ASI Series, Vol. F17
Fundamental Algorithms for Computer Graphics
Edited by R. A. Earnshaw
© Springer-Verlag Berlin Heidelberg 1985

(i) Single-valued curve interpolation

Suppose a scientist collects data values (x_i, y_i), i=1,2,..n, where the values y_i can be regarded as realisations of some underlying function of the independent variable x. The scientist wishes to construct some interpolant $f(x)$ such that

$$f(x_i) = y_i \ , \ i = 1,2, \ .. \ n.$$

The curve $f(x)$ is displayed as an estimate of the underlying function. The term 'single-valued' is used to highlight the fact that the underlying function is a single-valued function of x (i.e. it does not loop back on itself) and this property must be preserved by the interpolant.

(ii) Single-valued curve approximation

If the data values are known to be in error, the scientist requires an approximating function $f(x)$ such that

$$\| f(x_i) - y_i \|$$

is minimised, where $\|.\|$ is some suitable norm.

(iii) Parametric curve interpolation

The cartographer with a set of boundary positions (x_i, y_i), i = 1,2, .. n, has to construct a smooth curve through the data points. But this time the curve may be multivalued or even closed. In this case it is convenient to construct a parametric function $(x(t), y(t))$ such that

$$x \ (t_i) = x_i \ ; \ y(t_i) = y_i \quad i = 1,2, \ .. \ n$$

The values of t_i can be assigned in some convenient way, the simplest being $t_i = i$, i = 1,2, .. n. Parametric curves have the flexibility of being multivalued or closed if appropriate – just the flexibility that is not wanted in the single-valued case.

In the computer animation example, suppose the animator has drawn a sequence of three-dimensional pictures, showing a scene at times $t = t_i$, $i = 1,2, .. n$. These are called key frames. He records the position of a selected point in the scene in each key frame, giving a sequence of data points (x_i, y_i, z_i), $i = 1,2, .. n$. To construct 'in between' frames that give a smooth transition between key frames, the animator has to construct a 3D parametric function $(x(t), y(t), z(t)$ such that

$$x(t_i) = x_i , y(t_i) = y_i , z(t_i) = z_i , i = 1,2,...n.$$

The interpolant will give the position of the selected point at any time t, and so if the process is carried out for a representative set of selected points, the entire image at any time t can be automatically created.

(iv) Curve_design

The designer typically works with a parametric curve, $(x(t), y(t))$ say, whose shape depends in a well-defined way on a set of control positions (x_i , y_i), $i = 1,2, .. n$. For example, the curve might interpolate the control positions as in (iii) above. By modifying the control positions interactively, different shapes of curve are produced.

This paper considers each of the above problems in turn, looking for a mathematical representation of a curve that will satisfy the requirements of the problem. The paper is in fact dominated by a discussion of problem (i), single-valued curve interpolation; this is influenced to a large extent by the author's experience which lies in providing a computer graphics service to a mainly scientific user base. The other problems are discussed more briefly, with references to important papers in the literature. A final section looks at ways of realising the curve on a graphics display surface.

2. SINGLE-VALUED CURVE INTERPOLATION

Given a set of data values (x_i , y_i), $i = 1,2, .. n$, draw a smooth curve $y = f(x)$ through the data points. The problem is simple — yet fascinating. Consider for example the data of Table 1, illustrated in

Figure 1.

x	0.05	0.15	0.2	0.25	0.3	0.4	0.6	0.8	0.9	1.0
y	5.0	10.0	25.0	30.0	30.0	21.0	20.0	20.0	10.0	5.0

<u>Table 1</u>

Clearly there is an infinite number of ways of drawing an interpolating curve through the points. Some solutions are 'bad' - see Figure 2 - in fact there is an infinite number of bad solutions. Equally there is an infinite number of good solutions - but is there a <u>best</u> solution? What is needed is a set of criteria to help judge in an objective way the quality of a curve.

Let us try to identify then some possible criteria :

<u>(i) Order of interpolation method :</u> This indicates the maximum order of polynomial that is exactly recreated from sampled data by the interpolation method. Lagrange interpolation through n points, for example, has order n; cubic spline interpolation, which will recreate a single cubic polynomial, has order 4.

<u>(ii) Continuity :</u> This indicates the mathematical smoothness of the curve. Straight lines joining the data points give a C^0 interpolant (i.e. continuous in function value only) while a natural cubic spline gives a C^2 interpolant (second derivatives continuous throughout).

<u>(iii) Global versus local :</u> A global method requires knowledge of all the data points before construction of the interpolant can begin ; for example, Lagrange interpolation and cubic splines are global methods. In the case of a local method, the interpolating function in any interval between data points depends only on a small set of neighbouring data points ; it can therefore be constructed as the data is gathered - for example, trivially, straight lines joining data points is a local method.

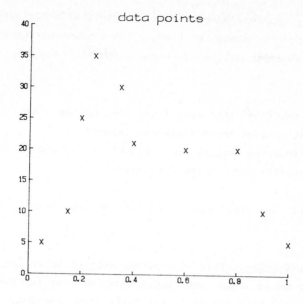

Figure 1

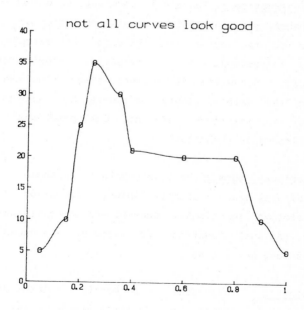

Figure 2

(iv) Linearity : Suppose bore-hole measurements of a coal-seam are made at a number of points along a line. The top and bottom of the seam are recorded. The depth of the coal seam along the line can be estimated in two ways :

- by subtracting the top from the bottom, and constructing an interpolant through the differenced values;
- by constructing interpolants through the bottom and top values, and taking the difference of the two interpolants.

If the answers are the same, the method is linear ; otherwise it is nonlinear.

(v) Visual appearance : This is a purely subjective criterion. Generally speaking, one would like the appearance of the interpolated curve to resemble the curve that one would naturally draw freehand. The difficulty here is that often a person drawing the curve has some preconceived idea of the shape of the curve - for example, that it be monotonically increasing - in addition to his knowledge of the data points.

(vi) Shape preservation : To help in constructing a curve of the expected visual appearance, one can ask that the interpolation method infer details of the shape of the curve from the data. For example, if the data is monotonically increasing, the interpolant should be monotonically increasing too. Convexity is another shape requirement that can be inferred from the data. (Note of course that shape preservation is a property that is sometimes relevant, but sometimes an unacceptable constraint to impose on the data.)

(vii) Computational form : Most interpolants in common use are piecewise polynomials of low order - usually cubics. Evaluation is therefore easy. Other interpolating functions, however, are sometimes used : exponential functions or rational functions, for example. The expense of evaluating such functions must be assessed.

(viii) Symmetry : This applies primarily to local methods where the interpolant is constructed as the data is collected. A method is symmetric if the same interpolant is constructed when the points are collected in reverse order.

(ix) __Invariance__under__scaling__transformation__: A fundamental transformation in computer graphics is the window-viewport mapping, where data in world coordinates is scaled to fit the graphics display surface. This will typically involve unequal scaling in x and y. It is of interest to know whether the same curve results from interpolating the points in world coordinates, and in device coordinates.

These criteria give us some way to judge different curve drawing methods.

Lagrange interpolation, where a single polynomial is fitted to the data points, has high order and continuity, it is invariant under scaling, it is linear, but it tends to produce dramatic fluctuations between data points. It loses out on visual appearance so seriously that it need not be considered further.

A numerical subroutine library is likely to recommend cubic spline interpolation - indeed it might well be the only interpolation method provided. So we should examine cubic splines closely against our set of criteria.

A spline is simply a piecewise polynomial, the pieces joined together at points called knots. In particular, a cubic spline is a piecewise cubic polynomial, constructed so that second derivative continuity is preserved at the knots. Visually, therefore, a cubic spline is continuous not only in position and slope but also in curvature.

For computational purposes, a cubic spline is best represented as a linear combination of B-splines. A cubic B-spline is itself a cubic spline, with the same set of knots as the original spline, but having the property that it is non-zero only over four adjacent knot intervals. These B-splines act as basis functions. A cubic spline with k knots can be represented as a linear combination of (k+4) cubic B-splines

$$s(x) = \sum_{j=1}^{k+4} a_j N_j (x)$$

For interpolation, we require

$$y_i = s(x_i) = \sum_{j=1}^{k+4} a_j N_j(x_i), \quad i=1,2,..n$$

giving n equations in (k+4) unknowns a_j. The usual strategy is to select the central (n-4) interior data points as knots, to give a fully determined linear system to solve.

A more detailed discussion of cubic splines in curve drawing can be found in Brodlie (1980), which also contains some useful references. The relevant routines in the NAG Library (NAG Ltd. 1984) are E01BAF and E02BBF. Cubic splines may be drawn using the NAG Graphical Supplement (NAG Ltd 1985) routine J06FAF.

Cubic spline interpolation has order 4, because a cubic polynomial is recreated. The method is linear and invariant under scaling, and the interpolant is C^2. The computational form is piecewise cubic - easy to evaluate at any point. However there are disadvantages too. It is a global method, requiring all the points to be available before interpolation can begin. The visual appearance is sometimes criticised, because a rather free-flowing curve tends to be produced - see Figure 3. Sometimes this is fine, but on some occasions a tighter curve is required. In particular, cubic spline interpolation has no shape preservation in the cases where the data is monotonic or convex.

To overcome the objections to the global nature of cubic splines, a number of local methods, essentially simulating cubic splines, have been proposed. The idea of a piecewise cubic is retained, but second derivative continuity is discarded in order to derive an interpolant that depends only on local data. The loss of second derivative continuity is not regarded as too serious in computer graphics ; continuity of slope (i.e. first derivative) usually ensures a reasonable visual smoothness.

These local piecewise cubic methods all work in a similar way. An estimate of the slope is made at each data point, the estimate depending only on a small number of neighbouring points. Within each interval between data points, the unique cubic is constructed matching the values

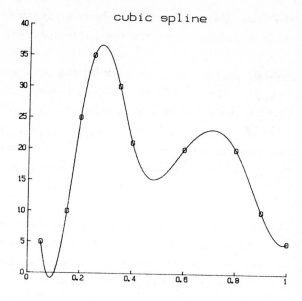

Figure 3

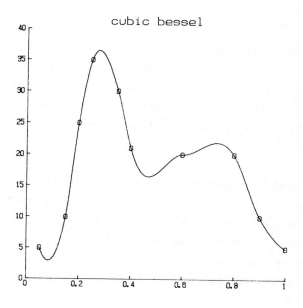

Figure 4

and slopes at the two end-points. The common slope at each data point ensures first derivative continuity of the piecewise function.

Different ways of estimating the slopes at the data points give rise to different methods. The oldest is the osculatory, or cubic Bessel, method (Ackland, 1915). The slope at a data point x_i is taken as the slope of the quadratic drawn through the points (x_{i-1}, y_{i-1}) , (x_i, y_i) and (x_{i+1}, y_{i+1}). The curve produced by this method is shown in Figure 4. It is a little tighter than the cubic spline curve of Figure 3, but still fairly free-flowing.

Apart from reducing the continuity of the interpolant to c^1 from the cubic spline c^2 , the order is also reduced to 3 —only quadratics are recreated. Ellis and McLain (1977) have suggested a variant where the slope at x_i is the slope of a cubic passing through (x_{i-1}, y_{i-1}) , (x_i, y_i), (x_{i+1}, y_{i+1}) and giving a best least-squares fit to the next data point on either side. This gives a method of order 4, but in practice it seems the visual appearance is little different from the cubic Bessel method (Brodlie, 1980 ; Fritsch and Carlson, 1980). Thus the NAG Graphical Supplement just uses the cubic Bessel method in its curve drawing routines JO6CAF and JO6CBF.

Although the cubic Bessel method solves the 'global' objection to cubic splines, there remains the problem of visual appearance – the curve produced is too free-flowing for some applications. There has been great interest recently, therefore, in methods which give improved visual appearance, and in particular preserve monotonicity or convexity of the data.

We shall consider monotonicity first. Suppose we seek a means of estimating slopes at the data points such that the resulting piecewise cubic preserves monotonicity. Immediately we find that one useful property must be jettisoned. De Boor and Swartz (1977) show that the only _linear_ method which preserves monotonicity is that obtained by setting all derivative estimates to zero. This is an order one method, and Figure 2 shows how unsatisfactory it is.

Thus a nonlinear method is certainly needed. Fritsch and Carlson

(1980) pinpoint exactly what conditions must be satisfied by the estimated slopes if monotonicity is to be preserved. Consider the interval

$$x_i \leq x \leq x_{i+1}$$

and let the estimated slopes at x_i, x_{i+1} be m_i, m_{i+1} respectively.

Suppose $y_{i+1} \geq y_i$. Then a sufficient condition for the interpolating cubic polynomial to be monotonic is

$$m_i \leq 3 d_i \ , \ m_{i+1} \leq 3 d_i \quad \text{where } d_i = (y_{i+1} - y_i)/(x_{i+1} - x_i) \quad (2.1)$$

that is, neither slope must exceed three times the slope of the straight line joining the data points. Fritsch and Carlson describe a means of modifying an initial set of estimates so that the above condition is satisfied. Unfortunately their method is not symmetric.

However, Butland (1980) shows that the required condition can be satisfied directly by choosing the estimate of the slope to be the harmonic mean of the slopes of the straight lines drawn to the adjacent points — that is,

$$1/m_i = 0.5 * (1/d_{i-1} + 1/d_i) \qquad (2.2)$$

In fact, with this formula, the stronger result

$$m_i \leq 2d_i \ , \ m_{i+1} \leq 2d_i$$

is achieved. An intuitive flaw in the Butland formula is that it fails to take account of the relative spacing of data points: the weighting in (2.2) does not take account of the relative closeness of x_{i-1} and x_{i+1} to x_i. Thus Brodlie (1980) suggested the following variation:

$$1/m_i = a_i /d_{i-1} + (1-a_i)/d_i \qquad (2.3)$$

where $a_i = 1/3 (1 + h_i /(h_{i-1} + h_i))$, with $h_i = x_{i+1} - x_i$, which still satisfies (2.3).

Often a data set will not be globally monotonic, but instead switches between regions of monotonic increasing and monotonic decreasing. Thus one requires the interpolant to follow the behaviour of the data (be co-monotone with the data), and increase where the data increases, and decrease where the data decreases. This property can be achieved by extending either (2.2) or (2.3) by the stipulation

$$m_i = 0 \quad \text{if} \quad d_{i-1} * d_i \leqslant 0.$$

Figure 5 shows the curve drawn through our sample data by method (2.3), which might be termed a weighted harmonic method. Note how co-monotonicity is preserved at the expense of sharp corners, and indeed in this example a rather unnatural curve is generated. On the other hand for other data sets where the preservation of monotonicity is more obviously appropriate the visual effect is often quite good. For example, consider the monotonically increasing data of Table 2 and the corresponding curve drawn by this method, shown in Figure 6. The weighted harmonic method is included as a monotonic option in the NAG Graphical Supplement curve drawing routines.

x	1.0	2.0	3.0	4.0	5.0	6.0	7.0	8.0	9.0	10.0
y	10.0	11.0	12.0	12.0	30.0	70.0	95.0	98.0	99.5	99.9

Table 2

Next we consider convexity. None of the methods described so far will guarantee to preserve convexity of the data. (The data can be said to be convex if straight lines joining the data points form a convex function). Indeed Handscomb (1981) has proved that a necessary condition for convexity when interpolating with piecewise cubic polynomials is :

$$(d_{i+1} - d_i) \geqslant 1.5 * (d_i - d_{i-1})$$

Note this is a condition on the data, not the estimates of the slopes, and so there will be convex data sets for which no piecewise cubic polynomial

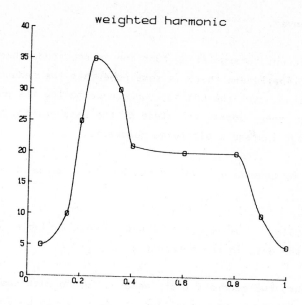

Figure 5

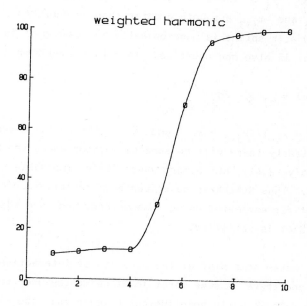

Figure 6

interpolant is convex.

Thus a different interpolating function is required. One possibility is a quadratic spline, where there is some hope that the reduced order will allow more control over the shape. Suppose we follow the usual approach and estimate by some means the slope at the data points, but fit not a piecewise cubic but instead a piecewise quadratic.

The paper by Schumaker (1983) shows how this can be done. There are two cases :

(i) if $0.5(m_i + m_{i+1}) = d_i$, then a single quadratic will interpolate the data in the interval $x_i \leqslant x \leqslant x_{i+1}$;

(ii) otherwise, two quadratics are needed, joined with common slope at a knot — the position of the knot can be anywhere in the interval.

Both monotonicity and convexity are considered. Take monotonicity first. Suppose $y_{i+1} \geqslant y_i$. Then, in case (i), the quadratic is monotonically increasing if m_i and m_{i+1} are both greater than or equal to zero. In case (ii), the quadratic spline is monotonically increasing if in addition the slope at the knot is also non-negative. This last condition reduces to:

$$am_i + (1-a) m_{i+1} \leqslant 2d_i \tag{2.4}$$

where $a = (\hat{x} - x_i)/(x_{i+1} - x_i)$ and $\hat{x}$ is the knot. Given values of m_i and m_{i+1} , clearly there will be some situations where the knot $\hat{x}$ can be chosen to satisfy (2.4) , but others where it is impossible — say, if $m_i = m_{i+1} = 3 d_i$. Thus Schumaker describes an interactive procedure whereby the slopes are first estimated using some method, and then adjusted so that the condition (2.4) is satisfied.

Schumaker makes some play of the benefits of interactive construction of the curve, and there is some merit in allowing the user to 'design' his own interpolant. It is worth pointing out however that the Butland formula (2.2) will yield values of m_i and m_{i+1} which directly satisfy condition (2.4) for _every_ choice of x.

Consider convexity next. In case (i), the quadratic is convex provided $m_i < m_{i+1}$. In case (ii), the quadratic spline is convex if in addition the slope at the knot, $\hat{m}$ say, satisfies

$$m_i \leqslant \hat{m} \leqslant m_{i+1}.$$

This last condition reduces to a requirement that the knot $\hat{x}$ lie in a specific interval between x_i and x_{i+1}. It is always possible to find such an interval, no matter what the size of the estimated slopes.

So this quadratic spline method gives a means of constructing an interpolating curve which preserves both monotonicity and convexity.

3. SINGLE-VALUED CURVE APPROXIMATION

Often in practice (perhaps more often than is admitted) the data points collected are subject to error. We assume here that the errors are only in the dependent variable, y, and that again the function underlying the data is single-valued. The problem is to find an approximating function f(x) such that

$$|| f(x_i) - y_i ||$$

is minimized. Normally the L_2 norm is used, and so the problem is to minimize

$$\sum_{i=1}^{n} (f(x_i) - y_i)^2$$

Here there is one well-established method of solution, using cubic splines (Cox, 1974). An initial set of knots is selected (generally far fewer knots than data points), and the spline based on these knots which best fits the data is calculated. Then interactively, the knot set is adjusted until a satisfactory fit is achieved.

The NAG Library routine E02BAF calculates a best least-squares cubic spline fit, and the companion Graphical Supplement routine J06FAF will plot the resultant spline. The use of interactive computer graphics to adjust the knot positions is valuable. McLain (1980) discusses how to judge whether a fit is acceptable or not.

This of course is a global method. A possible local method, using piecewise cubic polynomials continuous only in first derivative, is described in Ichida et al (1977).

4. PARAMETRIC CURVE INTERPOLATION

In the single-valued case, the data points (x_i, y_i) are such that the y-values are implicitly dependent on the x-values. The data is in fact defined in terms of a particular x-y coordinate system. There is the quite different case where the data points (x_i, y_i) are simply a collection of points in the plane − here x and y are independent variables, and the points are significant in their position relative to one another rather than to a particular axis system. This is common in cartography, and in design applications.

It seems that interpolation is far more common than approximation in this situation, and therefore we consider only the drawing of a smooth curve <u>through</u> the data points (x_i, y_i), i = 1,2, .. n. The variables x , y are considered separately as functions of a parameter t. The data points (x_i, y_i) are assigned parameter values t_i (for some monotonically increasing sequence t_i) and interpolants x(t) , y(t) are constructed so that

$$x (t_i) = x_i \; ; \; y (t_i) = y_i \; ; \quad i = 1,2, .. n.$$

This allows the curve to be multivalued.

Methods for single-valued curve interpolation extend quite naturally to the parametric case: single-valued interpolants x(t), y(t) are constructed separately and then combined to give a parametric curve. All the methods discussed in section 2 carry over : for example, a parametric cubic spline has x(t), y(t) each as cubic splines in t:

$$s_x(t) = \sum_i a_i N_i(t)$$

$$s_y(t) = \sum_i b_i N_i(t)$$

Some strategy is needed for the choice of parameter t. The simple parametrisation

$$t_i = i \quad , \quad i = 1,2, \ldots n$$

is sometimes used. It is better, however, to choose a parametrisation which reflects the distance between successive points - for example, the chord length parametrisation:

$$t_{i+1} = t_i + \left((x_{i+1} - x_i)^2 + (y_{i+1} - y_i)^2 \right)^{1/2},$$

(see for example, Brodlie, 1980).

5. CURVE DESIGN

Curve design is far too large a topic to be covered properly here, but it is possible to give an outline of the general approach.

In designing a curve, a design engineer will typically mark a number of points to indicate the outline of the shape he wishes to construct. He can then use a parametric curve interpolation method to generate an initial trial curve. There is then an iterative process in which the designer modifies the curve until it has the desired shape.

There are a number of ways in which this modification phase can be carried out. Suppose a parametric cubic spline is used as the interpolant. The designer can modify his initial set of trial points, and repeat the interpolation. This method tends not to be favoured, as it is difficult to judge how the points should be adjusted to obtain a particular shape of curve; that is to say, it is hard to control the shape of the curve between two points by making changes to the points themselves.

However parametric cubic splines have a remarkable duality property. Recall that a parametric cubic spline can be written as linear combinations of a set of B-splines

$$s_x(t) = \sum_i a_i N_i(t)$$

$$s_y(t) = \sum_i b_i N_i(t)$$

It turns out that the B-spline coefficients, taken as points (a_i, b_i), form the boundary points of a polygon which is closely related to the spline itself. By adjusting the 'coefficient points' (a_i, b_i) the designer can tease the curve into the desired shape.

For some general reading on curve design, see the book by Faux and Pratt(1981).

6. DRAWING OF CURVES

Once the mathematical representation of the curve is constructed, the remaining step is to realize that representation as a curve on the graphics display surface. The way this is done will depend on the interface available to the graphics programmer.

Most users access a graphics device through a basic graphics package, such as in the UK GHOST80 or GINO-F. Here the interface is at the level of straight lines, and so the problem reduces to one of approximating the curve by straight line pieces. In the single-valued case, we saw that for most purposes piecewise cubic polynomials provided a suitable mathematical representation.

Marlow and Powell (1973) describe a good algorithm for approximating a cubic polynomial by straight lines. Long segments are used where the function is relatively straight, and short segments where the curvature is great. A similar algorithm could be derived for plotting the quadratic splines that were seen to be useful from the shape preservation aspect.

As far as parametric curves are concerned, a satisfactory approach for parametric cubics is to use the Marlow and Powell algorithm on each of the cubic polynomials x(t) , y(t) and take the smaller of the two step-lengths in t that are calculated.

A quite different strategy is required when the interface to the graphics device is at the level of individual plotter increments or raster points. This case is described by Pitteway elsewhere in these proceedings.

7. CONCLUSIONS

This paper has illustrated some of the curve drawing problems that occur in computer graphics. In this final section, we summarize the conclusions reached on the solution of these problems.

For single-valued curve interpolation, cubic splines give an adequate curve for most situations. If the global nature of cubic splines is a problem, then a number of local methods are available, also based on piecewise cubics - the osculatory or Ellis and McLain methods being recommended. If the interpolant is to retain the shape of the data, special methods are needed. For monotonicity, the weighted harmonic method, again a piecewise cubic interpolant, is suitable. For convexity, piecewise quadratics must be used.

For single-valued curve approximation, cubic splines are recommended. Parametric curve drawing is seen as just an extension of single-valued methods, with some suitable parametrisation. Curve design uses parametric cubic splines in their B-spline formulation.

It is noticeable that piecewise cubic polynomials form a suitable basis for nearly all curve drawing. When using a conventional graphics package, adequate algorithms exist for decomposing piecewise cubics into straight line pieces that can be handled by the underlying system.

There are good reasons, however, for carrying out this decomposition separately for each device, so that the resolution of the device can be taken into account. The straight line approximation can be coarse for devices of low resolution, and fine for higher resolution devices.

The ISO graphics standard GKS makes provision for 'special' output primitives through its Generalised Drawing Primitive (GDP) function. It is planned that certain commonly used GDPs will be registered with a Registration Authority, so that they are implemented in the same way across all implementations of GKS. It would seem sensible to define two GDPs – one for drawing single-valued piecewise cubic polynomials, given the function value and slope at a sequence of data points; the other for drawing parametric piecewise cubic polynomials. This would have a number of benefits: it would allow the representation of curves to be handled differently for different devices, and more importantly, it would encourage the manufacturers of graphics devices to include a standard curve drawing capability within the firmware of the device.

REFERENCES

Ackland, T.G. (1915) "On osculatory interpolation, where the given values of the function are at unequal intervals."
J. Inst. Actuar., 49, 369-375.

Brodlie, K.W. (1980) " A review of methods for curve and function drawing" in "Mathematical Methods in Computer Graphics and Design" (K.W. Brodlie, ed.), pp 1-37. Academic Press, New York and London.

Butland, J. (1980) "A method of interpolating reasonable-shaped curves through any data", in Proc. Computer Graphics 80, pp 409-422. Online Publications Ltd, Middlesex, UK.

Cox, M.G. (1974) " A data-fitting package for the non-specialist user", in "Software for Numerical Mathematics" (D.J. Evans, ed), pp 235-251, Academic Press, London.

De Boor, C and Swartz, B. (1977) "Piecewise monotone interpolation", J. Approx. Theory, 21, 411-416.

Ellis, T.M.R. and McLain, D.H. (1977) "Algorithm 514- a new method of cubic curve fitting using local data" ACM Trans. Math. Soft., 3,

175-178.

Faux,I.D. and Pratt, M.J. (1981) "Computational Geometry for Design and Manufacture". Ellis Horwood, Chichester.

Fritsch, F.N. and Carlson, R.E. (1980) "Monotone piecewise cubic interpolation" Siam J. Numer. Anal., 17, 238-246.

Handscomb, D.C. (1981) Private communication.

Ichida, K, Kiyono, T, and Yoshimoto, F. (1977) "Curve fitting by a one-pass method with a piecewise cubic polynomial" ACM Trans. Math. Soft., 3, 164-174.

McLain, D.H. (1980) "Interpolation methods for erroneous data" in "Mathematical Methods in Computer Graphics and Design" (K.W. Brodlie, ed) pp 87-104. Academic Press, New York and London.

Marlow, S. and Powell, M.J.D. (1973) "A FORTRAN subroutine for plotting a cubic spline function". Report No. R7470, AERE Harwell.

NAG Ltd (1984) NAG Fortran Library Manual, Mark 11, NAG Central Office, 256 Banbury Road, Oxford.

NAG Ltd (1985) NAG Graphical Supplement Manual, Mark 2, NAG Central Office, 256 Banbury Road, Oxford.

Shumaker, L.L. (1983) "On shape preserving quadratic spline interpolation" Siam J. Nuner. Anal. 20, 4, 854-864.

Generation of β-spline curves
using a recurrence relation

by

T.N.T. Goodman and K. Unsworth
Department of Mathematical Sciences
University of Dundee
Dundee DD1 4HN
Scotland

ABSTRACT

The use of β-splines to produce design curves in the field of computer aided geometric design has recently been developed by B.A. Barsky, together with colleagues at the University of Waterloo. They have stated however that changes in the knot parameters will not "easily" lead to purely local changes in the shape of the curve. In an earlier paper, one of the authors (TNTG) has shown this statement to be incorrect, and this paper shows how β-spline curves may be generated using Goodman's formulation together with a recurrence relationship based upon the familiar B-spline recurrence relationship. Reference is also made to β2-spline curves, which may be evaluated more efficiently, with little loss of flexibility.

NATO ASI Series, Vol. F17
Fundamental Algorithms for Computer Graphics
Edited by R. A. Earnshaw
© Springer-Verlag Berlin Heidelberg 1985

1. Introduction

In computer-aided geometric design it is useful to represent a design curve in two dimensions in the form $Q(t) = (Q_1(t), Q_2(t))$, where Q_i $(i = 1,2)$ are cubic spline functions in the parameter t. If we require Q_i to be C^2 continuous then a convenient basis for these splines is given by the well-known cubic B-splines. However it was pointed out by Sabin [9] and Manning [8] that in order for the design curve to appear visually smooth, it is sufficient for Q to satisfy the weaker condition of second degree geometric continuity G^2, i.e. continuity of the curve, the unit tangent vector and the curvature vector. In [8] conditions were derived on $Q(t)$ for G^2 continuity. In [1] these were independently derived by Barsky who then constructed a basis of functions called β-splines which ensured second degree geometric continuity of Q, while generalizing B-splines by introducing shape parameters β_1 and β_2 called the bias and tension parameters respectively. In his work these parameters were initially taken to be constant throughout the curve. In order to provide a further means of local control of the shape of the curve, he also considered varying the parameters using an interpolating polynomial. Under certain circumstances though, this method produced curves that contained "kinks" which were visually unsatisfactory. Work by the first-named author [7], and independently by Bartels and Beatty [4], have shown however that you may allow β_1 and β_2 to take different values at different specified points of the curve, without using an interpolating polynomial. In addition it is shown in [7] that the curve cannot contain "kinks" because it must satisfy the variation-diminishing property. Although β-splines can be defined for arbitrary degree, it is found that the eye cannot detect a geometric discontinuity of degree higher than two and thus it is sufficient in practice to consider splines of degree three. Therefore this paper will restrict attention to the case of cubic β-splines.

In §2 we give a brief introduction to β-splines and their use in constructing a design curve. We then study the effect on the design curve of varying a single parameter, $β_1$ or $β_2$, while keeping the control vertices and the other parameters fixed. This will explain why a designer can easily modify the shape of the design curve by varying just the tension parameter, see [3].

When evaluating B-splines it is found convenient to use the recurrence relation of Cox and de Boor [5], [6], which is both efficient and stable. In §3 we generalise this recurrence relation to a stable recurrence relation for cubic β-splines, by expressing these β-splines in terms of quadratic B-splines. In §4 we use this relation to construct an algorithm for the evaluation of a design curve. A brief discussion of end conditions is included in §5, with particular reference to the design of closed curves. The algorithm can be made particularly efficient for the case in which only the tension parameters are allowed to vary. This case is of particular interest for the reasons indicated above, and is discussed in §6. Illustrations of curves generated by the algorithm are included in the paper.

2.　β-splines

Take $k \geq 4$ and an increasing sequence $\underset{\sim}{t} = (t_j)_{-2}^{k+1}$ whose elements we call knots. (Initially we will assume the sequence to be strictly increasing, but it will later be relaxed to allow coincident knots.) For $j = -1, \ldots, k$, take numbers $β_1(j) > 0$, $β_2(j) \geq 0$ called respectively the bias and tension parameters at the knot t_j. For $i = 0, \ldots, k-1$, we let N_i denote the β-spline with knots $t_{i-2}, \ldots, t_{i+2}$, which is the unique function satisfying the following properties,

$$N_i(t) = 0, \ t \notin (t_{i-2}, t_{i+2}),$$

$$N_i(t) > 0, \ t \in (t_{i-2}, t_{i+2}),$$

$$N_i|[t_j, t_{j+1}) \text{ is a cubic polynomial } (j = i-2, \ldots, i+1),$$

$$\left.\begin{array}{l}
N_i^{(\nu)}(t_{i-2}^+) = N_i^{(\nu)}(t_{i+2}^-) = 0 \quad (\nu = 0, 1, 2), \\[6pt]
N_i(t_j^+) = N_i(t_j^-) \quad (j = i-1, i, i+1), \\[6pt]
N_i'(t_j^+) = \beta_1(j) N_i'(t_j^-) \quad (j = i-1, i, i+1), \\[6pt]
N_i''(t_j^+) = \beta_1(j)^2 N_i''(t_j^-) + \beta_2(j) N_i'(t_j^-) \quad (j = i-1, i, i+1),
\end{array}\right\} \quad (2.1)$$

and the normalising condition

$$\sum_{i=0}^{k-1} N_i(t) = 1, \ t_1 \le t \le t_{k-2} . \tag{2.2}$$

If $\beta_1(j) = 1$, $\beta_2(j) = 0$ for $j = -1, \ldots, k$, the β-splines reduce to the usual normalised cubic B-splines. Now for $i = 0, \ldots, k-1$, let V_i be points in $\mathbb{R}^2$ which we call control vertices. The polygon gained by joining consecutive control vertices by straight line segments is called the control polygon. Now define a curve in $\mathbb{R}^2$ called the design curve by

$$Q(t) = \sum_{i=0}^{k-1} V_i N_i(t) \quad (t_1 \le t \le t_{k-2}) . \tag{2.3}$$

The conditions (2.1) ensure that Q satisfies second degree geometric continuity, i.e. it is continuous and has continuous unit tangent vector and continuous curvature vector. The curve approximates the control polygon and, in a sense, mimics its shape. The shape of the curve can be changed locally by changing either a control vertex, a knot, a bias or a tension parameter, although it should be noted that (2.3) is in fact independent of t_{-2}, t_{k+1} and of $\beta_\nu(j)$ for $\nu = 1, 2$, $j = -1, k$. If we require Q to be a closed curve satisfying second degree geometric continuity, we must have $V_j = V_{j+k-3}$ $(j = 0, 1, 2)$,

$\beta_\nu(j) = \beta_\nu(j+k-3)$ $(\nu = 1,2; \ j = 0,1,2)$, $\ t_j - t_{j-1} = t_{j+k-3} - t_{j+k-4}$ $(j = 0,1,2,3)$.
For further details on β-splines and the design curve see [1], [2].

Now the design curve $Q(t)$ is unaffected by a transformation in the parameter t. Thus by making a linear transformation in each interval $[t_j, t_{j+1})$ $(j = -2, \ldots, k)$, there is no loss of generality in considering either of the following cases:

a) $t_j = j$ $(j = -2, \ldots, k+1)$,

b) $\beta_1(j) = 1$ $(j = -1, \ldots, k)$.
$$\left.\right\} \qquad (2.4)$$

In [7] an explicit formula was given for N_i in case a). For simplicity we introduce the notation

$$\alpha_j = \beta_1(j)^2 + \beta_1(j) + \tfrac{1}{2}\beta_2(j) \qquad (j = -1, \ldots, k),$$

$$\beta_j = \beta_1(j) \qquad (j = -1, \ldots, k),$$

$$\delta_j = \alpha_j(\beta_{j+1}^3 + \beta_{j+1}^2) + \alpha_{j+1}(\beta_j + 1) + \alpha_j\alpha_{j+1} \qquad (j = -1, \ldots, k-1).$$

Then the formula is:

$$N_i(t) = \delta_{i-1}^{-1}\alpha_i u^3, \ u = t - i + 2, \ i - 2 \le t \le i - 1,$$

$$= \delta_{i-1}^{-1}\alpha_i + \delta_{i-1}^{-1}3\alpha_i\beta_{i-1}u + \delta_{i-1}^{-1}3\alpha_i(\alpha_{i-1}-\beta_{i-1})u^2$$

$$+ \delta_{i-1}^{-1}(\alpha_i\beta_{i-1}+\alpha_{i-1}\beta_i^2-2\alpha_{i-1}\alpha_i)u^3 - \delta_i^{-1}\alpha_{i+1}u^3,$$

$$u = t - i + 1, \ i - 1 \le t \le i,$$

$$= \delta_i^{-1}\alpha_i\beta_{i+1}^3 + \delta_i^{-1}3\alpha_i\beta_{i+1}^2 u + \delta_i^{-1}3\alpha_i(\alpha_{i+1}-\beta_{i+1}^2)u^2$$

$$+ \delta_i^{-1}(\alpha_{i+1}\beta_i+\alpha_i\beta_{i+1}^2-2\alpha_i\alpha_{i+1})u^3 - \delta_{i-1}^{-1}\alpha_{i-1}\beta_{i+1}^3 u^3,$$

$$u = i + 1 - t, \ i \le t \le i + 1,$$

$$= \delta_i^{-1}\alpha_i\beta_{i+1}^3 u^3, \ u = i + 2 - t, \ i + 1 \le t \le i + 2.$$
$$\left.\right\} \qquad (2.5)$$

We now consider the effect on the design curve of increasing one or more tension parameters $\beta_2(j)$ while keeping the control vertices and the other parameters fixed.

First suppose we vary only $\beta_2(j)$ for some j , $1 \le j \le k - 2$. Now from (2.2) and (2.3),

$$Q(j) - V_j = \sum_{i=0}^{k-1} (V_i - V_j) N_i(j)$$

$$= (V_{j-1} - V_j) N_{j-1}(j) + (V_{j+1} - V_j) N_{j+1}(j)$$

and so $|Q(j) - V_j| \le |V_{j-1} - V_j| N_{j-1}(j) + |V_{j+1} - V_j| N_{j+1}(j)$.

But $N_{j-1}(j) = \delta_{j-1}^{-1} \alpha_{j-1} \beta_j^3$ and $N_{j+1}(j) = \delta_j^{-1} \alpha_{j+1}$ which both decrease

with increasing $\beta_2(j)$ and are of order $\beta_2(j)^{-1}$. So $|Q(j) - V_j|$ decrease

with increasing $\beta_2(j)$ and is of order $\beta_2(j)^{-1}$. Thus the effect of

increasing $\beta_2(j)$ is to pull part of the design curve towards the control

vertex V_j .

Next suppose we vary both $\beta_2(j)$ and $\beta_2(j+1)$ for some j , $1 \le j \le k -$

Take $j \le t \le j + 1$ and define

$$P_t = V_j[N_{j-1}(t) + N_j(t)] + V_{j+1}[N_{j+1}(t) + N_{j+2}(t)] .$$

Then P_t is on the line segment joining V_j to V_{j+1} and

$$|Q(t) - P_t| = |(V_{j-1} - V_j) N_{j-1}(t) + (V_{j+2} - V_{j+1}) N_{j+2}(t)|$$

$$\le |V_{j-1} - V_j| N_{j-1}(t) + |V_{j+2} - V_{j+1}| N_{j+2}(t) .$$

Now $N_{j-1}(t) = \delta_{j-1}^{-1} \alpha_{j-1} \beta_j^3 (j+1-t)^3$ which is independent of $\beta_2(j+1)$,

decreases with increasing $\beta_2(j)$ and is of order $\beta_2(j)^{-1}$. Similarly

$N_{j+2}(t)$ is independent of $\beta_2(j)$, decreases with increasing $\beta_2(j+1)$ and

is of order $\beta_2(j+1)^{-1}$. So $|Q(t) - P_t|$ decreases with increasing $\beta_2(j)$

and $\beta_2(j+1)$ and is of order $\beta_2(j)^{-1} + \beta_2(j+1)^{-1}$. Thus the effect of

increasing both $\beta_2(j)$ and $\beta_2(j+1)$ is to pull a section of the design curve

towards the line segment joining V_j to V_{j+1} .

Next we consider the effect of increasing just a bias parameter $\beta_1(j)$, $2 \le j \le k-2$. Take $j - 1 \le t \le j$ and define

$$P_t = V_{j-2}N_{j-2}(t) + V_{j-1}(N_{j-1}(t) + N_j(t) + N_{j+1}(t)) \ .$$

Then we have

$$Q(t) - P_t = (V_j - V_{j-1})N_j(t) + (V_{j+1} - V_{j-1})N_{j+1}(t) \ .$$

From (2.5) we see that $N_j(t)$ and $N_{j+1}(t)$ are of order $\beta_1(j)^{-1}$ and $\beta_1(j)^{-2}$ respectively. Now $P_j = V_{j-1}$ and $P_{j-1} = \lambda V_{j-2} + (1-\lambda)V_{j-1}$, where $\lambda = \delta_{j-2}^{-1}\alpha_{j-2}\beta_{j-1}^3$. Thus the effect of letting $\beta_1(j) \to \infty$ is to pull a section of the design curve towards part of the line segment joining V_{j-2} to V_{j-1}, an effect which is in a sense less 'local' than that of letting $\beta_2(j) \to \infty$. The result of letting $\beta_1(j) \to \infty$ is unaltered if we also allow $\beta_2(j)$ to vary provided $\beta_1(j)^3/\beta_2(j) \to \infty$. However if $\beta_1(j) \to \infty$ and $\beta_1(j)^3/\beta_2(j) \to \ell < \infty$, then a similar analysis shows that $Q(j)$ approaches $\mu V_{j-1} + (1-\mu)V_j$, where $\mu = \ell(a+\ell)^{-1}$ for a constant $a > 1$.

Finally we mention the effect of letting $\beta_1(j) \to 0$. If $\beta_2(j) > 0$ then $Q(j)$ approaches $(1-\sigma)V_j + \sigma V_{j+1}$, where $\sigma = (1 + b\beta_2(j))^{-1}$ for a constant $b > 1$. If $\beta_2(j) = 0$ then the section of the design curve from $Q(j)$ to $Q(j+1)$ approaches part of the line segment from V_{j+1} to V_{j+2}.

The effects described above are illustrated in §4.

3.   A Recurrence Relation

We recall that in describing the design curve (2.3) it is sufficient to consider one of the cases a) or b) in (2.4). Henceforward we shall employ case b) for two reasons. Firstly it results in the formula for β-splines reducing to that for B-splines in the case $\beta_2(j) = 0$ $(j = -1,\ldots,k)$ thus enabling us to express cubic β-splines in terms of quadratic B-splines. Secondly it allows our recurrence relation to include, without modification, the case of coincident knots. We can transform the above equation for N_i from case a) to case b) as follows. For $j = i-2,\ldots,i+1$ we transform the interval $[j,j+1)$ to the interval $[t_j,t_{j+1})$ by replacing $t - j$ by $(t-t_j)/(t_{j+1}-t_j)$ and we replace $\beta_1(j)$ by $(t_{j+1}-t_j)/(t_j-t_{j-1})$ and $\beta_2(j)$ by $\beta_2(j)(t_{j+1}-t_j)^2/(t_j-t_{j-1})$.

Now for $m = 0,1,2$ and $i = -2,\ldots,k-m$, let N_i^m denote the normalised B-spline of degree m with knots $t_i,\ldots,t_{i+m+1}$. These can be given by the Cox - de Boor recurrence relation [5], [6] :

$$\left.\begin{array}{l} N_i^0(t) = \begin{cases} 1, & t_i \le t < t_{i+1} , \\ 0, & \text{otherwise}, \end{cases} \\[2em] N_i^1(t) = \dfrac{t-t_i}{t_{i+1}-t_i} N_i^0(t) + \dfrac{t_{i+2}-t}{t_{i+2}-t_{i+1}} N_{i+1}^0(t) , \\[2em] N_i^2(t) = \dfrac{t-t_i}{t_{i+2}-t_i} N_i^1(t) + \dfrac{t_{i+3}-t}{t_{i+3}-t_{i+1}} N_{i+1}^1(t) . \end{array}\right\} \qquad (3.1)$$

We recall that N_i has support on $[t_{i-2},t_{i+2}]$. Since N_j^2 has support on (t_j,t_{j+3}) we would hope to express N_i in terms of N_{i-2}^2 and N_{i-1}^2 . More precisely we look for an equation of the form

$$N_i(t) = A_i(t)N_{i-2}^2(t) + B_i(t)N_{i-1}^2(t) , \qquad (3.2)$$

where A_i is linear on each of the intervals $[t_j,t_{j+1})$, $j = i-2,\ldots,i$, and B_i is linear on $[t_j,t_{j+1})$ for $j = i-1,\ldots,i+1$. By equating coefficients of powers of t in each of these intervals it is straightforward to calculate formulae for A_i and B_i. These are simplified by introducing the notation

$$\left.\begin{aligned}
\psi_j &= \beta_2(j) \frac{(t_{j+1}-t_j)(t_j-t_{j-1})}{2(t_{j+1}-t_{j-1})} \quad (j = -1,\ldots,k), \\[2mm]
\delta_j &= t_{j+2} - t_{j-1} + (t_{j+2}-t_j)\psi_j + (t_{j+1}-t_{j-1})\psi_{j+1} \\[2mm]
&\quad + (t_{j+1}-t_j)\psi_j\psi_{j+1} \quad (j = -1,\ldots,k-1).
\end{aligned}\right\} \quad (3.3)$$

Then the formulae can be written as

$$\left.\begin{aligned}
\frac{A_i(t)}{1+\psi_i} &= \frac{t-t_{i-2}}{\delta_{i-1}}, \quad t_{i-2} \le t < t_i, \\[2mm]
&= \left\{ \frac{t_i-t_{i-2}+(t_i-t_{i-1})\psi_{i-1}}{\delta_{i-1}} + \frac{(t_i-t_{i-1})\psi_{i+1}}{\delta_i} \right\} \frac{t_{i+1}-t}{t_{i+1}-t_i} \\[2mm]
&\quad + \left\{ \frac{t_{i+2}-t_{i-1}+3(t_{i+1}-t_{i-1})\psi_{i+1}}{\delta_i} \right\} \frac{t-t_i}{t_{i+1}-t_i}, \quad t_i \le t < t_{i+1},
\end{aligned}\right\} \quad (3.4)$$

$$\left.\begin{aligned}
\frac{B_i(t)}{1+\psi_i} &= \left\{ \frac{t_{i+2}-t_i+(t_{i+1}-t_i)\psi_{i+1}}{\delta_i} + \frac{t_{i+1}-t_i}{\delta_{i-1}} \right\} \frac{t-t_{i-1}}{t_i-t_{i-1}} \\[2mm]
&\quad + \left\{ \frac{t_{i+1}-t_{i-2}+3(t_{i+1}-t_{i-1})\psi_{i-1}}{\delta_{i-1}} \right\} \frac{t_i-t}{t_i-t_{i-1}}, \quad t_{i-1} \le t < t_i, \\[2mm]
&= \frac{t_{i+2}-t}{\delta_i}, \quad t_i \le t < t_{i+2}.
\end{aligned}\right\} \quad (3.5)$$

Writing the equations in this form makes it clear that A_i and B_i are positive and so the recurrence relation (3.1), (3.2) is stable in the sense that it requires addition of only positive terms. We note that the recurrence relation continues to make sense if we allow coincidence of two knots $t_{j-1} < t_j = t_{j+1} < t_{j+2}$ or of three knots, $t_{j-1} < t_j = t_{j+1} = t_{j+2} < t_{j+3}$. However in the former case the design curve (2.3) will satisfy only first degree geometric continuity at t_j and in the latter case merely continuity at t_j . From (2.2) and (2.3) we see that at a triple knot t_j we have $Q(t_j) = V_j$ and so the design curve passes through the control vertex V_j .

4. **Algorithm for the generation of the β-spline curve**

In this section we describe an algorithm for calculating the coordinates of points which lie on a β-spline curve using the recurrence relation derived in §3. The algorithm is based upon that used for the generation of B-spline curves, described in de Boor [6], simultaneously generating the four cubic β-splines which are possibly non-zero at a given value of t .

Consider an arbitrary interval $[t_j, t_{j+1}]$ ($1 \le j \le k - 3$). From (2.3) and (2.5) we have

$$Q_j(t) = \sum_{i=j-1}^{j+2} V_i N_i(t) \quad (t_j \le t \le t_{j+1}) \tag{4.1}$$

where $Q_j(t)$ denotes the jth segment of the β-spline curve. Clearly, the coordinates of the points lying on the jth segment depend only upon the values of the four cubic β-splines which are non-zero in the given interval, and the coordinates of the corresponding control vertices. To evaluate (4.1) at a given t , we require, from (3.2), the evaluation of the non-zero quantities from amongst $A_i(t)N_{i-2}^2(t)$ and $B_i(t)N_{i-1}^2(t)$ for $i = j-1, j,$ $j+1, j+2$.

Referring to de Boor [6], the algorithm for the calculation of the values of the quadratic B-splines $N_i^2 (i = j-2, j-1, j)$ at a given $t \in [t_j, t_{j+1}]$ is as follows,

```
    b  = 1 ;
     1

    for k:=1 to 2 do

    begin saved:=0;

        for ℓ:=1 to k do

        begin term:=b / (t    -t      );
                     ℓ    ℓ+j  j+ℓ-k

                b :=saved + (t   -t) * term;
                 ℓ            ℓ+j

                saved:=(t-t      ) * term;
                         j+ℓ-k

        end;

            b   :=saved;
             k+1
    end;
```

On completion of this algorithm, b_1, b_2 and b_3 will store the values of $N^2_{j-2}(t)$, $N^2_{j-1}(t)$ and $N^2_j(t)$ respectively. From (3.2) and using b_1, b_2, b_3 from above, we calculate the values of the four non-zero cubic β-splines in a similar manner;

```
        saved:=0;

        for ℓ:=1 to 3 do

        begin term:=b ; b :=saved + B      (t) * term;
                      ℓ   ℓ          j+ℓ-2
                saved:=term * A     (t);
                               j+ℓ-1

        end;

        b :=saved;
         4
```

Now b_1, b_2, b_3, b_4 will store the values of $N_{j-1}(t), N_j(t), N_{j+1}(t)$ and $N_{j+2}(t)$ respectively.

Clearly, this calculation must be repeated at each specified evaluation point on each segment of the curve in order to generate the entire β-spline curve. Details of the complete calculation procedure are now given.

Firstly, we note that from (3.4) and (3.5) the evaluation of $A_j(t)$ and $B_{j+1}(t)$ will involve two multiplication operations for each $t \in [t_j, t_{j+1}]$.

This may be reduced to one multiplication by a reformulation of the expressions representing these two quantities. Details of the reformulations are given in the appendix, suffice to say that we may now redefine the $A_i(t)$ and $B_i(t)$ as follows,

$$A_i(t) = \begin{cases} 0 & (i = j-1) \\ \gamma_i^A(t-t_i) + \epsilon_i^A & (i = j) \\ (1+\psi_i)(t-t_{i-2})/\delta_{i-1} & (i = j+1, j+2) \end{cases},$$

$$B_i(t) = \begin{cases} (1+\psi_i)(t_{i+2}-t)/\delta_i & (i = j-1, j) \\ \gamma_i^B(t_i-t) + \epsilon_i^B & (i = j+1) \\ 0 & (i = j+2) \end{cases},$$

where $\gamma_i^A, \gamma_i^B, \epsilon_i^A, \epsilon_i^B$ are positive functions of $t_{i-1}, t_i, t_{i+1}, t_{i+2}$, $\psi_{i-1}, \psi_i, \psi_{i+1}, \delta_{i-1}, \delta_i$ only, and therefore remain constant on the interval $[t_j, t_{j+1}]$.

For the jth curve segment, (4.1) is repeatedly evaluated at the P_j values given by $u_1, u_2, \ldots, u_{P_j}$, where $u_1 = t_j$, $u_{P_j} = t_{j+1}$ and $u_i < u_{i+1}$.

Thus the overall calculation procedure consists of evaluating the coefficients which remain constant for a particular segment, and then computing the value of (4.1) at the evaluation points for that segment. This is repeated for all segments. A study of (3.4), (3.5) and the appendix shows that many of the terms that constitute the "constant" coefficients referred to above may be easily obtained by a simple change in the values of the subscripts, which in turn may be thought of as a shift of the coefficients between segment. Thus, we first initialise certain coefficients in the following procedure,

```
1 procedure INITIALISE (ψ̄,t̄,d2,t4,t5,t6,t7,t8,t9,t10,ψ1,ψ2,ψ3,ψ1d1,ψ2d2,
                                                         ψ2d1,ψ3d2);

2 local variable:d1;

3 begin t4:=t₀-t₋₂; t5:=t₀-t₋₁; t6:=t₁-t₋₂;

4        t7:=t₁-t₋₁; t8:=t₁-t₀; t9:=t₂-t₋₁;

5        t10:=t₂-t₀; ψ1:=ψ₋₁; ψ2:=ψ₀; ψ3:=ψ₁;

6        d1:=t6+t7*ψ1+ψ2*(t4+t5*ψ1);

7        d2:=t9+t10*ψ2+ψ3*(t7+t8*ψ2);

8        ψ1d1:=(1+ψ1)/d1; ψ2d2:=(1+ψ2)/d2;

9        ψ2d1:=(1+ψ2)/d1; ψ3d2:=(1+ψ3)/d2;

10 end;
```

Note that in this procedure $\bar{\psi},\bar{t}$ denote the set of $\{\psi_i\}$ (see (3.3)) and $\{t_i\}$ (the knots) respectively, while d1,d2 represent δ_{-1},δ_0 respectively.

The coefficients that remain constant for a particular segment are generated in the procedure COEFFICIENT, either following a call of INITIALISE, or a previous call of COEFFICIENT, or a call of SHIFTCOEFF (See later),

```
1 procedure COEFFICIENT (ψ̄,t̄,d2,t4,t5,t6,t7,t8,t9,t10,ψ1,ψ2,ψ3,ψ0d0,ψ1d1,
              ψ2d2,ψ1d0,ψ2d1,ψ3d2,j,γⱼᴬ,γⱼ₊₁ᴮ,εⱼᴬ,εⱼ₊₁ᴮ);

2 local variables: t1,t2,t3,d1,ψ0,num,term0,term1;

3 begin t1:=t4; t2:=t5; t3:=t6; t4:=t7; t5:=t8; t6:=t9;

4        t7:=10; t8:=tⱼ₊₁-tⱼ; t9:=tⱼ₊₂-tⱼ₋₁; t10:=tⱼ₊₂-tⱼ;

5        ψ0:=ψ1; ψ1:=ψ2; ψ2:=ψ3; ψ3:=ψⱼ₊₁;

6        d1:=d2; d2:=t9+t10*ψ2+ψ3*(t7+t8*ψ2);

7        ψ0d0:=ψ1d1;ψ1d1:=ψ2d2;ψ1d0:=ψ2d1;ψ2d1:=ψ3d2;
```

continued....

8       $\psi 3d2:=(1+\psi 3)/d2;$ $\psi 2d2:=(1+\psi 2)/d2;$

9       $term0:=t1*t2*\psi 0;$ $term1:=\psi 1*term0;$

10      $num:=t5*(t6*(1+\psi 0)+t4+t3)+t2*term1+\psi 2*(t4*(t3+t4*\psi 0+2*(t5*\psi 0+term1))$

11      $\gamma_j^A:=num*\psi 1d0/(d1*t5);$

12      $\epsilon_j^A:=term0*\psi 1d0+t2*\psi 2*\psi 1d1;$

13      $term0:=t10+t8*\psi 3;$ $term1:=\psi 2*term0;$

14      $num:=t5*(t6*(1+\psi 3)+t7+t9)+t8*term1+\psi 1*(t7*(t9+\psi 3*t7+2*(t5*\psi 3+term1))$

15      $\gamma_{j+1}^B:=num*\psi 2d1/(d2*t5);$

16      $\epsilon_{j+1}^B:=term0*\psi 2d2+t8*\psi 1*\psi 2d1;$

17 end;

Here, lines 9-12 of the procedure are concerned with the evaluation of γ_j^A, ϵ_j^A and lines 13-16 with $\gamma_{j+1}^B, \epsilon_{j+1}^B$. The other lines are concerned with the reassignment of the remaining variables.

The case in which knots are coincident, i.e. $t_j = t_{j+1}$, was referred to in §3 as having no effect upon the recurrence relation. Clearly in this case no new points on the curve will be generated, however certain terms must still be "shifted" so that future calls of the procedure COEFFICIENT will use the correct values. Hence, in this case, the only operation that is necessary is a call of the procedure SHIFTCOEFF as follows,

1 procedure SHIFTCOEFF $(\bar{\psi},\bar{t},d2,t4,t5,t6,t7,t8,t9,t10,\psi 1,\psi 2,\psi 3,\psi 1d1,\psi 2d2,\psi 2d1,$
                            $\psi 3d2,j);$

2 begin $t4:=t7;$ $t5:=t8;$ $t6:=t9;$ $t7:=t10;$

3      $t8:=t_{j+1}-t_j;$ $t9:=t_{j+2}-t_{j-1};$ $t10:=t_{j+2}-t_j;$

4      $\psi 1:=\psi 2;$ $\psi 2:=\psi 3;$ $\psi 3:=\psi_{j+1};$

5      $d2:=t9+t10*\psi 2+\psi 3*(t7+t8*\psi 2);$

continued....

6 $\quad \psi 1d1:=\psi 2d2;\psi 2d1:=\psi 3d2;\psi 2d2:=(1+\psi 2)/d2;$

7 $\quad \psi 3d2:=(1+\psi 3)/d2;$

8 end;

Now suppose $\bar{p}$ denotes the set $\{p_i\}$, the number of evaluation points per segment, $\bar{c}$ the β-spline curve (i.e. the set of points on the curve), $\bar{V}$ the control vertices and $\bar{u}$ the set of all evaluation points. We now have the overall calculation for a curve of m segments as follows;

1 procedure CURVECALC $(\bar{\psi},\bar{t},\bar{p},\bar{c},\bar{V},\bar{u},m)$;

2 local variables: $\bar{x},\bar{y},\bar{b},i,j,k,\ell$,temp1,temp2,term,d1,d2,

$\qquad$ t4,t5,t6,t7,t8,t9,t10,$\gamma_j^A,\gamma_{j+1}^B,\epsilon_j^A,\epsilon_{j+1}^B$,

$\qquad$ saved,w,$\psi 0d0,\psi 1d1,\psi 2d2,\psi 1d0,\psi 2d1,\psi 3d2,\psi 1,\psi 2,\psi 3$;

3 begin INITIALISE $(\bar{\psi},\bar{t},d2,t4,t5,t6,t7,t8,t9,t10,\psi 1,\psi 2,\psi 3,\psi 1d1,\psi 2d2,\psi 2d1,\psi 3d2)$;

4 $\quad$ temp1:=0, for j:=1 to m do

5 $\quad$ begin if $t_j=t_{j+1}$ then

6 $\quad\quad$ SHIFTCOEFF $(\bar{\psi},\bar{t},d2,t4,t5,t6,t7,t8,t9,t10,\psi 1,\psi 2,\psi 3,\psi 1d1,\psi 2d2,\psi 2d1,\psi 3d2,j)$ else

7 $\quad\quad$ begin

8 $\quad\quad\quad$ COEFFICIENT $(\bar{\psi},\bar{t},d2,t4,t5,t6,t7,t8,t9,t10,\psi 1,\psi 2,\psi 3,$

$\qquad\qquad\qquad \psi 0d0,\psi 1d1,\psi 2d2,\psi 1d0,\psi 2d1,\psi 3d2,j,\gamma_j^A,\gamma_{j+1}^B,\epsilon_j^A,\epsilon_{j+1}^B)$;

9 $\quad\quad$ for k:=1 to p_j do

10 $\quad\quad$ begin temp2:=k+temp1; $b_1:=1$;$w=u_{j,k}$

11 $\quad\quad\quad$ for i:=1 to 2 do

12 $\quad\quad\quad$ begin $y_i:=t_{j+i}-w$; $x_i:=w-t_{j+1-i}$; saved:=0;

13 $\quad\quad\quad\quad$ for ℓ:=1 to i do

14 $\quad\quad\quad\quad$ begin term:=$b_\ell/(y_\ell+x_{i+1-\ell})$;

15 $\quad\quad\quad\quad\quad$ b_ℓ:=saved + y_ℓ*term;

16 $\quad\quad\quad\quad\quad$ saved:=$x_{i+1-\ell}$*term;

continued....

```
17          end;

18            b_{i+1}:=saved;

19          end;

20          saved:=t_{j+1}-w;  y_1:=saved*ψ0d0;

21          y_2:=(t_{j+2}-w)*ψ1d1;  y_3:=γ_{j+1}^{B}*saved+ε_{j+1}^{B};

22          saved:=w-t_j;  x_1:=γ_j^{A}*saved+ε_j^{A};

23          x_2:=(w-t_{j-1})*ψ2d1;  x_3:=saved*ψ3d2;  saved:=0;

24          for ℓ:=1 to 3 do

25          begin term:=b_ℓ;  b_ℓ:=saved + y_ℓ*term;

26            saved:=term*x_ℓ;

27          end;

28            b_4:=saved;

29          for i:=1 to 2 do

30          begin saved:=b_1*V_{j,i};

31            for ℓ:=2 to 4 do

32            saved:=saved+b_ℓ*V_{j+ℓ-1,i};

33            c_{temp2,i}:=saved;

34          end;

35        end;

36        temp1:=temp2;

37      end;

38    end;

39 end;
```

The main loop in the procedure is between lines 4 and 38 inclusive. A ch
is first made for coincident knots (lines 5-6). If they are not coincident,
the coefficients that are constant on a segment are calculated (line 8), and t

values of the quadratic B-splines at a point on the segment are computed.
(lines 10–19). Lines 20–28 then calculate the corresponding value of the
β-spline, and the coordinates of the point on the curve are then computed
(lines 29–34). The calculation between lines 10 and 34 are then repeated
for each evaluation point on the segment.

Sample output for the case in which $m = 7$ is given in figures 1–7
inclusive. In each figure the '+' symbols indicate the locations of the
control vertices, the straight line segments joining them forming the
control polygon. Also in each figure, except fig. 3, the dashed curve
represents the corresponding B-spline design curve, and the continuous
curve the β-spline curve with the stated parameter values. The '0'
symbol indicates the locations of the knots for each curve. Note that
as stated earlier, the calculations are performed assuming $\beta_1 = 1$ at
each knot. However, for ease of comparison with previous work on the
subject, and in order to more readily isolate the effects of changes in
β_1 and β_2, the equivalent β_1, β_2 values for the case in which the
knots are uniform have been given for fig. 1–6.

The anticipated effect upon the shape of the curve due to a change
in the value of either $\beta_1(j)$ or $\beta_2(j)$ was discussed in §2. The
conclusions drawn in that discussion are supported by fig. 1–6.

Fig. 1–3 cover cases in which certain β_1 values are allowed to
vary, $\beta_1(j) > 1$ in fig. 1 and 2, and $\beta_1(j) < 1$ in fig. 3.

Fig. 4–6 cover the cases in which certain β_2 values are allowed
to vary. Figure 6 is of particular interest because of the large
difference between some of the adjacent β_2 values. In Barsky and
Beatty [2, §5], the parameters are allowed to take different values at
different knots using a quintic Hermite interpolating polynomial resulting in
a design curve whose components are ratios of polynomials of degree 18 and 15.
The construction of the polynomial means that "kinks" appear in the curve if

there are large enough differences between adjacent parameter values. As mentioned in §1 in the present method no such "kinks" would be expected to appear for any parameter values, and indeed this is supported by fig. 6.

In fig. 1-6, the local control of the shape of the curve is demonstrated, since a change in just one parameter value only affects four segments of the curve.

Fig. 7 demonstrates the effect of having coincident knots. As stated at the end of §3, at a triple knot, t_j, $Q(t_j) = V_j$, so that the design curve passes through the control vertex. The visual effect is in fact very similar to that obtained by having a very large $\beta_2(j)$, as seen in fig. 6. One important difference between the two situations however is that in the case of large $\beta_2(j)$, the curve still possesses G^2-continuity, while in the case of a triple vertex only continuity of the curve itself is retained.

An indication of the execution time necessary to generate a β-spline curve of m segments may be obtained by taking a count of the number of operations performed during execution of the procedure CURVECALC. Let us suppose that SHIFTCOEFF is called n_1 times, and COEFFICIENT n_2 times, then clearly $n_1 + n_2 = m$. Counting the number of additions/subtractions, multiplications and divisions in each procedure, we obtain the following expressions for the total number of such operations during execution of CURVECALC;

additions/subtractions: $17 + 8n_1 + 27n_2 + 26 \left(\sum_{j=1}^{m} p_j\right)$

$$= 17 + 19n_2 + 8m + 26mp \ , \tag{5.1}$$

multiplications : $6 + 3n_1 + 34n_2 + 26 \left(\sum_{j=1}^{m} p_j\right)$

$$= 6 + 31n_1 + 3m + 26mp \ , \tag{5.2}$$

divisions : $4 + 2n_1 + 4n_2 + 3 \left(\sum_{j-1}^{m} p_j\right)$

$$= 4 + 2n_2 + 2m + 3mp \ , \tag{5.3}$$

where p is the average density of evaluation [1,p.58] given by

$$p = (\sum_{j=1}^{m} p_j)/m \ .$$

5.   End Conditions

As we can see from the figures, and as discussed in [2], the β-spline curve does not in general begin at a control vertex, or even at a point along the line segment joining the first two control vertices. Barsky and Beatty explain in detail a number of ways in which better control of the beginning (end) of an open curve may be obtained, either by using a double or triple first (last) vertex, or by introducing phantom vertices. As mentioned in §2, in order to obtain a G^2-continuous closed curve, the first three control vertices and β_1, β_2 values must be identical to the last three, and the lengths of the intervals between the first four adjacent knot values must be the same as for the last four. The closed curve conditions are also discussed in [2].

Figures 8 and 9 compare the situation in which different end conditions have been used for a closed curve, fig. 8 using a triple first and last vertex, showing that G^2-continuity is not obtained. Fig. 9 demonstrates the improvement when the technique as described above is employed.

6.   β2-splines

In §2, attention was paid to the effect upon the β-spline curve following a change in one or more of the tension parameters, while keeping the bias parameters and control vertices fixed.

The particular case in which all bias parameters are unity, the knots are uniform and the β_2 values are the same throughout the curve has been studied by Barsky and De Rose [3]. They refer to this as the β2-spline curve. In our case β2-spline curves are obtained by enforcing both 2.4(a) and 2.4(b), while still allowing the β_2 values to vary between knots.

The evaluation of β2-spline curves may be performed in fundamentally the same manner as described in §4, although under certain assumptions simplifications may be introduced which enable the curve to be evaluated much more efficiently. In order to achieve this we must suppose that each segment of the m segment curve is evaluated at the same p values of u , given by $u_1, u_2, \ldots, u_p$, where

$$u = (t-t_j)/(t_{j+1}-t_j) \quad (t \in [t_j, t_{j+1}], \ 1 \le j \le m) \ .$$

Then clearly the values of the quadratic B-splines used in the recurrence relation will depend only upon the values of the $\{u_i\}$, and not on the segment being considered. Hence, these B-splines need only be evaluated once, and may then be stored for later use when evaluating points on the β2-spline curve Briefly this means that lines 9-19 of CURVECALC may be removed from the main loop commencing at line 4 of that procedure. Taking this into account, together with the fact that SHIFTCOEFF is no longer required, and making various simplifications in INITIALISE and COEFFICIENT, we obtain an operation count for the entire calculation as follows;

    additions/subtractions: 10 + 9p + 21m + 15mp,

    multiplications: 4 + 6p + 18m + 20mp,

    divisions: 4 + 3p + 4m .

If we use the β-spline algorithm as described in §4 under the same conditions, i.e. same evaluation points per segment, with equally spaced knots then (5.1) - (5.3) become

    additions/subtractions: 17 + 27m + 26mp,

    multiplications: 6 + 34m + 26mp,

    divisions: 4 + 4m + 3mp

respectively. Clearly the gain in runtime will depend upon m and p , but on the assumption that the 'mp' product terms are dominant, an approximate 30% gain may be expected. This is supported by the execution times obtained by generating the curves in fig. 10, in which m = 15 and p = 11. In this figure the continuous line is the same curve as in fig. 9, while the dotted line is the corresponding B-spline curve. Again the expected effect of varying β_2 is in evidence.

7.   Conclusion

We have presented here an algorithm for generating β-spline design curves using a recurrence relation based on that of Cox and de Boor. It has been shown that the values of the parameters β_1 and β_2 may vary between knots, and that the effect of any change in these parameters is of a local nature. Attention has also been given to the β2-spline curve in which only the β_2 parameter is allowed to vary. The loss of flexibility in restricting ourselves to manipulating just β_2 is minimal, while offering a particularly easy and efficient way of generating a design curve.

References

1.   Barsky, B.A., The Beta-spline: A Local Representation Based on Shape Parameters and Fundamental Geometric Measures, PhD dissertation, Department of Computer Science, University of Utah, 1981.

2.   Barsky, B.A. and Beatty, J.C., Varying the Betas in Beta-Splines, Report no. CR-82-49, Department of Computer Science, University of Waterloo, 1982. (also available as Report no. TR CSD-82-112 from the Computer Science Division, University of California at Berkeley).

3.   Barsky, B.A. and De Rose, T.D., The Beta2-spline: A Special Case of the Beta-spline curve and surface representation, Report no. TR CSD-83-152, Computer Science Division, University of California at Berkeley, 1983.

4. Bartels, R.H. and Beatty, J.C., Beta-splines with a difference, Report no. CS-83-40, Department of Computer Science, University of Waterloo, 1984.

5. Cox, M.G., The Numerical Evaluation of B-Splines, J. Inst. Maths. Applics., Vol. 10, 134-149, 1972.

6. de Boor, C., A Practical Guide to Splines, Applied Mathematical Sciences Vol. 27, Springer-Verlag, 1978.

7. Goodman, T.N.T., Properties of β-splines, J. Approx. Theory. (to appear).

8. Manning, J.R., Continuity Conditions for Spline Curves, Comp. Jnl., Vol. 17, No. 2, 181-186, 1974.

9. Sabin, M.A., Spline Curves, Unpublished report VTO/MS/154, British Aircraft Corporation, Weybridge, 1969.

Appendix

Reformulation of $A_j(t)$ (see (3.4))

$$\frac{A_j(t)}{1+\psi_j} = \{(t_{j+1}-t_j)(t_{j+2}-t_{j-1})(1+\psi_{j-1}) + (t_j-t_{j-1})\psi_j[t_j-t_{j-2}+$$

$$(t_j-t_{j-1})\psi_{j-1}] + (t_{j+1}-t_{j-1})\psi_{j+1}[t_{j+1}-t_{j-2}+(t_{j+1}-t_{j-1})\psi_{j-1}]$$

$$+ (t_{j+1}-t_j)\psi_{j+1}[t_{j+1}-t_{j-1}+t_{j+1}-t_{j-2}] +$$

$$2(t_{j+1}-t_{j-1})\psi_{j+1}[(t_{j+1}-t_j)\psi_{j-1}+(t_j-t_{j-2})\psi_j+(t_j-t_{j-1})*$$

$$\psi_{j-1}\psi_j]\} * (t-t_j)/(\delta_{j-1}\delta_j(t_{j+1}-t_j))$$

$$+(t_{j+1}-t_{j-2}+(t_j-t_{j-1})\psi_{j-1})/\delta_{j-1}$$

$$+(t_j-t_{j-1})\psi_{j+1}/\delta_j \ .$$

Reformulation of $B_{j+1}(t)$ (see (3.5))

$$\frac{B_{j+1}(t)}{1+\psi_{j+1}} = \{(t_{j+1}-t_{j-1})(t_{j+2}-t_{j-1})(1+\psi_{j+2}) + (t_{j+2}-t_{j+1})\psi_{j+1}[t_{j+3}-t_{j+1}$$

$$+(t_{j+2}-t_{j+1})\psi_{j+2}] + (t_{j+2}-t_j)\psi_j[t_{j+3}-t_j+(t_{j+2}-t_j)\psi_{j+2}]$$

$$+(t_{j+1}-t_j)\psi_j[t_{j+2}-t_j+t_{j+3}-t_j]+$$

$$2(t_{j+2}-t_j)\psi_j[(t_{j+1}-t_j)\psi_{j+2}+(t_{j+3}-t_{j+1})\psi_{j+1}+(t_{j+2}-t_{j+1})$$

$$* \psi_{j+1}\psi_{j+2}]\} * (t_{j+1}-t)/(\delta_j\delta_{j+1}(t_{j+1}-t_j))$$

$$+ (t_{j+3}-t_{j+1}+(t_{j+2}-t_{j+1})\psi_{j+2})/\delta_{j+1}$$

$$+ (t_{j+2}-t_{j+1})\psi_j/\delta_j \ .$$

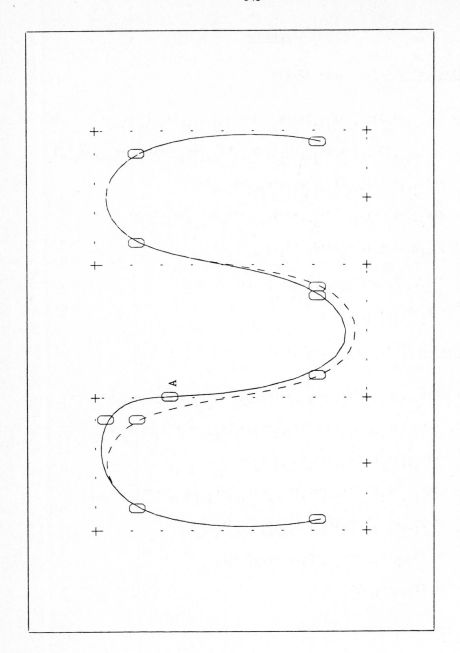

Fig.1   All $\beta_2 = 0$.   All $\beta_1 = 1$ except at A, where $\beta_1 = 8$.

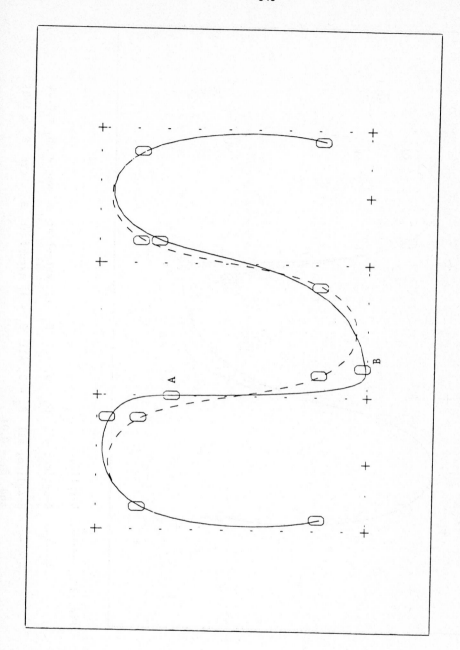

Fig.2　All $\beta_2 = 0$.　All $\beta_1 = 1$ except at A and B, where $\beta_1 = 8$.

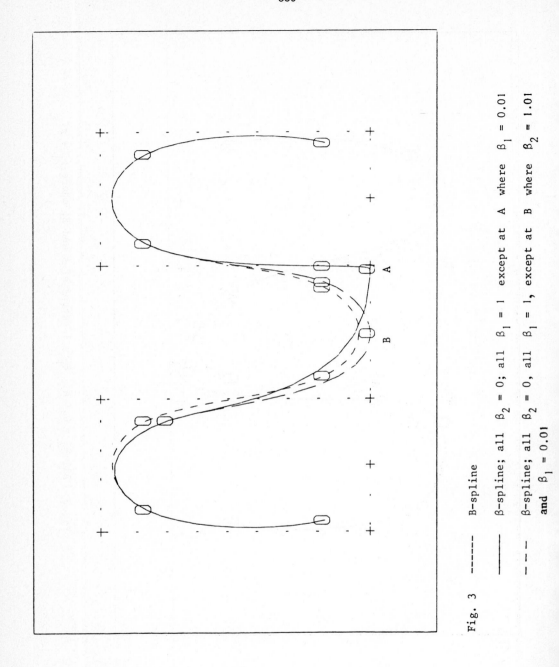

Fig. 3   ------   B-spline

——————   β-spline; all $\beta_2 = 0$; all $\beta_1 = 1$ except at A where $\beta_1 = 0.01$

— — —   β-spline; all $\beta_2 = 0$, all $\beta_1 = 1$, except at B where $\beta_2 = 1.01$ and $\beta_1 = 0.01$

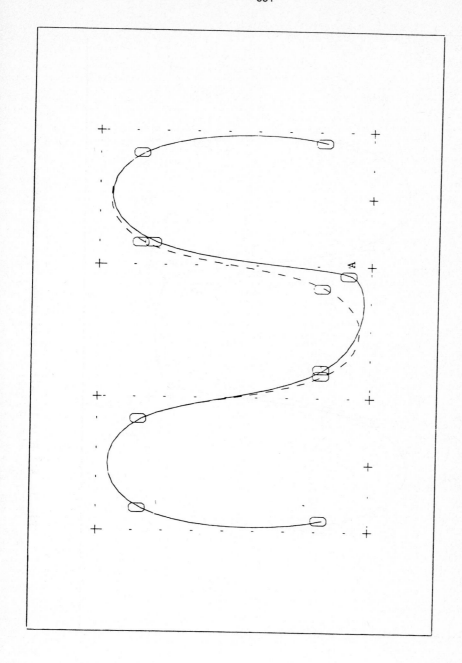

Fig.4   All $\beta_1 = 1$.   All $\beta_2 = 0$, except at A where $\beta_2 = 8$.

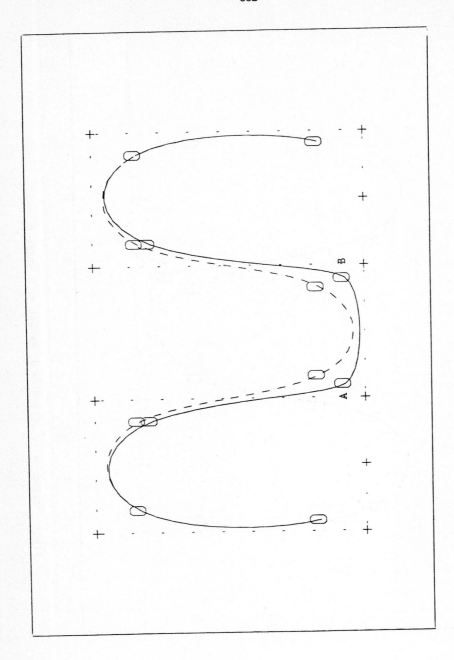

Fig. 5   All $\beta_1 = 1$. All $\beta_2 = 0$, except at A and B where $\beta_2 = 8$.

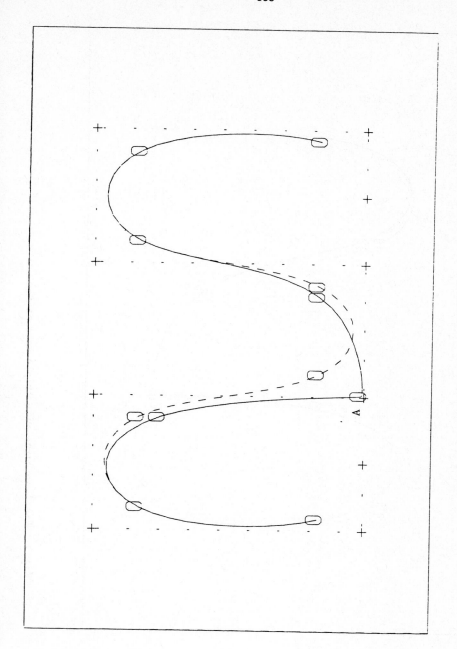

Fig.6 All β_1 = 1. All β_2 = 0, except at A where β_2 = 100.

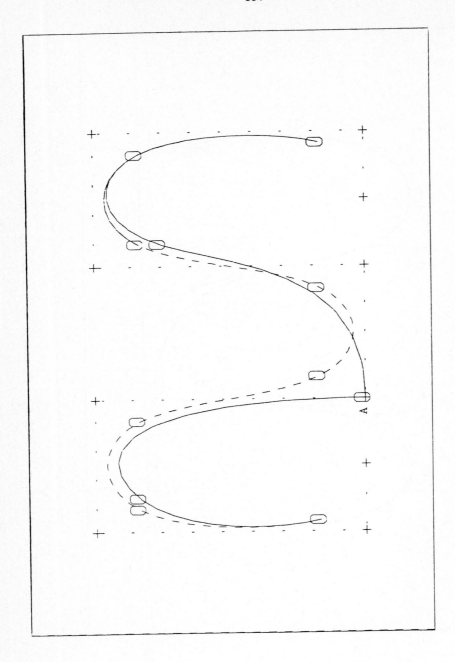

Fig.7 β-spline curve with triple knot at A.

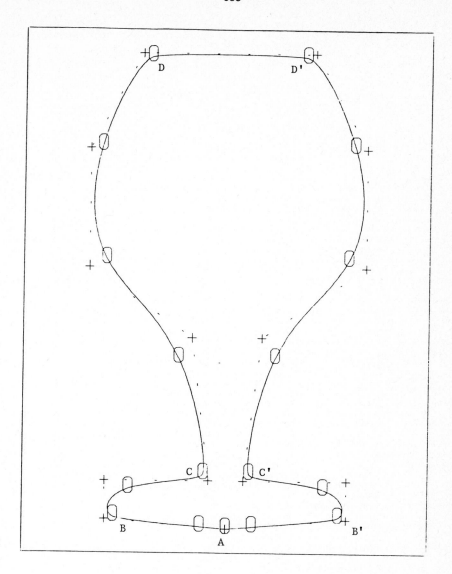

Fig. 8   β-spline curve using open curve end conditions,
i.e. triple first and last vertex at A.
All β_1 = 1. All β_2 = 0 except at B, B' (β_2 = 8),
C, C' (β_2 = 16), D, D' (β_2 = 20).

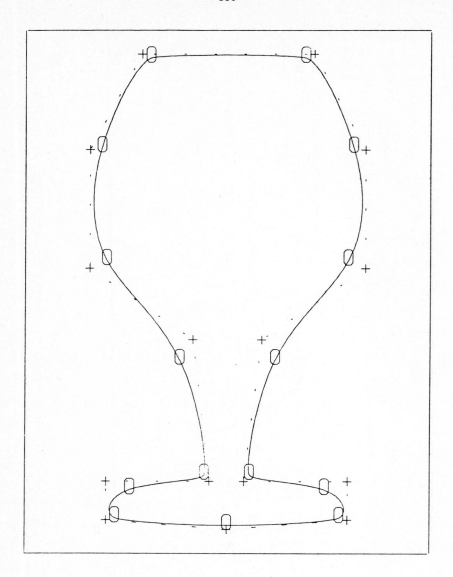

Fig.9   β-spline curve using closed curve end
conditions. Shape parameter values as
in Fig. 8.

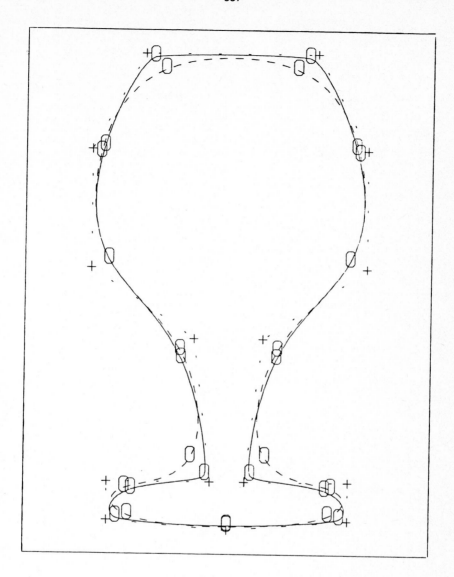

Fig.10   Output from β2-spline algorithm.

Section 4
Character Generation and Display

CHARACTER GENERATION AND DISPLAY

Philippe COUEIGNOUX
Data Business Vision, Inc.
3510 Dunhill Street, Suite B
San Diego, California 92121

1 - Introduction

The commercial success of high resolution digital screens and laser printers has put pressure on firmware developers to come up with attractive characters to represent the letters of the alphabet, by far the bulk of the matter output. Font, a once obscure term used by typographers to mean a homogenous set of characters (Fig. 1) [1-2], has quickly become a key word of computer graphics.

Character generation and display should not be perceived only as a passing fad. The shapes in question, one of the oldest and most perfected tools of the human intellect [3], remain central to any human interface, icons notwithstanding. From a more technical point of view, beyond the deceiving simplicity of processing mere black and white planar blobs, lies the illustration of many major topics of computer graphics.

In a tutorial way, this contribution first reviews character generation, then concentrates on its relation to some of these topics, namely:

- contour specification and drawing

- outline filling and windowing

- pixel scaling and antialiasing

- graphical data bases

NATO ASI Series, Vol. F17
Fundamental Algorithms for Computer Graphics
Edited by R. A. Earnshaw
© Springer-Verlag Berlin Heidelberg 1985

2 - Design Considerations

Given the task of reconstructing two-dimensional black and white patterns from a matrix of elementary dots, one really faces two distinct problems: the actual output of the characters for production and the initial encoding of the characters into the generator. Encoding should not be construed as identical to input: encoding can be, in fact should be, interactive and thus include some kind of output, albeit under constraints very different from normal production.

Analyzing the creation stage further, one can decompose it into three tasks. The noblest is of course free creation, whereby the artist is working with the direct assistance of the computer. More trite, but of immense economic interest, is slave creation, whose goal is to obtain the best copy of an available master drawing. Intermediate in scope, the third task is to obtain new variations from a known shape, for instance a bold character from a light original.

Production is readily divided according to the different output devices used for visualizing type. Among them the digital phototypesetter is the best in speed and quality, whether it uses a cathode-ray tube or a laser beam to insulate a bromide film or paper. But typesetting is no longer restricted to phototypesetters. The rise of office automation has pushed the use of a whole range of high quality dot printers, either electrolytic, thermal, electromagnetic, electrostatic, ink jet or laser. Though their physical resolution (200 to 400 dots/in) cannot be compared to that of phototypesetters (600 to 1200 dots/in), it is high enough to generate similar problems and solutions. Digital type should be designed to match this broad spectrum of possibilities, including in the extreme television screens and computer displays (30 to 80 dots/in).

Resolution is the most important design factor: for each character, not only code length increases with the resolution but the number of available distinct designs jumps in the thousands, making space efficient encoding all but necessary. Akin to spacial resolution, the ability to specify each dot or pixel according to a grey scale is specific to television output.

Besides resolution, another fundamental characteristic is the kind of scan which is allowed by the output process. The dot matrix which composes one character may be read independently of the other characters, generally in a one-pass sweep from left to right over its columns, or may have to be read a line at a time in conjunction with all other characters set across the same line of text. The latter restriction is typical of television and will be called the video scan, as opposed to the former, henceforth, called the free scan.

With respect to the creation and the production of type, a coding scheme can itself be characterized by five criteria: speed, space, flexibility, cost and quality. Speed is a double standard: speed of creation may range from a few minutes to a few hours, while speed of production can go beyond 1000 characters/sec depending on type size and device resolution. Space refers to the average size of the code for one character as well as the size of the internal buffers often needed for decoding. Flexibility refers to the different automatic modifications which are supported by the code: scaling, rotating, family variations (as going from light to bold). Cost is self-explanatory.

Quality is a more elusive factor [4-6]. Objectively, it is proportional to the largest dot matrix which can be reconstructed from the code without noticeable degradation. For a given resolution, this determines the largest type which can be represented faithfully. Arrays can go as high as 2000 X 2000 and often correspond to the initial sampling of the masters. However quality is ultimately assessed by the well-trained eye of the artist, a process not easily cast in a mathematical formulation. One can only offer guidelines. First, the quantizing noise inherent to digital processing should be de-emphasize whenever possible. Second the quality to optimize is in the eye of the beholder, not in the external physical shape: any optical illusion and device distortion should then be precompensated in the matrices output and any detail too small to be perceived should be eliminated. Last, visual accuracy gauges relative measurements better than absolute ones: hence, regularity is more important than precision.

It is essential at this point to remember that a character is never considered alone but in relation with all other characters on a page or a screen. Regularity in the typeface, in the character and line spacing, in the handling of the noise is at the root of readability, a basic factor of comfort for the user.

Obviously, the five criteria above are not independent (Fig. 2). The design of a digital character generator is an engineer's task whose goal is to strike the appropriate balance between the specifications for those five criteria combined with the characteristics of the production device, resolution and scanning, and the necessity of operating the corresponding creation station.

3 - Methods

Using a single method to match the entire range of resolutions at which physical devices output digital characters would be ideal but this idea, whether ever entertained, is unrealistic: no single coding mechanism can remain efficient from a 5 X 7 array to a 2000 X 2000 grid and still produce an acceptable quality. Device independency, a major goal in computer graphics, does not eliminate device dependency, it simply hides it from the end user. In the case under study, the user is able to specify the text matter to be set and the characteristics of the font in which to set it, but must leave the entire job of character generation to some hidden firmware, very much device dependent.

The present section reviews the main methods developed to cover the different classes of devices [7-8].

3.1 - Bit Map Coding

A digital character is nothing but a binary matrix. Hence the simplest code is to use a bit map representation [9]. Decoding speed is maximum, buffering is unnecessary, but the code grows as the square of the matrix size. These characteristics make bit map coding the best suited for low resolution, low quality generation. An annoying feature, though, is the limited flexibility it offers. For such low matrix sizes, typically from 5 X 7 to 15 X 20, scaling means scaling up: each original dot is thus replaced by a rectangular array of dots whose dimensions correspond to the scaling factors in x and y. This method grossly exaggerates the staircase effect of the quantization (Fig. 3). Whereas normal production devices usually run with fixed size characters, screens and printers dedicated to composing and proofreading tasks can take advantage of this crude scaling to simulate better methods at little cost.

Creation of original bit maps in low matrix size is done by turning on or off the individual squares of a grid. Such a painstaking approach is rendered necessary by the fact that noise and signal having comparable strength at this resolution, each square has to be optimized by hand. To ease the drudgery, one can lay the working grid over a high resolution model and create a library of useful parts.

On the other hand, slave creation frequently uses a bit map coding at very high resolution and quality. For space is not a problem and the bit map can be directly obtained from a precision scanner, viewed on a graphic screen and corrected on a bit per bit basis by an artist. In this case, the bit map is an intermediate step before final encoding. The bit editing is still necessary though, because many encoding schemes are very sensitive to the presence of noise in the masters.

3.2 - Run-Length Coding

Digital characters appear to be made of a few simple strokes, especially at medium or high resolution. It is therefore tempting to encode a character as the union of rectangular areas or other primitive patterns whose description is shorter than the number of bits they cover [10-16]. The most frequent choice is run-length coding, which uses rectangular areas one bit thick called runs [14]. If n is the size of the matrix, run-length coding grows as k n $\log_2 n$, k being the average number of runs per matrix line or column. This factor k is really a measure of the simplicity of the character shapes: for Roman body-text fonts, k is approximately 4, while it is higher than 10 for Chinese.

Run-length coding makes economical matrix sizes up to 100. The quality is enough to cover most type sizes on medium resolution. Decoding speed is not impaired and buffering can be avoided or kept at minimal cost. A strong point is that horizontal runs fit nicely into video scanning across a line of text. Indeed this coding method was developed in part by compressing facsimile signals for text and graphics. Flexibility remains limited, however, and most of the variations are better made electronically rather than digitally. The reason behind this comes from the low level at which the variations are made. For example, when digital scaling is performed on digital runs bordering a straight edge, the final rendition of the edge is likely to be more ragged than if scaling had taken place before digitization. This is especially true for slopes not perpendicular to the direction of the runs when the scaling factor is above 1/2, and even worse for any shape when upward scaling is attempted [17].

Theoretically, the distribution of the runs used to describe characters is far from random among all possible runs and statistical coding techniques can be applied to further reduce the current character code [13,14,16]. This method however further decreases code flexibility and is not believed to be in practical use.

3.3 – Differential Run-Length Coding and Chain-Link Coding

As far as code compactness is concerned, run-length coding really works in one direction only, namely the direction of the runs. A possible extension is to seek compaction also along the perpendicular. This is achieved through differential run-length coding [14], which only records variations in run extremities from one row to the next. Under the latter process, the two ends of one particular run can be dealt with separately, leading to two different lists of end variations. Eventually, what counts are not the runs across the character pattern but the edges shaping the contour of the pattern. Hence one way to implement the method is to use a chain-link coding of the contour [18].

The code length of chain-link codes can be approximated as $6 k n$, n being the matrix size and k the average number of intersections of the contour with either rows or columns. Indeed the chain code is 3 bits long per contour point and the number of contour points is around $2 k n$. This does not make the method very attractive with respect to run-length coding, for its theoretical benefits occur for n

already too high. Even worse, pure chain-linked characters must be entirely decoded in an n^2 buffer before they can be output.

On the other hand, differential run-length coding is adjusted to a one-pass sweep generation, thereby needing no more than **n** bits of buffer space. This advantage is not free, though. For provisions must be made in the code to signal the birth of new runs or the death of old ones.

Typically adjusting to a one-pass sweep requires a little more decoding time and adds **b** $(\log_2 n + c)$ bits to the length of the chain code, where **b** is the number of birth points in the character and **c** a constant taking care of the bookkeeping. For Roman body text fonts, **b** is rather low, 4 on the average, and **c** is of the order of 16 bits. The increase in length is therefore very modest, around 100 bits.

Though differential run-length coding appears better than chain-link coding, it can hardly be found satisfactory since the total code space, **6 k n + b** $(\log_2 n + c)$, is not shorter than for run-length coding itself at a reasonable **n**. Adopting the so-called raster-scan chain-code [19] does shrink this code space, as it takes 2 bits per contour point instead of 3 at the lower level. For us, the main interest of differential run-length coding lies in its being a convenient intermediate step between bit map coding, as obtained from slave creation, and more powerful contour coding schemes. For its structure is ideal to decompose the task of contour approximation into as many independent problems as there are sides in the structure, in a way which ensures a proper one-pass sweep decoding (Fig. 4) [20,21].

3.4 - Spline Encoding

Notwithstanding the information about births and deaths, differential run-length coding remains very local in scope: individual points on the contour are still recorded as such. The next step is to replace a point by point coding by a more global specification. Three main advantages can be sought in the process. First, a mathematical description is much more concise than a list of points which represent its digitization on a grid, at least as soon as the number of points is above a dozen: in theory, the code length increases as $\log_2 n$ with the size n of the matrix. Second, its flexibility under scaling, to name but the simplest of interesting variations, is enhanced for it enables scaling to precede digitizing, which reduces the noise. Last, specifying a character shape in terms of contour arcs brings the encoding closer to human understanding, hence to free creation.

The most common mathematical description is spline encoding, whereby the contour is approximated as a piecewise polynomial, with continuity conditions at the ends of each piece, the knots [22]. Spline encoding itself can be subdivided according to the way knots and pieces are determined and to the degree and nature of the polynomials used. The importance of this subject is such that its discussion is differed to a later section (4.1). Among the many schemes available, the most popular ones center around polynomials of degree one (polygonal encoding) [23-25] or three (cubic splines) [20,27-31]. The former is unbeatable for speed, the latter better in quality.

Contour encoding is not limited to polynomial splines. Original schemes have adopted rational fractions [32], circular arcs [21,33,34] and spirals [35]. The term spline is thereafter loosely used to cover these cases as well.

Spline encoding, as a direct descendant of chain-link coding, can always be designed to accommodate the one-pass sweep requirement. There exists still another family of contour coding techniques which do not respect this requirement. The patch code represents a character as a union of subareas, or patches, which are themselves defined in terms of contour coding [36,37]. Akin to run-length coding (Section 3.2) in its structure, the patch code presents space characteristics similar to normal contour coding: 600 bits for a 40 X 60 matrix [36], 400 bits for over 150 X 150 in [37].

Patch coding cannot be output without a bit map buffer or a randomly addressed cathode-ray tube. Though spline encoding behaves better and allows one-pass sweep generation, there still remains an obstacle towards full video scanning ability. As long as no computation had to be made to recover current points of living sides on a row, as with pure run-length coding, any number of characters could be dealt with at once on a whole line of text. As soon, however, as the computation is more than a mere memory lookup, it becomes intractable to operate on more than a few characters at once. Hence spline encoding is tuned to a vertical sweep of the spot over consecutive characters on a horizontal line of text, one character at a time. Video scanning requires either a page or text line buffer, to do scan conversion, or an a priori decoding of each character in the line into its run-length equivalent. The latter operation is rather economical is the same font is used for many lines since a priori decoding takes place only once per character, and if the resolution wanted is not so high as to make run-length coding prohibitive, even for temporary storage.

3.5 - Structural Encoding

As it is, spline encoding satisfies most commercial needs: the code is compact enough, decoding speed acceptable, scaling possible with little additional noise, video scanning can be generated, all at a reasonable cost. Yet two factors warrant higher levels of encoding at the expense of speed and cost. First it is difficult to control the quality of spline encoding at a precision better than one pixel. For medium resolution devices, however, a lapse of one pixel can potentially destroy the visual regularity of the print. There is a need to constrain the output further so as to ensure this will not occur. Second, scaling is the only variation that can be easily expected from spline encoding. A slanted version of the upright Roman can be generated, but this is not the true Italic. Variations in weight (bold to light) and set (extended to compressed) are even harder to come by in artistic quality.

The coding methods presented so far have all in common their generality: they apply to all black and white planar blobs, not just to characters. It is not surprising that they cannot deal with requirements which stem from the very nature of characters. The solution is to take this nature into account within the definition of the code. Such methods are called structural and fall into two broad categories: contour-oriented [38,32] and skeleton-oriented [27]. The former is more practical for Roman fonts, wherein the outline defines the shape. The latter is more accurate for fonts derived from brush, reed or quill handwriting like Arabic. Both are dual approaches of the same problem. For the sake of an example, we develop a contour-oriented presentation.

A layman will think that all body text fonts are alike while a type designer will say that no two of them are the same. Both opinions are legitimate. The explanation lies in a careful study of Fig. 9. There the similarity of four typefaces has been enhanced by that of the four letters chosen for the display: E, F, L, T. Both kinds of similarities can be attributed to the recurrence of common, primitive blocks throughout the 16 characters. Those primitives, respectively called, stem, arm and nose, using obvious analogies, help to formulate five fundamental rules:

 - (0) characters are made of primitives,

 - (1) the shape of a primitive is very stable among all characters it contributes to,

 - (2) shape variations are circumscribed to a few parameters, whose values depend mostly on the font they characterize and very little on the letter they embellish,

 - (3) the description of a character in terms of primitives depends only on the letter it represents and not on the font it belongs to,

 - (4) a primitive usually occurs within the specification of more than one letter.

As these rules can be verified to hold on a general basis, it is understandable that the layman is satisfied to see each letter always follow the same description while the artist relishes the small variations whose cumulative impact makes the identity of the font.

The list of primitives for the 52 upper and lower case letters is given in Fig. 10 and illustrated in Fig. 11. Figure 12 details the parameter lists for the primitives "stem" and "bow". Rule (2) has not been strictly observed inasmuch as some of these parameters may vary significantly within one font. For the stem, for instance, slope, thickness and serif type are not constant: slope is part of the letter specification; thickness and serif type are mere embellishments. To some extent the primitive "stem" is but a convenient gathering of real primitive shapes, strongly related but not identical. This freedom being granted, we find a remarkably low number of primitives, or families of primitives: thirteen, nine of which are used repeatedly throughout the alphabet.

Repetition does not exhaust the structure of Roman fonts, though. For there also exist strong relationships between the different primitives which make the basis for this repetition. Those relationships are of two kinds.

First, there are rules of proportion which link together the values of parameters of the same nature, whichever primitive they belong to. For example, vertical primitives are related in height and all primitives are related in thickness. Related values may not be all equal. Fonts may distinguish between thick and thin, for instance. Even when identity is sought, it may be distorted to take an optical factor into account: the physical height of the O is always bigger than that of the I (see Fig. 13). Nevertheless the primitive parameters fall into a tight net of proportions which also include the parameters necessary to describe the relative location of primitives within one character, such as character width.

The second kind of relationship occurs between primitives which make up the same character. Far from all combinations may be used. For instance, the small number of serif-primitive pairs has led us to lump the serif type as a primitive parameter. Stems rule out bays while bows admit bays only. A character has at least one basic stroke, and at most three, where a basic stroke is a thick stem or a bow. Concise rules, called rules of disposition, can be designed to generate all valid combinations and only those.

Given the structure of Roman fonts, several levels of encoding can be considered. At the very least rules of proportion can be enforced to ensure maximum regularity. Of capital importance for example is to constrain each letter to rest within its baselines and each stroke to have the appropriate thickness expressed in pixels independently of the letter to which it belongs. Next, primitive repetition can be used to generate each character in a type face from a library of building blocks. Last, the independency of letter structures with respect to fonts as well as the rules of disposition can be the basis for a meta-encoding of each letter.

While quality and code compactness are increased, the closeness of the code to the intrinsic structure of the fonts [39-41] also builds flexibility inside the coding method. For rules of proportion make clear the partition of all parameters within a font, be they for primitive shapes or relative disposition, into a small number of related families: heights, thick and thin thicknesses, types of serifs, squareness, slopes and character widths. From this classification, the definition of type series appears operational:

- "bold: a thickness of stroke appreciably greater than normal: [40],

- "condensed: rather narrower than standard" [40],

- "Italic: the reduced width of the individual characters usual to this style...."

All these quotations, and their obvious opposites for light and extended versions, call upon a simple affinity in one of the above parameter families. It is even possible to take into account the secondary influence of one family on another: for instance, an increase of weight will increase the set, hence the character widths. Another useful example is the possibility of distinguishing thick and thin strokes when scaling down significantly, since thick thicknesses will be more reduced than thin ones to avoid the disappearance of the latter.

Unfortunately structural coding may not be very efficient with respect to speed and buffering requirements. A buffer space in $2n^2$ is typical for decoding a n X n matrix, and speed enbarrassingly slow. Structural methods have so far found their way only in interactive encoding systems, whether experimental [38,32,27] or commercial [28,29]. Here they provide an interface acceptable to the artist and are used to create or rectify master drawings prior to spline encoding. One should notice that structural coding of outlines or skeletons is itself based on splines but these in general are not suited to fast output.

As a summary for this section, Figure 14 gives the main characteristics of the coding methods just discussed in tabular format. It appears than none is universal in performance, leaving room for the ingenuity of the engineer.

4 - Character Generation and Computer Graphics

The previous sections were intended to give an engineer the information he needs to specify a character encoding and decoding scheme optimized for his particular requirements. Few algorithms if any have been presented so far though! The reason is that character generation, albeit central to the implementation of human interfaces, is but an application of more fundamental topics in computer graphics and image processing. To get his tools, the engineer is thus forwarded to the wealth of material available from specialized surveys of these topics. However, the emphasis of any of these surveys might not be geared to the unique features of character generation and display. The purpose of the present section is to provide a critical approach to some of the most important topics from this specialized point of view.

4.1 - Contour Specification and Drawing

Numerous algorithms have been published for spline encoding [22,42-45]. One can reasonably be chosen based on speed of decoding and encoding and overall code compactness. Yet the issues which are most relevant to character generation are more subtle, namely the way in which the intermediate knots are derived and the choice between interpolation and smoothing [46].

Both issues have in common that they influence the quality of the result to a large extent, by determining where the residual errors occur. In general, better control is achieved around the knots and the errors smoothly distributed in the intervening pieces. Since artistic quality puts a premium on regularity at specific places, the algorithms will succeed if they ensure knots end up in these places and will fail otherwise.

This seems to favor interpolation, wherein an operator edit blending functions between selected knots: it is easy in this case to place the knots by hand in the right places. However this does not take into account the fact that characters are designed by artists, not engineers. The former are more likely than not to tell the computer the shape they want by actually drawing it rather than entering numbers or writing a program: what the computer gets is what is sees! A fortiori slave encoding of past designs does not fit well in a CAD/CAM environment. The best compromise is therefore to use smoothing procedures adjusted to accept an initial set of knots in specific places. Of course the whole scheme becomes extremely sensitive to noise present in these very places on the master drawing, hence the necessity to edit by hand even large bit maps, prior to encoding.

As long as quality gets the attention it deserves, the ultimate choice of splines becomes almost a matter of taste. It is even possible to replace an initial choice: this often happens when a font is licensed in digital form by a company which has already encoded it under a proprietary method.

Work done in character generation at Ecoles des Mines de Saint-Etienne [21,33,34] places knots at extrema in **x** and **y** in the default orientation, and at points of remarkable curvature: inflections (change in sign), cusps (infinite) and corners (multivalued). This set is then doubled by considering the points P_i at which the tangent T_i is parallel to the line joining the two adjacent knots P_{i-1} P_{i+1}. Points like P_{i-1}, P_{i+1} monitor the main division of the contour while points like P_i specify the degree of squareness of the interpolating curve (see Figure 15). Rational conics [32] or circular arcs [47-48] can be used to interpolate or smooth between the points while fitting the tangents. Additional subdivision may occur if the resulting shape is still in error.

In the decoder, speed is the essential factor, which favors lower degree curves. Drawing algorithms use general incremental techniques but the cases of the straight line, the circle and the conic have inspired specialized and powerful methods. In evaluating the literature, one should remember that simplification can occur when generating an outline for a one-pass sweep. Assume for example a sweep in increasing **x**. The popular Bresenham algorithm for the straight line [49] **ax + by = 0 (b>0)** from the origin to abscissa x_0 **(x_0>0)** becomes:

```
na=-|a| ; s=b/2 ; x=0 ; y=0 ;
while x<x_0 |  do:  x=x+1 ; s=s+na ;
           |            while s<0 | do:  y=y+1; s=s+b ;
           |                      | end-do;
           |         mark (x,y) ;
           | end-do ;
```

Care should be taken however to ensure the intersections with the scan lines computed by the drawing algorithm are recorded with their order of multiplicity, since any error in so doing would invalidate any fill routine use to ink in the outline of the character. The algorithm mentioned above for example marks only one point per abscissa.

4.2 - Outline Filling and Windowing

Spline encoding makes no explicit reference to the inside of a shape, as run-length encoding. Hence it must be complemented by a filling algorithm, which recovers the inside from the outline. There exist three types of such algorithms respectively dubbed the on/off, seed and fast fill.

In the on/off fill, the outline is first decoded in some blank buffer. The buffer is then read out in scan line order. Assuming the outline is strictly contained in the buffer, the status of successive points is "outside" at the buffer limit and switches each time an outline point is read out. Since the data is processed in scan line order, the buffer may be as small as one scan line if allowed by the decoding of the outline. The on/off fill is thus straightforward enough but has the disadvantage of requiring access to all points in the bit map. Also it cannot deal gracefully with overlapping objects, granted, a defect not very relevant to character generation.

The seed fill [50] requires the a priori knowledge of one point inside the outline called the seed. From this point, the "inside" status is propagated to the neighboring points in a progressive flood contained by the outline. It follows that only inside points are visited, a considerable advantage for skinny shapes such as characters. The price paid however is significant. First a seed has to be computed, often by an on/off trial. Second some bookkeeping has to be performed to ensure that all inside points are flooded. Third and foremost it requires full buffering because there is no control over the direction of the flood. Last overlapping objects are forbidden.

The fast fill [33-51] is closely related to differential run-length coding with which it shares its overhead. Essentially the outline is decoded in a one-pass sweep and the runs are identified from the ordered sequence of the intersections between the outline and each scan line. The overhead mentioned is strictly equivalent to the bookkeeping required by the seed fill. However, it is already justified any time the one-pass sweep is necessary, which further reduces the buffer to one scan line. Moreoever, the runs across the inside are recovered at once without individual bit reading. Finally, this is the only algorithm which can deal fairly with overlapping, textured objects.

The fast fill thus appears to suffer from only one drawback: its overhead. For character generation, however, this is a minor point. For the size of the overhead is very reasonable (aroung 100 bits) and its computation is entirely off line, at encoding time. At decoding time it is enough to order the intersections between the outline and the scan line, a light job considering this order changes only when a new birth has to be registered, an infrequent event. In fact, even this task can be eliminated by pre-assigning a rank to each side, the fraction of contour between a birth and a death (Fig. 16). This is because the ordering of the intersections on each scan line is consistent from scan line to scan line (assuming the contour is not self-intersecting) and determines a partial ordering on the sides themselves. Such considerations reinforce the link between the fast fill, which appears as an ordering problem on the sides in the direction of the scan, and the one-pass sweep encoding, which calls for an ordering on the birth points in the direction perpendicular to the scan.

Viewed as an ordering problem, the fast fill bears some striking similarities to priorities pre-assigned to objects for hidden surface removal in 3D. More directly, the power of the fast fill combined with the one-pass sweep makes it a precious tool for clipping spline-encoded objects against spline-encoded windows in a 2D environment. Last because the one-pass sweep fast fill makes the actual decoding very simple to organize, it is fit for a highly parallel VLSI implementation.

4.3 - Shape Theory

Shapes can be specified by their outlines, generally recorded as a sequential list of arcs, a fact emphasized in spline encoding. This is only one point of view however. The two-dimensional ordering borne by births and sides and studied in section 4.2 offers another one. Two shapes are said to be equivalent if they share the same ordering. This type of classification is neither entirely metric: large metric variations can happen within a given class; nor entirely topological: a number of constraints are expressed in metric terms. It is thought to offer a useful modeling, for many real life problems are neither purely metric nor purely topological in nature.

To put this new approach on a firmer basis, three questions should be examined:

- given the sequential description of the outline of a shape, how can the two-dimensional ordering of its births and sides be derived?
- can an appropriate representation be found for the problem?
- how can this two-dimensional ordering vary under rotation?

To be truly interesting, the answer to the first question should not require the decoding of the outline. Certainly, if the outline is fully decoded, the ordering can be derived from a few comparisons. However, if the ordering can be simply computed from a spline encoding, this holds also for the overhead associated with the fastest form of a one-pass sweep fast fill, since ordering and overhead share the same information. This in turn allows to drop the overhead from the code, adding to its compactness without decrease in speed. It also allows transformations on the code such as rotation which prevents the overhead from being computed in advance, thus adding to flexibility.

In view of the nature of the problem, semi metric, semi topological, the method is mixed. First the method assumes births are already recorded as knots. This is true if the splines are of degree 1; if they are circular arcs, it is still very easy to generate all the births without decoding. In this case one pass over the knots in sequential order is enough to find all the births and sort them by abscissa. Next, sequential relationships between sides bring a lot of information about the relative ordering of the sides under consideration, free of computation (Fig. 17). This information is not in general enough to derive a total ordering of all sides and, most of the time, a few metric comparisons performed on the coordinates of the knots are needed to complete the task. Unfortunately, some cases will not be solved without what amounts to a partial decoding.

In order to detail the method, one needs an appropriate representation of the result. We introduce the priority graph as a directed colored graph whose vertices are the births or bumps of the original shape and whose sides stand for the two "parallel" relationships between bumps, "to the left of" and "above". Traversing the priority graph in depth-order gives the ordering on the sides (Fig. 18).

One derives the priority graph by recreating the shape incrementally, introducing the bumps in birth order, one by one (Fig. 19). For each intermediate shape, two sequential relationships link the new bump to its neighbors on either side, which partially orders the new bump against the list of ordered sides already processed. The new bump is finally tested against the sublist of sides for which no information is known. Since this sublist is itself sorted, a binary search is recommended. The test itself involves the new bump and two sides meeting to a common death (Fig. 20).

Let **yn-Yn** be the extent in ordinate of the new bump in the strip determined in abscissa by the birth and the death. Let **yl-Yl** (resp. **yr-Yr**) the extent of both sides sharing the death in the same strip. Then:

if **yn$\leq$ max (yl, yr)** : new bump -> sides
if **min (Yl, Yr)** $\leq$ **Yn** : sides -> new bump
if **max (yl, yr)** < **yn** $\leq$ **Yn** < **min (Yl, Yr)** : undetermined

The undetermined case arises especially when no knots happen to fall in the strip besides the birth and the death themselves (Fig. 21). In this case, only a partial tracing of the sides in the strip can bring the information.

Given the importance of the extrema in abscissa on the outline, the births, it is to be expected the description of the shape in terms of births and sides is not invariant under rotation. The surprise is that in fact the contrary holds true to a point. As long as the rotation angle stays between some limits, the description is indeed invariant, in the sense that the positions of the births and deaths vary continuously with the angle, leaving the whole ordering structure intact. Catastrophes happen only in two cases (Fig. 22). First when the angle of rotation becomes parallel to a tangent of inflection, a pair of sides either appears or disappears.

Second when the angle of rotation becomes parallel to a bi-tangent with respect to which the shape is on both sides, the ordering between the sides needs to be updated. These results are true at least if all cusps and corners are smoothed out and when the shape is simply connected.

It is too soon to assess the practical interest of this aspect of shape theory which has just been sketched. However any demand for quick overhead computation prior to a one-pass sweep fast fill is likely to heighten it.

4.4 - Pixel Scaling and Antialiasing

The previous discussion of spline encoding (subsection 4.1) emphasized the importance of eliminating noise in selected places to achieve artistic quality. The purpose of this subsection is to make this requirement more explicit.

Broadly speaking, it means that the rules of proportions which are part of the structure of a given font (see section 3.5) have to be followed exactly. For example all characters have to be precisely aligned with respect to the reference lines of the font: base line, x-height line, X-height line, bottom line of descenders. It is thus unacceptable that the two stems of an H do not appear to be on the same horizontal line; it is likewise unacceptable that two successive I would present the same discrepancy. The same is true of the thickness of the thick stem: any unintended irregularity between characters or worse, internal to characters will lower the quality markedly. This explains why master drawings are bit-edited by hand to ensure absolute regularity at the outset. Subsequent encoding would not filter out this type of noise. The difficulty, though, is not entirely eliminated for scaling is likely to re-introduce an uncontrollable one bit error.

Remedies can come from three levels.

First it is good practice to specify the outline of each character with respect to a frame whose origin lies on the base line and in vertical alignment with the left side of the leftmost vertical stroke. At least the heights of the different reference lines and the thickness of the leftmost stroke will be handled consistently.

A more serious attempt would require the code to carry enough structural information so as to enforce consistency wherever needed.

Last one can resort to antialiasing whenever possible [52-55]. Indeed the importance of one bit errors is an abnormality in terms of signal processing and reflects an inadequation of the output device to its mission: the representation of the signal only at those frequencies where it dominates the noise. Antialiasing is the name given to the methods which filter out the high frequencies which are corrupted by the quantizing noise; it requires the ability to display grey values and is so far available only on certain screens. Though antialiasing blurs the high frequencies of the signal as well, such as sharp corners and edges, it brings about a definite increase in quality. Note that antialiasing per se does not modify significantly encoding schemes since it is applied a posteriori on a decoded bit map several times more precise than the target grid.

4.5 - Graphic Data bases

The use of structural information in the coding of characters has been mentioned in several places to improve quality, flexibility and, secondary, code compactness. Its introduction brings about a significant change in the organization of data. So far most font libraries are organized as a set of independent, randomly accessible characters. By enforcing relationships on these characters, structural encoding transforms a font library into a genuine graphic data base wherein constraints link graphic objects together and modify their representation according to a context. It is in this context that the spacing information needed to put characters together on a line should be created and recorded. More work in this area should bring as much understanding of it as enjoyed say by display list structures. The particular mixture of exacting constraints and loose reproductions of common parts altered under artistic judgment, which characterizes the structural information of fonts, would probably apply to other applications such as architecture.

5 - Conclusion

The purpose of this contribution was two-fold: on the one hand giving the engineer the basic information he needs to design a character generator or font encoding scheme adapted to his problem; on the other rooting character generation and display into the traditional concerns of computer graphics.

Though unstated, another goal was certainly to bring about some awareness about type for its own sake. It is my belief that the personal computer will soon enable enlightened amateurs to try their hands at type design, were it only to supplement a font with a missing symbol, and my wish that their future tools reflect a concern for quality more than 4000 years old.

Acknowledgement:

Parts of this contribution have been freely borrowed from an earlier publication [7] by the author, copyrighted by Academic Press, Inc.

Bibliography

To get acquainted with commercial implementations, we recommend reading the Seybold Report, available from Seybold Publications, Inc., and attending some major trade shows (DRUPA, ANPA, NCC, Comdex, NCGA, Siggraph). Membership in the ATYPI (Association Typographique Internationale) is also relevant.

Reference [46] contains a more extensive bibliography on contour specification and drawing as well as outline filling.

REFERENCES

1. J.I. Biegeleisen, Art Directors' Book of Type Faces, Arco, New York, 1967.

2. "Monotype," Specimen Book of Monotype Printing Types, Monotype, England.

3. C. Bigelow and D. Day, Digital Typography, Scientific American, Vol. 249, No. 2, 1983, 106-119.

4. C. Bigelow and J. Seybold, Technology and the Aesthetics of Type, The Seybold Report, Vol. 10, No. 24, 1981, 3-16.

5. C. Bigelow, The Principles of Digital Type, Quality Type for Low, Medium and High Resolution Printers, Part I, The Seybold Report, 11(11):3-23, 1982.

6. C. Bigelow, The Principles of Digital Type, Quality Type for Low, Medium and High Resolution Printers, Part II, The Seybold Report, 11(12):10-19, 1982.

7. Ph. Coueignoux, Character Generation by Computer, Computer Graphics and Image Processing 16, 1981, 240-269.

8. Lynn Ruggles, Letterform Design Systems, Stanford University, Computer Science Dept., Stan-CS-83-971, April, 1983.

9. R. Reddy et al., XCRIBL, A Hardcopy Scan Line Graphics System for Document Generation, Carnegie-Mellon University, Computer Science Dept., April 1973.

10. M. V. Mathews, C. Lochbaum, and J. A. Moss, Three fonts of computer-drawn letters, J. Typogr. Res. 1, No. 4, 1967, 345-356.

11. A. V. Hershey, Calligraphy for Computers, Technical Report No. 2101, Computation and Analysis Laboratory, United States Naval Weapons Laboratory, Dahlgren, Virginia, August 1, 1967.

12. A. V. Hershey, A Computer System for Scientific Typography, Computer Graphics and Image Processing, 4, 1972, 373-385.

13. A. J. Frank, High fidelity encoding of two-level, high resolution images, IEEE Intern. Conf. on Communications, June 1973, pp. 26.05-26.11.

14. T. S. Huang, Run-length coding and its extensions, in Picture Bandwith Compression (T.S. Huang and O.J. Tretiak, Eds.), pp. 231-264, Gordon & Breach, New York, 1972.

15. A. Pringle, P. Robinson, and N. Wiseman, Aspects of quality in the design and production of text, Computer Graphics 13, No. 2, 1979, 63-67.

16. H.E. White, M.D. Lippman, and K.H. Powers, Dictionary look-up encoding of graphics data, in Picture Bandwith Compression (T.S. Huang and O.J. Tretiak, Eds.), pp. 265-281, Gordon and Breach, New York, 1972.

17. Ph. Coueignoux, A posteriori scaling of run-length encoded polygons, Computer Graphics and Image Processing 17, 1981, 84-89.

18. H. Freeman, Computer processing of line-drawing images, Comput, Surv. 6, No. 1, 1974, 57-97.

19. R.L.T. Cederberg, Chain-link coding and segmentation for raster-scan devices, Computer Graphics and Image Processing, 10, 1979, 224-234.

20. Ph. Coueignoux, Compression of Type Faces by Contour Coding, M.S. thesis, MIT, Dept. Elec. Eng., January 1973.
21. M. Hourdequin, Generation de polices d'imprimerie pour photocomposeuse digitale, Doct. Ing. Thesis, Ecole Nationale Superieure des Mines de Saint-Etienne, France, Nov. 1978.
22. C. de Boor, A practical guide to splines, Springer-Verlag, 1978.
23. Evans et alii, Character Generating Method and System, U.S. Patent No. 4,029,947 filed May 11, 1973.
24. B.G. Baumgart, Image Contouring by Comparing, Stanford University, Art. Int. Lab., Memo AIM-199, STAN-CS-73-398, Oct. 1973.
25. J.C. Beatty,, J.S. Chin, and H.F. Moll, An interactive documentation system, Computer Graphics 13, No. 2, 1979, 71-82.
26. P. Baudelaire, The Fred User's Manual, Internal Report, Xerox Palo Alto Research Center, Palo Alto, California, 1976.
27. D.E. Knuth, Mathematical Typography, Stanford University, Computer Science Dept., Stan-CS-78-648, Feb. 1978.
28. P. Karow et al., Ikarus-System: computer-controlled font production for CRT and Lasercomp, Karow Rubow Weber GmbH of Hamburg, Germany, September 1979.
29. P. Karow et al., Ikarus-System: computer-controlled font production for Photocomp, Karow Rubow Weber GmbH of Hamburg, Germany, March 1979.
30. L. Ramshaw and K. LaPrade, Prepress Manual, version 2.1, Xerox Corporation, September 1980.
31. M. Plass and M. Stone, Curve-Fitting with Piecewise Parametric Cubics, Imaging Sciences Laboratory, Xerox Palo Alto Research Center, March 1983.
32. Ph. Coueignoux, Generation of Roman Printed Fonts, Ph.D. thesis, MIT, Dept. Elec. Eng., June 1975.
33. M. Bloch, Generation de taches bicolores - application aux caracteres d'imprimerie - problemes de nature ordinale, Doct. Ing. Thesis, Ecole Nationale des Mines de Saint-Etienne, France, July 1981.
34. C. Sico, Generation de taches bicolores - application aux caracteres d'imprimerie - problemes de nature geometrique, Doct, Ing. Thesis, Ecole Nationale des Mines de Saint-Etienne, France, March 1982.
35. P. Purdy and R. MacIntosh, PM Digital Spiral, <Journal Unknown>, Britain in Print, Forward Thinking, 1978.
36. M.V. Mathews and J.E. Miller, Computer editing, typesetting and image generation. Proc. AFIPS, FJCC 1965, 389-398.
37. A.J. Frank, Parametric font and image definition and generation, Proc. AFIPS, FJCC 1971, 135-144.
38. H.W. Mergler and P.M. Vargo, One approach to computer assisted letter design, J. Typogr. Res. 2, No. 4, 1968, 299-322.
39. R.R. Karch, How to Recognize Type Faces, McKnight and McKnight, Bloomington, Ill., 1952.

40. F.C. Avis, Type Face Terminology, Glenview, London, 1965.
41. M. Jacno, Anatomie de la lettre, Ecole Estienne, Paris, 1978.
42. C. de Boor and J. Rice, Least Squares Cubic Spline Approximation, Part I, Fixed Knots, Part 2. Variable Knots, Purdue University, Computer Science Dept., TR-20, TR-21, April 1968.
43. W. Boehm, On Cubics: a survey, Computer Graphics and Image Processing, 19, 1982, 201-226.
44. J.E. Midgley, Isotropic four-point interpolation, Computer Graphics, 11, 1979, 192-196.
45. K. Harada and E. Nakamae, An isotropic four-point interpolation based on cubic splines, Computer Graphics, 20, 1982, 283-287.
46. Ph. Coueignoux and R. Guedj, Computer generation of colored planar patterns on TV-like rasters, Proc. IEEE 68 July 1980, 909-922.
47. M. Hourdequin and Ph. Coueignoux, Specifying arbitrary planar smooth curves for fast drawing, Proc. for Eurographics, Bologna, Italy, Oct. 1979, pp. 193-211.
48. W.S. Rutkowski, Shape completion, Computer Graphics and Image Processing 9, 1979, 89-101.
49. J.E. Bresenham, Algorithm for computer control of a digital plotter, IBM Syst. J. 4, No. 1, 1965, 25-30.
50. H. Lieberman, How to color in a coloring book, Computer Graphics, 12, No. 3, 1978, 111-116.
51. D.T. Lee, Shading of Regions on Vector Display Devices, Computer Graphics, 15, No. 3, Aug. 1981, 37-44.
52. F.C. Crow, The use of grayscale for improved raster display of vectors and characters, Computer Graphics 12, No. 2, 1978, 1-5.
53. J.E. Warnock, The display of characters using gray level sample arrays, Computer Graphics, 14, No. 3, 1980, 302-307.
54. A.J. Wilkes and N.E. Wiseman, A soft-edged character set and its derivation, University of Cambridge Internal memo, July 1981.
55. J. Kajiya and M. Ullner, Filtering high quality text for display on raster scan devices, Computer Graphics, 15, No. 3, Aug. 1981, 7-15.

Garamond No.2
ABCDEFGHIJKLMNOPQRSTUVWXYZ&
abcdefghijklmnopqrstuvwxyz
1234567890 (.,:;!?''—/$-%)

Garamond Italic No.2
ABCDEFGHIJKLMNOPQRSTUVWXYZ&
abcdefghijklmnopqrstuvwxyz
1234567890 (.,:;!?''—/$-%)

Fig. 1   A sample font

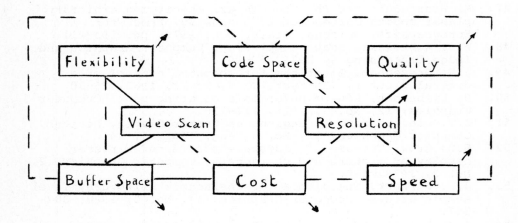

Fig. 2   Interrelationship of criteria in designing a character
generator

↗ : desirable improvement
___ : agreement   — — — : contrariness

Fig. 3   Scaling a bit map code
(a) original dot; (c) extension;
(b) compression; (d) enlargement

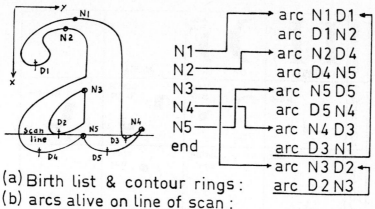

Y
X
N1
N2
D1
N3
D2
N5
N4
D3
D4
D5
Scan line
N1
N2
N3
N4
N5
end
arc N1 D1
arc D1 N2
arc N2 D4
arc D4 N5
arc N5 D5
arc D5 N4
arc N4 D3
arc D3 N1
arc N3 D2
arc D2 N3
(a) Birth list & contour rings:
(b) arcs alive on line of scan:
before: N1D3 N2D4 N3D2 N3D2 N4D3 N4D5
after : N1D3 N2D4 N5D4 N5D5 N4D3 N4D5

Fig. 4 Recording structure for one-pass generation

Fig. 5-8 Wrong numeration

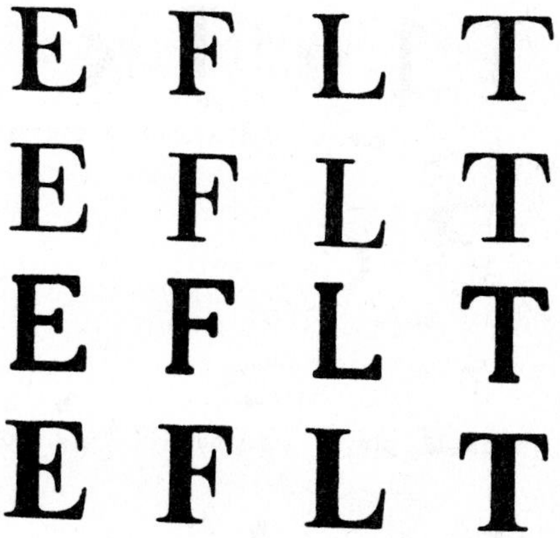

E F L T
E F L T
E F L T
E F L T

Fig. 9 Characters along letter and font dimensions (from [32])

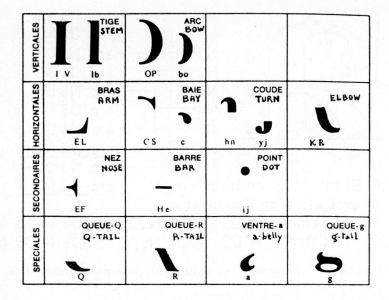

Fig. 10   Primitives for Roman body text

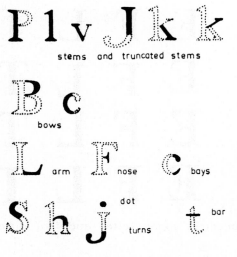

Fig. 11   Examples of primitives in context

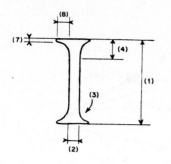
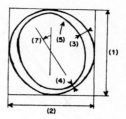

Fig. 12   Primitives stem and bow within letters I and O

I: (1) height, (2) thickness, (3) squareness, (4) height of fillet
     (5) slope, (6) type of serif, (7) serif thickness
     (8) serif width
     (5,6) not shown

O: (1) height, (2) 2 × width, (3) thick, (4) thin thicknesses,
     (5) inside, (6) outside squareness
     (7) inside, (8) outside tilts.
     (6,8) not shown

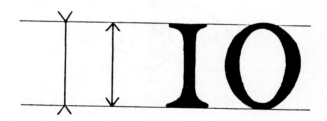

Fig. 13   Compensating for optical illusions

Method	Code space (in bits)	Buffer space (in bits)	Flexibility	Video Scan	Resolution (n)	Qual.	Speed
Bit Map	n^2	0	−	+ +	≤ 50	− −	+ + +
Run-length	$k \cdot n \cdot \log_2 n$	n	−	+ +	≤ 100	−	+ +
Chain-link	$6 \cdot k \; n$	n^2	−	−	≤ 100	−	+
Differential run-length	$6 \cdot k \cdot n + b[\log_2 n + c]$	n	−	+	≤ 100	−	+
Spline	$k \cdot \log_2 n$	$k_m \cdot \log_2 n$	+	+	≤ 2000	+	+
Structural	$k' \cdot \log_2 n$	n^2	+ +	−	≤ 2000	+ +	−

Fig. 14   Comparative Performances

394

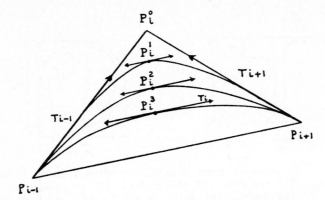

Fig. 15   An interpolating/smoothing scheme

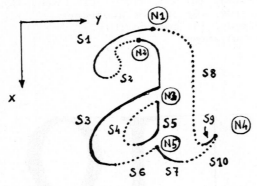

Fig. 16   Ordering the sides for fast fill

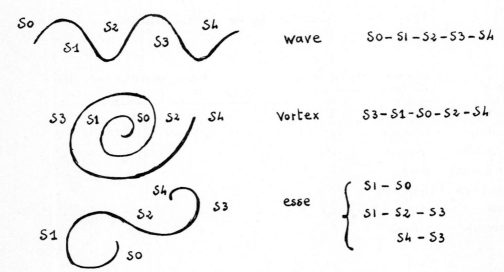

Fig. 17   Sequential relationships and side order

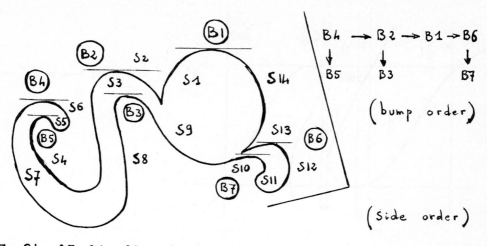

$$B4 \rightarrow B2 \rightarrow B1 \rightarrow B6$$

$$\downarrow \qquad \downarrow \qquad \qquad \downarrow$$

$$B5 \qquad B3 \qquad \qquad B7$$

(bump order)

(side order)

$$S7 - S4 - S5 - S6 - S3 - S8 - S9 - S2 - S1 - S14 - S13 - S10 - S11 - S12$$

Fig. 18   The priority graph

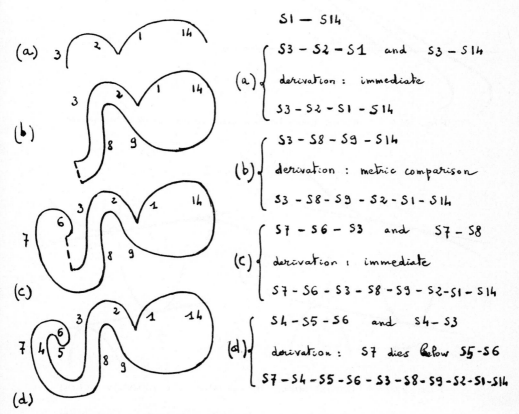

$$S1 - S14$$

(a) { $S3 - S2 - S1$ and $S3 - S14$

derivation : immediate

$S3 - S2 - S1 - S14$ }

(b) { $S3 - S8 - S9 - S14$

derivation : metric comparison

$S3 - S8 - S9 - S2 - S1 - S14$ }

(c) { $S7 - S6 - S3$ and $S7 - S8$

derivation : immediate

$S7 - S6 - S3 - S8 - S9 - S2 - S1 - S14$ }

(d) { $S4 - S5 - S6$ and $S4 - S3$

derivation : $S7$ dies below $S5 - S6$

$S7 - S4 - S5 - S6 - S3 - S8 - S9 - S2 - S1 - S14$ }

Fig. 19   Incremental derivation of the priority graph

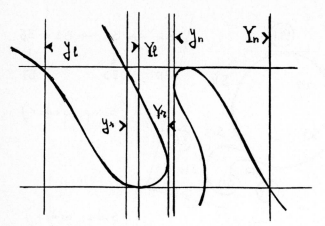

old sides → new bump

Fig. 20   Metric comparisons when ordering a new bump

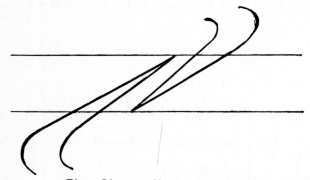

Fig. 21   Knots coordinates can leave undetermination

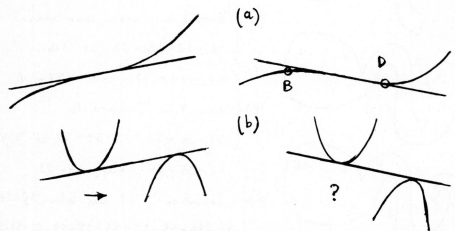

(a)

(b)

Fig. 22   Catastrophes in rotating the priority graph

Font information and device-independent output

Heather Brown
University of Kent at Canterbury

Computer typesetting systems have traditionally sent their output directly to a particular typesetter or printer. Typically these systems provide high quality output and allow access to all the facilities of their output device. They also reflect all the quirks and limitations of their output device, thus limiting their use and making it difficult to transport documents between systems.

A few widely available typesetting systems, however, are designed to be *device-independent*. Two notable examples are the new typesetter-independent version of TROFF and the TEX system for technical text. These two systems keep all device-dependent information separate from their main text formatting functions. In practice, this means that they keep all font information in a separate *font library*. Their output is a device-independent description of the final document — giving the exact position of each character on each page. Further processing is necessary to convert the output into the form necessary to drive a particular device.

This paper describes the techniques used in device-independent document preparation. It concentrates on the font information required for high quality text formatting and the form of the device-independent output. TROFF and TEX are used as the main examples; their output format is described briefly and compared to the new page description language, POSTSCRIPT.

Introduction

Computer typesetting systems have grown up in two separate worlds. In the printing and publishing world the emphasis has always been on good design and high quality printing. Many excellent computer typesetting systems have been developed, but they often rely on manual cut-and-paste for making up pages, and they are generally designed to drive a particular typesetter. In the office and computing world, on the other hand, the emphasis has been on flexibility and ease of use, but the output is generally destined for a poor quality printer. Unfortunately, each world tends to despise the other for its deficiencies rather than learning from its strengths.

The ideal system, of course, combines the good features of the two worlds. It retains all the typographical excellence of the printing world, but is also flexible, easy-to-use, and capable of driving a wide range of output devices — typesetters, laser printers, and high-resolution screens. Unfortunately, this ideal has not been achieved. There are, however, a number of techniques that can be used to create device-independent systems which at least approach the ideal. This paper describes how the new typesetter-independent version of TROFF [1] and the TEX system for technical text [2] make use of these techniques.

NATO ASI Series, Vol. F17
Fundamental Algorithms for Computer Graphics
Edited by R. A. Earnshaw
© Springer-Verlag Berlin Heidelberg 1985

Device-independent typesetting

Instead of driving an output device directly, a typesetting system can be designed to produce an intermediate form of output that gives a detailed — but device-independent — description of the final document. This description includes details of the character fonts used and specifies exactly where each character is to be placed on each page. It needs to be processed again to turn it into the form needed to drive a specific output device, and thus provides an intermediate stage between the original document manuscript and the final printed result.

There is a fundamental problem in providing both high quality and device-independence. It is impossible for the typesetting system to produce a high quality result unless it knows something about the character fonts available on its target output device. As an absolute minimum, it must know what fonts are available and the width of each character in each font. The vital point is that this knowledge should not be bound into the typesetting system. It should, instead, be available from an outside and readily changeable source. In practice a *font library* is set up containing all the necessary information in some systematic fashion. The typesetting system uses this during the first stage of the transition from the document manuscript to the printed result.

The second stage of the transition is performed by programs known as *device drivers* (or sometimes as *back-ends* or *raster image processors*). If several device drivers are provided, the device-independent output can be printed on a number of different typesetters and printers or, indeed, displayed on high-resolution screens. To cater for a new printer it is only necessary to provide the font library and device driver for it. The overall picture of the two-stage process is as shown below.

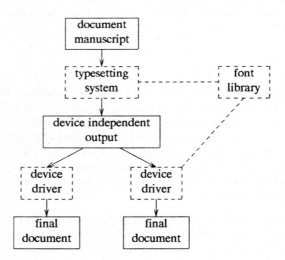

The font library is always needed during the first stage of the transition; it may also be needed during the second stage. In the first stage, the typesetting system uses it to provide all the detailed information it requires about the size and positioning of characters. In the second stage, the device driver may need it to provide information on the width and shape of characters. Whether or not it is required at this second stage depends on the exact form of the device-independent output and also on the amount of intelligence provided locally by the output device.

To achieve good results it is important that the correct font library is used for both stages in the translation process. There is, however, one exception to this general rule. This is when the document is destined eventually for a high quality device, but proof copies are required first on lower quality — and cheaper — devices. The first stage of the translation can be done using the font library for the eventual high quality device, and the resultant device-independent output can then be processed by the driver for the proof device. Proof copies obtained in this manner may look rather strange, but they should give an accurate picture of the line-breaks, page-breaks, and spacing that will be used in the final high quality document. In some cases there may be strange substitutions for missing characters or fonts. The proofs should, however, give the best representation they can within the physical limitations of the device used.

An ideal situation is to have three levels of output: a graphics screen for previewing the document without printing it, a laser printer for medium-to-good proof copies, and the target high quality typesetter.

Font information

The amount of font information required by a typesetting system depends very much on the quality of the formatting job it does. The higher its typographical standards the more information it needs. TROFF requires little more than character widths, but TEX requires all the information discussed below.

For each character

- The height, width, and depth of the character. The typesetting system does not know the *shapes* of the characters it handles. Instead it regards them as rectangular boxes. When setting the letters of a word, it places the boxes representing the characters adjacent to one another with their baselines along the baseline of the current line. The example below shows how the word 'Type' might appear to the typesetting system.

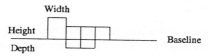

The height and depth of the character refer to its height and depth relative to the baseline. The rectangle defined by these values can be thought of as an enclosing box for the character shape. This is not always true, especially for italic characters which tend to extend beyond the edges of their character boxes, but is near enough to the truth to provide a convenient picture.

- Ligature information. Certain character pairs look uncomfortable next to one another and are therefore replaced, in some fonts, by composite characters known as ligatures. The most commonly used ligatures are made up of 'f' followed by 'i' or 'l' or another 'f'. The font library tells the typesetting system whether it should make ligature substitutions automatically or not. If necessary it identifies the ligature pairs and gives the position of the corresponding ligature characters in the font.

- Kerning information. As already mentioned, the typesetting system does not know the actual shapes of the characters it is handling. Sometimes, however, careful spacing is needed between certain character pairs because of their relative shapes. A common example is that the capitals 'A' and 'V' may need to be placed closer than normal to each other, otherwise there appears to be a gap between them. Similarly, pairs such as 'AY', 'AW', and 'Te' may need to be moved together. The example below shows the effect kerning might have on the way the word 'Type' is set.

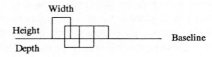

The rectangle representing the short letter 'y' has been moved closer to the rectangle representing the 'T'. The font library identifies all such *kerning pairs* and tells the typesetting system exactly how much to change the spacing between the pairs. In practice, the boxes representing the characters are overlapped (as shown above) or moved apart slightly instead of just touching.

- Extension pieces. For mathematical and other specialised fonts, it may be necessary to identify similar characters in different sizes or to build large characters out of a number of separate pieces. Large brackets often require this sort of treatment.

The information described above is needed for individual characters. In addition, some information is required about each font as a whole. The main items are

- The x-height and h-height of the font. This gives the height of short and tall characters in the font. It is needed for placing accents over characters.

- The slant of the font (if any). This can be important for the fine positioning of accents, subscripts, and superscripts.

- The normal, minimum, and maximum width of a space in the font. This tells the typesetting system about the allowable sizes of word spaces for the font.

- The design size of a font. This says, for example, whether it is a normal 10-point font or a small 5-point font.

The information given above is sufficient for a typesetting system which maintains very high typographical standards. It is important to realise, however, that nothing so far has defined the actual shapes of the characters. Even the ligature and kerning information only gives sets of rules to help with character selection and positioning.

The font library may also include some definition of the shapes of the characters. This could be in the form of a pattern of dots to be printed on a raster device, a vector definition, or some other outline information defining the shape. Shape information is for use by the device driver, not by the typesetting system.

Device-independent intermediate output

The intermediate output takes the form of a simple command language describing exactly where each character is to be positioned. It almost always embodies the ideas of a *current font* being used and a *current position* on the page. The output retains no information about the structure of the document; it simply records how the page image can be formed by placing characters at given positions on the page. Editing the intermediate output does not make sense, edits should always be made to the original document manuscript.

Commands are generally provided to

- start a new page;
- change the current font;
- change the current position (horizontally, or vertically, or both);
- set a given character from the current font at the current position.

One very common need is to set a character and then move the current position right by a short distance, ready to set the next character in the line. It is important to have concise commands for doing this.

Simple commands like those described above are easy to interpret and are similar to those provided by the manufacturers of typesetters for driving their devices. As a result the device driver for a particular typesetter may be a relatively simple program to convert from one command language to a similar one. If, on the other hand, the device driver is for an unintelligent laser printer it may have to do all the hard work of producing the actual pattern of dots to be printed. In this case, the device driver must have access to the character shapes (from the font library).

In addition, the intermediate output may well include other concepts familiar to programmers — a stack and some variables are common examples — and further commands may be provided for drawing simple graphics like lines, arcs, and curves. Graphics commands can demand quite a lot of intelligence from the device driver to produce the required effect on the output device.

The following sections provide a brief introduction to the intermediate output produced by TROFF and TEX.

TROFF intermediate output

TROFF output is relatively simple to read and interpret. Its overall form is simple and it consists almost entirely of visible ASCII characters. The example below shows part of the output for a document containing the line 'Typesetting can be fun'

```
H232
V160
cT
23y17p18e16s13e16t11t11i10n19gw28c15a17nw30b18ew27f12u19nn40 0
```

The 'H232' and 'V160' lines are commands to move to an absolute horizontal and vertical position on the page. The page origin is at the top left-hand corner so in this case the horizontal position is set to 232 units from the left of the page, and the vertical position is set to 120 units from the top. 'cT' means set character 'T' from the current font at the current position. '23y' means move 23 units right then set a 'y'; '17p' means move 17 units right then set a 'p', and so on. The 'w's indicate variable word spaces; they are there purely for information, and are useful mainly to device drivers for proofing devices which are not capable of fine spacing. (Similarly, the 'n40 0' at the end of the example is just an end-of-line marker; like the word space marker, it is useful to drivers for proofing devices. The two integers give information about space before and after the line.)

Other commands are available for font information and drawing graphics: lines, circles, ellipses, arcs, and β-splines. The command *Dl dh dv*, for example, draws a line from the current position to the current position plus *dh dv*. Thus *Dl 300 0* draws a horizontal line 300 units long, and *Dl 100 100* draws a diagonal line from the current position to a position 100 units right and 100 units down the page.

The majority of text, however, translates into commands like those shown above. Characters to be set usually translate into three-byte sequences like '23y' or '17p'. An extra large move is given before the first character after a word space because this includes both the width of the previous character and the width of the space. Explicit moves like this help the device driver, which does not need to use the font library to find the width of the characters. This makes the device driver simpler to implement, but tends to create very large output files.

One important point to note is that the 'units' used for the moves described above are actually 'device units'. In other words, TROFF needs to be told the resolution of the output device and it translates distances into these device units before producing its intermediate output. The output is therefore not really device-independent at all! (The example above was produced for a laser printer with a resolution of 240 dots/inch so '10n', for example, means move 1/24 of an inch to the right before setting the 'n'.)

TEX intermediate output

TEX intermediate output is known as DVI. It is more complex in form than TROFF output but it embodies most of the same ideas. One important difference is that it is binary in nature, rather than ASCII, and is designed to be concise. Another significant difference is that distances are measured in very small units called *scaled points* (65536 scaled points = 1 point). This is a real distance and as such is truly device-independent. The size of the unit is intended to allow fine positioning of characters, and to prevent accumulated rounding errors from having a visible effect.

TEX output uses the notions of *current font* and *current position* described previously. It also embodies the notion of a *stack* and six variables: *h*, *v*, *w*, *x*, *y*, and *z*. The current position on the page (measured from the top left-hand corner) is given by the contents of the two variables *h* and *v*. *w* and *x* are used for horizontal spacing; *y* and *z* for vertical spacing.

The example on the next page shows the DVI form of the same 'Typesetting can be fun' line used in the previous section to explain TROFF output. DVI is not as readily interpreted as TROFF output, so some explanation of the representation used is needed first. DVI commands are one byte long. They may, however, be followed by arguments which bring the total command length to more than one byte. Commands with values in the range $0 \leq n \leq 127$ are reserved to mean 'set character *n* from the current font at the current position and then move right by the width of the character'. These are one-byte commands with the value of the character they represent; they are shown in the example as single characters. Commands in the range $128 \leq n \leq 255$ are shown as *<name>*$_i$. The names used are taken from the official description of DVI [3], and the subscript shows the total number of bytes occupied by the command — including any arguments.

Using this representation the DVI output for the 'Typesetting can be fun' line is as follows

> *<push>*₁
> Typesetting *<w3>*₄ can *<w0>*₁ be *<w0>*₁ fun
> *<pop>*₁*<down3>*₄

The initial *<push>*₁ command saves the six registers on the stack, thus ensuring that the original position can be restored later. The letters of the word 'Typesetting' are then set using the one-byte command to set each character and move right by its width. The *<w3>*₄ command sets *w* to a three-byte value and then moves right by the contents of *w*. This is generally used for the first word space in a line. The *<w0>*₁ command moves right by the contents of *w*; this one-byte command can be used for subsequent word spaces of the same size. The *<pop>*₁ command retrieves the registers from the stack, thus restoring *h* and *v* and the original position. Finally, the *<down3>*₄ command moves down the page ready to start the next line.

One very important point to notice is that nothing in this DVI gives the character widths. The device driver must have access to these from the font library in order to perform the necessary move to the right each time it finds a 'set character' command. The advantage of this form is that, in straightforward text, each character translates into a single byte of output. The use of the one-byte *<w0>*₁ command means that many word spaces also only occupy one byte. The DVI output is therefore relatively compact, but it requires a more complex device driver to interpret it.

The example shown above is oversimplified. TEX maintains high typographical standards, and performs kerning of characters. This leads to further move commands appearing in the DVI. The real picture is as shown below.

> *<push>*₁
> T *<right2>*₃ yp *<x2>*₃ esetting *<w3>*₄ can *<w0>*₁ b *<x0>*₁ e *<w0>*₁ fun
> *<pop>*₁*<down3>*₄

The additional commands represent kerning after the initial 'T' and between the letter pairs 'pe' and 'be'. The *<right2>*₃ command simply moves right by a given two-byte value. (For kerning this value is often negative, and thus represents a small left movement.) The second two occurrences of kerning in the line happen to require the same amount of movement, so the *x* register is used to preserve the amount and thus allow a one-byte command to be used for the second occurrence. The *<x2>*₃ command sets *x* and moves right by its contents; *<x0>*₁ simply moves right by its contents. This use of *x* for kerning movements is similar to the use of *w* for word space movements.

Device drivers

A device driver performs two basic tasks. The first is to read the device-independent output and interpret the commands contained in it. The problems involved in this depend heavily on the form of the output. The second task is, of course, to drive the output device — either directly or indirectly via another command language.

The device driver is essentially a conversion program which has to reconcile all the many and varied formats used by typesetting systems and output devices. In theory this should be a relatively simple task. In practice, there can be a number of incompatible assumptions made in the different formats and the device driver has to go to great lengths to knit them together in an intelligent fashion. If the device provides its own low-level command language (like the Slave Input Language for the Monotype Lasercomp [4], for example) it is simple to perform the mechanical translation of one set of commands to the other. The difficulty lies in font compatibility and availability.

A typical problem area is the use of specialised mathematical characters. TEX, for example, expects to find the necessary characters in a set of mathematical fonts, and to have certain characters available in a number of different sizes. But the fonts containing the equivalent characters for the typesetter may be set up quite differently, possibly in the form of special 'mathematical superiors' fonts, and may not always be available in the desired sizes. The device driver has to cope with such problems by providing complex translation tables to pick out the correct character for the device. This could involve a number of tricky operations like changing the point size and adjusting the position of characters used as accents, subscripts and superscripts.

Sometimes a device driver is required to drive a completely unintelligent raster device. In this case the driver probably needs to create the complete page in bit-map form. While this is a tedious job, and one which involves handling large amounts of information, it can be an easier job than trying to convert between two essentially incompatible forms.

Rather than trying to describe the problems of specific device drivers in detail, this paper looks instead at the development of a new range of *page description languages* which could in the long run make device drivers almost redundant.

Page description languages and raster image processors

The rapid spread of laser printers has been responsible for an upsurge of interest in ways of controlling raster devices. Although these printers do not match the quality of typesetters, they do produce good quality documents and they have the flexibility to combine multiple character sets, graphics, and images on a page.

The printers themselves are driven by a signal corresponding to the bit-map that represents the page. This extremely low-level interface is quite unusable and is therefore supplemented by some form of intelligent controller which provides a higher level interface. The printer and controller are then seen as a single intelligent unit driven by an interface language. An interface language of this nature is often called a page description language, and the controller that implements the language for a particular device is known as a raster image processor (or RIP).

There are a number of interesting new page description languages now coming into widespread use for laser printers. These include the Xerox *Interpress Electronic Printing Standard* [5,6], the Adobe *PostScript* language [7], and the Chelgraph *ACE* language [8]. These languages are themselves device-independent, and they rely on their raster image processors to implement them on different devices. All three provide flexible facilities for handling multi-font text and complex graphics. Indeed, they represent a big step forward in the integrated handling of text and graphics.

The capabilities of these languages are impressive. They allow text to be scaled and rotated so that it can appear in any size and at any angle. Diagrams and images can be incorporated into documents, and these too can be scaled and transformed in various ways. Shapes can be defined, filled with patterns, overlaid, clipped to size, and combined.

The importance of the page description languages for device-independent typesetting is twofold. They may be used directly by the typesetting systems as their device-independent output. In this case the raster image processor that implements the language acts as the device driver. Alternatively, the device driver for a particular intermediate device-independent output format might translate into one of these page description languages. In this case the device driver can leave most of the problems to the raster image processor. This is particularly true of the graphical facilities. Problems of font compatibility will not disappear completely, but the availability of the same page description language for a variety of devices should help to cut down the number of different device drivers — and thus the number of font translations — needed.

The ACE language is based heavily on GKS [9] and uses many of the concepts found in GKS metafiles. This applies to the text handling as well as the graphics. ACE mirrors the GKS notions of *text path* and *character up vector* as well as such things as *polyline* and *polymarker*.

Interpress and POSTSCRIPT are both stack-based languages and they have much in common. In addition to a number of graphics primitives, they both provide many of the facilities associated with high level programming languages. POSTSCRIPT is the language chosen for the examples that follow in the next section. This is mainly because it is written in a readily understandable fashion using visible ASCII characters, while Interpress uses a coded form. Before leaving Interpress behind, however, it is worth noting one very important facility it provides that has no direct equivalent in POSTSCRIPT. Interpress allows font substitutions to be made (for missing or incompatible fonts) in such a way that the inevitable differences in character widths are handled as gracefully as possible. As font compatibility is one of the biggest problems in device-independent typesetting, this is particularly useful.

POSTSCRIPT

The Preface to the POSTSCRIPT Language Manual begins as follows: 'POSTSCRIPT is a simple interpretive programming language with powerful graphics primitives. The primary application of POSTSCRIPT is to describe the appearance of text, images, and graphic material on printed pages'. POSTSCRIPT does indeed provide many of the trappings of a programming language, including conditional statements, loops, and the ability to define procedures, but its main strengths lie in its flexible and high quality operations for handling text and graphics.

POSTSCRIPT maintains a current page which starts off completely white and then accumulates marks placed on it by the *imaging operators*. Marks may be characters, lines, curves, filled shapes, or images. One of the most important concepts in POSTSCRIPT is the *current path*. This defines shapes to be used by the imaging operators. When the entire page image has been built up, the **showpage** operator prints one copy of it on the attached device and clears the page to white ready to start again.

Returning to the 'Typesetting can be fun' example used previously, the POSTSCRIPT equivalent of this might be

```
144  576  moveto
(Typesetting can be fun) show
144  576  12  sub  moveto
```

The two numbers 144 and 576 are pushed onto the stack ready for the **moveto** operator which uses them as (x,y) coordinates to set a new current position. The character string 'Typesetting can be fun' is then pushed onto the stack, and the **show** operator images the characters in the string — starting at the current position and using the current font size and orientation. The **sub** operator subtracts the top item on the stack from the second item, so the final line of the example represents a move to position (144,564) ready to start the next line.

In the simple example given above, POSTSCRIPT itself is providing the word spaces. If necessary further **moveto** operators could have been used to force different spacing and to provide kerning. Special help with kerning is available in the form of the **kshow** operator (meaning **kern-show**) which makes provision for a user-defined procedure to be called between the imaging of each character in the string. This procedure can examine the preceding and following characters and adjust the spacing between them if necessary.

To give a very brief flavour of POSTSCRIPT's graphical abilities, this section finishes with an example showing how a shape can be defined as a path and then imaged in different ways. The examples are oversimplified and interested readers are referred to the POSTSCRIPT manual for further details.

The following commands define a POSTSCRIPT procedure called **box** which simply sets up a path representing the unit square.

```
/box
{ newpath
    0 0 moveto
    0 1 lineto
    1 1 lineto
    1 0 lineto
  closepath
} def
```

Using this definition a one-inch black square can be placed with its bottom left-hand corner 2 inches from the left of the page and 5 inches from the bottom of the page as follows

```
2 inch 5 inch translate
1 inch 1 inch scale
box fill
```

The **translate** and **scale** operators change the coordinate system to give the correct size and position ready for the call of **box**. The **fill** operator then fills the current path with the current grayscale colour.

A one-inch by two-inch rectangle can be placed at a different position and orientation as follows

```
3.5 inch 4 inch translate
1 inch 2 inch scale
–60 rotate
box stroke
```

In this case the scaling is different in the x and y directions, and the axes are rotated. The **stroke** operator draws a line round the current path (using the current line style).

Conclusion

The discussion above is necessarily sketchy. It does, however, attempt to pick out the essential ideas and problems of device-independent typesetting. One point that stands out is the wide variety of incompatible formats and languages used. At present a device driver is needed somewhere in the middle to reconcile all the many inconsistencies. With more careful design, and an eye to standardisation, the need for device drivers could be virtually eliminated.

Much effort has been put into the 'front-end' problems of typesetting and text formatting in the form of standard markup languages. There are encouraging signs that the corresponding 'back-end' problems are now beginning to receive the attention they deserve. Page description languages like Interpress, PostScript, and ACE are visible results of this. Their integrated approach to text, graphics, and images is long overdue.

References

1. B. W. Kernighan, 'A Typesetter-independent Troff', Computer Science Technical Report, **97**, Bell Laboratories, Murray Hill, New Jersey (1982).

2. D. E. Knuth, *The TeXbook*, Addison-Wesley (1984).

3. D. Fuchs, 'The Format of TeX's DVI Files', *TUGBOAT: the TeX users group newsletter*, **3,2**, pp 14–19 (1982).

4. D. R. S. Hedgeland and A. D. Lloyd, *Lasercomp Interface Manual: The Slave Input Program*, Monotype International (1981).

5. *Interpress Electronic Printing Standard*, XSIG 048404, Xerox Corporation, Stamford, Connecticut (1984).

6. R. F. Sproull and B. K. Reid, *Introduction to Interpress*, XSIG 038404, Xerox Corporation, El Segundo, California (1984).

7. *PostScript Language Manual*, Adobe Systems Incorporated, Palo Alto, California (1984).

8. *ACE (ASCII Coded Escapement Language) Specification*, Chelgraph Limited, Cheltenham, England (1984).

9. F. R. A. Hopgood, D. A. Duce, J. R. Gallop and D. C. Sutcliffe, *Introduction to the Graphical Kernel System (GKS)*, Academic Press (1983).

Section 5
Contouring and Surface Drawing

Contouring — the State of the Art

M.A. Sabin   Fegs Ltd.   March 1985

These notes are an expanded and updated version of a paper on Contouring of Scattered Data presented at the IMA conference on Mathematical Methods in Computer Graphics and Design, held in Leicester in 1978. [Sabin 1980] The view is taken (as in the original paper), that the contouring problem has two loosely coupled aspects. The first is deciding what surface to contour, the second how to draw the contour lines across it.

The first main section describes the kinds of data patterns which actually occur in the many applications which require contouring facilities and the traps which these data patterns provide for contouring methods. It then identifies some mathematical properties which might be desirable in interpolation methods.

The second section, which provides the bulk of the material, addresses the surface interpolation aspect. It lists the various methods which have been invented in these application communities, categorising them and noting their properties. Regular grid methods are included at the appropriate place here, as are the new methods of Natural Neighbour Interpolation and of Multivariate B-Splines.

The third describes the techniques for drawing the contours once a surface has been interpolated, together with the threading techniques which are not strictly rigorous. Short additional sections deal with the display of three-dimensional functional data and with other aspects which contouring software should address.

The notes close with a fairly full bibliography. Other surveys taking their authors' different points of view are by Crain [1970], by Rhind and Barrett [1971] and by Walters [1969]. Schumaker's survey [1976] includes an extensive bibliography focussing on the approximation theory viewpoint. Franke [1979] and Bashayan [1983] have carried out experimental comparisons of methods.

NATO ASI Series, Vol. F17
Fundamental Algorithms for Computer Graphics
Edited by R. A. Earnshaw
© Springer-Verlag Berlin Heidelberg 1985

I   PATTERNS OF DATA

There   are   almost   as many patterns of data   as   there
are applications   giving   the requirement for   its   contouring.
Land surveying,   aeromagnetic   surveys,   weather   forecasting
and   many others all give their own typical patterns.

(i)   Regular grid data

This   special case is in some ways regarded as the   ideal,
and   there   are methods which exploit the known   regularity   to
give   good   properties.   It   should be a   requirement   of   a
general   scattered   data   method that it   should   give   good
results on   regular   data.

Few do.

In   fact   there are variants of the regular   grid   methods
which   permit   their   good   properties to be   gained   on   a
rather   wider universe than   that of strictly   regular   data.
The cases   worth noting are:-

(i.i)   regular rectangular grid   (fig 1)
(i.ii)   tartan grid   (fig 2)
(i.iii)   regular triangular grid   (fig 3)

each of which has its methods, described in section II   below.

```
+ + + + + +        ++ + ++ + ++      +   +   +   +   +
                   ++ + ++ + ++
+ + + + + +                         +   +   +   +   +   +

+ + + + + +        ++ + ++ + ++       +   +   +   +   +

+ + + + + +        ++ + ++ + ++     +   +   +   +   +   +
                   ++ + ++ + ++
+ + + + + +        ++ + ++ + ++       +   +   +   +   +

+ + + + + +        ++ + ++ + ++     +   +   +   +   +   +
```

        fig 1   fig 2   fig 3

(ii) Almost regular data

This can arise in an experimental situation, where the control of the independent variables is not precise, but where they can be measured accurately. A nominally rectangular grid will then give this pattern of data, illustrated in fig 4. Each of the regular grids has its corresponding almost regular version.

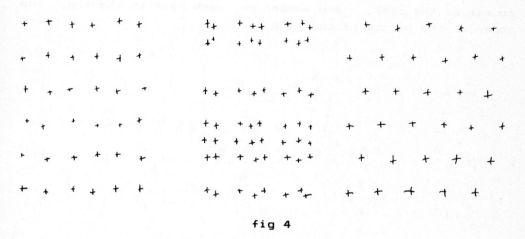

fig 4

(iii)   Even data

Here there is no pattern visible at all, the data being spread randomly, but with uniform density over the region to be contoured. Comparisons of methods against this kind of data are somewhat artificial, since it rarely occurs in practical situations.

(iv)   Data with voids

A void is a region, of diameter substantially greater than the mean distance between data points, containing no data. Voids may arise in surveying because of the physical inaccesibility of certain regions. They also arise where the surveyor can see that there is no feature of interest.   (fig 5)

(v)   Data with clusters

A cluster is a region containing a significantly higher
than average density of data points. They arise either
because it is cheaper for some reason to take a large number
of measurements in one locality,   or because there is a
local   concentration   of information needing many points to
capture its fine detail.   (fig 6).   For example, a surveyor
may survey a bank by recording pairs of points along the
course of the bank,   one member of   each pair at the top,   the
other at the bottom of the slope.

fig 5   fig 6

Clusters   and   voids   are extreme   examples   of
statistical irregularity of distribution which can occur in
less   extreme forms.   Measures of the amount of clustering
are considered by Morrison [1970] and by McCullagh and Sampson
[1972]

(vi)   Tracked data

A   particular kind of cluster is the linear   cluster
or 'track' which occurs when measuring equipment is being
moved,   and can cheaply take many readings along its path.
Obvious   examples are   echo-sounding marine surveys   and
airborne gravimetric and magnetic anomaly surveys.   (Swindle
and van Andel [1979] and Wren [1975]).   Laser scanning of
objects also gives this kind of representation.

Again, there are variants giving more or less difficulty to the interpolation process:-

(vii.i)   'Clean' tracks

Like even data, this pattern does not actually occur too often in practice unless the perturbations actually there remain unmeasured.

(vii.ii)   'Ragged' tracks

Much more typical is the situation where the data points lie in a fairly narrow band lying either side of the nominal track (fig 7). This causes particular problems in that lateral first derivatives cannot easily be distinguished from longitudinal second derivatives. (Ewen-Smith [1971])

(vii.iii)   Contour Input

One situation giving rise to ragged tracks occurs when the data actually lies along contours. Photogrammetric machines often give this kind of input, or contours may be digitised from existing maps in order to feed calculations such as cut and fill or visibility assessment.

Contours are typically ragged tracks, but with the known property that the first derivative across a given track has constant sign. Boots [1974], Christiansen and Sederberg [1978] and Ganapathy and Dennehy [1982] have addressed this case. Their work includes the full three-dimensional case where the 'contours' are cross sections of a solid object.

(vii.iv)   Crossing tracks

Just about the worst data pattern to handle is that where tracks cross (fig 8). Interpolation along the two tracks independently may give inconsistent values at the crossing point, implying spurious high slopes. This is a real challenge, since there are theoretical reasons for believing that this pattern gives more information per data point about the underlying surface than, for example, even data or even a regular grid. [Gordon 1971]

fig 7   fig 8

Spatial frequency and feature wavelength.

Most of these patterns have data spacings which vary very significantly either with position in the plane or with direction. A useful concept, derived from information theory, is that of the 'wavelength' of a feature.

Wavelengths longer than twice the distance between data points are justified by the data and may be regarded as telling the truth about the underlying surface provided that the data is sampled from a surface not containing any higher frequencies. This condition will be satisfied in the case where a human surveyor is taking readings where he sees that they are needed. It will not where physical inaccessibility is the reason for voids.

Shorter wavelengths are not justified by the data, but must be regarded as artifacts of the interpolation method, even when there are known to be short wavelength features in the underlying surface. Whenever such short wavelength features are known to be present (though not sampled adequately densely), it is to be expected that artifacts will appear due to aliasing.

Other Properties of interpolation methods

Four mathematical concepts are useful for classifying interpolation methods:-

(i)　　　Invariance

Under what transformations does the interpolated surface remain the same shape ?

(ii)　　　Continuity

Is there any circumstance in which a small change of some aspect of the data causes a big change in the resulting surface ?

(iii)　　　Linearity

Does a given change in the data always have the same effect on the surface ?

(iv)　　　Precision

If the data points all lie on a low order surface, does the interpolant return that surface ?

(i)　　　Invariance

If we restrict ourselves to the context where the abscissae (x and y) are regarded as different in kind from the ordinate (z), the interpolation problem can be regarded as a mapping function from the cartesian product of

　　a)　　the data point abscissae
　　b)　　the data point ordinates
and　　c)　　the interpolation point abscissa
　　　　　　　　(the 'probe position')

to the interpolation point ordinate (the 'probe value').

The invariance here is essentially that associated with the transformation commuting with the interpolation process. The interpolation is invariant under some transformation if applying the transform to the data points and probe abscissae and then interpolating gives exactly the same result as interpolating first and then applying the transformation to the probe abscissae and ordinates.

Unless there is a good reason to the contrary (such as the data lying on or near a regular grid), we should not expect the surface to be dependent on the orientation of the data with respect to a coordinate system. We expect invariance with respect to rotations and scaling of the abscissae. (In the three dimensional case, where abscissae and ordinates are not different in kind, the interpolated surface should be independent of rotation in three dimensions.)

It is a moot point whether we should also expect invariance under affine transformations (shears and non-isotropic scaling).

Scaling of the ordinates should also leave the interpolated shape invariant, since it should not matter whether our heights are measured in inches or miles.

Another arguably desirable property is that the addition of an extra point to the set of data points, with the value obtained by interpolation there, should not alter the interpolated surface. This argument stems from the surface design community, who regard it as important to be able to increase the local control of shape without losing whatever has been achieved at the coarser grain, but it is very plausible that having the method's guess confirmed as to the value at one point should not alter its predictions elsewhere. This is related to the concept of idempotence.

(ii)   Continuity

There are three questions of continuity, one related to
each of the three factors of the input to the interpolation.

a)   Continuity with respect to interpolation point abscissa

This is the easiest to grasp, as it is this kind of
discontinuity which may cause kinks in the contours.   There is
some debate as to whether this kind of continuity is necessary,
and,   if so,   of how many derivatives ?   If there are
discontinuities, where do they occur, and of what derivative ?
It is possible for discontinuities to occur across curves in
the surface, and also at isolated points.

It can reasonably be argued that there are circumstances
in which the interpolation of a discontinuous surface may be
quite acceptable.   However, this is a question which should
always be asked, as even small discontinuities can give extreme
effects on the contours in parts of the surface which are
almost flat.   If the interpolation is to be used for numerical
differentiation as well as evaluation,   unexpected small
discontinuities may be most undesirable.

Further, consideration of just where the discontinuities
appear leads to understanding of the actual behaviour of the
methods.

b)   Continuity with respect to data point ordinate

This is clearly desirable, since if it does not hold, it
is possible for rounding errors in the data to cause relatively
large changes in the interpolated surface.   Since two
alternative interpolations with a relatively large difference
cannot both be close to best, it can safely be argued that a
method without this kind of continuity is dangerous. Note that
the typical example plots at the ends of papers describing new
contouring methods cannot show the presence of this property.

c)   Continuity with respect to data point abscissae

By a like argument this property should be regarded as
essential. It is now amazing to my mind that this was not
pointed out until the early 1980's [Sibson 1981] .   The whole
of the contouring community including myself had missed it for
twenty years because we had only looked at one plot at a time.

Unfortunately, many good methods fail this test.

(iii)   Linearity

Linear variation of result with interpolation abscissa
would mean that we could only interpolate planes, and linear
variation with respect to data point abscissae would give even
stranger behaviours.

The important aspect of linearity is that the resulting
ordinate should vary linearly with data ordinates, because this
is a property which opens the door to some sharp analytic tools
for probing the behaviour of a method over a wide class of
problems.

Note that linearity implies continuity, and so a method
linear in this sense does not need to be checked even cursorily
for continuity with respect to the data ordinates.

(iv)   Precision

It is essential that, given data which actually lie in a
plane, an interpolation method should return only points lying
in that plane. It is desirable that if the given data lie in a
quadratic surface, all interpolated points should too.

Note that it is always possible to achieve a required
precision set by first fitting a best fit surface of the
required precision (a 'trend surface') to the data, then
applying the interpolation to he residuals and finally adding
the interpolant to the trend surface.

II   INTERPOLATION METHODS

So many methods have been devised for this kind of interpolation that some classification is necessary to make any sense of them.   This section introduces such a classification, together with criteria by which methods can be compared and the performance of new methods predicted.

This classification is depicted in fig 9, and appears as a full variant tree in Appendix 1.

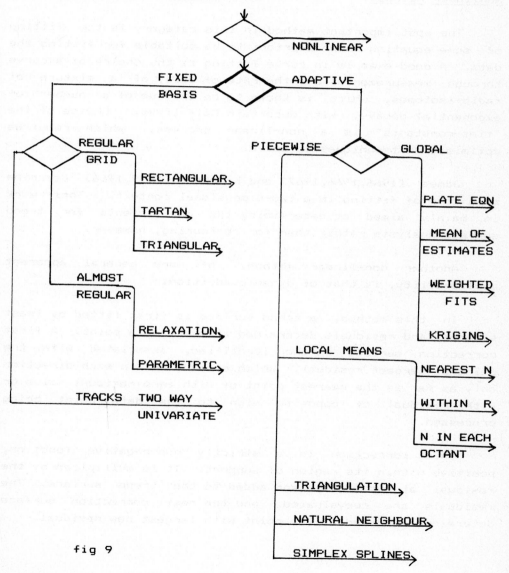

fig 9

The first classification property, linearity in the ordinates, was described in the previous section. It may not be obvious why it is chosen as the root property. The reason is that almost all methods are linear in this sense, and that separating those which are not linear allows us to use some fairly powerful mathematical concepts in classifying the rest.

Nonlinear Methods

The most important method in this category is the fitting of some equation known a-priori to be suitable for fitting the data. A good example in curve fitting is the choice of a curve through measurements of the rate of decay of a mixture of radio-isotopes, which is known to be the sum of a number of exponential decays, with uncertain half-lives. Choice of the 'time-constants' is a non-linear process, which requires optimisation techniques to solve.

James [1966,1966,1967] and Krumbein [1959,1966] describe this kind of fitting in a two-dimensional context. Their work is mainly aimed at determining the coefficients for trend surface analysis rather than for contouring, however.

Another non-linear method, of more general apparent applicability, is that of dynamic addition:-

In this method, a trend surface is first fitted by least squares, and residuals determined at every data point. A first correction surface is then identified, associated with the point of largest residual, which spreads out in each direction only as far as the nearest point of with zero residual value or with residual of opposite sign to the data point being processed.

This correction is a strictly non-negative function, positive within its region of support. It is multiplied by the residual at its focus, and added to the trend surface. The residuals are reevaluated, and the next correction surface determined focussed at the point with largest new residual.

Since at least one data point has its residual reduced to zero at each step, and no residual is ever increased in absolute value by a correction surface, the method converges to a surface interpolating all the data points.

Since the region of support of each correction function depends on the sequence in which the data points have their residuals cancelled, which in turn depends on the data ordinates, this method is non-linear in the ordinates. It is not difficulat to show that it is also discontinuous in the ordinates.

If the correction surfaces have zero slope at the edges of their region of support the resultant surface will be slope continuous in the probe abscissae.

The shortest wavelengths appearing in the surface appear from the final few correction surfaces which have very small regions of support. This wavelength is one cycle per data point spacing, half the minimum desirable, but it must be noted that since the correction surface amplitudes reduce monotonically with the correction sequence, it is likely that the amplitudes of these components will be small.

A better version requiring a little more computation uses at each stage a surface bounding all the data from one side. The initial fit is chosen to be the best fit of a simple surface subject to the value at each data point not exceeding the data value itself. The amplitude of each correction is chosen to be the greatest possible which maintains this property.

This is better because in both methods once a data point is matched, the tangent plane of the surface will not be altered there. In the second method the limits of the correction surfaces are more likely to be extrema where the slope should not alter: in the first they are crossing points where the slope is likely to need adjustment.

The amplitudes of the short wavelength components will therefore be smaller for the second method.

Linear Methods

Since the process of looking at the data to choose which method to apply is essentially non-linear, I suspect that it is always possible to find a non-linear method which will outperform any given linear one on a given set of data and with a given criterion of goodness. However, the difficulty of enumerating enough such methods to find a good one means that for general purpose work the linear techniques are the state of the art.

The important property of linearity which we shall use in further classification is that the surface can be represented by the equation

$$z = \sum_i a_i f_i(x,y)$$

where only the a_i depend on the data ordinates.

The f_i are termed <u>basis functions</u>, the a_i the <u>coefficients</u> and the possible surfaces which can be fitted form a <u>vector_space</u> <u>spanned</u> by the basis functions.

The same vector space is spanned by other linear combinations of the basis functions, and in general there is a basis which has the property that at each data point one of the basis functions takes the value 1, and the rest the value 0. These combinations are usually called the <u>cardinal_basis</u>, and denoted by $g_j(x,y)$

Now

$$z(x,y) = \sum_j z_j g_j(x,y)$$

$$= \sum_i a_i f_i(x,y)$$

Since

$$z_j = \sum_i a_i f_i(x_j, y_j)$$

we have

$$a_i = \sum_j z_j [f_i(x_j, y_j)]^{-1}$$

and so

$$g_j(x,y) = \sum_i [f_i(x_j, y_j)]^{-1} f_i(x,y)$$

These cardinal basis functions always exist, though they are seldom evaluated. They are important because they define the sensitivity of the surface to perturbations of the data values.

If $\sum_j g_j^2(x,y)$ is large, the surface will be very sensitive to uncorrelated noise on the data (experimental or quantisation errors), and is likely to show random artifacts.

If $\max_{x,y}(\sum_j |g_j(x,y)|)$ is large, the surface will have sensivity to some worst case combination of errors on the data.

Where high order polynomials are being used, orthogonal polynomials are recommended. There are a number of orthogonal bases for a vector space, and their use avoids some numerical problems. However, each vector space has only one cardinal basis, and so orthogonal bases do not avoid the problems which are inherent in the vector space.

For interpolation there must be as many basis functions in the set as there are data points: for approximation there may be fewer.

The next stage in the classification depends on whether the vector space chosen depends on the abscissae of the data points. By linearity it cannot depend on their ordinates. Procedures in which the abscissae control the vector space are termed <u>adaptive</u>, those in which the vector space is chosen a priori are termed <u>non-adaptive</u>.

Two non-adaptive methods which have been tried for scattered data have involved the fit of global high order polynomial or Fourier series solutions to all of the data. By and large, polynomials do not work, and Fourier solutions, although ideal in the case where there are no significant components present at spatial frequencies approaching the data spacing, are little better.

This poor behaviour may be expected for interpolation because the expression for g(x,y) above involves the inverse of the matrix

$$[f_i(x_j,y_j)]$$

The determinant of this matrix can be changed in sign by interchanging two of the data points by paths which nowhere become geometrically singular. Alternatively, we may see that the determinant, viewed as a function of the position of one of the data points, has a zero locus which passes through all of the other data points and is therefore fairly dense.

There are thus many configurations of the data points which give a close to singular matrix and thence poor cardinal functions.

Non-adaptive techniques are therefore appropriate only for specific data patterns, for which they are known to be non-singular.

There is an analogous analysis for approximation which evaluates the influence of each data value on the surface. Again, non-adaptive methods give surfaces which are much more sensitive to noise than need be. It is quite easy to produce examples of least squares fitting with low order interpolants, where small amounts of noise on the data can give larger errors in the fitted surface.

Pattern-Specific Methods

The regular grid methods are the obvious example, though any known pattern could have a good set of basis functions worked out for it once and for all.

Regular grids

The regular rectangular grid can be fitted by a wide variety of methods. The simplest uses bilinear functions to fill each grid square, but this leaves slightly more complication at the contouring stage, and so the variant with four triangles in each grid square, each edge being joined by a triangular (plane) facet to the centroid (fig 10), is typically preferred.

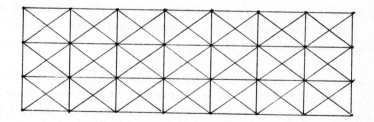

fig 10

This is only position continuous, of course, and higher order tensor product splines are sometimes used to give better continuity.

Advantage in the contouring can be gained by replacing the quadratic tensor product with basis functions defined on a tesselation reminiscent of the four triangles per cell method mentioned above.

Such methods are described by Powell [1974] and by Sibson and Thompson [1981]. Chui and Wang [1983] and Sablonniere [1982] relate these ideas to multivariate B-spline theory.

All of these methods typically give the ideal half-wavelength per data spacing in the main axis directions, with possibly one wavelength per data spacing diagonally if sufficiently pathological data is provided.

Regular triangular grids can be fitted by plane facets in the cells, or by higher order surfaces to give higher order continuity. C1 continuity can be given by single quintic pieces, or by dividing each cell into three cubic pieces (the Clough Tocher element) or six quadratic pieces [Powell and Sabin 1977].

In these C1 cases it is necessary to estimate the tangent plane at each data point. This can be avoided by the use of triangular B-splines, first described by Frederickson [1970,1971], and also recorded by Sablonniere [1982] and Sabin [1978]. These require the solution of a set of as many simultaneous equations as there are data points, but give surfaces of arbitrarily high continuity. The first of these is in fact the plane facetting, the second has cubic pieces, giving slope continuity.

An alternative, which gives quadratic pieces and slope continuity, requiring fewer pieces than the Powell-Sabin formulation, uses a conjugate tesselation, whic is also triangular, oriented at right angles to thd data point grid, and positioned so that the original data points lie one third of the way along the edges of this tesselation. (fig 11)

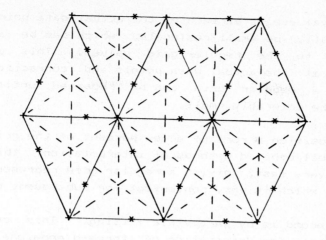

fig 11

Division of these triangles into six, Powell-Sabin style, gives a splinelike surface which has only four pieces of surface per data point, compared with twelve for the original Powell-Sabin version and six for the cubic Clough-Tocher element.

It is a source of some annoyance that similar piece-efficiencies are not possible on a lattice with rectangular symmetries.

Almost Regular Data

There are two ways in which the regular grid methods can be applied to almost regular data.

The first is by relaxation. Clearly each actual data point is near its regular counterpart, and so the surface value at the regular point will not be very different from the actual data value. Ignore the position errors, and fit a regular grid surface.

Then evaluate it at each of the actual data points. There will typioally be small residuals, which can be applied as corrections to the regular grid values. This process of evaluation at the actual data points and correction of the values on a regular grid can be repeated until all the residuals are tolerably small.

For position errors of a few percent of the grid spacing, and with well behaved methods of interpolation, this process converges very fast, giving a regular grid representation of the surface which is very convenient for subsequent contouring.

The second is by parametric fitting. This concept was first devised for description of three-dimensional surfaces [Ferguson 1964], but is a valuable tool here also. The idea is simply that the abscissae are handled in the same way as the ordinates and a regular grid method applied to all three. The contours are 'pushed sideways' to match the actual positions of the data points.

The amount of computation is trebled, because for each contour point evaluated during tracing, the abscissae need to be computed as well as the ordinate, and there is some complication of the actual contouring process where marching methods with step length control are being used.

However, this method is very powerful. It can handle position errors much larger than the relaxation approach, and also regular coordinate transformations. Approximate polar coordinates (as long as the pole itself is not included) can be handled with exactly the same code as approximate cartesians. All translations, rotations, scaling (and indeed affine transformations) can be carried out by the parametrisation [Hessing et al 1972].

Two-way Univariate Interpolation

For tracked data where the tracks are running more or less parallel, a fairly obvious technique is to interpolate along the tracks to give fully defined track curves, then to interpolate across them to fill in the surface in between [Done 1965].

Sometimes this will work well, but there are two sources of misbehaviour which should be checked for before it is definitely chosen:-

(i)   Raggedness on the tracks will cause problems if the lateral derivatives are at all large, as it will cause the interpolated curves to wiggle.

(ii)   Unless there is a definite theoretical reason to choose a specific direction for the transverse interpolation, it is difficult to make a good choice.   The symptom of a bad choice is that a feature in the underlying surface which actually runs at an angle to the transverse interpolation direction will not appear as an angled feature, but as a series of features aligned with the transverse interpolation, growing and shrinking to match the places where it crosses the tracks. This gives the effect of steps appearing in a bank, for example. (fig 12)

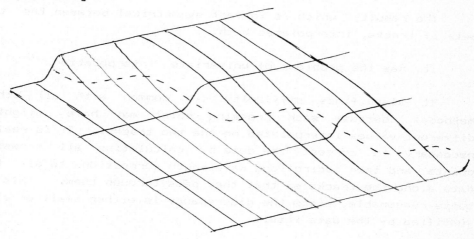

fig 12

Tracked data is probably better handled by a triangulation method which takes account of the track structure [Fuchs et al 1977],[Gannapathy and Dennehy 1982]. (and see below)

Blending

Crossing tracks are difficult for all methods, but a method which appears appropriate is that of blending. This may best be described as two simultaneous two-way Univariate interpolations.

The construction may be visualised as:-

(i)   Carry out a two way univariate interpolation for one set of tracks, using the direction of the other as the transverse interpolation direction.

(ii)   This will interpolate one set of tracks exactly, but leave a residual along the other set. Carry out a two way univariate interpolation through these residuals, and add this correction to the original.

The result, which is in fact symmetrical between the two sets of tracks, interpolates both.

It has the problems of univariate interpolation.

It also finds difficulty (in common with all other methods) because each crossing point may have slightly different values interpolated on the two tracks. It is really necessary to correct the data by calculating all crossing points and then adding long wavelength corrections to all the data along the tracks so that they pass through them. This is quite reasonable, since the discrepancy is either small or else justified by the data itself.

However, triangulation also has problems with crossing tracks and so it is not quite such a strong contender. Further, Gordon [1971] maintains that blending extracts more data about the surface per sample point than, for example, a regular grid, and it may be regarded as optimal when there are no extremely short wavelengths present.

Adaptive Methods

These methods are in principle applicable to any distributions of data, though some may hit specific difficulties, which will be noted. The methods are listed in two groups, those which are continuous in all derivatives everywhere except possibly at the data points, and those which have discontinuities of some derivative across boundaries within the abscissa plane.

Continuous Methods

Plate Equation

An analogue of the spline curve is the surface which minimises the bending energy subject to passing through all the data points. this leads to a set of basis functions of the form

$$f_i(x,y) = r_i^2 \log r_i^2 \quad \text{where} \quad r_i^2 = (x-x_i)^2 + (y-y_i)^2$$

together with three other functions, 1 x and y.

The coefficients are calculated by solving the interpolation conditions together with the auxiliary equations

$$\sum_i a_i = \sum_i a_i x_i = \sum_i a_i y_i = 0$$

This is described by Harder and Desmarais [1972] and analysed in deep mathematical terms by Meinguet [1979]. A variant which is slightly faster and has marginally better extrapolation behaviour uses the functions

$$f_i(x,y) = r_i^3$$

Other equations can be derived by minimizing other integrals over the surface. They will all have basis functions which are radially symmetric about the data points, and they will all have singularities of some derivative at the data points.

Determination of the coefficients of these forms requires solution of a large linear system. Briggs [1974] uses a relaxation technique to evaluate the interpolant on a regular grid prior to using a regular grid interpolant in a two-stage process.

Weighted Means

All linear methods are in some sense weighted means since the cardinal functions are effectively weights applied to the ordinates at the data points to give the interpolated value.

However, some methods explicitly use this concept, being based on the idea that the mean of data ordinates weighted inversely with distance of each data point from the probe must give a surface interpolating the data.

Unfortunately this simple concept gives a method with the disadvantage that the immediate neighbourhood of each data point is conical (with discontinuity of slope at the data points) if linear weighting is used, and horizontal if quadratic or higher weighting is used. It is also impossible for the surface to have a maximum higher than any of the data points. Indeed, if two data points lie just on either side of a hill top, the method puts a dip between them.

There are, however, two reasonably successful variants, which overcome these disadvantages:-

(i)   Mean of Estimates

Here the mean is taken, not of the data ordinates themselves, but of estimates based on ordinates and derivatives at the data points. It may also be regarded as applying correction terms based on the derivatives. These derivatives are typically calculated by using a least squares fit of a low order polynomial to the points around each data point.

The correction terms may either use that polynomial itself to give the estimates or may use carefully designed functions which cannot give estimates far outside the actual range of the data ordinates.

Methods of this kind are described by Connelly [1971], Hardy [1971] and Shepard [1968] with whose name these methods are usually associated. Recently it has been reported [Stead 1984] that Hardy's 'Multiquadrics' perform rather better, especially when a negative exponent is used, than Shepards method. Franke [1982] suggests the use of the plate equation to give the local estimates

(ii)   Local Fit

The weighted mean of ordinates can be regarded as a weighted least squares fit of a constant function to the data points. This can be generalised by fitting at each interpolation point, a higher order expression. The value of that expression at the interpolation point then gives the value of the interpolant at that point only. Any other point has different weights and therefore a different expression. Typically the fit of a quadratic with inverse quadratic weighting gives reasonable results. [Falconer 1971], [Lodwick and Whittle 1970], [McLain 1974], [Palmer 1969] and [Pelto et al 1968] report this method.

The basis functions for both variants are very high order rational polynomials with positive definite denominators. The order of the second variant is the lower, and one would therefore predict that the surface would be less prone to have short wavelength ripples, but there is no experimental evidence for this conjecture.

Kriging

This is based on the theory of random variables. It uses the relationships between the ordinates of the data to determine the statistical properties of the surface, and then gives a mean and a variance for the ordinate of each interpolated point. A contour map of height uncertainty is therefore available as well as that of height.

Because the theory is based on the surface being statistically stationary, it may be inappropriate for surface survey, where short wavelength features locally are marked by increased density of data. It may also give very pessimistic estimates of accuracy in the voids between tracks.

It is described by Matheron [1970] and by Olea [1974]. Akima [1975] raises some critical questions. Schagen [1979,1982] describes another statistically based method, and there is a paper [Dowd 1985] being presented in this study institute focussing specifically on this kind of method.

Piecewise Methods

The plate equation and weighted mean methods above are expensive for large sets of data. For n data points the plate equation solution requires n-squared logarithms and a matrix inversion costing n-cubed operations. For each interpolated point a further n logarithms need to be evaluated. The mean of estimates requires an initial setup of order n-squared, followed by a cost of order n per interpolation. The local fit avoids the setup cost, but takes roughly twice as many operations per interpolation point.

Various attempts have been made to reduce these costs by ignoring all those points which can be predicted to have very small weights (i.e. most of the data for large n) and therefore to have little influence of the final value interpolated. This idea is applicable to both variants of the weighted mean method.

Each attempt has in fact reduced the cost, but has introduced problems with certain kinds of data. This is because of a fundamental change which is made as soon as certain of the data points are ignored when interpolating in part of the abscissa plane.

Consider the surface which is fitted when all the ordinates except one are zero. This surface is in fact the corresponding cardinal basis function $g(x,y)$. If there is a part of the abscissa plane where that point is ignored, the $g(x,y)$ must be identically zero there. As there is presumably a region where $g(x,y)$ is non-zero, there must be a boundary between th two, and across this boundary there is a discontinuity of at least some derivative. The basis functions are no longer analytic, and may have piecewise equations. The non-zero region is termed the region of influence and its boundary the planform of the basis function.

The selection of which data points are to be taken into account for any given interpolation point may be made in a number of ways.

Simplest is to use the nearest m where m is typically about 20 for fitting a quadratic. A surface of the desired continuity may be fitted by using weighting functions which become zero at the distance of the farthest point and with enough zero derivatives there.

Then $(d^2 - r^2)/r^2$ will give value continuity, $((d^2 - r^2)/r^2)^2$ position and slope continuity etc.

This is satisfactory for even data, but gives bad results when voids are present because planforms congregate in the middle of the void, causing rapid changes of influences there. The effect is particularly bad with tracked data.

Not to be recommended at all is the use of all points within a fixed distance. Although the simplest method to code, the distance will be wrong in some part of the interpolation region for all except even data.

The problem of clustering of planforms can be avoided by taking the nearest m/8 points in each octant from the interpolation point. This, however, introduces discontinuities of position which cannot be avoided by tuning of the weighting functions.

The latest version of this approach uses the Voronoi neighbours: this will be described below after the explicitly piecewise interpolations.

Triangulation

Once the step to a piecewise surface has been made, an obvious possibility is that of explicitly dividing the abscissa plane into regions along some deliberately chosen boundaries, and fitting some equation into those regions with known continuity across all boundaries. Triangles are the most convenient such regions.

In early version of this method the triangulation had to be imposed manually [Bengtsson and Nordbeck 1964], [Heap 1972], but it may be calculated automatically by applying some optimality criterion. There are many possible criteria, but almost all of the plausible ones turn out [Lawson 1977] to give the Delaunay triangulation. [Rhynsburger 1973] This is most simply defined by the Voronoi tesselation:-

Round each data point construct the region which is closer to that data point than to any other. Join each data point to those others with which its region has a common frontier (fig 13).

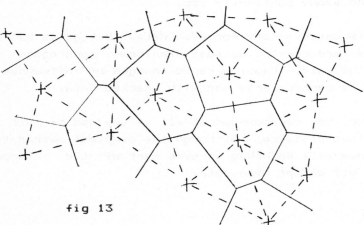

fig 13

An important property used in the algorithm of Green and Sibson [1978] is that the interior of the circumcircle of each triangle contains no other data point.

When contours are being used as data (and probably other examples of tracked data) it is best to avoid the possibility of a triangle having three vertices on the same track. This can be done easily by working along each inter-contour stripe, using the circumcircle property to decide which of the tracks to take the next point from, but always maintaining at least one vertex on each track. (fig 14)

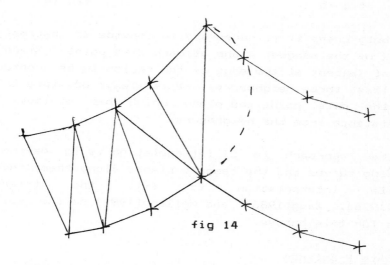

fig 14

What surface equation inside each triangle ?

Just as in the regular triangular grid case, the first obvious possibility is to fill each triangle with a plane triangular facet. This gives an extremely cheap to run algorithm, ideal for taking a first look at data.

If a smoother fit is required, each triangle may be filled by some higher order surface. The Clough Tocher element is fairly well known which uses three cubic pieces meeting at the centroid to fill each facet, giving continuity of value and first derivative. (fig 15) The Powell Sabin element of six quadratic pieces (fig 16) has the advantage that the pieces of contour have a parametric form, and are thus more easily generated. Farin [1982,1983] discusses some alternatives.

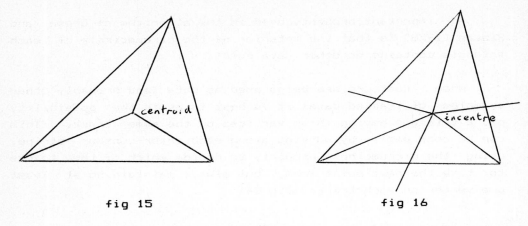

fig 15   fig 16

In both cases it is necessary to provide an estimate of the slopes of the tangent plane at each data point. Since each data point (except at the edge of the region to be contoured) has at least three neighbours, it is always possible to fit through the data point the plane which has minimum least squares distance from the neighbours.

Another approach to C1 interpolation is to define the partitioning curves and the tangent planes along them; then use transfinite interpolation to fill the triangles. Barnhill[1976], Wang[1983] and Neilson[1983] define suitable traingles for this purpse.

Multivariate B-Splines

In the regular triangular grid case it is possible to reduce the number of pieces necessary for a slope-continuous fit to four per data point. This is a special case of Multivariate Spline interpolation [de Boor 1976], but as yet the theory for this is not sufficiently developed to provide a recipe for the irregular case.

When it is developed the method will choose groups of five knot points, one group per data point, and fit basis functions given by the shadow on the abscissa plane of the four dimensional simplex joining the knots. This shadow is a piecewise quadratic.

Knots will be shared between the groups of different data points, so that the simplices fill a four dimensional region which is the outer product of the region of interpolation and a fixed triangle.

What we do not yet know for the general case is how to position the knots and to partition them into groups.

Natural Neighbour Interpolation

It is fairly easy to show that any method based on filling the facets of a triangulation cannot be continuous in the data abscissae. A recent proposal going beyond the simple facetting of the triangulation uses the topology of the triangulation to define neighbourhoodness [Sibson 1981].

The data points neighbouring a probe point are those to which it would be joined if it were added to the data set, and the closeness of that relationship depends on the contribution which each neighbour's Thiessen region makes to that of the new point. By definition this gives a set of weights which is used to give a weighted mean of estimates based on the surface local to those neighbours.

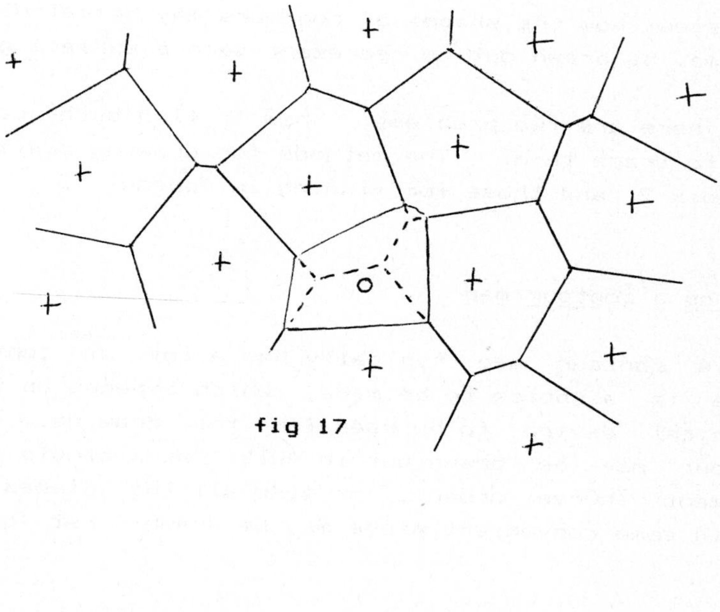

fig 17

This method is local, and invariant under rotation, translation and scaling of the data. It has the nice property of being continuous in the data point abscissae as well as potentially in the probe position, and it sounds plausible that it may have the idempotence property if good rules are used for estimating derivatives at the data points (though I have not checked this). To maintain both locality and continuity in the data abscissae requires care in slope estimation, as this process can easily violate one or the other.

The problem of running the interpolation along features mentioned above under two-way unvariate interpolation is still a problem with all these adaptive methods. It is a good example of the need for either a non-linear method which can look at the ordinates to detect the feature, or else manual intervention to select a suitable affine transformation for the abscissa plane.

III   DRAWING IT OUT

Previous sections have identified possible surfaces with which to interpolate between points of known data. This section addresses how the shapes of contours may be calculated so that they may be drawn out to represent such a surface graphically.

There are two problems, how to find such contours, and how to trace them. The methods for drawing are summarised in Appendix 2, and those for finding in Appendix 3.

Drawing a contour map

A contour map typically has a lot of contour curves. There is a choice to be made, which depends on the kind of graphical device to be used for the drawing. Either each contour may be drawn out in full, as a single flowing pen movement (curve order), or else all the pieces of contour within some convenient piece may be drawn first (grid order).

CRT displays nowadays are very tolerant, and will perform reasonably well with either strategy. Moving-pen plotters take time to move in air, and may misbehave in terms of the ink drying in the pen or by the line showing intensification at the beginning of a piece of curve where the ink has been loosened by the vertical pen motion. Raster plotters require much less store for storage of the image if it is created in stripes.

In fact there are three possible strategies, since it would be possible in some cases to draw each contour in grid order, independently of the others. I see no circumstances in which this would be advantageous except that if a sufficiently large computer is available, it may be a good strategy to compute the contour pieces in grid order, linking the pieces together in a data structure as they are determined, spooling the complete curves to the plotter when all pieces have been linked together.

Drawing a contour

We distinguish two classes of surface:-

(i) those which are easy to contour by algorithmic construction of pieces of contour curve of significant length.

and (ii) those which rely on construction of the contour point by point, with the points closely enough spaced to be joined by straight lines.

Easy Surfaces

In the first category come the simpler regular grid methods, and some of the scattered data methods based on triangulation, namely those whose surfaces consist of triangular pieces with linear or quadratic equation.

The linear triangle is trivial to contour: just join the points in which the contour level cuts the edges of the triangle, which may be found by linear interpolation. There is no finding problem in this case, as comparison of the triangle vertex values with the contour level identifies all pieces of contour.

The quadratic triangle has the property that its contours are conic section curves, which have a parametric form whose coefficients may be determined from those of the triangle. Once these coefficients have been determined, the contour may be traced out by substituting successive values of the parameter into the parametric equation to give successive points.

The first stage of this needs rather more complex code than the linear triangle, as it is possible for the contour level to be tangent to the surface at a saddle point, giving a contour consisting of two straight lines, crossing if the saddle point is within the triangle. (fig 18) This case should be considered and tested for. Where the contour level is close to a saddle point the contour equation may be close to singular.

It is also possible for the contour across the piece of surface to consist of up to three pieces of curve (fig 19). Depending on whether curve order or grid order tracing is being used to generate the entire map, this may be more or less of an embarrassment. If all contours across a single triangle are being determined at once it is not too difficult to draw all pieces of each one.

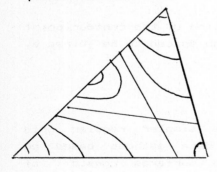
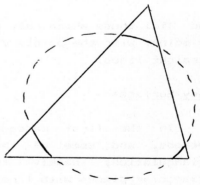

fig 18   fig 19

The routine published in [Marlow and Powell 1976] is a reliable one for drawing quadratic triangles, and I recommend it for this purpose.

Not-so-easy surfaces

There are a number of approaches which may be used. Six useful ones are:-

> Raster shading
> Two stage contouring
> Threading
> Progressive approximation
> Marching
> Recursive subdivision

Raster shading

One of the simplest ways to create a contour map (in terms of code, if not of computing time) is to evaluate the interpolant at every pixel of the screen area, and choose an appropriate colour depending on the value at that point.

This has been used since the earliest days of contouring, when 'line printer plots' (or even teleprinter plots) were a way of getting some kind of graphical representation. In this case different characters were used instead of different colours, but the principle was the same.

This is mentioned in [Schumaker 1976] but is much, much older.

An improvement worth considering is to sample the value not at the centre of each pixel, but where two consecutive scan lines pass from one pixel to the next. When the four samples are in the same range the pixel between can be painted with the colour for that range. When they are in different ranges, their values can be used to determine an intermediate colour which will give an anti-aliasing effect.

The interpolation methods which give polynomial pieces (of any order) lend themselves to this display mode, since the values at successive pixels along a scan line within a piece may be evaluated relatively quickly using differences instead of repeating the entire evaluation.

Two stage contouring

A favourite method for driving plotters has been to evaluate the interpolant on a regular grid, and then use a regular grid method to create the contours themselves. There is a major choice here, whether to use a fine grid with a simple regular interpolant or a coarse one with a more complex interpolant.

Obviously it will be cheaper with some of the more expensive interpolations to evaluate the scattered data interpolant at as few points as possible, but this runs the risk of the second interpolation not honouring the original data. Contours may pass on the wrong side of data points even though the fit is nominally an interpolation, not an approximation.

The wavelength concept suggests that a regular grid of spacing no more than the minimum original data spacing, with a linear or quadratic fit at the highest is probably the safest version of this approach. I do not really recommend it unless there are specific reasons (such as the provision of a full suite of contouring software in minimum programming time).

Threading

This is another dangerous shortcut. The principle is that instead of interpolating a complete surface, a network of curves joining the data points is constructed. The points where these curves cut the contour levels are computed, and smooth curves are then threaded through the points so found. [Haverlik and Kchro 1973]

Quite often the curves joining the data points are just straight lines. If high order curves such as cubic splines are then threaded, the first impression of the contour map may be thoroughly misleading. It appears smooth, but the surface implied by the map will have cone-vertex-like singularities of slope at all the data points.

A less subtle problem is that there is no guarantee that contours (independently interpolated) will not cross, giving a most visible and undesirable effect.

Cheap and Nasty, and I do not recommend it, though it does have the advantage over some better methods of being provably robust. It will always generate complete curves, though it will possibly miss loops not cutting the network of links.

Progressive approximation

There is, however, a variant of threading which is quite respectable and reliable. This uses a full surface interpolation to control it, but may succeed in evaluating that surface fairly seldom.

Like threading, this method starts by calculating the points where the contour level cuts a network of curves, either the edges of the pieces from which the interpolant is built, or links on the surface joining the data points.

If surface derivatives are not available, these points are linked by straight lines, and the interpolant is evaluated at the midpoint of each such link. If the value is in fact within tolerance of the contour level, the link is accepted and drawn. If it is not within tolerance, a search is made perpendicular to the link to find a contour level point.

The distance of this point from the original link gives an indication of how many straight line pieces will be needed to draw a visually smooth contour, a local parabola is defined through the three known points of the curve, and used as a base for estimating further contour points. These are in turn evaluated and corrected until they lie on the true contour.

If surface derivatives are available, it is possible to bypass the first trial at the midpoint, by setting up a cubic with the correct directions at both ends as a first approximation instead of the parabola.

Provided that the check is made that the parabola or cubic stays inside the piece of surface to which it is supposed to refer, this method should be as robust as threading, and although slower will give far better results.

Its main disadvantage is that loops entirely within one piece of surface are not detected. Extra links need to be added to the network to ensure that it includes all extrema of the surface.

Marching

One of the fastest methods is based on the idea of evaluating as few points as possible, which must therefore be close to the contour. There are two major variants of this idea, depending on whether it is possible to evaluate derivatives of the surface cheaply.

If derivatives are available, it works like this:-

Suppose the point has been found where a contour crosses the boundary of the region to be contoured. The tangent plane to the surface at this point is evaluated and is intersected with the contour level to give the direction of the contour. A step is made in this direction, and the value and derivatives evaluated again.

If the value is close enough to the contour level the contour is drawn to it and another trial step made in the direction of the contour here. If the value is not sufficiently close, the intersection line of the local tangent plane and the contour level is determined and a perpendicular dropped on to it.

This correction procedure is repeated until a point close enough to the contour level is found, when the next step can be taken. The marching process is repeated until the step taken falls off the edge of the region to be contoured.

Two enhancements to this which may be used are:-

(i) to use the distance of each evaluated point from the estimated direction to control the length of step actually taken at each point. This enables the density of points along the contour curve to vary with the local curvature, thus keeping low the number of points evaluated and the number of steps to be passed to the plotting software.

(ii) to use second derivatives or the last few points and their derivatives to improve the initial estimate of each step, thus reducing the number of corrections which need to be made.

On reasonably smooth surfaces this gives a very economical method. Although fast, this method has iterative loops deep within it which may not converge. The code has to be prepared to cover this possibility.

When derivatives are not available, the method described by Lodwick and Whittle [1970] can be used. Again an initial point is required, but also an estimate of direction. Two probe points are evaluated, one ten degrees to the left of the estimated direction, one ten degrees to the right. If these two values span the contour level, linear interpolation between them (iterated if necessary) gives the next point along the curve. If they do not, a closer pair of points is tried. (fig 20)

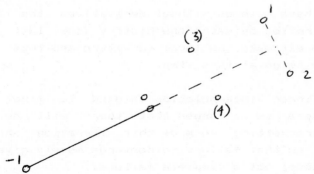

fig 20

An enhancement of this uses previous points to give as good an estimate as possible of where the next point will be. If the actual value here is not within tolerance, the known relationship of high ground to the contour (left or right) is used to choose a probe point on one side or the other. If this is on the opposite side of the contour, linear interpolation gives the contour point: if it is on the same side, a third probe point close to the last known point is evaluated and iterated linear interpolation used between this and the second. (fig 21)

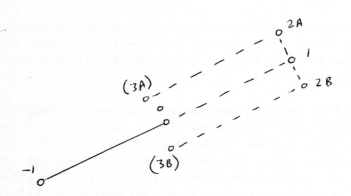

fig 21

In both of these methods without derivatives the step length can be controlled by using the history (the last few accepted points) to estimate the local curvature and thus the appropriate distance to go at this step.

If iterated linear interpolation is used to find the contour points, there is a danger that there will be no convergence. The bracketting form of this iteration should therefore be used, so that failure to converge merely gives a local bump on a contour, not a complete failure.

Recursive subdivision

Where the surface to be contoured can be represented by polynomial pieces, each local piece can be described by a network of control points, coefficients of the Bernstein polynomials. The Benstein polynomials are all positive within the region, and so the value of the surface always lies within the range of these coefficients. It is possible therefore to determine quickly and cheaply whether a piece contains a contour.

It is also possible fairly cheaply to determine the coefficients for each piece of surface within some further subdivision.

The combination of these two gives a robust and fairly economical method:-

(i)   If a piece to be contoured does not contain a contour ignore it.

(ii)   If it does contain a contour and is close enough to an easily contoured surface contour it.

(iii) If it is too complex to contour directly, subdivide it and apply this algorithm to each of the pieces.

Literal application of this recipe generates the contours in fragments, but if the above is interpreted as a way of calculating a set of chains of points which are returned as a result to the calling procedure, the sewing together of the pieces can be carried out within the return from the recursion.

This approach is most easily coded for regular grid contouring, but it can also be applied to an irregular grid, when the recipe for the new coefficients is the definition of the surface rather than just a property derived from some other definition.   [Catmull and Clark 1979],[Doo 1978],[Nasri 1984] These methods are inherently parametric. They have been developed by those interested in surfaces in three dimensions, but work in the two-dimensional context.

In any case benefit is obtained by using the culling procedure at as high a level of definition as possible, so that whole multi-piece regions are dismissed as early as possible from the search for contours.

While this method is not quite as fast as merching, it has the great advantage that it is fully robust, and guarantees to find every piece of contour.

Finding the Contours

Particularly with the marching methods, it is necessary to find where the contours are, and it can be quite a subtle problem to ensure that none are omitted.

The systematic scan of a grid order strategy means that the only problem is looking hard enough at each piece. It is easy to code a method which detects only those loops which cross mesh edges or which enclose at least one data point.[Sutcliffe 1980] If the interpolation method used can give regions higher than any data point, the tracing of the contours should take due note of this and estimate the highest (and lowest) point of each cell before reporting that there is no contour.

Curve order marching methods require that a contour which cuts the boundary should be traced from one end to the other. This can be achieved by a scan first round the boundary of the region to be contoured. If this scan is clockwise round the region, and transitions increasing through the contour level are detected, the contours from those points can be followed with high ground on the left (fig 22). Each such contour will emerge at a point where the clockwise scan has a transition decreasing through the contour level.

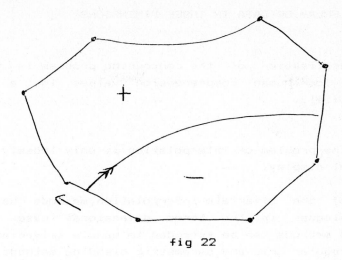

fig 22

Loops within the region must be found by some other process. Lodwick and Whittle use a grid for this purpose. It is worth noting that when many contours are being drawn, there are simple theorems proving that it is unnecessary to scan the whole grid for every contour. If the contours are drawn in increasing sequence of height, regions beneath the previous contour need not be scanned.

Another alternative for preprocessing the entire map is to determine a spanning tree, joining all the maxima and minima within the region or on its edge, to the corners of the region. Every contour must cut this spanning tree somewhere, and so iterated linear interpolation (bracketting) on every edge of the spanning tree will give all loops of each contour. A minimal spanning tree also gives a good set of places for labelling of the contours.

IV   DISPLAY OF DATA IN THREE DIMENSIONS

A generalisation of the contouring problem is that of
displaying   for human comprehension values in a three-
dimensional field.

Again the problem of interpolation is only loosely coupled
to the actual display.

Most of the bivariate interpolation methods have more
complex analogues in the three dimensional case.   Tensor
product grid methods can be extended to handle trivariate data,
as can the regular grid and parametric blending methods.

Weighted means can clearly be generalised, as can weighted
fits.   The   Delaunay triangulation can be generalised to three
dimensions [Bowyer 1981],[Watson 1981], and so there are
tetrahedron   filling   methods   and   also   natural   neighbour
weighting methods.

A new pattern of data appears in three dimensions,
particularly when one of the abscissae is time, when the data
may be distributed along lines of constant position which are
scattered in two dimensions.

If the data appear at the same time at all positions, a
mixed tensor product is clearly worth considering, the tensor
product of any of the bivariate methods in two of the
dimensions with linear, quadratic or cubic splines in the third
dimension.

Data   at   non-coherent times can still be handled by the
product of linear interpolation along the time axis with a
bivariate method in space.   This may be regarded as the
generalization of two-way linear interpolation.

The   question should always be asked as to what rotations are sensible in the total abscissa space. If it is sensible to scale one axis independently from the others (because the coordinates are masured in different units) some kind of mixed method is likely to be appropriate. If all three coordinates are of similar kind and so rotations in three space are meaningful, a method invariant under such rotations should be considered.

Display of a trivariate field on a two-dimensional image brings new questions. Contours on many sectioning planes as separate images is a reasonable approach. Another possibility for displays intended to give qualitative understanding rather than quantitative readability is to treat the surfaces of constant value as sheets of different colour material.   The interior of each sheet is made visible either by cutting holes in it [Butland 1985], or by using colour transparency simulation.

In some cases, the gradient of the field may be more important than the value, or may convey the nature of the variation of the field more evocatively.   In this case display of a regular array of oriented symbols gives a good presentation.[Baden Fuller and dos Santos 1980][Nassif and Silvester 1980]

Because it is most unlikely that the image conveying most information can be predicted before it is seen, interactive graphics becomes an essential tool.   In this context approximate interpolation has an important role in making it possible to produce many images quickly as the operator of the graphics device homes in on the image which makes the message most obvious.   In this context two stage contouring or even threading could be valuable quick options, provided that more rigorous contouring was also provided for the final hard copy version.

V   OTHER ASPECTS

Making software to do a general contouring job requires consideration of the entire task as seen by the user, not just the interesting mathematics.

Some specific points are:-

(i) Labelling of contours

Which contours should be labelled, and where should the labels be posted ? The spanning tree is convenient for this purpose.

(ii) Distinction of contours by use of dotted or dashed lines or different colours.

(iii) Redrawing of a part of the whole map.

Although some displays now offer 'pan and zoom' computed locally within the display, many do not, but the operator may well find this function valuable. Think about the interaction of this with labelling and distinction of the contours.

(iv)   Use of the interpolated surface for purposes other than contouring.

Cut and Fill is a frequent survey requirement, and Visibility Analysis significant in military mapping.

(v)   Presentations other than contours

Other representations also helpful to give the viewer an understanding of the shape of the surface are skew views with vertical sections shown as well as horizontal [Butland 1979]. High performance graphics devices can present rendered views with no lines drawn as such, only surface facets.

All of these may require hidden surface or hidden line removal, and there is information present in this kind of data which can be used to speed the removal process.

The use of an array of oriented symbols was mentioned above in the context of trivariate data, but a simpler version is just as valuable in two dimensions.

It is important in considering what facilities to provide in any general purpose software to take all of these requirements and more into account.

VI   APPENDICES

Appendix 1   Variant tree of interpolation methods

Linear in Ordinates ?
        No   – Dynamic Addition
                                        – Choice of nonlinear parameters

        Yes
            Adaptive Basis Functions ?
            Pattern Specific
                    What pattern ?
                    Regular grid
                        Which Pattern ?
                        Rectangular
                            What continuity ?
                            position   – bilinear in facets
                                       – four triangles per grid cell
                            slope   – Sibson
                                       – tensor product B-splines

                        Triangular
                            What continuity ?
                            position   –   plane facets
                            slope   –   Clough Tocher cubics
                                       –   Powell Sabin quadratics
                                       –   Sabin quadratics

                    Almost regular grid
                        –   relaxation
                            what pattern ? as for regular grid above
                        –   parametric fit
                            what pattern ? as for regular grid above
                    Two-way univariate interpolation
                            What directrix interpolation ?
                            What correspondance rule ?
                            What generator interpolation ?
                    Blending
                            What directrix interpolation ?

Adaptive

   Continuity ?

   Yes   (except maybe at data points)

       —   Plate Equation

         How evaluated ?

         relaxation on grid — Briggs

         solution of linear form — Harder and

                                     Desmarais

       —   Weighted mean of estimates

         What weights ?

       —   Weighted local fit

         What weights ?

       —   Kriging

   Piecewise continuous only

       —   Local weighted means

         What locality rule ?

           — nearest m

           — within radius r

           — nearest m in each octant

           — Thiessen neighbours

         What weights ?

       —   Triangulation

         What triangulation ?

           — Delaunay/Voronoi/Thiessen

           — between tracks

           — Other

         What fit in triangles ?

           — plane facets

           — Powell Sabin quadratics

           — Clough Tocher cubics

Appendix 2   Variant Tree for Contour Drawing

Easy surface ?

Yes   - triangular facets

     What order ?

       Linear   - draw straight lines from edge intercepts

       Quadratic   - construct conic sections

     What sequence ?

       Grid order

       Curve order

No

     What method ?

       Raster Shading

       Two stage

          What lattice ?

            Rectangular

            Triangular

          What density ?

          What fit as second stage ?

                   - see interpolation tree (App 1 above)

       Threading   - Approximate only !

       What curves between data points ?

                   - see curve drawing paper

       Progressive approximation

          Derivatives available ?

            No   -   linear approximations

            Yes   -   cubic approximations

       Marching

          With derivatives ?

            Yes   - Newton iteration

            No   - Lodwick and Whittle

       Recursive subvdivision

Appendix 3   Variant tree for Contour Finding

What method ?

   Lattice   - Approximate !!

   Convex Hull property

   Spanning tree.

VII   BIBLIOGRAPHY

Adams.J.   and Gary,J.   Compact representation of contour plots
for   phone line transmission.
            CACM vol 17 no 6 (June 1974) pp333-336

Akima,H.   A method of bivariate interpolation and smooth
            surface fitting based on local procedures.
            CACM vol 17 no 1 (Jan 1974) pp18-20,26

Akima,H.   Comments on   'Optimal Contour Mapping using
            Universal Kriging' by Ricardo A.Olea. (and reply)
            Journal of Geophysical Research
            vol 80 no 5 (Feb 10 1975) pp 832-836

Akima,H.   A method of bivariate interpolation and smooth
        surface fitting for irregularly distributed data points.
and   Algorithm 526.
            ACM ToMS vol 4 (1978) pp 148-159 and pp160-164

Anderson,W.L.   Application of Bicubic Spline functions to two
            dimensional gridded data.
            US geological Survey Report
            USGS-GD-71-022   (1971) 87pp

Atkins, M.J.   Objective Analysis of upper air height and
            humidity data on a fine mesh.
            Meteorological Magazine 99,(1970) pp 98-110

Bacchelli-Montefusco,L.   and Casciola,G.   Using   Interactive
            Graphics for Fitting Surfaces to Scattered Data.
            IEEE Computer Graphics and its Applications
            July 1984 pp43-45

Barnhill,R.E.,Birkhoff,G.   and Gordon,W.J. Smooth Interpolation
                            in Triangles.
            Research note (about 1970)

Barnhill,R.E.   Smooth Interpolation over Triangles.
            pp 45-70 in Computer Aided Geometric Design
            Barnhill and Riesenfeld (eds)
            Academic Press (1976)

Barnhill,R.E.   and Gregory,J.   Compatible Smooth Interpolation
                              in Triangles.
             Journal of Approximation Theory
             vol 15 no 3 pp 214-225

Baden Fuller,A.J. and dos Santos,M.L.X.   Computer   generated
                              display of 3D vector fields
                       CAD vol 12 no 2 (March 1980) pp 61-66

Bash-Ayan,A.B.   Algorithms for the Interpolation of Scattered
                              Data on the Plane.
             Dissertation, Brighton Polytechnic. (1983)

Batcha,J.P.   and   Reese,J.R.   Surface determination   and
                   automatic contouring for mineral exploration,
                          extraction and processing.
             Colorado School of Mines Quarterly
             vol 59 no 4 (1964)   pp 1-14

Bedient,H.A.   and   Neilon,J.R.   Automatic production   of
                                 meteorological charts.
             Conference on data handling, reduction
              and interpretation in geophysics.
             Yorktown Heights, New York   (1962)

Bengtsson,B.E. and Nordbeck,S.   Constructon of isarithms and
                              isarithmic maps by computers.
                BIT vol 4 (1964) pp 87-105

Bhattacharyya,B.K.   Two dimensional harmonic analysis as a tool
                          for magnetic interpretation.
             Geophysics vol 30 no 5 (Oct 1965) pp829-857

Bhattacharyya,B.K.   Bicubic Spline Interpolation as a method
                   for the treatment of potential field data.
             Geophysics vol 34 no 3 (June 1969) pp 402-423

Biggin,M.J.   Computer generated contours from numerical data.
                       37th annual meeting
             American Society of Photogrammetry   (1971).
             Falls Church , Virginia, USA pp668-682

Birkhoff,G. and Garabedian,H.L. Smooth surface interpolation.
Journal of Maths and Physics vol 39 pp258-268 (1960)

Boehm,B.W. Tabular representations of multivariate
functions with applications to topographic modelling.
Proc 22nd ACM Nat. Conf. (1967) pp 403-415

de Boor,C. Bicubic Spline Interpolation.
Journal of Maths and Physics
vol 41 (1962) pp212-218

de Boor,C. Splines as Linear combinations of B-splines
pp 1-48 in Approximation Theory II
(ed Lorentz, Chui, and Schumaker)
Academic Press 1976

Boots,B.N. Delaunay Triangles: an alternative approach to
point pattern analysis.
Proc. Assn. of Amer. Geographers vol 6 (1979) pop 26-29

Boville,S. Objective analysis of the atmospheric field using
Tchebtcheff minimization criteria
Inst. Roy. de Met. de Belg.
Pub. Ser.A no 69 (1969)

Bowyer,A. Computing Dirichlet Tesselations
Computer Journal vol 24 (1981) no 2 pp 162-166

Bradley,J.H.S. On the application of statistical methods to
scalar interpolation.
Arctic meteorology research group,
Dept. of Meteorology, McGill University, Montreal.
Meteorology no 100 (1971)

Briggs,I.C. Machine contouring using minimum curvature.
Geophysics vol 39 no 1 (Feb 1974) pp39-48

Butland,J. Surface drawing made simple.
CAD vol 11 no 1 (Jan 1979) pp 19-22

Butland,D. and Butland,J. private communication (1984)

Cadwell,J.H.   A least squares surface fitting program.
                Computer Journal vol 3 (1961)   pp266-269

Cadwell,J.H.   and   Williams,D.E.   Some orthogonal   methods   of
                     curve and surface fitting.
               Computer Journal vol 4 (1961) pp260-264

Cain,J.C. and Neilon,J.R. Automatic mapping of the
                     geomagnetic field.
               Journal of Geophysical research
               vol 68 no 16 (Aug 15 1963) pp4689-4696

Carlson,R.E.   and   Hall,C.A.   On   piecewise   polynomial
                interpolation in rectangular polygons.
                     WAPD-T-2160   (Nov 1969)

Catmull,E.   and   Clark,J.   Recursively Generated B-Spline
                Surfaces on Arbitrary Topological Meshes.
                CAD vol 10 (1978) pp 350-355

Cherin,P.,Madigan,R. and Martin,T.   A computer program for
                plotting a crystallographic fourier synthesis.
                Nature vol 207 pp391-392

Christiansen,H. and Sederberg,T.W.   Conversion of Complex
             Contour Line definitions into Polygonal Element Mosaics.
                Computer graphics XIII, 2 (Aug 1978) pp 187-192

Chui,C.H. and Wang,R.H.   Multivariate B-splines on
                     triangulated rectangles.
                J.Math. ANalysis vol 92 (1983) no 2 pp 533-551

Cole,A.J.,Jordan,C. and Merriam,D.F.   Fortran IV program for
                progressive linear fit of surfaces to a quadrate
                base using an IBM 1620 computer.
                Kansas Geological Survey,
                Computer Contribution 15

Cole,A.J.   Algorithm for the production of contour maps from
                scattered data.
                Nature vol 220 (Oct 5 1968) pp92-94

Cole,A.F. and Davie,A.J.T.   Local smoothing by polynomials
                         in N dimensions.
                Computer Journal (1969) pp72-76

Cole,A.J.   An iterative approach to the fitting of trend
                         surfaces.
                Kansas State Geological Survey
                Comp.Contr. 37   (1969)

Connelly,D.S.   An experiment in contour map smoothing on the
                ECU automated contouring system.
                Cartographic Journal vol 8 no 1   (1971)   pp59-66

Coons,S.A.   Surfaces for the computer aided design of space
                         forms.
                M.I.T. report MAC-TR-41   (1967)

Cox,D.D.   Multivariate Smoothing Spline Functions
                SIAM Journal of Numerical Analysis vol 21 no 4
                         (Aug 1984) pp 789-813

Cottafava,G. and le Moli,G.   Automatic Contour Map
                CACM vol 12 no 7 (July 1969) pp386-391

Crain,I.K.   Computer interpolation and contouring of two
                         dimensional data; a review.
                Geoexploration 8 pp71-86   (1970)

Crain,I.K. and Bhattacharyya,B.K.   Treatment of non-equispaced
                two dimensional data with a digital computer.
                Geoexploration vol 5 (1967) pp173-194

Crane,C.M. Contour plotting for functions specified at nodal
             points of an irregular mesh based on an arbitrary
             two-parameter coordinate system.
                Algorithm 75 Computer Journal
                vol 15 no 4 pp382-384

Dayhoff,M.O.   A contour map program for X-ray crystallography.
                CACM vol 6 no 10 (Oct 1963) pp620-622

Demirmen,F.   Mathematical procedures and Fortran IV program for
                    description   of   three   dimensional   surface
                    configurations.
                Geologic Research Section.
                University of Kansas, Lawrence, Kansas. (1972)

Dierckx,P.   A   fast   algorithm   for   smoothing   data   on   a
                    rectangular grid while using spline functions.
                SIAM   Journal   of Numerical Analysis   vol 19 no   6
                    (Dec 1982) pp 1286-1304

Dixon,R.   Orthogonal polynomials   as   a   basis   for   objective
                    analysis.
                Meteorological Office Scientific paper no 30
                HMSO, London (1969)

Dixon,R.   and Spackman,E.A.   The three dimensional analysis   of
                    meteorological data.
                Met. Off. Sci. Pap. No 31 HMSO London (1970)

Dixon,R. and Spackman,E.A.   Towards a four dimensional analysis
                    of meteorological data.
                Nature vol 226 (April 11 1970) pp131-133

Dixon,R.,Spackman,E.A.,Jones,I. and   Anne   Francis   The   global
                analysis   of meteorological data using   orthogonal
                    polynomial base functions.
                Journal of Atmospheric Sciences
                vol 29 no 4 (May 1972) pp609-622

Done,G.T.S.   Interpolation   of   mode shapes: a matrix   scheme
                    using two way spline curves.
                Aeronautical quarterly
                vol 16 pt 4 (1965) pp333-349

Doo,D.W.H.   A   Recursive   Subdivision Algorithm   for   fitting
                    Quadratic Surfaces to Irregular Polyhedrons.
                    Dissertation. Brunel University   (1978)

Dowd,P.A.   A   review   of   Geostatistical   Techniques   for
                    contouring.
                These proceedings   (1985)

Downing,J.A.   The automatic construction of contour plots with
                    application to numerical analysis.
                TNN-58 University of Texas,
                Austin Texas USA

Eddy,A.   Two dimensional statistical objective analysis of
                        isotropic scalar data fields.
                Atmospheric science group report no 5 (May 1967)
                Univ. of Texas College of Engineering,
                Austin, Texas

Ellis,T.M.R.   Some routines for plotting three dimensional
                        surfaces.
                Computing services report U3
                University of Sheffield (1975)

Ewen-Smith,B.M.   Algorithm for the production of contour maps
                        from linearised data.
                Nature vol 234 (Nov 5 1971) pp33-34

Falconer,K.J.   A general purpose algorithm for contouring over
                        scattered data points.
                NPL   report NAC 6
                National Physical Laboratory,
                Teddington, Middx   (1971)

Farin,G.   Subsplines Uber Dreiecken
                Dissertation Braunschweig   (1979)

Farin,G.   Designing C1 Surfaces consisting of Triangular
                            Cubic Patches.
                CAD vol 14 no 5 (Sept 1982) pp 253-256

Farin,G.   Smooth Interpolation to Scattered 3D data.
            pp 43-63 in Surfaces in CAGD (Barnhill and Boehm eds)
                North Holland   (1983)

Farin,G.   A Construction for the visual C1 continuity of
                    polynomial surface patches.
                Comp.Graphics and Image Processing

Feng,D.Y. and Riesenfeld,R.F.   Some new surface forms for
                        computer aided geometric design.
            Computer Journal vol 23 (1980) no 4 pp 324-331

Ferguson,J.   Multivariable curve interpolation
            JACM vol 11 no 2 (April 1964) pp221-228

de Floriani,L. and Dettori,G. An Interpolation Method for
                        Surfaces with Tension.
            Advances in Engineering Software
              vol 3 no 4 (Oct 1981) pp 151-154

Forgotson,J.M.Jr.   How computers help find oil.
            Oil and Gas Journal
            vol 16 no 11 (March 18 1963) pp100-109

Forsythe,G.E. Generation and use of orthogonal polynomials for
              data fitting with a digital computer.
            JSIAM vol 5 (1957) pp74-88

Franke,R.   Locally determined smooth interpolation at
            irregularly spaced points in several variables.
            Journal of Institute of Maths and Applics.
            vol 19 (1977) pp 471-482

Franke,R.   A critical comparison of some methods for
              interpolation of scattered data.
            NPS-53-79-003 Naval Postgraduate School, Monterey,
            California. December 1979.

Franke,R.   Smooth Interpolation of Scattered Data by Local
                  Thin-Plate Splines.
            Comp. and Maths with Applications
              vol 8 no 4 (1982) pp 273-281

Franke,R.   Scattered data interpolation: tests of some
                      methods
            Math. Comp. vol 38 no 157 pp 181-200 (1982)

Franke,R. and Neilon,G. Smooth Interpolation of large sets of
                        Scattered Data.
            Intl. Journal of Numerical Methods in Engineering
            vol 15 (1980) pp 1691-1704

Frederickson,P.O.   Triangular Spline Interpolation
                Report 6-70, Lakehead University (1970)

Frederickson,P.O.   Generalized Triangular Splines
                Report 7-71, Lakehead University (1971)

Frederickson,P.O.   Quasi-interpolation,   extrapolation   and
                approximation on the plane
            Conf. Numer. maths., Winnipeg (1971) pp159-167

Fritsch,M.J. Objective analysis of a 2D data field by the cubic
                spline technique.
            Dept of Atmospheric Science report 143 (1969)
        Colorado State University, Fort Collins, Colorado.

Fuchs,H. et al   Optimal Surface reconstruction from Planar
                Contours.
            CACM XX-10 (Oct 1977) pp 693-702

Ganapathy,S. and Dennehy,T.G.   A new general triangulation
                method for planar contours.
            Computer Graphics vol 16 no 3 (July 1982) pp 69-75

Gordon,W.J.   Blending function methods of bivariate and
            multivariate interpolation and approximation.
            SIAM Journal of Numerical Analysis
            vol 9 (1971) pp 158-177

Grant,F.S. A problem in the analysis of geophysical data.
            Journal of Geophysical Research
            vol 22 (1956) pp309-344

Green,P.J. and Sibson,R.   Computing Dirichlet Tesselations in
                the plane.
            Computer Journal, vol 21 no 2 (1978) pp168-173

Harbaugh,J.W. and Merriam,D.F.   Computer Applications in
                Stratigraphic Analysis.
            John Wiley, New York (1968)

Harbaugh,J.W. and Preston,F.W.   Fourier   series   analysis   in
                                   geology.
            Symposium on computers and computer applications
              in mining and exploration.
            College of Mines University of Arizona.
            vol 1 pp R-1 to R-46 (1965)

Harder,R.L. and Desmarais,R.N.   Interpolation using surface
                                   splines.
            Journal of Aircraft vol 9 no 2 (Feb 1972) pp 189-191

Hardy,R.L.   Multiquadric equations of topography and other
              irregular surfaces.
            Journal of Geophysical Research
            vol 76 no 8 (March 10 1971) pp 1905-1915

Hartwig,G.W.Jr.   CONTUR - a Fortran   IV   subroutine   for   the
                   plotting of contour lines.
            USA Ballistic Research Laboratories
            Mem.Rep.   2282   NTIS AD-760   437   (1973)

Haverlik,I. and Krcho,J.   Automatizacia tvorby vrstenicovych a
        izogradientovych   map   hl   adiska   primarnych   a
        sekundarnych azociarovych poli.
            Geodeticky a Kartyograficky obzor
            vol 19/61 no 6 (1973) pp151-158

Hayes,J.G. Available algorithms for curve and surface fitting
            NPL report NAC 39
            National Physical Laboratory,
            Teddington, Middx. (1973)

Hayes,J.G.   New   shapes   from   bicubic   splines.
            CAD 74 International conference, fiche 36G-37A
            IPC Science and Technology Press, (1974)

Hayes,J.G. and Vickers,T.   The fitting of polynomials to
                               unequally spaced data.
            Phil Mag. series 7 vol 42 (1951) pp1387-1400

Heap,B.R.   Algorithms for the production of contour   maps   over
                        an   irregular   triangular mesh.
                NPL   report DNAC 10,
                National Physical Laboratory,
                Teddington, Middx. (1972)

Heap,B.R. and Pink,M.G.   Three   contouring   algorithms
                NPL report AM 81
                National Physical Laboratory,
                Teddington, Middx. (1969)

Hebin,O.   Computer Drawn Isarithmic Maps.
                Geografisk Tidsskrift vol 68 no 2 pp 50-63   (1969)

Heindl,G.   Interpolation and approximation by piecewise
                    quadratic C1 functions of two variables
                in Multivariate Approximation Theory, ISNM 51
                    Birkhauser Verlag, Basle, (1979)

Hessing,R.C.,Lee,H.K.,Pierce,A.   and   Powers,E.N.   Automatic
                    contouring using bicubic functions.
                Geophysics vol 37 no 4 (Aug 1972) pp669-674

Hsu,M.L. and Robinson,A.H.   The fidelity of isopleth maps, an
                        experimental study.
        University of Minnesota Press, Minneapolis, Minnesota (1970)

ICA   ICA report on automation in cartography.
                Surveying and Mapping vol 31 no 4 (Dec 1971) pp595-602

Inman,R.L.   Papers on operational objective analysis schemes at
                    the national severe storms forecast center.
                NOAA Technical Memo ERL TM-NSSL51
                US Dept. of Commerce.

James,W.R.   The fourier series model in map analysis.
                Office of Naval Research Geography branch.
                Northwestern University, Evanston Illinois,
                Technical report 1   (1966)

James,W.R.   Fortran IV program using double Fourier series for
              surface fitting of irregularly spaced data.
              Kansas Geological Survey
              Computer Contribution 5 (1966)

James,W.R.   Non-linear models for trend analysis in geology.
              Kansas Geological Survey,
              Computer Contribution 12 pp26-30   (1967)

Jones,R.L.   A generalized digital contouring program.
              NASA   TN D-6022   (1971)
              NASA Langley Research Center,
              Hampton, Virginia.

Junkins,J.L.,Miller,G.W. and Jancaitis,J.R.   A   weighting
          function approach to modelling of irregular surfaces.
              Journal of Geophysical Research
               vol 78 no 11 (April 10 1973) pp1794-1803

Keppel,E.   Approximating complex surfaces by triangulation of
              contour lines.
              IBM Journal of Research anbd Development
              XIX (Jan 1975)   pp 2-11

Klucewitz,I.M.   A piecewise C1 interpolant to arbitrarily
                                 spaced data.
              Computer Graphics and Image Processing
              vol 8 (1978) pp 92-112

Kruger,H.B.   General and Special approaches to the problem of
              objective analysis of meteorological   variables.
                  Quarterly Journal of Meteorology
                  vol 95 (Jan 1969) pp21-39

Krumbein,W.C.   Trend surface analysis of contour type maps with
                     irregular control point spacing.
              Journal of Geophysical Research
              vol 64 no 7 (July 1959) pp 823-834

Krumbein,W.C. A comparison of polynomial and Fourier models in
                    map analysis.
             Office of Naval Research, Geography Branch,
             Northwestern University, Evanston, Illinois.
             Technical report 2   (1966)

Krumbein,W.C. and Graybill,F.A. An introduction to statistical
                         models in geology.
             McGraw Hill, New York, (1965)

Lawson,C.,Bloch,N. and Garrett,R.D.   Computer subroutines for
                              Contour Plotting.
             NASA IPL SPACE Programs.
             Summary no 37-32 (April 30 1965) pp18-22

Lawson,C.L. Generation of a triangular grid with application to
                    contour plotting.
             California Institute of Technology.
             Jet Propulsion Lab.
             Technical Memorandum 299   (1972)

Lawson,C.L. C1-compatible interpolation over a   triangle.
             California Institute of Technology.
             Jet Propulsion Lab.
             Technical Memorandum 33-770   (1976)

Lawson,C.L.   Software for C1 surface interpolation.
         pp 161-194 in Mathematical Software III (ed J.Rice)
             Academic Press 1977

Legg,M.P.C. and Brent,R.P.   Automatic contouring.
             Proc 4th Australian Computer Conference
             vol 1 pp 467-468   (1969)

Lewis,B.A. and Robinson,J.S.   Triangulation of planar regions
                     with applications.
             Computer Journal vol 21 no 4 pp 324-332

Liebenberg,E.   SYMAP; its uses and abuses.
             The Cartographic Journal
             vol 13 no 1 (June 1976) pp26-36.

Lintner,M.A.   Proj-algorithm and computer program for the
                hidden line problem for single valued surfaces.
                Idaho Nuclear Corporation. (Dec 1969)

Lodwick,G.D.and Whittle,J. A technique for automatic contouring
                field survey data.
                Australian Computer Journal.
                vol 2 no 3 (Aug 1970)   pp104-109

Lym,W.R.   The plotting of equipotential lines of a potential
                field.
                Simulation vol 9 (1967) pp81-85

Maine,R.   Automatic Numerical Weather analysis   for   the
                Australian region.
                Commonwealth of Australia.
                Meteorological study no 16   (1966)

Maine,R.,Hinksman,D.R. and Seaman,R.S. Computer Graphic display
                of analyses.
        Australian Meteorological Magazine. vol 15 (1967) pp190-204

Margerison,T.A. Computers and the Renaissance of Cartography.
                Natural Environment Research Council.
available from Experimental Cartography Unit.
                Kensington, London.   (1976)

Marlow,S. and Powell,M.J.D.   A Fortran subroutine for plotting
                the part of a conic that is inside a given triangle.
                Rep. R-8336 Atomic Energy Research Establishment
                Harwell, England (1976)

Matheron,G.   The theory of regionalised variables and its
                application.
                Cahiers du centre de Morphologie Mathematique de
                Fontainebleu. No 5
                Ecole national Superieure des Mines.

Maude,A.D.   Interpolation - mainly for graph plotters.
                Computer Journal vol 16 (1973) pp64-65

McCullagh,M.J. and Sampson,R.J.   User desires and graphics
                    capability in the academic environment.
                The Cartographic Journal
                vol 9 no 2 (Dec 1972) pp109-122

McIntyre,D.B.,Pollard,D.D. and Smith.R.   Computer Programs for
                    Automatic Contouring.
                Kansas Geological Survey.
                Computer Contribution 23

McLain,D.H.   Drawing Contours from arbitrary data points.
            Computer Journal vol 17 no 4 (Nov 1974) pp318-324

McLain,D.H.   Two dimensional interpolation from random data.
            Computer Journal vol 19 no 2 (May 1976) pp178-181

Meinguet,J.   Multivariate interpolation made simple
                ZAMP vol 30 pp292-304

Merriam,D.F. and Cocke,N.C. (Eds) Computer Applications in the
                earth sciences.
            in Colloquium on trend analysis.
                Kansas Geological Survey
                Computer Contribution 12   (1967)

Merriam,D.F. and Sneath,P.H.A.   Quantitative comparison of
                    contour maps.
                Journal of Geophysical Research
                    vol 71 (1966) pp1105-1115

Milly,S.M.   PLOTR; a two dimensional contouring and area
                    calculating routine.
                Sandia Labs. Albuquerque, New Mexico
                Research report SC-RR-69-685

Morrison,J.L.   A link between cartographic theory and mapping
                    practice; the nearest neighbour statistic.
                Geographical Review vol 40 no 4 (1970) pp494-510.

Morrison,J.L.   Method-induced error in isarithmic mapping.
                Amer. Confr. on Surveying and Mapping.
                Cartography Division.
                Technical Monograph nop CA-5   (1971)

Morse,S.P.   A mathematical model for the analysis of
                    contour line data.
               JACM vol 15 no 2 (April 1968)   pp205-220

Morse,S.P.   Concepts of use in contour map processing.
               CACM vol 12 no 3 (March 1969) pp147-152

Murray,F.W.   A method of objective contour construction.
            Rand Corporation Memorandum RM-5564-NRL   ONR 6   (1968)

Nagy,N.J.(III)   The graphical rep@resentation of two variable
                    data.
               Los Alamos Scientific Laboratory.
               Report no. LA 4796   (Nov 1971)

Nasri,A.H.   Polyhedral Subdivision Methods
                         for Free-Form Surfaces.
            Dissertation. University of East Anglia   (1984)

Nassif,N. and Silvester,P.P.   Graphic representations of three-
                    component vector fields.
               CAD vol 12 no 6 (Nov 1980) pp 289-294

Neilson,G.   A method for interpolating scattered data   based
               upon a minimum norm network.
               Maths. of Comp. vol 40 (1983) no 161 pp 253-272

Newton,R.   Deriving contour maps from geological data.
               Canadian Journal of the Earth Sciences.
               vol5 pp165-166   (1968)

Noma,A.A. and Misulia,M.G.   Programming Topographic Maps for
                    automatic terrain model construction.
               Surveying and Mapping vol 19 no 3 (1959) pp355-366

Nordbeck,S.   Location of areal data for computer processing.
               Lund studies in geography, C2, Lund, Sweden   (1962)

Ojakangas,D.R. and Basham,W.L. Simplified computer contouring
                    of exploration data.
               Stanford University Publ.Geol. Sci.
               vol 9 (1964) no 2 pp757-770

Oldham,C.H.G. and Sutherland,D.B. Orthogonal Polynomials; their
            use in estimating the regional effect.
        Geophysics vol 20 no 2 (April 1955) pp295-306

Olea,R.A.   Optimal contour mapping using universal   kriging.
        Journal of Geophysical Research
        vol 79 no 5 (Feb 10, 1974) pp695-702

Palmer,J.A.B.   Automated Mapping.
        Proc. 4th Australian Computer Conference
        vol 6 pp463-466   (1969)

Palmer,J.A.B.   An economical method of plotting   contours.
        Australian Computer Journal vol 2 no 1 (1970) pp27-31

Pelto,C.R.,Elkins,T.A. and Boyd,H.A. Automatic contouring of
            irregularly spaced data.
        Geophysics vol 33 no 3 (June 1968) pp424-430

Pincus,H.J.   Some vector and arithmetic operations on two
        dimensional orientation variates with   application
            to geological data.
        Journal of Geology vol 64 no 6 (Nov 1956) pp533-557

Powell,M.J.D. Piecewise quadratic surface fitting for contour
            plotting.
        pp 253-271 in Software for Numerical Mathematics.
        (ed. Evans,D.J.) Academic Press, London   1974

Powell,M.J.D.   Numerical methods for fitting functions of two
            variables.
        Report CSS 30 Computer Science and Systems Division.
        A.E.R.E., Harwell, Oxfordshire, England.   (1976)

Powell,M.J.D. and Sabin,M.A. Piecewise quadratic approximations
            on triangles.
        ACM transactions on Mathematical Software
        vol 3 no 4 (Dec 1977) pp316-325

Preston,F.W. and Harbaugh,J.W.   BALGOL programs for geologic
          application for single and double Fourier series.
               IBM 7090/7094 computers.
               Special Distribution Publication
               Kansas Geological Survey   (1965)

Rae,A.I.M.   A program to contour Fourier Maps by use of an
               incremental CRT display.
               Acta Crystallogr. vol 21 (1966) pp618-619

Read,W.A.   A new technique of trend surface analysis and some
               geological applications.
               Systematics Association vol 3
               Data Processing in Biology and Geology.
               ed Cuthill,J.L.   (1970)

Rens,F.J.   A Fortran Program for coordinate Mapping using IBM
               7090 computer.
               Office of Naval Research, Geography Branch
               Technical report 10   (1965)

Rhind,D.W.   Automatic Contouring — and empirical evaluation of
               some differing techniques.
               The Cartographic Journal vol 8 no 2 (1971) pp145-158

Rhind,D.W. and Barrett,A.N.   Status and problems of automated
                    contouring.
               Experimental Cartography Unit   (April 1971)

Rhynsburger,D.   Analytic delineation of Thiessen Polygons.
               Geographical Analysis vol 5 no 2 (1973) pp133-144

Rivara,M-C.   Mesh Refinement Processes based   on   the
               generalised bisection of simplices.
               SIAM Journal of Numerical Analysis
               vol 21 no 3 (June 1984) pp 604-613

Roberts,A.   Smooth interpolation between randomly located
               collocation points. private communication (1973)

Robinson,J.E.   Spatial Filtering of Geological Data.
               Int.Stat Inst. 37th session (1969)

Rosing,K.E.   Computer Graphics
               Area vol 1 no 1 (1969) pp2-7

Sabin,M.A.   The use of piecewise forms for the numerical
              representation of shape.
              Tanulmanyok 60/1977   (1977) 125pp

Sabin,M.A. Contouring - a Review of Methods for Scattered Data
     pp 63-86 in Mathematical Methods in Computer Graphics and
            Design.   (ed K.Brodlie) Academic Press 1980

Sablonniere,P.   Bases de Bernstein et Approximants Splines
                Dissertation,   Lille 1982

Sampson,R.J.   Surface II graphics system.
             Kansas Geological Survey,   Lawrence, Kansas   (1975)

Sasaki,Y.   Some basic formalisms in numerical variational
             analysis.
         Monthly Weather Review.   vol 98 no 12 (Dec 1970) pp875-883

Sasaki,Y.   Numerical variational analysis formulated under the
            constraints as determined by longwave equations and
            low-pass filter.
         Monthly Weather Review vol 98 no 12 (Dec 1970) pp884-898

Schagen,I.P.   Interpolation in Two Dimensions - a New Technique
         J.Inst Maths Applics (1979) vol 23 pp 53-59

Schagen,I.P.   Automatic Contouring from Scattered Data Points
         Computer Journal vol 25 no 1 (1982) pp 7-11

Schumaker,L.L.   Fitting Surfaces to Scattered Data.
               pp 203-268 in Approximation Theory II
               (ed by Lorentz, Chui and Schumaker)
               Academic Press 1976

Shepard,D.   A two dimensional interpolation function for
              irregularly spaced data.
           Proc. 23rd ACM National Conference (1968) pp517-524

SIA   Surface models produced by the rectangular grid or
       triangulation technique.   Draft   (1976)

Sibson,R.   Locally Equiangular Triangulations
            Computer Journal vol 21 no 3 (1978) pp 243-245

Sibson,R.   A brief description   of   Natural   Neighbour
                                Interpolation.
                pp 21-36 in Interpreting Multivariate Data
                    (ed Barnett) John Wiley 1981

Sibson,R. and Thompson,G.D.   A seamed quadratic element for
                                contouring.
                Computer Journal vol 24 no 4 (Nov 1981) pp 378-382

Slack,H.A.,Brunton,G.D.,Lee,H.C.,Rosenfeld,M.A.and Cram,I.H.Jr.
                Now - map making made accurate, objective.
                    Oil and Gas Journal
                vol 61 no 31 (Aug 5, 1963) pp158-170

Smith,F.G.   Three programs for contouring map data.
                Canadian Journal of the Earth Sciences
                    vol 5 (1968) pp324-327

Sowerbutts,W.T.C.   A surface plotting program suitable for
                                microcomputers.
                CAD vol 15 no 6 (Nov 1983) pp 324-328

Spitz,O.T.   Generation of orthogonal polynomials for trend
                    surfacing with a digital computer.
        Proc. Symp. Short course operations research Minerals Industry
                Pennsylvania State University 3:2-7   (1966)

Sprunt,B.F.   Geographics; a computer's eye view of terrain.
                Area vol 2 no 4 (1970) pp54-59

Stead,S.   verbal   presentation
            at Oberwolfach workshop on Computer Aided Geometric Design
                    (November 1984)

Stearns,F. A method of estimating the quantitative reliability
                    of isoline maps.
                Annals of Assocn. of Amer. Geog.
                    vol 58 no 2 (1968) pp371-385

481

Sutcliffe,D.   Contouring   over   rectangular   amd   skewed
                rectangular grids - an introduction.
    pp 39-62 in Mathematical Methods in Computer Graphics and
                    Design.   (ed K.Brodlie) Academic Press 1980

Swindle,G. and van Andel,Tj.H. Computer Contouring of deep sea
            bathymetric data.
            Marine Geology vol 7 (1969) pp347-355

Taylor,D.R.F.   bibliography of computer mapping.
    Council of planning librarians exchange bibliography no 263
                Monticelli Illinois (1972)

Thomas,A.L.   The automated contouring of block models.
            Area vol 4 (1972)

Tobler,W.R.   Automation in the production of thematic maps.
            Cartographic Journal vol 2 no 1 (1965) pp32-38

Tobler,W.R.   Geographical filters and their inverses.
            Geographical Analysis vol 1 no 3 (1969) pp234-253

Tobler,W.R.   Regional Analysis, time series extended to two
                dimensions.
            Geographia Polonica vol 25 (1973) pp103-106

Tobler,W.R.   Linear operators appled to areal data
        in   Display and Analysis of Spatial Data.
                eds Davis,J. and McCullagh,M.
                John Wiley, New York, (1974)

Tobler,W.R.   Geographical interpolation program.
                Cartographic Laboratory report 2
                Dept. of Geography, University of Michigan,
                Ann Arbor, Michigan (1974)

Walden,A.R.   Quantitative comparison of automatic contouring
                algorithms.
                Kansas Oil Exploration Decision System technical
                    report pp1-115
                Kansas Geological Survey, Lawrence, Kansas.

Walters,R.F.   Contouring by Machine; a users guide.
                Amer.   Assocn   of Petroleum Geologists Bulletin
                vol 53 no 11 (Nov 1969) pp2324-2340

Wang,C.Y.   C1 rational interpolation over an arbitrary triangle
                CAD vol 15 no 1 (Jan 1983) pp 33-36

Watson,D.F.   Computing the n-dimensional Delaunay tesselation
                with application to Voronoi polytopes.
                Computer Journal vol 24 no 2 (1981) pp 167-172

Wray,W.B.   Fortran IV CDC computer programs for constructing
                isometric   diagrams.
                Kansas Geological Survey Computer Contribution 44

Wren,A.E.   Contouring and the contour map, a new perspective.
                Geographical Prospecting vol 23 no 1 (1975) pp1-17

Zwart,P.B. Multivariate splines with non-degenerate partitions.
                SIAM Journal of Numerical Analysis
                vol 10 (1973) pp 665-673

A REVIEW OF GEOSTATISTICAL TECHNIQUES
FOR CONTOURING

by

P. A. Dowd

Dept. Mining and Mineral Engineering
University of Leeds, Leeds, U.K.

ABSTRACT

This paper is a summary of the geostatistical techniques which have been applied to contouring. The various forms of the estimation procedure known as kriging are introduced in the order of their historical development together with corresponding assumptions and hypotheses. One of the most recent developments, known as dual kriging, is also introduced, and its advantages and applications are discussed. Methods of contouring with unreliable data using kriging are also discussed.

Keywords: contouring, direct contouring, dual kriging, generalised covariances, geostatistics, kriging, universal kriging, variogram.

1. INTRODUCTION

Geostatistics has been widely applied in many fields for over twenty years. It has found major application in the mining and related industries and has been used in contouring applications in mining, geology, meteorology, geophysics, geochemistry, soil science, hydrology and environmental sciences.

Most of this paper deals with *indirect* contouring, i.e estimating values at the nodes of a regular grid from irregularly spaced data. The regularly gridded values are then contoured using a standard commercial package. Direct contouring by means of *dual kriging* is discussed in

NATO ASI Series, Vol. F17
Fundamental Algorithms for Computer Graphics
Edited by R. A. Earnshaw
© Springer-Verlag Berlin Heidelberg 1985

section 5.

1.1 Interpolation for contouring

All linear methods of interpolation are variants of weighted average or weighted moving average techniques. Weights are assigned to data values in a manner which is intended to reflect the relative influence each value has on the point to be interpolated. The simplest forms are means obtained by weighting by the inverse of a function of the distance of each datum from the interpolation point. More complicated methods include least squares fits of polynomial surfaces to weighted data values within some specified radius of the interpolation point.

In assessing an interpolation method it would seem logical to state the desired characteristics of an interpolator and to define some objective criterion (or criteria) for assessing its performance.

A very thorough treatment of the properties and characteristics of different interpolators is given in the paper by Sabin in this volume. For the purposes of this present paper the desirable characteristics of interpolation are taken to be:

 (i) data location (abscissae) adaptive (ie. the interpolator will perform equally well on any data co-ordinate pattern and will be influenced by that pattern)

 (ii) data value (ordinate) adaptive (ie. although a global model may be used the model will depend upon the data set and the value of the interpolator at any given point will depend upon the local data)

 (iii) exact interpolation (ie. interpolation at a known location will produce the data value at that location)

 (iv) contours should "honour" data points (ie.

contour lines should lie on the correct side of data values)

(v) contours should be continuous (except where discontinuities are explicity called for eg. faults)

(vi) precision, as defined by Sabin (1985): for data which actually lie on a particular surface, the interpolation method should return only points which lie on that surface.

Ideally, the interpolation method should also embody some criterion of performance and should return some measure of this criterion.

Almost without exception the interpolation methods used for contouring are deterministic and the weighting techniques used are based on data coordinates with respect to the interpolation point. Very few methods recognise the importance of the location of data values with respect to other data values or incorporate any of the structure in the data values themselves. For example, in figure 1a both data configurations show four data located at exactly the same distances from the interpolation point. Intuitively, the weight assigned to sample no 3 in the second configuration should be less than in the first configuration because the information conveyed by sample no 3 has been made somewhat redundant by sample no 2; the degree of redundancy will be determined by the behaviour of the data values. In addition, clustered data, as for example in figure 1b, convey less information than data more uniformly spread around the interpolation point (unless, of course the data values are completely random).

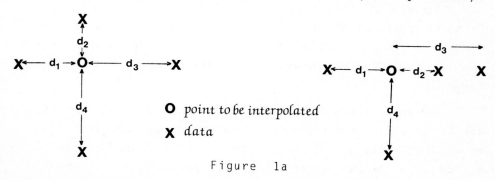

Figure 1a

O point to be interpolated

X data

Figure 1b

Amongst the deterministic methods, only some of the polygonal methods (eg. natural neighbourhood interpolation) attempt to take relative data locations into account and only the analytical methods (eg. least squares surface fits) make any attempt at modelling the behaviour of the data values.

The remainder of this paper is a summary of the geostatistical techniques which have been applied to contouring. In their most general form these techniques are a combination of statistical and deterministic methods which have all of the properties listed above (although honouring of data points can only be guaranteed with direct contouring).

The criteria for assessing the performance of the geostatistical interpolator are that it should be an unbiased estimator and should in some sense minimise the error of estimation. The measure of error of estimation is taken to be the mean squared error although attempts have been made to specify other measures such as absolute error.

By way of illustration two data sets are used. The first consists of measurements of the thickness of a Permian formation recorded at 83 locations. The second data set consists of 326 measurements of the depth of the same formation.

Contour plots of these data sets by the routine RANCON from the proprietary software package GINOSURF will be used as a basis for comparison. RANCON uses Falconer's method of a least squares fit of a paraboloid surface to

weighted data points. The weight assigned to data value
i is:

$$w_i = \frac{(s - d_i)^2}{d_i}$$

where d_i is the distance of data value i from the
interpolation point and s is the radius of the circle
centred on the interpolation point and within which data
are selected. The radius s is chosen so that, on average,
n data points are within the circle (with $n \geqslant 6$).

Provided that s is kept constant, the surface defined
by RANCON will be continuous with continuous first
derivatives. However, for erratically located data the
value of s may have to be altered several times and
discontinuous surfaces are a highly likely result.

Note that the use of the circle of radius s is an
empirical attempt to define a range of influence. Note
also that the range of influence is assumed to be isotropic
whereas in many applications this is patently not the
case. The geostatistical approach allows the data to be
checked for the existence of a range of influence. If
the range of influence does exist, it is then quantified
in as many directions as are necessary.

The GINOSURF routine was chosen for no other reasons
than that it is typical of weighted moving average techniques
and is widely used (at least in the U.K.).

As a comparison of indirect contouring, geostatistical
techniques will be used to by-pass the interpolation stage
of the GINOSURF routine. The regularly gridded,
geostatistically interpolated values will then be contoured
using only the contouring elements of GINOSURF.

Figures 2 and 3 show both the data locations and
the contour plots produced by RANCON from the thickness
and depth measurements respectively. Note, in particular,
the creation of artefacts in areas of sparse data (north-east
and north-west quadrants of figure 2 and south east quadrant
of figure 3) and, occasionally, even in areas of reasonable

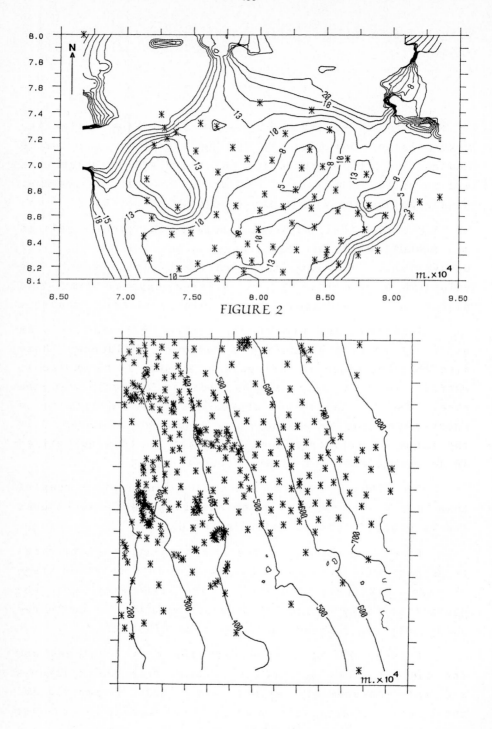

FIGURE 2

FIGURE 3

data density.

1.2 Notation

Upper case letters are used to indicate random variables and random functions. Lower case letters indicate particular values of random variables. Letters in bold type, eg. **x**, denote vectors.

For example, $Z(\mathbf{x})$ denotes the random variable Z at the vector location **x**; $z(\mathbf{x})$ is a particular value of the random variable $Z(\mathbf{x})$. In the real plane, $\mathbf{x} = (x,y)$; in three dimensions $\mathbf{x} = (x,y,z)$.

1.3 Interpretation

The value z measured at a geographical location **x** is interpreted as a particular value of a *random variable* $Z(\mathbf{x})$ at that location. The family of all such random variables at all locations (sampled or not) over the geographical region is a *random function*.

Without some form of stationarity, statistical inference would require multivariate distributions which, for most applications, is clearly impossible.

2. THE STATIONARY CASE

The first and widest hypothesis of stationarity is that the distributions of all the random variables are identical. For linear estimators only the first two moments of the distribution are required and the stationarity hypothesis reduces to:

(i) $E[Z(\mathbf{x})] = m$ (a constant)

(ii) the covariance between the $Z(\mathbf{x_i})$ and $Z(\mathbf{x_j})$ can be expressed as:

$$(1..)$$

$$\text{Cov}[Z(\mathbf{x_i})Z(\mathbf{x_j})] = E[Z(\mathbf{x_i})Z(\mathbf{x_j})]-m^2$$

$$= C(\mathbf{h})$$

$$\text{where } \mathbf{h} = |\mathbf{x_i}-\mathbf{x_j}|$$

i.e. the covariance depends only on the vector distance $\mathbf{h}$ which separates $Z(\mathbf{x_i})$ and $Z(\mathbf{x_j})$ and not on the particular locations $\mathbf{x_i}$ and $\mathbf{x_j}$.
Note that the variance of $Z(\mathbf{x})$ is $C(0)$.

$(..$

In many cases, especially in geological applications, the random variable does not have a finite variance. In these cases the stationarity hypothesis is replaced by the so-called *intrinsic* hypothesis under which stationarity is limited to first order differences or increments:

$$Z(\mathbf{x_i}) - Z(\mathbf{x_j})$$

and the two previous conditions are replaced by the corresponding moments of the first order difference:

(i) $\quad E[Z(\mathbf{x_i})-Z(\mathbf{x_j})] = 0$

(ii) The variance of the differences:

$$\text{Var}[Z(\mathbf{x_i})-Z(\mathbf{x_j})] = 2\ \gamma(\mathbf{h})$$

$$\text{with } \mathbf{h} = |\mathbf{x_i} - \mathbf{x_j}|$$

(2)

exists and depends only on the vector distance $\mathbf{h}$ which separates $Z(\mathbf{x_i})$ and $Z(\mathbf{x_j})$ and not on the particular locations $\mathbf{x_i}$ and $\mathbf{x_j}$
This variance is known as the *variogram*

When the variance exists it is related to the variogram by:

$$C(\mathbf{h}) = C(0) - \gamma(\mathbf{h})$$

(3)

Throughout the paper $\gamma(\mathbf{h})$ will be called the variogram, i.e the variogram is one-half the variance of the increments in (2).

2.1 Kriging

Kriging is a minimum variance, unbiased, linear method of estimating the value of a random variable at one location from values available at surrounding locations. (It is possible to provide estimates of values over areas or volumes but this is beyond the scope of this paper).

The estimated value of the random variable $Z(\mathbf{x})$ at the location $\mathbf{x_0}$ is:

$$Z^*(\mathbf{x_0}) = \sum_{i=1}^{n} \lambda_i Z(\mathbf{x_i})$$

where $\mathbf{x_i}$, $i=1,...n$ are locations at which data are available.

The weights λ_i are found by minimising the estimation variance:

$$Var\ [Z(\mathbf{x_0}) - \sum_{i=1}^{n} \lambda_i Z(\mathbf{x_i})]$$

subject to the unbiasedness constraint:

$$E[Z^*(\mathbf{x_0})] = E[Z(\mathbf{x_0})] = m$$

The result is a set of simultaneous linear equations (see for example, Journel and Huijbregts (1978)):

$$
\left.
\begin{aligned}
\sum_{j=1}^{n} \lambda_j C_{ij} + \mu &= C_{oi} \quad \text{for } i=1, \ ...n \\[2ex]
\sum_{i=1}^{n} \lambda_i &= 1
\end{aligned}
\right\}
$$

(4)

where C_{ij} denotes $C(|x_i - x_j|)$

and C_{oi} denotes $C(|x_o - x_i|)$

The minimum estimation variance, known as the kriging variance is:

$$\sigma_K^2 = C(0) - \mu - \sum_{i=1}^{n} \lambda_i C_{oi}$$

Using the covariance/variogram relationship in (3) these equations can be written as:

$$\left. \begin{array}{c} \sum_{j=1}^{n} \lambda_j \gamma_{ij} - \mu = \gamma_{oi} \quad \text{for } i=1.,\ldots n \\[2em] \sum_{i=1}^{n} \lambda_i = 1 \\[2em] \sigma_K^2 = \sum_{i=1}^{n} \lambda_i \gamma_{oi} - \mu \end{array} \right\} \quad (5)$$

In practice, the covariance or variogram has to be estimated from the available data. The usual approach is to estimate the variogram and then, if necessary, deduce the covariance. The covariance form of the kriging equations will always give maximum elements on the diagonal of the left hand matrix which is more efficient for matrix inversion. In practice, when the covariance is not defined it is advisable to use a *psuedo-covariance* for kriging:

$$C'(h) = A - \gamma(h)$$

where A is an appropriately large value.

Two major advantages of the kriging approach are immediately apparent from (4) and (5):

(i) kriging is an exact interpolator, i.e when $z(x_o)$ is included in the data set:

$$z^*(x_o) = z(x_o)$$

(ii) Each estimation yields an estimation variance. Each contour map can thus have an associated estimation variance map or, by making assumptions about the distribution of the error, an error map.

2.2 Estimating the variogram

The standard variogram estimator is:

$$\gamma^*(h) = \sum_{i=1}^{n(h)} \frac{[z(x_i) - z(x_i + h)]^2}{2n(h)} \tag{6}$$

where $n(h)$ is the number of pairs separated by h

Other more robust and resistant estimators have been suggested, cf Armstrong (1982), Cressie and Hawkins (1980), Dowd (1984).

For a discussion of the relationship between theoretical and experimental variograms see Matheron (1965).

One of the major problems in experimental variogram calculation is irregularly spaced data. However, intelligent use of widely published approximation techniques usually yields satisfactory results, see, for example, David (1975), Journel and Huijbregts (1978). There are many efficient programs published in the literature [eg. Journel and Huijbregts (1978)] and many general packages available eg. Dowd (1983).

Variograms are calculated in as many directions as are necessary to quantify anisotropies. They are usually plotted and the various features of the graph can very often be related to physical and/or geographical features.

Experimental variograms take many forms and some

typical examples are shown in figure 4.

Figure 4(a) shows the type of variogram which is produced by stationary, uncorrelated data. The other variograms display various amounts of correlation and continuity.

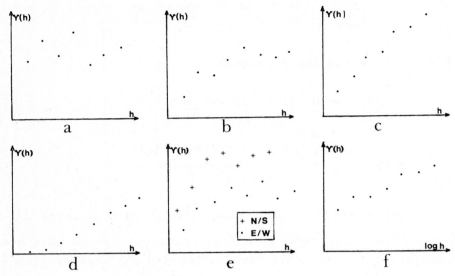

FIGURE 4: Typical variograms

2.2.1 Variogram/Covariance Models

Covariance or variogram values substituted in the kriging equations must be such that positive variances are always obtained. This is achieved by fitting positive definite models to the experimental variograms. Examples of models fitted to experimental variograms are shown in figure 5; the values of a define ranges of influence.

These variograms were calculated from measurements of the thickness of a Permian formation recorded at 83 locations irregularly scattered over a 30000m (East-West) x 20000m (North-South) field.

A complete account of variogram modelling can be found, for example, in Journel and Huijbregts (1978)

Model:

$$\gamma(h) = 2.5 + 12.0 \; \gamma_1(h) + 16.0 \; \gamma_2(h_z)$$

$$\gamma_1(h) = \begin{cases} \dfrac{3}{2} \dfrac{h}{a_1} - \dfrac{1}{2} \dfrac{h^3}{a_1^3} & h \leqslant a_1 \\[2mm] 1.0 & h > a_1 \end{cases} \qquad \gamma_2(h) = \begin{cases} \dfrac{3}{2} \dfrac{h_z}{a_2} - \dfrac{1}{2} \dfrac{h_z^3}{a_2^3} & h_z \leqslant a_2 \\[2mm] 1.0 & h_z > a_2 \end{cases}$$

$a_1 = 7500m \qquad a_2 = 5000m \qquad\qquad h_z \quad$ distance in NW/SE direction

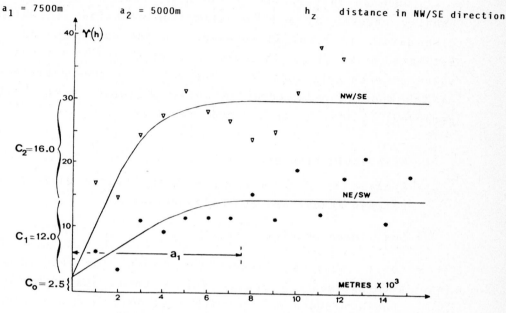

FIGURE 5:   Variogram Models

Models can be fitted by hand or by automatic techniques such as weighted non-linear least squares.

Some commonly used models are

$$\gamma(h) = C_0 + C|h|$$

$$\gamma(h) = C_0 + C\log|h|$$

$$\gamma(h) = \begin{cases} C_0 + C\left(\dfrac{3}{2}\dfrac{h}{a} - \dfrac{1}{2}\dfrac{h^3}{a^3}\right) & \text{for } |h| \leqslant a \\[2mm] C_0 + C & \text{for } |h| > a \end{cases} \tag{7}$$

the constant term C_0 is referred to as a *nugget effect* and is itself a legitimate model strictly defined as:

$$\gamma(\mathbf{h}) = \begin{cases} 0 & \text{for } |\mathbf{h}| = 0 \\ C_o & \text{for } |\mathbf{h}| > 0 \end{cases}$$

2.2.2 Verifying Models

Once an initial fit of the model has been made it is usually checked by a back estimation technique in which each datum, in turn, is removed from the data set and is estimated by kriging. This gives an actual and an estimated value at each data location. The values of the parameters of the model can be adjusted until the best results are achieved. Criteria for a "good" model are:

* Mean estimation error ≈ 0

* Average kriging variance $\approx$ mean squared difference between actual and estimated values

* Small mean absolute error

* Least squares linear regression (or a robust alternative) of actual values on estimated values should produce a line with a slope acceptably close to 1.0 and a relatively small ordinate axis intercept.

This procedure can be repeated with each datum, together with all other data within a specified radius removed. An example for the verification of the model in figure 5 is shown in figure 6.

When the model has been fitted and verified it is used to estimate the values at the nodes of a specified grid. These estimated grid values can then be entered as data to a standard contouring package (eg. GINOSURF) effectively overiding any regular gridding step.

In practice, a customised contouring program is used with the kriging of the regular grid as an integral part.

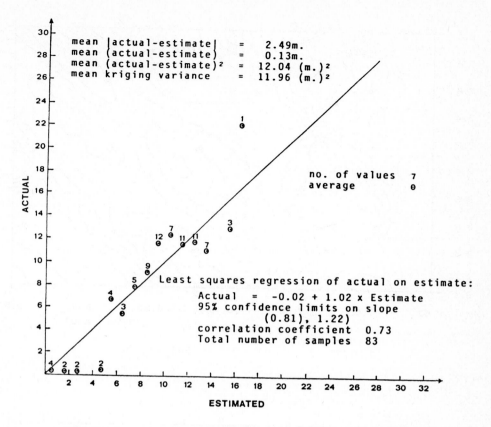

FIGURE 6 : MODEL VALIDATION WITH 1000m OF DATA REMOVED

2.3 Example

The variogram in figure 5, was used to estimate the values of formation thickness on a regular 2000m x 2000m grid. The regularly gridded values were then contoured using the proprietary software package GINSOSURF. Contours are shown in figure 7 with the associated error variance map in figure 8. Note, in particular, the much clearer structure in figure 7 compared to figure 2 and the absence of artefacts.

3. NON STATIONARITY

In the more general case stationarity cannot be assumed and:

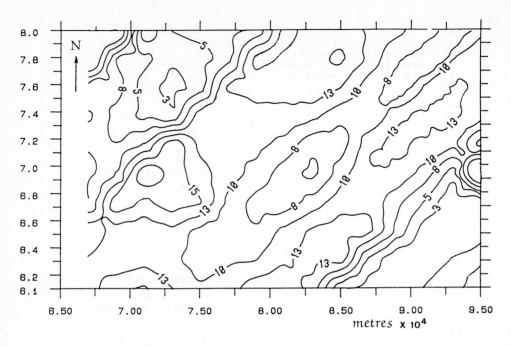

FIGURE 7 : CONTOURS OF THICKNESS

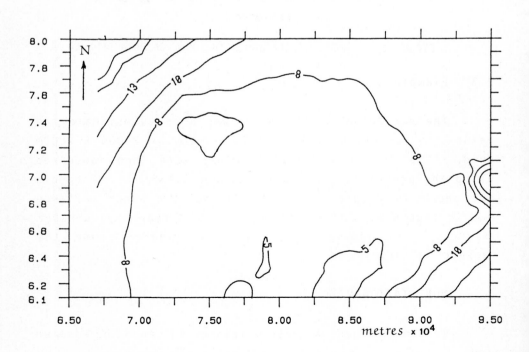

FIGURE 8 : ESTIMATION VARIANCES

$$E[Z(\mathbf{x})] = m(\mathbf{x}) \tag{8}$$

The geostatistical approach (cf. Matheron 1969) is to assume that $m(\mathbf{x})$ is a continuous and regular function which is expressed as a linear combination of K known functions, $f_k(\mathbf{x})$, with unknown coefficients, a_k:

$$m(\mathbf{x}) = \sum_{k=0}^{K} a_k \, f_k(\mathbf{x}) \tag{9}$$

The functions are usually restricted to polynomials and, in practice, it is seldom necessary to use any orders higher than K = 2. The polynomials in the real plane for k = 0,1,2 are summarised in table 1.

K	Polynomials
0	1 (i.e. constant mean)
1	1 x y
2	1 x y xy x^2 y^2

Table 1

The random function $Z(\mathbf{x})$ is considered to be the sum of the *deterministic* trend or *drift* term $m(\mathbf{x})$ and a random function $Y(\mathbf{x})$ sometimes called a *residual* random function:

$$Z(\mathbf{x}) = m(\mathbf{x}) + Y(\mathbf{x}) \tag{10}$$

To make any statistical inferences about $Z(\mathbf{x})$ the same types of hypotheses of stationarity made in (1) and (2) must be made about $Y(\mathbf{x})$:

(i)   *Stationary Hypothesis*

$$\text{Cov}\,[Y(\mathbf{x}_i)\,Y(\mathbf{x}_j)] = E[Y(\mathbf{x}_i)\,Y(\mathbf{x}_j)]$$

$$= C(\mathbf{h})$$

$$\text{where} \quad \mathbf{h} \quad = \quad |\mathbf{x}_i - \mathbf{x}_j|$$

(ii) *Intrinsic Hypothesis*

$$\text{Var}[Y(\mathbf{x}_i) - Y(\mathbf{x}_j)] \quad = \quad 2\gamma(\mathbf{h})$$

$$\text{where} \quad \mathbf{h} \quad = \quad |\mathbf{x}_i - \mathbf{x}_j|$$

Note that by construction: $E[Y(\mathbf{x})] = 0$

Note also that $C(\mathbf{h})$ and $\gamma(\mathbf{h})$ now refer to the covariance and variogram respectively of the *residual* random function $Y(\mathbf{x})$ and *not* $Z(\mathbf{x})$

3.1 Universal Kriging

For kriging, the value of $Z(\mathbf{x}_0)$ is estimated by:

$$Z^*(\mathbf{x}_0) \quad = \quad \sum_{i=1}^{n} \lambda_i \, Z(\mathbf{x}_i)$$

where λ_i are such that the estimation variance:

$$\text{Var} \, [Z(\mathbf{x}_0) - Z^*(\mathbf{x}_0)]$$

is a minimum subject to the constraint:

$$E[Z^*(\mathbf{x}_0)] \quad = \quad Z(\mathbf{x}_0)$$

A sufficient set of conditions for this minimisation is:

$$\left.\begin{aligned} \sum_{j=1}^{n} \lambda_j \, C_{ij} + \sum_{k=0}^{K} \mu_k f_k(\mathbf{x}_i) &= C_{i0} \qquad \text{for} \quad i=1,2,\ldots n) \\[2mm] \sum_{i=1}^{n} \lambda_i \, f_k(\mathbf{x}_i) &= f_k(\mathbf{x}_0) \qquad \text{for} \quad k=0,1,\ldots,K \end{aligned}\right\} \quad (11.
$$

The minimum estimation variance, or kriging variance is:

$$\sigma^2_K = C(\mathbf{0}) - \sum_{i=1}^{n} \lambda_i C_{io} - \sum_{k=0}^{K} \mu_k f_k(\mathbf{x_o}) \qquad \left\} \quad (..11) \right.$$

This form of kriging is usually referred to as *universal kriging* because it purportedly accounts for all cases whatever the values of the coefficients.

The universal kriging equations can also be expressed in terms of the variogram in exactly the same way as for the stationary case:

$$\left. \begin{aligned} \sum_{j=1}^{n} \lambda_j \gamma_{ij} - \sum_{k=0}^{K} \mu_k f_k(\mathbf{x_i}) &= \gamma_{io} \quad \text{for } i=1,\ldots n \\ \sum_{i=1}^{n} \lambda_i f_k(\mathbf{x_i}) &= f_k(\mathbf{x_o}) \quad \text{for } k=0,1,\ldots,K \\ \sigma^2_K &= \sum_{i=1}^{n} \lambda_i \gamma_{io} - \sum_{k=0}^{K} \mu_k f_k(\mathbf{x_o}) \end{aligned} \right\} \quad (12)$$

Note that for K=0 the simultaneous equations and kriging variance in (11) and (12) reduce to those for the stationary case given in (4) and (5).
Note also that Universal Kriging is an exact interpolator.

3.1.1 Estimating the drift

Under the hypothesis of stationarity of the Y(**x**) the drift itself can also be estimated by universal kriging. The estimate is:

$$m^*(\mathbf{x_o}) = \sum_{i=1}^{n} \lambda_i Z(\mathbf{x_i}) \qquad (13..)$$

where the λ_i are such that:

$$\sum_{j=1}^{n} \lambda_j C_{ij} + \sum_{k=0}^{K} \mu_k f_k(\mathbf{x_i}) = 0 \text{ for } i=1,\ldots,n$$

$$\sum_{i=1}^{n} \lambda_i f_k(\mathbf{x_i}) = f_k(\mathbf{x_o}) \quad \text{for } k=0,1,\ldots,K \qquad (..13)$$

The estimation variance is:

$$\sigma_m^2 = - \sum_{k=0}^{K} \mu_k f_k(\mathbf{x_o})$$

Under the *intrinsic* hypothesis for the Y(**x**) only *increments* $[m(\mathbf{x_i}) - m(\mathbf{x_j})]$ of the drift can be estimated and not the drift itself. The estimate and the kriging equations are:

$$m^*(\mathbf{x_o}) - m^*(\mathbf{y}) = \sum_{i=1}^{n} \lambda_i [Z(\mathbf{x_i}) - Z(\mathbf{y})]$$

$$= \sum_{i=1}^{n} \lambda_i Z(\mathbf{x_i})$$

where the λ_i are such that:

$$\sum_{j=1}^{n} \lambda_j \gamma_{ij} = \mu_0 + \sum_{k=1}^{K} \mu_k [f_k(\mathbf{x_i}) - f_k(\mathbf{y})]$$

$$\text{for } i=1,\ldots n$$

$$\sum_{i=1}^{n} \lambda_i [f_k(\mathbf{x_i}) - f_k(\mathbf{y})] = f_k(\mathbf{x_o}) - f_k(\mathbf{y})$$

$$\text{for } k=1,2,\ldots,K$$

$$\sum_{i=1}^{n} \lambda_i = 0$$

(14)

with estimation variance:

$$\sigma_m^2 = \sum_{k=0}^{K} \mu_k [f_k(\mathbf{x_o}) - f_k(\mathbf{y})]$$

Note that:

$$m(\mathbf{x_o}) - m(\mathbf{y}) = \sum_{k=0}^{K} a_k f_k(\mathbf{x_o}) - \sum_{k=0}^{K} a_k f_k(\mathbf{y})$$

$$= \sum_{k=1}^{K} a_k [f_k(\mathbf{x_o}) - f_k(\mathbf{y})] \qquad\qquad (15)$$

and the constant term a_0 is cancelled. Thus, under the intrinsic hypothesis the constant term will remain unknown.

3.1.2 Estimating the coefficients of the drift

Under the hypothesis of stationarity of the $Y(\mathbf{x})$ the coefficients of the drift can also be estimated by universal kriging. The universal kriging equations for the estimation of the coefficient a_ℓ are:

$$a_\ell^\star = \sum_{i=1}^{n} \lambda_i \, Z(\mathbf{x_i})$$

and the λ_i are such that:

$$\sum_{j=1}^{n} \lambda_j C_{ij} + \sum_{k=0}^{K} \mu_k f_k(\mathbf{x_i}) = 0 \quad \text{for } i=1,\ldots n$$

$$\sum_{i=1}^{n} \lambda_i f_k(\mathbf{x_i}) = \begin{cases} 1 & \text{if } \ell = k \\ 0 & \text{if } \ell \neq k \end{cases} \quad \text{for } k=0,1,\ldots,K \qquad (16)$$

The universal kriging variance is:

$$\sigma_{a_\ell}^2 = - \mu_\ell$$

Under the intrinsic hypothesis the coefficient a_ℓ, for $\ell > 0$, is estimated by:

$$a_\ell^\star = \sum_{i=1}^{n} \lambda_i \, Z(\mathbf{x_i}) \qquad\qquad (17..)$$

$$\sum_{j=1}^{n} \lambda_j \, \gamma_{ij} - \sum_{k=0}^{K} \mu_k f_k(x_i) = 0 \qquad \text{for } i=1,\ldots n$$

$$\sum_{i=1}^{n} \lambda_i \, f_k(x_i) = \begin{cases} 1 & \text{if } \ell = k \\ 0 & \text{if } \ell \neq k \end{cases} \qquad \text{for } k=1,\ldots,K$$

$$\sum_{i=1}^{n} \lambda_i = 0$$

$$\sigma^2_{a_\ell} = \mu_\ell$$

$$(..17)$$

and a_0 cannot be estimated

3.1.3 Practical Problems

The problems of applying universal kriging in practice have been summarised in a recent paper by Armstrong (1984a). These problems arise from the theoretical impossibility of estimating the underlying variogram or covariance of $Y(x)$ from the variogram or covariance of $Z(x)$. The variogram of $Y(x)$ is:

$$\gamma(h) = \tfrac{1}{2} \, \text{Var} \, [Y(x_i) - Y(x_j)]$$

$$= \gamma'(x_i, x_j) - \tfrac{1}{2} \, \text{Var}[m(x_i) - m(x_j)] \qquad (18)$$

where γ' denotes the variogram of $Z(x)$ and
$$h = |x_i - x_j|$$

In brief, the practical problems are:

(i)   in the intrinsic case the constant term a_0 in the drift cannot be estimated

(ii)   the universal kriging equations in (11) and (12) cannot be solved without first estimating the covariance or variogram. To estimate the covariance or variogram requires an estimate of the drift. But to estimate the drift requires an estimate of the covariance or variogram, cf. (13), (14) and (15), (16).

(iii) Even if a solution to (ii) is found (iteratively or directly as shown, for example, in Sabourin 1975) the variogram or covariance of the residuals cannot be inferred without considerable bias.

Notwithstanding the objections raised above, universal kriging in the form outlined here can prodouce satisfactory results if properly and intelligently applied.

The major drawback for contouring applications of Universal Kriging in this form is that it is by no means automatic and requires a considerable amount of manual input and subjective assessment. Subjectivity can be somewhat reduced by judicious use of such techniques as described, for example, in Sabourin (1975) and Olea (1972 and 1974) together with the back estimation techniques described earlier for the stationary case. However, a drift and variogram which produce good results is only one possible combination among an unknown number which may produce equally acceptable results.

The most advantageous situation is the one in which the drift is totally absent in one direction. Assuming isotropy, the variogram in this direction is taken as the true underlying variogram of the residuals. In other cases, the usual practice is to assume that the variogram model for the residuals is linear:

$$\gamma(\mathbf{h}) = b_0 + b_1 |\mathbf{h}|$$

and the coefficients b_0, b_1 and the drift are adjusted iteratively along the lines suggested in (ii) above together with back estimation.

Examples of variograms with drift are shown in figure 9. These variograms were calculated from 326 depth measurements at irregularly spaced locations over a 30000m (East-West) x 20000m (North-South) field. A summary of the verification of the models fitted to the experimental

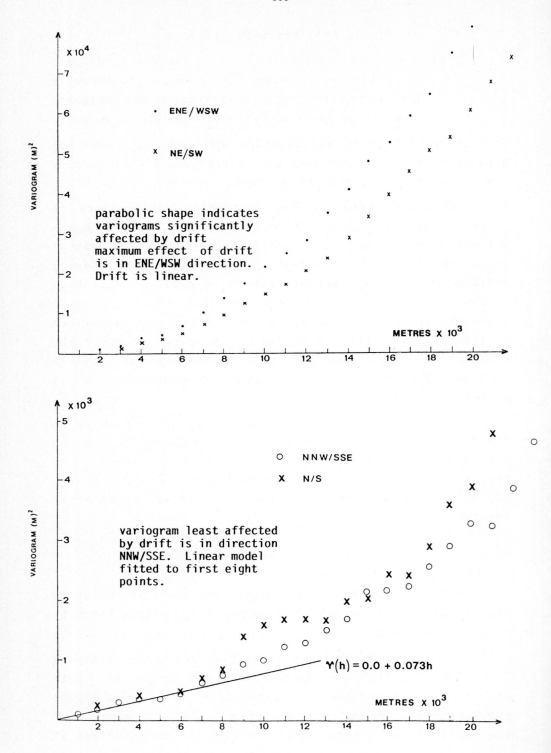

FIGURE 9

variograms in figure 9 is shown in figure 10. The variograms were used to estimate the depths at the nodes of a regular 2000m x 2000m grid. The regularly gridded values were then contoured using the proprietary software package GINOSURF. The results are shown in figure 11. The strong NNW/SSE alignments highlight the cause of the drift in the ENE/WSW direction: depth is fairly constant within the bands but changes significantly from one band to another. Note the absence of the artefacts which appear on figure 3.

The associated error variance map is shown in figure 12.

3.2   Generalised Covariances

The variogram can be written in a more general form as:

$$\text{Var}[Z(x_i) - Z(x_j)] = \text{Var}[\sum_{i=1}^{2} \beta_i Z(x_i)] \text{ with } \beta_1 = 1$$

$$\beta_2 = -1$$

$$= \sum_{i=1}^{2} \sum_{j=1}^{2} \beta_i \beta_j C(|x_i - x_j|)$$

In the stationary case the first order difference, or increment, $Z(x_i) - Z(x_j)$, filters out the constant drift. In the non-stationary case higher order differences would be required to filter out the higher orders of the polynomial drift. This approach, used in time series analysis, leads to *generalised increments* and *generalised covariances*, cf. Matheron (1973, 1976), Delfiner (1976).

The first order difference $Z(x)-Z(x+h)$ is a particular case of a generalised increment. If $Z(x)$ is a function in the real plane then a linear combination:

$$\sum_{i=1}^{m} \beta_i Z(x_i)$$

(19)

of m values is a generalised increment of order K if, and

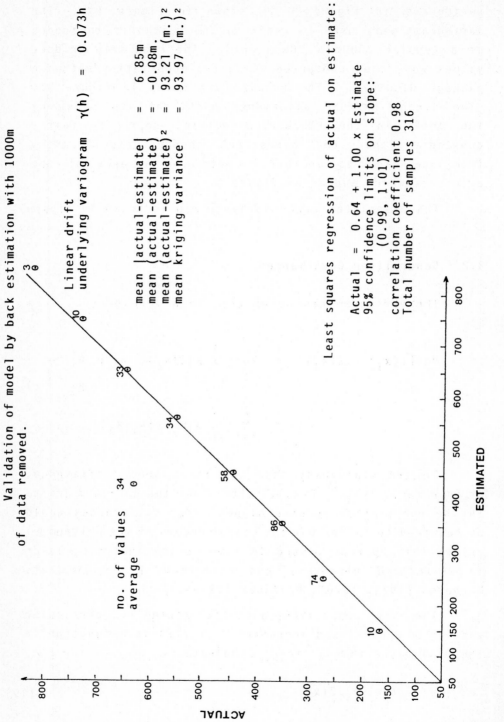

Validation of model by back estimation with 1000m of data removed.

Linear drift
underlying variogram $\gamma(h)$ = 0.073h

mean |actual−estimate|	=	6.85 m
mean (actual−estimate)	=	−0.08m.
mean (actual−estimate)^2	=	93.21 (m.)^2
mean kriging variance	=	93.97 (m.)^2

no. of values   34
average   0

Least squares regression of actual on estimate:

Actual = 0.64 + 1.00 x Estimate
95% confidence limits on slope:
              (0.99, 1.01)
correlation coefficient 0.98
Total number of samples 316

ACTUAL

ESTIMATED

FIGURE 10

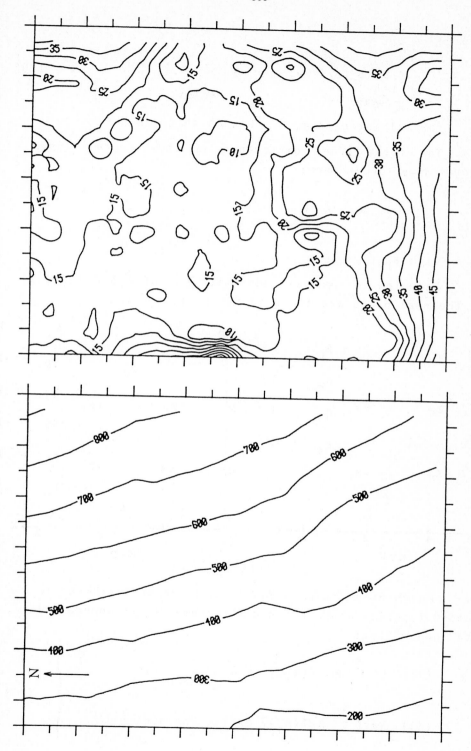

metres x 10^4

FIGURE 12 : ESTIMATION VARIANCES

FIGURE 11: CONTOURS OF DEPTH

only if:

$$\sum_{i=1}^{m} \beta_i \, x_i^{\, j} \, y_i^{\, \ell} \; = \; 0 \tag{20}$$

for all integers j, $\ell \geqslant 0$ such that $j + \ell \leqslant K$

The first order difference is thus a *generalised increment* of order zero:

$$\sum_{i=1}^{2} \beta_i \; = \; 0$$

with $\beta_1 = 1$ and $\beta_2 = -1$

Examples of generalised increments of order 1 and 2 in the real plane are shown in figure 13.

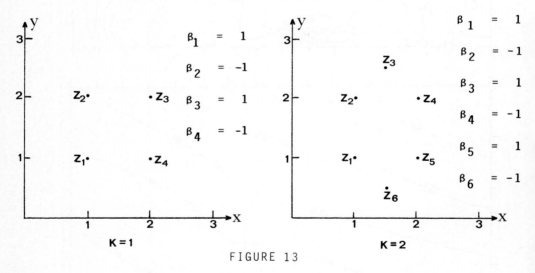

FIGURE 13

An *Intrinsic Random Function* of order K (IRF-K) is a random function whose K^{th} order increments are second order stationary i.e.:

$$\text{(i)} \quad E\left[\sum_{i=1}^{m} \beta_i \, Z(x_i) \right] \; = \; 0$$

$$\text{(ii)} \quad \text{Var}\left[\sum_{i=1}^{m} \beta_i Z(x_i) \right] \text{ exists and does not} \tag{21}$$

depend on the locations x_i

Just as the intrinsic random function of order zero (IRF-0):

$$Z(x) - Z(x+h)$$

filters out the constant mean so higher order differences, or increments, filter out polynomials.

The variance of an IRF-K can be defined as:

$$Var[\sum_{i=1}^{m} \beta_i Z(x_i)] = \sum_{i=1}^{m} \sum_{j=1}^{m} \beta_i \beta_j C(|x_i - x_j|) \qquad (22)$$

which again is a generalisation of the case K=0 in which (22) reduces to (3):

$$VAR[Z(x_1) - Z(x_2)] = 2C(0) - 2C(|x_1 - x_2|)$$

$C(h)$ is now called a *generalised covariance*. The left hand side of (22) defines a *generalised variogram* although to be consistent with the definition used in this paper it should be divided by

$$\sum_{i=1}^{m} \beta_i^2$$

The relationship between the generalised variogram and the generalised covariance for K>0 is more complex than that given in (3), cf. Chiles (1979).

3.2.1 Models for generalised covariances

The most widely used models for generalised covariances [cf. Matheron (1973) and Delfiner (1976)] are polynomials of the form:

$$C(h) = b_0 + \sum_{j=0}^{K} (-1)^{j+1} b_{j+1} |h|^{2j+1}$$

where the coefficients are such that $C(\mathbf{h})$ is conditionally positive definite. These conditions, together with the corresponding covariances for values of K used in practice are:

$$K=0 \quad : \quad C(\mathbf{h}) = b_0 - b_1 |\mathbf{h}| \qquad b_0 \geqslant 0, b_1 \geqslant 0$$

$$K=1 \quad : \quad C(\mathbf{h}) = b_0 - b_1 |\mathbf{h}| + b_2 |\mathbf{h}|^3$$

$$b_0 \geqslant 0, b_1 \geqslant 0, b_2 \geqslant 0 \qquad (23)$$

$$K=2 \quad : \quad C(\mathbf{h}) = b_0 - b_1 |\mathbf{h}| + b_2 |\mathbf{h}|^3 - b_3 |\mathbf{h}|^5$$

$$b_0 \geqslant 0, b_1 \geqslant 0, b_2 \geqslant 0, b_3 \geqslant 0, b_2 \geqslant -2\sqrt{b_1 b_3}$$

3.2.2 Estimation using Generalised Covariances

Minimisation of the estimation variance subject to the unbiasedness constraints leads to:

$$Z^*(\mathbf{x_0}) = \sum_{i=1}^{n} \lambda_i Z(\mathbf{x_i})$$

$$\sum_{j=1}^{n} \lambda_j C_{ij} + \sum_{k=0}^{K} \mu_k f_k(\mathbf{x_i}) = C_{io} \qquad \text{for} \quad i=1,2,..n$$

$$\sum_{i=1}^{n} \lambda_i f_k(\mathbf{x_i}) = f_k(\mathbf{x_0}) \qquad \text{for } k=0,1...,K \qquad (24)$$

$$\sigma_K^2 = C(0) - \sum_{i=1}^{n} \lambda_i C_{io} - \sum_{k=0}^{K} \mu_k f_k(\mathbf{x_0})$$

and C_{ij} denotes the *generalised covariance* $C(|\mathbf{x_i}-\mathbf{x_j}|)$

Note that the solution no longer requires the estimation of the drift. The only requirement in (24) is the generalised covariance; the $f_k(\mathbf{x})$ are assumed to be known polynomials as before.

3.2.3 Fitting Models

In practice it is seldom necessary to consider any values of $K > 2$.

The problem is to fit a generalised covariance $C(\mathbf{h})$ such that:

$$Var[\sum_{i=1}^{m} \beta_i Z(\mathbf{x_i})] = \sum_{i=1}^{m} \sum_{j=1}^{m} \beta_i \beta_j C(|\mathbf{x_i} - \mathbf{x_j}|)$$

where the β_i satisfy the constraints in (20)

The most widely used approach is to fit one of the polynomials in (23) by weighted least squares; other approaches involve optimisation or iterative techniques.

For example, for $K=0$, the weighted least squares approach is to minimise the weighted sum of squares:

$$SS = \sum_{\ell} w_{\ell} \left\{ [z(\mathbf{x_i}) - z(\mathbf{x_j})]^2 - b_0 - b_1 |\mathbf{h}| \right\}^2$$

where the summation ℓ is taken over all data configurations ie. over all pairs of data $z(\mathbf{x_i})$, $z(\mathbf{x_j})$ for which $|\mathbf{x_i} - \mathbf{x_j}| = h$. This is simply a weighted least squares fit of the data to a linear variogram.

For $K=1$ the weights β_i must be chosen such that:

$$\sum_{i=1}^{4} \beta_i = 0$$

$$\sum_{i=1}^{4} \beta_i x_i = 0$$

$$\sum_{i=1}^{4} \beta_i y_i = 0$$

To find a solution one weight must be arbitrarily set to a value (eg. to 1).

Once the weights are determined the following sum of squares must be minimised

$$SS = \sum_{\ell} w_{\ell} \left\{ \left[\sum_{i=1}^{4} \beta_i z(x_i) \right]^2 - \sum_{i=1}^{4} \sum_{j=1}^{4} \beta_i \beta_j C(|x_i - x_j|) \right\}^2$$

where $C(|x_i - x_j|) = b_0 + b_1|x_i - x_j| + b_2|x_i - x_j|^3$

and the summation ℓ is taken over all data configurations.

For K=2, the weights β_i are first found by solving the simultaneous equations:

$$\sum_{i=1}^{7} \beta_i = 0$$

$$\sum_{i=1}^{7} \beta_i x_i = 0$$

$$\sum_{i=1}^{7} \beta_i y_i = 0$$

$$\sum_{i=1}^{7} \beta_i x_i y_i = 0$$

$$\sum_{i=1}^{7} \beta_i x_i^2 = 0$$

$$\sum_{i=1}^{7} \beta_i y_i^2 = 0$$

after first arbitrarily setting one weight (eg. to 1) The next step is to minimise the weighted sum of squares:

$$SS = \sum_{\ell} w_{\ell} \left\{ \left[\sum_{i=1}^{7} \beta_i z(x_i) \right]^2 - \sum_{i=1}^{7} \sum_{j=1}^{7} \beta_i \beta_j C(|x_i - x_j|) \right\}^2$$

where:

$$C(|x_i - x_j|) = b_0 - b_1|x_i - x_j| + b_2|x_i - x_j|^3 - b_5|x_i - x_j|^5$$

with the coefficients satisfying the constraints given in (23) and the summation ℓ is taken over all data configurations.

In practice all combinations of polynomials in (23) are fitted and those with coefficients which do not satisfy the constraints in (23) are rejected.

For large data sets it may not be feasible to use all data configurations. An alternative is to select subsets at random.

In all cases the weights ($w_ℓ$) should, ideally, be chosen to equalise the variances for each data configuration, i.e for a given data configuration:

$$w_ℓ = 1/Var[\sum_{i=1}^{m} \beta_i z(x_i)] \quad \text{for configuration } ℓ$$

As this is not possible, suggested alternatives (cf. Delfiner, 1978) are:

$$w_ℓ = 1 / \sum_{i=1}^{m} \sum_{j=1}^{m} \beta_i \beta_j |x_i - x_j|$$

or

$$w_ℓ = 1 / \sum_{i=1}^{m} \sum_{j=1}^{m} \beta_i \beta_j |x_i - x_j|^3$$

As a criterion for goodness of fit the normalised residual sum of squares:

$$\frac{SS}{Var[\sum_{i=1}^{m} \beta_i z(x_i)]}$$

can be compared to the value of 2/3 which would be obtained under assumptions of normal distributions. Values close to 1.0 indicate a poor fit.

The only remaining problem is to determine the order, K, of the IRF.

This could be done by fitting all possible models in (23) and choosing the model which gives the best fit. However this can be cumbersome as there are 15 possible models in (23) obtained by setting various coefficients to zero. In addition there is no statistical test available for testing the significance of the goodness of fit criterion above.

The recommended practice is (cf. Delfiner, 1976):

(i)   Determine the order K by *assuming* a model and applying the back estimation technique using the universal kriging equations in (24)

(ii)   fit a generalised covariance of order K using weighted least squares

(iii) check the generalised covariance model by back estimation using (24). Adjust the coefficients if necessary.

Step (i) may seem a little dubious but it should be remembered that it is only the *order* of the drift which is required and, provided that a resistant method of assessment is used, the relative performance of the estimators should be the same regardless of the model, i.e. if a linear drift is present, estimation using any other order of drift, including zero, should be consistently worse than using a linear drift, whatever the covariance model.

The usual practice is to use a linear model

$$C(h) \quad = \quad b_1 |\mathbf{h}|$$

or a pure nugget effect

$$C(h) = b_0$$

In the latter case universal kriging is simply piecewise least squares linear regression.

Although the procedure of fitting the generalised covariance function can be made automatic, care should be taken to ensure that the data are homogeneous; a "black box" approach can give meaningless results.

The two previous examples of depth and thickness were identified by the generalised covariance procedure as:

thickness : $K=0$ $C(h) = 4.1 - 0.003|h|$

depth : $K=1$ $C(h) = -0.091|h|$

The model for thickness, although correctly identifying the absence of drift, is inadequate to describe the type of anisotropy clearly indicated by the data and the variograms in figure 5. Contours produced by the generalised covariance function are significantly different from those in figure 7.

As expected, the model for depth produces identical contours to those in figure 11; estimation variances are slightly higher (by a constant factor).

The example for thickness indicates a failing in the technique which is particularly marked for the case $K=0$: the generalised covariance models are all isotropic. For $K>0$ it is assumed that any anisotropies are filtered out along with the drift. For $K=0$ variogram calculation and modelling in the usual manner appear to almost always give better results. This step is recommended for all applications even if only as a preliminary to fitting a generalised covariance.

3.2.4 Kriging and Splines

A significant recent development is the demonstration by Matheron (1980) of the formal equivalence of cubic spline interpolation and kriging in a global neighbourhood (i.e using all data for each estimation - cf. section 5) with a linear trend and the generalised covariance:

$$C(h) \;=\; h^2 \log h$$

Watson (1984) gives a clear demonstration of the equivalence for the one-dimensional case and shows that the Green's function used in cubic spline interpolation is the uncentred covariance of some random function. Thus, the spline solution could always be derived via kriging but the converse is not necessarily true. The covariance function inherently assumed in the spline interpolation will usually not be the same as that provided by a rigorous geostatistical analysis and may not even be compatible with the data.

Dubrule (1983) gives a method of combining kriging and spline interpolation.

4.   UNRELIABLE DATA

Suppose that some or all of the data are subject to error or some degree of uncertainty. The random function representation is:

$$Y(\mathbf{x}) \;=\; Z(\mathbf{x}) + \mathcal{E}(\mathbf{x})$$

where $Y(\mathbf{x})$ is the observed random function

$Z(\mathbf{x})$ is the error free random function

and $\mathcal{E}(\mathbf{x})$ is an error random function

4.1 Unbiased Data Errors

Let $\mathcal{E}(x)$ be such that

(i) $E[\mathcal{E}(x)] = 0$ i.e., the errors are unbiased or non-systematic

(ii) $Cov[\mathcal{E}(x_i)\mathcal{E}(x_j)] = 0 \quad \forall i \neq j$

i.e. errors are uncorrelated

(iii) $Cov[Z(x)\mathcal{E}(x_i)] = 0 \quad \forall i, x$

i.e. $\mathcal{E}(x)$ is independent of $Z(x)$

Then the kriging equations become (Matheron 1971, Delhomme 1974, Dowd 1984):

$$
\left.
\begin{aligned}
Z^*(x_0) &= \sum_{i=1}^{n} \lambda_i Y(x_i) \\[2mm]
\sum_{j=1}^{n} \lambda_j C_{ij} + \lambda_i s_i^2 + \sum_{k=0}^{K} \mu_k f_k(x_i) &= C_{io} \quad \text{for } i=1,\ldots n \\[2mm]
\sum_{i=1}^{n} \lambda_i f_k(x_i) &= f_k(x_0) \quad \text{for } k=0,1,\ldots K \\[2mm]
\sigma_K^2 &= C(0) - \sum_{i=1}^{n} \lambda_i C_{io} - \sum_{k=0}^{K} \mu_k f_k(x_0) \\[2mm]
s_i^2 &= Var[\mathcal{E}(x_i)] = E[\mathcal{E}(x_i)]^2 \\[2mm]
\text{and} \quad C_{ij} &= Cov[Z(x_i)Z(x_j)]
\end{aligned}
\right\} \quad (25)
$$

In practice, s_i^2 will usually be derived from the likely range of the error for the data value at x_i. If the data value at x_i is not subject to error then $s_i^2 = 0$.

4.2 Biased Data Errors

Assume that:

(i) $\quad\quad E[\mathcal{E}(\mathbf{x})] = e_0 \quad$ (unknown)

(ii) $\quad\quad E[\mathcal{E}(\mathbf{x_i})\mathcal{E}(\mathbf{x_j})] = 0 \quad \forall i \neq j$

(iii) $\quad\quad E[\mathcal{E}(\mathbf{x_i})Z(\mathbf{x})] = 0 \quad \forall i, x$

In this case there must be at least one of the $Z(\mathbf{x_i})$ which can be measured free from error or uncertainty otherwise e_0 cannot be separated from $E[Z(\mathbf{x})]$.

Let S_0 be the set of locations $\{\mathbf{x_i}\}$ at which data are free of error and S_1 be the set of locations $\{\mathbf{x_j}\}$ at which data measurements are subject to error. The kriging equations are

$$Z^*(\mathbf{x_0}) = \sum_{i \varepsilon S_0} \lambda_i Z(\mathbf{x_i}) + \sum_{i \varepsilon S_1} \nu_i Z(\mathbf{x_i})$$

$$\sum_{j \varepsilon S_0} \lambda_j C_{ij} + \sum_{j \varepsilon S_1} \nu_j C_{ij} + \sum_{k=0}^{K} \mu_k f_k(\mathbf{x_i}) = C_{io} \quad\quad i \varepsilon S_0$$

$$\sum_{j \varepsilon S_0} \lambda_j C_{ij} + \sum_{j \varepsilon S_1} \nu_j C_{ij} + \nu_i s_i^2 + \sum_{k=0}^{K} \mu_k f_k(\mathbf{x_i}) + \mu_{K+1} = C_{io} \quad\quad i \varepsilon S_1$$

$$\sum_{i \varepsilon S_0} \lambda_i f_k(\mathbf{x_i}) + \sum_{i \varepsilon S_1} \nu_i f_k(\mathbf{x_i}) = f_k(\mathbf{x_0})$$

$$\text{for } k = 0, 1 \ldots K$$

$$\sum_{i \varepsilon S_1} \nu_i = 0$$

$$\sigma_K^2 = C(0) - \sum_{i \varepsilon S_0} \lambda_i C_{io} - \sum_{i \varepsilon S_1} \nu_i C_{io} - \sum_{k=0}^{K} \mu_k f_k(\mathbf{x_0})$$

(26)

5. THE DUAL FORM OF KRIGING

If the kriging equations are solved in parametric form for the $\{\lambda_i, \mu_k\}$ and these are substituted back into the kriging equations a *dual* system of kriging equations is obtained in a manner analogous to the dual and primal forms of a linear program, see, for example, Matheron (1982), Galli et al. (1984), Royer and Vieira (1984). The two forms are summarised in table 2.

Primal   **Dual**

$$Z^*(x_o) = \sum_{i=1}^{n} \lambda_i Z(x_i) \qquad\qquad Z^*(x_o) = \sum_{1=1}^{n} d_i C_{io} + \sum_{k=0}^{K} P_k f_k(x_o)$$

$$\sum_{j=1}^{n} \lambda_i C_{ij} + \sum_{k=0}^{K} \mu_k f_k(x_i) = C_{io} \qquad\qquad \sum_{j=1}^{n} d_j C_{ij} + \sum_{k=0}^{K} P_k f_k(x_i) = Z(x_i)$$

$$\text{for } i=1,\ldots n \qquad\qquad\qquad\qquad \text{for } i=1,\ldots n$$

$$\sum_{i=1}^{n} \lambda_i f_k(x_i) = f_k(x_o) \qquad\qquad \sum_{i=1}^{n} d_i f_k(x_i) = 0$$

$$\text{for } k=0,1,\ldots K \qquad\qquad\qquad \text{for } k=0,1,\ldots K$$

Table 2: Primal and dual kriging systems

Unfortunately, there is no such duality for the kriging variance. The matrix expression for the kriging variance is:

$$\sigma_K^2 = C(0) - [C_{io} \mid f_k(x_o)] \begin{bmatrix} C_{ij} & f_k(x_i) \\ \hline f_k(x_j) & 0 \end{bmatrix}^{-1} \begin{bmatrix} C_{io} \\ \hline f_k(x_o) \end{bmatrix}$$

The matrix of covariances and drift polynomials must be inverted to solve both the primal and dual kriging systems. There are a number of more efficient alternatives to direct inversion usually involving decomposition of the matrix, eg. Cholesky decomposition or the factorisation suggested by Davis and Culhane (1984).

There are two major advantages of the dual kriging system for automatic contouring, both of which arise from the fact that the solutions $\{d_j, p_k\}$ are independent of the location of the value which is to be interpolated. Each data value has an associated d_j which does not change when the location to be estimated or interpolated changes.

5.1   Kriging in a Global Neighbourhood

If all data values are included in the dual kriging system the equations need only be solved once and the value at any location can be interpolated or estimated. Such an approach, besides being more computationally efficient than the primal form, avoids the discontinuities sometimes produced by the traditional moving neighbourhood approach which uses different subsets of the data to estimate the value at different locations.

In applications with large data sets the only major problem is to invert a very large matrix. However, very efficient solutions, involving decomposition and reduction of the matrix to symmetric band form, have been proposed by Davis and Culhane (1984) and Davis and Grivet (1984).

5.2   Direct Contouring

In the dual formulation of the kriging equations, the kriging estimator appears as a direct interpolator cf. Matheron (1971) Galli et al. (1984). In this form it can be used to contour directly rather than being used simply as a means of producing a set of estimated values at the nodes of a regular grid. Contours can thus be made to pass through data points and inconsistent contours near data points can be avoided. In this form kriging can be seen as an exact interpolator (cf. Matheron (1971) p.168f). Further work needs to be done to fully automate the method but initial results presented by Galli et al. (1984) are encouraging.

6.   SMOOTHING

In common with other contouring methods, kriged contours may require smoothing for a number of reasons, chief among which are:

(i) discontinuities arising from the use of different data subsets for estimation at each location

(ii) interpolation in areas of sparse data

(iii) interpolation near the boundaries of two areas with significantly different densities of data

(iv) extraploation, especially around borders

The first case is best dealt with by using the global approach discussed in section 5.

Filters are often used for smoothing contours. These may be of the standard type (eg. Royle et al., 1981) or be a function of the estimation variance at a particular location. In the latter case the amount of smoothing to be applied may be proportional to the magnitude of the estimation variance.

Methods for obtaining smoothed, extrapolated contours are discussed in Renard and Yancey (1984)

7. SUMMARY AND CONCLUSIONS

Geostatistical techniques provide methods of direct and indirect interpolation which are founded on sound statistical theory and are based on the individual character- istics of each data set. In addition, they provide an estimation variance for each estimated value.

Kriging is a weighted moving average method in which the weights assigned to data values depend on:

(i) the inherent variability of the variable as exhibited by the data and expressed in the variogram or covariance

(ii) the position of the data values relative to the point to be estimated or interpolated as expressed by the C_{io} and Y_{io} terms in the kriging equations

(iii) the position of each data value relative to all others as expressed by the C_{ij} and γ_{ij} terms in the kriging equations. For example, kriging distinguishes between the cases shown in figure 1.

Kriging also satisfies all of the properties listed in 1.1. Kriging in a global neighbourhood gives a surface which is continuous with continuous first derivatives. Note that there is no restriction on the weights to be positive; the more continuous the variogram model the more likely it is that some of the weights will be negative. Note also that stationarity is a property of the random function model and **not** of the data.

Although only linear kriging techniques have been discussed in this paper, kriging has been extended to various non-linear forms. In general, non-linear kriging techniques involve some type of transformation of the data to normal (gaussian) values. Estimation is done using the transformed values and a variogram/covariance derived from the normal data. The estimate is then transformed back to the original data space. See, for example, Matheron (1976b), Rendu (1979), Dowd (1982).

The techniques can also be extended to the multivariate case in which kriging is known as co-kriging. See, for example Journel and Huijbregts (1978), Myers (1982, 1984).

Some of the criticisms often levelled at geostatistical techniques are discussed below.

When a variogram or covariance has a nugget effect greater than zero, contours may appear on the wrong side of data points. Note, however, that if a datum location coincides with a grid node the kriged value will be equal to the true value. Although there are statistically valid reasons for the "violation of data points" it can be avoided by direct contouring using the dual form of kriging in section 5. It should never be avoided artificially by setting a non-zero nugget effect to zero.

The criteria of minimum variance and unbiasedness may not always be the best criteria for estimation. Much current research in geostatistics is devoted to such alternatives as minimum absolute deviation, see for example Dowd and Scott (1982), Dowd (1984) and Journel (1984).

To the uninitiated, variogram model fitting often appears, at best, subjective and at worst, dubious. However, estimates are generally very robust with respect to models and careful data analysis and scrutiny can eliminate many problems in variogram interpretation. A very good summary of common problems encountered in variogram interpretation and calculation is given in Armstrong (1984c).

The need to fit a model is often seen as a drawback. However, besides offering a critical assessment of the data, model fitting is a crucial element in an adaptive technique.

8.   REFERENCES

Armstrong, M. (1984) Problems with universal kriging. Journal Int. Assoc. Math. Geol. Vol 16 No 1 pp. 101-108.

Armstrong, M. (1984b) Improving the modelling and estimation of the variogram. Geostatistics for Natural Resources Characterisation NATO ASI Series C: Mathematical and Physical Sciences Vol 122 part 1. Ed. Verly et al., pub. D. Reidel Publishing Co. Dordrecht Holland pp 1-20.

Armstrong, M. (1984c) Common Problems seen in variograms. Journal of the Int. Assoc. Math. Geology vol 16 No 3 pp 305-313

Chiles, J.P. (1979) Le variogramme généralisé. Note Interne No N-612 Centre de Morphologie Mathematique (CGMM) Fontainebleau, France.

Cressie, N. (1984) Towards resistant geostatistics. Geostatistics for Natural Resources Characterisation NATO ASI Series C: Mathematical and Physical Sciences vol 122 part 1. Ed. Verly et al., pub. D. Reidel Publishing Co, Dordrecht Holland pp 21-44.

Cressie, N. and Hawkins, D. (1980) Robust estimation of the variogram. Journal Int. Assoc. Math. Geology. vol 12 pp 115-125.

Davis, M.W. and Culhant, P.G. (1984) Contouring very large data sets using kriging. Geostatistics for Natural Resources Charact-erisation. NATO A.S.I. Series C: Mathematical and Physical Sciences vol 122 part 2 Ed. Verly, G. et al., pub. D. Reidel Publishing Co. Dordrecht Holland pp 599-618.

Davis, M.W. and Grivet, C.L. (1984) Kriging in a global neighbourhood. Journal of the Int. Assoc. for Math. Geology. vol. 16 No 3 pp 249-265.

Delfiner, P. (1976) Linear estimation of non-stationary spatial phenomena. Advanced Geostatistics in the Mining Industry NATO ASI Series C: Mathematical and Physical Sciences vol. 24 Ed. Guarascio et al. pub. D. Reidel Dordrecht Holland pp 49-68

Dowd, P.A. (1982) Lognormal Kriging - the general case. Journal of the Int. Assoc. for Math. Geol. vol 14 No 5 pp475-499.

Dowd, P.A. (1983) GEOSTAT3 - Users Manual. Dept. Mining and Mineral Eng. University of Leeds pp 400

Dowd, P.A. (1984) The variogram and kriging: robust and resistant estimators. Geostatistics for Natural Resources Characterisation. NATO ASI Series C: Mathematical and Physical Sciences

vol 122 part 1 Ed. Verly et al., pub. D. Reidel
Publishing Co. Dordrecht, Holland, pp 91-106.

Dowd, P.A. and Scott, I.R. (1982) Geostatistical application
in stratigraphic orebodies. Sixth Australian
Statistical Conference. Melbourne University,
August 1982.

Dubrule, O. (1983) Two methods with different objectives:
splines and kriging. Journal of the Int. Assoc.
for Math. Geology vol. 15 pp 249-261.

Galli, A., Murillo, E. and Thomann J. (1984) Dual kriging
- its properties and its uses in direct contouring. Geostatistics for Natural Resource Characterisation NATO ASI Series C: Mathematical and
Physical Sciences vol. 122 part 2 Ed. Verly et
al., pub. D. Reidel, Dordrecht, Holland pp
621-634,

Journel, A. (1984) MAD and Conditional quantile estimators.
Geostatistics for Natural Resources Characteri-

sation NATO ASI Series C: Mathematical and
Physical Sciences vol 122 part 1 Ed. Verly et
al., pub. D. Reidel, Holland pp 261-270.

Journel, A. and Huijbregts, C. (1978) Mining Geostatistics
Academic Press, London.

Matheron, G. (1965) Les variables régionalisés at leur
estimation Doc. Eng. Thesis. Masson, Paris
306p.

Matheron, G. (1969) Le Krigeage Universel Frascicule No 1
Cahiers du Centre de Morphologie Mathematique
(CGMM) Fontainebleau, France 83 pp.

Matheron, G. (1971) The theory of regionalised variables
and its application. Fascicule No 5 Cahiers
du Centre de Morphologie Mathematique,
Fontainebleau, France 212 pp.

Matheron, G. (1973) The intrinsic Random Functions and their applications. Advances in Applied Probability. Dec. 1973 No. 5 pp 439-468.

Matheron, G. (1976a) Le choix des modèles en geostatistique. Advanced geostatistices in the mining industry. NATO ASI Series Ed. Guarascio, David and Huijbregts. pub. D. Reidel Publishing Co. Dordrecht, Holland pp 3-10.

Matheron, G. (1976b) A simple substitute for conditional Expectation: disjunctive kriging. In Advanced Geostatistics in the Mining Industry, NATO ASI Series C: Mathematical and Physical Sciences vol. 24 Ed. Guarascio et al., pub. D. Reidel, Dordrecht, Holland. pp 221-236.

Matheron, G. (1980) Splines et krigeage: Leur equivalence formelle Note Interne CGMM Fontainebleau, France.

Myers, D.E. (1982) Matrix formulation of cokriging Journal of the Int. Assoc. for Mathematical Geology Vol. 14 No 3 pp 249-257.

Myers, D.E. (1984) Co-kriging - new developments. Geostatistics for Natural Resources Characterisation NATO ASI Series C: Mathematical and Physical Sciences Vol 122 part 1. Ed Verly et al., pub. D. Reidel, Dordrecht, Holland pp 295-305.

Olea, R.. (1972) Application of regionalised variable theory to automatic contouring. Special Report to the American Petroleum Institute, Research Project 131.

Olea, R.A. (1974) Optimal contour mapping using universal kriging. Journal of Geophysical Research Vol. 79 pp 695-702.

Renard, D. and Yancy, J.D. (1984) Smoothing discontinuities when extrapolating using moving neighbourhoods. Geostatistics for Natural Resources Characterisation NATO ASI Series C: Mathematical and Physical Sciences, Vol 122 part 2 Ed. Verly et al., pub. D. Reidel, Holland, pp679-690.

Rendu, J.M. (1979) Normal and lognormal estimation Journal of the Int. Assoc. for Math. Geol. Vol 11 pp 407-422.

Royer, J.J. and Vieira, P.C. (1984) Dual formulation of kriging Geostatistics for Natural Resources Characterisation. NATO ASI Series C: Mathematical and Physical Sciences Vol 122 part 2 Ed. Verly et al. pub. D. Reidel, Dordrecht, Holland, pp 691-702.

Royle, A.G., Clausen, F.L. and Frederikson, P. (1981) Practical Universal Kriging and automatic contouring. Geo-Processing Vol. 1 pp 377-394.

Sabin, M.A. (1985) Contouring NATO A.S.I. on fundamental algorithms for computer graphics Ilkley U.K.

Sabourin, R. (1976) Application of two methods for the interpretation of the underlying variogram. Advanced Geostatistics in the mining industry. NATO ASI Series C: Mathematical and Physical Sciences. Vol. 24 Ed. Guarascio et al., pub D. Reidel Dordrecht, Holland, pp 101-109.

Watson, G.S. (1984) Smoothing and interpolation by kriging and with splines. Journal of the Int. Assoc. Math. Geol. Vol. 16 No. pp 601-616.

ALGORITHMS FOR THREE-DIMENSIONAL
INTERPOLATION BETWEEN PLANAR SLICES

by

P.A. Dowd

Department of Mining and Mineral Engineering
University of Leeds, Leeds. U.K.

ABSTRACT

The general problem is introduced by way of a particular application. An unknown, three-dimensional object is sampled discretely on parallel planar slices. The problem is to interpolate the shape of the object between the "known" planar slices. An algorithm is introduced for the solution of the problem and is illustrated by examples. Other possible approaches are discussed. The algorithm is used for the three-dimensional display of the object and to provide cross-sectional views from specified perspectives.

Keywords: Fischler's algorithm, interpolation, orebody, shape function, three-dimensional display.

1.   INTRODUCTION

The aim of this paper is to present an algorithm and some additional suggestions for the solution of a problem which arises in geological and mining applications of computer graphics, modelling and estimation. Although it is presented here as a particular problem it undoubtedly has much wider application and part of the reason for this presentation is to attract a wider interest.

As a general problem it can be posed as the three-dimensional interpolation of arbitrary surfaces. An unknown, three-dimensional object is sampled at a number

NATO ASI Series, Vol. F17
Fundamental Algorithms for Computer Graphics
Edited by R. A. Earnshaw
© Springer-Verlag Berlin Heidelberg 1985

of points on a series of parallel planes, usually vertical; on each plane a surface can be interpolated. The problem is to interpolate surfaces between the "known" planar surfaces. The purpose of the interpolation may be as a first step in the three-dimensional representation of the object, to display the object from another perspective or simply to display a cross-sectional view of the object at a particular location.

1.1   The object

In this particular application the object is an orebody or mineral deposit beneath the earth's surface.

In general, the object may be of any shape from very regular to very erratic; its cross-sectional outline may be convex on one planar slice and non-convex on the next. Its orientation is defined by the general orientation of its three major axes. The axis of maximum extent in the horizontal plane is called the *strike axis* and its orientation, or *strike*, is measured clockwise from north. The general axis in the vertical plane perpendicular to the strike axis, is called the *dip axis* . The dip of the object is usually specified from 0° to ± 90°. The plane containing the dip and strike axes is called the *dip-strike plane* and can also be defined as the median plane through the object and which is inclined to the horizontal. If the major axis in the general strike direction is inclined to the horizontal plane this inclination is referred to as the *plunge* and the axis is the *strike-plunge axis*. An example is shown in figure 1.

The strike, dip and plunge may vary throughout the object as much as from one cross-section to the next or even on a particular cross-section.

1.2   Sampling the object

In the initial stages of development the orebody

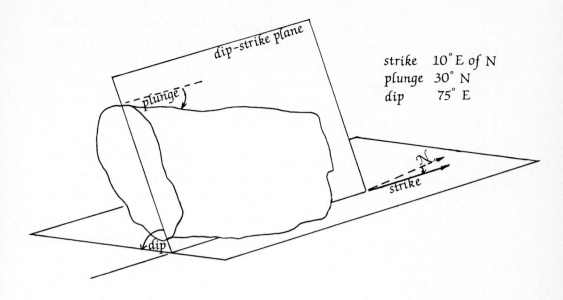

strike   10° E of N
plunge   30° N
dip   75° E

FIGURE 1

will be intersected by drill holes from the surface. At
later stages the intersecting drill holes will originate
beneath the surface either close by the orebody or actually
within it; the holes will be more or less on vertical
cross-sectional planes perpendicular to the strike of the
orebody.   The drill holes can be thought of as lines in
the plane of the cross-section. A simplistic illustration
is shown in figure 2.

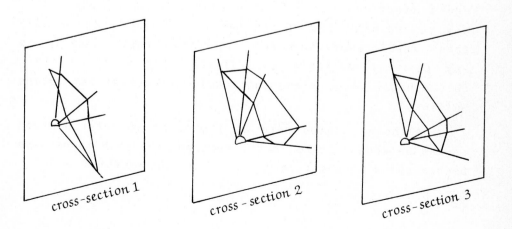

cross-section 1   cross - section 2   cross- section 3

FIGURE   2

The outlines on the vertical cross-sections are formed by joining the drill hole intersection points by straight lines. In general, smoothing of these outlines is not required and is not desirable.

1.3   Interpolation

In general, the problem can now be stated as: given a number of polygonal outlines of the object on vertical cross-sectional slices interpolate the shape of the object on any other specified cross-section.

The easiest way to do this is simply to extend each cross-sectional shape half-way to the next cross-section. However, this leads to discontinuities at the half-way point and does not, in general, produce a realistic model.

Another way is to identify pairs of defining points on two neighbouring cross-sections and interpolate linearly between these points as shown in figure 3. It is usually a simple matter to identify the pair of points by hand but rather more difficult to devise an algorithm to do this automatically.

The algorithms presented here are attempts at automatic interpolation methods which have been found to work well in practice. It is assumed that cross-sectional outlines are defined by an ordered set of co-ordinates x (east-west) and z (vertical) for fixed y (north-south). Obviously, any co-ordinate system can be rotated so as to satisfy these requirements and the algorithms apply equally to any pair of variable co-ordinates for a fixed third co-ordinate (e.g. long-sectional or horizontal plane outlines).

Although stated here as a problem of interpolation on and between vertical cross-sections the techniques have been adapted to cross-sections of any orientation.

2.   THE ALGORITHM

(i)   Select the nearest known cross-sections either side of the cross-section to be interpolated.

(ii)   Calculate the centre of gravity of each cross-sectional outline on the two known cross-sections. The co-ordinates of the centre of gravity are calculated as the weighted average of the co-ordinates of each line segment; the weights are the lengths of the line segments. This method partly overcomes the problem associated with unequal spacings of defining points. Note that this centre of gravity is, by definition, the point which minimizes the weighted sum of squares of distances from the point to the mid-point of all boundary defining line segments.

(iii) Check the position of each centre of gravity. If one centre of gravity lies outside the boundary of its cross-sectional outline, redefine its position as the point which minimises the weighted sum of squares of distances from the point to the mid-points of all boundary defining line segments, *subject to the condition* that it lies inside the boundary. If both centres of gravity lie inside or outside their respective boundaries, omit this step.

(iv)   On each cross-section join the centre of gravity to each point defining the cross-sectional boundary outline. Define each point by:
   (a)   If the connecting line crosses an odd number of boundaries the point is labelled as an "n-point". If the connecting line does not cross a boundary or crosses an even number of boundaries it is labelled as a "p-point".
   (b)   the direction of the connecting line as measured in the plane of the cross-section anticlockwise from the horizontal.

(v)   Select the cross-sectional outline with the greater number of boundary defining points. Take the first

defining point for this outline and connect it to a
point on the second cross-sectional outline. The
point on the second cross-sectional outline is chosen
such that:

(a)   only like points are joined i.e. p-point to
       p-point, n-point to n-point.

(b)   its direction is closest to that of the point
       on the first outline.

If both cross-sections have the same number of defining
points, choose the first cross-section arbitrarily.

(vi)   Repeat step (v) for each point in turn on the first
       outline *subject to the condition* that once a direction
       of movement on the second cross-sectional outline
       is established this direction must be maintained.

(vii) In the case of step v(a) preventing a match for a
       given point on the first outline, the last point
       connected on the second outline is chosen.

(viii) Any cross-section between the two defining
       cross-sections can now be interpolated by linear
       interpolation along the connecting lines.

2.1   Notes

(a)   The method is not necessarily an exact interpolator
       for both defining cross-sections but is always an
       exact   interpolator   for   the   first   defining
       cross-section.   Exact   interpolation   on   both
       cross-sections is only achieved when all co-ordinates
       on each cross-section are joined.

(b)   The method is sensitive to the position of the "centre
       of gravity". This point must lie inside the boundary
       so as to provide an unambiguous directional definition
       of locations of the defining boundary co-ordinates.

(c)   An algorithm to generate a point which lies inside
       a closed boundary and is such that the sum of squares
       of distances from the point to the co-ordinates

defining the boundary is a minimum is still under development. In most cases the centre of gravity will automatically satisfy both criteria. For the case in which one centre of gravity lies outside the boundary an approximate solution which seems to work well in practice is to shift the centre of gravity to the nearest boundary co-ordinate. In this case the boundary co-ordinate is defined as a p-point.

(d) Classification of n and p points in step iv(a) is made to ensure that similar shape elements are matched and to prevent opposite boundaries being joined.

(e) The direction of movement defined in step (vi) must be maintained so as to prevent re-entrant interpolated boundaries.

(f) The co-ordinates on the defining cross-sections do not have to be defined in the same direction i.e. one may be clockwise and the other anticlockwise.

(g) Some points on the second cross-section may not be joined.

(h) A point on one cross-section may be joined to more than one point on the other cross-section.

(i) The interpolated shape is only one possibility and may not be the "desired" shape.

(j) Very complex shapes which differ radically from one cross-section to another may produce unacceptable interpolations and unclosed boundaries.

(k) For very regular, convex shapes the classification of n- and p-points in step v(a) is not required.

(l) The method for determining whether the centre of gravity lies inside the shape is to sum the angles subtended by the centre of gravity joined to each boundary defining point. A sum equal to 360° indicates that the centre of gravity lies inside while a sum equal to 0° indicates that it lies outside.

2.2 Examples

Two simple examples are shown in Figures 3 and 4.

The example in figure 3 is straightforward and in this case the method is an exact interpolator for both cross-sections.

On cross section No. 1 the points are defined as follows:

Point No.	angle	boundary condition
1	225°	P
2	90°	P
3	315°	P

On cross section no. 2 the points are defined as follows:

Point No.	angle	boundary condition
1	45°	P
2	135°	P
3	225°	P
4	315°	P

Begin with the cross-section with the most points, i.e. cross-section no. 2. On cross-section 2 begin with point no. 1 defined by the angle 45°. On cross section 1 search for the angle closest to 45°. The required angle is 90° and point 1 on cross section 2 is joined to point 2 on cross section 1. Now move to point no. 2 on cross-section 2 and find the angle on cross-section 1 which is closest to 135°. The required angle is 90° and point 2 on cross-section 2 is joined to point 2 on cross-section 1. Move to point 3 on cross-section 2 and find the angle on cross-section 1 which is closest to 225°. The required point is no 1 and point no 3 on cross-section 2 is joined to point no 1 on cross-section 1. Note the joining sequence on cross-section 1 has now been defined as anticlockwise and joining must continue in this direction so as to avoid crossed lines. Finally

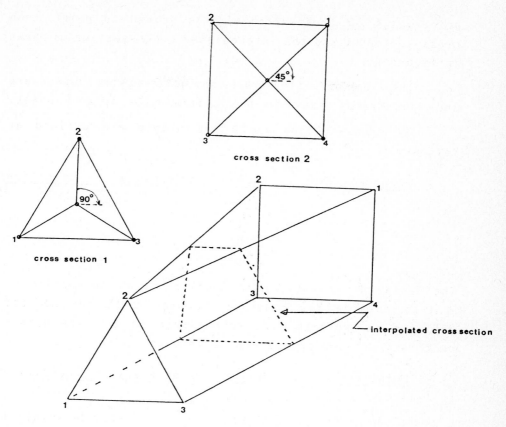

FIGURE 3

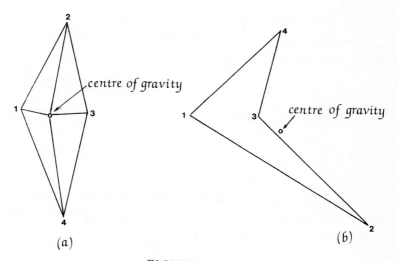

(a)

(b)

FIGURE 4

point no 4 on cross-section 2 is joined to point 3 on cross-section 1 and the interpolated cross-section is shown in figure 3.

The example in figure 4 is not quite so straightforward and illustrates some of the points made in the notes.

On cross-section no 1 the points are defined as follows:

Point No	angle	boundary	condition
1	167°	P	
2	81°	P	
3	10°	P	
4	275°	P	

The centre of gravity of the outline on cross-section no 2 lies outside the boundary. Move it to the nearest defining co-ordinate i.e. co-ordinate no 3. The points on this cross-section ae now defined as

Point no.	angle	boundary	condition
1	180°	P	
2	315°	P(by definition)	
3	0°	P	"
4	76°	P	"

As the number of points on both cross-sections is the same it is irrelevant which cross-section is selected first. The points connected are:

cross section 1	cross-section 2
1	1
2	4
3	3
4	2

Some practical examples are now shown in the following figures in which the cross-sectional outlines are taken from a nickel orebody.

In the first example an outline is to be interpolated midway between the two cross-sectional outlines shown in figure 5.

On cross-section no. 1 the points are defined in Table 1.

Point no.	angle	boundary condition
1	255.8	P(crosses 2 boundaries)
2	250.8	P
3	246.1	P(crosses 2 boundaries)
4	244.6	n
5	248.1	P
6	247.1	P
7	237.8	P
8	134.4	P
9	106.5	P
10	83.2	P
11	75.3	P
12	62.7	P
13	57.8	P
14	17.6	P
15	253.7	P
16	255.6	n
17	258.4	n
18	260.5	n
19	258.7	P(crosses 2 boundaries)

Table 1 : Points on Cross-section 1

On cross-section 2 the points are as defined in Table 2.

Begin with the cross-section with most points, i.e. no. 1. On cross-section 1 begin with point no. 1. The point on cross-section 2 with the closest direction is point no. 13. Similarly, point 2 on cross-section 1 is joined to point 14 on cross-section 2. The direction of movement on cross-section 2 has now been established. Point no. 3 on cross-section 1 is also joined to point no. 14 on cross-section 2. Point no. 4 on cross-section

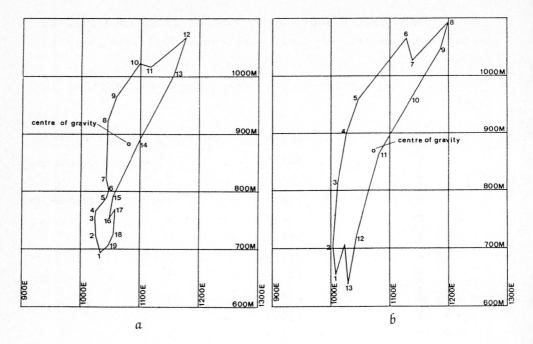

FIGURE 5

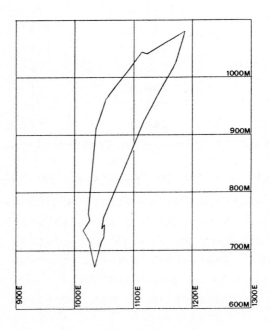

FIGURE 6

1 is an n-point and, as there are no n-points on cross-section 2, it is joined to the last point connected on cross-section 2, i.e. point no. 14 (cf step vii).

point no.	angle	boundary	condition
1	252.6	p	
2	246.6	p	
3	221.5	p	
4	149.9	p	
5	108.4	p	
6	75.0	p	
7	68.1	p	
8	61.1	p	
9	57.9	p	
10	55.9	p	
11	311.6	p	
12	258.0	p	
13	257.9	p	
14	252.4	p	

Table 2 : Points on cross-section 2

The points connected are shown in Table 3.

The interpolated cross-sectional outline is shown in figure 6.

This example illustrates a case in which the classification of n- and p- points is of no great advantge although it has ensured that the two different and distinctive shapes on the bottoms of both outlines in figure 5 have not been projected very far from their respective cross-sections. An example, in the same orebody, in which the classification is critical is shown in figure 7. The cross-section interpolated midway between these two outlines is shown in figure 8.

544

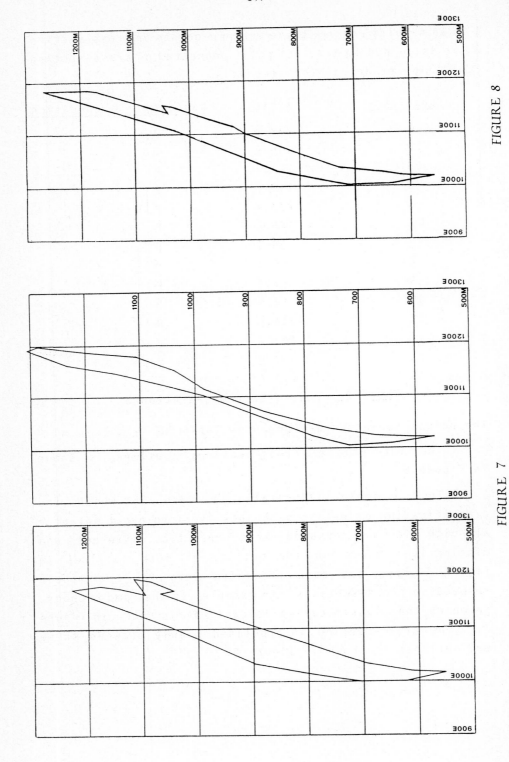

FIGURE 8

FIGURE 7

cross-section 1	cross-section 2
1	13
2	14
3	14
4	14
5	2
6	2
7	2
8	4
9	5
10	6
11	6
12	8
13	9
14	10
15	12
16	12
17	12
18	12
19	13

Table 3 : Connecting points

2.3 Orientation of planar slices

The algorithm described above does not explicitly take into account the possibility of different orientations of the object on the two confining planar slices. eg. the angle of dip of each cross-sectional outline may be significantly different as, for example, if the outline in figure 5(b) is rotated through, say, 30°.

It is possible to preface the algorithm with a re-orientation step so as to align the two outlines in the same sense. Two methods are suggested here.

2.3.1 Least squares orientation

For each cross-section, assume that the centre of

each intersecting drill hole lies in the strike-dip plane. The line of intersection of the strike-dip plane with the cross-sectional outline can be estimated by the least squares fit of a straight line through the drill hole mid points. This is illustrated in figure 9.

One cross-sectional outline is then rotated until its fitted dip line coincides with that of the other cross-sectional outline.

2.3.2 Fischler's algorithm

The second method uses Fischler's algorithm to find the maximum diameter of each outline. cf Fischler (1980), Lin (1983).

On each cross-section:

(i) define an origin at the lower left hand corner of the outline

(ii) define a unit reference vectors evenly spaced between 0 and π ; ten vectors should be sufficient.

(iii) calculate the projection length of each boundary defining point **p** in the direction of each **v**. This is done by taking the dot product, **p.v**, of **v** with each point **p**.

(iv) for each **v** store the minimum and maximum dot product. The difference between minimum and maximum values gives an estimate of the "diameter" in direction **v**

(v) the largest diameter for all **v**'s is the longest major axis.

A modification is to replace the reference vectors in (ii) by a set of unit vectors defined by joining the origin to each boundary defining point.

The largest major axis for each outline defines the orientation of the outline. The outlines are rotated until their major axes coincide.

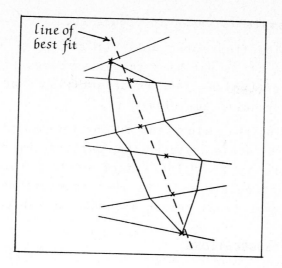

FIGURE 9

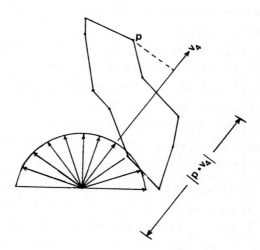

FIGURE 10

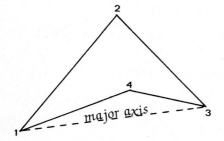

FIGURE 11

An example is shown in figure 10.

The algorithm works well for convex or near convex outlines but it is not hard to devise cases of non-convex outlines for which the re-orientation would produce undesirable results eg. figure 11.

Applying this algorithm to the interpolation problem in figure 5 would rotate the outline in figure 5(b) anticlockwise by 2°. The effect of this rotation would be to connect point no 11 in 5(a) to point no 7 in 5(b); all other connections remain as shown in table 3.

3.   OTHER SUGGESTIONS

A second algorithm, still under development, uses the Zahn and Roskies shape function, cf. Zahn and Roskies (1972), Lohmann (1983).

(i)   Assume that each cross-sectional outline is defined in the clockwise direction and define the shape function $\phi(\ell)$ as the net angular change in direction (ϕ) between the starting point and the point represented by perimeter length ℓ. For example, consider the two shapes in figure 4 reproduced (and re-numbered clockwise) in figure 12.

By definition, $\phi(0) = 0$. On cross-section 1 there is a change in direction of -139° at point 2 i.e., after a perimeter length of ℓ = 2.4cms. Thus $\phi(2.4)$ = -139°. At point 3 there is a change in direction of 26° giving a net angular change of -165° from the starting point. The graph of $\phi(\ell)$ for cross-section 1 is shown in figure 13.

(ii)   The domain of definition of $\phi(\ell)$ is [0,L] where L is the total perimeter length.
Define a normalised shape formation $\phi*(t)$:

$$\phi*(t) = \phi(\frac{Lt}{2\pi}), + t$$

such that $\phi*(0) = 0; \; \phi*(2\pi) = 0$

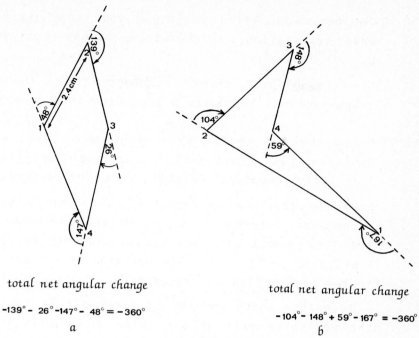

total net angular change

$-139° - 26° - 147° - 48° = -360°$

a

total net angular change

$-104° - 148° + 59° - 167° = -360°$

b

FIGURE 12

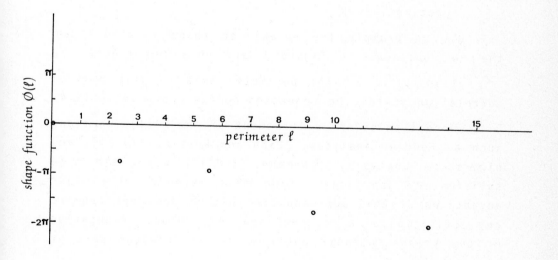

FIGURE 13 : Shape function for shape in figure 12a plotted as discrete points

The domain of $\phi^*(t)$ is $[0, 2\pi]$ and it is invariant under translations, rotations and charges of parameter L.

The normalised shape functions for the two cross-sections in figure 4 are shown in figure 14.

(iii) Match the two shapes by moving their $\phi^*(t)$ shape functions to positions of maximum correlation. This step requires further work for automation.

Lohman (1983), in an application to microfossil shapes, recommends interpolation of outline perimeters to the same number of equal length segments to obtain a point to point comparison but this is not possible in the application discussed here.

A technique which appears to work well is to slide the perimeter axis of one shape along that of the other until maximum correlation of points, in the least squares sense is achieved. Pairs of joining points are then as defined by the $\phi^*(t)$ shape functions.

As an example, the normalised shape functions for the two outlines in figure 5 are shown in figure 15.

Translation of the perimeter axis to give maximum correlation yields the connected points shown in table 4.

More sophisticated treatment of the $\phi^*(t)$ function, such as Fourier analyses, [Zahn and Roskies (1972)], and eigershape analysis, [Lohmann (1983)], may yield more satisfactory approaches using this method. The major advantages of this approach are that it does not require any definition of a "centre" and that mutual orientation of the cross-sectional outlines is an integral part of the algorithm.

Note that the total perimeter length of the interpolated outline must also be interpolated; this may simply be a linear interpolation between the known perimeter lengths of the two confining outlines.

cross-section 1	cross-section 2
1	1
2	2
3	2
4	2
5	3
6	3
7	4
8	4
9	5
10	6
11	7
12	8
13	9
14	11
15	12
16	12
17	12
18	14
19	14

TABLE   4

4.   CONCLUSIONS

The algorithms, as presented here, will not necessary provide workable solutions in all cases.

Point-by-point matching (possibly with the elimination of superfluous points) is preferred to methods which generate a new set of defining co-ordinates on one cross-section as this can lead to incompatible and unrecognisable shapes.

The first algorithm is in routine use in several modelling programs at Leeds University and is capable of producing interpolated images on an IMLAC terminal screen, connected to an Amdahl VM580, without user-observable delay after the interpolating location has been specified.

Work is still progressing on adapting the Zahn and Roskies shape function approach to the problem.

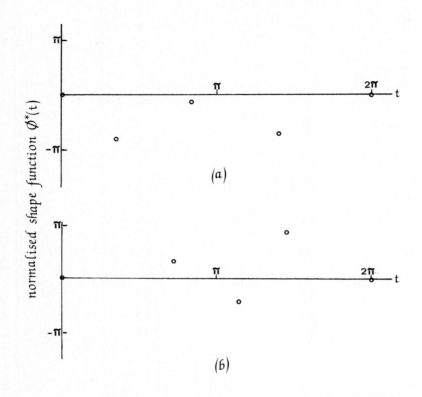

FIGURE 14

5.   REFERENCES

Dowd, P.A. (1984) Two algorithms for geometrical control control in kriging and orebody modelling. Science de la Terre, Séries Informatique Geologique No. 19 : Quelques Etudes Gèostatistiques. Nancy.

Fischler, M.A. (1980) Fast algorithms for two maximal distance problems with applications to image analysis. Pattern Reconition vol. 12, pp35-40.

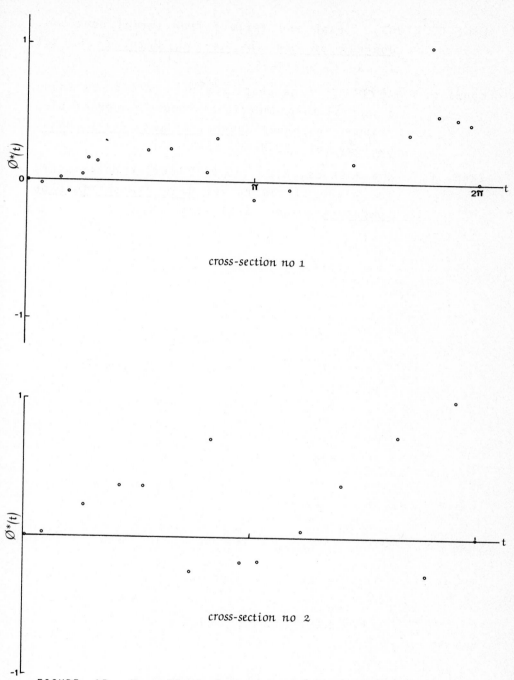

FIGURE   15 : Normalised shape functions for shapes in figure 5
standardised to unit amplitude

Lin, C. (1983) Shape and texture from serial contours. _Journal of the Int. Assoc. Math. Geol_. Vol 15, No. 5 pp617-632.

Lohmann, G.P. (1983) Eigenshape analysis of microfossils: a general morphometric procedure for describing changes in shape _Journal of Int. Assoc. Math. Geology_ Vol 15, No 6, pp659-672.

Zahn, C.T. and Roskies, R.Z. (1972) Fourier descriptors for plane closed curves _IEEE Transactions on Computers_ volumes C-21 pp269-281.

GENSURF: A SYSTEM FOR GENERAL SURFACE DEFINITION AND MANIPULATION

D. Catley, G.H. Davison, M.B. Okan, C. Whittle and
P. Thornton
The British Ship Research Association,
Wallsend on Tyne,
United Kingdom

Paper to be presented to NATO ADVANCED STUDY INSTITUTE; Conference on Fundamental Algorithms for Computer Graphics

SUMMARY

The paper reviews the mathematical background to surface definition and describes a general surface definition, fitting and manipulation system called GENSURF, developed at the British Ship Research Association. The system combines desirable attributes such as user-friendliness, flexibility and robustness with a sound mathematical background on surface modelling.

The basic design philosophy of the organisation of the software within the user and graphic interfaces and the mathematical library is discussed. Considerations are made of hardware-software compatability, hardware requirements and anticipated future trends with special regard to single user graphics workstations.

The paper explains how GENSURF is used, as well as outlining its advantages, and the salient features are illustrated. Simple geometries can be generated semi-automatically, general surface to surface intersection is available and surface patches can be blended and/or filleted.

NATO ASI Series, Vol. F17
Fundamental Algorithms for Computer Graphics
Edited by R. A. Earnshaw
© Springer-Verlag Berlin Heidelberg 1985

CONTENTS

1   INTRODUCTION

Surface definition and manipulation at the design stage is fundamental to numerous industries. At the British Ship Research Association an advanced general purpose surface definition system, GENSURF, has been developed which is based on bi-cubic, B-spline surface patches.

Advances in hardware processing power and interactive computer graphics facilities over the past decade have been significant. Single-user, graphics workstations now provide the required attributes of a surface definition system at reasonable cost; price/performance is improving. As a consequence, widespread use of computing and CADCAM systems on single user workstations should be considered as a serious option.

With the advent of computerised technology, several commercial packages have become available; these tend to be based on Coons patches, Bézier patches or various types of spline surfaces. In particular, spline surfaces offer a formulation which is most suitable for interactive design and manipulation. These may be B-splines of a certain order, rational, exponential or periodic splines. Appropriate continuity conditions can be defined across patch boundaries.

GENSURF is based on a bi-cubic, B-spline formulation and can be implemented on either a mainframe or a turn-key micro. The system is based on several fundamental algorithms and in-built graphics routines. A unique definition of the surface is obtained and this may be manipulated and interrogated in a user-friendly manner.

Whilst the authors have their experience mainly in the shipbuilding industry[1] and have addressed the particular requirements of a good hydrodynamic surface design using HULL-SURF, a customised version of GENSURF, the system which has evolved is applicable to quite general surfaces and a broad spectrum of industry. Fig.1 illustrates a typical surface which has been defined (see also Section 4.1). This form is, in part, based on simple geometrical patches and the general surface to surface intersection facility. Section curves and patch boundaries are shown.

2   OUTLINE OF GENSURF

The general surface definition system, GENSURF, is a computer aided system for the mathematical definition of a surface using interactive graphics facilities. By use of a current datastore, the master version of the surface definition may be updated as required and in a continual manner, both during and at the end of a run. No knowledge of the spline mathematics is required by the user of the GENSURF system. The GENSURF system is a true surface modeller with which the surface may be uniquely defined at every point. The system is most suitable for interactive design work and sufficient for production purposes. The surface definition may be controlled efficiently and the results of any changes made are observed from any arbitrary viewpoint and at a required scale via a specified view box.

The purpose of the GENSURF system is to allow the designer to define a surface quickly and accurately. To achieve this the user defines and manipulates a series of surface patches. There is no practical limit to the number of patches that may be defined and the interactive system is designed for efficient user response. The size of the system datastore compares favourably with the storage requirements of, for example, a two-dimensional definition system.

The individual surface patches are created from input files containing data points lying on the surface. Each patch is given a unique name and continuity conditions on adjoining boundaries may be specified.

There is a great deal of flexibility in the allowed data input procedures. Input is via sets of data points lying on "defining curves" on the surface. Each curve so defined may be represented by a different number of input data points and each patch may be defined by a different number of curves. Furthermore, the orientation of the defining curves of adjacent patches is not restricted.

Geometrical patches can be defined using special input data formats and patches can be copied, edited, translated, rotated and/or scaled to generate further patches at the required position of the surface.

2.1 Logical Structure

The user communicates with the GENSURF system via a single level command interface which has, in common with several other BSRA products, been produced using a syntax generator program. A Typical GENSURF workstation is shown in Fig.2.

Certain tolerances and system flags are set to default values at the commencement of a run of GENSURF and the datastore is copied to a scratch (i.e. work) file. Thus any patches which have already been created are copied into the scratch file.

The philosophy of GENSURF is based upon a current patch and/or current curve. All manipulations are applied to the current object. Commands are provided to store the current object in the datastore and to retrieve from the datastore objects which are then considered as the current object. To manipulate a specific patch, the patch must become the current patch. This is achieved by using the command SELECT. The information defining this patch is read from the scratch file and stored in a common area. To manipulate a particular curve in the patch, the curve must be similarly selected.

Once access to the GENSURF system has been achieved, the user will be prompted for each command. By typing the word HELP the user is given a command menu. Each command to the system has a HELP file associated with it. By entering HELP followed by the command name, the appropriate HELP file is listed on the user's terminal.

The user is given the choice of controlling the system from a keyboard or from a tablet. When entering commands from the keyboard it is necessary only to enter sufficient characters of the command to make the command unique. When in tablet mode, cursor input is controlled by the tablet pen, whereas in terminal mode cursor input can optionally be controlled by the thumbwheels of the terminal keyboard or the puck of the tablet.

2.2 Software Organisation

As illustrated in Fig.3 the GENSURF system can be split into three main areas as follows:

• The Interface Library Routines

These routines interpret the commands input by the user, check the validity of the command information and call the appropriate routines in the mathematical library to carry out the command.

• The Mathematical Library Routines

The Library contains:

· Routines to read and write information to the datastore file and the scratch (i.e. work) file.

- Routines which generate the required surface definitions, intersections, manipulations and interrogations.

- Routines which set up graphical information for display.

- Routines to scale and manipulate the display area.

- The Graphical Library Routines

These routines are used to display the surface information on the graphics screen or alternatively on a plotter.

The Interface and the Mathematical Libraries have individual common blocks where all the common information is stored.

Fig.3 shows how the routines link the user terminal devices and the various data files.

2.3 Hardware Considerations

GENSURF has been implemented on a VAX 11/780 and an ICL PERQ. Other implementations, for example IBM 4341 and APOLLO, are currently in-hand. Hardware requirements of any interactive graphics system are:

- Guaranteed processing power
- Sufficiently large, immediate access memory
- Interactive graphics input/output
- Sufficiently large, fast access secondary storage.

Software development requires the availability of operating systems and compilers which make effective use of the hardware.

Single user graphics workstations such as VAX STATION 1, APOLLO, MG1, PERQ and SUN provide these attributes at reason-

able cost and price/performance is improving. Processing
power is guaranteed by virtue of their being dedicated to a
single user. Their large memory permits the use of multiple
graphics windows, while screen resolution of some 2000 pixels
per square centimetre provides adequate resolution. Pointing
devices such as tablets, mice etc., allow effective user
interaction when augmented by the use of screen or tablet
menus. Plotters may be used to give higher quality drawings
of the defined surface held in the datastore.

User interaction depends upon the hardware facilities available. The minimum requirement is for a graphics VDU and
keyboard, together with a means of cursor input. With this
configuration, commands and other alphanumeric information,
e.g. patch names are entered via the keyboard; co-ordinates can
be specified via the cursor controls. When commands are
entered via the keyboard, it is necessary only to enter
sufficient characters to make the command unique. Multiple
commands may be entered in a single record.

If a digitising tablet is available, commands may be input via
a menu placed upon the tablet and co-ordinates information
input via the same device. Command parameters such as patch
names or file names are always entered via the keyboard.
Tablet menus may be created by the user; up to 400 entries can
be assigned either single or multiple commands. A tablet menu
for HULLSURF, the customised version of GENSURF is shown in
Fig.4.

2.4 Special Features of GENSURF

Shape changes to B-spline curves can be achieved by manipulating the defining polygon points. For planar curves this
provides a very powerful yet simple means of control. For
surfaces, however, the polygon points are necessarily two-

dimensional projections. This causes considerable difficulty in visualising the relationship between the surface and the polygon points and results in an inability to achieve accurate and predictable surface control. This problem has been recognised for some time and is stressed by Clark[2].

The solution to this difficulty is achieved by manipulating the surface directly through surface section lines, e.g. conventional orthogonal intersection views. Techniques have been developed to displace any selected point on the surface to a new position, with the necessary changes to the polygon points to effect the "offset", being automatically generated. This technique is essentially identical to conventional two-dimensional fairing procedures except that necessary cross-fairing between different orthogonal views is eliminated due to the surface definition. A further advantage of this technique is that it is equally applicable to any surface section and is not restricted to sets of curves in a particular othogonal view.

B-spline surface knuckles may be defined in two distinct ways; via coincident knots or coincident polygon points. The latter method has been adopted in the GENSURF system since the relationship between the knot distribution and the surface shape has been chosen in a particular way so as to provide a smooth surface interpolation.

The mathematical model is completely general, it allows for the definition of a large variety of free-form surfaces so that unconventional designs may be modelled. Features of the GENSURF system are as follows:

- A patch can be defined by a grid of a minimum of 4 defining curves, each containing at least 4 points and a maximum of 30 curves each containing at most 30 points. (This upper limit has been chosen based on experience but could easily be increased if necessary so as to suit a particular user's requirements.) The data points can be irregularly spaced along and across the defining curves.

* Special types of patches are permitted which are based on a reduced input data format and patch data generation facilities exist for geometrically defined patches, e.g. planar, ruled, conical, cylindrical, spherical, axisymmetrical patches and patches obtained by transformations applied to established patches.

* Infinite slopes in particular views require no special handling.

* The shape of the surface can be altered without affecting the boundaries' positions.

* Two or more patches can be matched identically along adjacent boundaries. The B-spline tangency matching across the patch boundary region retains the smooth characteristics of the surface or else knuckle lines can be defined to represent surface discontinuities.

* Blending, filleting and offsetting are available.

* Basic geometrical details and contour plots of positions of equal Gaussian curvature can be obtained.

* Intersection of the surface with a plane or other general surface is available.

* Input data files are of a simple structure and there is no practical limit to the number of patches.

* An efficient disk storage scheme has been adopted for the surface definition.

- The surface definition can be interrogated for geometrical details.

3 MATHEMATICAL BACKGROUND

3.1 Comparison of Available Techniques

The process of defining a surface interpolating or approximating to surface data $\{x_{ij}, y_{ij}, z_{ij}\}$ consists of defining a mapping from a three-dimensional $\{x,y,z\}$ space to a two-dimensional $\{s,t\}$ surface:

$$\underline{r}(s,t) = \sum_{i=1}^{N} \sum_{j=1}^{M} \underline{R}_{ij} \; f_i(s) \; g_j(t)$$

In this equation,

$$\underline{r}(s,t) = x(s,t)\underline{e}_x + y(s,t)\underline{e}_y + z(s,t)\underline{e}_z$$

is the position vector of the surface, $f_i(s)$ and $g_j(t)$ are predefined approximating functions and

$$\underline{R}_{ij} = X_{ij}\underline{e}_x + Y_{ij}\underline{e}_y + Z_{ij}\underline{e}_z$$

are the constants to be determined.

Several methods have been developed by using various types of approximating functions (See Refs.[3,4] for example). The first, and the simplest of these, is the Coons patch where $f_i(s)$ and $g_j(t)$ are chosen to be ordinary polynomials. However, the polynomials are restricted to be fourth order polynomials to avoid oscillations on the surface and only

(4x4) data is used at a time. By making use of continuity considerations across the patch boundary one obtains a matrix equation:

$$\{\underline{r}_i\} = \{s^3 \ s^2 \ s \ 1\} \ [\underline{B}] \ \{t^3 \ t^2 \ t \ 1\}^T$$

where the matrix $[\underline{B}]$ consists of quantities such as the position vector, its first derivative and cross derivatives. In general one can define the position vector and its first derivatives, but the cross derivatives, which are called twist vectors of the surface, are rather difficult to visualize and consequently can not be easily estimated. Furthermore, the storage space required is extensive. There is a lack of detailed control facilities available for making modifications to the surface shape within the patch boundaries. In order to define the surface patches one has to assemble the $\underline{B}$ matrix.

Another method used is to adopt exponential splines where the functions $f_i(s)$ and $g_j(t)$ are exponential functions of the form $e^{\lambda_i s}$ and $e^{\mu_j t}$ [5]. Here one needs only the position vectors for the solution of the problem. However, in addition to the $[\underline{R}_{ij}]$, solution of the $\{\lambda_i\}$ and the $\{\mu_j\}$ is required. This necessitates the solution of M+N nonlinear equations and tends to be rather time consuming. The only advantage of the exponential splines is that, regardless of the irregularity of the data, oscillations of the resulting surface are avoided.

The choice of $f_i(s)$ and $g_j(t)$ as the ratio of two polynominals leads to a rational spline representation of the surface. However, the problem again tends to be time consuming and also one is left with the task of defining a minimum of 16 weighting functions[3]. The storage requirement is increased. These cited disadvantages tend to outweigh the advantage of precise fitting to conic surfaces which is achieved by using rational splines.

In recent years, techniques which allow a fast definition of the surface as well as efficient manipulations have been developed based on the particular choice of $f_i(s)$ and $g_j(t)$ functions. The first technique was developed by Bézier where $f_i(s)$ and $g_j(t)$ were chosen to be Bernstein polynomials:

$$f_i(s) = J_{n,i}(s) = \binom{n}{i} s^i (1-s)^{n-i}$$

where n defines the order of the Bernstein polynomial. By using only the position vector values and an inversion process one obtains the solution of the matrix $[\underline{R}_{ij}]$ which is in this case a matrix of control points; by changing the values of $\underline{R}_{ij}$ the surface can be easily modified in a predictable manner.

Although Bézier's method yields a powerful tool for manipulating the surface, one is faced with the problem of oscillating solutions while handling dense data. This is because of the relation between the number of data points and the order of the Bernstein polynominal. To overcome this problem one has to generate more patches and this in turn causes the expansion of the datastore and an increased time consumption to achieve the continuity across the boundaries.

An alternative to the resolution of the problems of a Bézier curve is the use of B-spline functions as approximating functions for each of the two defining parameters.

B-splines were first intoduced by Schoenberg in 1946 [6]. Their usefulness in the field of CAD however was not fully realised until Reisenfeld, 1973, extended the Bézier technique utilising B-splines [7]. Cox [8] and De Boor [9], 1972, in-dependently developed a recurrence relation for generating the basis functions (the $N_{i,j}$) with required properties.

$$f_i(s) = N_{i,n}(s) = \frac{s - \lambda_{i-n}}{\lambda_{i-1} - \lambda_{i-n}} N_{i-1,n-1}(s) +$$

$$+ \frac{\lambda_i - s}{\lambda_i - \lambda_{i-n+1}} N_{i,n-1}(s) \qquad n > 1 \; , \quad \lambda_{i-1} < s < \lambda_i$$

$$f_i(s) = N_{i,1}(s) = \left\{ \begin{array}{ll} 1 & \lambda_{i-1} < s < l_i \\ 0 & \text{Elsewhere} \end{array} \right.$$

This relationship is both computationally fast and numerically stable and can be used as the fundamental definition for the normalized basis functions of the surface. Using these basis functions, an approximating or alternatively an interpolating spline can be constructed for a given set of data.

Again, the problem is reduced to taking the inverse of a matrix , where the position vectors are given and the matrix of control points is required. Since the B-spline functions have compact support, the order of the function is independent of the number of data points used. This feature of the B-splines overcomes the problems of increased storage and time consumption faced in Bézier surface construction.

Several initial evaluations were made some years ago into the use of B-spline surfaces for hull surface definition. Examples are Refs.[10, 11, 12]. The results reported were encouraging to the development of a practicable system. In a B-spline surface representation, the shape control is achieved by manipulating the spatial control points (not necessarily lying in the surface). The surface defined by these "polygon points" has an inherent high degree of 'fairness' and is not limited to patch boundary control as in the Coons technique.

It is generally acknowledged that the B-spline formalism offers the most flexible approach for the design of an advanced surface system.

3.2 Mathematical Basis of GENSURF

In GENSURF, the representation of general splines in terms of B-splines has been generalised to surfaces and techniques have been developed for transforming general bi-parametric patches (e.g. Coons, Bézier, etc.) into a B-spline surface.

A GENSURF patch is by default based on a 10 by 10 grid of polygon points. However, the user has the option of changing the "netsize" to any integer between 6 and 30 so as to reflect the density of the available data and/or the complexity of the surface. The adopted bi-cubic, B-spline formulation is based on an integer knot set (the λ_i of Section 3.1) with three duplicate knots being placed at the patch boundaries for each defining curve. The basis functions are themselves splines with zero value, shape and curvature at their ends and are constructed over four spans, see Fig.5. The use of multiple knots alters the shape of the basis functions but they are still properly defined.

The data for a GENSURF patch lie on defining curves which are fitted with B-splines. New data values are then taken to lie at the node positions of the knot set λ_i using Schoenberg's technique[6] and an interpolating spline is defined on the same knot set. Inversion of the matrix of B-spline basis function coefficients then gives the polygon point co-ordinates. As a consequence of the knot selection scheme, the first and last polygon points of each defining curve lie on the curve.

Having fitted the patch data along the defining curves, a semi-regular grid of points has been formed. It is then

necessary to consider the surface in the direction across the
defining curves and to calculate the polygon points of the
patch. This step is based on a similar approach to the interpolation of the defining curves. The corner data points are
the corner points of the surface patch.

If bounding patches of the surface have already been established in the datastore then the boundary polygon points of
the primary patch are replaced by the adjoining boundary patch
polygon points. Where cross-boundary tangency is required
then the interior polygon points of the primary patch are
modified. Tangency and curvature is controlled by respectively the first one and the first two interior rows/columns
of polygon points.

These properties form the basis of the blending functions
which may be defined to create patches where only boundary
information is available, see Fig.6. Filleting of adjacent
patches is based on the repositioning of polygon points,
optionally involving changes to one or both of the patches.

The various commands to manipulate the surface are based on
modifications to optionally

- the data sets
- the polygon points of the defining curves
- the surface polygon points.

The "offset" facility whereby the user may displace a general
point of the surface to a new position involves the
repositioning of either four (local offset) or sixteen (global
offset) polygon points to accommodate the change. The
B-spline formulation is most powerful for manipulating and
fairing a complex surface.

Planar intersections, e.g. the traditional lines in orthogonal
views may be generated readily and efficiently by intersecting

the mathematical definition with a series of planes without adding to the size of the datastore. Furthermore, a complex algorithm has been written and incorporated to achieve the intersection curve of any two general surface patches. This is based on addressing the problem of sub-patch intersections using the convex hull property[3] of B-spline surfaces, taking curves from one patch and intersecting the other patch where an overlap is indicated.

4   ILLUSTRATIVE APPLICATIONS OF GENSURF

The examples given in this section illustrate the following facilities of GENSURF:

- Patching
- Continuity at patch boundaries including partial continuity
- Calculation and drawing of planar intersections based on a minimum of stored information
- General surface to surface intersections
- Blending and filleting of surface patches
- Contour plotting of a scalar variable, for example the gaussian curvature of the surface
- Manipulation and fairing of the surface
- Interrogation of multi-body configurations.

Some of the figures have been reproduced directly from TEKTRONIX screens; improvement of quality can be achieved using a plotter device for which GENSURF can be prompted to supply a general plot file representing specified drawings from the screen. Furthermore, with GENSURF one may "window-in' to a surface region of interest and improve the resolution of the lines drawings.

4.1 Design and Fitting of a Ship Bulbous Bow

This exercise illustrates the applicability of GENSURF to
special geometries; the form studied was being considered for
its hydrodynamic characteristics.

The conventional ship forebody was defined as a standard
GENSURF patch. The sections of the basic form are shown in
Fig.7. The bulb was constructed from geometrical patches and
then fitted to the forebody patch using surface to surface
intersection.

As shown in Fig.8 the bulbous bow was formed from four
geometrical patches:

- Part of a sphere
- Part of a cone
- Part of a cylinder
- A flat patch

The intersection curve was calculated between the forebody and
the bulb and then excess data (i.e. data beyond the intersection curve) was removed. The waterlines were each terminated at the appropriate point on the intersection curve. A
similar process was carried out for the bulbous bow patches.

The region above the bulbous bow is a region of double curvature. To enable a patch to be blended across this region the
surface was interrogated at specified waterline heights. New
stem patches were defined and the form was completed using
blended patches. See Fig.9. Sections of the completed form
are shown in Fig.10 in section view; waterlines and buttocks
(intersections with respectively horizontal and longitudinal
planes) are shown in Fig.11.

4.2 Basic Pontoon Form

The symmetric half of a hemisphere, cylinder and after patch were used as the basic form to define a typical SWATH pontoon. The after patch was based on a 4-point B-spline curve rotated about the longitudinal axis. To the basic form was added a vertical strut having a NACA aerofoil cross-section. This was intersected with the basic form, using the general surface to surface intersection facility of GENSURF, to produce the pontoon. The surface patch mesh-lines are shown in Fig.12. These are lines of constant parameter value (either s or t) and are the most rapid visualisation of the surface.

An enhancement to the form is to fair-in the aerofoil patch. Figure 13 shows sections through the pontoon after the FILLET command has been used to remove the knuckle line at the inter-section with the main cylindrical body. Figure 14 shows a faceted definition which could be used as geometrical data for conventional hydrodynamics analysis programs; the points shown are output to a named file. The density and/or aspect ratio of the facets can be readily altered.

4.3 Definition of Internal Structure of a Ship

Nominal definitions of a deck and a transverse bulkhead were used to calculate intersection curves with the hull surface.

Patches of simple geometry were used which, as shown in Fig.15, extended beyond the hull patch boundaries. The intersections of the example structural components with the shell were obtained as shown. The number of points obtained and the description of the intersection curves is dependent on a crown height tolerance which can be reset by the user of GENSURF and depends also on the selected view and the viewing window.

Note that the intersection curve in the case of the transverse
bulkhead could have been obtained directly from the surface
definition using a planar intersection, i.e. without recourse
to an additional patch.

4.4   Submarine Form

A section lines data file was used to generate the patch data
for a submarine form which is shown in Fig.16.   The after
region, see Fig.17, contains also some blended patches which
were required because there was a lack of definition over this
region.   An application of partial continuity across patch
boundaries is also illustrated in Fig.17 where a knuckle line
is terminated within the surface along the keel line.

4.5   Geometrical Benchmark

As a demonstration of GENSURF applied to a bench mark test
example [13], four flat patches were formed based on boundary
data points and the intermediate regions of the surface
defined by blending patches, see Fig.18.   The blending
functions used are based on cubic B-splines.   Section lines
are shown through the blended region and illustrate the preservation of the surface features, i.e. two straight lines and
a curved section.   Although an exact parabolic fit cannot be
achieved without recourse to rational B-splines, the final
surface is considered to be satisfactory for all practical
purposes.   Blending is a powerful tool in creating and maintaining a fair surface over regions of sparse data.

4.6 Other Examples

Figure 19 shows a propeller blade modelled using two surface patches, Fig.20 shows part of a tyre modelled using a single axi-symmetrical patch and gives two examples of the surface to surface intersection facility, Fig.21 illustrates how a surface can be manipulated in a sculptured design using the offset facility and Fig.22 shows how GENSURF may be used to fit general data.

5   FURTHER DEVELOPMENTS

5.1 Possible Enhancements to GENSURF

A variety of surface properties could be obtained by interrogating the defined form and utilizing the uniqueness of the definition. A few areas of current interest are listed.

- Area and volume calculations
- Plate definition and development
- Generate offsetting capabilities
- Calculation of principal curvature and drawing of lines of principal curvature
- Definition and drawing of distributions of a general scalar function, e.g. velocity potential.

5.2 Projected Hardware Developments and their Influence

Apart from a general increase in processing power and memory size, there are two developents in hardware design which are likely to have a dramatic effect on programs for surface design and manipulation.

- Hardware Support

Increased hardware support for graphical output devices including higher resolution, graphical transformations and clipping and anti-aliasing.

- Parallel Processing

Surface design using multiple patches is ideally suited to parallel processing. Current developments in computer architecture will provide support in this area.

6   CONCLUDING REMARKS

The paper has described a general surface definition, fitting and manipulation system, GENSURF, its mathematical foundations, software architecture and hardware requirements. Illustrative examples of the use of GENSURF have been given. Whilst many of the illustrations are taken from the ship and offshore industries, the GENSURF system is applicable to a broad range of industries where rolled or sculptured surfaces are used. GENSURF may also be used to fit experimental data.

ACKNOWLEDGEMENTS

The authors would like to thank the Chairman and Research Council of BSRA for permission to publish this paper. As the work described has been progressed over several years, acknowledgement is due to a number of colleagues at BSRA, both past and present.

REFERENCES

[1]   "Unique Mathematical Definition of a Hull Surface, its
      Manipulation and Interrogation". CATLEY, D., OKAN, M.B.
      and WHITTLE, C.   Western European Conference on Marine
      Technology (WEMT), Paris, July 1984.

[2]   "Spline Methods for Computed Aided Definition of Ships'
      Lines". CLARK, A.P. BSRA SRD Report, Feb.1981.

[3]   "Computational Geometry for Design and Manufacture".
      FAUX, I.D. and PRATT, M.J.   Ellis Harwood Publishers,
      1979.

[4]   "Mathematical Elements for Computer Graphics.
      ROGERS, D.F. and ADAMS, J.A. McGraw Hill Company, 1976.

[5]   "Theory, Computation, and Application of Exponential
      Splines". McCARTIN, B.J. New York University R&D Report
      DOE/ER/03077-171, 1981.

[6]   "Contributions to the Problem of Approximation of
      Equidistant Data by Analytic Functions".
      SCHOENBERG, I.J. Quart. Appl. Math. Vol.4, 1946.

[7]   "Applications of B-Spline Approximation to Geometric
      Problems of Computer Aided Design".   REISENFELD, R.
      1973.

[8]   "The Numerical Evaluation of B-Splines". COX, M.G. J'.
      Inst. Maths. Applications, 10, 1972.

[9]   "On Calculating with B-Splines".   De BOOR, C.   J'.
      Approx. Theory, 6, 1972.

[10] "The Role of Splines in Computer-Aided Ship Design".
      THEILHEIMER, F. and McKEE, J. Proceedings of the First
      International Symposium on Computer-Aided Hull Surface
      Definition. Annapolis, 1977.

[11] "B-Spline Curves and Surfaces for Ship Hull Definition".
      ROGERS, D.F. Proceedings of the First International
      Symposium on Computer-Aided Hull Surface Definition.
      Annapolis, 1977.

[12] "Computer Aided Ship Design and Numerically Controlled
      Production of Towing Tank Models". ROGERS, D.F. 16th
      Design Automation Conference, San Diego, 1979.

[13] "On The Limitations of Surface Modelling Systems".
      BALL, A. Article, CADCAM International, Jan 1984.

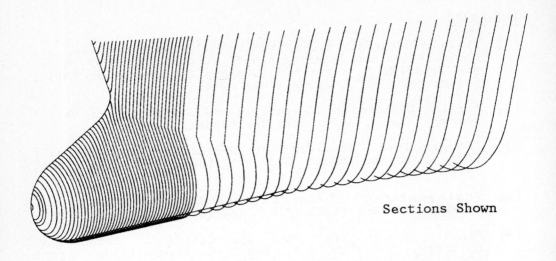

Sections Shown

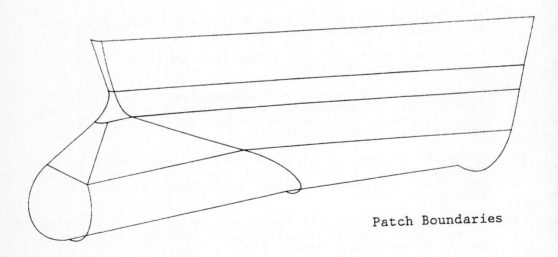

Patch Boundaries

Fig. 1 A Ship with a Bulbous Bow Fitted.

Fig. 2　A GENSURF Workstation.

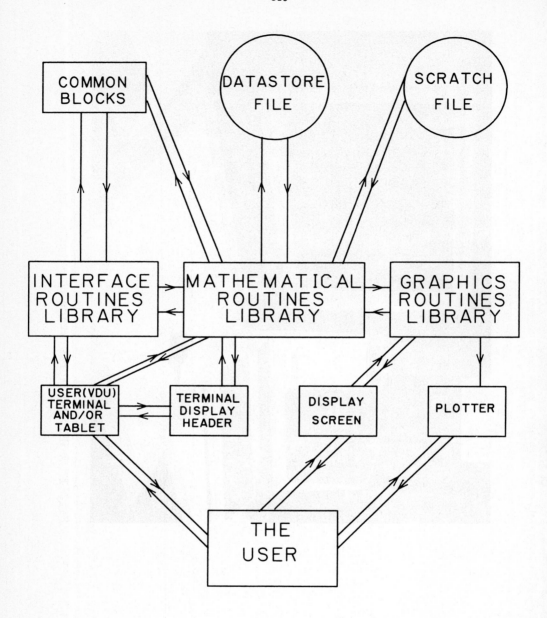

Fig. 3 Organisation of GENSURF.

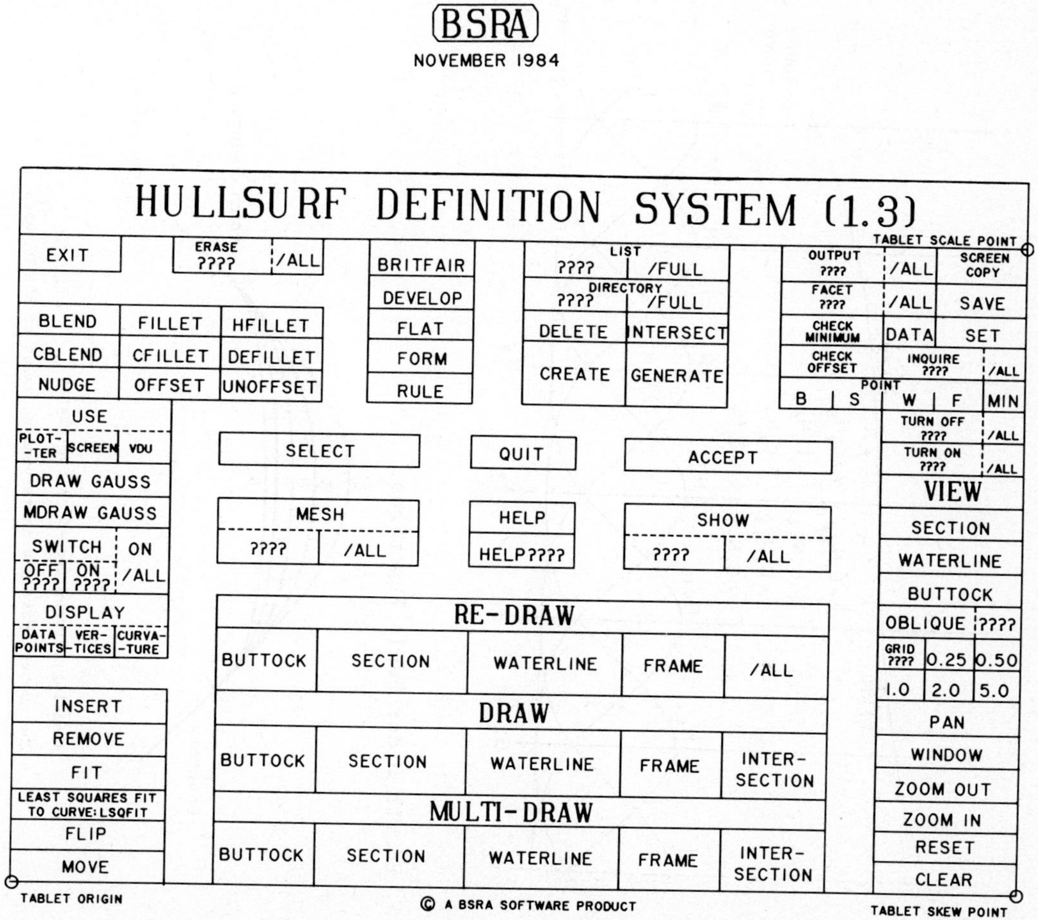

BSRA

NOVEMBER 1984

HULLSURF DEFINITION SYSTEM (1.3)

TABLET SCALE POINT

OUTPUT ????	SCREEN COPY
FACET ????	/ALL	SAVE
CHECK MINIMUM	DATA	SET
CHECK OFFSET	INQUIRE ????	/ALL
POINT B	S	W	F	MIN
TURN OFF ????	/ALL
TURN ON ????	/ALL

LIST ????

????	/FULL
DIRECTORY ????	/FULL
DELETE	INTERSECT
CREATE	GENERATE

BRITFAIR

DEVELOP | FLAT | FORM | RULE

ERASE ???? | /ALL

EXIT

BLEND | FILLET | HFILLET
CBLEND | CFILLET | DEFILLET
NUDGE | OFFSET | UNOFFSET

USE

PLOT-TER | SCREEN | VDU
DRAW GAUSS
MDRAW GAUSS
SWITCH ON | OFF ???? | ???? | /ALL

DISPLAY

DATA POINTS | VER-TICES | CURVA-TURE

SELECT
MESH ???? | /ALL

QUIT
ACCEPT

HELP | HELP????
SHOW | ???? | /ALL

VIEW

SECTION
WATERLINE
BUTTOCK
OBLIQUE ????

GRID ???? | 0.25 | 0.50
| 1.0 | 2.0 | 5.0

PAN

WINDOW
ZOOM OUT
ZOOM IN
RESET
CLEAR

RE-DRAW

BUTTOCK | SECTION | WATERLINE | FRAME | /ALL

DRAW

BUTTOCK | SECTION | WATERLINE | FRAME | INTER-SECTION

MULTI-DRAW

BUTTOCK | SECTION | WATERLINE | FRAME | INTER-SECTION

INSERT
REMOVE
FIT
LEAST SQUARES FIT TO CURVE: LSQFIT
FLIP
MOVE

TABLET ORIGIN

© A BSRA SOFTWARE PRODUCT

TABLET SKEW POINT

Fig. 4   Tablet Menu for HULLSURF, a Customised Version of GENSURF.

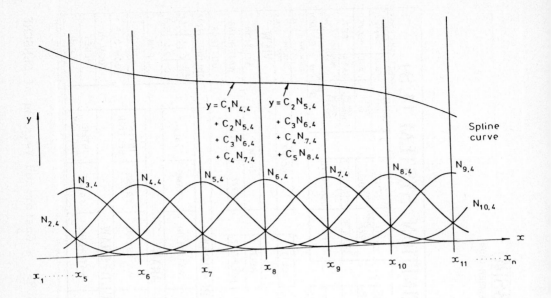

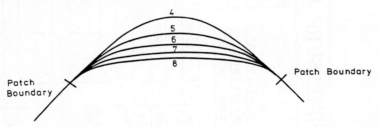

Fig. 5   Fourth Order Basis Functions.

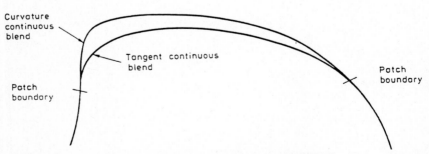

Fig. 6   Alternative Blending Functions used in GENSURF.

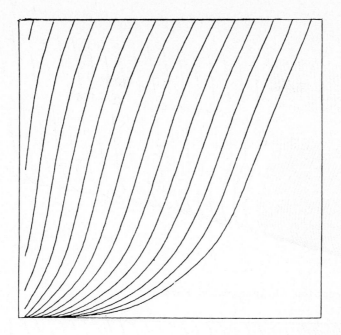

Fig. 7   Sections of Conventional Ship Form.

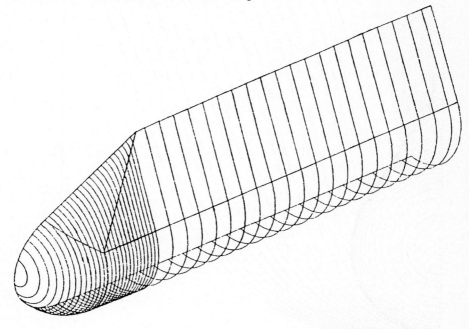

Fig. 8   Geometrical Patches used to Define Bulb.

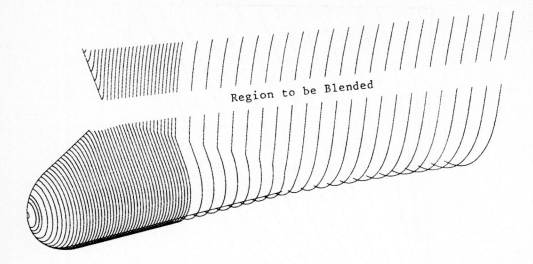

Region to be Blended

Fig. 9   Construction of Integrated Form.

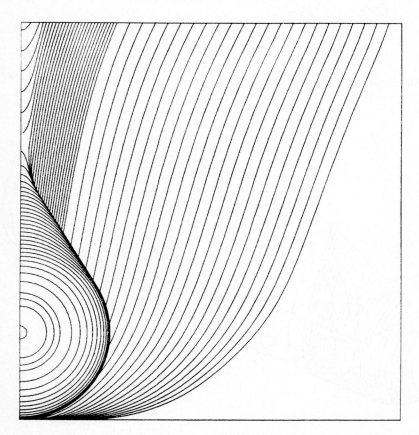

Fig. 10 Sections of Integrated Form; Bulbous Bow.

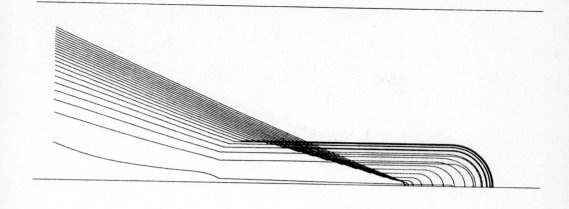

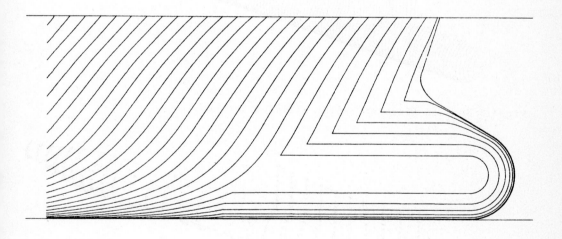

Fig. 11 Longitudinal Section Lines Through Bulbous Bow.

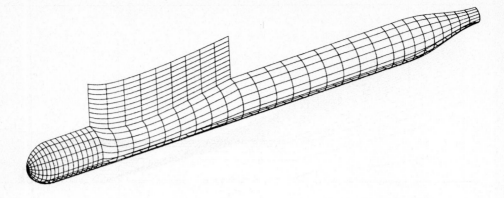

Fig. 12 Mesh Lines of SWATH Pontoon.

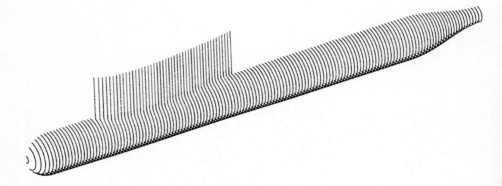

Fig. 13 Section Lines of SWATH; Filleted Patches.

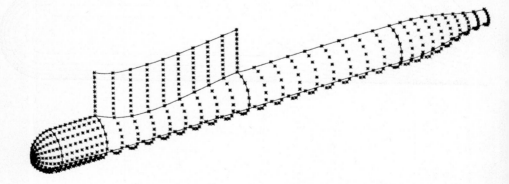

Fig. 14 Facet Points of SWATH.

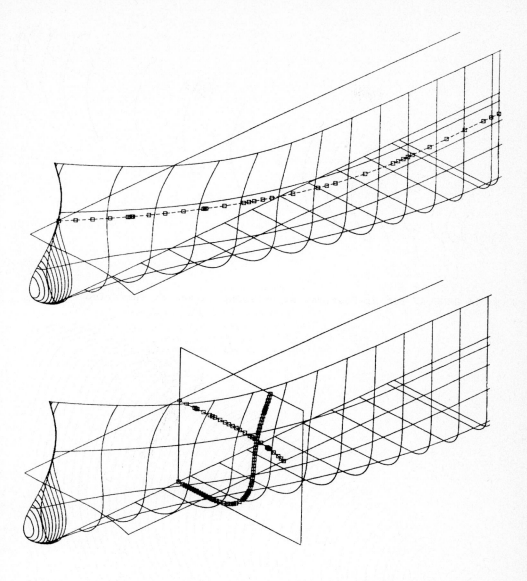

Fig. 15 Internal Structure Profiles obtained using Surface to Surface
Intersection.

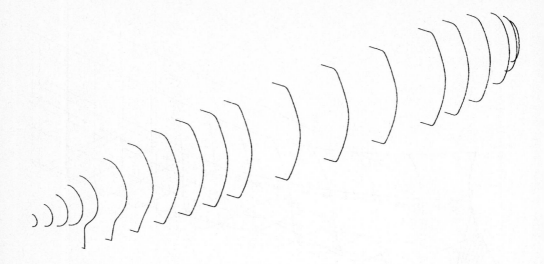

Fig. 16 GENSURF Fit at Postions of Defining Curves of Submarine.

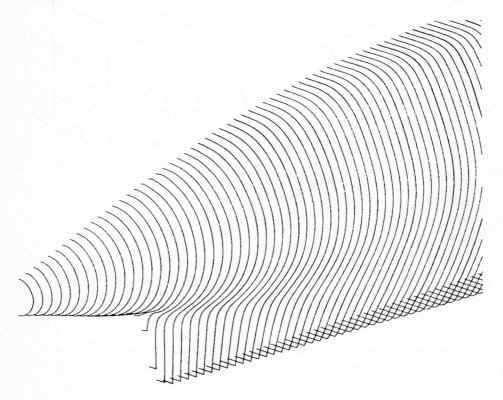

Fig. 17 Section Lines over Aft End of Submarine.

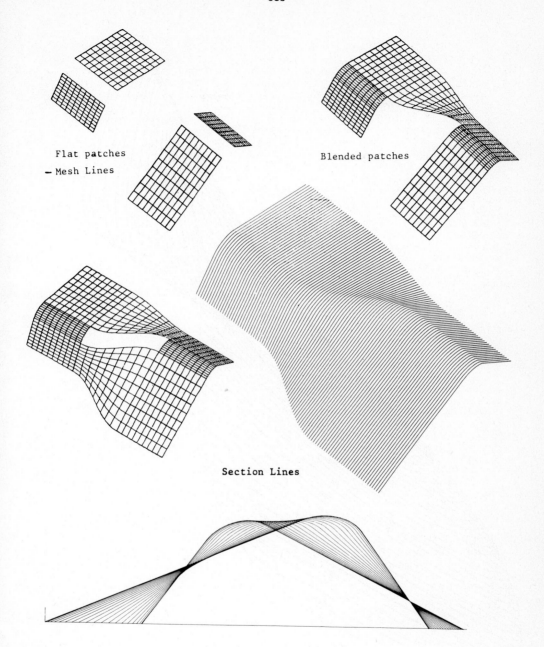

Flat patches

— Mesh Lines

Blended patches

Section Lines

Fig. 18 Benchmark test using Blending of Patches.

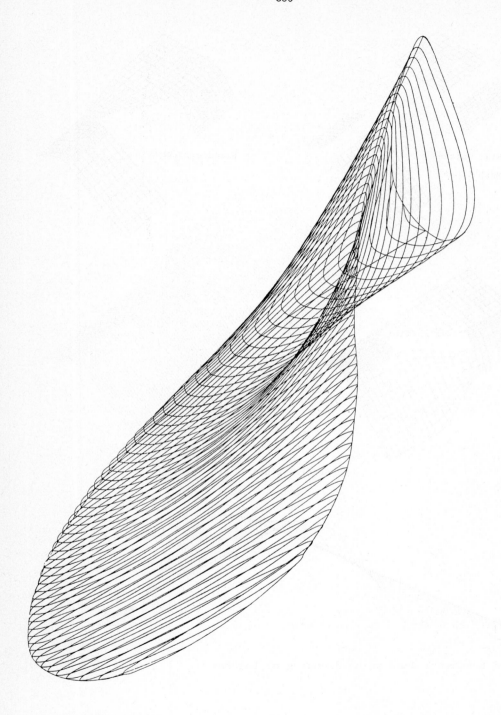

Fig. 19 Propeller Blade Defined using two GENSURF Patches.

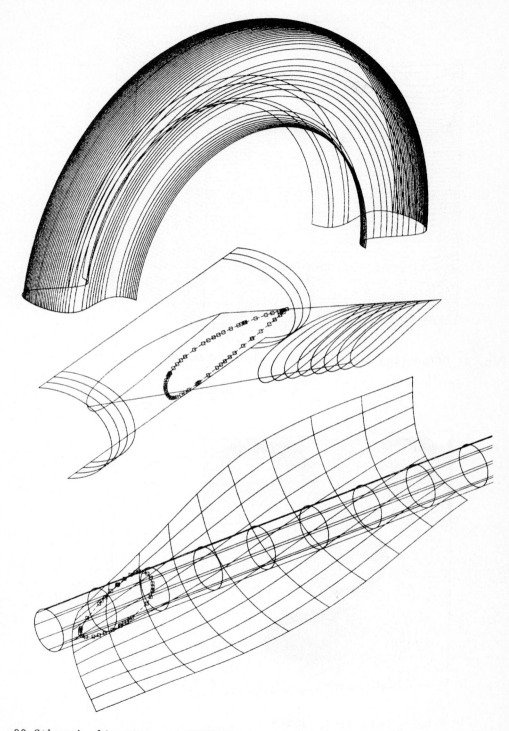

Fig. 20 Other Applications of GENSURF; Intersection Curves Shown.

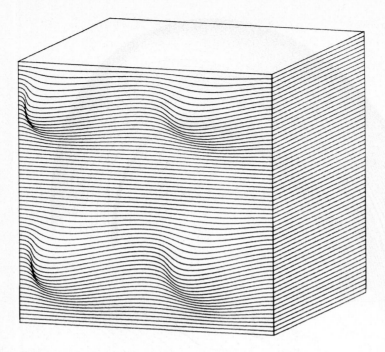

Fig. 21 Offsetting a Surface in Sculptured Design.

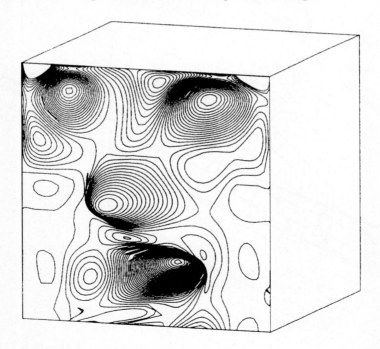

Fig. 22 Fitting Data using GENSURF.

An Interesting Modification to the Bresenham Algorithm for Hidden-Line Solution

Václav Skala

Department of Technical Cybernetics
Technical University, Nejedlého sady 14
306 14 PLZEŇ, CZECHOSLOVAKIA

1. Introduction

The solution of many engineering problems have as a result functions of two variables, that can be given either by an explicit function description, or by a table of the function values. The functions, that can be given either by an explicit function description, or by a table of the function values. The functions have been usually plotted with respect to visibility. The subprograms for plotting the functions of two variables were not so simple ([6]-[7]) although visibility may be achieved by the relatively simple algorithm at the physical level of the drawing, if we assume raster graphics devices are used. The Bresenham algorithm for drawing line segments can be modified in order to enable the drawing of explicit functions of two variables with respect to the visibility.

Though the order of curve drawing is essential for the method used the algorithm has not been published yet. Williamson [7] solved the problem by fixing the position of the view-point, Watkins [6] only pointed out that some rotation angles can cause wrong hidden-line elimination and Boutland's method [1] can use only one angle.

Therefore the algorithm that ensure the right order of the curve's drawing is presented here.

2. Problem specification

Let us have an explicit function of two variables x and y

$$z = f (x , y)$$

where: $x \in \langle ax, bx \rangle$ and $y \in \langle ay, by \rangle$

and we want to display that function by using the graphical raster display or plotter. For many scientific problems is enough to show the behaviour of that function by drawing the function slices according to the x and y axises, e.g. curves

$$z = f (x , y_i)   i=1,\ldots,n$$

NATO ASI Series, Vol. F17
Fundamental Algorithms for Computer Graphics
Edited by R. A. Earnshaw
© Springer-Verlag Berlin Heidelberg 1985

where: $x \in \langle ax, bx \rangle$ and $ay = y_1 < y_2 < \ldots < y_n = by$
and curves:

$$z = f (x_j , y)$$ $$j = 1, \ldots, m$$

where: $y \in \langle ay, by \rangle$ and $ax = x_1 < x_2 < \ldots < x_m = bx$

   The given function can be represented either by a function
specification or by a table of the function values for the grid
points in the x-y plane. If the function is complex it can be
very difficult to imagine the function behaviour because some
parts are in the reality invisible. The problem has been solved
by Watkins [6], Williamson [7] and Boutland [1] relatively very
successfully. The principle of the solution is generally very
simple. If we have drawn the first two slices parallel to the x
axis we have produced two curves and the space between them is
the strip of invisibility. Let us suppose that we draw the lines
in the direction from foreground to background. Now if we want
to draw the third curve it is obvious that those parts which are
passing through the strip of invisibility are invisible and therefore ought not to be drawn, see figure 1.

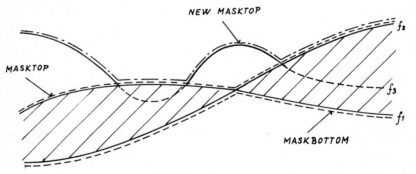

Figure 1.

   If we analyze the problem in detail we will realize that we
need to represent the borders of the strip of invisibility. It
can be done by the MASKTOP and MASKBOTTOM functions. The real
representation of the MASKTOP and MASKBOTTOM functions we will
omit temporarily. Now the problem of drawing curves with respect
to the visibility becomes simple, see algorithm 1., because we
will draw the next function slice only if and only if the curve
points are outside of the strip of invisibility.

   The visibility problem has been solved by Watkins [6] by
introducing mask vectors for the representation of the MASKTOP
and MASKBOTTOM bounds. Several problems had to be solved because
all computation was done in the floating point representation:

- the first problem is how to decide if we have set up MASK[i]
  or MASK[i+1] if the coordinate x is between values i and i+1
  e.g. $i < x < i+1$
- the second problem is that the MASKTOP and MASKBOTTOM arrays
  have to be set up for all point of the curve. That means that
  an interpolation procedure has to be employed, with some suitable interpolation step length.
- the third problem is that special case has to be solved: when
  the curve is parallel with the z axis, the usual line segment
  slope computation can fail.

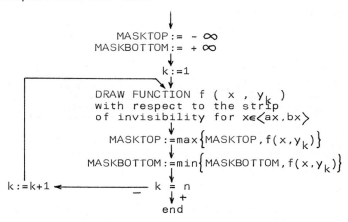

Algorithm 1.

3.Proposed method

In [6] the functions MASKTOP and MASKBOTTOM are represented by
vectors with values in floating point representation. We can imagine the whole proces of hidden-line drawing as follows in figure 2.

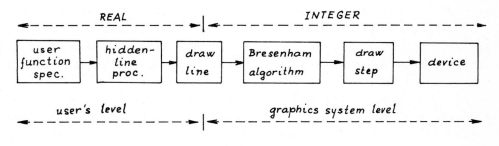

Figure 2.

Now we can ask ourselves if there is any possibility of increasing the efficiency of the hidden-line solution. One possibility is

to combine the complete Watkin s algorithm with the Bresenham algorithm directly at the physical level. Because we are dealing with
the raster devices at the physical level we have got rid of all
these above mentioned problems.

The solution of the hidden-line problem is now relatively very
simple, becausy we have to change only the procedure DRAW-STEP,
that generates code for the physical movement, in order to take
account of the strip of invisibility. Because DRAW-STEP draws only
one step we have to check only if the next end-point in the raster
is inside of the strip of invisibility or not. The structure of the
proposed method is shown on figure 3.

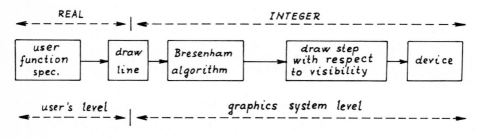

Figure 3.

It is obvious that we need only integer representation for the
MASKTOP and MASKBOTTOM masking arrays. The simplified solution is
shown by the algorithm 2.

It was find out that the lines (on the physical level) which
are parallel to y axis cause some problems with setting of the masks
arrays, see figure 4. Suppose that we have defined the strip of invisibility and we want to draw the line segment $x_1 x_2$. The problem
is that if we want to draw the segment between the points 1 and 2
we have to change the strip of invisibility so the future points
3 and 4 become inner points in the strip of invisibility; but that
is not true. Therefore in the complete algorithm the content of the
mask´s arrays is changed only if dx<>0. The whole algorithm can be
found in [4], where the clipping is realized too.

Watkin´s original method and proposed solution have one common
problem, that has not been published yet. Because of rotation sometimes the foreground and background can be altered and the order in
which the curves are drawn cause a violation of the masking premi-
ses. The second problem is how to select the scales for scaling in
order not to lose any part of the picture and use the full screen
area. The first problem seems to be more complicated and it is more
fundamental. The proposed solution is presented bellow. The second

problem can be solved easily by finding maximal and minimal values
for the screen coordinates.

```
{ GLOBAL VARIABLES }
VAR xO,yO: REAL;
    masktop,maskbottom: ARRAY [O..1024] OF INTEGER;
PROCEDURE draw ( dx,dy: INTEGER );
VAR flag5: BOOLEAN;
BEGIN xO:=xO+dx; yO:=yO+dy;
      flag5:=FALSE;
      IF masktop[xO] <= yO THEN
      BEGIN flag5:=TRUE; masktop[xO] :=yO; END;
      IF maskbottom[xO] >= yO THEN
      BEGIN flag5:=TRUE; maskbottom[xO] :=yO; END;
      IF flag5 THEN physline(dx,dy)
               ELSE physmove(dx,dy)
END;


PROCEDURE bresenham (u,v: INTEGER );
VAR j,d,a,b: INTEGER;
BEGIN a:=v+v; d:=a-u; b:=a-u-u;
      FOR j:=1 TO u DO
          IF d<O THEN BEGIN draw(1,O); d:=d+a; END
                 ELSE BEGIN draw(1,1); d:=d+b; END
END;
```

Algorithm 2.

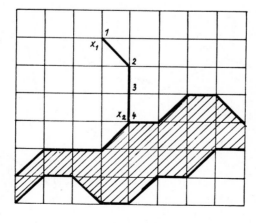

Figure 4.

4.Design of the drawing order

If we rotate the function or have a look at the function from different points, we have to keep the basic rule of the drawing. We have to draw at first the function slices that are nearer to us. Watkins [6] pointed out this problem, but the problem solution has not been published yet and many users have real difficulties to ensure that. Therefore when the function is rotated many pictures are drawn wrong. Let us try to find the solution.

Assume that the points:

$$X_1 = (ax, ay, 0) \qquad X_3 = (bx, by, 0)$$
$$X_2 = (bx, ay, 0) \qquad X_4 = (ax, by, 0)$$

are the corner-points of the grid in the x-y plane. We want to know the order of the drawing of the drawing slices.

Assumes that the points:

$$X_1' = T(X_1) \qquad X_3' = T(X_3)$$
$$X_2' = T(X_2) \qquad X_4' = T(X_4)$$

are the corner points of the grid after the rotation transformation. Now we have to pick up two margines from which we will start to draw the picture. We have to select the end-points of these margines that has the smallest z´ coordinate. We will mark that point by the index r. In general there are two basic possibilities that are shown on figure 5.

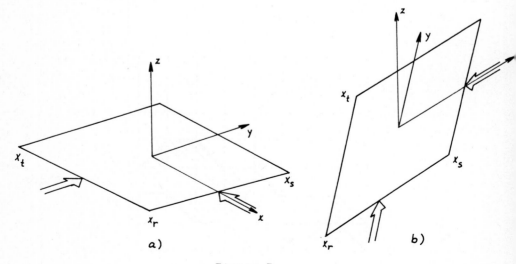

Figure 5.

The direction in which the slices are to be drawn are marked by ⇐

In the case ad a) we can see that the margins from which we will start to draw line segments belongs to the end-points $X_r X_s$ and $X_t X_r$. In the case ad b) we can see that we will fail. Therefore we have to test if

$$x_t^{'} <= x_r^{'} <= x_s^{'} \qquad \text{or} \qquad x_s^{'} <= x_r^{'} <= x_t^{'}$$

If the boolean expression has value false then we have to find the second point which has minimal $z^{'}$ coordinate and which is different from the original point. The new point will be remarked by the index r.

The whole procedure can be described by the algorithm 3.

1. Find the index $r \in \langle 1,4 \rangle$ so that
$$z_r^{'} = \min \{ z_i^{'} \} \qquad i=1,\ldots,4$$
2. Find the indices of neighbours and mark them by indices t,s
3. If condition
$$x_t^{'} <= x_r^{'} <= x_s^{'} \qquad \text{OR} \qquad x_s^{'} <= x_r^{'} <= x_t^{'}$$
   has value FALSE then
   begin
         Find index $u \in \langle 1,4 \rangle$ so that
   $$z_u^{'} = \min \{ z_i^{'} \} \qquad i=1,\ldots,4 \quad \text{and} \quad i \neq r$$
         r := u
         Find the indices of neighbours and mark them by indices t,s
   end

Algorithm 3.

Now we can draw the function by drawing the slices according to the selected margins, which are defined by line segments with the end-points $X_r X_t$ and $X_r X_s$.

But if we draw a function whose behaviour is wild enough then we receive a picture which is wrong, see figure 6 It seems to be more convenient in this situation to apply the Zig-zag method 1 and we will then obtain the correct results, see figure 7

The Zig-zag method can be described by:
1. Initialize the mask's arrays
2. Draw the margins that are defined by the end-points $X_r X_s^{'}$ and $X_r^{'} X_t^{'}$ (steps 1,2)
3. Draw the function values according to the grid and according to the directions on figure 8 (steps 3-12)

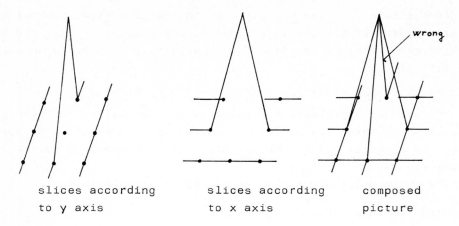

slices according   slices according   composed
to y axis   to x axis   picture

Figure 6.

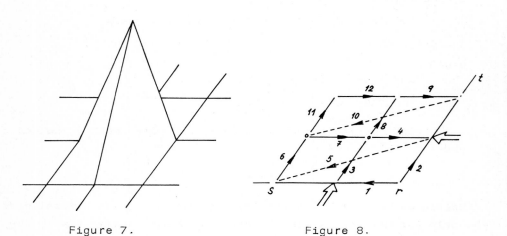

Figure 7.   Figure 8.

Let us suppose that the function is given by the values
$$f[i,j] \quad i=1,\ldots,n \quad \text{and} \quad j=1,\ldots,m$$
in the grid - points those coordinates are given by values
$$x[j] \quad j=1,\ldots,m$$
$$y[i] \quad i=1,\ldots,n$$
Then after transformation (rotation, translation) we receive
values
$$x'[j] \;,\; y'[i] \;\;,\; f'[i,j] \quad i=1,\ldots,n \text{ and } j=1,\ldots,m$$
Now the whole process of drawing can be made in the integer representation without using a floating point processor.

5.Conclusion

The algorithm presented for drawing functions of two variables with respect to visibility is intended for the use with microcomputers. Because the basic algorithm for visibility respectation can be realized by about ten assembly instructions it seems to be convenient to build it directly into the algorithm for a drawing straight lines. Now we can see that the basic graphics menu can be extended by the operations:

- initialize mask's arrays
- draw line with respect to the visibility,

that means, that the intelligence of graphic devices can be easily and significantly improved by adding several assembly instructions into the algorithm for the drawing lines. If the graphics display with grey scale is used the algorithm can be easily improved by using algorithm [3] for drawing straight lines.

We can ask ourselves whether primitive-level instruction for drawing lines which takes account of visibility, should be a part of any basic graphics software system, e.g. GKS.

6.Acknowledgement

I would like to thank Prof. L.M.V. Pitteway and Dr.J.P.A. Race for their many helpful discussions and suggestions that enabled me to finish this project succesfully.

7.Literature

[1] Boutland J.: Surface Drawing Made Simple. Computer Aided Design 11(1) January 1979, pp.19-22

[2] Bresenham J.E.: Algorithm for Computer Control of Digital Plotter, IBM Syst. J. 4(1) 1965, pp.25-30

[3] Pitteway M.,Watkinson D.: Bresenham's Algorithm with Grey Scale, Comm. of ACM 23(11), November 1980, pp.625-626

[4] Skala V.: Hidden-Line Processor, CSTR/29, Computer Science Dept., Brunel University, Uxbridge, Middlesex, 1984

[5] Sowerbutts W.T.: A Surface-Plotting Program Suitable for Microcomputers, Computer Aided Design 15(6), November 1983, pp.324-327

[6] Watkins S.L.: Masked Three-Dimensional Plot Program with rotation, Comm. of ACM 17(9), September 1974, pp.520-523

[7] Williamson H.: Hidden-Line Plotting Program, Comm. of ACM 15(2), February 1972, pp.100-103

EFFICIENT HIDDEN LINE REMOVAL FOR SURFACE PLOTS UTILISING RASTER GRAPHICS

D. J. Boller,
Royal Signals and Radar Establishment,
St. Andrews Road,
Great Malvern,
Worcs. WR14 3PS

Introduction

Graphic illustrations are frequently used in the course of scientific research to investigate the form of a function of one or more independent variables. The existence of a repeatable and systematic relationship is most readily verified by inspecting the graphical illustrations resulting from the outcome of suitably controlled experiments since they allow the large quantity of numerical data obtained to be presented in a form which is easy to comprehend. Whilst a two dimensional graphic medium naturally accomodates a function of one independent variable, some artifice will be necessary to accomodate functions of more than one independent variable.

The two techniques most commonly used for the graphic representation of the surface described by a function of two independent variables are contour plots and planar projections. Whilst the contour plot emphasises the quantitative aspect and thus readily lends itself to interpolation of the function value at some arbitrary point on the surface, the function is depicted in a more readily visualised form by a planar projection. The contour plot can only be used to describe a single valued function of two independent variables due to its inability to describe those parts of the surface which form an overhanging region. Although a planar projection of the surface is not subject to this restriction, removing hidden lines is considerably more difficult if the function is not single valued (solid modelling, for example). For this reason, only single valued functions of two independent variables are considered.

Although algorithms do exist for computer generated contour plots or planar projections representing the surface described by a single valued function of two independent variables, they are not as widely utilised as might be expected due to the punitive amount of memory and CPU resources needed to implement them. As a result, most researchers are quite adept at assimilating families of curves, where each curve corresponds to some constant value of the second independent variable. However, there is much to be gained by exploiting some artifice to make use of a third dimension since it often provides a more profound understanding of the problem than a more conventional plot [1]. At present, it appears that contour plots or planar projections are used only when it is unavoidable.

The work reported in this paper has arisen from the need to readily visualise the spatial distribution of sample data obtained at locations which are distributed at regular intervals in orthogonal axes across the surface of a processed semiconductor wafer. At each location there are a variety of electrical test structures, each designed to yield specific

NATO ASI Series, Vol. F17
Fundamental Algorithms for Computer Graphics
Edited by R. A. Earnshaw
© Springer-Verlag Berlin Heidelberg 1985

information concerning the material attributes of the various layers that are formed during processing and the characteristics of the devices which are the outcome of the overall process. Planar projections offer the most satisfactory artifice for revealing the underlying trends. The function values correspond to the measured parameter value at each location whilst the corresponding values of the two independent variables can be derived from the coordinates of the location. Since the axes along which the test sites are located are generally not optimised to facilitate assessment of the spatial distribution, it is imperative that there are no restrictions upon the choice of projection. Whilst only parallel projections have been implemented to date there is no reason why perspective projections should not be employed other than that the resolution of the graphic device used does not warrant the additional computation. Another application specific problem addressed arises from the need to be able to accomodate partially populated rectangular data arrays since the semiconductor wafers, which are entirely covered by test locations, are circular and the need to be able to delineate those locations at which the data value is suspect.

Most published algorithms utilise the boundary visibility solution to remove hidden portions of the planar projection of a mesh which consists of a pair of mutually orthogonal families of curves, where each curve is approximated by a series of straight line segments drawn between adjacent mesh nodes in X and Y. Because they were devised to suit a direct-writing graphic device, they do not exploit the local processing capabilities of bit-mapped graphic devices which are gradually superseding direct-writing devices.

An efficient algorithm for the realisation of surface plots, wherein the hidden line removal task is effectively offloaded to the processor of the bit-mapped graphic device, is described. Hidden lines are removed by utilising the area fill and independent bit-plane manipulation functions provided by the internal processor of a DEC VT125 graphic VDU, via its native command language ReGIS. Although most bit-mapped graphic devices offer similar functionality, it might not be possible to implement this algorithm on certain look-alike replacements for direct-writing devices.

The Boundary Visibility Solution

The surface is represented by the planar projection of the mesh which consists of a pair of mutually orthogonal families of curves. Each curve is approximated by the series of straight line segments drawn between the adjacent mesh nodes in X or Y, whose Z values are stored in a rectangular array. The corresponding X and Y values for the mesh nodes can be derived from the array indices. The surface is thus approximated by the set of butting surface elements whose boundaries correspond to the mesh of straight line segments.

All straight line segments connecting mesh nodes are visible if the surface thus approximated is considered to be of a transparent nature, regardless of the choice of planar projection employed. However, the plot is likely to be confused where some part of the mesh lies behind another part of the mesh, because both parts will be superimposed in the plane of projection. This confusion can be resolved by considering the surface approximated by the mesh to be opaque rather than transparent. Figure (1) illustrates the confusion that arises when all line segments are drawn whilst figure (2) illustrates how this confusion is resolved by removing those portions of the mesh obscured by the opaque surface approximated by the mesh. Obviously, when determining whether an arbitrary point on the surface is visible or hidden from view by the opaque surface, it will be necessary to take into consideration which side of the surface this point lies on; points lying on the upper side of the surface and points lying on the lower side of the surface have to be considered separately.

Approximating the surface in the manner described leads to difficulty when attempting to construct a readily manipulated approximating function for any given surface element which can be used to determine whether an arbitrary point is visible or hidden from view by the opaque surface. The problem arises from the conflict between the use of straight lines to delineate the boundaries of each surface element when the points between which these straight lines are drawn are generally not coplanar. Whilst each element of the surface can be approximated by two butting triangular planar facets, it is not evident which diagonal should be specified as the common boundary. Obviously, such an approach is ambiguous. Although techniques which approximate the surface in a consistent fashion do exist (for example, B-spline surfaces), the computing resources required to implement them are considerable.

The boundary visibility solution circumvents this difficulty, simply by considering the set of unique segments of either the constant X value plane or the constant Y value plane in which each line segment defines a boundary. The mesh defined on the upper side of the surface will be drawn with hidden portions removed if for each straight line segment, the plane segment in which it defines a boundary is considered to be opaque below the boundary and transparent above it. Similarly, the mesh defined on the lower side of the surface will be drawn with hidden portions removed if these opaque and transparent attributes are reversed. That this is true when drawing only the family of curves in constant X value planes or when drawing only the family of curves in constant Y value planes is evident by inspection of figures (3a) and (3b). However, the display required can not be realised merely by superimposing the two families of orthogonal curves derived on this basis, since some portions of the set of straight line segments drawn in constant X value planes may also be obscured by the opaque regions defined by the set of boundaries in constant Y value planes and vice-versa. Since it is quite straight-forward to determine which plane segments lie between the observer and the line segment of interest, a suitable sequence of boundaries, consisting of line segments with either a constant X value or a constant Y value, can be determined for a given planar projection such that proper hidden line removal is assured regardless of the Z values stored in the rectangular array.

Algorithms For Direct-Writing Graphic Devices

The algorithms in common use [2,3,4] have been devised to be suitable for direct-writing graphic devices, where it is not possible to erase any portion of the mesh once it has been physically drawn. They utilise the boundary visibility solution, progressively moving the boundaries so that plane segments further into the background are included as those portions

of the mesh which are visible are identified, adding to the list of lines
to be physically drawn and updating the boundaries to include the areas
of the projection plane obscured by the opaque regions thus defined. Two
separate boundaries are necessary; one for the lines drawn on the upper
side of the surface, below which all portions of these lines subsequently
added are hidden from view, and another for the lines drawn on the lower
side of the surface, above which all portions of these lines subsequently
added are hidden from view.   Although the plane segments are taken into
account in the same order irrespective of which side of the surface is
being considered, the two boundaries overlap such that an area defined to
be opaque by both boundaries will develop as the mesh is constructed.

    Although minor variations in the precise order in which these plane
segments are taken into account are possible, the principal differences
between the various algorithms are: whether both the upper and the lower
boundaries are constructed concurrently or each constructed in turn, the
method employed to represent these boundaries and whether the choice of
projection is restricted in order to allow some degree of simplification
or not.

    Twice as much array space is required to allow both the upper boundary
and the lower boundary to be constructed concurrently, whilst repetitive
computation is necessary if the boundaries are constructed consecutively.
Different colours may be utilised to provide the means whereby lines that
are drawn on the upper side of the surface and lines that are drawn on
the lower side of the surface can be distinguished from each other. When
a pen-plotter is to be driven, it usually pays to minimise the number of
pen changes necessary. Also, it is possible that only one of the meshes
is required. Consequently, it is usual to construct the mesh on one side
of the surface and then the mesh on the other side if required, making
use of the same array for each boundary in turn.

    Each boundary can be represented by an ordered list of points on the
projection plane, connected implicitly by straight line segments or by
exploiting the finite resolution of the graphic device and representing
the boundary as an array of vertical ordinates with one array element for
each horizontal ordinate possible. The former requires that the points
which define the boundary are sorted into an ordered list and that the
position of any intermediate point on the boundary is interpolated as
required whereas the latter requires that all array elements are updated
to include the opaque areas defined by each visible portion of the mesh
as it is identified. Both approaches result in sufficient demands being
made on CPU time and core storage to stimulate the development of a more
economical approach.

    One such approach [5] restricts the choice of the planar projection
used to a parallel projection such that the horizontal ordinates of the
(MxN) array of mesh nodes are aligned to one of (M+N-1) possible values,
thus dividing the projection plane into a series of "stripes" which can
be considered in sequence. Within each stripe, the plane segments are
taken into account in a zigzag order, working from the segment closest to
the observer towards the segment furthest away. Thus, the array required
to store the boundary data in the form of an array of vertical ordinates,
one for each horizontal ordinate possible, is not as large as it would be
in the general case.

There are also a variety of algorithms which restrict the projection in a similar manner but only consider whether the mesh nodes are visible or not. They trivialise the problem to the extent that they can be relied upon to fail to achieve proper hidden line removal if they are applied to any function that is not moderately smooth, since they fail to remove the hidden portions of lines drawn between visible mesh nodes, fail to reveal visible portions of lines drawn between hidden mesh nodes and often fail to correctly compute the point at which a line connecting a visible mesh node to a hidden mesh node ceases to be visible.

An Efficient Algorithm For Bit Mapped Graphics

Whilst a bit mapped graphic device can usually be driven as though it is a direct-writing device and is therefore suitable for use with one of the algorithms already described, they have additional functions which can be exploited to minimise the involvement of the host-processor in the task of hidden line removal. The principal objection to utilising the additional functionality afforded by a bit mapped graphic device is the lack of a standard, whereas the basic "move" and "draw" commands are universally available.

Where only the family of constant X value curves is required, hidden line removal is easily achieved if each curve is considered to define the boundary between transparent and opaque portions of the plane in which it is drawn. The constant X value curve in the plane which is furthest into the background is drawn first, since the opaque portion of this plane can not obscure any other curve. The remainder are drawn in sequence, drawing the curve in the plane which lies furthest into the background when all planes considered to date have been discounted, after having first erased the area defined to be opaque by the boundary thus delineated. Erasure is readily achieved by filling the area between the boundary and the top or bottom of the screen as required, using the background pixel value.

This erase-before-draw process removes all portions of the lines drawn to date that will become hidden by the opaque region defined by the boundary about to be drawn. Where macro definitions can be stored in the graphics processor, the sequence of instructions necessary to define the series of straight line segments which approximate to the curve can be stored and invoked once, having selected the area fill mode, to erase the portion of the screen area that will be obscured and invoked a second time, having disabled the area fill mode, to draw the boundary itself.

As previously stated, the display required cannot be obtained merely by superimposing the two families of orthogonal curves thus derived since some portions of the set of straight line segments drawn in constant X value planes may also be obscured by the opaque regions defined by the set of boundaries in constant Y value planes and vice-versa. However, the mesh can be realised with the hidden portions properly removed, if the plane segments in which the boundary is defined are taken into account in the appropriate order.

Figure (4) shows the mesh that would be drawn for a surface described by a constant Z value and shows the order in which the plane segments are used to define the boundary. The first boundary is delineated in the two plane segments furthest into the background. The boundary is then brought closer to the observer, defining a set of plane segments which lie on the "zigzag" from left to right. The process continues until all of the plane segments have been accounted for. For an (MxN) rectangular array, a total of (M+N-2) boundaries are necessary. The sequence of coordinates required to construct each boundary can be assembled in arrays of (M+N-1) elements using pointers to indentify the left-most and right-most index values for the current zigzag, so that successive boundaries can be obtained simply by modifying alternate array elements. Now, the order in which the plane segments are taken into account depends only upon the quadrant into which the surface is rotated. This is easily accomodated by generating notional indices for one of the four quadrants and mapping these indices to those of the Z array, according to the quadrant required.

Note that the boundaries for lines drawn on either the lower or upper side of the surface are now identical. The mesh on the upper side of the surface is drawn with hidden portions removed by erasing the area between the boundary and the bottom of the screen before the boundary is drawn. The mesh on the lower side of the surface is drawn with hidden portions removed by erasing the area between the boundary and the top of the screen before the boundary is drawn. Evidently, the visible portions of the mesh drawn on the upper side of the surface and the visible portions of the mesh drawn on the lower side of the surface must be realised in separate pixel planes; otherwise, the entire screen will be erased before each of the series of boundaries is drawn. Since the two meshes are each realised in separate pixel planes, the mapping from pixel value to screen colour/intensity can be manipulated to reveal only the visible portion of the mesh drawn on the upper side of the surface, only the visible portion of the mesh drawn on the lower side of the surface or both, making use of different colours or intensities to differentiate between them. Changes in the pixel value to screen intensity/colour mapping are subjectively instantaneous. Figure (5a) shows a surface where the visible portions of both meshes are drawn. Figures (5b) and (5c) show only the lines visible on the upper and lower side of the surface respectively.

Because all line segments are drawn and hidden portions subsequently removed, the observer has the opportunity to gauge whether a different projection would yield a more informative view during the course of an interactive dialogue. There are dot matrix printers that can be attached to raster scanning bit mapped graphic VDUs to provide hard copy where required.

Restrictions on the Projection Employed

The boundary visibility solution implicitly assumes that the Z axis appears vertical when projected. This facilitates the simple division of the plane of projection into regions which lie either above or below the boundary. This restriction can be satisfied without detriment. The area fill function provided within ReGIS only allows the filling of areas which lie between a specified horizontal line and the series of straight line segments which delineate the other boundary. There should be no problem providing an equivalent area fill when using a device with a more versatile area fill capability.

A parallel planar projection has been implemented with all projectors normal to the plane of projection. The surface is first rotated about its Z axis and then tilted about the horizontal axis of the screen. The array of Z values are pre-scaled and the same scaling factors are used for all subsequent views. Hidden line removal is correctly implemented regardless of the rotation and tilt angles chosen.

Embellishments

In some cases, lines drawn on the lower surface are not meaningful. A "skirt" dropped vertically around the periphery, either to the bottom of the screen or to some constant Z value, to produce a planar projection of an imaginary solid object can be readily added. If the skirt is dropped below the smallest value of Z stored in the rectangular array, no part of the mesh drawn on the lower side of the surface can possibly be seen. The operations necessary to draw the visible portion of this mesh can then be omitted; only one pixel plane is then required. The visible portion of a grid which corresponds to the base value of Z completes the construction of the imaginary solid object.

The ability to superimpose one image onto another can be exploited to allow a grid which corresponds to a constant Z value to be moved through the imaginary solid without the need to redefine the planar projection of the surface, defining the grid in another pixel plane as required.

Partially Populated Z Arrays

Most surface plotting algorithms make no provision for a partially populated array of Z values. Where the Z value corresponds to a measured value of some function of X and Y, there are occasions when a meaningful value can not be obtained. Where no meaningful Z value is available, then the straight line segments normally drawn to the corresponding mesh node can be omitted, replacing the "draw to" command with a "move to" command in the string of commands used to define the boundary, moving to the next known position on the surface rather than drawing to an arbitrary point. Even though the line segments are omitted, the surface on which the mesh is drawn is still considered to be opaque. That is, the mesh lines form the boundary of an enlarged, opaque surface element which includes the mesh node for which the Z value is unknown, as illustrated by figure (6). The observer can usually interpret this effect provided that the surface appears moderately smooth.

It is a straight-forward matter to draw lines in some constant Z base plane until a valid Z value is reached, making an abrupt transition from the base plane to the surface with constant X and Y, follow the boundary on the surface until the last valid Z value is reached, making an abrupt transition from the surface to the base plane and draw lines on the base plane again. Not only does this allow for a non-rectangular distribution of Z values due to "missing" data outside the periphery, it represents a missing mesh node as a "hole" whose sidewalls consist of constant X or Y value plane segment as illustrated by figure (7).

Conclusions

The algorithm described successfully offloads the hidden line removal task to the local processor of a bit-mapped graphic device when a planar projection of a rectangular array of Z(X,Y) points is used to graphically represent a single valued function of two independent variables. The host processor is relieved of all computation other than that which is needed to project the set of sample values obtained onto the plane of projection and the memory requirement is reduced to a minimal amount. This brings the use of planar projections within the scope of a wider range of users than hitherto, since it is suitable for implementation on computer systems with relatively meagre resources.

References

(1) Stanley L. Grotch, "Three-Dimensional and Stereoscopic Graphics for Scientific Data Display and Analysis", IEEE CG and A, November 1983, pp 31-43.

(2) Thomas J. Wright, "A Two-Space Solution to the Hidden Line Problem for Plotting Functions of Two Variables", IEEE Transactions on Computers, Vol. C-22, No. 1, January 1973, pp 28-33.

(3) Hugh Williamson, "Algorithm 420, Hidden-Line Plotting Program [J6]", Communications of the ACM, Vol. 15, No. 2, February 1972, pp 100-103

(4) Steven L. Watkins, "Algorithm 483, Masked Three-Dimensional Plot Program with Rotations [J6]", Communications of the ACM, Vol. 17, No. 9, September 1974.

(5) J. Butland, "Surface Drawing Made Simple", Computer-aided Design, Vol. 11, No. 1, January 1979.

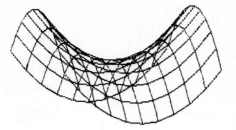

PARAMETER RANGE

Maximum: 1.000E+00
Minimum: -1.000E+00

PROJECTION ANGLES

Rotation: 20.00
Tilt: 80.00

Figure (1): Example of a surface where all lines are drawn

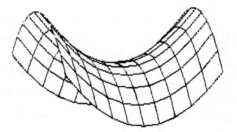

PARAMETER RANGE

Maximum: 1.000E+00
Minimum: -1.000E+00

PROJECTION ANGLES

Rotation: 20.00
Tilt: 80.00

Figure (2): Example of a surface with hidden lines removed

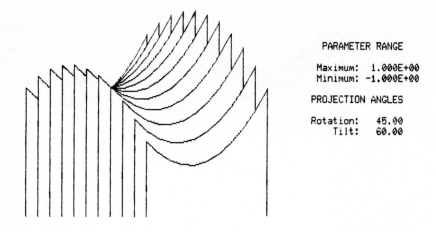

PARAMETER RANGE

Maximum: 1.000E+00
Minimum: -1.000E+00

PROJECTION ANGLES

Rotation: 45.00
Tilt: 60.00

Figure (3a): Drawing curves only in planes with constant X value

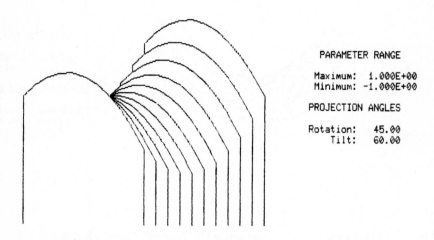

PARAMETER RANGE

Maximum: 1.000E+00
Minimum: -1.000E+00

PROJECTION ANGLES

Rotation: 45.00
Tilt: 60.00

Figure (3b): Drawing curves only in planes with constant Y value

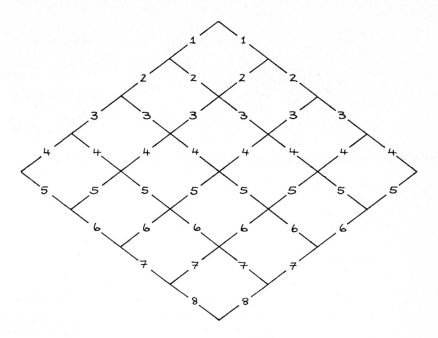

Figure (4): The plane segments included in successive boundaries

<u>Sequence of operations for N boundaries:</u>

(a)   *Draw boundary 1 in both pixel planes 0 and 1*

(b)   *For boundaries 2 to N repeat steps (c) to (f) inclusive*

(c)   *Define next boundary in macro store*

(d)   *Erase between boundary and top of screen in pixel plane 0*

(e)   *Erase between boundary and bottom of screen in pixel plane 1*

(f)   *Draw boundary in both pixel planes 0 and 1*

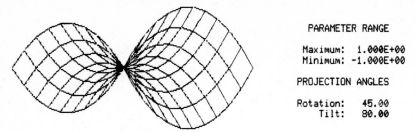

PARAMETER RANGE

Maximum: 1.000E+00
Minimum: -1.000E+00

PROJECTION ANGLES

Rotation: 45.00
    Tilt: 80.00

Figure (5a): Example of surface showing meshes on both sides

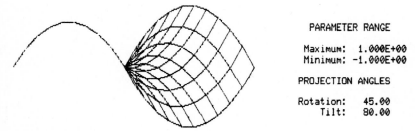

PARAMETER RANGE

Maximum: 1.000E+00
Minimum: -1.000E+00

PROJECTION ANGLES

Rotation: 45.00
    Tilt: 80.00

Figure (5b): Example of surface showing mesh on upper side only

PARAMETER RANGE

Maximum: 1.000E+00
Minimum: -1.000E+00

PROJECTION ANGLES

Rotation: 45.00
    Tilt: 80.00

Figure (5c): Example of surface showing mesh on lower side only

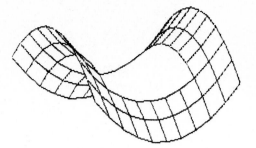

PARAMETER RANGE

Maximum: 1.000E+00
Minimum: -1.000E+00

PROJECTION ANGLES

Rotation: 30.00
Tilt: 70.00

Figure (6): An example of an opaque "hole"

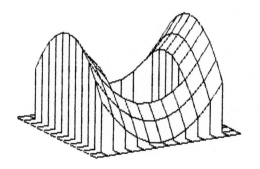

PARAMETER RANGE

Maximum: 1.000E+00
Minimum: -1.000E+00

Base: -1.000E+00

PROJECTION ANGLES

Rotation: 30.00
Tilt: 70.00

Figure (7): An example of an imaginary solid

Section 6
Hardware Architectures and Algorithms

Graphics Software Standards and
Their Evolution with Hardware Algorithms

James H. Clark
Silicon Graphics, Inc.

ABSTRACT

Graphics systems have repeated a cycle of evolution at least twice in the last fifteen years -- the first time with vector displays and now again with raster displays. Recent changes in computing systems allow this cycle to be broken and provide the opportunity for creating a better solution to the problem of graphics software interfaces, or graphics standards. This paper presents a view of the evolution of graphics hardware algorithms and these standards. After presenting this view and some deficiencies in existing graphics standards such as GKS, CORE and proposed standards such as PHIGS and the 3D extensions to GKS, the presentation then outlines a simple but powerful set of software concepts and primitives that accommodate hardware functionality that has emerged in recent years and also allow for future hardware developments.

Evolution of Software and Hardware

General-purpose programming languages and operating systems usually evolve in a de facto manner. The best known example is FORTRAN, but LISP, C, and UNIX are other de facto standards in their own limited domains. Attempts at "legislated", or committee-defined, standards have yielded languages such as ALGOL60, ALGOL68, and Ada, but these languages have not found widespread acceptance (although Ada may, if the US Government stays on its present course).

Graphics standards are problematic for more reasons than this "legislative" difficulty, however. Among them are

* Algorithms for making renderings of geometric objects have evolved significantly over the last fifteen years.

* Hardware is required to reduce the time necessary for repetitive calculations in rendering images of geometry. Thus, graphics systems architectures that incorporate new algorithms potentially change the software interface.

NATO ASI Series, Vol. F17
Fundamental Algorithms for Computer Graphics
Edited by R. A. Earnshaw
© Springer-Verlag Berlin Heidelberg 1985

* Technology has recently made it feasible for every user of a computer system to have their own color raster graphics display -- hence interface standards are a much bigger issue than before.

Once Around the Wheel of Reincarnation

Ivan Sutherland wrote a paper in about 1970 that outlined a cycle of thinking that took place at Harvard and the University of Utah. It concerned the role of display processors in vector graphics systems. The following few sections are a modern version of this paper, updated to include current thinking on graphics standards and raster displays.

The Basic Image Memory.

The most fundamental component of a raster graphics system is a raster-scan CRT and a frame-buffer memory that holds an image that is refreshed on this CRT. Enabled by declining memory costs, it is a very general display medium, since the computer system to which it is connected may create arbitrary images by generating suitable pixel values. A special controller to refresh the CRT is essential, since the general-purpose processor cannot operate at the speeds required to supply memory values to the CRT.

The software interface to such an image memory can be as simple as as mapping the entire image memory into the address space of the processor, thereby giving the processor random access to it. On the other hand, it might require access via several subroutines. In either case, the color maps and other refresh related hardware require certain conventions if they are to be changed. These conventions form the start of the software interface standard.

Creeping Functionality.

Frame buffers are used in two main categories of application: 1) representing image data proper (an array of pixels) 2) rendering geometric data (higher-level geometric representations).

The first is to hold an image that has been either created or captured in pixel form. In this form, the array of pixel values is the object of interest, and the user makes sense of the image only when all pixels are viewed in this array form. Examples are scanned images of photographs and television pictures, or human generated images, such as from "paint" systems. Thus, in a raster graphics system, software conventions must be defined to allow manipulation of pixel data. Although it is sufficient to map the image memory into the address space of the host processor, the processor will often spend a great deal of time computing the (x,y) address of a pixel in the memory. It is faster to build this address translation mechanism in hardware. In either case, a convenient software interface would allow (x,y) address specification.

The second category of frame buffer application is to hold an image that has been generated from geometric data. For this type of usage, the frame buffer is usually quite slow in generating images. Geometric objects are often defined as collections of lines, polygons, characters, points, or higher-order representations such as curves, surfaces or volumes that may be reduced to collections of these primitives. Drawing these primitives into a frame-buffer may be costly if the frame buffer is simply connected to a "host" processor that must employ a simple but repetitive algorithm executed by the general-purpose processor.

It is natural to "off-load" the host processor by giving the frame-buffer an "intelligent" microprocessor. This "intelligent" frame-buffer may then receive higher-level commands that, for example, specify the endpoints of lines in the coordinate system of the screen, which are then drawn using Bresenham's algorithm or other technique. Likewise, it might accept character codes which cause retrieval of icons for the characters from a bit-map, and polygon vertices which define regions in screen coordinates that are filled with definable colors, textures or both. The list of possible functions to embed in this intelligent device grows as we ensure that the renderings generated from the primitives are sufficient to represent the objects required by the applications.

Software conventions are required to modify and specify these primitives. Conventions for accepting sequences of points that are connected with lines, changing colors, loading and selecting character fonts, defining and selecting line-styles and textures, etc. are a few examples of the required interface conventions.

What started as a simple CRT controller with memory in the address space of the CPU has evolved into a more complex system. The reason for increasing its complexity in this way is to make it faster. Specialized hardware speeds the task of drawing the primitives, often by more than a factor of ten, over the speeds of the general-purpose processor in the host computer. Thus its additional cost yields better response time, which makes the user more productive.

User Coordinates and Screen Coordinates.

The primitives supported by the "intelligent" frame buffer have thus far been relative to the coordinates of the output device. In most applications, however, the geometric data to be represented on the screen is originally in a different coordinate system -- one more appropriate to the application. For example, a two dimensional collection of objects composing a drawing held in the computer memory might be represented in inches or other units -- the screen image is only an artifact, created from a particular view of the drawing. This view is specified by a class of operations that includes defining a window onto the drawing and mapping the geometric objects within the window to the screen. Included in this class of operations are those allowing the creation of "instances" of symbols and objects, rotations, scalings and translations of these instances and representing a hierarchy of objects.

These windowing and mapping functions at this point must be done in software algorithms running in the "host" processor. Because this simple set of operations is always performed on a small set of drawing primitives, it is natural to wish to "off-load" the processor by "migrating" this functionality to the microprocessor in the frame-buffer. That is, by giving the graphics system the ability to accept user-defined coordinates and windows onto a user's drawing space, the intelligent device can further off-load the host processor. It can then do the repetitive tasks of transforming the user's drawing under the window, manipulating objects to create a hierarchy of instances, determining what is in the window and clipping out those portions that are not, and mapping the results to a suitable rectangle on the screen.

This set of operations applies to 3D objects as well, if we postpone for the moment any discussion of hidden-surface removal, shading, etc. That is, renderings of both 2D drawings and 3D objects and collections of objects can be produced with one simple set of transformation, windowing and mapping operations. By incorporating these operations in the intelligent terminal, it is transformed into a device suitable for rendering both 2D and 3D objects, although presumably the 3D renderings are at this point only line-drawings or simple sets of polygons that do not obscure each other.

A four by four matrix of numbers will accomplish all of the manipulations for rotation, translation, and other manipulation of views in both two and three dimensions. Including a matrix stack further enables the hierarchy of instances. Other support for a clipping mechanism and the arithmetic means for mapping the window to the viewport is also easily included.

Incorporating these operations in the graphics system allows its interface to be application coordinates rather than screen coordinates, simplifying the software interface. Building them in hardware makes the graphics system many times faster. Likewise, since various pointing and input devices usually work in screen coordinates, and now the user interface is in user-space coordinates, software and hardware in the graphics system must provide conventions for mapping screen coordinates to user-coordinates, to assist in inputing data.

The main point here is that conventions suitable for both 2D and 3D displays must be chosen for communicating the transformation information to the intelligent terminal, specifying the "windows" onto the drawings and specifying the screen destination to which they are to be mapped (viewports). In addition, the system should be able to derive applications-coordinates from screen coordinates. Thus, the graphics standard grows with the complexity of the system. But up to this point, the increase in complexity decreases response time, which translates to higher productivity on the part of the user.

Giving the Intelligent Terminal Local Memory.

An intelligent graphics system, or terminal, with no significant local memory must rely on the host computer system to maintain all of the original geometric data. The "host" computer must retrieve all, or most, of the data each time a new image is to be generated from it -- it must be directly involved. It seems natural to "off-load" this task from the host by giving the intelligent terminal its own complement of local "display-list" memory. Then, all geometry for the application can be stored there, and the host need only determine when a new view is to be displayed, tell the graphics device which portions of it to display and then do other more important and presumably more computing related things.

This is the most insidious transition in the wheel of reincarnation. The difficulty arises because applications always have more than just graphical and geometrical data in their databases; mass properties, formatting information, electrical characteristics, composition materials, relations to other components, etc. are all examples of data that is related to an application but not necessarily to graphical renderings of it (although it sometimes must be displayed in textual form). In addition, local "display-list" memory requires conventions for defining it and modifying it. Thus we are required to define a "dynamic" mechanism for modifying graphic data held remotely.

In making this transition there are two extremes: either the entire database is moved to the remote intelligent terminal, thereby inducing the further requirement that the terminal be a substantial database handler, or only the geometric and graphical portion is moved. In both cases, significant software conventions must be adopted to provide for manipulation and display of this remote data.

Note that "remote" here means under the control of an "intelligent" device that may be located elsewhere. The problems arise even if the graphics microprocessor is on the same backplane (not physically remote), potentially sharing the same memory. If the system allows the creation of remote display-lists and insists that they be editable, problems await. Before proposing a solution, let us continue around the wheel.

Programming the Terminal.
Having made all of the foregoing transitions, the next step along the wheel is to give the user the ability to program the intelligent terminal.

Several forces are at work here. First, we have put substantial data in the "terminal" and the complexity of the interface software that manipulates this data has grown to the point that we inevitably want to manipulate and control the terminal's behaviour in ways that were not provided by the interface standard. Second, as we moved these display-lists to the remote device, no easy mechanism was provided for embedding in them the ability to do conditional branches -- making the "terminal" programmable eliminates this, since we can program the conditionals as necessary on the basis of data embedded in the display lists. Finally, conventions that allow editing the remote data in the finest detail are required if the system is to be completely flexible. By making the terminal programmable, many of these objections can be eliminated.

In making this choice, however, we must confront a whole new set of systems issues. For example, the terminal must be programmable in one or more languages. Moreover, the compilers for these languages must run on the "host" computer, since the terminal cannot compile programs for itself. And since we would normally expect the terminal to be interfaced to a variety of host computers, the compilers that generate executable code for the terminal might also be expected to run on a variety of hosts. These are very difficult systems implementation issues, and in general they are very difficult to accomplish.

Completing the Cycle.

The final step in the wheel of reincarnation is to give the remote device a local operating system with compilers, editors, and otherwise means for developing and executing programs independent of any outside host. Note that this may or may not imply that the device have a disk, since it might access disk storage via a file server located on a network. If this capability is coupled with the ability to behave and communicate as a terminal with a remote "host", everything that was possible in the above sequence is still possible, but the result is considerably more flexible. It is also, in many ways, easier.

At this point, if the local microprocessor is powerful enough, we might wish to migrate the entire application to this new system. We will call this new system a "workstation", since this is the term commonly used in the computer industry for such a system (not to be confused with the GKS term). The former host might then be relegated to the task of a database server, or file server. Optionally, the application might be split between the original host and this workstation.

This completes the cycle of reincarnation. A new system has been created that is capable of standing alone and running the application, if it has sufficient secondary storage access. The "host" has become the microprocessor of the workstation.

Existing Graphics Standards and the Cycle.

A wheel of reincarnation scenario of this type was originally outlined for vector graphics systems by Ivan Sutherland in about 1970. Ivan Sutherland, Bob Sproull and colleagues at Harvard and E&S Computer Corporation had gone through this cycle in the process of creating first the LDS-1 display system and later the LDS-2. Both the LDS-1 and the LDS-2 were vector graphics controllers, but the LDS-2 was a general-purpose processor that fetched and executed general-purpose computing instructions. After designing it and partially confronting the problems associated with programming it, Sutherland and colleagues abandoned giving vector graphics systems local display-list storage ability, since doing so starts a trend that results in making the complete cycle around the wheel, and moving the problem rather than solving it.

The same cycle has been repeated today, but whereas then only a few companies could contemplate the intelligent display processor, now because of the microprocessor, many more companies can implement it. We make the following observations:

* In the early 1970's, microprocessors were not available. Thus, going the complete distance around the wheel did not make as much sense as it does today. Going only part of the way yielded many problems. The availability of microprocessors and solid-state memory and fifteen years of progress have seduced us to repeat previous errors. We should not.

* The workstation of today is a combination of a graphics system with a computing system. It allows us to have both an intelligent terminal and a standalone computing and graphics environment in the same system -- thus, the isolated intelligent terminal notion has evolved into the workstation concept.

* Standards in current use were derived from the requirements of remotely intelligent terminals, and these standards suffer from the difficulty of defining means for editing remote data. Many of us proposing graphics standards have not yet recognized the insidious character of the cycle. Graphics standards should not try to encompass database management (PHIGS and to a lesser degree GKS). The complexity of these standards arises partly as a result of this.

The Principles of a Graphics Standard.

Graphics software interfaces usually adhere to certain guiding principles. We believe that the following principles yield the best set of objectives for a standard.

1. **Simplicity.** Keep the system' as simple as possible, but no simpler, to implement the desired functions. (This principle continues to prevail in all aspects of system design.)

2. **Realizable.** Use only standard features of high-level languages to implement. (We restrict ourselves to scientific languages.) No proposed standard will ever become one unless it can be implemented in FORTRAN, no matter how much we dislike this language. A very disagreeable imposition of this language is that all variables and subroutines must be uniquely identified by the first six letters of the name.

3. **Geometric.** Provide geometric, user-space coordinates, with rotations, translations, and other affine transformations carried out automatically as specified on all drawing primitives. This requirement is one of making the system interact with the user in the user's frame of reference, or coordinate system, independent of the resolution of the output device. In general, this implies that the graphics system must provide a coordinate transformation mechanism, such as a 4x4 matrix. In addition, this requires a means of specifying windows, clipping to these windows and mapping to a destination viewport on the screen.

4. **Generalized.** Provide pixel primitives for image manipulation, and for geometric manipulations, treat 2D and 3D drawing instructions in the same manner. In general, there is very little difference between the concepts of viewing and manipulating 2D geometry and 3D geometry. Thus, the system should treat them with a consistent interface.

5. **Graphics State.** Provide current state, such as graphics position, current coordinate system, etc. as well as means to change, save and restore it. Some proposed graphics standards, such as PHIGS, require that there be no current graphics position. Some state, however, is unavoidable in a graphics system, so that a better proposal is to allow the state to be saved, restored, and in general handled by the application, except where the state is operating-system related.

6. **Queued Input.** Channel all inputs from input devices through and event queue. An event queue removes the necessity to poll input devices, provides a more lucid interface that polling, and requires less processor time in a multi-tasking environment.

7. **Multiple Graphics Processes.** Provide for concurrent multiple windows in the graphics system. The user interface standard of graphics workstations is the multi-window environment. It gives a user the ability to keep several things

active at once.

8. **3D Shaded Pictures.** Provide for renderings of shaded three-dimensional objects using simple light-sources and with hidden surfaces removed automatically.

A Graphics Library will be presented in the talk according to the following outline.

1. **Drawing Primitives.** Commands whose execution cause geometric information or text to be sent to the graphics system. These include points, lines, polygons, characters and cubic curves and surfaces.

2. **Coordinate Transformations.** Routines for changing the viewing window, rotations, projections for 3D, etc.

3. **Textures and Fonts.** Setting and Changing linestyles, character fonts, and raster-fixed texture patterns.

4. **Display Modes and Color.** Commands that control modes of display, color maps, refresh synchronization, buffer swapping, cursor glyphs, etc.

5. **I/O Commands.** Using the event Queue, polling devices, etc.

6. **Graphical Objects.** Limited display-list commands.

7. **Picking and Selecting.** Selecting objects pointed to by a screen-oriented pointing device.

8. **Shaded, 3D Objects.** Providing 3D, shaded, visible surfaces.

Summary and Conclusions.

The wheel of reincarnation scenario points out the difficulty in having "remote intelligence graphics" while maintaining the locus of control for the graphics in a separate host computer. Software standards have become too complex in trying to serve these difficult ends. Because the microprocessor is the main controller in intelligent terminals and the same microprocessor is the processor of microcomputers, the principal difference between them is the presence of a disk and local operating system. Given the advantages of "local" control and the presence of networking technology in workstations, it is natural that the intelligent terminal be replaced by the workstation.

Graphics "terminal" functionality is still necessary; where necessary, however, workstations will serve the role previously served by remote intelligent terminals. If a workstation is to behave as a terminal to another host, where the locus of control is in the host, the desired portion of the application can easily be put in the workstation. In so doing, one has the option and flexibility of replacing the lower-level set of subroutine calls that might be used in the host-terminal scenario with higher-level commands for transferring data between the "host" and the workstation, perhaps using established network protocols.

Graphics standards typically have two parts -- one part dealing with database manipulations, display-list editing, and so forth, and the other part dealing with the algorithmic manipulations for making pictures of various data held in the data structures. The database management should not be part of the standard.

Hardware Enhancements for Raster Graphics

Andrew Glassner
Henry Fuchs

Department of Computer Science
University of North Carolina at Chapel Hill
Chapel Hill, North Carolina 27514 USA

Abstract

Great strides have been made in the field of fast, realistic image generation in the last 20 years. A generally acknowledged goal of the field called the Ultimate Display has been guiding the field all that time, and may very well be guiding us for the next 20 years. But with the recent advent of VLSI technology the Ultimate Display may finally be less of a dream and more of an achievable goal.

Most of the recent advances toward the Ultimate Display have been in the fields of image synthesis and generation. The development of these fields has taken place on at least two major fronts in recent years. One research direction has been to place a premium on the realism of the generated images, regardless of the clock time required to create the image. Another major research direction has been to build highly interactive, dynamic systems that must produce successive images within some fixed period of time, usually 1/30 second or less.

This paper examines approaches that have been used to squeeze the maximum realism out of an image generated on a real-time system. Most of these approaches have begun as insights into the nature of the algorithms, permitting a speedup through strategic and tactical improvements. Recently, the powers of multiple processors have been brought to bear on the problem, exploiting parallelism inherent in the image synthesis procedure. Very Large Scale Integration (VLSI) techniques have proven to be a very useful way to develop these multiple-processor systems. VLSI is helping not only with the generation of images but with many other problems involved in the Ultimate Display, such as hand and eye tracking, and a miniaturized head-mounted display. This paper discusses each of these subjects.

This work was supported in part by the Defense Advance Research Project Agency , Contract number DAAG29-83-K-0148 (monitored by U.S. Army Research Office, Research Triangle Park, NC) , the National Science Foundation, Grant number ECS-8300970, and the National Institutes of Health (NIH), Grant R01-CA39060.

I. Introduction

The field of computer graphics has grown rapidly in the last several years. One subfield of special interest to many people is real-time graphics. The term real-time is usually applied to systems that must react interactively by updating the image on the screen to reflect changes desired by the user.

In this paper we will restrict our attention to real-time, three-dimensional shaded graphics systems. These systems have been used for many years as flight simulators and trainers. More recently, real-time systems have started helping doctors, architects, engineers, and others who work with complex three-dimensional scenes. As the range of applications grows, so does the range of operations requested by these users. Thus the designer of a real-time graphics system must support an ever-increasing range of operations, always working within the constraint of producing a new image at least 30 times each second. Some of today's applications are so complex that current systems are unable to meet this demand, and users must tolerate slower update rates. But the goal of 30 frames per second remains.

In addition to the increasing range of operations and complexity of data, users are also demanding increased realism in their images. Many techniques have been developed for generating images that appear so realistic they seem to be photographs of natural, complex scenes. But these techniques have generally been developed with little consideration for their real-time applications. The more realistic an image appears the more work must go into its synthesis, and in general this work costs time. Thus the graphics architect must supply even more function in the ever-constant 1/30 of a second. The job of the real-time graphics system architect does not end with the synthesis of the image. The other aspects of the man-machine interface also must be considered and gracefully incorporated into the whole system.

In this paper we will consider how some real-time computer graphics systems have been designed to respond to these demands of increased performance and realism.

In Section II we present the overall goals of real-time computer graphics systems in their most general form. We then identify four key topics important to reaching that goal: image generation, display techniques, tracking techniques, and database interaction. The next four sections examine these key topics in more detail, with special emphasis on past attempts to speed up or improve the results.

Section III examines the key topic of image generation, and begins with a brief history of the development of some key ideas in that field. We then present a summary of the image generation process as we perceive it, and analyze the different approaches that might be taken to speed it up. The rest of the section presents several such approaches, characterized by the terms identified in the analysis.

Section IV involves the key topic of display techniques, and how the image may be best presented to the user. This issue is critically related to the perception of the image and its effectiveness as a conveyor of information to the user.

Section V considers the issue of key topic of tracking. The goal is to make the transfer from user to computer of information describing the user's position and gaze direction as natural and effective as possible.

Section VI concerns the key topic of control and modification of the database. As the user interacts and modifies the data it reacts and changes. As the number of applications of real-time graphics increases this dynamic element is becoming increasingly important.

Section VII offers our acknowledgements.

II. Overall Goals of Real-time Graphics Systems

In 1965 Ivan Sutherland presented a seminal paper describing his vision for the future of computer graphics [Suth 65]. His goal was the creation of an "ultimate display" to present the graphical output of a computer to a user. This display would be so portable that it would travel with the user all the time he or she was using the machine. To present its graphical information it displayed images in front of the user's eyes; thus it seemed natural to mount the device on a helmet on the user's head. The family of techniques that have risen to approximate this goal are thus referred to as "head-mounted displays." The head-mounted display may indeed take the form of a helmet, or miniaturization of video display tubes and optics may give it the form of a lightweight pair of glasses. The display itself need not obscure the user's environment. Indeed, half-silvered mirrors have been used for many years to combine two images; they could certainly be used to combine a synthetic image with a user's environment.

One goal of the head-mounted display vision was that the images created by the computer should be so realistic and natural that they are indistinguishable from actual objects. Thus, the computer is able to present a new environment to the user, one that is a smooth mixture of the simulated and the real.

Another goal in the head-mounted display is the ability to track and respond to the user's actions. For example, let us imagine a surgeon wearing a head-mounted display. The surgeon might be presented three-dimensional data from a CAT or NMR scan of a patient, displayed to give the surgeon the illusion that she is a small visitor inside the patient's body. For example, the surgeon may suspect a tumor inside some body part, so she walks over to the part in question. Unfortunately, she may find that the body part completely surrounds the suspected tumor. The surgeon could reach her hand out, sweep the extra material to the side, and look into the hole she just made. Of course, the surgeon actually didn't push any real thing; the computer saw, recognized, and reacted to the movement by manipulating the database in the correct way to preserve the illusion and help the surgeon do her work.

So in its full form the head mounted display allows the ultimate computer-generated video experience. The wearer can be placed into any visual surroundings with any degree of correlation to the "real world," including none at all! The actions of the user are interpreted as interactions with the real and simulated worlds, and the computer adjusts the simulated world accordingly. Actually, the original "ultimate display" idea went even further, providing inputs to all five senses, not just sight. In particular, the sense of feel would also receive synthetic input from force feedback equipment. Thus, a user could sit in a virtual chair, or climb a virtual tree! Except in passing we won't consider the other senses again in this paper.

To bring about the head-mounted display we have many problems to solve. In this paper we have isolated four critical issues. These consist of algorithms for synthesizing images, techniques for displaying images, methods for tracking the user's gaze and actions, and ways to control the database to reflect the user's actions.

III. Real-Time Realistic Image Generation

The generation of realistic images has been one of the central research issues of computer graphics for many years. The general approach has been to isolate the critical aspects of natural scenes that give them the quality of "reality," and study how synthesis algorithms may include that information in the images they generate. The first pictures made that exhibit this new information are usually made at great expense in computer resources, including rendering time. Only after the effects are well understood are we able to search for faster implementations.

The critical constraint in real-time image generation is the persistence of vision of the human eye. If the eye is presented with successive images too slowly, the human peceptual system will not fuse them into one continuous stream. The required interval between frames varies among observers and conditions; for instance the interval in a dark room is not the same interval in a light room. For a variety of technical and psychophysical reasons the value chosen as the "real-time threshold" is usually 1/30 of a second. Thus the goal of the real-time systems architect is to completely finish the rendering of a picture and get it presented to the viewer in no more than 1/30 of a second.

In general, to increase the quality of the image requires an increase in the amount of computer power used to create the image. In a single processor system this means a higher-quality picture (more realistic, more detailed, or superior in some respect to another picture) requires more time. Multiple-processor systems offer the promise of better pictures without an increase in time by applying their computing power in parallel.

In the next part of this section we will briefly review some highlights in the history of computer image generation. This history is extremely biased; no attempt was made to give a comprehensive review of the field. Rather, we simply mention those contributions which will be relevant later in this paper.

Early History

When Sutherland proposed the "Ultimate Display" in 1965 no one had yet rendered a shaded image with hidden surfaces removed (or at least if he did, he didn't publish it widely). The core of computer graphics was vector screens and light pens; realism was a dream.

Two years earlier in 1963 Roberts described a method for removing the hidden lines from a vector image [Robe 63]. It wasn't until four years after Sutherland's paper that the first two real-time hidden surface techniques emerged, in rapid succession. In 1969 Schumaker et al. described the General Electric real-time shaded graphics system [Schu 69]. In 1970 Watkins described his real-time scan-line algorithm for visible surface generation [Watk 70]. His algorithm was later incorporated into the real-time flight simulator produced by the Evans & Sutherland Computer Corporation. The GE and the E&S systems were the first two real-time shaded graphics displays. They were able to produce an apparently continuous stream of 3D shaded images from a changing viewpoint.

These systems gave high performance, but they had price tags to match. It was clear that small systems could not afford the extensive hardware routinely employed by these large-scale simulators. Efforts continued at finding ways to find more efficient methods for rendered image generation. In 1972 Newell et al. published a paper which suggested a very elegant technique called the "painter's algorithm" [Newe 72]. Polygons were simply drawn on the screen one after the other, starting with the polygon farthest away and working forward toward the user. Unfortunately, there are a myriad of special cases that the unadorned painter's algorithm doesn't handle. The authors suggested an hierarchy of techniques to be applied in order, starting with the bare algorithm and increasing in complexity and required computation. Thus, the simplest cases went fastest, and extra time was only spent when needed.

In 1974 Sutherland et al. published a classic paper comparing ten published hidden surface algorithms [Suth 74]. In this paper they describe the common and differentiating features of the various algorithms, and offer analyses of their performances. They also mention in passing that a large array of memory can be used to store the depth at each sample point in an image. This is the germ of the idea of the z-buffer, which appeared again in the description of a frame buffer [Kaji 75].

Later History

In this subsection we describe some important advances that either have not yet been implemented in specialized hardware, or are currently being tested in different implementations. There have been several persistent problems in computer-generated images that confront the designer of a graphics system. Some of these problems are algorithmic and due to insufficient knowledge or study (such as a simulation of mixing liquids), while others are inherent in the medium (such as sampling artifacts).

In 1977 Weiler and Atherton presented what is essentially an inverse painter's algorithm [Weil 77], commonly known as the "cookie cutter" algorithm. The algorithm simply draws polygons sorted from nearest to farthest, testing each new polygon against those already in the pixel. Those parts of the polygon that are already covered in the pixel are simply removed prior to adding that polygon in. This algorithm has a great advantage in that the area contributions of all fragments within a pixel sum to unity. We can use this information to assign a pixel's color in such a way that it correctly combines the contribution of each object in the pixel, a process known as "anti-aliasing."

In 1980 Whitted presented an extension of the ray-tracing algorithm originally presented by Appel [Appe 67]. Whitteds's algorithms incorporated shadows, reflections, and transparency [Whit 80]. The techniques based on ray tracing yield pictures of extremely high realism, but at a correspondingly high computational cost. The subject of ray tracing has received a great deal of attention recently, including a description of distributed ray tracing by Cook et al. [Cook 84]. This formulation combines solutions to many traditionally hard problems in graphics into one unified and elegant model.

A paper presented in 1984 by Carpenter described an extension of the z-buffer called the A-buffer [Carp 84]. The A-buffer is similar to several other techniques in that it collects subpixel fragments which are combined to determine a final shade for the pixel. The A-buffer has the advantage that fragments can arrive in any order; final color resolution is performed when all visible surfaces have been scan converted, shaded, and entered into the A-buffer.

Lighting and Shading

Calculating the proper shade at each pixel once the visible surface is known was once thought to be simple. However, techniques which produce increasingly realistic images require increasingly more computer time to perform this operation.

A variety of techniques exist for computing shading. These also follow the pattern that more realism costs more computing time. Three shading models are most commonly used in real-time systems today. The models can be applied to any kind of surface element, but for clarity of comparison they will all be discussed with reference to polygons. We will also note that these models are used to determine the illumination of a surface, not necessarily the color of the surface at any point.

The Lambert (or faceted) model simply assigns a single color to an entire polygon based on the angle the polygon's surface normal makes with the light source. The Lambert model is the simplest lighting model used. Next in complexity and expense is the Gouraud (or smooth-shading) model, which computes the correct shading for the polygon at each vertex and blends the shades across the face of the polygon. Most expensive in time and complexity is the Phong (or normal-interpolating) model. This model computes the shade for each point on the polygon as a function of the location of the point and the average normal for the composite surface at each vertex of the polygon. The Phong model requires a square root for each pixel in the final display; this is a very costly operation.

Summary of Real-time Image Generation

We have given our view of the generic real-time image generation process in the model in Figure 1. The process of generating a frame begins anew from the top for each object, creating the images of objects one by one to build up the entire picture. Objects are stored in the database, and are retreived at the appropriate time by the database accessor. The object is then subjected to a series of transformations, possibly including rotation, scaling, skewing, and other geometric operations. The object is then projected to the screen by a process called scan conversion. This basically consists of determining which pixels might need to be altered to add this object to the final image. After this step each pixel is considered independently.

Each pixel which might be affected by this object must determine whether the object is truly visible, or if it is obscured by other objects at that pixel. This determination of visible surfaces is followed by a shading step. Each pixel which does include some of the object must determine the correct coloring for the section of the object within the pixel. This step is referred to as .shading, although it may also include operations such as texturing.

When a piece of object has been colored it is sent to the image build store, where this fragment of the object is combined with all other current and previous object fragments. The image resolver then combines these fragments in some way to produce a composite picture. The picture is actually displayed by the video generator, which may employ algorithms for display correction of the image, including color adjustment and compensation for a particular observer's color biases.

This process can be viewed as a classic pipelined algorithm, where each box is simultaneously working on the results of the previous box. If each step in the pipeline takes the same amount of time the system can be clocked synchronously and thus achieve maximum efficiency.

We suggest that there are two main techniques for speeding up this pipeline. The first technique is based on classic parallelism; the application of many identical processors to solve a given task. To achieve this we isolate a step in the pipeline and design a processor to execute it. We then amass a set of these processors under control of a supervisory processor and use this organization as a pipeline step. In essence, we simply assign many identical processors to a single task. The other way to speed up the pipeline is to consolidate pipeline steps into a single chip. We can then take advantage of the extreme ratio of on-chip to off-chip signalling times and increase the throughput between those steps of the pipeline. This approach is especially fruitful when used with high-bandwidth pipeline elements.

Relative to the pipeline boxes of Figure 1 we can consider the first approach as an extension of a given box in the horizontal direction, and the latter approach as a combination of boxes vertically. Thus the column of processors in Figure 1 may become either wider or shorter.

In the classic paper comparing hidden surface algorithms, Sutherland et al. [Suth 74] distinguish between those algorithms that work in image space (i.e. the screen) and those that work in object space (i.e. the 3D world where we define objects). In a similar vein, speedup techniques can be viewed as operating in either image space, object space, or both. An examination of Figure 2 will also show an interesting correlation: object-space speedups are implemented with pipelining, while image-space speedups are implemented with parallel processing.

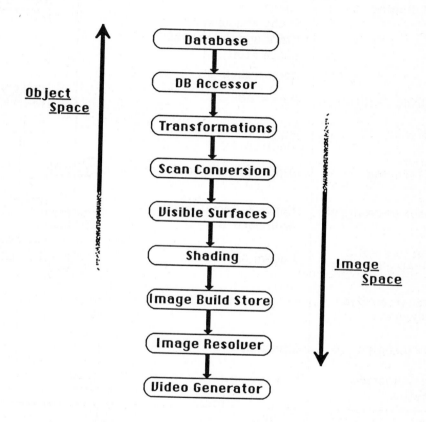

The Image Generation Pipeline

Figure 1

The Image Generation Pipeline

Technique	References	Pipelining	Splitting in Object Space	Splitting in Image Space	Classical Parallelism
8-by-8 display	Fuchs '77 Fuchs and Johnson '79 Clark and Hannah '80 Gupta et al. '81 Demetrescu '85			☑	☑
Distributed Z-Buffer	Parke '80			☑	☑
Pixel-planes	Fuchs '81 Poulton '85			☑	☑
Sub-volume Ray-Tracing	Dippé & Swenson '84	☑	☑		
Processor per Polygon	Cohen & Demetrescu '80 Weinberg '81	☑	☑	☑	☑
Constructive Solid Geometry Machine	Kedem & Ellis '84	☑	☑	☑	☑
E&S Transformation Hardware		☑			
Geometry Engine	Clark '82	☑			
Weitek Rendering Pipeline	Weitek '84	☑			
TI 4161 Row-Scan Memory Chip	TI '83				
NEC 7220 Raster Fill and Scan Chip	NEC '83				

A Characterization of Hardware Speedup Techniques

Figure 2

A Characterization of Hardware
Speedup Techniques

Hardware Speedup Summary

In this subsection we will look at a variety of speedup techniques that have been reported in the literature. Figure 2 summarizes the characteristics of each technique in terms of object vs. image space, and parallelism vs. pipelining.

There are two general approaches to hardware speedup: custom hardware designed to replace a general processor, and special-purpose chips designed to replace common aggregates of smaller chips. Most of this discussion will be concerned with the former, though we will consider special-purpose chips at the end.

Image-Space Approaches

A powerful, general-purpose processor at every pixel would be ideal. Unfortunately, it would also be expensive to make and maintain, hot to run, and very difficult to justify. But the processor-per-pixel idea is so seductive that various approximations to it have been tried.

One generic approach was described in various forms in [Fuch 77], [Fuch 79], [Clar 80], and [Gupt 81]. This approach is usually referred to as the 8-by-8 display. In general, the 8-by-8 display consists of a square matrix of processors, 8 processors on a side, for 64 processors in all. An example of one of the 8-by-8 architectures is given in Figure 3. The other common feature of all but the most recent 8-by-8 proposals is a picture memory buffer interlaced in both x and y by a factor of 8. Thus, each of the 64 processors can speak to a unique pixel simultaneously. The 8-by-8 displays can therefore offer a maximum theoretical speedup of a factor of 64 above a single-processor framebuffer. The most recent 8-by-8 display proposal [Deme 85] differs from the others in that each processor addresses not a single pixel, but an entire scan line. Thus, its relative power is much greater than 64 over a single processor; it is in fact the product of 64 and the width of a scan line.

Rather than taking our 8-by-8 array and assigning each processor to one pixel, we might want to take an array of some other size and assign each processor some small piece of the screen. We can then send descriptions of our surface elements to all the processors at once and let them take care of the job of checking whether or not they should be placed in the display.

Another good solution to determining which objects are visible is called the z-buffer. The z-buffer algorithm is a very common, very effective brute force solution to the hidden surface problem. With just one processor sitting on top of the z-buffer we must wait for that processor for every pixel of our object. In 1980, Parke published a comparison of several schemes for distributing control of a z-buffer among several processors [Park 80]. It was found that if many processors are each given a small piece of the z-buffer to monitor and control some significant time savings can be achieved.

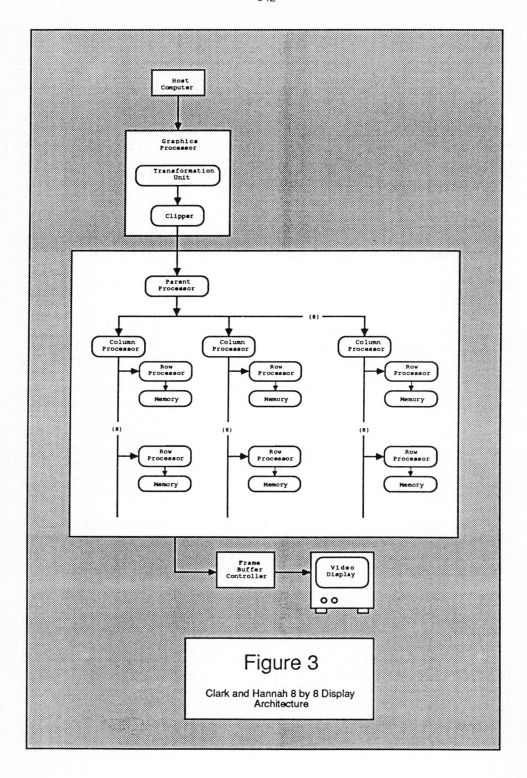

Figure 3

Clark and Hannah 8 by 8 Display
Architecture

The ultimate image space machine, as we mentioned above, is a powerful processor at each pixel. The 8-by-8 display compromises on the number of processors by providing a powerful processor for each pixel in a subregion of the screen. The other compromise is to provide a processor at every pixel but vastly reduce the power of that processor. This latter approach is used in the Pixel-planes system [Fuch 81], [Poul 85], [Fuch 85], which is shown in Figure 4.

In Pixel-planes, a unique architecture is exploited to perform scan conversion of a polygon in parallel over a large segment of the screen. Each Pixel-plane chip addresses a subset of the screen and provides a very small, very limited processor at each pixel. Each of these processors is supported with a large, dedicated memory (72 bits in the fourth-generation chip). A tree structure is imposed on this chip providing the solution to the plane equation of a polygon at all points on the screen simultaneously. Each edge of the polygon is sent to the chip, and each processor determines which side of the edge the pixel it controls is on. Processors that are on the side of the edge that is "outside" the polygon effectively turn themselves off until the first edge of the next polygon. Processors whose pixels are inside the polygon then compare the pixel's current z value with the z value of the polygon at that pixel. If the polygon is farther away than the z value stored at the pixel the processor turns itself off until the first edge of the next object. Only processors still on after all edges have been checked actually end up contributing to the final image for that polygon. These processors then update their z value to represent the new object. At the conclusion of all the edges of a polygon the processors are reset and the process begins anew.

Object-Space Approaches

When rendering an image on a fixed time budget you must decide how much time you're willing to pay for various attributes of the final image. If realism is highly desired then you'll have to get the time for the processing from somewhere. If you want Phong shading, for example, you'll have to take a square root at every pixel. You can build the fastest square root extractor ever, but you still have to wait for it and no amount of parallel processing will speed that up. You can buy some time in late pipeline stages (like shading) by speeding up early pipeline stages (like visible surfaces). This is exactly the benefit of object-space speedup.

A good example of pure object-space speedup is the parallel ray tracer described by Dippe & Swensen [Dipp 84]. The three-dimensional space is subdivided into a large number of tetrahedra, each of which holds some number of objects. When a ray is sent into the scene, it passes from volume to volume until the ray-object intersection completes. Each processor is assigned a tetrahedral volume and a ray and is asked to perform the ray-tracing algorithm in that volume. When the rays are intersected and returned the visible surface problem has been solved. In this case the Transformation and Visible Surface steps have been combined in the ray-tracing processor (the ray-tracing algorithm side-steps the scan conversion step).

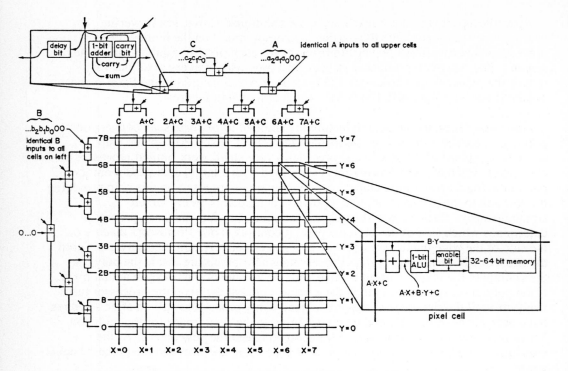

Conceptual design of an 8 x 8 pixel PIXEL-PLANES image-buffer memory chip.
Scan conversion, hidden-surface elimination and color-rendering commands are translated
outside the memory system into A,B,C coefficients and associated PIXEL-PLANES commands.

Figure 4

Pixel Planes Organization

Combined Approaches

Several researchers have combined image and object space approaches in the same system to realize the benefits of both worlds.

In 1980 Cohen & Demetrescu presented a system which can be characterized as having a processor for each polygon along a given scan line [Cohe 80]. Each processor scan converts its polygon for a given scan line, as shown in Figure 5. The processor then examines the scan line that has been built up so far and adjusts it where necessary to include the object for which that processor has responsibility. The adjusted scan line is then output from the processor. A chain of these chips arranged in a pipeline outputs the nearest z and associated shade for each pixel in scanline order.

In 1981 Weinberg suggested adding coverage information to each message sent by the scan converting processors [Wein 81]. This information helped the combining processor compute an average coloring for the pixel and thus facilitated anti-aliasing of the image.

In 1984 Kedem presented a description of a Constructive Solid Geometry machine [Kede 84]. The machine stored objects in the leaf nodes of a processor tree, as shown in Figure 6. The objects were combined according to the rules of CSG at node processors to find the final result at a pixel. The distribution of objects into leaf nodes is an object-space division; the CSG nodes manipulate rays which corresponded to pixels, placing those processors in image space.

Support Hardware

In 1968 the Evans&Sutherland Computer Corporation completed the LDS-I, a 3D vector pipeline. The LDS-I had a hardware 4-by-4 matrix multiply unit which performed geometric transformations.

The Geometry Engine described by Clark in 1982 [Clar 82] is a general-purpose mathematics chip for graphics applications, particularly transformations. The IRIS system marketed by Silicon Graphics uses 12 of these chips to compute the geometrical and perspective transformations on 3D image data.

The Weitek WTE6000 Tiling Engine (1983) is a tiling and shading pipeline for high-speed image generation. It's basically a very specialized architecture using very fast mathematics chips.

The Texas Instruments 4161 memory chip (1983) is a dual-ported RAM designed for frame-buffer applications. It supplies two ports for chip addressing, allowing the CPU and refresh circuitry to operate independently. It also provides a 256-bit serial shift register which can be clocked off-chip to easily support transmission of chip data

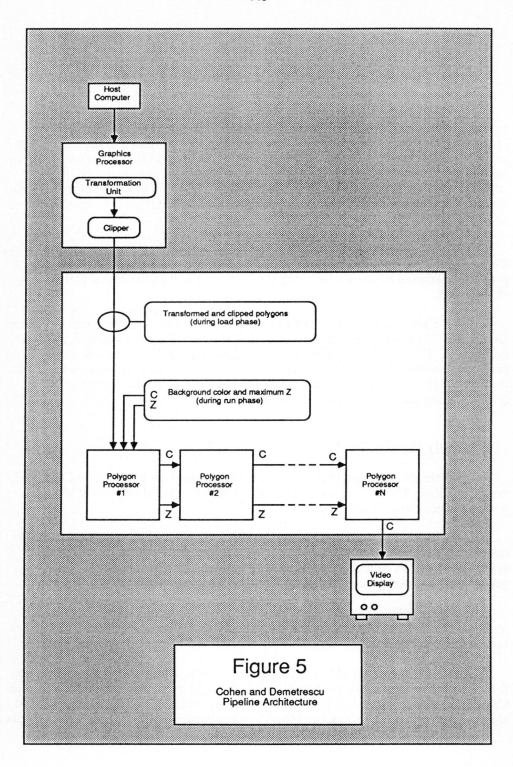

Figure 5

Cohen and Demetrescu
Pipeline Architecture

647

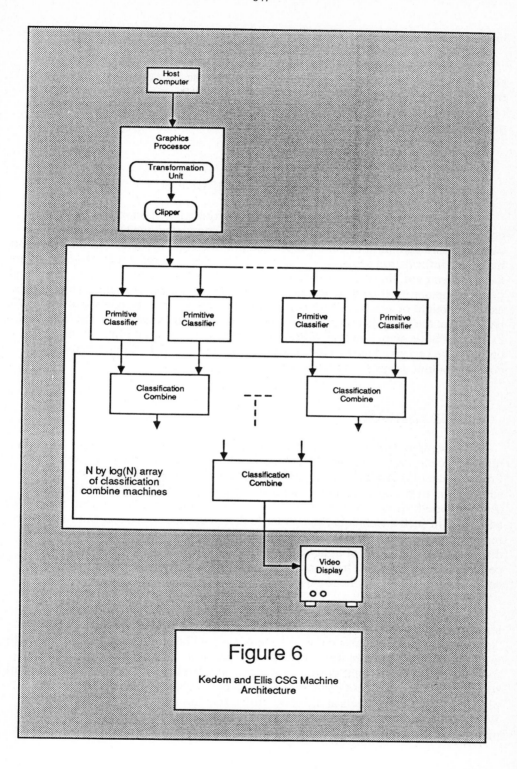

Figure 6

Kedem and Ellis CSG Machine
Architecture

to raster generating hardware.

The NEC 7220 (1983) also provides several high-level functions. Intended as a general-purpose frame-buffer controller, it is able to scan-convert polygons into a frame buffer, and provides functions for drawing lines, arcs, and other graphic primitives. The chip also serves as a video generator, which supports zooming, panning, windowing, and light-pen tracking.

IV. Display Techniques

So far we have concerned ourselves with the formation of an image inside the computer. When the image rendering pipeline is completed, we have a two-dimensional matrix of colors expressed in some color system. Our next job is to make this information accessible to the user. The classic computer output devices are the punched card, line printer, and cathode ray tube. These devices are all peripheral to the computer itself, and are usually used in a deliberate way. That is, a terminal is usually thought of as a means for controlling a computer, not the computer itself. We believe that the most natural and efficient forms of communication do not involve this extra translation step, however widespread it may be. We would like our input and output to be perceived as directly associated with the machine. In this chapter we consider output devices for presenting images to users.

Dream Displays

If we were to dream of any devices for output, our dreams would be of the ultimate head-mounted display. Here the word "ultimate" is used advisedly. Probably the ultimate display in purely technical terms would be direct cortical stimulation, in which computer-generated stimuli could not be distinguished from sense-reported stimuli. We feel that there are important social and ethical issues to be addressed in such a technique, and prefer to dream about devices that can be easily removed by the wearer at any time. In that context, we envision the head-mounted display to look like a set of lightweight, attractive eyeglasses. The display would contain no high voltages, frequencies, or radiators, and would not be physically coupled to any object in the room except the wearer.

In one configuration the lenses of the glasses would be several layers deep. The lenses would be high-resolution color matrices dot-addressable by layer, where "transparent" is an available color. The lenses would have fast switching times, on the order of 33mS (to achieve frame rates of 1/30 second). The lenses would also have the ability to generate light as well as absorb and reflect it, so they could work in dark rooms. The images would consititute a stereo pair, enhancing the stereopsis by placing synthesized objects at different virtual foci through some system of optics. We would like to point out that the head-mounted display is not simply a matter of placing synthetic images in front of the user. There is a problem of hidden surfaces that has been in computer graphics since the start, and it returns in this context as well.

Imagine that you are holding a coil of rope in your hand. Your hand is stretched out in front of you, the coil is grasped in your fist and is resting on the inside of your elbow. Clearly you cannot see your elbow through the opaque rope; the rope obscures your elbow. Now think about where your hand is grasping the rope. Your fingers are coiled around the rope, so you can see your fingers but not the rope. Now let us return to the head-mounted display. You are looking at the world through half-silvered lenses that are displaying computer-synthesized images along with the outside world. The rope will be a computer-generated object. Your hands are real; they are the outside world. Now consider what you actually see. Since the images on your half-silvered lenses are merged everywhere with the real world scene, you have to somehow compensate for the hidden surfaces we mentioned just above.

How do we obscure the rope by the hand? We need to know where the hand is in relation to the rope and in relation to the viewer. Anywhere we decide the rope is behind the hand we just do not draw in the rope. Because the image of the rope suddenly stops at the edge of your fingers and starts again at the other edge, and the stereo cues make you think it is just about where your fingers are, you will probably decide that your hand is obscuring the rope. Now consider the rope sitting on your elbow; you see the rope and not your elbow. But how do we stop you from seeing your elbow? As we've described things so far there's no way; the synthetic image is merged with the real image at every point. The only way to make the elbow invisible is to opaque those points on your glasses through which you see your elbow. Now you can't see your elbow, but you still see the image of the rope; thus you may decide that the rope is obscuring your elbow.

The conclusion we can draw from this is that the glasses need to be more than just transparent glass or even colored glass; they need to be light-generating on the side near your eye and controllably transparent on the side away from your eye.

The glasses would come with a set of lightweight headphones to connect up to computer-controlled sound synthesis equipment, to provide yet another dimension of sensory illusion. The head-mounted display would become a universal tool for interacting with one's environment. In the office, a virtual desk would extend in front of the wearer, with an arbitrary number of papers and books; anything can be brought to the "real" desk where all interactions are monitored and recorded by the computer. An object changes as it is manipulated, and effects of that change, if any, propagate throughout the simulated environment. Thus, taking a book from the bottom of a stack may cause the remaining books to topple, but a spoken word or gesture will get them to re-stack themselves with no trouble.

Surgeons could be supplied with projections of the patient upon whom they are considering surgery. They can plan and even practice the surgery, and watch computer simulations of the results in a greatly accelerated time frame. When real surgery is being performed any information the surgeon desires, from a magnification of the work being done to x-ray views of the patient, can be supplied instantly. The artistic and entertainment possibilites are open to the imagination. Giant networks of people interacting with each other's virtual images all over the globe could gather to see cultural events or synthesize their own. With the distributed home computer network now growing the future of such a display could change nature every few years.

Today's Displays

Recent work by Shiffman and Parker [Schif 84] and Vuilleumier et al [Vuil 84] have shown that it's possible to construct very small high resolution displays using IC fabrication technology for both the driving electronics as well as for the display substrate itself. Such work encourages us in the belief that displays can be constructed with sufficient size, speed, and resolution for useful head-mounted displays.

Today's Problems

The displays mentioned above are all relatively new technology that will certainly have to go through several design iterations until all the bugs are worked through, if indeed all the bugs can be solved. These new displays also suffer from some common problems. They are not very powerful light sources, so either the light must be used very carefully or a light "repeater" will have to be used between the display and the eye. Additionally, they are all physically very small. To generate a display large enough to operate as a head-mounted display their image must be magnified in some way.

V. Tracking

The goal of tracking is to make the computer responsible for maintaining information describing where the user is looking and what he or she is doing with respect to the database. For example, in the head-mounted display paradigm we require that the computer know where we are looking. This is the opposite philosophy from sitting in front of a display tube with joysticks and sliders and manually entering your position and gaze; we want the computer to keep track and do the work itself.

There are two major reasons we want to track the user: to provide the correct images to the head-mounted display, and to modify the database correctly to respond to the user's movements. For the purpose of accurate viewpoint determination, we need to know at a minimum where the user's head is located and in what direction the eyes are looking. To dynamically modify the database when interacting with the user, we can progress from gross physical motions to subtle cues depending on our expertise, goals, and funding.

A minimum tracking system would keep track of the user's position and gaze, and the tip of a wand held in the user's hands. We suggest that the first improvement to make to this system would be to track the user's hands. Gestures constitute a large part of our everyday communication, and our hands are a major mechanism of interaction with our surroundings.

The next two subsections will investigate the two major approaches to tracking: the machine tracking the user, and the user tracking himself.

Machine Tracking User

The head-mounted display requires that we know where the user is located and in what direction the user is looking. Database interaction requires that we know how the user is interacting with the world. We will first look at a device that enables tracking of the user's head and gaze, and then we will look at two devices that allow the user to interact with the database.

Viewpoint via Mechanical Coupling: The Sword of Damocles

In 1968 Sutherland published an account of the first interactive head-mounted display [Suth 68] (also described in [Vick 70]). The means of tracking the user was via a device formally named the "Head Position Sensor." This was a shaft of nested cylindrical tubes that ran between two pivots: one on the ceiling of the room and one on the top of a helmet-like contraption the user wore on his or her head. The computer determined where the head was located and the angle at which it was oriented by measuring the overall length from ceiling to head and the values of the angles at the two pivots.

Ivan Sutherland is said to have referred to this device as "The Sword of Damocles," in reference to the overhead contraption. The optics in the headpiece projected the synthetic image to a focus point apparently several feet in front of the viewer.

Interaction via Visual Coupling: The Wand

The first device to be used with the Utah head-mounted display was a wand. This was simply a stick with a light at the end, which was driven by some light-camera synchronization circuitry. The blinking light was sensed by cameras mounted on the walls of the room, which were also controlled by the synchronization circuits. Although the implementation of such a scheme is simple, it suffers from some severe problems. First, the light must always be visible by the cameras. Thus, the system builder must either buy many cameras and mount them throughout the room, or severly modify where the wand may be held and where the user may stand. Another problem is that since the light must be differentiable from the image of the room, it must be sufficiently bright to be easily distinguishable. This implies either that the room be dark (which may be troublesome to the user), or that the light be very bright (and possibly irritating). There are also other drawbacks. So although the problems with this scheme are manifold, it does represent a first step towards virtual interaction.

Interaction via Mechanical Coupling: The Arms

In 1976 Kilpatrick reported on a system called GROPE [Kilp 76], built at the University of North Carolina at Chapel Hill. GROPE consisted of two mechanical arms, a master arm grip and slave arm tongs. The system was able to perceive the location of the user's hand by measurement of the geometry of the arm mechanics, much like Utah's Sword of Damocles. The UNC system was able to provide force feedback through the arm, to simulate the actual resistance objects in the database would present to changes in their inertia.

Kilpatrick reports on a series of experiments he ran with a set of subjects. The subjects were placed in front of a computer-controlled vector CRT which presented them with an image of the database. Included in this image was a robot arm similar to the master arm. The subject then placed his hand into a grip on the end of the master arm and interacted with the database, using the force feedback in the arm and the image in the vector tube as cues.

This system also had its drawbacks. Most important was the potential harm to the user in case of system failure. Large, powerful metal arms driven by computer-controlled motors may be dangerous or even lethal in the hands of hardware or software error. Also, the force feedback in the master arm may go too far and hurt the user. Although many safety devices and interlocks were built into the system, there is always the possibility that something could go wrong.

Viewpoint via Visual Coupling: Gaze Following

In 1981 Bolt described a system which reacted to the perceived location of the user's gaze. The user was constrained to sit in a chair located in the center of a large room. A TV camera sensitive to infrared light was zoomed into a close-up of the user's eyes. Mounted fairly high up in the room was an infrared light source. The light was unobtrusive to the user, yet the reflections of the light on the user's eye provided sufficient cues to determine the gaze angle to within 1 degree. The combination of the gaze angles of the two eyes yielded the three-dimensional point upon which the user's eyes were focused. As in all the other schemes mentioned so far, the user was restricted in how far he or she could wander in the room. This system also limited the range of gazepoints to within 10 to 30 degrees off of some reference axis. However, this system was superior to the others above in terms of the unobtrusiveness of the measuring device.

User Tracking Self

An alternative solution to the tracking problem is to reverse the location of the responsible hardware from the above schemes. This statement implies that tracking responsibility should move away from the computer and back to the user, which seems to defeat the entire notion of tracking. The approach is not to make the user himself responsible, but to attach some hardware to the user which will make itself responsible for accurate tracking of the user.

There is a significant implication in this statement. In the previous schemes the user was restricted in some critical ways because of the nature in which measurements were being taken of him or her. But if the user is measuring his own position, then there should be no restrictions. Thus, when a user tracks himself, many of the range restrictions on the parameters of interest are relaxed or eliminated.

Decoupling: The Self-Tracker

In 1984 Bishop presented information on a custom VLSI chip he called the Self-Tracker [Bish 84a], [Bish 84b]. The chip consisted of a one-dimensional array of photosensors, control circuitry, and a processor. The chip performed tracking by analyzing successive images falling on its 1-dimensional photosensor array. By mounting several of the chips in a cluster at angles to each other, Bishop was able to show that his system could determine its own movement between successive sample intervals. By maintaining a small sampling interval the Self-Tracker was able to hold numerical problems in check and effectively track its own motion - translation and rotation - in virtually any environment.

The Self-Tracker as presented did not completely solve all the problems associated with a device tracking itself, but it did solve many of them and it was a major conceptual and technical step forward. By mounting a Self-Tracker cluster on a user's head, the front sensors would be looking very nearly where the eyes would be looking. The only communication needed out of the cluster would be successive transformation information.

VI. Interactive Databases

When the head-mounted display paradigm comes of age we will have solved many of the problems mentioned so far throughout this paper. But the freedom and versatility of the head-mounted display will cause a new pressure to arise in the user community: interactive databases. The study of databases is a well-established field, and complex databases are common in sophisticated systems such as flight and space simulators. But although there may be a great deal of interaction between a user and a database in such a system, there has so far been little work on graphics databases that support user-user, user-object, and object-object interaction.

When a user in a head-mounted environment interacts with some piece of data, he or she will naturally expect the rest of the environment to conform to the change. For example, consider a user wearing a head-mounted display which places her on a dirty field, standing next to a marbles game. The user pitches a virtual marble forward into the ring, and watches as the marble strikes other marbles, which in turn strike other marbles, and so on until all the marbles roll to a halt. If one of the marbles happens to fly through the air and hit the windshield of a nearby car, the windshield may shatter and the marble pass through into the car, possibly rolling around a bit before setting down. The bits of windshield glass would then be scattered on the ground, and may affect future shots in the marbles game. This contrived example only indicates the difficulties that a self-interacting database will have to solve. The issues of a shattering windshield and real-time, interacting marbles are beyond the capabilites of almost all graphics database managers today.

It is our opinion that graphics databases are going to soon be modelled with intelligent, communicating objects, very much like objects in the language Smalltalk. We suggest that distributed intelligence is the best tool computer science has right now for coping with the incredible complexity of environments on the order of natural environments.

Happily, these techniques are the object of great study by many people in computer science today, who are looking to them for applications from artificial intelligence to parallel processing. The architectures and techniques for managing large numbers of intelligent, communicating objects will be critical to the success of a head-mounted display environment.

VII. Acknowledgements

Several of the figures in this paper were adapted from similar figures created by Greg Abram for publication in [Abra 84]. We gratefully acknowledge his permission to use them in this paper. The authors extend their thanks to Jeff Hultquist for his many contributions to this project, including Figures 1 and 2, help on wording critical passages, a very thorough critical review, a tolerant ear, and an intolerant blue pencil. Thanks also go to Bobette Eckland, who found many textual errors in the original manuscript and offered thoughtful editorial advice.

X. References

[Abra 84]   "VLSI Architectures for Computer Graphics", G. Abram,
              H. Fuchs, Proceedings of the NATO Advanced Study
              Institue on Microarchitecture of VLSI Computers,
              July 1984

[Appe 67]   "The Notion of Quantitative Invisibility and the Machine
              Rendering of Solids", A. Appel, Proceedings of the ACM
              National Conference, Washington DC, 1967

[Bish 84a]   "The Self-Tracker : A Smart Optical Sensor on Silicon", Gary
              Bishop and Henry Fuchs, 1984 Conference on Advanced
              Research in VLSI, M.I.T.

[Bish 84b]   "Self-Tracker : A Smart Optical Sensor on Silicon",
              Gary Bishop, Ph.D. thesis, UNC-CH, 1984

[Bolt 81]   "Gaze-Orchestrated Dynamic Windows", Richard A. Bolt,
              Siggraph Volume 15 Number 3, August 1981

[Carp 84]   "The A-buffer, an Antialiased Hidden Surface Method",
              Loren Carpenter, Siggraph Volume 18 Number 3, July 1984

[Clar 80]   "Distributed Processing in a High-Performance Smart
              Image Memory", J. Clark, M. Hannah, VLSI Design,
              Volume 1 Number 3, 4th Quarter, 1980

[Clark 82]   "The Geometry Engine: A VLSI Geometry System for Graphics",
              James Clark, Siggraph Volume 16 Number 3, July 1982

[Cohe 80]   Presentation at Siggraph 80, D. Cohen, S. Demetrescu

[Cook 84]   "Distributed Ray Tracing" R. Cook, T. Porter, L. Carpenter,
              Siggraph Volume 18 Number 3, July 1984

[Deme 85]   "High Speed Image Rasterization Using Scan Line Access
              Memories", Stefan Demetrescu,
              1985 Chapel Hill Conference on VLSI Proceedings,
              Computer Science Press

[Dipp 84]   "An Adaptive Subdivision Algorithm and Parallel Architecture
             for Realistic Image Synthesis", Mark Dippe and John
             Swenson, Siggraph Volume 18 Number 3, July 1984

[Fium 83]   "A Parallel Scan Conversion Algorithm with Anti-Aliasing,
             for a General-Purpose Ultracomputer", E. Fiume,
             A. Fournier, L. Rudolph, Siggraph 83, Volume 17, Number 3
             July 1983

[Fuch 77]   "Distributing A Visible Surface Algorithm Over Multiple
             Processors", H. Fuchs, Proc. 1977 Annual ACM Annual
             Conference, October 1977

[Fuch 79]   "An Expandable Multiprocessor Architecture for Video
             Graphics", H. Fuchs, B. Johnson, Proc. of 6th Annual
             ACM-IEEE Symposium on Computer Architectures,
             April 1979

[Fuch 81]   "PIXEL-PLANES: A VLSI-Oriented Design for a Raster Graphics
             Engine", H. Fuchs, J. Poulton, VLSI Design, Volume 2,
             Number 3, 3rd Quarter, 1981

[Fuch 85]   "Fast Spheres, Shadows, Textures, Transparencies, and
             Image Enhancements in Pixel Planes", H. Fuchs,
             J. Goldfeather, J. Hultquist, S. Spach, J. Austin, J. Eyles,
             J. Poulton, to appear in Siggraph Volume 19, Just 1985

[Fuss 82]   "A VLSI-Oriented Architecture For Real-Time Raster Display
             of Shaded Polygons", D. Fussell, Graphics Interface '83,
             May 1982

[Gupt 81]   "A VLSI Architecture for Updating Raster Scan Displays",
             S. Gupta, R. Sproull, I. Sutherland, Siggraph 81,
             Volume 15, Number 3, August 1981

[Kaji 75]   "A Random-Access Video Frame Buffer", J. Kajiya, I. Sutherland,
             E. Cheadle, Proc. IEEE Conference on Computer Graphics,
             Pattern Recognition and Data Structure, May 1975

[Kede 84]   "Computer Structures for Curve-Solid Classification in
             Geometric Modelling", Gershon Kedem and John Ellis,
             Rochester Institute of Technology TR 137, May 1984

[Kilp 76]   "The Use of A Kinesthetic Supplement in An Interactive
             Graphics System", Paul Jerome Kilpatrick,
             Ph.D. thesis, UNC-CH, 1976

[Newe 72]   "A New Approach to the Shaded Picture Problem",
            M. Newell, R. Newell, T. Sancha,
            Proc. ACM National Conference, 1972

[Park 80]   "Simulation and Expected Performance Analysis of Multiple
            Processor Z-Buffer Systems", F. Parke, Siggraph 80,
            Volume 14 Number 3, July 1980

[Poul 85]   "PIXEL-PLANES: Building A VLSI-Based Raster Graphics
            System", J. Poulton, H. Fuchs, J. Austin, J. Eyles,
            J. Heinecke, C. Hsieh, J. Goldfeather, J. Hultquist,
            S. Spach, to appear in 1985 Chapel Hill Conference
            on VLSI Proceedings, Computer Science Press

[Robe 63]   "Machine Perception of Three-Dimensional Solids",
            L. Roberts, MIT Lincoln Lab TR 315, May 1963

[Schu 69]   "Study for Applying Computer Generated Images to Simulation",
            R. Schumacker, B. Brand, M. Gilliland, W. Sharp,
            AFHRL-TR-69-14, Air Force Human Resources Lab,
            Wright-Patterson AFB, OH September 1969

[Shif 84]   "An Electrophoretic Image Display With Internal NMOS Address
            Logic and Display Drivers", R.R. Shiffman and R.H. Parker
            Proceedings of the Society forInformation Display, 25(2), 105-152

[Suth 65]   "The Ultimate Display", I. Sutherland, Proceedings of
            1965 IFIP Conference

[Suth 68]   "A Head-mounted Three Dimensional Display", I. Sutherland,
            FJCC 1968, Washington DC, 1968

[Suth 74]   "A Characterization of Ten Hidden-Surface Algorithms",
            Ivan Sutherland, Robert Sproull, Robert Schumaker,
            Computing Surveys, Volume 6 Number 1, March 1974

[Vick 70]   "Head Mounted Display", Donald L. Vickers. utechnic magazine,
            Volume 10, Number 4, May 1970

[Vuil 84]   "Novel Electromechanical Microshutter Display Device",
            R. Vuillemier, A. Perret, F. Porret, P. Weiss, Proceedings
            of the 1984 Eurodisplay Conference, Society for Information
            Display, July 1984, Paris.

[Watk 70]   "A Real Time Visible Surface Algorithm", G. Watkins,
            Ph.D. dissertation, TR 70-101, University of Utah, June 1970

658

[Weil 77]   "Hidden Surface Removal Using Polygon Area Sorting",
            K. Weiler, P. Atherton, Siggraph 77, Volume 11 Number 2
            Summer 1977

[Wein 81]   "Parallel Processing Image Synthesis and Anti-Aliasing",
            Richard Weinberg, Siggraph Volume 15 Number 3,
            August 1981

[Whit 80]   "An Improved Illumination Model for Shaded Display",
            T. Whitted, CACM Volume 23 Number 6, June 1980

Systolic Array Architectures for High Performance CAD/CAM Workstations

Peter M. Dew
Department of Computer Studies

John Dodsworth
Geometric Modelling Project
Department of Mechanical Engineering

David T. Morris
Department of Computer Studies and
Department of Mechanical Engineering

The University
Leeds LS2 9JT
England

Abstract

The purpose of this paper is to describe progress in the theory and implementation of systolic arrays, and to explore its possible application to the design of highly parallel architectures for future CAD/CAM workstations. Such workstations will not only need to display objects but also have the capability to manipulate and analyse solids in reasonable time. In the paper we concentrate on the use of constructive solid geometry (CSG) to represent solids as this representation offers conciseness, completeness, boundedness and validity. CSG algorithms are computationally intensive and therefore a good candidate for mapping onto highly parallel VLSI structures.

After a brief description of the architectural requirements of CAD/CAM workstations, we outline the basic properties of a systolic array architecture and its implementation with particular reference to the CMU systolic array computer, INMOS transputer and the NCR GAPP (geometric arithmetic parallel processor) chip. In the second half of the paper we concentrate mainly on two CSG algorithms, ray casting and octree spatial subdivision, and discuss their potential for parallelism. We identify common features between CSG algorithms and show that systolic array architectures are effective in solving these problems.

1. Introduction

Computer aided design and manufacture (CAD/CAM) systems are designed to improve the productivity of engineers allowing him to evaluate design tradeoffs at an early stage of the design process. Such

NATO ASI Series, Vol. F17
Fundamental Algorithms for Computer Graphics
Edited by R. A. Earnshaw
© Springer-Verlag Berlin Heidelberg 1985

systems provide tools to:

(1) test ideas without the need to build physical prototypes (simulation),

(2) compose several ideas (synthesis), and

(3) understand the effect of design decisions (analysis).

In more advanced systems we need to add manufacture, inspection and maintenance to this list, [1]. Such systems will be needed if the goal of factory automation is to be achieved.

Todays CAD/CAM workstations are not powerful enough to provide the engineer with the capability to evaluate fully all the possibilities open to them. Current research is therefore directed towards: (1) provision of more intelligent user interfaces to increase productivity by ensuring that what is intended actually happens, (2) design and analysis of algorithms for the important computations and (3) developing techniques and computer architectures to exploit parallelism. Although more intelligent user interfaces will put much greater emphasis on textual input, graphics will still play an important role in design verification. The visualisation of an object is also useful in both marketing and educating people about the product. In this paper we will be describing research that is directed towards improving performance by the provision of highly parallel computer architectures.

An overview of a software architecture for a CAD/CAM workstation is shown in figure 1-1. The application modules (only a few of which are shown) interface with the user and more importantly with the engineering (product) database. The database includes information on both the geometry and material of the object. A major unresolved issue is the choice of representation of the object to suit the requirements of the application modules. The need to automate the design and manufacturing process has meant that constructive solid geometry (CSG) representation is often used because it provides a complete, bounded and concise description of a object. The appropriate algorithms to operate on a CSG representation is application dependent. A popular choice for a number of applications is *boundary evaluation* where the CGS representation is transformed into a boundary representation. For example this used in the NONAME system developed at Leeds University, [2]. Since CSG algorithms are computationally expensive and have a direct bearing on the user response time it natural to consider the design of parallel architectures to improve the performance of these algorithms. At the same time we would like to speed up the linear algebra operations involved in the finite element analysis of CSG objects.

The demand for more intelligent and comprehensive software coupled with the need for real and "reasonable" time response makes the design of a parallel computer architecture to support CAD/CAM software a particularly rich area for architectural research. It is possible to identify three principle areas of research:

(1) imaging architectures to provide the increased bandwidth needed for higher resolution displays with non-interlaced 50-60 frames per second refresh,

(2) highly parallel architectures for computationally intensive algorithms arising from the need to manipulate and analyse 3D objects, and

(3) architectures to efficiently support large databases, rule-based and logic languages, and other IKBS software tools.

Currently hardware developments have concentrated on *imaging* from hierarchical display lists of vectors or polygons (see below the contributions by H. Fuchs and J. Clarke in these proceedings), whereas the real cost of producing graphical displays of solid models is in *generating* the display list. Thus in this paper we focus on providing a highly parallel architecture for CSG-based computations but one which is also sufficiently general that it can be used for other applications like basic

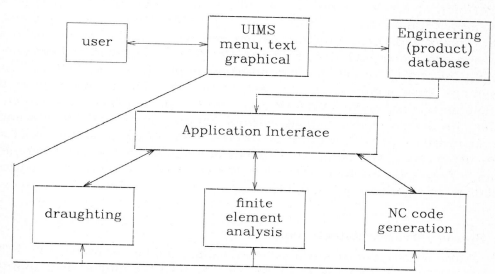

Figure 1-1 Software Architecture for a CAD/CAM System

linear algebra (e.g. finite element analysis). We shall not concern ourselves with the design of architectures to support IKBS tools as the applications of these techniques is not yet sufficiently mature.

In recent years there has been a growth of interest in the use of highly parallel architectures to solve many compute bound problems in numerical computation, signal and image processing and computer graphics (see the January 1982 Special Issue of IEEE Computer on highly parallel structures). There are today a number of commercial products available that incorporate highly parallel, special-purpose structures. For example, in computer graphics there are number of products available for displaying a solid represented by polygon mesh: (1) Solidview from Lexidata, (2) the Weitek tiling and solid modeling engines, and (3) the IRIS workstation with its linear array of geometry engines. Of the three the geometry engine is of most interest to us in this paper because it is an example of a sophisticated floating point processor being tailored to a particular application. Closely related are the products available for image processing and computer vision (e.g. [3]).

There are a large number of ways of mapping algorithms onto highly parallel structures. In this paper we focus on one particular design methodology, namely the *systolic array methodology* and investigate its application to algorithms that operate on a constructive solid geometry (CSG) representation of a 3D solid. There are already a large number of systolic array algorithms for regular compute-bound algorithms and experimental machines are being built at a number of University and Research Establishments. In Section 2 we outline the ideas behind systolic arrays and their implementation and in particular we describe a systolic array computer which has recently been designed at Carnegie-Mellon University for solving computer vision problems. We believe that a systolic array computer is also well suited for many of computational problems arising in the CAD/CAM area. In Section 3 of the paper we consider the design of systolic algorithms for displaying CSG objects and compare them with other attempts at designing hardware structures for CSG algorithms, including the Kedem and Ellis Ray casting machine. Finally a systolic array architecture is described for the octree spatial subdivision algorithm given in [4].

2. Systolic Array Architectures

Systolic arrays were invented at Carnegie-Mellon University by H.T. Kung and C.E. Leiserson in the late 70's, [5], as a technique for mapping regular, compute-bound algorithms onto VLSI structures. The general concept of systolic arrays is shown in Figure 2-1, where "pe" denotes a processing element. The idea is to improve performance by using an array of processor elements which make multiple use of each input data item. For compute-bound problems (e.g matrix computations) this removes the I/O bottleneck between processor and memory. For example, suppose that the memory can read/write a data item every 100ns then one processor can perform a maximum of 5 mops (million operations per second) whereas an array of n processors with the same I/O bandwidth can perform a maximum of $5n$ mops. The price we pay for increased throughput is an increase in *latency* (the number of cycles between the input of a data item and receiving the results from processor array). There are a large number of one and two dimensional systolic arrays for a wide variety of computations. Two dimension arrays are effective when the bandwidth of the processing elements is less than the I/O bandwidth.

The main applications of systolic arrays have been in the signal and image processing area and recently a systolic array computer, [6], has been designed at Carnegie-Mellon University as an experimental machine for vision processing. On the commercial side International Robomation/Intelligence Ltd market a systolic co-processor for their MC 68000 based workstation and NCR have produced the GAPP chip which is a 6x12 systolic array of 1 bit processors.

The efficient mapping of algorithms onto architectures is an important element of VLSI research and there have been several studies to apply formal transformations from a high-level representation to a low-level hardware description. The recent paper by Li and Wah, [7], gives a summary of the relevant papers for systolic array design. The authors present a *systematic methodology* for the design of optimal pure planar systolic arrays for algorithms that are representable as linear recurrence processes (such as convolution and matrix multiplication). In the following we outline a systolic array methodology proposed by Leiserson and Saxe, [8], because this theory is most closely connected

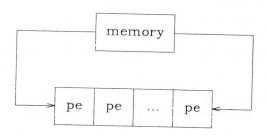

Figure 2-1 Concept of a Systolic Processor Array

with the systolic array work at Carnegie-Mellon University.

2.1. Synchronous Systems

An important contribution to the formalism and understanding of the principles of systolic array design has been made by Leiserson and Saxe, [8]. They outline a systolic array methodology that allows the designer to specify a processor network in its most convenient and natural form. This can include global broadcasting and the use of a ripple carry between processors. The system is then transformed into a systolic system by the addition of registers to delay data flowing between neighbouring processors. Their approach is based on graph-theoretic arguments. The principal advantages of a systolic system are that:

(1) it is a simple and regular design

(2) it exploits parallelism by pipelining, and

(3) the processing elements communicate only with their neighbours in a synchronous fashion.

These advantages mean that systolic systems are particularly well suited for VLSI implementation.

To model a synchronous system Leiserson and Saxe partition it into *function elements* (combination logic) and *registers* (clocked memory). Such a system S can be modelled as a finite edge-weighted directed graph which is referred as a *communication graph*. The nodes denote the function elements and the weights denote the number of registers between two nodes. The data is clocked synchronously through the registers. It is now possible to formalise the meaning of synchronous and systolic systems.

Definition
A system is said to be *synchronous* if every cycle in its communication graph has positive weights and *systolic* if each weight is strictly greater than zero. ▪

An example of a synchronous system for the 1D convolution computation

$$y_i = w_0 x_i + w_1 x_{i+1} + w_2 x_{i+2} + w_3 x_{i+3}$$

is given in Figure 2-2, where the ip-nodes compute the *inner product step* (linear recurrence relation)

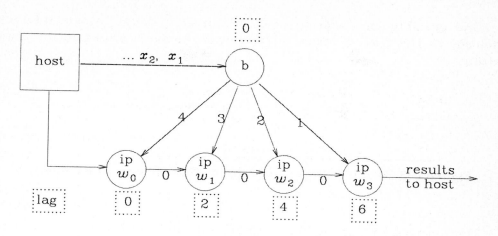

Figure 2-2 Synchronous System for 1D Convolution

$$s_{out} = s_{in} + x_{in} * w$$

and the constant w is stored within the node during the initialisation phase. Each data item in the input stream is **broadcast** (via the "b node" - see Figure 2-2) to each of the ip-nodes and associated with each edge is a weight denoting the number of registers the input data is clocked through before it arrives at the ip-node. This ensures that x_1 arrives at the first node at the same time as x_4 arrives at the last node. The reader should also note that a **ripple carry** chain is used to accumulate the results (i.e. the edges of the path connecting the ip-nodes have zero weights).

Although it is easy to verify that the synchronous system shown above computes the required 1D convolution, the use of a ripple carry and the need to broadcast data makes the circuit inefficient and expensive to build. These problems can be removed by transforming the synchronous into a systolic system using the Leiserson and Saxe **retiming lemma**. Briefly each node in the graph is assigned an integer (called a lag) and the edge-weights are reassigned according to the formula:

$$W + lag(v) - lag(u)$$

where W is the weight on the edge from node u to node v. To avoid negative weights the data can be **k—slowed** by arranging that a new data item is "pumped in" every kth beat. The effect of k-slowing a synchronous system is to multiply all the edge weights by k.

One possible lag function is shown in Figure 2-2, by the number enclosed in the dotted boxes. Applying the above retiming formula we obtain:

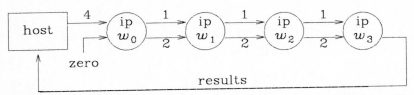

Figure 2-3 Retimed System with Input Data Passed Systolically

The new system can be shown to be equivalent in the sense that the behaviour to the host is the same, except the latency has increased. Notice that the broadcast node (i.e. b node) has been removed and the input data is passed *systolically* between cells. The above systolic system is not unique, other systems can be derived by a different choice of the lag function. For example, a systolic system with input data and results flowing in opposite directions can be derived by first twice-slowing the system. Li and Wah, [7], show that the systolic system shown in Figure 2-3 is optimal in the sense that both T and $\#PE * T^2$ are minimised, where T is the total computational time and $\#PE$ denotes the number of processors.

A more formal and general justification of the Leiserson and Saxe retiming lemma has been given by Brookes, [9], using fixed-point theory. Formal semantic theory has also been applied by Chen and Mead [10].

2.1.1. Two Level Pipelines and Fault Tolerance

The ideas of Leiserson and Saxe have recently been extended in an interesting paper by Kung and Lam, [11]. The paper deals with two important issues:

(i) the need to reconfigure an array when processors are found to be faulty, and

(ii) the need to handle two-level pipelining (see below) when the processor itself supports pipelined floating point chips.

The main result in the paper is the *cut theorem*. A cut is defined to be a set of edges that "partitions" the nodes into two disjoint sets, the *source set* and the *destination set*, with the property that these edges are the only ones crossing the (cut) boundary and are all directed from the source to the destination set.

Cut Theorem

For any design, adding the same delay to all the edges in a cut and to those pointing from the host to the destination set of the cut will result in an equivalent design. ∎

The cut theorem can always be applied when there are no cycles in the graph. For example it can be applied directly to the 1D convolution example considered above. A fragment of the systolic system is shown in Figure 2-4, assuming zero delays for the arithmetic units. To allow for pipelining in the arithmetic units we need to make two cuts, as shown by the dotted lines in Figure 2-4. If we assume that both the adder and multiplier have p pipeline stages then we need to add $p-2$ units at the vertical cut p units at the horizontal cut. The incoming data must be p-*slowed* from the original design. The final circuit is shown in Figure 2-5, for the case when $p=4$, [12].

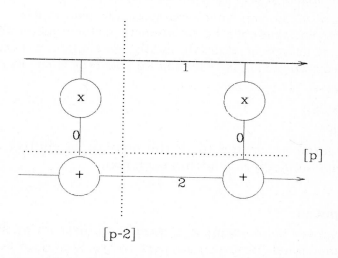

Figure 2-4 Application of the Cut Theorem

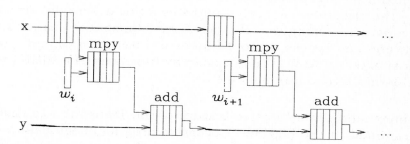

Figure 2-5 Two-Level Pipelining for 1D Convolution (taken from [12])

2.1.2. Example of Matrix Multiplication

Systolic arrays have been developed for a wide variety of compute-bound algorithms in numerical linear. The following example taken from Kung, [12], illustrates one possible systolic design for matrix multiplication. It could, for example, be used for computing the product of homogeneous transformation matrices arising in computer graphics and robotics.

The original systolic algorithm is shown in figure 2-6 for n = 8. The reader should note that the results are accumulated in the cell and then transferred along the output bus systolically. We refer to this as a *stationary systolic design*. The cell layout with two level pipelining is shown in Figure 2-7. These diagrams have been taken from Kung(1984), [12], The reader is referred to the paper for further details.

2.2. Implementation of a Programmable Systolic Cell

The design of a high performance, programmable systolic cell involves the classic tradeoffs between cost, performance and generality, inherent in the design of algorithmically specialised processor arrays, [13]. To contrast the designs tradeoffs we consider three examples

(1) Transputer

(2) CMU Warp Cell

(3) GAPP chip

These are ordered according to to the amount of control and address generation capability there is within each cell.

2.2.1. Transputer

The Transputer is an example of a reduced instruction set computer (RISC) with additional hardware support to transfer data between Transputers along serial links. The Transputer (IMS T242) is a 32 bit system with a maximum processing power of 10 mips (million instructions per second). The user manual, [14], illustrates a linear array of Transputers used as a personal computer add-on. Each Transputer has its own control unit and can access up to 4K bytes of internal RAM and a massive 4G bytes of external RAM. The linear array functions as a MIMD (multiple instruction-multiple data) machine.

An important and attractive feature of the Transputer is that it can be programmed in the high level programming language called OCCAM, [15], which is an implementation of Hoare's Communicating Sequential Processes (CSP) model of computation. The language allows the programmer to explicitly express communication between processes by

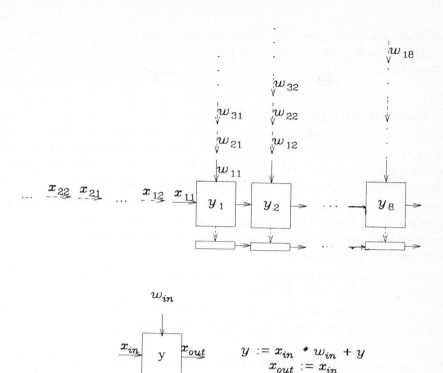

Figure 2-6 A Systolic Algorithm for Matrix-Matrix Multiplication

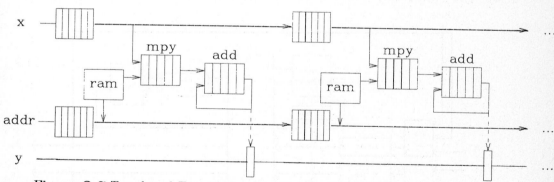

Figure 2-7 Two-level Pipelining for Matrix-Matrix Multiplication

modelling the "handshake method" used in hardware. Another important feature is that the programmer can use an arbitrary number of processes without the programmer needing to know how many physical processors are available. However for high performance applications the lack of hardware support for floating point arithmetic and serial communication links makes it uncompetitive with the CMU Warp processor described below.

2.2.2. The CMU Warp Processing Cell

The CMU Warp cell is the most advanced processor tailored specifically for systolic computation. It will be incorporated in the CMU systolic array computer, [6]. shown in figure 2-10. From an application view point the most significant features of the warp cell are:

(i) the addresses to the data memory within each warp cell are passed systolically (along with 2 bits of systolic control) - the cell has only a limited capability to generate data-dependent addresses for its data and control memories,

(ii) the cell supports two processing elements: the Weitek 32-bit floating point multiplier and alu chips.

(iii) the control unit is based on a AMD 2910A micro sequencer supporting branching, one-level looping and nested subroutine calls.

The data path for the Warp cell is shown in Figure 2-8. All data paths are 16 bits wide but functionally it can be considered as a 32-bit processor with a (major) cycle time of 200ns and each cell is capable of 10 MFLOPS (million floating point operations per second). The data path can divided into two units, the *functional unit* and the *systolic timing unit*. The functional part includes a full crossbar, processing elements

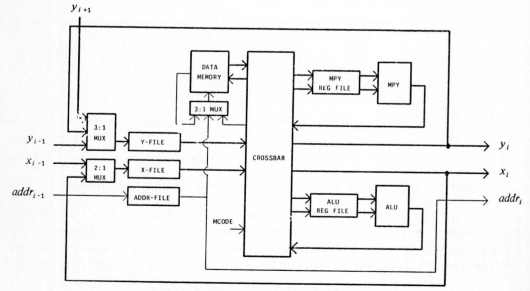

Figure 2-8 The CMU Warp Cell

and data memory, and the systolic timing unit consists of the three input files (x-file, y-file and addr-file). The input files can be used as FIFOs (queues) to generate the delays that arise when a synchronous system is retimed to a systolic system. Alternately they may be used as additional registers. The input multiplexers allow two-way systolic flow (e.g. for the QR algorithm, [12]).) They also allow the cell to be used in local mode (see below).

The major saving in hardware complexity is made, at the expense of generality, by passing the cell's memory addresses systolically and providing only a limited support for data dependent computations that require to compute dynamically the cell's memory and control addresses. An interface unit (see Figure 2-10) is responsible for the generation of address patterns and for handling data-type conversions (e.g. integer-to-real). The Warp processor is very effective for a number of compute-bound problems including FFTs (a 10-cell array can process 1024-point complex FFT at a rate of one every 600 μs) and work is underway at CMU to build a boundary cell which can compute special functions like divisions and square-roots at the same pipeline rate as an inner product step.

Two final points are worth mentioning. Firstly AMD have announced a new product range based around a 32-bit floating point alu and multiplier with a cycle time of 100 ns and no pipeline stages (over five-fold improvement on the Weitek chips). The use of this chip set would significantly improve the performance while only doubling the bandwidth between the array of systolic cells and the host. It would also ease the programming difficulties since there would be fewer pipeline stages. The second point is that CMU have a related project to design a Link and Interconnection Chip (LINC), [16], with the aim of significantly reducing the chip count of the Warp cell. The cell has a number of applications including an implementation of the 3D geometry system used in the IRIS workstation.

2.2.3. The GAPP Chip

Finally we contrast the above systolic cells with the NCR GAPP (Geometric Arithmetic Parallel Processor). The philosophy behind this chip is to use a cell that is sufficiently simple cell it is possible to place a large number onto one chip. In the present version of the chip there are 72 1-bit cells arranged in a 6x12 array. Each cell has 128 bit of RAM. To keep the cell simple the memory addresses and the control instructions are broadcast globally to all cells. This decision means that the chip should be more accurately classified as a SIMD machine (single instruction multiple data) but it differs from other machines like the ICL DAP in two important ways:

(1) there is no provision to enlarge the cell's memory by using off chip memory,

(2) an extra bus has been included so that I/O can be overlapped with computation in a similar way to the Warp cell.

The NCR GAPP chip is suitable for problems where it is possible to exploit spatial parallelism without the need to use a large amount of local memory (e.g. convolution).

2.3. System Organisation

The organisation of a suitable system to support a systolic processor has received very little attention at the present time. This is mainly due to the fact that the design of a suitable system is very application dependent. The simplest approach (used by IRA [3]) is to view the systolic processor as another co-processor attached to the system bus. However, this is generally not satisfactory because the system bus becomes a bottleneck. The IRIS workstation is, in this respect, similar except that the output of the geometry engine array is attached directly to the display hardware. In contrast the GAPP chip user manual illustrates a customised system to perform 2D convolution for real time vision processing applications.

The universal host organisation , shown in Figure 2-9, is an alternative solution see Kung, [17]. This architecture consists of a high bandwidth bus, a large (interleaved) mass memory and a number of microprogrammable interface processors (ip). Attached to the interface processors are the host, the algorithmically specialised (systolic) processors (asp), the display device(s) and mass storage devices. The host processor has overall control of the computation and provides a general purpose computing environment. A number of commercial systems are available (or will soon be) including an *Aptec 2400* designed to support the floating point system (FPS) array processor. The Aptec has a maximum bus capacity of 24 Mbytes per second and each interface processor is Unibus compatible. This system has proved to be adequate for a systolic implementation of a robot navigation problem, [18], using a 10-cell warp processing array. A variation on the universal host model is used in the systolic array computer shown in Figure 2-10. This is based on the 68020 processor and the VME bus (maximum throughput of 40 Mbytes/s).

The universal host is an example of a *loosely coupled multiprocessor* [19]. Many of the techniques used in the design of both loosely and

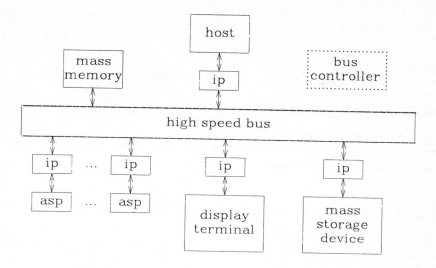

asp : algorithmically specialised processor
ip : interface processor

Figure 2-9 Universal Host Organisation and Supporting Modules

tightly coupled multiprocessors are relevant to the design of a system to support an array of high performance systolic processors. In the longer term, the elegant *paracomputer* model which allows any processor to access any memory cell in one cycle may be attractive. An experimental machine (Ultracomputer) based on this model is being built at NYU, [20].

2.4. Designing Algorithms for a Systolic Array Computer

The following are some brief notes on the design of algorithms for a systolic array computer. The remarks arise from one of the authors experience in mapping a complete application problem, the passive navigation of robot, 18], onto a systolic array computer of the type being built at Carnegie-Mellon University. An order of magnitude speedup is predicted using an Aptec 2400 as the universal host. For sake of definiteness we assume that the systolic processing cells have the same functionality of the CMU Warp processing (Figure 2-8) and can operate in *systolic* and *local* mode.

2.4.1. Systolic Mode

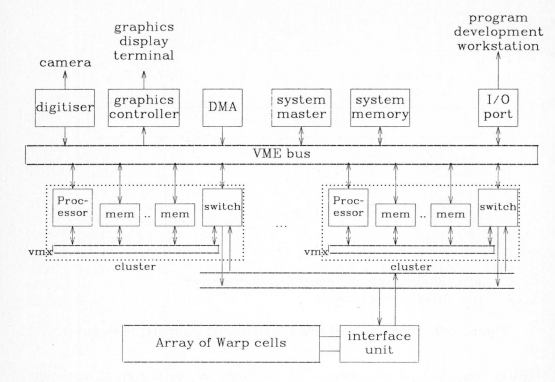

Figure 2-10 The CMU Systolic Array Computer (taken from [6])

This mode is appropriate when we wish to speed-up tight, data-independent loops, such as convolution or full matrix computation. In practise these often arise within a larger data dependent computation and our experience to date suggests that the controlling (master) processor must perform the following type of algorithm:

control algorithm

1. initialise data tables and setup the systolic processor for the required systolic computation

repeat

2. preload "target" data into each systolic cell

3. load "source" data and perform the systolic computation

4. save results from the systolic processor in a buffer

5. assemble new data tables (handle the data dependency)

until finished

Notes

(i) The data tables normally contain the start and end addresses of data in the main memory. These addresses are updated at the end of each iteration using the results from the systolic processors.

(ii) the systolic processor is essentially being used as a hardware sub-routine for the *data independent* part of the computation.

An algorithm of this type was used successfully for a binary search correlator computation. The purpose of this computation is to match a set of features distributed in a target image, with the corresponding features in the source image. The features were selected on the basis of having a high contrast and therefore likely to be easy to match, but meant that they were not uniformly spaced around the target image. The binary search correlator algorithm is a multi-resolution template matching procedure using images of increasing resolution. The control algorithm selects the required portions of the target and source images for all the features and passes them in a continuous stream through the systolic processor. The systolic processor is used to compute a normalised correlation function, [21]. The actual area of the image searched at each resolution depends on the results of the search at the next lower resolution giving rise to a data dependency. A similar control algorithm will be discussed in section 3-4 for the Octree spatial subdivision algorithm.

There are two types of systolic algorithms:

(1) *Stationary Systolic Algorithm* : the data and addresses move systolically but the results are assembled within each cell and output along one of the buses systolically (see the systolic matrix multiplication algorithm - Figure 2-6). In this mode one of the buses is normally devoted to input data and the other to output. The buses act in a similar way to a global bus except that they can transmit more than one piece of data at any one time with a corresponding increase in the latency. This style of systolic algorithm is easy to implement and we shall use it in the following sections.

(2) *Moving Systolic Algorithm* : the other style of systolic algorithm, which is generally more difficult to design, is to use each cell to compute a partial result. The required answer is then available from the last cell. The convolution example was implemented in this way. The main advantage of this mode is that the boundary cell can often be used to perform the more time consuming special mathematical functions such as division and square-roots. A number of the

systolic algorithms for matrix factorisation (e.g. LU, QR, singular-value decomposition) are of this type; the inner systolic cells compute the basic inner-product step computation and the boundary cell is used to perform the necessary divisions and square-roots. Used in this way we can afford to add extra hardware in the boundary cell to perform these computations at the same rate as the inner product step.

2.4.2. Local Mode

It is often difficult, in the absence of a suitable compiler, to devise effective systolic algorithms and for this reason the CMU Warp Cell has been designed to implement computations in a *stand-alone mode* or *local mode*. For example, many of the SIMD algorithms for image processing can be implemented in this manner. We first load the image data into the individual cell memories so that each cell operates on a particular segment of the image. The computation is performed in a "standard" serial manner and at the end all results are unloaded. The CMU Warp cells can be used very effectively in this manner given sufficient bandwidth to input and output results at its full rate of 40 Mbytes per second. An example of this style of programming is the Warp implementation of Moravec's interest operator [18].

Given the ability to program each cell in the array separately we can potentially use each cell to perform a different computation (MIMD) in a similar manner to a linear array of geometry engines. This could, for example, be useful for speeding up shading computation. The one major restriction on using a warp-like processor is that the addresses are passed systolically making it difficult to program individual cells separately. This is because it is hard to generate control and data memory addresses within the cell.

3. CSG Algorithms and their Potential for Parallelism

Section 1 of this paper identified the need to manipulate, analyse and display 3D objects using a CSG representation. Our purpose here is to demonstrate that a systolic array architecture is very effective for this class of problems. The design of parallel algorithms/architectures for CSG algorithms is still in its infancy and to keep the problem manageable we shall concentrate mainly on the problem of displaying a CSG description of a 3D solid.

We have investigated three CSG algorithms:

(1) boundary evaluation as used in NONAME and PADL-2, [22],

(2) ray casting, [23], and

(3) Woodwark-IBM Spatial Subdivision Algorithm used in Winsom, [24, 4].

Space does not allow us to describe these algorithms in detail and we refer the reader to the references mentioned above. The algorithms have been ordered as a hierarchy both in the complexity of the geometrical algorithms performed in the primitive classification, and the amount of information that we need to process within the CSG tree (see below). We decided early in our investigation that a complex algorithm like boundary evaluation would not be suitable for an initial investigation into parallel implementations of CSG algorithms. It involves explicitly calculating the boundary of the solid by analytic solid geometry techniques. In addition there is a need to process carefully the "on" set making the code very large and complex. The geometric modelling group at Leeds University is, in any case, investigating new algorithms to replace it. In the longer term we need to study and invent representations that are easy to implement in parallel and provide the necessary information to the application modules.

The basic theoretical ideas behind the CSG representations are well described in two important papers by A.A.G. Requicha, [25], and R.B. Tilove, [26]. A useful summary, particularly related to ray casting, can be found in a recent report on the computer structures for curve-solid classification in geometric modelling by G. Kedem and J.L. Ellis, [23]. This report is significant because it represents the first serious attempt to design a VLSI structure for a CSG algorithm.

3.1. Curve-Solid Classification

The essential idea behind the CSG algorithms is that solids can be represented *constructively* as (regularised) combinations of simple regular sets which serve as the basic building blocks. The representation can be defined recursively:

<csg-solid> :: <solid-primitive> | <solid-operator> <csg-solid> <csg-solid>

<solid-operator> ::= union | intersect | difference

where the set operators are regularised, [26].

The basic idea behind most of the algorithms that operate on a CSG representation is that of *set membership classification* (SMC). This takes as input a "candidate" set which is to be classified and a "reference" set which is to be classified against. It can be defined by a membership function which returns three sets: the subsets of the candidate set which are *in*, *out* and *on* the boundary of the reference set. It is a generalisation of clipping. Specific instances of SMC are PMC (point membership classification) which finds whether a point is *in*, *out* or *on* of a solid; and curve-solid classification which determines the *in*, *on* or *out* segments of a curve with respect to a solid. A special case of this is ray casting where the curves are simply straight lines.

In order to evaluate the edges of a solid defined in a CSG representation we need to produce a set of candidate edges that can be classified against the solid to produce the real edges of the solid. A sufficient set can be generated by intersecting every (infinite) surface in the solid with every other surface (this can be reduced to intersecting the primitive-solid faces). The curves are then classified using the divide-and-conquer algorithm:

function ClassifyCurveSolid (curve, solid)
return [in, on, out : set]

begin
case solid **of**

operator :
left := ClassifyCurveSolid (curve, left-subtree)
right:= ClassifyCurveSolid (curve, right-subtree)
return combine (left, right)

primitive :
return ClassifyCurvewrtPrimitive(curve, primitive)

end
end

Two fundamental requirements are to combine the segments which are *in*, *on* and *out*, and to be able to segment a curve with respect to a primitive solid (possibly a single halfspace). The first requires list merging utilities depending on the particular operators used. The second requires special code for each geometric case. If the domain consists of planes and quadric surfaces there are some difficulties in determining analytically if, for instance, the intersection of a cone and a sphere lies totally on a cylinder. For higher order domains the problems become even harder.

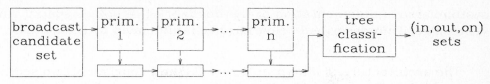

Figure 3-1 Stationary Systolic Algorithm for CSG classification

An outline of a *stationary systolic algorithm* for the basic CSG computation is shown in Figure 3-1. The majority of the computation time is used in classifying a member of the candidate set against a primitive, so we use a warp-like cell (possibly enhanced to support high performance units for special functions arising in computational geometry) for this part of the computation. In Figure 3-1 we have allocated one primitive per cell. The combine operations within the CSG tree are performed in a boundary cell. Thus instead of descending the tree to a primitive level and then ascending and combining the subtree results, all the combinations at a particular "level" in the tree can be performed independently and therefore concurrently. This is the essence of the ray casting machine described below.

3.2. Kedem–Ellis Ray Casting Machine

Ray casting is an extremely flexible technique for use with a CSG representation. It is capable of producing highly realistic shaded images with perspective, reflections and shadows. In addition it can be used for computing other properties of a CSG objects such as its volume. The CSG ray casting algorithm is well described in the report by Roth [27]. Briefly, to generate a shaded picture of a CSG object it is necessary to determine for every pixel on the screen which surface of the object lies nearest to the screen. A ray is fired from each pixel towards the object and the points where the ray enters and leaves the object are recorded in a sorted list. The surface nearest to the screen at a given pixel is the first point on the list of intersections.

The CSG algorithm is divided into two parts. The first part is the intersection of the ray with every primitive, *ray-primitive classification*; this returns two parameters where the ray enters and leaves the primitive defining the *in-segment*. The intersections for each primitive are combined together by the *classification-combine algorithm* using the rules of CSG set operators at the nodes of the CSG tree to merge two sorted lists of intersections. A VLSI architecture to support a simplified CSG ray casting algorithm has been proposed by Kedem and Ellis [23]. This machine has several interesting features and the systolic array implementation of the Woodwark-IBM octree spatial subdivision algorithm described below has been influenced by their ideas.

The architecture is shown in Figure 3-2 and consists of two sections: a set of *primitive classification (PC) processors* which compute the intersection of the primitives with the rays (lines), and a number of *classification combine (CC) processors* to implement the internal CSG tree operations. To improve the performance and reduce the hardware complexity Kedem and Ellis made three important simplifications:

(i) the rays are restricted to parallel straight lines;

(ii) the primitives are restricted to linear and quadratic halfspaces;

(iii) the *on* classification is not considered.

The first restriction allows us to exploit *spatial parallelism*, the second significantly simplifies the design of the primitive classifier processor and third reduces the complexity of the classification combine processors.

The PC processors classify a primitive half space (stored in local memory) against a regular lattice of parallel lines defined by

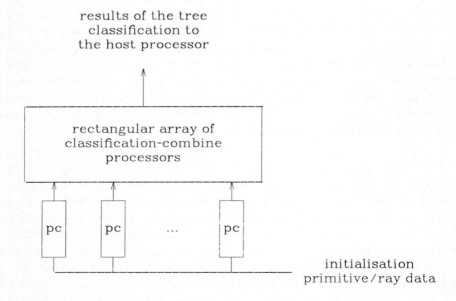

Figure 3-2 Overview of the Ray Casting Machine

$$P(s,h;t)=(x(s,h;t),y(s,h;t),z(s,h;t))$$

where x,y and z are linear expressions in s,h,t, e.g.

$$x(s,h;t)=x_0+a_2s+a_1h+a_0t$$

For each fixed value of s and h, $P(s,h;t)$, defines a straight line. A regular lattice of parallel lines is obtained by incrementing both s and h over a specified range. Kedem and Ellis show that for a constant incremental period (i.e. $h_i=h_0+i*dh$) four additions, one subtraction and one square-root are needed per parallel line (fixed s) classification against any quadratic halfspace. Four more additions are needed to make incremental computation in s possible. To keep the VLSI circuits simple they use bit-serial arithmetic. Each processing element consists a microcode memory and a customised 1 bit data path to support the above computation.

The restriction of using a regular lattice of parallel lines means that we can use a linear array of processors in *local mode* (see Section 2-4-2) since we only need to broadcast the initial coefficients of the rays to each processor. For a more general implementation of CSG ray casting we could use the stationary systolic algorithm discussed above. It is interesting to note that Kedem and Ellis could have simplified their design by broadcasting (systolically) the control to all the processors.

3.2.1. Embedding the CSG Tree

A significant feature of the ray casting machine is the design of the rectangular array of classification-combine (CC) processors to compute the CSG tree classification function once the results of the primitive/ray classification are known. Kedem and Ellis propose to embed directly the tree onto a rectangular array of processors allocating one tree node per processor. The general question of laying out a tree of processors on a VLSI circuit has been studied by a number of researchers, [28], and it is known that (assuming a processor has constant area)

(i) using a H-tree any binary tree can be laid in $O(n)$ area

(ii) if we make the restriction that leaves of the tree must lie on the border the lower bound on the area is $\Omega(n\log(n))$.

Kedem and Ellis extend these results by showing that a *right heavy* binary tree (i.e. a binary tree where the number of nodes in each right subtree is greater than or equal to the number of nodes in the corresponding left subtree) can be mapped onto a $\log(n)*n$ array of processors and further outline the following algorithm:

The root is in the upper left corner. The leaves are at the bottom edge. Left links of the tree point downward on the grid and the right links point to the right. The tree is embedded by traversing the tree in preorder. If the leaf is encountered before the bottom of the grid is reached,the last link is extended to the bottom. Each right link is extended according to following rule: Let K be the number of leaves that are before the current node (in prefix order). The right link is extended so that the node is in column $K+1$

A CSG can be made right heavy by interchanging one of its left and right subtrees,[23]. A mapping of a CSG tree onto a rectangular array of CC processors is shown Figure 3-3. The solid lines denote the actual computational path and some processors are used to simply pass the data straight through without performing any computation on it.

The actual operation of a CC processor (see figure 3-4) is to combine two streams of interval segments from the previous level and merge them into one stream according to the CSG operator at the node. For example, suppose we have the difference operator $(A-B)$ and input (x denotes the interval containing "in" set and o the "out" set)

    A: ooooooooxxxxxxxxoooooooxxxxxooo
    B: ooooooooooxxxooooooooooooxxxooooo

and output

    C: ooooooooxxxooxxoooooooxxoooxoooo

The CSG tree operators fragment the intervals and in the worst case the output stream contains double the information in either of the input streams, resulting in an exponential growth of information (worst case) as we ascend the tree. Although the information growth will be much less for a typical CSG object, we believe that this is likely to be a serious bottleneck limiting the performance of the machine. The octree spatial subdivision algorithm discussed below does not suffer from this problem as we only need to pass a three element classification, *in*, *out* or *partially-inout* (see below).

The CC processors used by Kedem and Ellis have sufficient hardware to compare and sort the intervals (min-max function), handle two, one or none input streams (the later case corresponds to the straight-through mode) and to be able to communicate its state to neighbouring processors using a standard handshake protocol.

3.2.2. General Remarks about CSG Tree Embedding

The combine-classification algorithm is *domain independent*, meaning that its operation is independent of the geometric properties of the primitives or the particular ray begin used (except that it must have an interval parameter t). The structure that Kedem and Ellis propose is potentially very general and applicable to other CSG algorithms. We

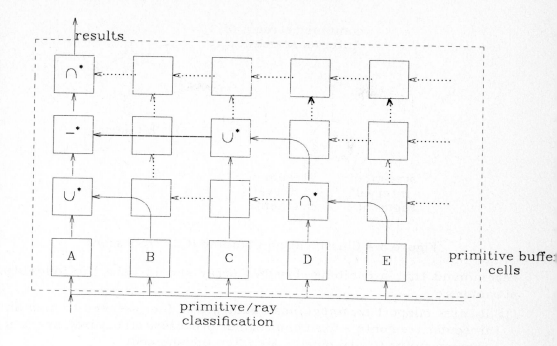

results

primitive buffer
cells

primitive/ray
classification

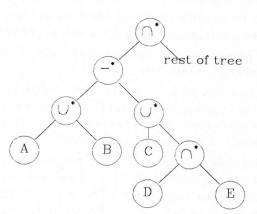

rest of tree

Figure 3-3 Embedding of a CSG Tree into a Rectangular Grid of Processors

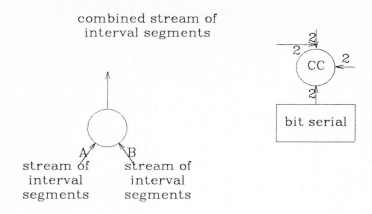

Figure 3-4 Classification-Combine (CC) Processors

recommend that a combine-classifier array should have the following attributes:

(1) it must support an *unbalanced binary tree* (i.e. we need to map an irregular tree onto a fixed and regular processor structure), as trees corresponding to real objects are often unbalanced;

(2) it must be able to handle an irregular flow of data through the processor array, i.e. message passing between processors;

(3) it must have provision for handling larger CSG trees than the number of processors available

(4) the final classification results must contain enough information to make the results immediately useful so that we avoid an excessive amount of post-processing in the other modules (e.g. the shader requires knowledge of the surface normal).

The Kedem and Ellis design has only the first two attributes. The third attribute is necessary because it is likely that the size of the CSG tree will outgrow the available hardware. The last attribute is important because if no provision has been made to identify the surface that has been intersected by the ray (or curve) it makes later processing like shading very expensive.

There are two obvious techniques for mapping a CSG tree onto an array of processors that is smaller than the number of tree nodes. The first is to group several tree nodes at each processor thus increasing the I/O requirements to each cell and the second is to compute the results for a set of subtrees leaving the controlling (master) processor to combine the results. The second option seems preferable since the complexity of the individual cells remains the same apart from some extra memory and a comparator to identify the subtree.

We can use the Kedem-Ellis design for the boundary cell in the stationary systolic algorithm discussed above, as shown in Figure 3-3. The primitives are stored in the buffers at the base of the array. Each buffer has a comparator so that the correct primitive can be loaded into the appropriate buffer. For later identification each primitive is tagged. The CC processors would be similar to those used by Kedem and Ellis except that we would support multiple subtrees (by tagging the particular subtree being processed) and pass the primitive identifications up the tree. The complexity of the CC processors would be increased but the results would be more useful. The same array structure can be used for the octree spatial subdivision algorithm discussed below, although the actual processors would be different as we need to support a *pruned tree* rather than process interval segments.

3.3. Woodwark-IBM Octree Spatial Subdivision

This algorithm, which was originally developed by J. Woodwark [29] and later extended by P. Quarendon at the IBM UK Scientific Centre [24], is fully described in the companion paper, [4], and only a brief outline will be given here. The algorithm has been used in the IBM WINSOM system written by Peter Quarendon and Plate 1 illustrates the primitives available and some simple composite solids. In Plate 2 a recursively defined solid object is shown. This object was defined in just a few lines of code.

The Woodwark-IBM algorithm operates in *image space* (rather than object space) and is based on the idea of recursively subdividing a cubic volume of space (called a voxel) into eight subspaces. This is known as octree spatial subdivision (see figure 2 of [4]). The recursion is terminated when a voxel contains either

empty space

one primitive

or the limiting resolution has been reached. If the voxel contains only one primitive it is sent to the shader subsystem and the appropriate area of the quadtree is marked for hidden surface elimination (see [4]). If the limiting resolution has been reached (i.e. at pixel resolution) we arbitrarily assign one of the primitives consistent with the surrounding pixels that have already been filled.

Importantly the algorithm has a running time $O(n)$ time compared with $O(n^3 log(n))$ for boundary evaluation, where n is the number of primitives in the object. This means that it can produce complex pictures of shapes with many primitives much faster than programs like NONAME which needs to evaluate the whole boundary. For example, to draw the camshaft pump with 400 primitives (see Plate 3) takes about 1 minute on a VAX 11/780 whereas NONAME would require approximately one hour. Our aim is to design parallel architectures that will draw in reasonable response time models with a very large number of primitives (e.g. 10^5 primitives which currently takes 3 hours on an IBM 4341 for a resolution of 512x512). Because the algorithm operates in image space the computation time is also dependent on the resolution required.

The details of the main computational modules are shown in figure 3-5. We comment briefly on each module and refer the reader to the companion paper in the proceeding [4]:

(1) *The subdivision controller* performs the recursive subdivision of the octree and has overall control of the computation. On the basis of the results from the tree/voxel classification it decides which primitive/voxel classification to process next and transfers a primitive-voxel pair to the shader/display module

(2) *The **primitive broadcaster*** stores the complete set of primitives (halfspaces) for the CSG tree and transfers them to the primitive-

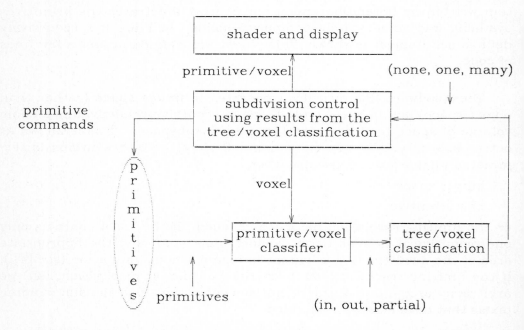

Figure 3-5 Software Architecture for Octree Spatial Subdivision

voxel classifier and the shading/display module, under commands from the subdivision controller

(3) *The primitive-voxel classifier* performs the actual primitive-voxel classification by testing to see if the primitive lies *inside, outside* or *partially inside* a given voxel. It is computationally intensive involving the use of floating point vector arithmetic.

(4) *The tree simplification module* inputs the results of the primitive-voxel classification and apply them to the CSG tree to generate a tree/voxel classification (empty, one primitive, many-primitives). It must contain sufficient storage for the entire CSG tree and any pruned trees that are generated during the subdivision of space.

(5) *The shading/display module* receives a description of a primitive to be shaded and a square region of screen to be filled. The surface normals on the primitives are computed and a lighting model used to compute the intensities at each pixel in the screen area. This module interfaces with the display hardware.

3.3.1. Parallel Algorithms/Architectures

For completeness, we mention some of the parallel algorithms that have been proposed for the octree spatial subdivision algorithms. The approach used by J. Woodwark, [30], and S. Goldwasser, [31], is to exploit *area-coherence*. For example in the Woodwark-IBM algorithm, within each voxel of the octree we maintain a *pruned tree* (figure 5 of [4]) which is independent of its neighbouring voxels. This leads to the obvious solution of dividing the screen into fixed areas of pixels and allocating one processor to each area block. This means each processor executes the same algorithm but on different data and without the need to transfer large amounts of data between processors. The processing elements would need to be quite complex as we need to compute: primitive/voxel classification, pruning the CSG tree and shading algorithms. The main criticism of this architecture is that real scenes are not sufficiently *homogeneous* across the picture to ensure approximately the same loading on each processor. For example, most engineering parts are drawn in the centre of the screen. The problems become worse as the number of processors is increased, thus limiting the degree of parallelism that can be achieved. Attempts to load share, by allocating more than one area of the screen to each processor can improve processor-utilisation but this leads to complex partitioning schemes and loss of area coherence. An adaptive solution to the loading sharing problem (in the context of ray casting) is discussed by M. Dippe and J. Swensen, [32].

Finally, it is worth mentioning that J. Woodwark and his colleagues at the University of Bath, [33], proposed an alternative network of multiprocessors to support the recursion. Essentially the "root" processor creates a list of operations to be performed on a stack, which neighbouring processors can "steal" and execute themselves. These processors also maintain a "waiting-for execution" stack which the neighbouring processors can "steal". Parallel architectures of this type for general divide-and-conquer algorithms have been studied recently by R. Sleep and his colleagues at the University of East Anglia, [34].

3.4. Systolic Array Architecture for Woodwark-IBM Algorithm

In this section we report on a preliminary study carried out at Leeds over the last six months aimed at mapping the Woodwark-IBM algorithm onto a systolic array computer. The main difference between our approach and the multiprocessor solutions discussed above is that we attempt to speed-up the *inner loop*, i.e. the primitive/voxel classification. We have also looked briefly at the design of a special-purpose tree classifier. Although we have no precise timings yet, we expect to achieve speed-ups of between 1 to 2 orders of magnitude depending on the number and power of the systolic processors.

The computationally intensive part of the Woodwark-IBM algorithm is the primitive-voxel classification which can be performed on an array of "warp-like" processing cells using a stationary systolic algorithm as shown in figure 3-6. For simplicity we allocate one voxel per processing cell. In practice it would be more efficient to allocate several voxels per processing cell as this would make it easier to keep the pipelines full (by interleaving computations) and would reduce the number of times we need to pass the primitives through the array.

Once the octree subdivision process has started we can maintain an "active queue" of voxels waiting to be classified. Each primitive/voxel classification is completely independent and can be performed in

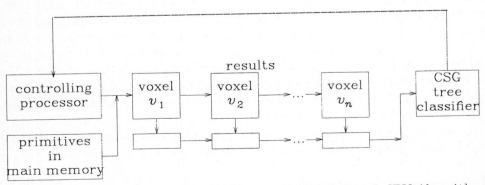

Figure 3-6 Stationary Systolic Algorithm for Woodwark-IBM Algorithm

parallel. The voxels are preloaded (target data) into the systolic cells and the primitives to be classified are passed systolically between cells. The primitives are stored in main memory and indexed according to their "primitive tag" number. The result of each primitive/voxel classification flows out systolically to the boundary cell (tree classifier). The controlling processor performs the algorithm (in outline only):

basic control algorithm

> **begin** initialise data structures and assign the root voxel (image space) to the active queue
>
> **while** active queue is not empty **do**
>
>> **begin**
>> preload the systolic cells with N visible voxels from the active queue;
>>> **for** all primitives "in" the N voxels **do**
>>> **begin**
>>> input primitive to the systolic processor and receive the output from the tree/classifier (results)
>>>
>>>> **case** results.kind **of**
>>>>
>>>> empty   : do nothing
>>>> one-primitive : **if** voxel is visible**then**
>>>>   mark quadtree and
>>>>   send primitive-voxel pair
>>>>   to the shader
>>>> many-primitives: subdivide by putting sub-voxels
>>>>   on the active queue
>>>
>>> **end**
>> **end**
> **end**

notes

(i) The results from the voxel/tree classifier consist of the voxel and primitive identifier and a 2-bit result indicating empty, one-primitive or many-primitives. For example, this information can be packed into a 32 bit word by using 16 bits for the primitive tag and 14 bits for the voxel tag. This allows us to use 64K primitives and maintain an active queue of 16K voxels.

(2) The parameter N refers to the number of systolic cells used in the array.

(3) The computational time for each systolic cell depends on the particular primitive being processed (see Table 3-1 and [4]). To ensure a smooth flow of data we propose to sort the primitives so that the pipeline is kept full of the *same* type of primitive. A systolic control would be used to configure the cells to handle a particular primitive type. Alternately a more general controller could be used in each processor to allow them handle different primitives in parallel.

(4) We have carried out some preliminary studies on the type of computation performed by the systolic cell and these are summarised in Table 3-1. The main requirement is to be able to perform simple vector arithmetic and special mathematical functions like square-root and division. These operations can be performed, for example, on a warp-like processor or a Transputer. We believe that the bandwidth to/from the systolic processor would be very modest. For a 10-cell array of Warp processors we estimate that it is less than 2 Mbytes per second. The number of bytes need to describe uniquely a primitive and its position in space, together with the processing needed can be seen in Table 3-1.

3.5. Supporting the Pruned Tree

The CSG tree classifier algorithm used in the Woodwark-IBM algorithm differs in two important aspects compared with the curve-solid tree classifier discussed above:

(i) at each combine process we need only to output the result (in, out, partial) which means that the information flowing up the tree is *constant*, and

(ii) we need to store the pruned tree for each voxel-solid classification.

The first difference is of importance because we can use the Kedem-Ellis processor array (with different CC processors) without incurring the

Prim kind	Storage (bytes)	3-vector		Scalar ops			total ops
		add	mult	add	mult	sqrt	
Plane	20	0	1	4	5	0	9
Sphere	20	1	1	8	4	0	12
Cone	40	1	2	7	8	1	15
Torus	40	1	2	12	12	1	24
Cylinder	40	1	2	11	8	0	29
Egg	76	1	3	18	15	0	33
Helix	76	1	4	17	19	2	36

Table 3-1 Primitive/Voxel Operations

penalty of an information bottleneck as we ascend the tree. The second difference means that it is necessary to support tree pruning for the subdivision algorithm. This is the process by which trees become successively simpler as subtrees that are outside the the voxel are pruned from the tree. As the voxel being classified is subdivided into successively smaller parts, the tree is pruned at each level until it is either reduced to one primitive or it is completely empty. This result is then returned to the subdivision module.

It is important to note that the subdivision algorithm is a *depth first traversal* of the octree space and this allows us to use a simple stack in the CC processors to store the pruned trees. This stack need only be the *depth* of the octree recursion. When a cube is subdivided a copy of the current tree on the top of the stack is made and pushed onto the stack after being pruned by the normal CSG rules. As the recursion unwinds, under the control of the subdivision controller, the stack is popped and the pruned tree exposed again ready for another subdivision.

Depending on the processor power available in the primitive classification process, the tree support hardware may not be needed at all. Its task could be performed by a general purpose processor, as long as the primitive classification pipeline is sufficiently slow.

4. Conclusions and Further Work

In this paper we have surveyed the progress being made in the theory and implementation of systolic array architectures and outlined possible systolic algorithms for two CSG methods (ray casting and octree spatial subdivision). Of the two, we believe that the Woodwark-IBM algorithm is the more suitable for a parallel (VLSI) implementation, particularly as the information content remains constant as we ascend the tree. The systolic approach appears to be promising but we must await detailed simulation results from the work currently being carried out by David Morris.

Further research is needed to find the most suitable CSG representations/algorithms for mapping onto a parallel architecture (e.g. a systolic array computer) and can be used by the application modules which may themselves use the warp-like processing array. Another question for investigation is the utility of systolic arrays for data dependent (compute-bound) computations like sparse matrices, CGS algorithms and middle vision problems (e.g. image segmentation).

5. Acknowledgements

The authors would like to acknowledge the help and guidance given by Professor A. de Pennington and two of the authors (PMD & DTM) would like to thank Professor H.T. Kung for the opportunity to visit Carnegie-Mellon University and to learn at first hand the progress being made in the design and implementation of a systolic array machine. The colour pictures where produced by the WINSOM system at the IBM UK Scientific Centre. Finally we would like to thank SERC and the IBM UK Scientific Centre for supporting David Morris.

References

1.   M.P. Groover and E.W. Zimmers (Jr.), *CAD/CAM: Computer-Aided Design and Manufacture*, Prentice-Hall (1984).

2.   J.R. Dodsworth, *Current Issues in Solid Modelling*, Geometric Modelling Project, Department of Mechanical Engineering, University of Leeds (October 1984).

3.   L.A. Goshorn, "Vision systems eye real-time speeds through multiprocessor architectures", *Electronics*, (December 1983).

4.   D.T. Morris and P. Quarendon, "An Algorithm for Direct Display of CSG Objects by Spatial Subdivision", *NATO Advanced Course on the Fundamentals of Computer Graphics Algorithms*, (April 1985).

5.   H.T. Kung and C.E. Leiserson, "Systolic Arrays (for VLSI)", pp. 256-282 in *Sparse Matrix Proceedings 1978*, ed. I.S. Duff and G. W. Stewart,Society for Industrial and Applied Mathematics (1979).

6.   E. Arnould, H.T. Kung, O. Menzilcioglu, and K. Sarocky, "A Systolic Array Computer", in *Proceeding of the IEEE Conf. on Acoustics, Speech and Signal Processing*, (March 1985).

7.   G.-J. Li and B.W. Wah, "The Design of Optimal Systolic Arrays", *IEEE Trans. on Computers* **c-34**(1)(Jan. 1985).

8.   C.E. Leiserson and J. B. Saxe, "Optimizing Sysnchronous Systems", *J. VLSI and Computer Systems* **1**(1) pp. 41-67 Computer Science Press, (1983).

9.   S.D. Brookes, *Reasoning about Synchronous Systems*, Department of Computer Science, Carngie-Mellon University (1984).

10.   M. Chen and C. Mead, "Hierarchical Simulator Based on Formal Semantics", in *Proc. Third Caltech Conference on VLSI*, (1984).

11.   H.T. Kung and M.S. Lam, "Fault-Tolerance and Two-Level Pipelining in VLSI Systolic Arrays", in *Proceedings of the Conference on Advanced Research in VLSI*, (Jan. 1984).

12.   H.T. Kung, "Systolic Algorithms for the CMU Warp Processor", in *Proceeding of the Seventh International Conference on Pattern Recognition*, (July 1984). Previously The Warp Processor: A Versatile Systolic Array for Very High Speed Signal Processing

13.   R. W. Hockney and C.R. Jesshope, *Parallel Computers*, Hilger (1981).

14.   Inmos, *IMS T424 transputer user manual*

15.   Inmos, *Occam Programming Manual*

16.   F.H. Hsu, H.T. Kung, T. Nishizawa and A. Sussman, *LINC: The Link and Interconnection Chip*, Department of Computer Science, Carnegie-Mellon University (May 1984).

17.   H.T. Kung and S.Q. Yu, "Integrating High-Performance Special-Purpose Devices into a System", pp. 205-211 in *VLSI Architecture*, ed. B. Randel and P.C. Treleaven, Prentice/Hall International (1983).

18.   P.M. Dew and C.H. Chang, *Passive Navigation by a Robot on the CMU Warp Machine*, Department of Computer Science, Carnegie-Mellon University (1984).

19.   K. Hwang and F.A. Briggs, *Computer Architecture and Parallel Processing*, McGraw-Hill (1984).

20.   A. Gottlieb et al, "The NYU Ultracomputer - Designing an MIMD Shared Memory Parallel Computer", *IEEE Trans. on Computers* c-**32**(2)(Feb. 1983).

21.   D. H. Ballard and C.M. Brown, *Computer Vision*, Prentice-Hall (1982).

22.   A.G. Requicha and H.B. Voelcker, *Solid Modelling: Current Status & Research Directions*, Prepared for IEEE Computer Graphics & Applications (July 1983).

23.   G. Kedem and J.L. Ellis, *Computer Structures for Curve-Solid Structures for Curve-Solid Classification in Geometric Modelling*, Production Automation Project (May 1984). (Ray Casting Machine)

24.   P. Quarendon, "Winsom Reference Manual", 176, IBM UK Scientific Centre (August 1984).

25.   A.G. Requicha, "Representations for Rigid Solids: Theory, Methods, and Systems", *ACM Computing Surveys* **12** pp. 437-464 (December 1980).

26.   R.B. Tilove, "Set Membership Classification: A Unified Approach to Geometric Intersection Problems", *IEEE Trans. on Computers* C-**29** pp. 874-883 (October 1980).

27.   S.D. Roth, "Raycasting for modelling solids", *Computer Graphics and Image Processing* **18** pp. 109-144 (Feb. 1982).

28.   J. Ullman, *Computational Aspects of VLSI*, Computer Science Press (1984).

29.   J.R. Woodwark and K.M. Quinian, "Reducing the effect of Complexity on Volume Model Evaluation", *CAD Journal* **14**(2) pp. 88-95 (1982).

30.   J.R. Woodwark, *A Multiprocessor Display Architecture for Viewing Solid Models*, School of Engineering, University of Bath (). preliminary version

31.   S. M. Goldwasser, "A Generalized Object Display Processor Architecture", pp. 38-47 in *The 11th Annual International Sysposium on Computer Architecture*, IEEE (1984).

32.   M. Dippe and J. Swensen, "An Adaptive Subdivision Algorithm and Parallel Architecture for Realistic   Image Synthesis", *SIGGRAPH '84* **18**(3)ACM Computer Graphics, (July 1984).

33.   A. Bowyer, P.J. Willis, and J.R. Woodwark, "A Multiprocessor Architecture for Solving Spatial Problems", *Computer Journal* **24**(4) pp. 265-278 (1981).

34.   F.W. Burton and M.R Sleep, "Communication in a Distributed Implementation of An Applicative Language", *Proc. of 6th ACM European regional conference on Systems Architecture*, Westbury House, IPC Business Press, (1981).

Parallel Architectures for High Performance Graphics Systems

Alistair C. Kilgour,
Computing Science Department,
University of Glasgow.

Abstract

A framework is proposed for categorising parallel display architectures, ranging from "polygon serial" (one processor per pixel) to "pixel serial" (one processor per polygon or object). A variety of proposed architectures is discussed in relation to this framework, including the Pixel-planes system of Fuchs et al, the 8x8 display of Sproull et al and the Zone Management Processor system of Grimsdale et al.

1. Required Operations for Rendering

Although systems have been designed which deal directly with surface patches, for present purposes the discussion is limited to the rendering of scenes defined as a set of polygonal facets. The operations required to render such a scene include:

> clipping;
> hidden surface removal;
> scan conversion;
> shading;
> anti-aliasing.

Simple (Gouraud) shading can be incorporated in the scan conversion algorithm, since it involves only linear interpolation between colours or intensities defined at polygon vertices. The more powerful shading models (Phong, Cook-Torrance, etc) required for accurate rendering of highlights are not considered further here, and anti-aliasing is referred to only incidentally. Attention is focussed on the operations of hidden surface removal and scan conversion.

2. Polygon Serial Versus Pixel Serial

When considering the introduction of parallelism to speed up the rendering process, two approaches suggest themselves:

(i) "polygon serial": for each facet in turn, find out where it is visible, and write its shade into the frame store at those points.

(ii) "pixel serial": for each pixel, probe the scene, find out what is visible there, and write its shade to the frame store.

In the first method the aim might be to use the processor per pixel (a "smart frame store") to achieve the scan conversion and hidden surface removal in real time. With the second approach, the idea could be to have one processor per polygon (or object), and for each of these processors to report in parallel the depth and shade of its polygon at the current pixel. The depths could then be compared and the polygon with the smallest depth would have its shade recorded.

If a shading model more complex than Gouraud is being used, computing the shade at each pixel of a polygon can be extremely time consuming, and the time is wasted if the polygon turns out not to be visible at that pixel.

NATO ASI Series, Vol. F17
Fundamental Algorithms for Computer Graphics
Edited by R. A. Earnshaw
© Springer-Verlag Berlin Heidelberg 1985

A useful improvement is therefore to record in the frame store the identity of the polygon visible at each pixel, rather than its shade, and then compute the shades only of visible polygons, in a second pass through the frame store. This approach has recently been proposed by Weghorst et al as a method of speeding up ray-tracing calculations [WEGH84].

The framework for categorising systems as "polygon serial" or "pixel serial" was first suggested by Cohen [COHE81], and although not all architectures fit easily, it nevertheless provides a useful starting-point for comparing systems. An analysis and simulation of various "polygon serial" architectures is given by Parke [PARK80].

A fundamental limitation of any polygon-serial system is that performance deteriorates linearly with the number of polygons. To maintain performance given increased scene complexity it is necessary to speed up the pixel processors. On the other hand, resolution can be increased just by increasing the number of processors.

With the pixel serial approach, increased scene complexity can be compensated for by adding more polygon processors. However, increased resolution requires faster processors to maintain performance. The processing times available per pixel at various resolutions are, as estimated by Finke [FINK83], as follows:

No. of lines	Pixels/line	Total no. of Pixels	Time/pixel
384	512	196K	66.5ns
512	640	328K	38.3ns
768	1024	786K	14.4ns
1024	1280	1310K	8.0ns

Particularly at the higher resolutions, these times are very demanding, and ·it is a tribute to the ingenuity of hardware designers that useful systems have been devised which meet these constraints.

3. Polygon Serial Systems

This type of system is perhaps more common than the alternative pixel serial structure. The approach is analogous in many ways to the structure of conventional high-performance calligraphic systems. The picture is defined by a "display file" consisting not of vectors but of 3D polygon definitions. (Often the polygon complexity is restricted to triangles or planar convex quadrilaterals). At each vertex of the polygon a depth and colour (or grey scale) is stored. As with the calligraphic refreshed display, the display processor traverses the "display file" performing clipping, transformation and conversion to device co-ordinates, ideally at video refresh rates, i.e. 50 (UK) or 60 (US) times per second, for a non-interlaced display.

The kind of algorithms required for these operations on polygons are well understood, and have recently been encapsulated in silicon in a flexible and powerful manner by Clark [CLAR80a, CLAR80b, CLAR82, CLAR85]. If that were all that were involved, the problem of real-time 3D image generation would be relatively straight-forward, and systems capable of handling 100,000 polygons would be not much harder to construct than calligraphic systems capable of handling 100,000 vectors. But the two operations omitted from consideration so far, namely scan conversion and hidden surface removal, alter matters dramatically. Either problem can be avoided or made relatively trivial, at the cost of complicating the other.

3.1 Avoiding Hidden Surface Removal

For designers of high-performance 3D graphics systems, the Z buffer has considerable attractions, because, at the cost of some additional memory to hold the minimum depth value so far at each pixel, it virtually abolishes the hidden surface problem. (Unfortunately, it doesn't abolish the aliasing problem, although supersampling with post filtering, as described by Crow [CROW82], is applicable in principle). The following sections describe a selection of the many "polygon-serial" systems which use the Z buffer approach. (An interesting discussion of the evolution and application of the Z buffer algorithm is given by Fuchs in [FUCH79]).

3.2 Whitted's Enhanced 3D System

This is an attempt to provide a low-cost hardware enhancement to a conventional scan-line hidden surface algorithm [WHIT82]. The enhancement takes the form of a one-dimensional Z buffer, which solves the hidden surface problem in parallel for all polygons crossing a given scan-line. It is still necessary to maintain by software an active polygon list containing all polygons intersected by the scan line, and to update this as necessary when moving from one scan line to the next (which in turn requires an initial sort of all polygons on maximum Y value).

Although not capable of real-time rendering of complex scenes, Whitted's system reduced image generation times from an hour or more to at most several minutes on a VAX 11/780, for typical scenes.

3.3 Fuchs's Pixel-planes System

This system represents the "polygon serial" approach in its pure form [FUCH79, FUCH81, FUCH82] and is described in more detail elsewhere in these proceedings [FUCH85]. Each pixel has a "Zmin" storage element as well as a colour value, and is capable of comparing a broadcast depth value with the previously stored minimum, setting a 1-bit register according to the result. Subsequently colour values are broadcast to each pixel, and those pixels where the minimum depth has changed accept and store the new colour value.

Prior to broadcast of the depth and colour values, details of the edges of the polygon are broadcast to each pixel, so that it can decide, after all edges have been distributed, whether it is inside or outside the polygon. Only pixels inside the polygon are eligible for subsequent depth comparison.

Conceptually, therefore, each pixel may be regarded as having a processor which, given a 3D polygon definition, is capable of:

(i) deciding if the pixel is inside or outside the polygon;

(ii) computing the depth of the polygon at the pixel, and storing it if it is less than the previous minimum;

(iii) computing the colour (or grey level) at the pixel, by linear interpolation between values stored at the polygon vertices, and storing it if the depth value has changed;

although in practice much of the computation is performed by the broadcast circuitry. All the pixel processors execute in parallel, so that both scan conversion and hidden surface removal are performed very quickly, within the frame store itself.

3.4   The 8x8 Display of Sproull et al

The early design of this system is described in [GUPT81], and an analysis of experience in building and evaluating the prototype is given in [SPRO83]. The basic idea of this system is to allow parallel access to an arbitrary group of 8x8 pixels in the frame store, representing a square area of the picture. Scan conversion algorithms need to be modified, of course, to take advantage of the parallel access, and Sproull has described the derivation of a suitable generalisation of Bresenham's algorithm for generating vectors on such a display [SPRO82]. The prototype system described in [SPRO83] has these and other scan-conversion algorithms stored in microcode.

The parallelism in the 8x8 display is at the pixel addressing level, and is intended primarily as a mechanism for speeding up operations which involve movement of rectangular areas around the screen (the so-called "rasterop" or "bitblt" operations). In this respect impressive figures are reported for the prototype, which is capable of copying a complete 768x1024x1 bit raster in 52 milliseconds. However, scan conversion and hidden surface removal must still be done in serial, although with a significant speedup due to working in terms of 8x8 blocks rather than single pixels when transferring to and from the frame store.

Whelan has described an architecture similar to but in some ways more general than the 8x8 display, in that it can fill any rectangular area of the frame store with a given value in constant time [WHEL82].

4.   Pixel Serial Systems

In this approach, in its pure form, there is a processor for each polygon which, given the position of the current pixel, reports the depth and intensity of the polygon at that pixel. The depths from all processors are compared and the polygon with the smallest depth values "wins", i.e. has its intensity value written to the frame store (or used to determine the beam voltage, if the frame store is bypassed). The polygon processors are synchronised so that all are considering the same pixel at the same time.

One of the earliest such systems was the Electronic Scene Generator [ROUG69, BUNK72] designed by GEC for the NASA manned space program. The initial design [ROUG69] allowed for forty objects, with a separate processor for each object. Each object processor was itself a sophisticated device, capable of generating a dynamically-changing view of the object at video frame rates. Output from the different object processors was merged, using precomputed interobject priorities for contention resolution, to produce the final scene. No explicit frame store was used.

Many of the recent "pixel serial" architectures proposed for high-performance graphics systems are based on principles derived from the GEC design, in particular the system described by Cohen [COHE81]. This consists of a pipeline of identical polygon processors, each of which decides whether the current pixel is inside or outside its polygon and if inside computes the depth and shade. The depth is compared with the minimum so far, passed from the previous stage in the pipeline. If the new depth is less it replaces the previous minimum, and the new shade is passed on.

Cohen's design appears to be capable of rendering scenes with up to 10,000 polygons at TV resolutions in real time, but reports of actual performance figures have not yet appeared in the literature.

4.1 Avoiding Scan Conversion

The problem of displaying a single simple polygon on a raster scan display can be reduced to a question of deciding when (and at what energy) to switch on and off the electron beam (or beams for a colour system) during each horizontal sweep of the raster. It should therefore be possible to generate a picture of the polygon directly from the polygon definition, without using a frame store. This is the basis of several designs, including the Zone Management Processor system described below.

The potential advantages of direct analogue scan conversion, which is what this approach amounts to, are considerable. The shape of a polygon, or its position, can be changed without the need to generate or move potentially large quantities of data in the frame store. However, the problem of contention between overlapping polygons, which is equivalent to the hidden surface problem, has to be solved before the technique is capable of generating useful 3D renderings.

4.2 The Zone Management Processor System

The common method of resolving contention is to allocate a priority to each polygon, based on its position in a linear list of polygons ordered, say, on minimum depth (over all vertices in the polygon). Depth sorting on its own does not fully define the correct viewing priority, and the auxiliary comparisons first enumerated by Newell, Newell and Sancha [NEWE72] are also necessary. To avoid the overheads of sorting, Willis has proposed an alternative method of assigning priority based on distance from the viewpoint [WILL77, WILL78], which has some similarities to the priority methods used with the GEC system [SUTH74]. Willis's method was designed for use with a hardware device known as the Zone Management Processor System, developed at Sussex University by Grimsdale and his colleagues [GRIM79].

Each Zone Management Processor is a polygon processing element, capable of handling a triangle or convex quadrilateral, and delivering output signals at the times when the CRT beam enters and leaves the polygon, on each scan line which intersects it. Within any scan-line, a separate Zone Management Processor is required for each polygon which can potentially contribute to the line. (Each processor can handle several polygons in a complete refresh cycle, provided they don't overlap in Y). The priority of each polygon is stored with its defining data, and contention-resolution hardware ensures that the processor with the highest priority gains control over the beam at each transition point on the scan line.

The Zone Management Processor system now forms the final stage of a successful flight simulator developed at Sussex University

4.3 Thomas's Boolean Expression Engine

An interesting pixel-serial system, which also operates without explicit scan conversion or frame store, has been designed and constructed by Adrian Thomas of Durham University (now at University of Sussex) [THOM83, THOM84]. The most unusual feature of this system is that the display is driven directly from a Boolean expression representing the object or scene to be displayed as the union of intersection of 3D half-spaces bounded by planes. This is in fact a CSG definition of the scene, using low-level primitives (half-spaces), and Thomas's system is in effect a simple ray-casting engine which, for each virtual pixel on the screen, computes the visible surface and its shade. There is a processor for each plane bounding a half-space, which computes the depth and shade incrementally for each pixel in turn. The outputs from the plane processors are merged according to the Boolean expression defining the scene, which is effectively re-evaluated at each pixel.

Thomas's system achieves both hidden surface removal and scan conversion in the hardware in real-time, but the prototype is limited in the complexity of scene it can display. However, since the design is modular, scene complexity may be increased by adding more units, without change to the basic design.

4.4   Wiseman's Rainbow Workstation

This is an example of a system with an unconventional framestore structure. It generates standard video output from a high-level description of the picture in terms of polygonal areas (basically rectangular in this case) [WILK84, STYN85]. The Rainbow workstation is designed primarily for efficient handling of 2D window management, but because the relative priority of overlapping windows may be defined, it is capable of dynamic hidden surface removal. However, the maximum number of polygons intersecting any scan line is restricted to ten in the current version.

Although window boundaries are rectangular, a masking function may be defined for every pixel within a window which controls how the colour values defined for the window are to be combined with those of other windows which it overlaps. In effect this permits irregular boundaries to be defined within the rectangular area, and one of the more impressive demonstrations of the capability of the workstation consists of dynamically moving overlapping star-shaped coloured regions, with polygon intersection and antialiasing at region boundaries being performed in real-time.

The above examples represent only a selection of proposed architectures which might be described as "pixel serial", although in some there may, as has been indicated, be no explicit frame store. Because, as Cohen has pointed out, pixel serial systems can in principle handle increased complexity by adding more processors, rather than, as with polygon serial systems, making the existing processors faster, these systems would appear to offer the best prospect for affordable real-time manipulation of complex pictures.

The discussion so far has been based on polygonal representations with a very simple shading model, which is severely limited in the realism of the pictures produced. For high realism ray tracing is currently the favoured technique, and several efforts are underway to build parallel systems aimed at speeding up the ray tracing process, which on serial machines typically requires of the order of hours of processor time to render a single frame. Discussion of these is beyond the scope of the present article.

5.   Hybrid Techniques

Given a processing element per polygon (or object), why should it be necessary to synchronise all these processors so that they are all considering the same pixel at the same time? Given a Z buffer incorporated with the frame store, it should be possible in principle to allow the polygon processors to produce their output in any order and at any time. Updating of the complete picture is then complete whenever the last polygon processor has terminated.

The difficulty with such a "free-for-all" approach arises from possible contention between several processors attempting to access the same pixel simultaneously. There must be a mechanism for ensuring exclusive access to the memory by one processor at a time, and for queuing requests from other processors so that they get satisfied eventually. Such a mechanism is built into the design of some general purpose parallel computer architectures, commonly known as "ultracomputers" [SCHW80].

Fiume, Fournier and Rudolph [FIUM83] have described an algorithm for parallel scan conversion of polygons, designed for implementation on the NYU ultracomputer [GOTT83]. The processing elements handling the polygons will share access to a frame store and associated depth buffer, on which an indivisible "replace minimum" operation will be provided, which replaces the current depth and shade values at a pixel by new values if the new depth value is less than the minimum. Unlike previous algorithms involving use of the Z buffer, the method of Fiume et al incorporates antialiasing using an approximate supersampling technique which takes further advantage of the parallelism available in the hardware.

The contest between solutions based on special-purpose hardware designed specifically for the rendering process, and methods such as that proposed by Fiume et al which utilise general purpose parallel computer architectures, will be interesting to watch. In the short term the special-purpose systems which gain a significant share of the market are bound to win out on cost, but in the longer term the added flexibility and adaptability of the general-purpose solution may prove a significant factor.

6. Conclusion

The "polygon serial" versus "pixel serial" characterisation of parallel display architectures has been described, and a number of existing and proposed systems discussed in relation to this framework. The aim has been not necessarily to provide a fully comprehensive account of the growing literature on parallel architectures for graphics, but to suggest a framework against which the interested reader may evaluate current and future systems.

Acknowledgement

I would like to thank Danny Cohen of the Information Sciences Institute of the University of Southern California, whose contribution to the raster graphics seminar at Leicester Polytechnic in August 1980 sparked off my interest in high performance graphics systems, and many of whose insights provide the foundation for the present paper.

REFERENCES

Entries marked with an asterisk (*) are reproduced in the compendium volume "Selected Reprints on VLSI Technologies and Computer Graphics" compiled by Henry Fuchs and published by the IEEE Computer Society [FUCH83].

[BUNK72]   BUNKER, W.M. Visual scene simulation with computer generated images. Proc Fifth Annual Simulation Symposium, Kay and McLeod (eds) (Progress in Simulation Vol 2) Gordon & Breach, New York (1972) 91-114.

[CLAR80a] CLARK, J.H. Structuring a VLSI system architecture. Lambda 1, 2 (Second Quarter 1980) 25-30.

[CLAR80b] CLARK, J.H. A VLSI geometry processor for graphics. Computer 13, 7 (July 1980) 59-68.

702

[CLAR82]*   CLARK, J.H.   The geometry engine: a VLSI geometry system for graphics.   Computer Graphics 16, 3 (July 1982) 127-133.

[CLAR85]   CLARK, J.H.   Graphics software standards and their evolution with hardware algorithms.   These proceedings (1985).

[COHE82]   COHEN, D. AND DEMETRESCU, S.   A VLSI approach to computer image generation.   Information Sciences Institute, University of Southern California (1981).

[CROW81]   CROW, F.D.   A comparison of antialiasing techniques.   IEEE Computer Graphics & Applications 1, 1 (Jan 1981) 40-48.

[FINK83]   FINKE, D.L.   Dynamic RAM architectures for graphics applications.   Proc. National Computer Conference Anaheim, California (May 1983) 479-485.

[FUCH79]*   FUCHS, H.   An expandable multiprocessor architecture for video graphics.   Proc. 6th IEEE Symposium on Computer Architecture (1979) 58-67.

[FUCH81]   FUCHS, H. AND POULTON, J.   Pixel-planes: a VLSI-oriented design for 3D raster graphics.   Proc. 7th Canadian Man-Computer Communications Conf. (June 1981) 343-347.

[FUCH82]*   FUCHS, H., POULTON, J., PAETH, A. AND BELL, A.   Developing Pixel-planes: a smart memory-based raster graphics system.   Proc. Conf. on Advanced Research in VLSI, MIT, Artech House Inc (1982) 137-146.

[FUCH83]   FUCHS, H. (ed)   Selected Reprints on VLSI Technologies and Computer Graphics.   IEEE Computer Society Press (IEEE Catalog No EHO 204-8) 1983.

[FUCH85]   FUCHS, H.   Implementation of image generation algorithms in VLSI.   These proceedings (1985).

[GOTT83]   GOTTLIEB, A., GRISHMAN, R., KRUSKAL, C.P., McAULIFFE, K.P., RUDOLPH, L. AND SNIR, M.   The NYU ultracomputer - designing an MIMD shared memory parallel computer.   IEEE Trans. on Computers C-32, 2 (Feb 1983) 175-189.

[GRIM79]   GRIMSDALE, R.L. HADJIASLANIS, A.A. AND WILLIS, P.J.   Zone management processor: a module for generating surfaces in raster-scan colour displays.   Computers and Digital Techniques 2, 1 (Feb 1979) 21-25.

[GUPT81]   GUPTA, S., SPROULL, R.F. AND SUTHERLAND, I.E.   A VLSI architecture for updating raster-scan displays.   Computer Graphics 15, 3 (April 1981) 71-78.

[NEWE72]   NEWELL, M.E., NEWELL, R.G. AND SANCHA, T.   A solution to the hidden surface problem.   Proc. ACM Nat. Conf. (1972) 443-450.

[PARK80]*   PARKE, F.I.   Simulation and expected performance analysis of multiple processor Z-buffer systems.   Computer Graphics 14, 3 (July 1980) 48-56.

[ROUG69] ROUGELOT, R.S. The General Electric computed color TV display. In Faiman and Nievergelt (eds) Pertinent Concepts in Computer Graphics, University of Illinois Press (1969) 261-281.

[SPRO82] SPROULL, R.F. Using program transformations to derive line-drawing algorithms. ACM Trans. on Graphics 1, 4 (Dec 1982) 259-273.

[SPRO83]* SPROULL, R.F., SUTHERLAND, I.E., THOMPSON, A., GUPTA, S. AND MINTER, C. The 8x8 display. ACM Trans. on Graphics 2, 1 (Jan 1983) 32-56.

[STYN85] STYNE, B.A., KING, T.R. AND WISEMAN, N. Pad structures for the Rainbow workstation. Computer Journal 28, 1 (Feb 1985) 68-72.

[SUTH74] SUTHERLAND, I.E., SPROULL, R.F. AND SCHUMACHER, R.A. A characterisation of ten hidden-surface algorithms. Computing Surveys 6, 1 (March 1974) 1-55.

[THOM83] THOMAS, A.L. Geometric modelling and display primitives: towards specialised hardware. Computer Graphics 17, 3 (July 1983) 299-310.

[THOM84] THOMAS, A.L. Synthetic image generation. University Computing 6, 3 (Winter 1984) 148-160.

[WEGH84] WEGHORST, H., HOOPER, G. AND GREENBERG, D.P. Improved computational methods for ray tracing. ACM Trans. on Graphics 3, 1 (Jan 1984) 52-69.

[WHEL82]* WHELAN, D.S. A rectangular area filling display system architecture. Computer Graphics 16, 3 (July 1982) 147-153.

[WHIT81]* WHITTED, T. Hardware enhanced 3D raster display system. Proc. 7th Canadian Man-Machine Communications Conf. (June 1981) 349-354.

[WILK84] WILKES, A.J., SINGER, D.W., GIBBONS, J., KING, T.R., ROBINSON, P. AND WISEMAN, N.E. The Rainbow workstation. Computer Journal 27, 2 (May 1984) 112-120.

[WILL77] WILLIS, P.J. A real time hidden surface technique. Computer Journal 20, 4 (1977) 335-339.

[WILL78] WILLIS, P.J. Proximity techniques for hidden surface removal. IEEE J. Computers and Digital Techniques 1 (1978) 171-178.

Section 7

Computational Geometry and CAD

COMPUTATIONAL GEOMETRY IN PRACTICE

A. R. Forrest
University of East Anglia
Computational Geometry Project
School of Information Systems
Norwich, NR4 7TJ, U. K.

Abstract

At a practical level, there are many important issues in computational geometry which are seldom discussed in the literature. In this paper we illustrate some of these by concentrating on a fundamental operation in geometric computing – the intersection of lines – drawing the reader's attention both to geometric and computational aspects. Geometric special cases and the importance of numerical accuracy, correctness and consistency are emphasised.

1. Introduction

The term *computational geometry* means different things to different groups of computer scientists. Historically, the term was coined independently by at least three different groups: the first mention is as the sub-title of the book *Perceptrons* by Minsky and Papert *[MiPa69]*. Unfortunately, as far as I can determine, computational geometry is mentioned nowhere else in that book so we must guess as to what the authors meant. The next definition is my own, stemming from work in the Computer-Aided Design Group in Cambridge in the late 1960's when I felt that the classical constructions and theorems of geometry had little relevance to "the computer based representation, analysis, synthesis (design) and computer-controlled manufacture of two- and three-dimensional shapes" *[For71]*. At

NATO ASI Series, Vol. F17
Fundamental Algorithms for Computer Graphics
Edited by R. A. Earnshaw
© Springer-Verlag Berlin Heidelberg 1985

that stage I was personally concerned rather more with problems of curve and surface design than with other forms of geometry and to some extent my definition has been taken to apply only to curves and surfaces. This was not my intention as I meant it to apply to geometry in general. This definition has become widespread in the computer graphics and computer-aided geometric design fields and indeed the term computational geometry appears under the graphics heading in ACM Computing Reviews categories.

Historically the third use of the term is due to Dobkin and Shamos [Sha74] working initially in the early seventies at Yale University. They were concerned largely with the design and analysis of algorithms, including complexity theory, and that branch of computational geometry has since blossomed enormously, providing an exceedingly fruitful arena for the more theoretical computer scientists. Lee and Preparata's recent survey paper [LePr84] is a witness to this growth. Geometry proves an appropriate area for study in the design and analysis of algorithms providing many interesting problems to be solved. Work in this area is concentrated largely on two-dimensional geometry with an emphasis on linear problems, that is to say points, lines and polygons. Whilst there has been the odd excursion into three dimensions, it is clear that many of the useful results from two dimensions do not readily extend to three, a phenomenon well known to geometric modellers. Perhaps due to the early emphasis on complexity, many of the problems tackled have been problems involving fairly large numbers of geometric items. For example, we might be interested in the problem of triangulating a set of points in the plane, where efficiency is particularly valuable for large point sets. The outcome of this work has been the development of sophisticated algorithms, based often on powerful data structures, and the understanding of several general strategies for tackling geometric problems including for example divide and conquer, and the plane sweep method. It is a fair comment on this aspect of computational geometry that many of the algorithms are paper algorithms and have not been seriously implemented for practical purposes. Indeed some of the algorithms have proved exceedingly difficulty to implement at all. Furthermore, for the sake of facility of argument and proof, certain simplifying assumptions are commonly made and these assumptions would be invalid in practical cases. As an example, an algorithm dealing with sets of line segments might impose the restriction that none of the line segments be vertical. Implicitly, in the design of geometric algorithms, not only is a particular machine architecture often assumed, but also the ability accurately and correctly to carry out certain basic geometric operations is taken for granted. This we shall see is a rather dangerous assumption.

In the field of computer-aided geometric design, and in particular in geometric modelling, that is to say the modelling of three-dimensional solid objects, considerable advances have been made both in theory of representation of solids, and in practical implementations of systems to design them. In this context, one thinks particularly of the pioneering work in boundary representation modellers by Baumgart and Braid [Bau75, Bra79], with the use of Euler operations and sophisticated face-edge-vertex data structures. One also points to the development of constructive solid geometry (CSG) by Voelcker and his co-workers [VoRe77, ReTi78] at Rochester and elsewhere, based on regular set theory. Geometric modellers are in everyday practical use but despite this apparent success, there remain many problems. Geometric modellers which can tackle realistic problems are large, often slow, and prone to occasional errors. They might not be based on the theoretically efficient algorithms developed by theoretical computer scientists, taking, as they do, a pragmatic approach to implementation, and they are certainly by no means as robust as their developers might claim (unless tackled in an unguarded moment).

In this paper we consider some of the practical problems of computational geometry from two particular points of view: that of resolving purely geometric problems and that of resolving numerical problems. If we wish to construct a geometric computing environment in which the development of geometric algorithms can be facilitated, then we should ask ourselves what are the fundamental operations of computational geometry, and how might these operators themselves be implemented correctly and accurately? Given that the fundamental operations are correctly implemented, we stand a reasonable chance of building robust geometric systems. We would scarcely contemplate the implementation of algorithms on computers whose basic constructions were not theoretically and practically correct, and it is surprising that both the theoretical computational geometers and the practical computational geometers appear willing to implement systems based on rather shaky foundations.

2. A Typical Geometric Algorithm: Point-in-Polygon Testing

One of the most common basic operations in geometric algorithms is the intersection of lines. We shall illustrate the problems arising from this basic operation by considering its use in a typical geometric algorithm and whilst we will highlight both the geometrical and the numerical problems, we will not attempt to offer complete solutions. The problem we select is to detect whether or not a given test point lies within a given closed polygon (*Point-in-Polygon Testing*) and the algorithm we shall use is sometimes called the *Parity Algorithm*. Briefly stated, the algorithm is as follows:

(1) From the test point construct a ray (a semi-infinite line). The ray may be in any direction; for sake of argument we shall make it extend horizontally to the right.

(2) Count the number of intersections between the ray and the sides of the polygon. If that number is odd, the test point lies within the polygon, and if that number is even the test point lies outside.

This is one of the oldest algorithms for point in polygon testing, and it is by no means the best for that purpose. Here it serves to illustrate the thesis that the basic operations of computational geometry are insufficiently investigated.

The basic operation in this case is seen to be testing whether a semi-infinite line, a ray, intersects a finite segment of a line, that is to say a line segment. We thus need to be rather more precise in our use of the phrase *line intersection*. Clearly, there is a difference between the intersection of infinite lines and the intersection of line segments since although lines may intersect, the point of intersection might not lie within line segments embedded in those lines. A further point to note is that in order to compute the point in polygon test, we need to establish whether or not the ray intersects a side but we do not need to know in detail the exact location of that intersection point. A general principal in computational geometry, first elucidated by Chazelle and Dobkin *[ChDo80]*, is that detection is easier than computation. That is to say it is easier to detect whether or not lines intersect than it is to evaluate that intersection. One is reminded of the predilection of mathematicians for existence proofs rather than concrete solutions! In other branches of computational geometry and computer graphics it is conventional to perform simple detection tests first to determine whether or not to proceed further. Examples can be found in Warnock's hidden surface removal algorithm [War68] and many other such algorithms. Unfortunately it seems the case in many geometric problems that the detection phase and the evaluation phase involve little in the way of common code. It would be convenient if it were possible to make an early exit from a segment of code for evaluation if nothing of interest were detected but it appears that in practice we have to implement detection and evaluation separately. We proceed now to study the point in polygon problem in more detail.

3. Geometric Problems

Tilove has written on the problem of line-polygon classification [Til81], which is essentially our point-in-polygon problem in disguise, and has identified the geometric problems found therein. We shall repeat that exercise, from a slightly different standpoint, since the results are not as widely known as they should be and a different emphasis is needed. As well as studying the basic operation of ray-line segment intersection, Tilove goes on to discuss the complexity of various implementations of the point-in-polygon algorithm. We shall not be concerned here with complexity issues.

The parity algorithm appears on the surface to be simplicity itself. Certain clearly identified cases pose no problems, for example see Figures 1a and 1b where the test point is respectively outside and inside the test polygon. The most

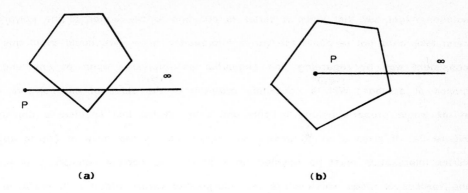

(a)   **(b)**

Figure 1: Point-in-Polygon Testing – Simple Cases

obvious special case is the case where the ray passes through a vertex of the polygon, Figures 2a and 2b. How do we count this intersection? Our first stab at a

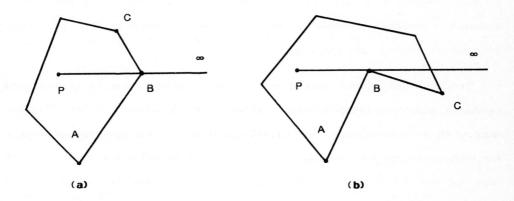

(a)   **(b)**

Figure 2: Point-in-Polygon Testing – Ray Interpolates Vertex

solution might say that since a vertex is common to two edges of the polygon we must take care not to count the vertex intersection twice. We could avoid this in a consistent way by regarding line segments as intervals, open at one end and closed at another. With a consistent ordering of the sides of the polygon, each vertex would properly belong to only one side. Whilst this solution is correct for Figure 2a, it gives a wrong answer for Figure 2b. In the case of Figure 2b, the vertex intersection must be counted as 2 or 0. The correct solution is to look at the vertices of sides which share the interpolated vertex and if both these vertices (A and C in Figures 2a and 2b) lie on the same side of the ray then we count the intersection with vertex B as 2 and if they lie on the opposite side as in Figure 2a we count the intersection as 1. In order to overcome this geometric problem we must adopt one of two strategies: either we ensure that vertex interpolation is impossible by some readjustment of the problem (this seems to the author a crude solution unworthy of a good computer scientist) or we require the ray-segment intersection detection primitive to return not two possible results, but three: intersecting, missing, and touching.

This particular special case is documented in several texts on graphics and geometric algorithms [NeSp79, FovD82, Sed83]. There is however a further special case which we must consider. In Figures 3a and 3b, the ray coincides with one of the sides of the polygon. How do we count *this* intersection? A first crude approach says that this is not really an intersection since the ray and the line segment do not intersect in a point. We would therefore count such intersections as 0, giving the wrong answer for Figure 3a and fortuitously the correct answer for Figure 3b.

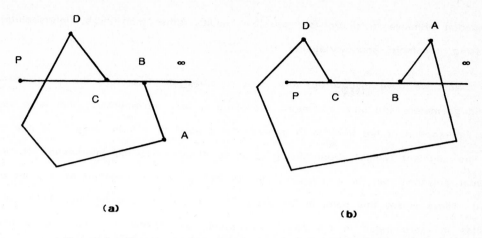

(a)   **(b)**

Figure 3: Point in Polygon Testing – Ray Coincides with Side

Our second approach says that we ought to consider the intersection as being equivalent to intersection of the ray with both end points of the line segment the side in question. Applying the solution we adopted for vertex intersection above, we are now left with a problem of deciding on which side of the ray the second interpolated vertex lies in each of the vertex intersection tests. Whatever we do should be consistent and there appears to be no correct way of carrying out this procedure. If, however, we treat intersection of the ray with the side as being the intersection of a single pseudo–vertex, then the rules we derived for vertex interpolation can be applied and we get the correct results since, in Figure 3a, the sides before and after the interpolated side lie on opposite sides of the ray and the segment ray intersection counts as one in this case, and in Figure 3b, as the sides before and after the interpolated side lie on the same side of the ray, this intersection therefore counts as two. Clearly in order to be able to carry out this particular part of the algorithm, we must require our ray–segment intersection detection primitive to return *four* possible results rather than three: intersecting, missing, touching, and overlapping.

What we have discovered here is a problem well known to the constructive solid geometers and other geometric modelling system implementers: that is to say the intersection of two lines is in general not a point or null but may be a line or a line segment [TiI80]. Generalising to three dimensions, the intersection of two planar polygons can be a polygon itself as well as a line segment or a point or null. Tilove makes this point in his paper on line polygon classification [TiI81] and writes in more detail in his paper on regular set theory. In implementing line intersection primitives in general, we see that the intersection of two infinite lines may return three possible results: the lines meet at a finite point, the lines are parallel and meet therefore at a point at infinity, and the lines are coincident. Using homogeneous co-ordinates [Max46], we can of course treat parallel and intersecting lines in a similar fashion, but coincident lines require rather separate treatment. Rays, semi-infinite lines, may intersect at a finite point or a point at infinity, they may miss, they may touch, and they may overlap either as rays or line segments. Segments may intersect at a finite point, touch, overlap, or miss. In view of the apparent complexity, it is a moot point whether we would implement a single line-ray-segment intersection primitive or specialise and provide more efficient primitives for line-line intersection, segment-segment intersection, ray-segment intersection, etc..

In implementing a geometric algorithm such as point in polygon detection, we must decide whether points on the boundary of the polygon are to be taken as lying inside the polygon or outside. Conventionally we might regard points on the boundary of the polygon as lying inside the polygon. However, in some circumstances we might well wish to know whether the point lies inside, on the boundary, or outside. Braid in his BUILD-2 geometric modelling system [Bra79] provided three-valued logic operations for identifying inside, outside and on boundaries. We have seen that in order to implement the point in polygon algorithm using ray-segment intersection as a primitive (not necessarily the best way to perform this operation), the ray-segment intersection detection primitive must return four possible cases so in this sense four-valued logic might be required.

Note that if the test point itself coincides with a vertex or lies on a side of the test polygon, we must take care to count the resulting ray-segment intersection correctly. If we are to include points on the polygon boundary as inside, then coincidence of the test point with a point on the boundary must count as 1, no matter what the configuration of the adjacent vertices. I.e. we must identify the case where the segment touches the ray at the start point of the ray, and distinguish this from the case where the segment touches the ray elsewhere.

It might seem pedantic to place stress on the special cases, but they do cause difficulties in implementing algorithms. Some authors advocate the simple expedient of shifting the polygon slightly in order to avoid vertex interpolation or co-incidence with sides [BuKo84]. This is at best an inelegant fudge, and at worst a dangerous procedure, since there is no guarantee that shifting the polygon a small amount will not cause similar problems with other portions of the polygon. In general there is no guarantee that special cases can be avoided and the best way forward is to ensure that the intersection detection primitive is implemented in a careful and accurate manner.

4. Numerical Problems

Computation of the point of intersection between two lines can be regarded as simply a matter of solving two linear equations [BoWo83]. It is well known from numerical analysis that the most accurate results will be obtained if the two lines are perpendicular and that there will be severe numerical problems when the lines are almost parallel. Transforming the geometry of the situation to provide better conditioned equations for solution is not necessarily the answer since the transformations may themselves be a source of considerable error. Careful choice of the line equations, including normalising their coefficients, and close attention to the order of evaluation of arithmetic operations can reduce the numerical problems. Discussion of suggested solutions is beyond the scope of this paper.

Line segment intersection detection is generally performed by evaluating the

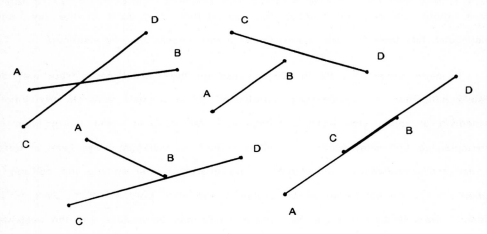

Figure 4: Line Segment Intersection Detection

following test. Line segments A→B and C→D, Figure 4, *intersect* if points **A** and **B** lie on opposite sides of the line C→D and points C and D lie on opposite sides of the line A→B. Note that this test fails if the segments overlap *[Sed83]*! Implementation of this test involves the use of yet another geometric primitive: the detection of on which side of a directed line a point lies. Adopting a suitable sign convention, we simply substitute the co-ordinates of the test point into the equation of the line with the convention that if the result evaluates to 0 the point lies on the line and say if it evaluates to negative the point lies to the left and positive to the right. Again, careful attention to the computation of both the coefficients of the line and the order and method of evaluation of side detection is needed to improve accuracy. Note that this operation is equivalent to evaluation of the signed area of the triangle formed by two points on the test line and the test point.

In contrast to detection of the intersection of line *segments*, intersection of *lines* may be detected by examining the line equations. Assuming those equations are normalised, then intersection is readily detected by inspection of the equation coefficients. *Line segment* intersection detection involving the side-of-line primitive, has little in common with the actual evaluation of the intersection point if one is detected. However, it would be possible to use the line segment intersection detection test in an iterative manner, much as Sproull's clipping divide *[SpSu68]*, to evaluate the intersection point. In general this would involve more arithmetic than direct solution of the line equations, but close inspection of the arithmetic operations in question might reveal that this approach was numerically more stable in awkward cases.

Whilst there are obvious numerical problems due to rounding and truncation, there are other more subtle numerical problems. For example, we might find that segment A→B intersects segment C→D, but if we reverse the direction of the segments, segment B→A does not intersect segment D→C. That is to say, the order of evaluation may determine the results. Similarly in view of the lack of common code between detection and evaluation operations, we might well find that a detection operation indicates that an intersection occurs but evaluation yields a point which is not a legal intersection point for, say, line segments. Worse, our detection algorithm might indicate no intersections and consequently we would not attempt to evaluate an intersection point although evaluation in this case might yield a legal intersection point! It is for this reason that many geometric modelling systems are inconsistent and in practice systems are known to blow up under certain circumstances whereas, if the geometric operations are performed in a different order, they may well succeed. In many cases this is regarded by both the users and the implementers as irritating and inexplicable. The solution lies in careful attention to numerical detail and in attempting to implement systems in which geometric operations are performed in a consistent order.

The root cause of many of the numerical problems in geometry is that geometric entities constructed from representable geometric objects such as line segments may not themselves be representable. It is perfectly possible, for example, that the intersection between two line segments whose end points are defined as lying on an integer grid simply cannot be represented in the floating point number system. In this case what we have to decide is how consistently to round or truncate to a unique floating point number. It might be thought that the case of intersection of line segments whose end points were defined as integers would be numerically simple. This is not the case, as Ramshaw [Ram82] discovered, and the solution to the problem in his case was to adopt carefully tuned double and single precision floating point arithmetic. This is an object lesson to us all: constructing geometric objects defined on a grid of points requiring ten bits for representation can lead to double precision floating point arithmetic!

As mentioned before, it is beyond the scope of this paper to offer solutions. Careful tuning of floating point arithmetic is obviously essential but is very much machine dependent. One hope for the future is the adoption of standardised floating point arithmetic in which case tested solutions might be applicable to a wider range of systems. Several other approaches have been suggested. Geisow, for example, has used algebraic manipulation for a great deal of the preliminary work in curve intersection [Gei83], and similarly algebraic manipulation is used extensively in the Alpha-1 system developed by Riesenfeld et al. [Rie83]. Performing as many of the operations as possible symbolically has clear advantages. A second approach suggested by Mudur and Koparkar [MuKo84] is to use interval arithmetic and this appears to be promising. A third approach often suggested is the use of rational arithmetic. Here it is possible to maintain precision in a controlled manner but we must realise that in generalising to other geometric operations, we again encounter perfectly legitimate geometric configurations which generate points, for example, which do not have a rational representation. Thus rational arithmetic can give *exact* results for lines and polygons defined on integer grids, but can only give *approximate* answers where circular arcs are involved.

5. Conclusions

Simply by examining an apparently trivial operation which must have been implemented thousands of times in practice, we have shown that such operations are by no means trivial. It is doubtful indeed whether any completely sucessful implementations exist or indeed can ever exist. We tend to take for granted in many algorithms the ability to implement these primitives successfully and we must realise that we do so at our peril. Implementation requires careful attention to the various geometric cases which must be correctly identified, and to all the arithmetic operations involved. The precision to which these operations must be carried out is considerably higher than many realise.

6. Acknowledgements

This work was funded in part by the U.K. Science and Engineering Research Council. Some of the work was carried out whilst the author was a Visiting Scientist in the Imaging Science Laboratory of the Xerox Palo Alto Research Center, where the author benefitted from discussions with Bob Sproull, John Warnock, Frank Crow, Leo Guibas and Lyle Ramshaw.

7. References

[Bau75]   B. G. Baumgart
    A Polyhedron Representation for Computer Vision. Proceedings of the ACM
    National Conference, 1975.
[BoWo83]   A. Bowyer and J. Woodwark
    A Programmer's Geometry. Butterworth, 1983.

[Bra79]   I. C. Braid
Notes on a Geometric Modeller. Cambridge University CAD Group Document 101, June 1979.

[BuKo84]   F. W. Burton, V. J. Kollias and J. G. Kollias
Consistency in Point-in-Polygon Tests. Computer Journal, Volume 27, Number 4, November 1984, pages 375-376.

[ChDo80]   B. Chazelle and D. Dobkin
Detection is Easier than Computation. Proc. 12th ACM STOC, Los Angeles, Cal., April 1980.

[For71]   A. R. Forrest
Computational Geometry. Proceedings of the Royal Society of London, A, Volume 321, 1971.

[FovD82]   J. D. Foley and A. van Dam
Fundamentals of Interactive Computer Graphics. Addison-Wesley, 1982.

[Gei83]   A. D. Gelsow
Surface Interrogations. Ph. D. Thesis, Computational Geometry Project, University of East Anglia, 1983.

[GuSt82]   L. J. Guibas and J. Stolfi
Computational Geometry. Stanford University, Lecture Notes for CS445, 1982.

[Hac62]   R. Hacker
Certification of Algorithm 112: Position of a point relative to a polygon. Comm. ACM, Volume 5, page 606, 1962.

[Har83]   S. Harrington
Computer Graphics: A Programming Approach. McGraw-Hill, 1983.

[LePr84]   D. T. Lee and F. P. Preparata
Computational Geometry – A Survey. IEEE Transactions on Computers, Volume C-33, Number 12, December 1984.

[Max46]   E. A. Maxwell
The Methods of Plane Projective Geometry based on the use of General Homogeneous Coordinates. Cambridge University Press, 1946.

[MiPa69]   M. Minsky and S. Papert
Perceptrons: An Introduction to Computational Geometry. M. I. T. Press, 1969.

[MuKo84]   S. P. Mudur and P. A. Koparkar
Interval Methods for Processing Geometric Objects. IEEE Computer Graphics and Applications, Volume 4, Number 2, February 1984.

[NeSp79]   W. M. Newman and R. F. Sproull
Principles of Interactive Computer Graphics. McGraw-Hill, 1979.

[Pav82]   T. J. Pavlidis
Algorithms for Graphics and Image Processing. Springer Verlag, 1982.

[Ram82]   L. H. Ramshaw
The Braiding of Floating Point Lines. CSL Notebook Entry, Xerox Palo Alto Research Center, October 14, 1982.

[ReTi78]   A. A. G. Requicha and R. B. Tilove
Mathematical Foundations of Constructive Solid Geometry: General Topology of Closed Regular Sets. Production Automation Project, University of Rochester, Report TM-27, March 1978.

[Rie83]   R. F. Riesenfeld
A View of Spline-Based Modeling. Proceedings of Autofact 5, American Society of Mechanical Engineers, 1983.

[Sed83]   R. Sedgewick
    Algorithms. Addison-Wesley, 1983.
[Sha74]   M. I. Shamos
    Problems in Computational Geometry. Notes, Yale University, June 1974.
[Shi62]   M. Shimrat
    Algorithm 112: Position of point relative to a polygon. Comm. ACM, Volume
    5, page 434, 1962.
[SpSu68]   R. F. Sproull and I. E. Sutherland
    A Clipping Divider. AFIPS Proceedings of the Fall Joint Computer Conference,
    November 1968.
[Til80]   R. B. Tilove
    Set membership Classification: A Unified Approach to Geometric Intersection
    Problems. IEEE Transactions on Computers, Volume C-29, Number 10,
    October 1980.
[Til81]   R. B. Tilove
    Line/Polygon Classification: A Study of the Complexity of Geometric
    Computation. IEEE Computer Graphics and Applications, Volume 1, Number 2,
    April 1981.
[VoRe77]   H. B. Voelcker and A. A. G. Requicha
    Geometric Modelling of Mechanical Parts and Processes. IEEE Computer,
    December 1977.
[War68]   J. E. Warnock
    A Hidden Line Algorithm for Halftone Picture Representation. University of
    Utah, Computer Science, Technical Report TR4-5, May 1968.

An algorithm for direct display of CSG objects by spatial subdivision

David T Morris

Departments of Computer Studies and Mechanical Engineering,
University of Leeds, England

Peter Quarendon

IBM United Kingdom Scientific Centre
Southgate St, Winchester Hants SO23,9DR.

1. INTRODUCTION

This paper describes an algorithm for displaying shaded images of Constructive Solid Geometry (CSG) objects. The algorithm was originally proposed by Woodwark [1] for planar surfaces and has been substantially extended in a Pascal implementation, WINSOM, by Peter Quarendon at the IBM UK Scientific Centre. [2] It uses an Octree subdivision technique to produce shaded images quickly and directly from CSG trees of quadric surfaces without the need for faceting or boundary evaluation. Boundary evaluation is an $O(N^4)$ algorithm where N is the number of primitive surfaces, and is a major bottleneck in the display of highly complex CSG solids. The runtime of the algorithm is dependent on the screen resolution and is approximately linear in the number of primitive objects to be displayed. This has made it practicable to display CSG objects containing tens of thousands of primitives which would take days to display by boundary evaluation.

Some other advantages include its inherent parallelism, which makes it suitable for implementation in VLSI hardware[3] ,and the range of geometric primitives it can support. A sophisticated lighting model is used to provide coloured, shaded images with surface highlights from multiple light sources. Surface texture and perspective effects are also supported.

2. An Introduction to Constructive Solid Geometry

An introduction to CSG and its advantages and disadvantages can be found in Requicha [4] but the fundamentals will be briefly described here.

NATO ASI Series, Vol. F17
Fundamental Algorithms for Computer Graphics
Edited by R. A. Earnshaw
© Springer-Verlag Berlin Heidelberg 1985

Constructive Solid Geometry (CSG) is a way of describing solid objects as combinations of *Primitive* solid objects such as cylinders and cones. Three *Solid Operators* are used to build up complex solids from the primitives, and combinations of primitives.

The *UNION* operator takes two CSG objects and adds the volume of the two together to form a new object. Therefore anything that is inside either object is inside the new object

The *DIFFERENCE* operator subtracts the volume of one object from another. The new object consists of anything inside the first object that is not inside the second.

The *INTERSECTION* operator gives the common volume of two solids : ie the resultant object consists of anything that is inside both objects.

A solid object can be described as a binary tree whose nodes are CSG operators and whose leaf nodes are the primitives. This is a *CSG Tree*. Figure 1 shows the CSG tree for an angle bracket.

The bracket is first constructed from two primitive blocks using the Union operator to give the tree $(A+B)$. A hole is then made in the bracket by subtracting the cylinder C from it to obtain the tree

$$(A+B)-C$$

For convenience the user builds solid objects using *bounded primitives* such as blocks and cylinders. In practice each bounded primitive is decomposed

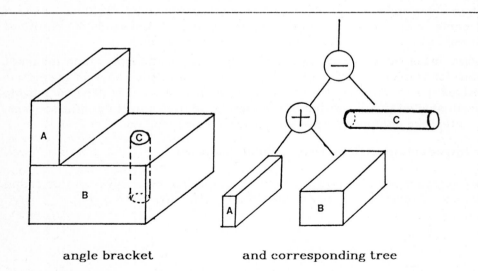

angle bracket   and corresponding tree

Figure 1 - An example of constructive solid geometry

into the CSG intersection of a set of unbounded *primitive halfspaces*. A halfspace is a surface that divides space into two disjoint parts, one part *inside* the halfspace and the other *outside*. A bounded cylinder such as C on the diagram is created from two infinite planar halfspaces and a cylindrical halfspace. The cylinder C is then the volume inside both the cylindrical halfspace and the two halfspaces defining its ends.

3. Coordinate Systems

A variety of coordinate systems are used when defining and drawing a CSG object. The first is the *Primitive Coordinate System* (PCS) in which individual primitives are conveniently defined. For instance a Cylinder may be defined in a PCS where its axis coincides with the Y-axis, its radius is one, and one end is at the origin. This basic cylinder is then transformed to obtain a cylinder of a given radius, origin or axis direction in the *Object space*, which is the space in which the entire CSG tree is defined.

A *Viewing Transformation* is then applied to the CSG tree to map it into *Normalised Device Coordinates* (NDC) which are bounded by a unit cube. When the object is drawn the screen is assumed to be coincidental with the front of the NDC cube and the viewing direction is perpendicular to the to the front of the cube looking inwards. Therefore the viewing transform must scale the CSG tree to the correct size relative to the NDC, translate it so it is in the correct place in the image, and rotate it to produce the correct viewing angle.

At the end of this process the CSG tree is a binary tree whose leaf nodes are primitive halfspaces described in NDC coordinates ready for shading.

4. Image Space, Octrees and Quadtrees

Images are drawn on a square display screen of size P pixels which lies on the front of a cube of size P : the *image space* . Before drawing , the CSG object must be transformed from the NOS space (a cube of size 1) into image space by scaling it by a factor of P known as the *screen resolution*. This is usually chosen to be a power of two, for reasons that will become apparent. The number N where $P=2^N$ is known as the *Image Depth*. A common choice for P is 512 pixels which gives a 512 * 512 image and a image depth of 9. Image space can be recursively subdivided into a set of smaller subcubes known as *Voxels* (Volume Pixels) as shown in Figure 2 .

This is known as an *octree* subdivision of space, which splits space into a tree of voxels of depth N with eight way branching at each node. At the lowest level of the octree is a 1×1×1 voxel which is the same size as a pixel on the screen.

The front face of the Octree, the display screen, is the two dimensional analogue of the Octree known as a *Quadtree*. Each square region of the quadtree is known as a *Quad* and is recursively divided into four smaller quads of equal size, orthogonal to the axes.

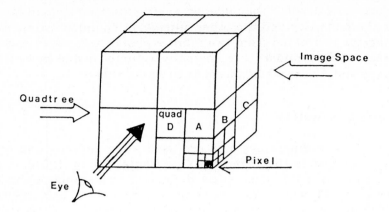

Figure 2 - The image space showing the quadtree and voxels.

Each Quad is the projection of the front face of the a set of voxels. In Figure 2 Quad A is the front face of Quads B and C.

5. The Drawing Algorithm

To produce a shaded image it is necessary to find which of the surfaces in CSG object is nearest to the front of the screen at each pixel. An important feature of the algorithm is that it exploits *locality* i.e a small area of the screen will contain a small part of the tree. This is exploited by a process known as *tree simplification* against voxels, which prunes the CSG tree to those parts of the object which lie entirely inside, or partially inside a voxel. Any parts of the tree entirely outside the voxel are discarded. It is therefore a form of clipping in three dimensions and is described in detail in a later section. A divide and conquer approach is used to draw the CSG object. Initially the algorithm has the CSG tree in image space coordinates and constructs the image space voxel of size 2^N. The tree is then *simplified* against this voxel and the pruned tree inspected. Three cases are possible:

(1) The simplified tree is completely empty : the voxel contains no objects so nothing is done.

(2) The simplified tree contains one primitive and can be is drawn using standard shading techniques described later.

(3) The simplified tree consists of two or more primitives and cannot be immediately drawn.

In the last case the voxel is divided into eight subvoxels and the above algorithm is applied to each voxel. Thus the algorithm recursively subdivides image space into successively smaller voxels until either there are no primitives, one primitive to be shaded, or the voxels have reached a limiting size. The effective limiting size of a voxel is the size of one pixel on the screen. Once that size has been reached subdivision would be pointless as the smallest voxels would be smaller than the smallest displayable area on the screen. If anti-aliasing is to be done then it may be necessary to subdivide beyond the size of one pixel to produce an average colour for the pixel, but for most images the expense is not justified. When subdivision cannot be used a different algorithm must be used to determine the topmost surface at the pixel.

A simple and effective technique is to choose a primitive in the CSG tree inside the pixel and assume it is the topmost surface. This works well in practice, as long as the same surface is chosen consistently in adjacent pixels so that there are no sudden discontinuities in shading. A more sophisticated technique is to use a ray-casting algorithm as described by Roth [5] to project a ray through the pixel centre into the image space to determine which surface it intersects first. Although Ray-casting is an expensive and slow technique for general CSG trees it is not particularly expensive here because the pruned trees contain only a few primitives. In practice the CSG tree that intersects a pixel sized area on the screen is rarely larger than three primitives, so raycasting is inexpensive.

Ray-Casting is only used on a small proportion of the screen area, most usually on the intersection of two primitive surfaces. The rest of the pixels are shaded in the standard manner.

6. Hidden Surface elimination

In any drawing algorithm it is necessary to draw only those surfaces that are visible,and to eliminate any objects that are hidden. A major advantage of the algorithm is that hidden surface elimination is done very cheaply, without the sorting that is required in standard polygonal hidden surface algorithms.[6] Hidden surface elimination in this algorithm is done by Octree subdividing the image space from the front to the back. As each voxel is subdivided into eight, the front four voxels are always processed first. The surfaces that are in the frontmost voxels will always be shaded onto the screen before any rearmost ones, and hide them from view. Before any voxel is considered, a check is made to see if the all the pixels on the front of the voxel have been filled in. If so, then the voxel is completely hidden from view and is discarded.

In order to implement the test efficiently, a Quadtree is used to test if a given voxel is hidden from view. Each Quad in the quadtree is a projection of the front faces of the set of voxels that lie directly behind it. As each pixel is written to the screen, the quad corresponding to that pixel is marked as being full. If all four adjacent quads are full then the Quad of size 2 by 2 at the next highest resolution is also full. In turn, this may make a Quad of size 4 by 4 full. This process will continue until a Quad is found with three or less of its sub-quads full. Therefore the test to see if a given voxel is hidden is therefore very simple, and is done by checking if the quad which lies in front of the voxel is marked as completely full.

7. The Tree simplification algorithm

The details of the tree simplification algorithm will now be discussed. It divides naturally into two parts.

(i) The *primitive/voxel classification* algorithm tests if *primitives* intersect with a given voxel in space and returns a result that states if the primitive entirely fills the voxel, partially intersects it, or does not intersect it at all.

(ii) The *tree/voxel simplification* algorithm uses the results of primitive/voxel classification and the rules of CSG in order to produce a simplified version of the tree containing only those subtrees that intersect the voxel. Each algorithm will now be described.

7.1. Primitive/voxel classification

This is the process by which primitive halfspaces are tested against a voxel to determine if they are inside, outside or partially inside a voxel. The results from the classifications are then used in the tree simplification algorithm.

This is the most computationally expensive part of Woodwarks Algorithm and care must be taken to implement it efficiently. The results of the algorithm are a 2 bit code giving the inside/outside classification which is independent of the kind of primitive. This property allows new primitives to be added without changing the tree-simplification algorithm. At present primitive/voxel classification algorithms have been implemented for planar half-spaces, cylinders, ellipsoids, toroids, spheres, cones and helices but others could easily be written.

In order to demonstrate how the classification is done, the cylinder against voxel test will be described in detail. It is expensive to test a cube against an arbitrary halfspace, so the the voxel is enclosed with a sphere touching all four corners, to give an approximation to its volume. Primitives are then classified against the sphere instead. The only effect that this will have on the classification results are that some primitives that are outside the voxel will be classified as partially inside the sphere. This somewhat decreases the efficiency of the tree-simplification but does not affect the results.

7.2. Cylinder/Voxel classification

Figure 3 shows how the Voxels and the primitive cylinder are defined. A cylinder is defined by a scalar radius r, a point on the centreline **o** and a direction vector **a** pointing along the axis of the infinite cylindrical halfspace. All of the coordinates are in image space.

The voxel is defined by its centre point in image coordinates **p** and half the length of its sides h. It is enclosed with a sphere whose origin is the

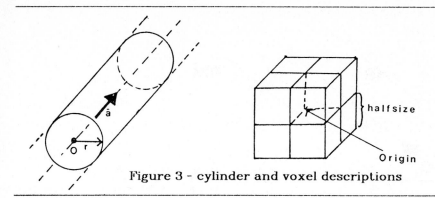

Figure 3 - cylinder and voxel descriptions

voxel origin and whose radius is

$$region\_radius = h * \sqrt{3}$$

The classification can be done as a simple test of the distance of the nearest part of the sphere to the nearest part of the cylinder. As the sphere is symmetric all geometry can be done in the plane of the axis and the line joining the origin of the spherical region and the cylinder axis, as is shown in Figure 4. The following points and distances are shown in Figure 4.

    a is a unit vector along the cylinder axis
    o is the cylinder origin
    r is the nearest point on the axis to the sphere origin
    i is the nearest point on the surface of the cylinder
           to the surface of the sphere
    d is the distance from **p** to **r**
    l is the distance from **o** to **r**
    e is the distance from **p** to **i** :the distance
           of the nearest point on the cylinder to the surface
           of the sphere.

Initially the distance d from the sphere centre to the cylinder axis is found. By the theorem of pythagoras in the triangle **opr**

$$d^2 = \left|(\mathbf{o}-\mathbf{p})\right|^2 - l^2$$

The distance *l* from **o** to **r** is

$$l = (\mathbf{o}-\mathbf{p})\,\mathbf{a}$$

After solving for *d* the distance *e* from the cylinder to the sphere is

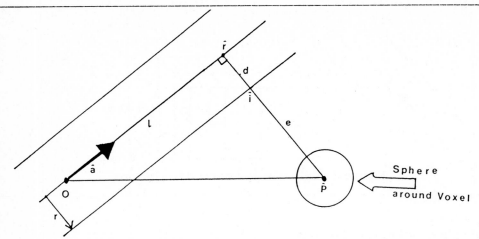

Figure 4 - Cylinder against voxel classification

$$e = d - r$$

The cylinder lies outside the sphere if

$$e > region\_radius$$

and intersects the sphere if

$$e \leq region\_radius$$

Similar techniques can be used to classify other kinds of primitive by finding the distance from the voxel centre to the nearest part of the primitive halfspace. For instance a sphere can be classified by finding the distance between the sphere and voxel centres and testing it against the sphere and voxel radii. In many cases it is possible to save time by comparing the squares of distances so that square roots are not required.

7.3. Tree/Voxel simplification

Once Primitive/Voxel classification as been completed the results are used to produce a *pruned tree* consisting of those parts of the tree that lie partially inside the voxel. The process is best illustrated by an example, shown in figure 5. The tree to be drawn is the bracket shape in figure 1. Initially the tree is the expression

$$O = (A + B) - C$$

which lies entirely inside the image space. The image space is then subdivided and the tree classified against Voxel X. The primitives are first classified against the voxel X and the results are then used at the leaf nodes of the CSG tree. If the primitive is Outside the voxel it is replaced by a special node called *empty* which marks that subtree as pruned. The results are then recursively combined at each node in the tree using the rules given in table 1, which state how to build the pruned tree. The results from each subtree are used to determine what the pruned version of the subtree will be. In figure 5.2, The Cylinder C has been classified as outside, and is therefore empty. A and B are partially inside, and are unchanged. At the node (A+B) the resultant pruned tree is therefore (A+B), unchanged. The node (A+B) - C is now (A+B) - empty. The Difference of a Partially full left tree and an empty tree is simply the left subtree,from the table so the tree (A+B) is the resultant pruned tree. The same technique may be used to prune this tree against the voxel Y.

8.   Shading Calculations

Once a voxel has been found that contains only one primitive halfspace, it is passed to the shading subsystem to be shaded. Initial input to the shading algorithm is a primitive definition and a description of the voxel and a description of the lights that are illuminating the surfaces. The output is a set of shaded pixels on the screen area , corresponding to the front face of the voxel.

The shading algorithm is split into two phases. In order to compute the intensity of light on the surface at each pixel, the *Surface Normal* must be computed ; the orientation of the surface with respect to the image space at that pixel.

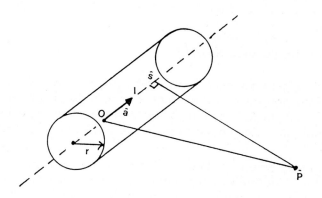

Figure 5 - tree against voxel simplification

The rules of CSG Classification			
	Left	Right	simplified tree
Union	Full	Full	Full
	Full	Partial	Full
	Full	Empty	Full
	Partial	Full	Full
	Partial	Partial	Left Union Right
	Partial	Empty	Left tree
	Empty	Full	Full
	Empty	Partial	Right tree
	Empty	Empty	Empty
	Left	Right	simplified tree
Difference	Full	Full	Empty
	Full	Partial	Right tree
	Full	Empty	Full
	Partial	Full	Empty
	Partial	Partial	Left Difference Right
	Partial	Empty	Left Tree
	Empty	Full	Empty
	Empty	Partial	Empty
	Empty	Empty	Empty
	Left	Right	simplified tree
Intersection	Full	Full	Full
	Full	Partial	Right tree
	Full	Empty	Empty
	Partial	Full	Left tree
	Partial	Partial	Left Intersect Right
	Partial	Empty	Empty
	Empty	Full	Empty
	Empty	Partial	Empty
	Empty	Empty	Empty

Table 1 - the rules of CSG classification-combine

This surface normal is then used to compute the intensity and shade of the pixel, using the standard surface information.

8.1. Computation of the Surface Normal

For simple surfaces such as spheres, a standard incremental scan-line algorithm may be used to compute the surface normals for each pixel in the voxel, providing very substantial optimisation due to area coherence. More complex surfaces such as helices need to have the normal computed at every pixel separately.

An example will be given of the surface normal computation for a cylinder. The cylinder is defined in the same way as for the primitive/voxel classification. As is shown in figure 6, the normal is computed by calculating the nearest point on the centreline of the cylinder to the voxel centre. The normal is then the line joining the points **s** and **p** The distance l along the axis of the cylinder is given by

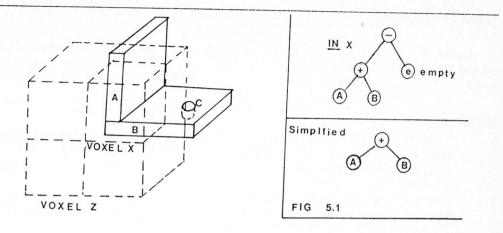

Figure 6 - surface normal computation

$$l = a \cdot (o - p)$$

as the Axis vector **a** is normalised. The coordinates of **s** are therefore

$$s = o + l a$$

and the normal is

$$n = p - s$$

which is the line joining **p** and **s**

This is then normalised for use in the lighting calculations.

9. Lighting Calculations

Once the surface normal has been calculated the pixel intensity and colour can be determined. Several pieces of information are stored with each primitive to determine its surface appearance. Each primitive has a basic colour and a glossiness which is used by the shading algorithm to compute intensities at any point on the surface. A texture may also be specified, which will modulate the surface intensity to provide patterns. Once the surface normal, colour and specularity are found for a given pixel the pixel intensity and colour can be computed using a standard specular reflection algorithm which will not be described here. The reader is referred to Blinn.[7] for details.

The last stage in the process is to write the pixel to the frame buffer for display.

Acknowledgements

David Morris would like to acknowledge the support of an SERC Case award in conjunction with the IBM UK Scientific Centre, under Dr Tom Heywood
–

References

1. WOODWARK J.R. , "The explicit quad tree as a structure for computer graphics", *Computer Journal* **25** (2) pp. 235-238. (February 1982.).

2. QUARENDON P, "Winsom Reference manual.", 176 IBM UK Science Centre Winchester. (1984).

3. DEW P.M , MORRIS D.T , DODSWORTH J. , "Systolic array architectures for High Performance CAD/CAM Workstations", *Proc. NATO Advanced Study Institute On Fundamentals Algorithms for Computer Graphics April 1985.*, (1985).

4. REQUICHA A.A.G. and VOELKER, H.B. , "Constructive Solid Geometry published as Technical Memorandum 25,", *Production Automation Project University of Rochester, Rochester, NY 14627.*, (1977).

5. ROTH S.D., "Ray casting for modelling solids ", *Computer Graphics and Image Processing* **18** pp. 109-144. (February 1982.).

6. SECHREST S. and GREENBERG, D. , "A Visible Polygon Reconstruction Algorithm ", *Computer Graphics* **15** (3) pp. 17-27. (August 1981.).

7. BLINN J.E, "Shading models for surfaces.", *ACM Computer Graphics and Image processing* **23**(1)(1980).

COMPUTATIONAL GEOMETRY AND PROLOG

Wm. Randolph Franklin
Electrical, Computer, and Systems Engineering Dept.
Rensselaer Polytechnic Institute
Troy, New York, USA, 12180.

Telephone: (518) 266-6077
Telex: 646542 RPI TRO
Arpanet: WRF%RPI-MTS.Mailnet@MIT-Multics

ABSTRACT

Prolog is a good tool for implementing computational geometry algorithms. This paper discusses its advantages and disadvantages, and gives examples, including linking chains together, boolean operations on polygons, and cartographic map overlay and reduction. An implementation of polygon intersection proves Prolog to be much more compact and easier to use than Fortran.

This material is based upon work supported by the National Science Foundation under grant no. ECS-8351942, the Rome Air Development Center, contract number, F30602-85-C-0008, subcontract 353-9023-7, and by the Data System Division of the International Business Machines Corp.

INTRODUCTION TO PROLOG

Prolog is a so-called fifth generation logic programming language based on Horn clauses. The standard Prolog reference is Clocksin and Mellish [8], accompanied by the exercises in Perreira [9]. Its chief characteristics are as follows.

a) Prolog is a declarative, rather that a procedural, language. Essentially, a formula that the solution must satisfy is stated, and the system generates possible solutions and tests them until a good one is found. Nevertheless, in real Prolog programs, there are some procedural steps, such as the assertion of facts, and I/O.

b) There are no assignments of values to variables, except the binding (unifying) of two formulae. If one formula is a free variable, and the other a known quantity, then the effect is similar to an assignment, except that the bound variable cannot have its value changed, except as described below.

c) Prolog proceeds by finding facts in its database that satisfy its current formula. If part of the formula fails, then the system backtracks, undoes bindings, and matches another fact.

d) There is only one data structure, the list, as in Lisp. The major control structure is the recursive procedure. This effects the same result as iteration in most other languages.

e) Prolog is often combined with other languages such as Lisp so that assignment, iteration, and other features can be used. Of course a Lisp assignment executed from Prolog does not get undone on backtracking. Another major limitation of Prolog is that it is not self-referential in the same sense as Lisp: it is difficult for a Prolog procedure to create another Prolog procedure.

Some other implications of automated deduction are given in Goos [17, 18]. Swinson [22, 23, 24] introduces the use of Prolog in architectural design.

The examples in this paper were implemented in Salford Prolog [21] on a Prime 750 computer in the Image Processing Lab at Rensselaer Polytechnic Institute.

COMPUTATIONAL GEOMETRY

Intuition verses implementation

Computational geometry is concerned with spatial relationships and geometric coincidences, such as which pairs of a set of objects intersect. There is frequently a wide gap between intuition and implementation. Consider for example performing boolean operations on two polygons, A and B.

When the intuitive algorithm given in the section Boolean Combinations of Polygons is implemented in Fortran by a typical graphics programmer, it will require 500 to 1000 lines of code, although it can be explained to another person in a few minutes. While this is true throughout computer science - people joke about the need for a DWIM (Do What I Mean) machine - nowhere is it more true than for geometry algorithms.

Algorithms which are difficult to understand, unlike the above, can be close to impossible to implement. An example is the recursive construction of a Voronoi diagram.

Special Cases

Special cases form another problem with graphics implementations. When all the special cases for the polygon combination problem are considered, the number of lines of code rises to 1000 to 2000. A simple example shows the problem. We wish to determine whether two finite line segments intersect. What do we do if the endpoint of one line lies on the other line? Note that in software engineering terms, this is a functional specification problem, not a design or implementation one. A failure to realize this is common and serious.

How this special case is handled does not matter much except that the line intersection routine will be incorporated into other routines, such as one to determine whether two chains of line segments intersect. The hope is that deciding the low level special case properly will mean that the high level algorithm will automatically work correctly. For example, we might define the half plane on one side of each line segment positive, and assume that an lying on a line lies on the positive side. Then if and vertex of one chain lies on an edge of another, then the chain intersection will automatically be correct.

However, the above fails if a vertex of one chain coincides with a vertex of another. It can be proved by exhaustion that that is no way to handle the special case of coincident vertices when two lines intersect so that two intersecting chains will be processed properly. The only solution is for the chain intersection algorithm to consider the line intersection special cases itself, at a considerable increase in complexity.

The above simple problem has been considered in some detail since it illustrates quite well the problem of special cases. Special cases in nontrivial problems are that much worse, and they occur in everywhere. The cases that occur in polygon combination include concident vertices, collinear edges, a vertex of A on an edge of B, and multiple components that may or may not intersect the other polygon.

SIMPLE PROLOG EXAMPLE - LINKING CHAINS

The thesis of this paper is the Prolog is an excellent tool for implementing computational geometry algorithms. Its power will be illustrated by a simple problem, that of linking isolated pieces of a into a chain. The data structure is a set of facts, one per chain piece:

chain(end1, end2, list)

'end1' and 'end2' are the names of the vertices at the two ends of the chain. 'list' is a list of all the vertices in the chain after end1, up to and including end2. This definition of list simplifies the algorithm. If the chain is only one edge, then list = [end2]. The complete Prolog program to combine chains segments into longer chains as long as this is possible is this:

```
join1 :-        /* Combine 2 chains
    chain(A,B,L1),
    chain(B,C,L2),
    retract(chain(A,B,L1)),
    retract(chain(B,C,L2)),
    append(L1,L2,L3),
    assert(chain(A,C,L3)).

joinall :- join1, fail.
joinall.

chain(a,b,[b]).                    /* Sample data
chain(c,d,[d]).
chain(b,c,[c]).
```

Join1 searches for two chains where the ending vertex of the vertex equals the starting vertex of the second. This search is built into Prolog. The lists of vertices for the chains are combined, then these two chains are deleted from the database, and the new chain added.

Joinall repeats join1 as long as join1 can find two chains to combine. After it is finished, the only remaining fact concerning chains is

chain(a,d,[b,c,d]).

This program, which is complete, compares quite favorably with, a Fortran program to accomplish the same goal. We will now consider in detail some of Prolog's advantages and disadvantages for computational geometry.

DETAILS OF PROLOG ADVANTAGES AND DISADVANTAGES

High Level Language

Prolog is a good high level language. It has dynamic data structures, lists, and the code and data can be interchanged.

Another HLL advantage is that Prolog is extensible: we can define new data structures and operators. This allows the creation of more powerful virtual machines. This can improve implementations of geometry algorithms that are bedeviled by numerical inaccuracies. For example, if a point is slightly inside a polygon, and you rotate the scene including the point and the polygon, then the point might now be outside. Also, although floating point numbers are a model for the real number system, almost none of the real field axioms are satisfied. There are computers, for example, where addition is not commutative. This lack of correspondence between what the user expects and what actually happens, is in SWE terms, a FAILURE. Using Prolog, a rational number package can be implemented with which to perform the arithmetic.

Pattern Matching

Much of geometry consists of processing patterns. If you split a line where another line intersects it, then you are pattern matching for the intersection of two lines. This matches the intuitive way people think about geometry.

In the chain linking example given above, we wish to search for the pattern which is two chains that can be linked, and then link them.

Unification

This is equivalent to strong connectivity in graph theory. This operation can be used in graphics to determine the connected components of a graph as follows.

a) Associate a different free variable with each vertex of the graph.

b) Process each edge of the graph by unifying the free variables corresponding to the vertices at the ends of the edge.

After all the edges have been processed, there remains exactly one free variable for each separate component of the graph. When the free variable corresponding to some vertex is bound to a value, such as that vertex's name, then all the variables corresponding to vertices in the same component are simultaneously bound. If this is repeated until there are no more free variables, then the graph components are determined.

Data Structures

Pure Prolog, at least, lacks the random addressing of local data. Thus the only efficient way to simulate an array is to implement balanced trees. This adds a log factor to the execution time.

Efficiency

There are two considerations here. First, a primitive operation in Prolog, such as A=B, can take an arbitrarily large time to execute, depending on the size of the two expressions being unified. This makes it more difficult to determine bounds for the execution time.

Second, defining algorithms declaratively, which Prolog executes with an exhaustive generate and test procedure, clearly hurts efficiency. Although it is simple to write a procedure that is satisfied for all intersections of two edges in the database, this will require time = O(N**2) where N = number of edges in the database.

There are two solutions to this, at least in the geometric case. The first is to impose a second data structure such as an adaptive grid. Franklin has implemented algorithms where this can be quite efficient for geometric intersection problems. [11] gives a hidden surface algorithm that when implemented on a Prime 500, a midicomputer, could determine the visible arcs of 10,000 random circles, packed ten deep, in 383 seconds. These techniques would transfer to Prolog. An even more robust data structure is a k-d tree invented by Bentley, [4]. However, these techniques are retreating somewhat from the declarative form of Prolog since they mean giving a detailed prodecure .

The more abstract answer is to notice that Prolog implementations can be good at using hashing to test for equality of the arguments of isolated facts. That is, given a database with facts of the form

person(height, weight).

they can return all facts matching

person(H, 200).

in constant time per fact returned. It is possible to imagine how searches such as

person(H1,W), person(H2,W)

might be performed in time proportional to the size of the data returned. However, what is really needed for geometry, and what no Prolog implementation can do is to execute the following search person(H,W), H > 5, H < 6, W < 200.

in time linear in the number of facts returned. This would require that k-d trees be used in the search mechanism.

Nevertheless, with Prolog, the user has the choice of the amount of efficiency desired. A purely declarative procedure will be easy to code, but slow to execute, while as procedural rules are added, the execution becomes faster. The user does not have this choice in many other languages.

Software Engineering Considerations

Prolog lacks certain nesting facilities that may make it difficult to properly modularize and structure large programs. The definition of a procedure is global; it is not restricted to the domain of another procedure. It is impossible to have separate domains or subdomains of facts apart from the global heap.

BOOLEAN COMBINATIONS OF POLYGONS

In this paper, our big example will be a polygon boolean combination algorithm, so a review of this problem is in order.

History

There have been many solutions to the polygon and polyhedron boolean combination problem, each with various advantages and disadvantages. Some of them are:

Eastman and Yessios [10] give a general algorithm for combining 2-D polygons. It works by finding all the intersections between the polygons' edges, and then "threading" or traversing around the pieces of edges to determine the resulting algorithm.

Maruyama [19] gives a procedure for determining whether two polyhedra intersect by comparing the faces pair by pair. However, he does not determine the intersection, only whether it is null.

Baer, Eastman, and Henrion [1] give a good summary of geometric modelling systems, which "shape operations" (i.e. intersection etc.) they perform, and how they do it.

Tilove [25] considers important questions of what intersection and so on mean in the abstract, and introduces "regularized set operators" to answer them. He also gives recursive methods of intersection and union of objects defined as as combinations from a small family of primitives. These methods are used in P.A.D.L., one of the best known geometric processors. P.A.D.L. also contains a non-CSG polyhedron combination algorithm that has been presented in short courses.

Boyse [5] gives an algorithm for determining whether two objects interfere, where one of the objects can be moving along a straight or circular trajectory. His objects are composed of vertices, straight edges, and flat faces, so for two objects to interfere it is necessary and sufficient for an edge of one object to pass through a face of the other object. This he tests for. However, this does not extend to producing the intersection.

If one of the objects is a convex polyhedron, then we can use the fact that it is the intersection of a number of semi-infinite half-spaces, one for each face, by intersecting them against the other polyhedron, one by one. This is easier if the other polyhedron is also convex. However, the only way that this method generalizes to non-convex objects is to partition them into convex pieces, which increases the complexity.

Baumgart [2, 3] has a good geometric manipulation system with polyhedron combination operators, using a different algorithm. Braid [6] has another polyhedron combination algorithm. Parent [20] describes another one.

Another independent similar algorithm is described in Turner [26]. Again, it does not include a means of handling complex objects. It has been implemented, but cannot handle two objects with a common face, or an edge of one lying in a face of the other.

A similar polyhedron boolean combination algorithm is a part of the design of the Kepler geometric manipulation system described in [12, 13]. An earlier algorithm for polygons was implemented in 1973. A similar planar graph overlay algorithm is described in [14].

Finally, Weiler [27] gives an excellent polygon comparison method that clips two polygons against each other. Its use of a graph data representation simplifies matters, and can compare concave polygons with holes.

Prolog Algorithm

A set theoretic definition of C = A intersect B is:

$$C = \{p \mid p \text{ in } A \ \& \ p \text{ in } B\}$$

This is not directly implementable if the universe has an infinite measure. A CSG (Constructive Solid Geometry) representation merely avoids the problem until it must determine whether the resulting object is empty, at which time it must perform some approximation to the algorithms described below.

We give an intuitive definition of C that includes all special cases and is implementable. It handles collinear edges, many edges incident on the same vertex, a vertex in the middle of another edge, a polygon with multiple separate components and holes with islands, and an infinite polygon that includes the whole plane except for a finite region. It is as follows.

a) Determine all the intersections of edges of A with edges of B.

b) Split all the edges at these intersections into smaller segments that do not intersect. If an endpoint of one edge lies on another, then split the other edge. This includes the case of two collinear edges; if either contains an endpoint of the other in its interior, then it will be split there.

c) Determine the relation of each segment to the other polygon. There are six cases:

i) A segment from a edge of polygon A may be inside polygon B.

ii) It may be outside B.

iii and iv) Ditto for segments of polygon B.

v) The segment results from an edge of A being collinear with an edge of B, and is part of a edge of both A and B. Both polygons are on the same side of the segment.

vi) As before, except that A and B are on opposite sides of the segment.

d) Use a decision table to select the segments appropriate to the boolean operation desired. For intersection, we want the segments from only cases (i), (iii), and (v).

This produces the set of segments in the output polygon. A planar graph traversal may be done to link them up, but this is not necessary since most desired operations, such as point inclusion testing, area measurement, cross-hatching, and further boolean operations, do not require the global topology.

Status

The program is implemented and working except for the collinear edges. In contrast to Fortran, the Prolog version has only 151 executable lines of Prolog. The lines are of a natural length, not packed to column 80.

CARTOGRAPHIC MAP OVERLAY AND REDUCTION

Franklin [15] describes the problem of map overlay in cartography. Here a difficult algorithm combines with numerical inaccuracies. Peter Wu is implementing a solution in Prolog where the two difficulties are decoupled. The algorithm is being implemented with an infinite precision rational number package in Prolog. Next the output will be reduced to floating point format with an expert system.

This reduction process involves moving the vertices to legal coordinate values one by one. After each vertex is moved, the topology of the map around it is checked for correctness and consistency. If an error has been produced, then the vertex must be moved to another legal place, or something else must be moved to correct the topology. In extreme cases, the topology must be changed while keeping its consistency. For example, a very small polygon might be combined with a neighbor.

SUMMARY

The pattern matching, backtracking, capabilities of fifth generation languages such as Prolog are particularly useful in geometry. Their correlation with the way that people think about geometry and their abstraction of unnecessary details allows us to spend more time on the creative aspects of the algorithms, which makes larger systems and more difficult algorithms practical to implement.

REFERENCES

[1] A. Baer, C. Eastman, and M. Henrion, "Geometric Modelling: A Survey", Computer Aided Design 11 (5), Sept. 1979.

[2] B.G. Baumgart. GEOMED: Geometric Editor, Stanford University STAN-CS-74-414, Also available as NTIS AD-780 452, (May 1974),

[3] B.G. Baumgart. Geometric Modelling for Computer Vision, Stanford University Artificial Intelligence Memo AIM-249, (Oct. 1974),

[4] J.L. Bentley and M.I. Shamos. "Divide And Conquer in Multidimensional Space", Proc. 16th Annual IEEE Symposium on the Foundations of Computer Science, (1975), pp. 220-230

[5] J.W. Boyse. "Interference Detection Among Solids and Surfaces", Comm. ACM 22 (1), Jan. 1979, pp. 3-9.

[6] I.C. Braid. "The Synthesis of Solids Bounded by Many Faces", Comm. ACM, (1975).

[7] K.L. Clark and S.-A. Tarnlund. Logic Programming, (1982), APIC Studies in Data Processing No 16, Academic Press.

[8] W.F. Clocksin and C.S. Mellish. Programming In Prolog, (1981), Springer-Verlag, New York.

[9] H. Coelho, J.C. Cotta, and L.M. Pereira. How to Solve it With Prolog, 2nd edition, Ministerio da Habitacao e Obras Publicas, Labatorio Nacional de Engenharia Civil, Lisboa, (1980).

[10] C.M. Eastman and C.I. Yessios, An Efficient Algorithm for Finding the Union, Intersection, and Differences of Spatial Domains, Carnegie-Mellon University, Dept. of Computer Science, (Sept. 1972).

[11] W.R. Franklin. "An Exact Hidden Sphere Algorithm That Operates In Linear Time", Computer Graphics and Image Processing 15, 4, (April 1981), pp. 364-379.

[12] W.R. Franklin. "3-D Geometric Databases Using Hierarchies of Inscribing Boxes", Proceedings of the 7th Canadian Man-Computer Conference, (10-12 June 1981), Waterloo, Ontario, pp. 173-180.

[13] W.R. Franklin. "Efficient Polyhedron Intersection and Union", Proc. Graphics Interface'82, Toronto, (19-21 May 1982), pp. 73-80.

[14] W.R. Franklin. "A Simplified Map Overlay Algorithm", Harvard Computer Graphics Conference, Cambridge, MA, (31 July - 4 August 1983), sponsored by the Lab for Computer Graphics and Spatial Analysis, Graduate School of Design,

[15] W.R. Franklin. "Cartographic Errors Symptomatic of Underlying Algebra Problems", Proc. International Symposium on Spatial Data Handling, vol. 1, (20-24 August 1984), Zurich, Switzerland, pp. 190-208.

[16] J.C. Gonzalez, M.H. Williams, and I.E. Aitchison. "Evaluation of the Effectiveness of Prolog for a CAD Application", IEEE Computer Graphics and Applications, (March 1984), pp. 67-75.

[17] G. Goos and J. Hartmanis. Lecture Notes in Computer Science 87: 5th Conference on Automated Deduction, (1980), Springer-Verlag, New York.

[18] G. Goos and J. Hartmanis. Lecture Notes in Computer Science 138: 6th Conference on Automated Deduction, (1982), Springer-Verlag, New York.

[19] K. Maruyama. "A Procedure to Determine Intersections Between Polyhedral Objects", Int. J. Comput. Infor. Sc. 1 (3), 1972, pp. 255-266.

[20] R.E. Parent. "A System for Sculpting 3-D Data", Computer Graphics (ACM) 11 (2), (Summer 1977), pp. 138-147.

[21] University of Salford. LISP/PROLOG Reference Manual, (March 1984).

[22] P.S.G. Swinson. "Logic Programming: A Computing Tool for the Architect of the Future" , Computer Aided Design 14, (2), (March 1982), pp. 97-104.

[23] P.S.G. Swinson, F.C.N. Periera, and A. Bijl. "A Fact Dependency System for the Logic Programmer", Computer Aided Design 15, (4), (July 1983), pp. 235-243.

[24] P.S.G. Swinson. "Prolog: A Prelude to a New Generaion of CAAD", Computer Aided Design 15, (6), (November 1983), pp. 335-343.

[25] R.B. Tilove. "Set Membership Classification: A Unified Approach to Geometric Intersection Problems", IEEE Trans. Comput. C-29 (10), 874-883, (October 1980).

[26] J.A. Turner. An Efficient Algorithm for Doing Set Operations on Two- and Three- Dimensional Spatial Objects, Architectural Research Laboratory, University of Michigan.

[27] K. Weiler. "Polygon Comparison Using a Graph Representation", <u>ACM Computer Graphics ACM Computer Graphics 14</u> (3), (Proc. SIGGRAPH'80), (July 1980), pp. 10-18.

[28] F. Yamaguchi and T. Tokieda. "A Unified Algorithm for Boolean Shape Operations", <u>IEEE Computer Graphics and Applications 4</u>, (6), (June 1984), pp. 24-37.

SUBDIVISION TECHNIQUES FOR PROCESSING
GEOMETRIC OBJECTS

P. A. KOPARKAR

S. P. MUDUR

NATIONAL CENTRE FOR SOFTWARE DEVELOPMENT AND COMPUTING TECHNIQUES
TATA INSTITUTE OF FUNDAMENTAL RESEARCH
HOMI BHABHA ROAD, COLABA, BOMBAY, 400005, INDIA.

Abstract

Geometric objects are basically described using curves and surfaces. The variety of applications that deal with geometric shape description demand different processing tasks to be performed on them. This paper describes new techniques developed for processing geometric objects based on the subdivision principle.

The methods handle parametrically defined bounded segments and patches in object space. The "divide and conquer" paradigm is used throughout. The more significant and origional results include:

(1) A method for estimating Euclidean bounds of curves and surfaces.
(2) The tests for linearity of curves and for planarity of surfaces.
(3) Interval methods for processing geometric objects.
(4) A general schema that describes the nature of the subdivision algorithms for processing curves and surfaces based on the evaluation of properties.
(5) Algorithms for often used operations like silhouette detection, detection of intersection, curve/surface rendering.

NATO ASI Series, Vol. F17
Fundamental Algorithms for Computer Graphics
Edited by R. A. Earnshaw
© Springer-Verlag Berlin Heidelberg 1985

Mathematical Forms and Algorithmic Strategies

Computational techniques for the processing of solid geometric objects today is largely restricted to simple shapes such as points, lines, conics, planes, cylinders, cones, and spheres. These have a wide application in the representation of a very large class of machined objects. In some particular cases this has been extended to include spun and swept surfaces, as well as quadric surfaces such as the ellipsoid, hyperboloids,paraboloids etc. All these shapes have been studied in classical mathematics and are expressible in the implicit equation forms shown below:

for plane curves:

$$ax^2+by^2+2hxy+2ux+2vy+k =0$$

and for surfaces:

$$ax^2+by^2+cz^2+2fyz+2gxz+2hxy+2ux+2vy+2wz+k =0.$$

These forms are suitable for checking whether any given point in space lies on the curve/surface. A number of applications require the generation of various points on the curves/surfaces. This can only be accomplished by solving the non-linear equations. For typical curves/surfaces like conics and quadrics, the resulting equations are simple enough so that they can be solved by inspection or by standard analytic methods. the problem arrises especially when the degree of the equation is quite high or when the functional form is not algebraic but contains functions such as trigonometric, exponential and logarithmic functions. In such a situation, numerical methods have been adopted.

Analytic methods of equation solving are global and find the entire solution in one shot. Numerical procedures are exactly opposite. They are local in nature in that they search for the solution only in the neighbourhood of some point. The process is iterative; given an initial guess for the solution it finds a better approximation to it. What is essentially needed is a repetitive process in which a sequence of more and more accurate solutions is determined and which is expected to converge to the actual solution. However, the convergence depends on the initial guess with which the process has started. Also the process may always converge to only one of a number of solutions, leaving other solutions undetected. The numerical process thus lacks in exhaustiveness and robustness.

Sculptured or free form curves and surfaces have been receiving considerable attention for their application in industries such as aircraft,ship and automobile construction. Sculptured curves/surfaces are defined in terms of some geometric handles which are more easily understood by shape designers. A curve is expressed in terms of some control points or positions and slopes of the end points. A surface patch is expressed by the data at its corners and boundaries or through a net of control points. These essentially represent bounded shapes. These are mathematically represented using the parametric form.

The curves and surfaces in the parametric form have different functions for x, y and z coordinates related to each other through their arguments u (and v) which are called parameters.

Curves:

$$x = f(u)$$

$$y = g(u)$$

$$z = h(u).$$

Surfaces:

$$x = f(u,v)$$

$$y = g(u,v)$$

$$z = h(u,v).$$

The main advantage of this over the implicit form is that the points on the curve/surface are obtained simply by the evaluation of the functions and do not require solution of equations. The functional form may be complicated and involve non-algebraic functions. An important point to note about the parametric form is that most of the standard engineering curves/surfaces like conics and quadrics can be suitably parametrized. This enables one to use the same methods (applicable to parametric form) for both the newly developed sculptured shapes and the classical shapes such as conics and quadrics.

In the recent past, a number of methods have been suggested which are based on the subdivision principle. This is algorithmicaly a differnt strategy in that instead of solving some equations (either analytically or numerically) to determine the solution set of points that satisfies a certain property, one evaluates the property for the entire segment/patch. The property is expressed using predicates constructed out of some mathematical functions whose arguments are the points varying on the given segment/patch. The range of the function cor- responding to the entire segment/patch is evaluated to check whether the property predicate is true or false. If it is true then the property holds for the entire segment/patch and we are through. Otherwise the segment/patch is subdivided suitably, generally at the midvalues of its parameter domains and the procedure is repeated for each subsegment/subpatch generated. This terminates when suitable criteria are satisfied by subsegment/subpatch.

The subdivision method searches for a solution in a global fashion. No solution goes undetected as long as sufficient levels of subdivision are carried out. Also a proper choice for termination allows one to obtain results to any desired accuracy.

This work discusses the parametric form for shapes and the development of algorithms for processing these shapes based on the subdivision principle. Major desirable features of subdivision method are:

(1) Fast rejection of unwanted portions
(2) Proper termination of subdivision process
(3) Identification of objects that can be directly processed (say using analytic methods) without any recourse to the subdivision methods
(4) fast and exhaustive methods of property evaluation needed in (1),(2) and (3) above.

Typical Algorithms

In this section we shall give a quick overview of algorithms based on the subdivision principle.

ALGORITHMS FOR CURVES

(1) Rendering a parametric curve

```
PROCEDURE draw(p:curve);
BEGIN
  IF linear(p)
  THEN drawline(p)
  ELSE
    BEGIN
      subdivide(p,pl..pm);
      draw(pl)
        .
        .
        .
      draw(pm)
    END
END{draw};
```

* linear(p) is a function that checks linearity of p within some prescribed tolerance.

* drawline(p) is a procedure to draw a straight line between two end points of p.

* subdivide(p,pl..pm) subdivides p into m subcurves pl..pm and returns them. Value of m depends on the implementation.

(2) Curve–Curve Intersection Detection

```
PROCEDURE intersect(p,q:curve);
BEGIN
  IF overlap(p,q)
  THEN
    BEGIN
      IF linear(p) AND linear(q)
      THEN linelineintersection(p,q)
      ELSE
        BEGIN
          IF NOT linear(p)
          THEN subdivide(p,pl..pm)
          ELSE rename(p,pl);
          IF NOT linear(q)
          THEN subdivide(q,ql..qn)
          ELSE rename(q,ql);
          intersect(pl,ql);
          intersect(pl,q2)
               .
               .
               .
          intersect(pm,qn)
        END
    END
    {overlap}
END {intersect};
```

* overlap(p,q) is a boolean function that checks whether two segements p and q have any potentials to overlap by examining their eucledian bounds. * linelineintersection(p,q) is the procedure to detect the intersection of two linear curves p and q using analytic methods. * rename(p,pl) renames p as pl.

ALGORITHMS FOR SURFACES

(1) Rendering a tessallated drawing

(2) Surface-surface intersection

These are similar to the algorithms for curves.

(3) Detecting (and drawing) silhouettes

```
PROCEDURE silhoutte (p:patch);
VAR
  a,b:REAL;
BEGIN
  { evaluate the range of the
  function N.E over the entire patch p
  and store it as an interval [a,b] }
  evaluateNdotE (p,a,b);
  IF a<=0<=b
  THEN
    IF planar (p)
    THEN drawplane (p)
  ELSE
    BEGIN
      subdivide (p,pl..pm);
      sillhouette (pl)

      .

      .

      .

      sillhouette (pm)
    END
END { sillhouette };
```

* planar (p) and

* drawplane (p) are similar to linear (p) and drawline (p) above.

This method draws sillhouette as an approximation by planes. At times, it turns out that the approximation is crude and the generated picture shows a wide strip instead of a fine line.

A remedy to this is to store the patches for which N.E > 0 or N.E < 0 holds together with the planar patches and then pair off the patches with N.E > 0 and N.E < 0 which share an edge. Such edges form the sillhouette curve. We shall not discuss this method in any detail here. See [Koparkar/Mudur -3] (4) Generating a Shaded Picture

```
PROCEDURE shade(p:patch)
  VAR
    a,b:REAL;
  BEGIN
    IF planar(p)
    THEN shadeplane(p)
    ELSE
      BEGIN
        calculateintensity(p,a,b);
        IF a > maxintensity OR b < minintensity
        THEN skip(p)
        ELSE
          IF b-a <= intensitylevel
          THEN display(p,round(a))
          ELSE
            BEGIN
              subdivide(p,pl..pm);
              shade(pl)
              .
              .
              .
              shade(pm);
```

```
                    END;
              END { nonplanar }
          END { shade };
```

* shadeplane(p) is a procedure that displays a planar patch p with appropriate intensity.

* calculateintensity (p,a,b) calculates the range of the intensity function using some standard illumination model. The range is returned as an interval [a,b].

* minintensity and maxintensity are the minimum and maximum permissible values of intensity level.

* skip(p) does nothing.

* display(p1) renders the entire patch with a constant intensity.

This procedure assumes that addressable values for intensity in the output device are bound by minintensity and maxintensity and change by intensitylevel. The range of intensity function is calculated as an interval [a,b]. For planar patches ,the intensity is constant.

All drawings in this paper are generated using these algorithms.

Fig. 1 shows constant parametric lines drawn on a surface.

Fig. 2 shows tessellated drawing of the same surface.

Fig. 3 shows the intersection between two surfaces. Only the boundaries are drawn for clarity.

Fig. 4 shows the silhouette line drawing
            (together with the boundaries).

Fig. 5 shows various stages in silhouette generation.

A Schema

It can be seen that the earlier described algorithms for processing curves and surfaces all fit into a single general schema. In describing the schema the following points must be noted.

(1) All operations evaluate intervals that include ranges of functions. The interval may be exactly equal to the actual range of the function or it may be wider than that. The evaluation of interval may be using any convenient method. The schema is independent of the particular method used.

(2) Every processing task requires the evaluation of one or more properties of the geometric object(s) under consideration. The functions which describe such properties we shall call as property functions. When a property function is evaluated the result interval provides the bounds to the values that the property can have for that object.

Examples of property functions are:

. the Euclidean bound-function (for detecting overlap).

. the visibility-function (N.E).

. the intensity-function.

. the deviation from linearity-function

. the deviation from planarity-function.

(3) Most properties will have absolute bounds to their values. These typically depend on the nature of the property. In the worst case these bounds will be set by the machine word length on which the computations are carried out. All interval function evaluations are clipped to these absolute bounds before further processing. For

example, intensity is relative, with a 0 intensity value being the lowest and a 1 intensity value being the highest. The intensity function value may thus be clipped to the interval [0,1].

(4) Depending on the values of properties of objects further actions are taken. The conditions which property values would have to satisfy we shall call as property-predicates. Note that predicates are on intervals.

Examples of property-predicates are:

. overlap predicate for bounds

. a 0 contained in the visibility (for silhouette)

. a positive value of the visibility (for local visibility)

. the width of the intensity-function value covering one

   intensity level

. deviation within tolerance.

(5) The actions on the objects/sub-objects may be categorized as below:

(i) reject action: the object is of no further interest. For example, non-overlapping objects in intersection processing or negative visibility elements in rendering with shades.

(ii) process action: the object is processed immediately. For example, the object with intensity range containing only one intensity level is rendered with all pixels covered by this object having the same intensity.

(iii) Simple action: the object is simple enough to be processed by a special set of procedures. For example, straight lines and planes are processed usually in a straightforward manner using analytic methods. Similarly if an object covers only a single pixel then it is considered simple.

(iv) subdivide action: the object is too complex for its property to satisfy any of the above three conditions. It is subdivided and the property function/predicate evaluated for each of the sub objects. (This course of action is based on the piecewise interval evaluation theorem which states that the range of any function may be evaluated in a piecewise manner and the resulting ranges may be merged together to get the entire range). For example in rendering with shading that object is subdivided which is not planar and for which the intensity function value covers more than one intensity level.

The Object Processing Schema

```
    overall-process(object)::=
    begin
      (* evaluate ranges of relevant, property functions
      and clip to the appropriate bounds *)
      if rejectable then reject (object)
      else if processable
           then process (object)
           else if simple
                then simple-process (object)
                else begin
                        subdivide(object, object1, object2
                                        .....objectn);
                        overall-process(object1);
                        overall-process(object2);
                                .
                                .
                                .
                        overall-process(objectn)
                     end
    end.
```

When the processing task involves more than one object, for example, intersection, then object in the above schema would stand for objects. It should be noted that not all processing tasks may require taking all the four actions listed in the general schema.

Simplifications

Piecewise linear approximation of a curve segment helps in reducing computational complexity; linear segments can be processed in a straightforward way. For all computational purposes, some tolerance is prescribed within which the linearity is checked. Linearity in this sense is a measure of the maximum deviation of the curve segment from a straight line. The reference line for the measurement of linearity is usually chosen to be the chord or one of the end tangents.

Fig. 6 shows the deviation of a point on a curve from its chord.

For parametric curves, which are modelled using Bezier or B-spline form, the segment lies within the convex hull of its control vertices. It therefore suffices to have a linear convex hull in order to get a linear curve segment. The test checks the control vertices, which are finite in number, for linearity.

Analogous to the linearity of the curves, planarity plays an essential role in simplifying operations on curved surfaces. Planarity is defined in terms of the maximum deviation of the surface from a plane which is chosen with some fixed relation to the surface. (For example, it may be a plane through three particular points on the surface). A surface is planar if its deviation is within the prescribed tolerance.

Deviation may be estimated by determining the extrema of the function defining the Euclidean distance of any point on the surface from the reference plane. This uses vector analysis. Another method is to estimate some upper bound to the deviation instead of measuring its maximum. For parametric surfaces expressed in Bezier or B-spline form, the test of planarity of the surface reduces to the planarity of the convex hull of the control vertices.

Fig. 7 shows the deviation of a point on a surface from a plane defined by three of its corners.

Euclidean bounds estimate in some way the extent of the curve or a surface in Euclidean space. If the object extends to a very small region which may be treated as a single point for all practical purposes, then it can be processed in a straightforward way. A surface patch that covers only one pixel of the final display device is an example. The Euclidean bounds define a region, of some typical shape, around the curve segment, which completely contains the curve segment. The boundary of such a shape is relatively easy and compact to store and evaluate. Circles (bubbles or balls) and rectangular boxes with or without their sides parallel to coordinate axes are two examples that have been used frequently. For a parametric curve in Bezier or B-spline form, the convex hull of their control vertices determine their Euclidean bounds. The box around any curve/surface is defined by the six values

$$<Xmin,Xmax,Ymin,Ymax,Zmin,Zmax>$$

where any point (x,y,z) on that curve/surface satisfies

$$Xmin <= x <= Xmax.$$

$$Ymin <= y <= Ymax.$$

$$Zmin <= z <= Zmax.$$

Fig. 8 shows the box around a curve.

Direct evaluation techniques for curves

In this section all coordinate functions are assumed to be twice continuously differentiable. The class of curves that can be handled using the techniques is very large, including conics, superconics, polynomial and rational cubics. The two properties that are commonly required are the Euclidean bounds and the linearity of curves. This section develops methods for estimating these properties.

Definition : Characteristic value of the first type

Let $f(u)$ be a well-defined and once continuously differentiable (C^1) function on $[u_0, u_1]$. Any value u_c in $[u_0, u_1]$ is its characteristic value of the first type iff the following conditions hold :

For every $d>0$ there exists u' satisfying

    (1) $u_c - d < u' < u_c + d$
    (2) $df/du(u_c) = 0$ and $df/du(u') <> 0$.

Fig. 9 shows various cases of characteristic values of the first type.

Definition : Characteristic value of the second type

Let $f(u)$ be a well-defined and twice continuously differentiable (C^2) function on $[u_0, u_1]$. Any value u_c in $[u_0, u_1]$ is its characteristic value of the second type iff the following conditions hold :

For every $d>0$ there exists u' satisfying

    (1) $u_c - d < u' < u_c + d$
    (2) $d^2f/du^2(u_c) = 0$ and $d^2f/du^2(u') <> 0$.

Definition : Characteristic point of the first type

Let $P(u)=[x(u),y(u),z(u)]$ $u_0<=u<=u_1$ be the parametric curve. A parametric value u_c is said to define a characteristic point of the first type on the curve if u_c is a characteristic value of the first type for either one of the three coordinate functions x,y or z

Definition : Characteristic point of the second type

Let $P(u)=[x(u),y(u),z(u)]$ $u_0<=u<=u_1$ be the parametric curve. A parametric value u_c is said to define a characteristic point of the second type on the curve if u_c is a characteristic value of the second type for either one of the three coordinate functions x,y or z.

The following theorem relates the Euclidean bounds of a curve segment to its characteristic points.

Theorem : "Endpoints Extrema Theorem"

If $P(u)$, $u_0<=u<=u_1$ is a curve such that no u satisfying $u_0<u<u_1$ is its characteristic point of the first type then one of the following holds:

(1) $X_{min} = x(u_0)$ and $X_{max} = x(u_1)$

(2) $X_{min} = x(u_1)$ and $X_{max} = x(u_0)$

X_{min} and X_{max} are the minimum and maximum values of X over $[u_0,u_1]$. Similar results hold for y and z.

The proof of this and all other theorems are discussed in [Koparkar], [Koparkar/Mudur-1] and [koparkar/Mudur-2].

This theorem asserts that if the curve is split at its characteristic points of the first type then the resulting segments have the property that their extreme points occur at the boundaries, i.e. the end points of the segment, and hence are quite trivial to compute. Further, this property is inherited by all their descendants resulting out of further subdivisions.

Linearity of a curve from a straight line is measured within some prescribed tolerance. If the maximum deviation of the curve from the line is less than the tolerance, the curve is linear. Below we present a number of theorems. These provide a simple method for estimating linearity of curves.

Theorem : "Chord Non-intercepting Theorem"

If $P(u)$, $u_0 <= u <= u_1$ is a curve such that no u^* with $u_0 < u^* < u_1$ is its characteristic point of the second type then the graph of the coordinate function $x(u)$ in the u-x plane does not cross its chord (except at the end points) and lies entirely on one side of the chord. Similar results hold for $y(u)$ and $z(u)$ functions.

Theorem : "Triangle Containment Theorem"

If $p(u)$, $u_0 <= u <= u_1$ is a curve such that any u, $u_0 < u < u_1$ is not a characteristic point of the second type of $p(u)$ then the x coordinate function curve lies entirely within the triangle formed by the intersection of the chord $\{(u_0, x_0) - (u_1, x_1)\}$ and the slope lines $dx/du(u_0)$ and $dx/du(u_1)$. Similarly $y(u)$ and $z(u)$ lie entirely in their respective triangles formed as above.

Theorem : "Curve Linearity Theorem"

Let $P(u)$ $u_0 <= u <= u_1$ be a curve. If $x(u)$, $y(u)$, $z(u)$ are linear within tolerance T, then $P(u)$ is linear within tolerance kT, where k is given by

$$k = 2\{|x(u1)-x(u0)|+|y(u1)-y(u0)|+|z(u1)-z(u0)|\}.$$

This theorem provides a test of linearity for curves which works in a coordinatewise fashion. If T is the tolerance within which the curve segment is considered linear then the maximum deviation permissible for each coordinate is easily determined using this theorem. It is therefore enough to consider deviations in the x-u, y-u, z-u planes individually. Each of these is computed easily through simple substitutions.

Direct evaluation techniques for Surfaces

In this section we develop techniques for processing parametric surfaces. The techniques presented are essentially for efficient computation of surface properties needed by the processing tasks. The two
properties considered are the Euclidean bounds and the planarity of
surface patches.

COMPUTING EUCLIDEAN BOUNDS

We now introduce the notion of a potential extremum. The set of
potential extrema contains all extreme values that define the box for a
surface. The equations defining potential extrema and their solutions
for various surface types are discussed below.

Consider a patch $p(u,v)$ where

$$p(u,v) = [x(u,v), y(u,v), z(u,v)], \quad u_0 <= u <= u_1, \quad v_0 <= v <= v_1.$$

We shall concentrate on a single coordinate x since methods for y and z
are analogous. The whole patch p is considered coordinatewise. We assume
that $x(u,v)$ has continuous derivatives.

Definition: Characteristic curve

The u-characteristic curve is the set of values (u_c, v_c) such that for
all $d > 0$ there exists $u_n <> u_c$, $u_c - d <= u_n <= u_c + d$ with $D_u(x(u_c, v_c)) =$
0 and $D_u(x(u_n, v_c)) <> 0$ where D_u represents first partial derivative
w.r.t. u.

v-characteristic curve is defined similarly.

Definition: Potential extrema

Let

$$C_u = \{\text{set of u-characteristic curves}\} \underline{\text{union}} \{x(u_0,v), x(u_1,v)\}.$$

$$C_v = \{\text{set of v-characteristic curves}\} \underline{\text{union}} \{x(u,v_0), x(u,v_1)\}.$$

where $x(u_0,v)$,...etc. are boundary curves obtained by setting $u=u_0$ etc. The potential extremum is the point of intersection of the curves f and g where f $\underline{\text{belongs to}}$ C_u and g $\underline{\text{belongs to}}$ C_v.

The name potential extremum is justified by the following theorem.

Theorem : "Potential Extrema Theorem"

The maximum and minimum values of $x(u,v)$ on the patch are attained at one (or more) of the potential extrema.

A potential extremum is the value (u,v) which simultaneously satisfies the following two conditions:

$$(D_u=0) \text{ or } (u=u_0) \text{ or } (u=u_1)$$

$$(D_v=0) \text{ or } (v=v_0) \text{ or } (v=v_1)$$

A potential extremum may lie on a corner (corner potential extremum) or on a boundary (excluding corners; boundary potential extremum) or may lie in the interior of the patch (interior potential extremum). See fig. 10.

The particular form of the solutions of $D_u(x) = 0$ and $D_v(x) = 0$ ensures that product surface subpatches do not have interior potential extrema once they are split at these solutions. This simplifies the processing of product surfaces considerably. (Product surfaces are adequately discussed in [Koparkar], [Koparkar/Mudur-2] and [Mudur/Koparkar-1].) Product surfaces include quadric surfaces. In fact the total operations required to be performed for each subpatch obtained after subdivision is quite small. If the subpatches have no boundary potential extrema then the box is obtained simply by evaluating the required patch corners and then doing a min-max search operation for each coordinate. If the subpatch does have boundary potential extrema then these have to be additionally evaluated and included along with patch corners in the min-max search operation. The complexity of evaluating the potential extrema depends on the nature of the $D_u = 0$ and $D_v = 0$ equations. In cases like the cubic or the rational quadratic this is fairly simple.

Thus, in general, after detecting the simultaneous solutions of $D_u=0$ and $D_v=0$ the patch is split at the solution points. The resulting subpatches contain these points at their corners and do not have any more interior extrema. The simultaneous equations may sometimes result not in isolated point solutions but in common curve segments. If the simultaneous solution consists of one or more curve segments, then these segments need no special attention [Koparkar],[Koparkar/Mudur-2].

Once the interior potential extrema points are determined and the surface split at these, for the rest of the subdivision process the total number of operations needed is fairly small. As in the case of product surfaces the required corners are evaluated. The boundary potential extrema now have to be evaluated both for u and v boundaries and then a min-max search operation done on all the above. Typically for bicubics a subdivision into four subpatches would require the evaluation of at most a quadratic equation in u and a quadratic equation in v. These are then added to the set of potential extrema for the appropriate subpatches. Compare this with the convex hull based method [Lane/Riesenfeld] which requires for each subdivision the evaluation of 45 new control points and then a min-max operation on 16 points for each patch.

CALCULATING INTERIOR POTENTIAL EXTREMA

Detection of interior potential extrema of a patch requires each and every solution to the simultaneous equations $D_u = 0$ and $D_v = 0$ to be detected. Numerical methods like Newton-Raphson based on the sequence of successive approximations converging towards the solution may not be of use as discussed earlier.

E.Moore introduces a method based on interval contractions for detecting all solutions to simultaneous non-linear equations [Moore]. The method checks the possibility for a solution to lie within the entire domain of the patch (considered as a 2-D interval). This is done by interval evaluation of the functions D_u and D_v. If both the evaluations contain 0 then there is some chance for the solution to exist. The patch is subdivided. The process is repeated for the subdivided patches and this continues in a recursive fashion. The recursion terminates when the patch under consideration can be treated as a single point for all practical purposes. Those patches for which one or both the evaluations fail to contain 0 are discarded from considerations. This method detects every solution that lies on the patch.

From the theoretical point of view, Moore's method appears to be very robust and sound for detecting each interior potential extremum of a patch. It works very well for the patches that have only point interior extrema. If the solution includes one or more curves that can not be written in the form u = constant or v = constant, then the method detects each of the curves as a collection of a large number of points. These points are quite close to each other. Splitting at every such point is impracticable for after splitting, a large number of patches are generated. Most of these are extremely small in size. These are difficult to handle, especially when their size is of the order of the tolerance used.

For Moore's method to be practical in detecting interior potential extrema, some method of identifying the curves from the collection of points is needed. Unfortunately, analytic methods are in general not available for arbitrarily defined parametric patches.

ESTIMATING PLANARITY

In this section we shall devise a planarity test,which is based on the linearity of curves (or functions of one variable).

Theorem: "Surface Planarity Theorem"

Let $P(s,t)=[x(s,t),y(s,t),z(s,t)]$ $s0<=s<=s1,t0<=t<=t1$ be the patch. If $x(s,t),y(s,t),z(s,t)$ are planar within some tolerance T then $P(s,t)$ is planar within tolerance KT where K depends on the coefficients.

Theorem: "Surface Sum Planarity Theorem"

If $x_1(s,t)$ and $x_2(s,t)$ are two functions which are planar within the tolerances T1 and T2 then the function $x(s,t)$ defined by $x= x_1+x_2$ is planar within the tolerance T1+T2.

Theorem: "Surface Product Planarity Theorem"

Let $x(s,t)= A(s)B(t)$. If $A(s)$ and $B(t)$ are linear within some tolerance T1 and the four corners of $x(s,t)$ are coplanar within some tolerance T2 then $x(s,t)$ is planar within the tolerance k_1T1+T2 where k_1 depends on the coefficients.

Theorem: "Patch Planarity Theorem"

If the patch $p(u,v)$ has the form

$$\sum_{i=0}^{m} \sum_{j=0}^{n} A_i(u)\, B_j(v)\, P_{ij}$$

and if

(1) A_i's B_j's are linear   and

(2) the four corners are coplanar

then the patch is planar. (Everywhere appropriate tolerances are assumed).

This theorem provides the planarity test for the surface patches for which the coordinate functions have well defined algebraic forms in terms of the blending functions $A_i(u)$ and $B_j(v)$. "The planarity of the patch is implied by the linearity of the blending functions together with the coplanarity of the four corners". The linearity test provided earlier uses mere substitutions and so is easy to compute. The functions $A_i(u)$ and $B_j(v)$ are not restricted except that they should be twice continuously differentiable. $A_i(u)$, $B_j(v)$ may be quadratic, cubic, trigonometric, polynomial or rational functions or any power thereof.

This test for planarity really decomposes into the flatness of the surface in two independent directions along the u and v parametric curves. Singly curved surfaces like cylinders are subdivided without having to subdivide along their generators. Doubly curved patches are thought of as combinations of two singly curved entities.

An important byproduct of this test is that all subdivisions ultimately result into planar quadrilateral patches bounded by straight lines. Once the planarity of a patch is confirmed, the linearity of its edges follows as a part of the planarity. Hence processing of these patches only needs techniques for the processing of planes and straight lines,which have been very well studied.

Interval Methods for Function Evaluation

In the subsequent sections we shall present interval based methods for geometric processing of objects. These methods work without the need to solve simultaneous non-linear equations. We, however, would like our readers to note that these methods do not prohibit us from using methods of estimating exact bounds whenever possible (for example, quadrics, product surfaces, and simple bicubic patches having only point interior potential extrema). These methods are discussed in detail in [Koparkar] and [Mudur/Koparkar-2].

Extensions of number systems involving ordered pairs of numbers from the given system are commonplace. The rational numbers are essentially ordered pairs of integers; complex numbers are ordered pairs of real numbers. In each case, operations are defined with rules for computing the components of a pair resulting from an arithmetic operation on two pairs. Pairs of some special form are equivalent to the numbers of the original type. Operations on intervals, may be defined in the same spirit. An interval is an ordered pair and also a set of real numbers as defined below:

$$[a,b] = \{x \mid a <= x <= b\}.$$

With this view, all set theoretic operations are well defined in case of intervals. We shall use the words belongs to, subset of, etc. in the usual sense of set theory. Degenerate intervals of the form [a,a] are equivalent to real numbers.

If @ represent one of the symbols +, -, *, /, then we define [a,b] @ [c,d]= {x@y| x <u>belongs to</u> [a,b] and y <u>belongs to</u> [c,d]}.

except that we do not define [a,b]/[c,d] in case 0 <u>belongs to</u> [c,d].]

This definition emphasises the fact that the sum, difference, product, or quotient of two intervals is just the set of sums, differences, products, or quotients, respectively, of pairs of real numbers, one from each of the two intervals.

An equivalent set of definitions of algebraic character in terms of formulae using end points of the two intervals can be easily constructed.

We have

$$[a,b] + [c,d] = [a+c, b+d]$$

$$[a,b] - [c,d] = [a-d, b-c]$$

$$[a,b] * [c,d]=[\min (a*c, a*d, b*c, b*d),$$
$$\max (a*c, a*d, b*c, b*d)]$$

$$[a,b] / [e,d] = [a,b] * [1/d, 1/c]$$

provided 0 <u>does not belong to</u> [c,d].

The main motivation in describing interval arithmetic comes from the need to express the range that results out of calculations that repeatedly involve arithmetic operations. The following theorem paves the way in relating the actual range of a rational function $f(x_1,...,x_n)$ to the interval obtained as a result of evaluation of its interval counterpart $F(X_1,...,X_n)$, for which x_i <u>belongs to</u> X_i.

Theorem: "Range Containment Theorem"

Let $f(x_1,..x_n)$ be a real rational function and let F be the corresponding interval rational function.

If for each $i, 1<=i<=n$, x_i ranges over $[a_i,b_i]$ then

$$F([a_1,b_1],... [a_n,b_n]) \underline{\text{superset of}}$$

$$\{ f(x_1,..x_n) \mid x_i \text{ belongs to } [a_i,b_i], 1<=i<=n \}$$

$$= \{ \text{ range of } f \}.$$

It is worth noticing that F gives a wider interval than the actual range of f. In other words we get loose bounds to the variation in the values of f whenever x_i have variations among $[a_i,b_i]$. In fact in most cases the interval that we get by evaluating the interval rational function F is much wider than what we desire it to be. An example will enlighten this point.

We restrict ourselves to a single variable x and define $f(x)=x-x$, with x varying in $[0,1]$. then $f(x)=0$ and the range is $[0,0]$. The interval expression gives rise to $[0,1]-[0,1]=[-1,1]$.

The development of interval arithmetic yields a direct and simple method of calculating bounds to the variation of any well defined rational function over a certain set of intervals within which the arguments of the function vary. Fig. 11 shows the interval for a 2-D curve (obtained as a rectangle) using interval arithmetic. Rational functions are not the only functions that are encountered in mathematical calculations. Irrational functions such as $\exp(x)$, $\log(x)$, $\cos(x)$, $\sin(x)$, $\arctan(x)$ as well as x^k are freely used throughout the domain of mathematics and computer science. Apart from these there are many other functions of several variables like vector functions. In computer science, especially in the areas that deal with geometric shape representation, spline functions are frequently used. These are piecewise analytic functions, and in most of the cases are piecewise polynomials. It is therefore necessary to develop interval methods -or extend interval arithmetic- in order to deal with all irrational and spline-like functions. Defining convergent sequences of intervals converging towards the ranges of such functions is of little use, as it is an infinite process. We choose another course for this. We shall now present a method for estimating ranges of piecewise continuously differentiable functions.

Theorem: "Piecewise Interval Evaluation Theorem"

Let $f(x)$ be any function defined on $[a_0, a_n]$.

Let

$$[a_0, a_n] = [a_0, a_1] \underline{\text{union}} [a_1, a_2] \underline{\text{union}} \ldots \underline{\text{union}} [a_{n-1}, a_n].$$

Then

$$\{f(x) \mid x \underline{\text{belongs to}} [a_0, a_n]\} =$$

$$\{f(x) \mid x \underline{\text{belongs to}} [a_0, a_1]\} \underline{\text{union}} \{f(x) \mid x \underline{\text{belongs to}} [a_1, a_2$$

$]\}$

$$\ldots \underline{m} \{f(x) \mid x \underline{\text{belongs to}} [a_{n-1}, a_n]\}.$$

This theorem enables us to define the range of a function in a piecewise manner. The ideal choice of splitting the given interval is one, that yields after merging the least width interval as the function value. The appropriate places for splitting the domain interval of any function are decided by the nature of the function. The following theorem gives rise to such points, where we can split the interval and calculate ranges of the function in each of the subintervals that result. The results are then merged to get the total range.

Theorem: "End Value Extrema Theorem"

If f is defined and continuously differentiable on [a,b] and no value xc with a<xc<b is a characteristic value of the first type of f, then one of the following two holds:

    (1) maxf = f(a) and minf = f(b)

    (2) maxf = f(b) and minf = f(a)

where minf and maxf denote, respectively the minimum and maximum values that f takes in [a,b].

This theorem essentially asserts that if we split the domain [a,b] of any continuously differentiable function f at its characteristic values then the range of f on each of the subintervals can be found out just by evaluating f at the end points of that subinterval (The end points that result may be in reverse order). All such sub-ranges may be merged in order to get the complete range of f over [a,b].

In view of the previous theorem, we may consider a piecewise continuously differentiable function over an interval [a,b]. Initially, this interval is split at the points of discontinuity of f and df/dx to result in a collection of subintervals such that f is continuously differentiable on each of the resulting subintervals. Characteristic values over each of these intervals are well defined, and each of the intervals is further subdivided to get a larger collection of narrower sub-intervals. Range of f is calculated on each of these by evaluating it at the end points; the total range is obtained, as before, by merging these sub-ranges.

Fig. 12 shows the evaluation of intervals after splitting. Compare this to Fig. 11.

Thus what we have presented above is a method that calculates the range of any function f which is piecewise continuously differentiable over the interval for which the range is to be evaluated. The method is applicable irrespective of whether the function f is an irrational function or a spline function or has any other functional form. Moreover, the range that we obtain using this method is exact!

We shall now present a few examples to illustrate applications of these methods in evaluating intervals.

Square root of an interval

Only non-negative roots are considered.

sqrt([a,b]) = square root of ([a,b])

    = [sqrt(a), sqrt(b)] if a>=0

    = [0, sqrt(b)] if a<0<=b

    =   undefined   if b<0.

Interval vector functions

A 3-D interval vector is a triple of intervals,representing a rectangular box whose sides are parallel to the coordinate planes In 2-D space, it corresponds to a rectangle whose sides are parallel to the coordinate axes. Any real vector that is in the given interval vector is represented by some point in the rectangular box or the rectangle.

Consider a function of a vector (x,y,z) defined by

$$norm = n[(x,y,z)] = sqrt(x^2+y^2+z^2)$$

$$D_x(n) = 2*x / sqrt(x^2+y^2+z^2)$$

where $D_x(n)$ is the partial derivative of n w.r.t. x.
$D_x(n) = 0$ is equivalent to x = 0. Similarly $D_y(n) = 0$ and $D_z(n) = 0$ are equivalent to y = 0 and z = 0. Thus we may split the domain intervals of x,y and z at 0 (if they contain it). For the resulting split domains, the extreme values of n[(x,y,z)] lie on one of the eight corners. These can be easily evaluated and searched for minimum and maximum values of n[(x,y,z)].

Note that this method produces exact bounds of the functions over its domain.

CLIPPING

In a number of applications the programmer knows the clipping limits in advance and may incorporate them into the program to restrict the ranges of functions. Clipping of resulting intervals speeds up computations whenever such intervals are used for further calculations.

An implicit application of clipping may be found in our definition of |[a,b]| in the previous section. The resulting intervals are clipped from below at zero to avoid negative numbers in the range of the absolute value function.

Applications of Interval Methods to Geometric Processing

In this section we show some examples of how interval computations can be used for estimating bounds to properties of curves and surfaces. Direct methods for estimating bounds to linear deviation, planar deviation and Euclidean bounds have been discussed previously. Readers are urged to compare those methods and their interval analogues to see for themselves the elegance and universal applicability of interval methods. Of course interval computations do result in looser bounds, but that does not prohibit their use in subdivision methods.

1) LINEARITY ESTIMATION

We now present a method for estimating the deviation of a curve from its chord using interval methods. This is based on formulating a single function for the Euclidean deviation.

Let $d(u)$ denotes the deviation vector, i.e. the vector perpendicular from the point $p(u)$ of the curve to the line with respect to which the linearity is measured (usually the chord of the segment), then the deviation of the point $p(u)$ is denoted by $|d(u)|$. Using interval evaluation of functions an appropriate condition for the linearity of the curve $P(u)$ turns out to be

$$|d([u_0, u_1])| \subseteq [0, T].$$

where T is the tolerance value.

$d(u)$ can be expressed using vector analysis in terms of $P(u)$:

$$d(u) = P-P0 - (P1-P0) \{ (P1-P0).(P-P0) \}/|P1-P0|^2$$

This equation has the same form as $P(u)$ when considered as a function of u. $|d([u_0,u_1])|$ can therefore be calculated. {as $P(u)$ is differentiable on $[u_0,u_1]$ so also is $d(u)$}.

It is important to note that in the conventional methods of real numbers, we cannot consider the range of $|d(u)|$ in this way. We have to seek the maximum deviation in order to find the range of $|d(u)|$. At the point of maximum deviation, the curve tangent is perpendicular to $d(u)$ so that $d(u).dP/du = 0$ where dP/du denotes the derivative of P w.r.t. u. This equation has the point of maximum deviation as one of its roots. At this root, $d(u)$ is calculated to get the maximum deviation. For a polynomial curve of nth degree this equation reduces to the equation of degree $2n-1$. Since $u-u_0$ and $u-u_1$ are two factors, it reduces further to an equation of degree $2n-3$. For cubics, it gives a cubic equation. In case of rational quadratics the degree is four while for rational cubics, the degree is seven.

Interval methods for estimating bounds of a property do not require the detection of extrema. Only evaluation of the corresponding interval function suffices. Testing of the property i.e. linearity in this case - reduces to the containment of the resulting interval into another prescribed interval.

2) LOCAL VISIBILITY

The points on the silhouette edges are the solutions of the equation $N.E=0$ where N is the surface normal at the point and E is the vector along the line of sight. N, for a surface $P(u,v)$ is given by $D_u(P) \times D_v(P)$ where D_u and D_v denote partial derivatives w.r.t. u and v. Interval methods may be used to evaluate $N.E$ over the entire patch so that the resulting interval contains the actual range of $N.E$. The resulting interval may be tested for visibility and existence of a silhouette edge.

Based on this test, suitable action may be taken. For subdivision methods, the patches containing silhouette lines —i.e. the one having 0 value included in the range of $N.E$— are considered further. Other patches are not further processed. The process is repeated for each of the subpatches that results from subdividing those patches for which the estimated range of $N.E$ contains the value 0. The subdivision process terminates when the $N.E$ interval for the patch contains 0 and the width of the interval is within tolerance or when the patch is planar within tolerance. Note that even though the $N.E$ real value is constant for a planar patch, the $N.E$ interval may be wider.

3) INTENSITY CALCULATION

In rendering solid objects, on a raster display, each pixel is required to be drawn with appropriate shade or light intensity. At any point on the surface $P(u,v)$, the final value of intensity or shade that is passed to the display hardware depends on several factors.

The simplest form of the equation is Lambert's law.

I = k(N.L) where

I = intensity at the required point on the surface

k = reflectance coefficient   0<k<1

L = unit vector along the direction of the light source

and N = the unit normal to the surface at the point

where the intensity value is to be calculated.

All other quantities in the above expression are constant except N, which is a function of u and v. Thus the intensity value turns out to be a function of u and v and evaluates to a subinterval of [-k,k]. If the result goes beyond this interval, then it is clipped at the limits -k and +k.

The display itself has a finite number of discreet intensity levels, say 0,1,2... lmax. In order to simulate the shading on a display, the computed intensity is mapped on the range of these levels. This is easily done by scaling with a factor lmax. If the resulting interval [a,b] overlaps with the range of intensity levels i.e. [0,lmax+1] then it is checked for containing one or more intensity levels. If the width of this interval w([a,b]) is < 1 or it contains exactly one of these levels, then the patch is rendered with the level of intensity given by trunc(b) (Where trunc(b) is the greatest integer <=b). If the interval contains more than one intensity levels then the patch is subdivided into a number of smaller patches, and each resulting subpatch is considered separately for determining its intensity. Figure 11-6 shows a picture of a shaded patch.

The interval method used for calculating a shading range over the entire patch at a time performs well and avoids unnecessary repetitions of the subdivision process as compared with the existing algorithms in which the patch is subdivided until it becomes planar[Lane/Carpenter, Lane et.al.], or covers one raster unit[Catmull],irrespective of whether it requires only one level of intensity or more. Once the patch is flat enough so that it can be shaded with only one level of intensity, there is no point in further subdividing it. Since most raster scan displays today are frame buffer displays and do region filling locally, this method turns out to be a very efficient method for generation of shaded pictures.

Implementation issues

These algorithms have been implemented on DEC-1077 and VAX-11/780 systems in PASCAL. All figures in this paper have been generated using these implementations.

Procedures for different functions reside in different libraries. Four such libraries have been constructed:

(1) Interval operations (+ etc.).

(2) Interval property evaluations (N.E etc.).

(3) Analytic procedures (for handling lines and planes).

(4) Visualization/Transformation procedures (rotation etc.).

The data base is in the form of subdivision trees which are created whenever required and traversed for generating the desired output.

These programs are very straight forward to use. However, our experience in their use has made us aware of one very important point which we would like to mention here. In the use of subdivision methods the choice of various tolerance values plays a very critical role. Inappropriate tolerances result in cracks in tessellated drawings and discontinuities in the intersection curves of two surfaces. These have to be removed by adjusting tolerances.

Acknowledgements

The authors are greatful to Prof.R.Narsimhan and Dr.M.V. Pitke of the Tata Institute of Fundamental Research and Dr.V.N. Joshi of the Bombay University for their encouragement. The first author was partially supported by University Grants Commission Research Fellowship.

References

[Catmull] Catmull A.A.: "A Subdivision Algorithm for Computer Display of Curved Surfaces", Ph.D. Thesis, University of Utah, 1974.

[Koparkar] "Computational Techniques for Processing Parametric Curves and Surfaces", Ph.D. Thesis, Bombay University, Feb 1984.

[Koparkar/Mudur-1] "A New Class of Algorithms for Processing Parametric Curves", Computer Aided Design, V 15, p 43, 1983.

[Koparkar/Mudur-2] "Computational Techniques for processing parametric surfaces", Computer Vision, Graphics, Image Processing, V28, No3, p33, (1984).

[Koparkar/Mudur-3] "Generation of Continuous and Smooth Curves Resulting from Operations on Parametric Surfaces", submitted for publication.

[Mudur/Koparkar-1] "Product Surfaces and Modulated Surfaces for 3-D Shape Representation in Computer Vision Systems", IEEE conference on Cybernatics and Society, held in Bombay and Delhi,Jan 3,1984.

[Mudur/Koparkar-2] "Interval Methods for Processing Geometric Objects",Computer Graphics and Applications, V3,No2, (1984).

[Lane/Carpenter] Lane J.F. and Carpenter L.C.: "A Generalized Scan Line Algorithm for the Computer Display of Curved Surfaces", Computer Graphics and Image Processing, V11, p290, 1979.

[Lane et. al.] Lane J., Carpenter L., Whitted T. and Blinn J.: "Scanline Methods for Displaying parametrically Defined Surfaces", Communications of A.C.M. V23, p23, 1980.

[Lane/Riesenfeld] Lane J.M., Riesenfeld R.F.: "A Theoretical Development for the Computer Generation and Display of Piecewise Polynomial Surfaces", IEEE Transactions on Pattern Analysis and Machine Intelligence, V2, p36, 1980.

[Moore] Moore R.E.: "Interval Analysis", Prentice Hall Inc., 1966.

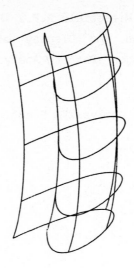

Fig 1

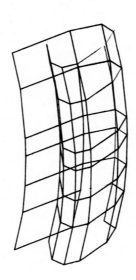

Fig 2

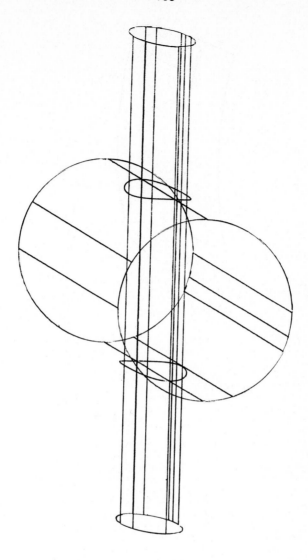

Fig 3

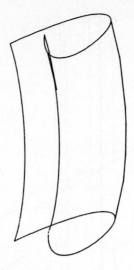

Fig 4

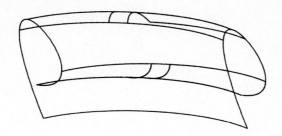

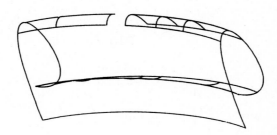

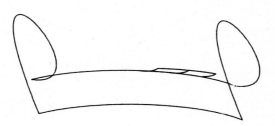

Fig 5

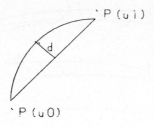

Fig 6

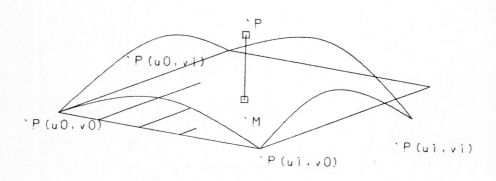

Fig 7

Fig 8

Fig 9

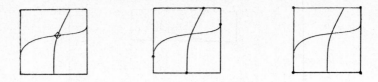

Fig 10

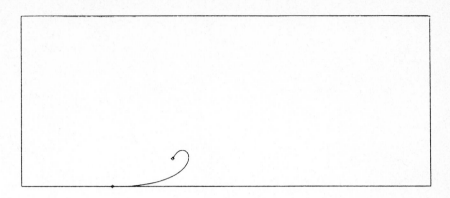

Fig 11

Fig 12

Section 8
Theoretical Aspects and Models

RANDOM FRACTAL FORGERIES

Richard F. Voss
IBM Thomas J. Watson Research Center
Yorktown Heights, NY 10598 USA

ABSTRACT

Mandelbrot's fractal geometry provides both a description and a mathematical model for many of the seemingly complex shapes found in nature. Such shapes often possess a remarkable invariance under changes of magnification. This statistical self-similarity may be characterized by a fractal dimension, a number that agrees with our intuitive notion of dimension but need not be an integer. In section I, a series of computer generated and rendered random fractal shapes provide a visual introduction to the concepts of fractal geometry. These complex images, with details on all scales, are the result of the simplest rules of fractal geometry. Their success as forgeries of the natural world has played an important role in the rapid establishment of fractal geometry as a new scientific discipline and exciting graphic technique. Section II presents a brief mathematical characterization of these forgeries, as variations on Mandelbrot's fractional Brownian motion. The important concepts of fractal dimension and exact and statistical self-similarity and self-affinity will be reviewed. Finally, section III will discuss independent cuts, Fourier filtering, midpoint displacement, successive random additions, and the Weierstrass-Mandelbrot random function as specific generating algorithms.

I. VISUAL INTRODUCTION TO FRACTAL FORGERIES

Figure C1, like all of the color illustrations accompanying this article (but collected elsewhere in this volume), is an example of a fractal forgery. It is actually composed of three separate forgeries which will be discussed in more detail below: the fractal landscape in the foreground, Fig. C2, its fractally distributed craters, Fig. C3, and the generalization of Brownian motion onto a sphere rising in the background, Fig. C4. The objects represented in the images exist only as arrays of pseudo-random numbers in a computer. Yet, the resemblance to the real world is unmistakable. My success with these forgeries and the extent to which they capture some of the essential characteristics of nature is due to a new branch of mathematics, *fractal geometry* [1], as conceived and developed by Benoit Mandelbrot.

NATO ASI Series, Vol. F17
Fundamental Algorithms for Computer Graphics
Edited by R. A. Earnshaw
© Springer-Verlag Berlin Heidelberg 1985

According to Galileo (1623),

> "Philosophy is written in this grand book - I mean universe - which stands continuously open to our gaze, but it cannot be understood unless one first learns to comprehend the language in which it is written. It is written in the language of mathematics, and its characters are triangles, circles and other geometrical figures, without which it is humanly impossible to understand a single word of it; without these, one is wandering about in a dark labyrinth".

Galileo was, of course, stating one of the basic tenets of modern science. In order to understand or simulate nature, one must first comprehend its language. To scientists, nature's languages are mathematics and geometry presents the specific structures for understanding and manipulating shapes. Galileo was, however, wrong in terms of the dialect used by much of nature. The inability of the triangles and circles of Euclidean geometry (the actual dialect to which he referred) to accurately describe the natural world has been unappreciated until recently. In retrospect it is obvious that, "clouds are not spheres, mountains are not cones, coastlines are not circles, and bark is not smooth, nor does lightning travel in a straight line" [Mandelbrot, ref. 1]. Fortunately, there is now a geometry that is appropriate for the irregular shapes of the real world.

mathematical monsters: some early fractals

The turn of the century coincided roughly with an upheaval in the world of mathematics. Minds conceived of strange monsters seemingly without counterpart in nature: Cantor sets, Weierstrass functions, Peano curves, curves without derivatives and lines that could fill space. Having once discovered these monsters (and congratulated themselves on a creativity superior to nature), mathematicians banished the beasts, mostly sight unseen, to a mathematical zoo. They could imagine no use for, nor interest in, their creations by natural scientists. Nature, however, was not so easily outdone. As shown by Benoit Mandelbrot, a mathematician at IBM and Harvard, many of these "monsters" do, in fact, have counterparts in the real world. Illuminated by computer graphics, they have finally been recognized as some of the basic structures in the language of nature's irregular shapes: the fractal geometry of nature.

Fractals (a word coined by Mandelbrot in 1975) have blossomed tremendously in the past few years and have helped reconnect pure mathematics research with both the natural sciences and computing. Within the last 5-10 years fractal geometry and its concepts have become central issues in most of the natural sciences: physics, chemistry, biology, geology, meteorology, and materials science. At the same time, fractals are of interest to graphic designers and filmmakers for their ability to create new and exciting shapes and artificial but realistic worlds. Computer graphics has played an important role in the development and rapid acceptance of fractal geometry as a valid new discipline. The computer rendering of fractal shapes leaves no doubt of their relevance to nature. Conversely, fractal geometry now plays a central role in the realistic rendering and modelling of natural phenomena in computer graphics.

fractals: self–similarity and dimension

What then are fractals? How are they different from the usual Euclidean shapes? The answer can be illustrated with one of the early mathematical monsters: the von Koch snowflake curve (first proposed around 1904). Figure 5 illustrates an iterative or recursive procedure for constructing a fractal curve. A simple line segment is divided into thirds and the middle third is replaced by two segments forming part of an equilateral triangle. At the next stage in the construction each of these 4 segments is replaced by 4 new segments with length 1/3 of their parent according to the original pattern. This procedure, repeated over and over, yields the beautiful von Koch curve shown at the top of Fig. 5 and demonstrates that the iteration of a very simple rule can produce seemingly complex shapes with some highly unusual properties. At each stage in its construction the length of the curve increases by a factor of 4/3. Thus, the limiting curve crams an infinite length into a finite area of the plane without intersecting itself. The curve has detail on all length scales. Indeed, the closer one looks, the more powerful the microscope one uses, the more detail one finds. More important, the curve possesses an exact *self-similarity*. Each small portion, when magnified, can reproduce exactly a larger portion. The curve is said to be invariant under changes of scale.

This property of self-similarity or *scaling* is one of the central concepts of fractal geometry. It is closely connected with our intuitive notion of *dimension*. An object normally considered as one-dimensional, a line segment, for example, also possesses a similar scaling property. It can be divided into N identical parts each of which is scaled down by the ratio $r=1/N$ from the whole. Similarly, a two-dimensional object, such as a square in the plane, can be divided into N self-similar parts each of which is scaled down by a factor $r=1/N^{1/2}$. A three-dimensional object like a solid cube may be divided into N little cubes each of which is scaled down by a ratio $r=1/N^{1/3}$. With self-similarity the generalization to fractal dimension is straightforward. A D-dimensional self-similar object can be divided into N smaller copies of itself each of which is scaled down by a factor r where $r=1/N^{1/D}$ or

$$N = 1/r^D. \tag{I.1}$$

Conversely, given a self-similar object of N parts scaled by a ratio r from the whole, its *fractal* or *similarity dimension* is given by

$$D = \log(N)/\log(1/r). \tag{I.2}$$

The fractal dimension, unlike the more familiar notion of Euclidean dimension, need not be an integer. Any segment of the von Koch curve is composed of 4 sub-segments each of which is scaled down by a factor of $1/3$ from its parent. Its fractal dimension $D = \log(4)/\log(3)$ or about 1.26.... This non-integer dimension, greater than one but less than two, reflects the unusual properties of the curve. It somehow fills more of space than a simple line (D=1), but less than a Euclidean area of the plane (D=2). Mandelbrot[1] gives many variations of the von Koch construction. As D increases from 1 toward 2 the resulting "curves" progress from being "line-like" to "filling" much of the plane. Indeed, the limit $D \rightarrow 2$ gives a Peano or "space-filling" curve. Although the von Koch curve has a fractal dimension $D = \log(4)/\log(3)$, it remains a "curve" with a topological dimension of one. The removal of a single point cuts the curve in two pieces.

statistical self-similarity

Although objects in nature rarely exhibit exact self-similarity, they do often possess a related property, *statistical self-similarity*. Perhaps the simplest example is a coastline. As with the von Koch curve, the closer one looks at a coastline, the more detail one sees. In a measurement of the length of a coastline, the more carefully one follows the smaller wiggles, the longer it becomes. A drive along a coast highway is shorter than a walk along the beach. Moreover, each small section of a coastline looks like (but not exactly like) a larger portion. This concept of statistical self-similarity can also be quantified in terms of fractal dimension as above. When using a ruler of size r to measure a coastline's length, the total length equals the ruler size r × the number of steps of size r, N(r), taken in tracing the coast

$$\text{LENGTH} = r \times N(r).$$

As with the snowflake, N(r) varies *on the average* as $1/r^D$ and

$$\text{LENGTH} \propto r \times 1/r^D = 1/r^{D-1}. \tag{I.3}$$

The variation of apparent coastline length with ruler size has been studied by Richardson as summarized in [1]. Real coastlines can, in fact, be characterized by fractal dimensions D of about 1.15 to 1.25, close to the $\log(4)/\log(3)$ of the von Koch curve.

The property that objects can look statistically similar while at the same time different in detail at different length scales, is the central feature of all of the random fractal forgeries presented here. Figure 6 shows a series of views, at increasing magnification, of a computer generated fractal landscape with just such a statistically self-similar coastline. The upper left image shows a section of the landscape. A small portion, outlined by a black box, is then magnified to fill the second frame. In each succeeding frame a portion about the coastline, indicated by a small box, is magnified to fill the next frame. The total magnification is given above each frame. This zooming process can be continued indefinitely. In Fig 6. the magnification is carried to a total of more than 16 million and the final frame repeats the starting view. Each frame is clearly a magnification of a portion of the previous, yet each frame also looks like a different part of the same landscape *at the same magnification*. This is the statistical self-similarity of a random fractal. It is random in the sense that (unlike the von Koch curve) a large scale view is insufficient to predict the exact details of a magnified view. The way in which the detail varies as one changes length scale is once again characterized by a fractal dimension. The irregular fractal surface is more than a simple surface (D=2) and the sample shown in Fig. 6 has D=2.2. The fractal dimension of the coastline is one less than that of the surface itself. Here the coastline D=1.2.

Mandelbrot landscapes

For the idealized Mandelbrot fractal landscape of Fig 6. the statistical self-similarity extends from arbitrarily large to arbitrarily small scales. Actual landscapes, on the other hand, can be statistically self-similar only over a finite (but often quite large) range of distances. The largest variations may be limited by the size of the planet or the force of gravity (the materials may not be strong enough to support arbitrarily high mountains). The smallest scales may be limited by the smoothing of erosion, the basic grain size of the rock and sand or, at the very least, by the atomic nature of the particles. The mathematical ideal is an approximation to the real world (or vice versa to some mathematicians). Mandelbrot's fractal geometry, however, remains by far the best approximation and, to date, the most widely successful mathematical model.

As discussed below, almost all algorithms for generating the fractal landscapes effectively add random irregularities to the surface at smaller and smaller scales similar to the process of adding smaller and smaller line segments to the von Koch curve. Once again, the fractal dimension determines the relative amounts of detail or irregularities at different distance scales. Surfaces with a larger D seem rougher. This effect is illustrated in Fig. C7 which shows the "same" surface but with different fractal dimensions. Figure C7(a) has a relatively low fractal dimension for the surface, D = 2.15, that is appropriate for much of the earth. An increase in the fractal dimension to D=2.5 is shown in Fig C7(b). A further increase to D=2.8 in Fig. C7(c) gives an unrealistically rough surface for an actual landscape. Fractal geometry specifies only the relative height variations of the landscape at different length scales. For the samples given here the color changes were based on height above water level and local slope.

The image in Fig. C7(a) does not, however, resemble many of the valleys on the Earth's surface which are significantly eroded. A flat bottomed basin can, however, be approximated mathematically by simply taking the height variations and scaling them by a power-law. This process is illustrated in Fig. C7(d) where the original landscape of Fig. C7(a) is "cubed". The effect of such a power greater than 1 is to flatten the lower elevations near near the water emphasizing the peaks. Scaling with a power less than one has the opposite effect of flattening the peaks while increasing the steepness near the water. A cube-root processing of Fig. C7(a) is shown in Fig. C7(e). This forgery gives the impression of river erosion into an otherwise fairly smooth plain.

fractally distributed craters

In order to give the impression of a lunar landscape, as shown in the foreground of Fig. 1, it is necessary to add craters to the "virgin" fractal landscape of Fig C7(a). Each crater is circular with a height profile similar to the effect of dropping marbles in mud. The trick in achieving realism is to use the proper distribution of crater sizes. For the moon, the actual distribution is fractal or power-law, with many more small craters than large ones. Specifically, the number of craters having an area, a, greater than some number A, $N(a>A)$ varies as $1/A$. The computer simulation is shown in Fig. C3. This is the same surface that forms the foreground of Fig. C1.

fractal planet: Brownian motion on a sphere

Rather than add increasing detail at progressively smaller scales, the rising fractal planet in Fig. C1 was generated by a different algorithm that is closer to an actual model for the evolution of the earth's surface. Its surface is a generalization of Brownian motion or a random walk on a sphere. A random walk is the sum of many independent steps, and the sphere's surface becomes the result of many independent surface displacements or faults. Each fault encircles the sphere in a random direction and divides it into two hemispheres which are displaced relative to each other in height. Inside the computer, the surface of the sphere is mapped onto a rectangular array similar to a flat projection map of the earth. Figure C8(a) shows the surface variations, as represented by regions of different color, both for the full and the flattened sphere after only 10 random faults. After 60 faults in Fig. C8(b), the flattened sphere gives the impression of a cubist painting. With 750 faults in Fig. C8(c), the sphere has developed a localized land mass and the effects of an individual fault are becoming lost. After more than 10,000 faults and the addition of polar caps in Fig C8(d), the sphere's surface becomes a plausible planet with $D=2.5$. Mapping the data of Fig. C8(d) back onto a sphere gives the fractal planet in Fig. 1 or the enlarged view of the rotated sphere shown in Fig. C8(e). Remarkably, the same sphere is also a good forgery of a much more arid generic planet. Fig. C8(e) shows the same data but with different coloring and without water.

fractal flakes and clouds

Up to now the fractal forgeries have been pretentious surfaces. The addition of irregularities on smaller and smaller scales raise their dimensions above a topological value of 2 to a fractal value $2<D<3$. It is, however, also possible to generate fractals with a topological dimension 3 whose scaling irregularities raise the fractal dimension to $3<D<4$. Rather than landscapes, which consist of random heights as a function of 2-dimensional surface position, such objects might represent a random temperature or water vapor density as a function of 3-dimensional position. The simplest means of viewing such constructions is with their *zerosets* (equivalent to the coastlines of the fractal landscapes) as shown in Fig. C9. For a temperature distribution $T(x,y,z)$ with fractal dimension $3<D<4$, the zerosets are all points for which $T(x,y,z)-T_0 = 0$ and have a fractal dimension of $D-1$. They can be displayed by treating all points for which $T(x,y,z)>T_0$ as opaque while all others are transparent. The resulting fractal flakes are shown in Fig. C9(a) where $D-1=2.5$ and Fig. C9(b) where $D-1=2.2$. A more accurate display is also possible by allowing the local light scattering to vary as $T(x,y,z)$. In this case, the flakes are transformed into realistic looking fractal clouds as shown in Figs C9(c) and (d). The correspondence to actual clouds is not surprising. Clouds and rain areas are the natural shapes where fractal behavior has been experimentally verified over the widest range of distance scales[1]. A combination of such a fractal cloud above a cratered fractal surface is shown in Fig. C9(e). Here light scattered by the cloud produces shadows of varying intensity on the landscape.

scaling randomness in time: $1/f^\beta$ noises

All of the above forgeries have been based on fractal randomness in space. The computer generated images show, the extent to which simple fractal constructions capture the essence of natural shapes. Changes in time, however, have many of the same similarities at different scales as changes in space. To the physicist, unpredictable changes of any quantity V varying in time t are known as *noise*. Graphical samples of typical noises V(t) are shown in Fig. 10. To the left of each sample is a representation of its *spectral density*. The spectral density, $S_V(f)$, gives an estimate of the mean square fluctuations at frequency f and, consequently, of the variations over a time scale of order $1/f$. The traces made by each of these noises is a fractal curve and there is a direct relationship between the fractal dimension and the logarithmic slope of the spectral density which will be discussed below. Indeed, it is the understanding and simulation of such noises that forms the basis for all of the fractal forgeries presented here.

Figure 10(a) shows a *white noise*, the most random. It could be produced by a pseudo-random number generator and is completely uncorrelated from point to point. Its spectral density is a flat line, independent of frequency. Alternately, a white noise contains equal amounts of all frequencies (like a white light). Figure 10(c) shows a Brownian motion or a random walk, the most correlated of the three noise samples. It consists of many more slow (low frequency) than fast (high frequency) fluctuations and its spectral density is quite steep. It varies as $1/f^2$. Formally, the Brownian motion of Fig. 10(c) is the integral of the white noise of Fig. 10(a). In the middle, in Fig. 10(b) is an intermediate type of noise known as *1/f noise* because of the functional form of its spectral density. In general, the term $1/f$ noise is often applied to any fluctuating quantity V(t) with $S_V(f)$ varying as $1/f^\beta$ over many decades with $0.5 < \beta < 1.5$. Although both white and $1/f^2$ noise are well understood in terms of mathematics and physics, $1/f$ noise, whose origin remains a mystery after more than 60 years of investigation, represents the most common type of noise found in nature.

There are no simple mathematical models that produce $1/f$ noise other than the tautological assumption of a specific distribution of time constants. Little is also known about the physical origins of $1/f$, but it is found in many[2] physical systems: in almost all electronic components from simple carbon resistors to vacuum tubes and all semi-conducting devices; in all time standards from the most accurate atomic clocks and quartz oscillators to the ancient hourglass; in ocean flows and the changes in yearly flood levels of the river Nile[3] as recorded by the ancient Egyptians; in the small voltages measurable across nerve membranes due to sodium and potassium flow; and even in the flow of automobiles on an expressway[4]. $1/f$ noise is also found in music.

fractal music

One of my most exciting discoveries[5,6] was that almost all musical melodies also mimic $1/f$ noise. Music has the same blend of randomness and predictability that is found in $1/f$ noise. If one takes a music score and draws lines between successive notes of the melody one finds a graph remarkably similar in quality to Fig. 10(b). Some of the actual measured spectral densities for different types of music is shown in Fig. 11. There is little to distinguish these measurements on widely different types of music from each other or from the $1/f$ noise of Fig. 10(b). This type of analysis is surprisingly insensitive to the different types of music. It emphasizes, instead, the common element in music and suggests an answer to a question that has long troubled philosophers[7]. In the words of Plato, "For when there are no words (accompanying music), it is very difficult to recognize the meaning of the harmony and rhythm, or to see that any worthy object is imitated by them". Philosophers generally agreed on the imitative nature of the arts. It seemed obvious that painting, sculpture or drama imitated nature. But what does music imitate? The measurements suggest that music is imitating the characteristic way our world changes in time. Both music and $1/f$ noise are intermediate between randomness and predictability. Like fractal shapes there is something interesting on all (in this case, time) scales. Even the smallest phrase reflects the whole.

It is, of course, possible to use fractals, in this case as $1/f^\beta$ noises, for music as well as landscape forgery. Fig. 12 shows samples of "music" generated from the three characteristic types of "noise" shown in Fig. 10. Although none of the samples in Fig. 12 correspond to a sophisticated composition of a specific type of music, Fig. 12(b) generated from $1/f$ noise is the closest to real music. Such samples sound recognizably musical, but from a foreign or unknown culture.

fractals and the return to nature

Man has always been confronted with a world filled with seemingly complex irregular shapes and random fluctuations. In the quest for understanding, natural science has progressed by concentrating primarily on the simplest of systems. In this process, it has moved away from the direct experience of nature to the electronically instrumented laboratory. After all, who could describe, let alone understand, the profile of a mountain or the shape of a cloud? With fractal geometry, the quest for scientific understanding and realistic computer graphic imagery can return to the everyday natural world. As these forgeries show, nature's complex shapes are only seemingly so.

II. MATHEMATICAL CONSIDERATIONS: fractional Brownian motion

This section presents an expository summary of the major mathematical definitions and relations used in the random fractal forgeries as condensed from Mandelbrot[1]. When no other reference is indicated [1] may be assumed as the source.

The most useful mathematical model for the random fractals found in nature has been the *fractional Brownian motion* (fBm) of Mandelbrot and Wallis[1,8]. It is an extension of the central concept of *Brownian motion* that played an important role in both physics and mathematics. Moreover, it forms the basis for all of the forgeries presented here and the standard by which various generating algorithms may be compared.

A fractional Brownian motion, $V_H(t)$, is a single valued function of one variable, t (usually time). Its increments $V_H(t_2)-V_H(t_1)$ have a Gaussian distribution with variance

$$<|V_H(t_2) - V_H(t_1)|^2> \propto |t_2 - t_1|^{2H}, \tag{II.1}$$

where the brackets $<$ and $>$ denote averages over many samples of $V_H(t)$ and the parameter H has a value $0<H<1$. Such a function is both stationary and isotropic. Its mean square increments depend only on the time difference t_2-t_1 and all t's are statistically equivalent. The special value $H=1/2$ gives the familiar Brownian motion with $\Delta V^2 \propto \Delta t$.

As with the usual Brownian motion, although $V_H(t)$ is continuous, it is nowhere differentiable. Nevertheless, many constructs have been developed (and are relevant to the problem of light scattering from fractals) to give meaning to "derivative of fractional Brownian motion" as *fractional Gaussian noises*. Such constructs are usually based on averages of $V_H(t)$ over decreasing scales. The derivative of normal Brownian motion, $H=1/2$, corresponds to the uncorrelated *white Gaussian noise* of Fig. 10(a), and Brownian motion is said to have *independent increments*. Formally, for any three times such that $t_1<t<t_2$, $\Delta V_1=V_H(t)-V_H(t_1)$ is statistically independent of $\Delta V_2=V_H(t_2)-V_H(t)$ for $H=1/2$. For $H>1/2$ there is a positive correlation both for the increments of $V_H(t)$ and its derivative fractional Gaussian noise in Figs. 10 (b) and (c). For $H<1/2$ the increments are negatively correlated. Such correlations, moreover, extend to arbitrarily long time scales.

As with coastlines, $V_H(t)$ shows a statistical scaling behavior. If the time scale t is changed by the factor r, then the increments ΔV_H change by a factor r^H. Formally,

$$<\Delta V_H(rt)^2> \propto r^{2H}<\Delta V_H(t)^2>. \tag{II.2}$$

Unlike statistically self-similar coastlines, however, a $V_H(t)$ trace requires *different* scaling factors in the two coordinates (r for t but r^H for V_H) reflecting the special status of the t coordinate. Each t can correspond to only one value of V_H but any specific V_H may occur at multiple t's. Such non-uniform scaling is known as *self-affinity* rather than self-similarity.

self–similar vs self–affine fractals.

The distinction between similarity and affinity is important. By way of summary[1], a *self-similar* object is composed of N copies of itself (with possible translations and rotations) each of which is scaled down by the ratio r in all E coordinates from the whole. More formally, consider a set S of points at positions $\vec{x} = (x_1, ..., x_E)$ in Euclidean space of dimension E. Under a *similarity* transform with real scaling ratio $0 < r < 1$, the set S becomes rS with points at $\vec{rx} = (rx_1, ..., rx_E)$. A bounded set S is *self-similar* when S is the union of N distinct (non-overlapping) subsets each of which is congruent to rS. *Congruent* means identical under translations and rotations. The fractal or *similarity dimension* of S is then given by

$$1 = Nr^D \quad \text{or} \quad D = \frac{\log N}{\log 1/r}. \tag{II.3}$$

It is useful to note that the fractal dimension D also characterizes the covering of the set S by E-dimensional "boxes" of linear size L. If the entire S is contained within one box of size L_{max}, then each of the $N = 1/r^D$ subsets will fall within one box of size $L = rL_{max}$. Thus, the number of boxes of size L, $N(L)$, needed to cover S is given by

$$N(L)/N(L_{max}) = (L_{max}/L)^D \quad \text{or} \quad N(L) \propto 1/L^D. \tag{II.4}$$

This definition of *box dimension* is one of the most useful methods for estimating the fractal dimension of a given set.

One can also estimate the "volume" or "mass" of the set S by a covering with boxes of linear size L. If one considers only distances of order L about a given point in S, one finds a single box of size L with E-dimensional volume L^E. If the distance scale about the same point is increased to $L_{max} = L/r$, one now finds a total of $N = 1/r^D = (L_{max}/L)^D$ boxes of the same size boxes. Thus, the mass within a distance L_{max} of some point in S, $M(L_{max}) = N \times M(L) = M(L) \times (L_{max}/L)^D$ or

$$M(L) \propto L^D. \tag{II.5}$$

The fractal dimension D, thus, also corresponds to the commonly used *mass dimension* in physics. Mass dimension also has a strong connection with intuitive notions of dimension. The amount of material within a distance L of a point in a one-dimensional object increases as L^1. For an E-dimensional object it varies as L^E. The mass dimension is another extremely useful method for estimating the fractal dimension of a given object.

The set S is also *self-similar* if each of the N subsets is scaled down from the whole by a different similarity ratio r_n. In this case, D is given implicitly by

$$1 = \sum_{n=1}^{N} r_n^D , \qquad (II.6)$$

which reduces to the familiar result in Eq. (II.3) when all of the r_n are equal.

The set S is *statistically self-similar* if it is composed of N distinct subsets each of which is scaled down by the ratio r from the original and is identical in all statistical respects to rS. The similarity dimension is again given by Eq. (II.3). In practice, it is impossible to verify that all moments of the distributions are identical, and claims of statistical self-similarity are usually based on only a few moments. Moreover, a sample of a random set (such as a coastline) is often statistically self-similar for all scaling ratios r. Its fractal dimension is usually estimated from the dependence of box coverings N(L) or mass M(L) on varying L as in Eqs. (II.4) and (II.5).

Under an *affine* transform, on the other hand, each of the E coordinates of $\bar{x}$ may be scaled by a different ratio $(r_1, ..., r_E)$. Thus, the set S is transformed to r(S) with points at $r(\bar{x}) = (r_1 x_1, ..., r_E x_E)$. A bounded set S is *self-affine* when S is the union of N distinct (non-overlapping) subsets each of which is congruent to r(S). Similarly, S is *statistically self-affine* when S is the union of N distinct subsets each of which is congruent *in distribution* to r(S). The fractal dimension D, however, is not as easily defined as with self-similarity.

the relation of D to H for self-affine fractional Brownian motion

The assignment of a fractal dimension D to a self-affine set can be illustrated with a trace of fractional Brownian motion $V_H(t)$ from above. It may be helpful to glance again at Fig. 10. Consider, for convenience, a trace of $V_H(t)$ covering a time span $\Delta t = 1$ and a vertical range $\Delta V_H = 1$. $V_H(t)$ is statistically self-affine when t is scaled by r and V_H is scaled by r^H. Suppose the time span is divided into N equal intervals each with $\Delta t = 1/N$. Each of these intervals will contain one portion of $V_H(t)$ with vertical range

$\Delta V_H = \Delta t^H = 1/N^H$. Since $0 < H < 1$ each of these new sections will have a large vertical to horizontal size ratio and the occupied portion of each interval will be covered by $\Delta V_H/\Delta t = (1/N^H)/(1/N) = N/N^H$ square boxes of linear scale $L = 1/N$. In terms of box dimension, as t is scaled down by a ratio $r = 1/N$ the number of square boxes covering the trace goes from 1 to $N(L)$ = number of intervals × boxes per interval or

$$N(L) = N \times N/N^H = r^{2-H} = 1/L^{2-H}. \tag{II.7}$$

Thus, by comparison with Eq. (II.4),

$$D = 2 - H \quad \text{for a } 1/f^\beta \text{ noise.} \tag{II.8}$$

Consequently, the trace of normal Brownian motion has $D = 1.5$.

The *zeroset* of fBm is the the intersection of the trace of $V_H(t)$ with the t axis, the set of all points such that $V_H(t) = 0$. The zeroset is a disconnected set of points with topological dimension zero and a fractal dimension $D_0 = D-1 = 1-H$ that is less than 1 but greater than 0. Although the trace of $V_H(t)$ is self-affine, its zeroset is self-similar.

self–affinity in higher E: Mandelbrot landscapes and clouds

The traces of fBm such as Fig. 10(c) bear a striking resemblance to a mountainous horizon. The modelling of the irregular Earth's surface as a generalization of traces of fBm was first proposed by Mandelbrot. The single variable t can be replaced by coordinates x and y in the plane to give $V_H(x,y)$ as the surface altitude at position x,y. In this case, the altitude variations of a hiker following any straight line path at constant speed in the xy plane is a fractional Brownian motion. In analogy with Eq. (II.1),

$$< | V_H(x_2, y_2) - V_H(x_1, y_1) |^2 > \propto [(x_2 - x_1)^2 + (y_2 - y_1)^2]^H. \tag{II.9}$$

Once again, the fractal dimension D must be greater than the topological dimension 2 of the surface. Here,

$$D = 3 - H \quad \text{for a fractal landscape.} \tag{II.10}$$

The intersection of a vertical plane with the surface $V_H(x,y)$ is a self-affine fBm trace with $D = 2-H$, smaller by one than the value of Eq. (II.10). Similarly, the zeroset of $V_H(x,y)$, its intersection with a horizontal plane, also has a fractal dimension $D_0 = 2-H$. This intersection, which produces a family of (possibly disconnected) curves, forms the coastlines of the $V_H(x,y)$ landscape. Since the two coordinates x and y are, however, equivalent, the coastlines of $V_H(x,y)$ are self-similar, not self-affine.

This generalization of fBm can continue to still higher dimensions to produce the self-affine fractal temperature distribution $T(x,y,z)$ as $V_H(x,y,z)$. Here, the temperature variations of an observer moving at constant speed along any straight line path in space generate a fBm and the fractal dimension

$$D = 4 - H \quad \text{for a fractal cloud.} \tag{II.11}$$

The zeroset $V_H(x,y,z) = $ constant now gives a self-similar fractal with $D_0 = 3$-H.

To summarize, a statistically self-affine fractional Brownian function, V_H of $\vec{x} = (x_1, \ldots, x_E)$ in E+1 Euclidean dimensions satisfies

$$<|V_H(\vec{x}_2) - V_H(\vec{x}_1)|^2> \propto |\vec{x}_2 - \vec{x}_1|^{2H}. \tag{II.12}$$

and has a fractal dimension

$$D = E + 1 - H. \tag{II.13}$$

The zerosets of $V_H(\vec{x})$ form a statistically self-similar fractal with dimension $D_0 = $ E-H.

spectral densities for fBm and the spectral exponent β

As mentioned in section I, random functions in time $V(t)$ are often characterized[9,10] by their *spectral densities* $S_V(f)$. If $V(t)$ is the input to a narrow bandpass filter at frequency f and bandwidth Δf, then $S_V(f)$ is the mean square output $V(f)$ divided by Δf, $S_V(f) = |V(f)|^2/\Delta f$. $S_V(f)$ gives information about the time correlations of $V(t)$. As shown in Fig. 10, when $S_V(f)$ increases steeply at low f, $V(t)$ varies more slowly. If one defines $V(f,T)$ as the Fourier transform of a specific sample of $V(t)$ for $0<t<T$,

$$V(f,T) = \frac{1}{T} \int_0^T V(t)e^{2\pi ift}dt, \text{ then } S_V(f) \propto T|V(f,T)|^2 \text{ as } T \to \infty. \tag{II.14}$$

An alternate characterization of the time correlations of $V(t)$ is given by the *2 point autocorrelation function*

$$G_V(\tau) = <V(t)V(t + \tau)> - <V(t)>^2.$$

$G_V(\tau)$ provides a measure of how the fluctuations at two times separated by τ are related. $G_V(\tau)$ and $S_V(f)$ are not independent. In many cases they are related by the Wiener-Khintchine relation[9,10]

$$G_V(\tau) = \int_0^\infty S_V(f) \, \cos(2\pi f\tau) \, df. \tag{II.15}$$

For a Gaussian white noise $S_V(f)$ = constant and $G_V(\tau) = \Delta V^2 \delta(\tau)$ is completely un-correlated. For certain simple power laws for $S_V(f)$, $G_V(\tau)$ can be calculated exactly. Thus, for

$$S_V(f) \propto 1/f^\beta, \text{ with } 0<\beta<1, \quad G_V(\tau) \propto \tau^{\beta-1}. \tag{II.16}$$

Moreover, $G_V(\tau)$ is directly related to the mean square increments of fBm,

$$<|V(t+\tau) - V(t)|^2> = 2[<V^2> - <V>^2] - 2G_V(\tau). \tag{II.17}$$

Roughly speaking, $S_V(f) \propto 1/f^\beta$ corresponds to $G_V(\tau) \propto \tau^{1-\beta}$ and a fBm with $2H=\beta-1$ from Eqs. (II.1) and (II.17). Thus, the statistically self-affine fractional Brownian function, $V_H(\vec{x})$, has a fractal dimension D and spectral density $S_V(f) \propto 1/f^\beta$, for the fluctu-ations along a straight line path in any direction in E-space with

$$D = E + 1 - H = E + \frac{3-\beta}{2} \tag{II.18}$$

This result agrees with other[1,8,11] "extensions" of the concepts of *spectral density* and *Wiener-Khintchine relation* to *non-stationary* noises where some moments may be unde-fined. Moreover, it provides an extremely useful connection between D, H and β for fi-nite simulations. For H in the range $0<H<1$, $E<D<E+1$, and $1<\beta<3$. The value $H \simeq 0.8$ is a good choice for many natural phenomena.

Although the formal definition of fBm restricts H to the range $0<H<1$, it is often useful to consider integration and an appropriate definition of "derivative" as extending the range of H. Thus, integration of a fBm produces a new fBm with H increased by 1, while "differentiation" reduces H by 1. When $H \to 1$, the derivative of fBm looks like a fBm with $H \to 0$. In terms of spectral density, if $V(t)$ has $S_V(f) \propto 1/f^\beta$ then its derivative dV/dt has spectral density $f^2/f^\beta = 1/f^{\beta-2}$. In terms of Eq. (II.19), differentiation de-creases β by 2 and decreases H by 1.

III. ALGORITHMS: approximating fBm on a finite grid

Section I established the visual connection between many, seemingly complex, shapes in the natural world and statistically self-similar and self-affine fractals. Section II reviewed some of the mathematical considerations and established the relation between fractal dimension D, the H parameter of fBm, and the spectral density exponent β. This section discusses various methods for producing a finite *sample* of fBm as a noise (E=1), a landscape (E=2), or a cloud (E=3). As with nature itself, this sample will typically be limited by both a smallest size or resolution λ and a largest scale L_{max}. Consideration will be given to sample statistics (mathematically, how well does it approximate fBm?), visual features (does it look natural?) and computation characteristics (how does computation time vary with sample size? can one magnify or extend the sample beyond its boundaries?). In general, the closer a given algorithm approximates fBm, the more "realistic" the resulting image looks. Although no specific consideration will be given to image rendering, it is important to note that in most cases rendering of a fractal sample requires far more computation than sample generation. This is particularly true for rendering packages based on Euclidean shapes which have an extremely difficult time with the "infinite" number of surface patches on a fractal surface.

Brownian motion as independent cuts

In the usual definition, Brownian motion, $V_B(t) = V_H(t)$ for H=1/2, is the integral of a Gaussian white noise W(t),

$$V_B(t) = \int_{-\infty}^{t'} W(t')dt'. \tag{III.1}$$

Brownian motion may also be considered as the cumulative displacement of a series of independent jumps. A pulse at time t_i causes a jump of magnitude A_i (a Gaussian random variable) in V(t). The response to such a pulse, $A_iP(t-t_i)$ has the form of a step function with P(t)=1 for t>0 and P(0)=1 for t<0. Thus, $V_B(t)$ can also be written as the sum of independent cuts at random (Poisson distributed) times t_i

$$V_B(t) = \sum_{i=-\infty}^{\infty} A_iP(t - t_i). \tag{III.2}$$

This latter formulation of Brownian motion is useful since it can be generalized to circles and spheres to produce the fractal planet of Fig. C8. The time coordinate t may be replaced with the angular position θ on a unit circle. A Brownian motion in θ must then have the periodicity that $V_B(\theta) = V_B(\theta + 2\pi)$. In this case, $V_B(\theta) = \int_{\theta-\pi}^{\theta} W(\theta')d\theta'$. The $P(\theta)$ correspond to half circles, $P(\theta)=1$ for $0<\theta<\pi$ and $P(\theta)=0$ for $\pi<\theta<2\pi$, and Brownian motion on a circle becomes the summation of independent "half-circles" uniformly distributed in θ_i,

$$V_B(\theta) = \sum_{i=-\infty}^{\infty} A_i P(\theta - \theta_i). \tag{III.3}$$

In the generalization to a sphere, V_B becomes a function of $\vec{r}$, the position on the unit sphere, and corresponds to the addition of random hemispheres whose positions $\vec{r}_i$ are uniformly distributed on the sphere surface,

$$V_B(\vec{r}) = \sum_{i=-\infty}^{\infty} A_i P(\vec{r} - \vec{r}_i). \tag{III.4}$$

Here, $P(\vec{r} - \vec{r}_i) = 1$ for $\vec{r} \cdot \vec{r}_i > 0$ and zero otherwise. The evolution of a Brownian sphere under this summation process is shown in Fig. C8.

A flat Brownian relief $V_B(x,y)$ can similarly be constructed from the addition of randomly placed and randomly oriented faults in the plane. The profile of such a fault corresponds to the step function of random amplitude A_i. Such a surface will have a fractal dimension D=2.5.

The independent addition of such step function faults is extremely expensive computationally. Each fault requires additions to roughly half of the surface elements. Moreover, the resulting fractal always corresponds to a fBm with H=1/2. Nevertheless, the procedure is straightforward and represents, historically, the first[1] method used for producing fractal landscapes.

random cuts with H ≠ 1/5: Campbell's theorem

The summation in Eq. (III.2) is a special case of Campbell's theorem (1909). Consider a collection of independent pulses occurring at random times t_i corresponding to an average rate $1/\tau$. Each pulse produces the profile $A_i P(t-t_i)$. The random function $V(t) = \Sigma A_i P(t - t_i)$, will then have a spectral density[9],

$$S_V(f) \propto \frac{1}{\tau}<A^2>|P(f)|^2, \tag{III.5}$$

where $P(f)$ is the Fourier transform of $P(t)$, $P(f) = \int P(t)e^{2\pi i f t}dt$. For normal Brownian motion, each excitation by the white noise $W(t)$ in Eq. (III.1) produces the step function response P(t) with P(f) $\propto$ 1/f and $S_V(f) \propto 1/f^2$. With a suitable power-law choice of P(t), one can generate an approximation to fBm with any H. In fact, fBm can be put in a form[1,8] similar to Eq. (III.1),

$$V_H(t) \;=\; \frac{1}{\Gamma(H + 1/2)} \int_{-\infty}^{t} (t - t')^{H-1/2} W(t') dt'.$$

Thus, fBm can be constructed from independent pulses with response $P(t) = t^{H-1/2}$ corresponding to $P(f) \propto 1/f^{H+1/2}$ from Eq. (II.16) and $S_V(f) \propto 1/f^{2H+1}$ in agreement with Eq. (II.18). This was the first method used for generating samples of fractional Gaussian noise and fractional Brownian landscapes. Unless only a few "pulses" or "faults" are acceptable, this process is, in general, too expensive computationally.

Fast Fourier Transform filtering

Another straightforward algorithm for fBm is to directly construct a random function with the desired spectral density $\propto 1/f^\beta$. For all practical purposes, the output of a pseudo-random number generator produces a "white noise" W(t). Filtering W(t) with a transfer function T(f) produces an output, V(t), whose spectral density,

$$S_V(f) \;\propto\; |T(f)|^2 S_W(f) \;\propto\; |T(f)|^2.$$

Thus, to generate a $1/f^\beta$ noise from a W(t) requires $T(f) \propto 1/f^{\beta/2}$.

A continuous function of time, V(t), may be approximated by a finite sequence of N values, V_n, defined at discrete times $t_n = n\Delta t$, where n runs from 0 to N-1 and Δt is the time between successive values. The discrete Fourier transform (DFT) defines V_n in terms of the complex Fourier coefficients, v_m, of the series:

$$V_n \;=\; \sum_{m=0}^{(N/2)-1} v_m e^{2\pi i f_m t_n}, \tag{III.6}$$

where the frequencies $f_m = m/N\Delta t$ for m=0 to N/2 - 1. For a fBm sequence with $S_V(f)$ varying as $1/f^\beta$ the coefficients must satisfy

$$<|v_m|^2> \;\propto\; 1/f^\beta \;\propto\; 1/m^\beta. \tag{III.7}$$

The relation between β and D and H is given by Eq. (II.18) with E=1. The v_m may be obtained by multiplying the Fourier coefficients of a white noise sequence by $1/f^{\beta/2}$ or by directly choosing complex random variables with mean square amplitude given by Eq.

(III.7) and random phases. One possible variation sets $|v_m| = 1/m^{\beta/2}$ and only randomizes the phases. With an FFT (Fast Fourier Transform) algorithm the evaluation of Eq. (III.6) requires of order NlogN operations[12] to produce a series of N points. As such it offers a significant improvement over the random cuts described above.

Since the FFT includes all possible frequency components over the range of distance scales from λ to $L_{max}=N\lambda$ it represents an accurate approximation to fBm. It has, however, several drawbacks. The entire sample must be computed at once and it is difficult to vary the degree of detail across the sample or to extend the sample across its original boundaries. In addition, the result is periodic in time, $V_n = V_{n+N}$. Such boundary constraints become more obvious as $B\rightarrow3$, $H\rightarrow1$, and $D\rightarrow1$. This effect may be reduced by generating a longer sequence and keeping only a portion (typically 1/4 to 1/2). Nevertheless, the FFT transform has been used to produce some of the most striking still images of random fractals (as shown in the color figures).

Although neither the random cuts nor the FFT filtering represent a *recursive* method of generating random fractals, the process of adding more and more frequencies is similar to the construction of the von Koch snowflake. Fig. 13 shows the increasing complexity in the FFT construction of a fBm sample with $H=0.8$ as higher frequencies are included.

The procedure is easily extended to functions of 2 coordinates to generate a fractal surface $V_H(x,y)$. $V_H(x,y)$ should have the same form for its autocorrelation function as a fBm. Eq. (II.15) can be extended to the xy plane

$$<V_H(\vec{r})V_H(\vec{r} + \vec{\delta})> = \int_0^\infty S(\vec{k}) \cos(2\pi\vec{k} \cdot \vec{\delta})2\pi kdk,$$

where $\vec{r}$ is a point in the xy plane and $\vec{\delta}$ is a displacement in the xy plane. Since all directions in the xy plane are equivalent, $S(\vec{k})$ depends only on $|\vec{k}| = k = (k_x^2 + k_y^2)^{1/2}$ and $|\vec{\delta}|$. For this δ dependence to correspond to the τ dependence of $<V(t)V(t+\tau)>$, $S(\vec{k})$ must vary as $1/k^{1+\beta}$ and $S(\vec{k}) \propto S_{cut}(k)/k$. The extra factor of k compensates for the 2 dimensional differential, $2\pi kdk$, in the integrand. For 3 coordinates, the spectral density of $V_H(x,y,z)$, $S(\vec{k}) \propto S_{cut}(k)/k^2$. and $S(\vec{k})$ varying as $1/k^{2+\beta}$ produces a $1/f^\beta$ noise for a sample V_H along any line.

The corresponding fractal surface is approximated on a finite N by N grid to give $V_H(x_n,y_m)$ where $x_n = n\lambda$ and $y_m = m\lambda$. The 2 dimensional complex FFT can be used to evaluate the series

$$V_{nm} = \sum_{qr}^{(N/2)-1} v_{qr} e^{2\pi i(k_q x_n + k_r y_m)},$$

where $k_q = q/(N\lambda)$ and $k_r = r/(N\lambda)$ are the spatial frequencies in the x and y directions. For a fBm surface corresponding to $\beta = 1+2H = 7-2D$, the coefficients v_{qr} must satisfy

$$<|v_{qr}|^2> \propto 1/k^{\beta+1} \propto 1/(q^2 + r^2)^{4-D}. \qquad (III.8)$$

The landscapes of Fig. C7 with 2<D<3 were generated with this process.

For a 3 dimensional fractional Brownian volume, $V_H(x,y,z)$, the Fourier coefficients v_{qrs} will satisfy

$$<|v_{qrs}|^2> \propto 1/k^{\beta+2} \propto 1/(q^2 + r^2 + s^2)^{(11-2D)/2} \qquad (III.9)$$

with 3<D<4. This method was used to produce the fractal flakes and clouds of Fig. C9.

random midpoint displacement

Random midpoint displacement is a recursive generating technique that was applied to normal Brownian motion as early as the 1920's by N. Wiener. It is a natural extension of the von Koch construction and figures in many of the fractal samples described by Mandelbrot[1]. Its use in computer graphics has been widely popularized by Fournier, Fussell, and Carpenter[13,14]. For $H \neq 1/2$ or $E > 1$, it sacrifices mathematical purity for execution speed in its approximation to fBm.

Consider the approximation to a simple fBm, $V_H(t)$, where the mean square increment for points separated by a time $\Delta t=1$ is σ^2. Then, from Eq. (II.1), for points separated by a time t, $<|V_H(t)-V_H(0)|^2> = t^{2H} \times \sigma^2$. If, for convenience, $V_H(0)=0$, then the points at $t=\pm 1$ are chosen as samples of a Gaussian random variable with variance σ^2 to satisfy Eq. (II.1). Given these initial conditions, one defines the midpoints at

$$V_H(\pm 1/2) = 0.5[V_H(0) + V_H(\pm 1)] + \Delta_1, \qquad (III.10)$$

where Δ_1 is a Gaussian random variable with zero mean and variance Δ_1^2 that is determined by the condition that the increments from 0 to $\pm 1/2$ must satisfy Eq. (II.1).

$$\Delta_1^2 = \frac{\sigma^2}{2^{2H}} - \frac{\sigma^2}{4} = \frac{\sigma^2}{2^{2H}}[1 - 2^{2H-2}]. \qquad (III.11)$$

The first term is the desired total variance from Eq. (II.1) while the second term represents the fluctuations already in $V_H(\pm 1)-V_H(0)$ due to the previous stage. As $H \to 1$, $\Delta_1^2 \to 0$, $D \to 1$, no new fluctuations are added at smaller stages, and $V_H(t)$ remains a collection of smooth line segments connecting the starting points. At the second stage, $V_H(\pm 1/4) = 0.5[V_H(0) + V_H(\pm 1/2)] + \Delta_2$ where Δ_2 has variance

$$\Delta_2^2 = \frac{\sigma^2}{4^{2H}} - \frac{\Delta_1^2}{4} = \frac{\sigma^2}{4^{2H}}[1 - 2^{2H-2}]. \tag{III.12}$$

At the nth stage, the length scale has decreased to $1/2^n$ and a random Gaussian variable Δ_n is added to the midpoints of the $(n-1)$th stage with variance

$$\Delta_n^2 = \frac{\sigma^2}{(2^n)^{2H}}[1 - 2^{2H-2}] \tag{III.13}$$

As expected for a fBm, at a length scale $r = 1/2^n$ one adds randomness with mean square variations varying as r^{2H}.

Although this process does produce a fractal, the result is, unfortunately, not stationary[1,15] for all H. Once a given point at t_i has been determined, its value remains unchanged in all later stages. All additional stages change $t < t_i$ independent from $t > t_i$ and the correlations required of fBm with $H \neq 1/2$ are not present. More specifically, by construction, the increments $<|V_H(\pm 1)-V_H(0)|^2> = \sigma^2$. For a stationary process, the same should be true of all increments with $\Delta t = 1$. However, the absence of correlation across an earlier stage requires that

$$<|V_H(1/2) - V_H(-1/2)|^2> = 2<|V_H(1/2) - V_H(0)|^2> = 2\frac{\sigma^2}{2^{2H}}.$$

This gives the desired result σ^2 only for the $H=1/2$ of normal Brownian motion.

Figure 14 shows the generation of a fBm sequence with $H=0.8$. Points generated at different stages have different statistical properties in their neighborhoods. This often leaves a visible trace that does not disappear as more stages are added. The effect is more pronounced as $H \to 1$. These visible artifacts, which are a consequence of the lack of stationarity of the mathematical approximation, are particularly visible on fractal surfaces. Figure 16 shows a zenith view of such a midpoint displacement surface with $H=0.8$. In the generation of a midpoint displacement surface on a square grid each step proceeds in two stages. First the midpoints of each of the squares is determined from its 4 corners and shifted by a random element Δ. This determines a new square lattice at 45 degrees to the original and with lattice size $1/\sqrt{2}$. In the second stage, the midpoints of the new lattice receive a random contribution smaller by $1/(\sqrt{2})^H$ from the first stage. This produces the new square lattice with a scale $1/2$ the original. The traces of early stages are readily visible in Fig. 16. These artifacts, which occur at all stages, can not be eliminated by local smoothing.

In spite of its mathematical failings, the speed of midpoint displacement, and its ability to add "detail" to an existing shape make it a useful fractal algorithm for some applications. To generate N points requires only order N operations. To extend the sequence by just one point at the smallest scale beyond its original endpoints, however, requires an additional $\log_2 N$ operations.

successive random additions

In many respects the non-stationary artifacts of midpoint displacement are similar to the staircase effect of aliased raster display lines. With midpoint displacement, once determined, the value at a point remains fixed. At each stage only half of the points are determined more accurately. If one imagines the process of magnifying an actual object, as the spatial resolution increases *all points are determined more accurately*. In terms of the Nyquist sampling theorem, to approximate N real points requires $N/2$ complex frequencies or $N/2$ sine and cosine components. When the resolution is doubled to 2N points, the additional high frequency components alter all of the original values. Midpoint displacement only adds the additional sine (or cosine) components. Conversely, in reducing the resolution of an image an anti-aliasing procedure will average over neighboring pixels. Simply keeping the same value as the center (the equivalent of midpoint displacement) produces the objectionable staircase edge.

I call the process of adding randomness *to all points* at each stage of a recursive subdivision process *successive random additions*. This enhancement reduces many of the visible artifacts of midpoint displacement and the generation still requires only order N operations to generate N points. The computation of the midpoints is the same as midpoint displacement. The only difference is in the number of random elements. For a sequence of N elements, $N/2$ points in the final stage had only one random addition. $N/4$ points in the previous stage had 2 random additions. $N/8$ had 3 and so on. The series converges to the 2N random additions for the N elements.

The zoom sequence of Fig. 6 was produced with successive random additions. The artifacts of the square lattice are not as visible as with the midpoint displacement surface of Fig. 15. Figure 16 shows the construction of a fBm sequence with H=0.8 by successive random additions.

With successive random additions, at each stage all points are treated equivalently. This has the additional advantage that the resolution at the next stage can change by any factor r<1. For midpoint displacement r must be 1/2. Thus, given a sample of N_n points at stage n with resolution λ, stage n+1 with resolution rλ is determined by first interpolating the $N_{n+1} = N_n/r$ new points from the old values. In practice, this can be accomplished using either linear or spline interpolation. A random element Δ_n is then added to all of the new points. At stage n with scaling ratio r<1, the Δ will have a variance

$$\Delta_n^2 \propto (r^n)^{2H}. \tag{III.14}$$

When 1/r is an integer, the generation of a sequence of N points requires order C(r)N operations. The coefficient C(r) varies as $\Sigma n(1 - r)^n$ over the number of stages.

The fractal dimension D for the generated objects is determined only by H, r can be varied independently. Variations in r change the *lacunarity* of the fractal. Figure 17 shows three samples of successive random addition surfaces (all with H=0.8, D=2.2) generated from differing r. The zoom sequence in Fig. 6 was generated with 1/r=2. As 1/r increases to 4 in Fig. 17(a) and 8 in Fig. 17(b) the few characteristic resolutions at which randomness has been added become visible and the lacunarity increases. As 1/r is decreased below 2 to √2 in Fig. 17(c) the lacunarity decreases and the surfaces approach the characteristics of the FFT samples. Empirically, a value of 1/r much smaller than 2 produces little observable change.

The free choice of a value for r is an important addition for filmmaking. The addition of irregularities to a surface can be accomplished continuously as the resolution is slowly increased from frame to frame.

Weierstrass–Mandelbrot random fractal function

Each stage in a midpoint displacement process increases the highest spatial frequency by a factor 1/r=2. Each stage of successive random additions increases this frequency by 1/r>1. Thus, both are related to Mandelbrot's generalization[1,11] of the Weierstrass non-differentiable function, $V_{MW}(t)$. Whereas the Fourier series of Eq. (III.6) involves a *linear* progression of frequencies, the Weierstrass function involves a geometric progression. In the notation of this paper,

$$V_{MW}(t) = \sum_{n=-\infty}^{\infty} A_n r^{nH} \sin(2\pi r^{-n}t + \phi_n), \tag{III.15}$$

where A_n is a Gaussian random variable with the same variance for all n and ϕ_n is a random phase uniformly distributed on 0-2π. The original Weierstrass function did not include the terms for n<0 which add small spatial frequencies and large scale fluctuations. As with successive random additions, the addition of a new term to the V_{MW} sum decreases the spatial resolution by r and adds new fluctuations with variance $A^2 r^{2H}$. In terms of spectral density, although V_{MW} contains only discrete frequencies $f_n = 1/r^n$, each component has a mean square amplitude $\propto r^{2Hn} \propto 1/f_n^{2H}$ in a bandwidth $\Delta f \propto f$. Thus, the spectral density

$$S_{V_{MW}}(f) \propto \frac{\text{amplitude}^2}{\Delta f} = \frac{1}{f^{2H+1}} \tag{III.16}$$

in agreement with Eq. (II.18).

Although the V_{MW} sum involves an infinite number of components, all practical applications introduce both low and high frequency cutoffs. For a range of distance scales from λ to L_{max} only $\log(L_{max}/\lambda)$ components are needed. Frequencies much higher than $1/\lambda$ average out to zero contribution over scales of size λ while frequencies much lower than $1/L_{max}$ contribute only an overall offset and slope. The V_{MW} random fractal function of Eq. (III.15) allows the direct computation of $V_{MW}(t)$ *at any t* from a stored set of order $\log(L_{max}/\lambda)$ coefficients A_n and ϕ_n. Figure 18 illustrates this process for H=0.8 as the number of terms is increased.

With the use of table lookup for sin(x), the V_{MW} fractal function can be made extremely fast. The fractal is represented by a only few stored coefficients and there is no penalty for calculating the function outside its original boundary. The resolution can easily be changed by changing the number of components used. A variable r allows changing lacunarity independent of D. Other periodic functions can be used in place of sin(x). For example, both midpoint displacement and successive random additions, correspond to a triangle function. In addition, midpoint displacement sets all ϕ_n = constant. Extensions to E>1 are possible with periodic functions in all E coordinates.

acknowledgement

This work was made possible by the help, encouragement, and inspiration of Benoit Mandelbrot.

suggested references

1. Mandelbrot, B.B. *The Fractal Geometry of Nature*, (Freeman, New York) 1982 and references therein. See also, *Fractals: Form, Chance, and Dimension*, W. H. Freeman and Co., San Francisco (1977).

2. Voss, R. F. "1/f (flicker) noise: a brief review", *Proc. 32rd Annual Symposium on Frequency Control*, Atlantic City, (1979), 40-46 and references therein.

3. Mandelbrot, B. B. and Wallis, J. R. "Some Long-Run Properties of Geophysical Records", *Water Resources Research 5*, (1969) 321-340.

4. Musha, T. and Higuchi, H. "The 1/f Fluctuation of a Traffic Current on an Expressway", *Jap. J. Appl. Phys. 15*, (1976), 1271-1275.

5. Voss, R. F. and Clarke, J. "1/f Noise in Music: Music from 1/f Noise", *J. Accous. Soc. Am. 63*, (1978), 258-263.

6. Voss, R.F. and Clarke, J. " '1/f noise' in music and speech", *Nature 258*, 317-8 (1975).

7. Gardner, M. "White and brown music, fractal curves, and one-over-f noise", Mathematical Games column in *Scientific American*, April 1978 p16.

8. Mandelbrot, B.B. and Wallis, J. W. "Fractional Brownian motions, fractional noises, and applications", *SIAM review, 10* (1968) 422-437.

9. For example see: Freeman, J. J. *Principles of Noise,* John Wiley & Sons, Inc., New York, (1958), Chapter 1, "Fourier Series and Integrals." or Robinson, F.N.H. *Noise and Fluctuations,* Clarendon Press, Oxford, (1974).

10. A good discussion is found in Reif, F. *Statistical and Thermal Physics,* McGraw-Hill Book Co., New York, (1965), Chapter 15, "Irreversible Processes and Fluctuations."

11. Berry, M.V. and Lewis, Z.V. "On the Weierstrass-Mandelbrot fractal function", *Proc. R. Soc. Lond. A, 370* (1980) 459-484.

12. Cochran, W. T. et al. What is the Fast Fourier Transform? *Proc. IEEE 55,* (1967), 1664-1677.

13. Carpenter, L. "Computer rendering of fractal curves and surfaces", *SIGGRAPH '80 Conference Proceedings,* (1980) 109.

14. Fournier, A., Fussell, D., and Carpenter, L. "Computer rendering of Stochastic Models", *Comm. of the ACM, 25,* (1982) 371-384

15. Mandelbrot, B.B. "Comment on Computer rendering of Fractal Stochastic Models", *Comm. of the ACM, 25,* (1982) 581-584, and the response by Fournier, Fussell, and Carpenter.

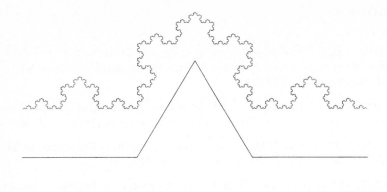

Figure 5. Construction of the exactly self-similar von Koch curve. At each stage in the construction a line segment (on the bottom) is replaced by 4 smaller segments of length 1/3 of its parent (as shown in the middle). The top figure shows the curve after 6 stages (4096 line segments) with a fractal dimension $D = \log(4)/\log(3) = 1.26... $.

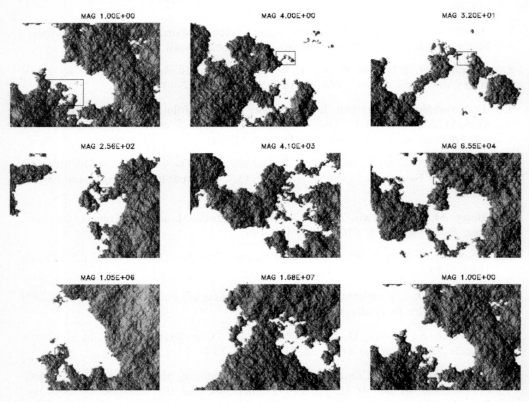

Figure 6. Zoom sequence of a statistically self-similar fractal landscape (D=2.2). Each succeeding picture shows a blowup of the framed portion of the previous image. As the surface is magnified, a small portion looks similar to (but not exactly the same as) a larger portion. The total magnification corresponds to 16 million.

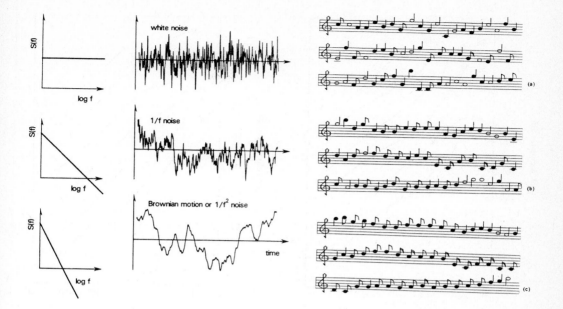

Figure 10. Samples of typical "noises", V(t), the random variations of a quantity in time. (a) White noise, the most random. (b) 1/f noise, an intermediate but very commonly found type of fluctuation in nature, its origin is, as yet, a mystery. (c) Brownian motion or a random walk. To the left of each sample is a graphical representation of that noises spectral density, $S_V(f)$, a measurement technique for characterizing the time correlations in the noise.

Figure 12. Samples of stochastically composed fractal music based on the different types of noises shown in Fig.10.(a) "white" music is too random. (b) "1/f" music is the closest to actual music (and most pleasing). (c) "Brown" or $1/f^2$ music is too correlated.

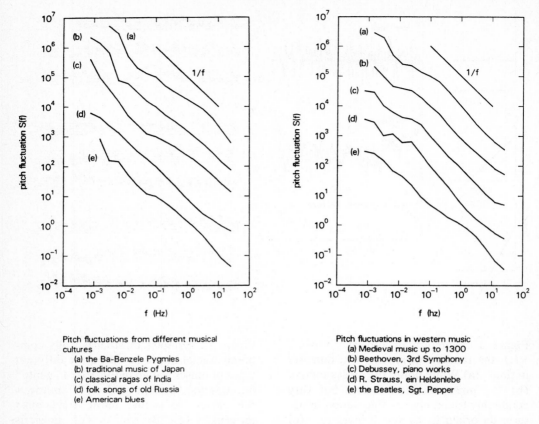

Pitch fluctuations from different musical
cultures
   (a) the Ba-Benzele Pygmies
   (b) traditional music of Japan
   (c) classical ragas of India
   (d) folk songs of old Russia
   (e) American blues

Pitch fluctuations in western music
   (a) Medieval music up to 1300
   (b) Beethoven, 3rd Symphony
   (c) Debussey, piano works
   (d) R. Strauss, ein Heldenlebe
   (e) the Beatles, Sgt. Pepper

Figure 11. Spectral density measurements of the pitch variations in various types of music showing their common correlations as $1/f$ noise.

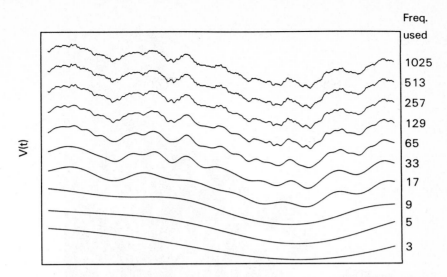

Figure 13. Increasing detail in a FFT generated sample (N=1024) of fBM for H=0.8, β=2.6, and D=1.2 as higher frequencies are included. To generate N points requires order NlogN operations.

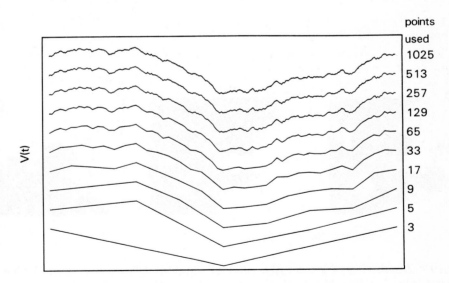

Figure 14. Increasing detail in a midpoint displacement generated sample of fBM for H=0.8 and D=1.2 as the number of stages is increased. At each stage a random displacement is added to each of the midpoints of between the previous values. Note that large fluctuations in an an early stage remain as "special points" in later stages. This sample is not stationary. To generate N points requires order N operations.

Figure 15. Zenith view of a midpoint displacement surface on a square lattice for H=0.8 and D=2.2. The illumination was along one lattice direction. The non-stationary character is visible as the prominent shadows. This may be compared with Figs. 6 and 17 which were also generated on a square lattice.

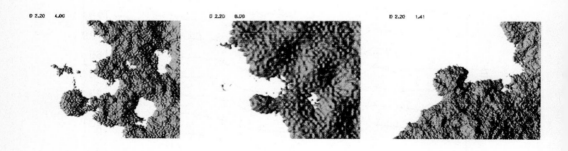

Figure 17. Zenith view of a successive random addition surfaces on a square lattice for H=0.8 and D=2.2. The illumination was along one of the axis. By varying the expansion factor 1/r before new randomness is added, the surface *lacunarity* (or texture) can be varied without changing D. (a) 1/r=4. (b) 1/r=8. (c) 1/r=1.41. The lacunarity increases as 1/r increases and for large 1/r only a few fluctuation scales are visible. As r→1 the lacunarity approches that of the FFT surfaces.

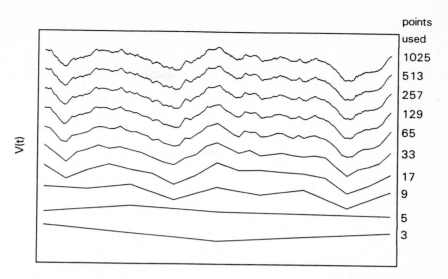

Figure 16. Increasing detail in a successive random addition sample of fBM for H=0.8 and D=1.2 as the number of stages is increased. At each stage a random displacement is added to each of the points, not just the midpoints. This sample is a better approximation to fBm than the midpoint displacement of Fig. 14 but the generation requires order N operations for N points.

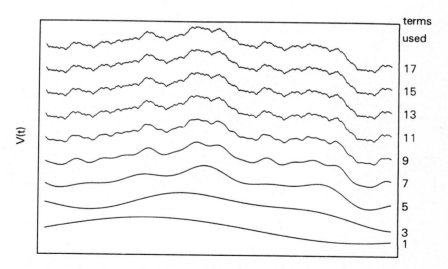

Figure 18. Increasing detail as more components are included in a pseudo-random V_{MW} fractal function based on the Weirstrass-Mandelbrot random series. Here $1/r = 2/(\sqrt{5}-1) = 1.618\ldots$. Computation of N points covering a spatial irregularity scale from λ to L_{max} involves order $N\log(L_{max}/\lambda)$ operations.

THE ALGEBRA OF ALGORITHMS

M.L.V. Pitteway
Department of Computer Science
Brunel University
Uxbridge
Middlesex UB8 3PH

ABSTRACT

Algorithms are worthy of study in their own right, and are not just programs of instructions describing processes for computer or human implementation. As shown by Sproull (1982), Bresenham's algorithm can be derived by applying program trans-formations to a simple, obviously correct algorithm, and simil-arly the octant change re-assignments for the incremental conic drawing algorithm can be derived simply and elegantly by program transformation, thus avoiding much tedious conventional algebra. It is suggested that this technique provides a powerful analytic tool - a new toy for the theoretician.

1.   INTRODUCTION

Most academic computer scientists, and many practising computer professionals, have experienced the chore of instruc-ting the innocent in the art of programming the local computer complex in some available high or low level language. Much demonstrator time and attention must needs be given to matters of syntax and other such trivia, counting and matching brackets to explain why some plausible looking algebra was unrecognised by the compiler, or explaining why divide-by-zero, or an attempted access to a non-existent file causes a run-time error.

Those who have suffered have their own horror stories to relate; the dreadful things that our students have required our poor, long suffering computers to do. One of my own favourites involved an eminent "professor of difficult sums", who asked me to hand-code part of his Atlas Autocode, so that it "wouldn't

NATO ASI Series, Vol. F17
Fundamental Algorithms for Computer Graphics
Edited by R. A. Earnshaw
© Springer-Verlag Berlin Heidelberg 1985

cost so much to run". His code included a statement of the form
"if f(x) < g(x) then go to (some labelled instruction
elsewhere in his code)".
His very next instruction (unlabelled, so not accessible by any
other route):
"if f(x) ≥ g(x) then .....".
These statements were nested six deep in do loops, with x remaining unchanged within the inner three, while f(x) and g(x) were
function calls to routines of similar poor quality which he had
also written. A simple tidying speeded his code by a factor of
more than a thousand, compared with the five or so he was looking for. But this man was supposed to be not unintelligent. He
would never think to publish the first formula which came into
his head for some algebraic expression without looking for
cancelling terms, factors or other simplifications. The thought
had just never occurred to him that, just as a formula can be
simplified by the judicial application of the rules of simple
algebra, so can an algorithm (or its practical realization as
a computer program).

Of course, many improvements of this sort can be achieved
by using optimising compilers, though for the most part even
the most sophisticated compilers achieve their savings through
very simple program manipulations, recognising common sub-
expressions, for example, or deleting redundant code. In my
own experience, I have never yet written a successful computer
program to achieve a task which I didn't know how to do by hand
(given time), and converting cruddy programming into god-like
code is no exception. Could anyone reasonably expect an optimising compiler to achieve the program simplifications used by
Sproull (1982) to derive Bresenham's algorithm from a simple,
obviously correct starting point? Given a simple Fourier transform routine, could it be expected to discover the FFT for
itself? Could it derive quicksort from a simple bubble sort,
or for that matter any of the N^2 to $N \ln(N)$ run time improvements? I think not.

Let me take another example, this time from the field of
computer graphics. I have seen published papers, five in fact,
in which the object is to find points situated on, or reasonably
close to, some given straight line or curve, in order to find

an adequately close representation using short straight lines
that can be generated by the hardware provided on some display.
The critical point in the code involves a test on some computed
quantity d, which represents the distance of the point in question from the intended line thus:

"Is |d| < tolerance ?" (if yes, to keep the point for sub-
sequent use), where "tolerance" is defined as some parameter
controlling the number of points selected. Naturally enough,
the computation of d usually involves a square root (because of
Pythagoras), and the rest of the learned article is given over
to a discussion of Chebychev polynomials and the like, explaining how much computer time can be saved by an appropriately
crude approximation. (Interestingly enough, it often turns out
that the approximation simply involves measuring distance by an
octahedral metric like that sketched in figure 1, a shape which

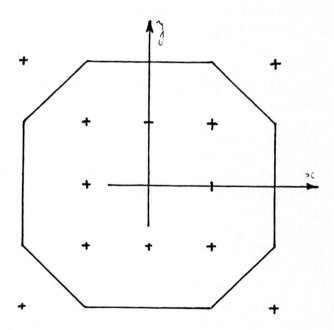

Figure 1   Distance metric for a crude square root

I have found to be extremely useful in thickening bounding
lines for polygonal shapes in applications such as computer-
aided architecture, since it can be slid around the inside of
a boundary more easily than the corresponding circular disc.)

It never seems to occur to the originating mathematician that
"is $|d| <$ tol ?" can simply be replaced by the algorithmically
equivalent "is $d^2 <$ tol^2?", where tol^2 is an alternate pre-
computed constant, and the squaring of d obviates the need for
the square root in the first place. An algorithm deserves at
least as much attention, of a human manipulation kind, as the
algebraic simplification of the formulae which led to the code
in the first place. This in itself, however, constitutes only
a simple starting point for the theoretical methodology which
this paper attempts to describe and advocate, through some
simple examples. One such is advanced in a companion paper on
"The Relationship between Euclid's algorithm and Run-length
Encoding", where it is shown that the derivation of an accelerated version of Bresenham's algorithm, which involves much
turgid mathematics in a conventional analysis, becomes almost
embarrassingly simple from the algorithmic standpoint. Further
examples are provided in the following sections of this paper.

2.   DRAWING CIRCLES, AND OTHER CONICS, FROM STRAIGHT LINE
      SEGMENTS

      The average mathematician, writing a program to construct
circles from straight line segments as suggested in figure 2,
soon realizes that, for a specified accuracy, the number of
lines required varies according to $\sqrt{R}$, where R is the radius
of the circle. (More specifically, if the lines are required
to stay within some given tolerance ε, the length of each line,
ℓ, is given by $\sqrt{8R\varepsilon}$ for an inscribed polygonal representation
of the circle, which can be increased by $\sqrt{2}$ to $4\sqrt{R\varepsilon}$ if the
polygon is allowed to deviate by as much as ε on either side.
The number of lines is then given by some convenient integer
near to $2\pi R/\ell$). His (or her) code next computes some angle
θ, being 360° (or 2π in Fortran) divided by the number of
vectors, and proceeds with a loop which looks like:

```
for i := 1 step 1 until N
    u := ℓ*cos(i*θ)
    v := ℓ*sin(i*θ)
    draw the line (u,v)
repeat.
```

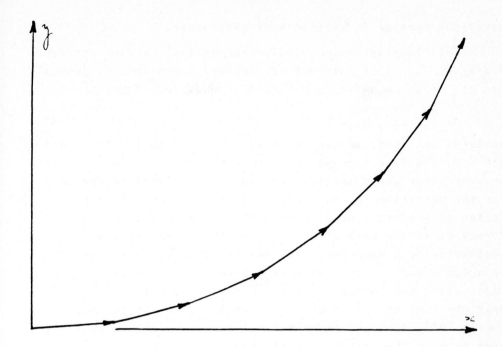

Figure 2   Constructing a circle from straight line segments

Maybe there will be a little sophistication, like buffering up the moves for the first quadrant, or octant, to be
repeated without further computation, but that is about all.
Very few mathematicians untrained in the ways of computer
science think on to realize that there are convenient trigonometric formulae involving sin(A+B) = sin A * cos B + cos A *
sin B, and similarly cos (A+B) = cos A * cos B - cos A * cos B,
which can be applied in this case to allow the computer to
increment the values of u and v from the previous values in
the loop without calling for the evaluation of a new cos function and a new sin function every time thus:

        u' := u*cos θ - v*sinθ
        v' := u*sin θ + v*cosθ

(The constants sin θ and cos θ being pre-computed and stored
before entering the loop).   The primes, u' and v', are introduced here simply to improve readability, to denote new values
for the variables u and v.   Variables really do vary in computer
science, a point which can cause much confusion, and which is

developed further in section 4 of this paper.

This loop involving simply four multiplications and two additions. It is of interest to computer scientists to generalize it, since no extra computation is required, thus:

u' := A*u + B*v

v' := C*u + D*v

It turns out that, if the determinant of the coefficients A*D - B*C = 1, the line segments u,v inscribe a polygon to an ellipse or some other conic section, and so, with a suitable choice for the parameters A, B, C and D, useful curves can be represented on a plotter or display with vector generating hardware. Moreover, in the case of an ellipse, the representation is aesthetically a good one, with shorter line segments being selected where the curvature is greatest near the ends of the major axis, and longer segments where the curvature is least, near the ends of the minor axis. In fact, it can be shown (Smith 1971) that the inscribed polygon is so chosen that the area between the polygon and its bounding ellipse is minimized.

If the determinant A*D - B*C is not equal to unity, the analysis is more difficult, but in fact the curve represented spirals in or out logarithmically (Cohen 1970), a log spiral being a case in point. This is a point to which I return in the next section.

In the early days of the Sketchpad project at M.I.T., much attention was given to the design of an efficient algorithm for the generation of circles or circular arcs, and in particular it was noted that, since θ is supposedly small for a reasonable representation, cos θ can be approximated to one, saving two further multiplies in the inner loop. Legend has it that it was as a result of an obvious programming error - or perhaps because it was unlikely to make much difference in any case - that, instead of implementing:

u' := u - α*v

v' := v + α*u

(where the parameter α controls the radius of the circle, as would sin θ) the programmer actually coded:

u' := u - α*v

v' := v + α*u',

i.e. the variable u was overwritten by the first assignment
before it was used in the second, rather than having the
computer write it away to some workspace. From an algebraic
viewpoint, the second assignment can be rewritten in terms of
the original u thus:

$$v' := v*(1-\alpha^2) - \alpha*u.$$

Thus the matrix of coefficients from the general form, A*D -
B*C, becomes unity, so in the form with u being overwritten
before the second assignment the algorithm avoids a tendency
to spiral in or out, and closes accurately. It often seems
to happen that the most natural form for the computer, the
overwriting of u in this case, turns out to be the better
behaved, again perhaps suggesting that the algorithms themselves are the more natural and elegant form for study?

3   INCREMENTAL CURVE DRAWING

If a plotter or display comes equipped with vector
generating hardware, it is sensible to use techniques like
those described in the previous section of this paper to
represent curves as a sequence of short, straight line segments.
If there is no such hardware, however, so that the straight
lines, too, must be software generated as by Bresenham (1965),
it is more sensible to develop the incremental software itself
at the pixel (pel, if you work for IBM) level, and this we
now consider from an algorithmic standpoint.

It is shown in a companion paper on the "Algorithms for
Conic Generation" that Bresenham's algorithm can be simply
extended to generate conic section curves by introducing new
parameters, K1, K2 and K3, which involves using simple addition operations in the inner loop to change the values of the
quantities b and a which control the gradient of the line
approximated, thus generating a curve. In the more general
form of figure 3 a fourth parameter, K4, is possible without
extra run-time costs in the inner loop, so again a practising
computer scientist may be led to wonder what can be achieved
with this extra degree of freedom? (The signs, incidentally,
were chosen to look for a reducing gradient, so that positive

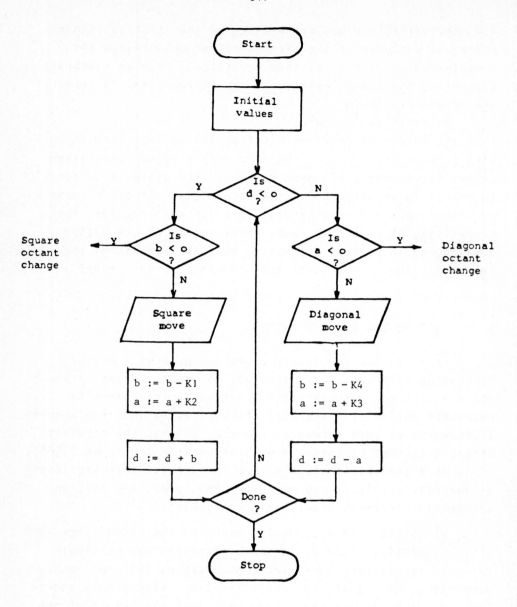

Figure 3   A generalized curve drawing algorithm following
            Bresenham (1965)

values can be introduced through K1, K2, K3 or K4 to cause a
reduction in the value of b, or an increase in a, and thus a
resultant decrease in the gradient b/(a+b), as the run proceeds).

As a first exercise, however, we can show that the algorithm itself suggests that perhaps the value of K2 should be
set equal to K4, without recourse to the underlying mathematics.
Suppose that, at some point in the run, we find that the control
parameter d is very nearly equal to zero, and consider the outcome of the next two passes round the loop: If we start with
d just less than zero, the algorithm will output first a square
move, then a diagonal move, and, in terms of their starting
values, the quantities b, a and d are changed to b -K1 - K4,
a + K2 + K3 and d + b - K1 - a - K2 - K3 respectively. Had d
been positive, on the other hand, the diagonal move would be
output before the square move, while b, a and d become b - K4 -
K1, a + K3 + K2 and d - a - K3 + b - K4 - K1. The change in
the quantities b and a is thus not affected by the change in
the order of the operations caused by a supposedly very small
change to the initial d, but d itself _is_ dependent upon the
order, _unless_ K2 and K4 have been set equal to one another.

And what happens if K2 is not set equal to K4? My study
of this vexing question has, over the last 18 years or so,
become somewhat notorious at Brunel. Basically, it turns out
that the curve represented tends to spiral in, or out, logarithmically (outwards if K4 < K2, so that the initial small
change to d is accentuated by the dual passage, and inwards if
K4 > K2), just as Dan Cohen's analysis of the "curves from
straight line segments" algorithm of the previous section
showed spiralling in or out according to the sign of A*D -
B*C - 1. There is, however, another difference: In the case
of the conics, with K2 = K4, it can be shown that the incremental approximation leaves the plotter pen, or chooses the
pixel centres, in such a way that we are never more than half
an increment away from the intended curve in a direction
measured parallel to the y axis (for the first, fourth, fifth
or eighth octants, x axis otherwise). With the log spiral,
this tolerance has to be increased to a full plotter increment
or pixel side, the extra range being occupied by a pseudo-
random wandering which is not fully understood - at least,

not by this author. Moreover, if K4 is chosen to be less than K2, so that the algorithm tends to spiral out, the equation of the log spiral matched can be determined only by running the algorithm, or its equivalent, again for reasons which seem difficult to understand.

Let us now return to safe ground with K2 = K4, and consider the octant change arithmetic which is required before we can use the algorithm of figure 3 to generate a complete ellipse, or more than one octant of an ellipse (or hyperbola). Conventional mathematical wisdom would suggest a change of axes, perhaps, so that we could first derive the initial conditions that would be required to set up the algorithm to operate in the eighth octant if b has become negative (so that a square octant change, with an associated re-specification of the meaning of "diagonal move", is called for), and similarly for the diagonal change into the second octant if a < 0, with "square move" needing to be changed from "x-step" to "y-step". Before rushing into code, however, we examine the quantities b, a, d, K1, K2 and K3 already computed and stored within our computer, and ask what arithmetic is required to compute the new values needed from the old ones already available? Then, hopefully, if we have coded the whole thing properly, it will handle subsequent changes into octants 3 through 7 properly without further analysis on our part, though the whole process seems frightfully tedious for the human originator.

Here, too, however, it turns out that a simple analysis of the algorithm itself can lead us to discover precisely what needs to be done, without going back to the underlying mathematics. The square octant change condition, for example, is sketched in figure 4, and let us assume, for simplicity, that we are working with the mid-point algorithm, choosing between the square and diagonal moves according to the sign of d evaluated at the mid-point $i+1$, $j+\frac{1}{2}$ as indicated. If the test, as shown in figure 3, picks up the condition b < 0, the computer currently has d evaluated at the point $i+1$, $j+\frac{1}{2}$, but now we need it at the point $i+1$, $j-\frac{1}{2}$, in order to decide instead whether it is better to move to $i+1,j$ (as we would by default in the absence of an octant change), or whether to make the new diagonal move downwards to $i+1$, $j-1$. We can

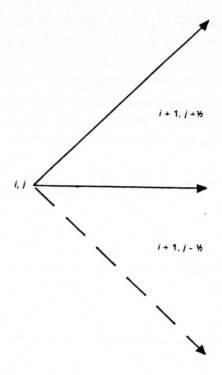

Figure 4   Specification for a square octant change

easily discover how to compute the new, mid-point value for d, which is to be evaluated at $i+1$, $j-\frac{1}{2}$, if we note that the algorithm of figure 3 is reversible, i.e. that it can be backtracked, as the arithmetic operations involved are them-selves all reversible.

Consider what happens if we suppose that the algorithm of figure 3 is driven <u>backwards</u> through a diagonal step, d being changed now to d+a, a to a - K3 and b to b+K2 (and note that we are <u>not</u> proposing to actually have the computer perform this reversed arithmetic - it is enough that it is showing us what is required for the program). We now have the plotter pen (or the centre of pixel attention) moved back from i,j to $i-1$, $j-1$, while the test variable d is now evaluated at the point i, $j-\frac{1}{2}$. Now we allow a square move in the forwards direction, stepping b from b+K2 to b+K2-K1, a from a-K3 to a-K3+K2, and then finally d from d+a to d+a+b+K2-K1. Apart from a sign change (because we will now be calling for a square move if d is <u>below</u> the intended curve), this is the new value for d required to restart the algorithm from the d test in the new octant. The new values required for K1, K2, K3, b and a are obtained similarly by differencing.

For many years I believed that the corresponding algorithmic derivation of the arithmetic required for the diagonal octant change, as shown in figure 5, was impossible, as we can-

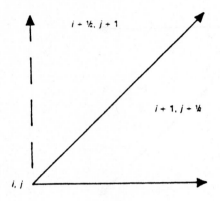

Figure 5 Specification for a diagonal octant change

not move d from the point i+1, j+$\frac{1}{2}$ to the new location required, i+$\frac{1}{2}$, j+1 by simple steps in either the forwards or backwards direction. We can backtrack one square step to find d at i, j+$\frac{1}{2}$, but now we need to move forwards just one half of a diagonal step to locate d at i+$\frac{1}{2}$, j+1. How do we follow the arithmetic through for half a step, passing downwards through the right hand branch of figure 3 just half a time? Surprisingly, perhaps, it turns out that there is no problem, if we accept that the arithmetic operations described by the right hand branch of figure 3 can be viewed as simply achieving a certain change in the values of the stored variables b, a and d. In passing through the operations one half of one time, we are simply seeking to define a corresponding computational operation which, if applied twice, will perform an exactly equivalent change to: b := b- K2, a := a + K3, followed by d := d - a' (where the prime is used to warn of the changed value for a, as in the previous section).

The half operations for b and a are trivial: b := b-½K2, and a := a + ½K3. But for d we require: d := d - ½a - ⅛K3, the interesting term being the extra ⅛K3, required to correct for the fact that a has only been stepped half-way the first time it is applied to do.

If this is accepted as reasonable, the rest of the work is straightforward. The gelrabra for a backwards square move, followed by the half diagonal move forwards, establishes that d at i+½, j+1 can be evaluated as d - b - ½a + ½K2 - ⅜K3 in terms of the original values, though a sign change is again required before restarting the algorithm in the second octant, and again, the new values for K1, K2, K3, b and a are obtained by differencing.

As is perhaps by now apparent, the point of these manipulations is not just to start with a simple, obviously correct algorithm, which can be transformed, moulded or manipulated into something more efficient and elegant. I am looking to start from an algorithmic definition, perhaps of a circle if the general conic case proves too difficult, and to establish its properties from the algorithmic definition, just as, in an exercise of classical mathematics, we may start with a differential equation, perhaps, or a power series defintiion, establishing subsequent properties from either starting point, and of course relating the two by proving either one from the other as starting point. I am not seeking, following Sproull, to establish a simple, incremental circle or conic generator from some mathematical expression of the properties of a circle or perhaps from the equation of an ellipse, but rather to suggest that the subsequent properties, such as setting K2 = K4, or the octant change arithmetic, can be established from the algorithm of figure 3, which suggests itself as the most obvious curve drawing extension of Bresenhem's algorithm, simply introducing extra addition operations to cause the gradient controlling parameters, b and a, to vary in the most natural way which occurs to me, in order to produce a curve. The process is guided by the kindness of nature, in that one expects the simplest possible curves, conic sections, to be generated by the simplest possible algorithm.

AN ALGORITHMIC DEFINITION OF THE NATURAL LOG FUNCTION

To derive the properties of the conic sections from the algorithmic definition of figure 3 (with K2 set equal to K4), as opposed to starting from the equation of a general quadratic form, or the concepts of projective geometry, is beyond me, but a similar exercise is to derive the basic properties of the natural log function, such as $\ln(1/x) = -\ln(x)$, or $\ln(x*y) = \ln(x) + \ln(y)$ from an algorithmic definition (Perlis 1962) sketched in figure 6. Note that figure 6 is <u>not</u> offered as an efficient algorithm for the computation of natural logarithms (which is more sensibly accomplished by using a polynomial approximation on the mantissa in floating point form, introducing the exponent by the subsequent addition of the appropriate multiple of ln 2). But it will suffice as a logarithmic <u>definition</u> of ln(x), just as well as the differential equation dx = 1/x, or the power series $\ln(1+x) = x - x^2/2 + x^3/3 - x^4/4....$ One further point involves the test for termination in figure 6, which I have expressed previously as "is b approximately equal to a?". It is simply that, as the continued square root approximation takes u ever nearer to one, so b approaches ln(x) to any accuracy that may, in principle, be required, and it seems sterile to labour the point through some more rigorous terminating count.

The idea, then, in establishing that $\ln(1/x) = -\ln(x)$, for example, is to move from our definition by assigning 1/x, instead of simply x, to u in our first function. Then we manipulate the code, one simple, logical step at a time, requiring that each new algorithm must manifestly perform a process roughly equivalent to the previous manifestation - "isomorphic automata" is a useful phrase from Cybernetics for those who like to confuse simple ideas with amorphous turns of phrase - until we are back to figure 6, apart from a change of sign to give output b'. (Actually, we come out with b' $\equiv$ - b*u', where u' = 1/u, but as u, and thus u', approaches 1, this is good enough).

As mentioned earlier, however, the exercise is more confusing than conventional, simple algebra in that, with algorithms or computer programs, the variables really do vary,

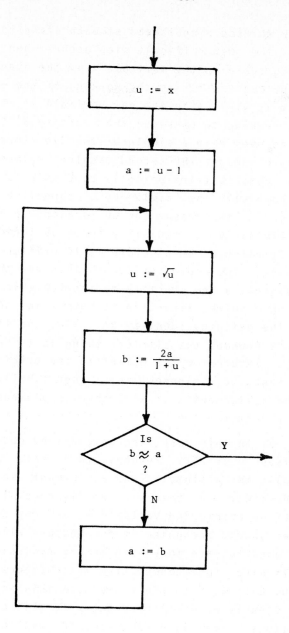

Figure 6   An algorithmic definition of the natural log function
            b = ln(x), following Perlis (1962).

and it is necessary to keep a cool head at each stage to see
the thing through. The most difficult step occurs when we
alter the program to scale up the variable x by the quantity u,
i.e. so that the new machine copies the working of the original
machine except that it works with the new variable x', instead
of the original x, seeking to preserve the identity x' ≡ x*u.
If the first machine uses x in a simple arithmetic expression,
it is straightforward enough; the second machine replaces x by
(x'/u), (and again, note that the prime is used only to improve
readability), and hopefully the "divide by u" cancels a "multiply by u" term which was the reason for our scaling up of x in
the first place. Similarly, any quantity to be assigned to x
is simply to be multiplied up by u before it is written away to
u' on the new machine. The confusion occurs whenever the
original program assigns a new quantity to the variable u, for
then the new version requires attention to both x and u' in
order to maintain the defining identity x' ≡ x*u, and it has
to "run to keep up". Perhaps the simplest thing is to have it
perform x := x/u (i.e. return for the moment to the original,
unscaled x), then make the assignment to u, then finally re-
establish x' by the assignment x := x*u, three statements
required to replace just the one.

   But suppose, as in this case, the originating code to
be modified comprises "u := √u"? Perhaps, to be safe, we
really ought to split the arithmetic and assignment uses of u
in the original thus: w := √u, then u := w; (my code always
involves the use of an overworked variable w, and any decent
optimising compiler should recognise it for me, and allocate
a special scratch pad, to save many main memory cycles). The
new machine then requires four consecutive instructions:
"w := √u; x := x/u; u := w; x := x*u". Perhaps this is too
heavy handed, for clearly we don't need the w in this case.
The three instructions: "x:=x/u; u:=√u; x:= x*u" will suffice.
But it is perhaps less obvious that these three are algorithmically identical to the two instruction sequence: "u := √u;
x := x/u"? It certainly seems a mite deeper than "change the
side and change the sign", or some such elementary rule of
schoolboy (or schoolgirl) algebra.

The full exercise involves the following sequential steps:
Replace the working variable u by u', defined by u' ≡ 1/u.
Replace the working variable a by a', defined by a' ≡ -a*u'.
Combine the two steps "a' := a'/u'; b := -2a'/(1+u')" into
"b := -2a'/u'(1+u')"

(note that a' is overwritten by -b*u' after the test, so is not used).

Replace the working variable b by b', defined by b' ≡ -b*u', and we have established an algorithm equivalent to the original definition of ln(x), except that the output is now b', thus ln(-x) is identical to - ln(x), apart from the u' which, as mentioned before, becomes equal to one, subject to the accuracy of the test. Similarly it can be shown that ln(x*y) = ln(x) + ln(y), though this is left as an exercise for the reader.

REFERENCES

J.E. Bresenham 1965 "Algorithm for Computer Control of a Digital Plotter, IBM Systems Journal $\underline{4}$, 25-30.

D. Cohen 1970 "On Linear Difference Curves", Proceedings of the International Symposium CG70 Volume 1, Brunel University and "Advanced Computer Graphics", Plenum Press 1971, 1143-1177.

A.J. Perlis 1962 "The Computer in the University", from "Management and the Computer of the Future", M.I.T. Press and Wiley, 190.

M.L.V. Pitteway 1979 "The Algebra of Algorithms - A New Toy for the Theoretician?", IUCC Bulletin $\underline{1}$, 139-144.

M.L.V. Pitteway 1985 "The Relationship between Euclid's Algorithm and Run-length Encoding", Proceedings of the NATO Advanced Study Institute "Fundamental Algorithms of Computer Graphics", Ilkley.

M.L.V. Pitteway 1985 "Algorithms of Conic Generation", Proceedings of the NATO Advanced Study Institute "Fundamental Algorithms of Computer Graphics, Ilkley.

L.B. Smith 1971 "Drawing Ellipses, Hyperbolas with a fixed number of points and maximum inscribed area", Computer Journal $\underline{14}$, 81-85.

R.F. Sproull 1982 "Using Program Transformations to Derive Line-Drawing Algorithms", ACM Transactions on Graphics, $\underline{1}$, 259-273.

THEORETICAL CONSIDERATIONS IN ALGORITHM DESIGN

B.C. Thompson and J.V. Tucker
Department of Computer Studies
University of Leeds
Leeds LS2 9JT
Britain

*In science nothing capable of proof ought to
be accepted without proof*

Richard Dedekind

INTRODUCTION

<u>Background</u>   What is an algorithm and how do we design an algorithm to accomplish a given task?

We will examine some theoretical considerations in the design of an algorithm that amplify these imponderable questions. We will discuss the formalisation of an algorithm and its task in terms of four considerations :

levels of computational abstraction involved in the algorithm;

specifications of task, algorithm, and algorithm complexity;

verification of specifications;

testing of specifications.

We belive that the process of designing an algorithm, and its implementation by means of a computer, can be organised as the production of a sequence of draft *algorithm designs*

$$D_1, D_2, \ldots, D_n$$

wherein each draft D_i is a formal characterisation of an algorithm in terms of the four considerations above. The sequence of algorithm designs is generated through cooperation and competition between these considerations with the designer as arbiter. The generation of the sequence *design decisions* can be partially formalised by means of various *algorithm transformations*.

Thus, we are interested in the study of a *methodological model* for the design of algorithms that is founded upon formal methods and involves the use of software tools. Actually, our methodology is intended for the design of VLSI systems, but its origin will not intrude unduly in this paper.

NATO ASI Series, Vol. F17
Fundamental Algorithms for Computer Graphics
Edited by R. A. Earnshaw
© Springer-Verlag Berlin Heidelberg 1985

Algorithm Designs   In this paper we will concentrate on the formal description of a stage in the design of an algorithm. In Section 1 we discuss the four considerations mentioned earlier and formulate general principles for the formal representation of a draft algorithm design. Noteworthy here is our insistence on a formal treatment of algorithm performance/complexity. We introduce the formal concept of a *level of computational abstraction* which is, in essence, an algorithmic language with a formally defined syntax and semantics, *and a complexity model involving time and space units that are intrinsic to the language*. In our work we are continually examining subtleties of the concept of time in an algorithmic context.

In the remainder of the paper we illustrate these ideas by considering a pair of parallel sorting algorithms. We contrast their informal description in Section 2 with their formal treatment in Sections 3-5. To accomplish this we introduce a new algorithmic language *PR*. *PR* is a functional notation based on the simultaneous primitive recursive functions of Richard Dedekind [1888] . In the course of the discussion we will glimpse several important components of our design methodology including optimising program transformations and multilanguage environments for the equivalent representation of algorithms .

Acknowledgements   This work forms part of a large project on the foundation of VLSI system design at Leeds. The notation *PR* is a fragment of a synchronous system definition language called *Dedekind* we are designing; *PR* was first studied in Tucker and Zucker [1985]. Material relevant to our concerns will be cited in due course   (in particular in subsection 1.4).

We thank C. Jervis, A. Martin, G. Megson for very useful conversations on some of the topics in this paper. One of us (JVT) is pleased to thank J.A. Bergstra for many critical discussions on design methodologies in software engineering which have helped shape the thinking on design presented here. Finally we thank Ms. J.A. Thursby for preparing this typescript.

1.   DESIGN OF AN ALGORITHM

1.1   What is a Well-Designed Algorithm?   We discern a number of basic characteristics of a good design of an algorithm A for a task T.

Logical Abstraction   The *level of logical abstraction* L of the algorithm should be clearly defined. This is determined by

(a)   the level of abstraction of data and basic operations in data used in A, which we will call the *data type* of A; and

(b) the constructs used to construct the algorithm from the data type, which we will call the *commands* of A.

The formalisation of these components of the algorithm is an important step in the design of A. We think of it as the formal definition of an algorithmic notation and its semantics or, in short, an *algorithmic or programming language*, in which A resides.

Correctness   The task T of the algorithm should be clearly defined although we allow its specification TSpec to be informal in certain circumstances. A formal *correctness specification* CSpec for the task and algorithm should be devised. This CSpec is intended to formally define relevant behaviour of A and should be written strictly in terms of the level of logical abstraction L. We expect to demonstrate that CSpec faithfully represents the task TSpec and, of course, to rigorously prove that A meets the specification CSpec. In this way we establish the sense in which A accomplishes the original task T.

Performance Abstraction   The performance or computational complexity of the algorithm should be analysed to assess, for instance, the computation time or memory space required by A. This analysis should be made strictly in terms of the level of abstraction L. Thus, we must add to the formal definition of L assumptions on, for instance, the time and space required for basic operations and commands. To measure the complexity of A in a way that is intrinsic to L requires us to take the data type as a basic *irreducible* level of data abstraction and to choose units to reflect this requirement. For example, the data and basic operations of the data type should determine unit costs. A *level of computational abstraction* consists of an independent and autonomous programming language that supports a correctness theory *and* a complexity theory.

Performance Speficiation   To establish the complexity of the algorithm A we must define relevant aspects of its performance in a formal specification PSpec. This specification should be written strictly in terms of the level of computational abstraction L. We expect that it can be rigorously proved that A meets the performance specification PSpec. (Notice that in real-time algorithms (after Wirth [1977]), and in VLSI systems generally, questions of performance arise in questions of logical correctness of algorithms).

Testing   The correctness and performance of the algorithm A should be
tested on appropriate data sets. Testing should be considered to be an
experimental process that aims to refute the formal specifications CSpec
and PSpec. In particular, testing should be undertaken as an empirical
study of computation strictly in terms of the level of computational
abstraction L. Thus, testing A involves the execution of A in a computer
simulation of L that represents the behaviour and performance of L.

1.2   The Concept of An Algorithm Design   Our considerations suggest that
the formalised algorithm, in insolation, is incomplete as a product of a
scientific design process. It is the formalised algorithm together with its
formally defined level of abstraction, specifications, proofs and experiments
that is to be designed and produced. We will term this formal package an
algorithm design.

An *algorithm design* D consists of the following five components :

(i)   A *level of computational abstraction* L that is formally definable as
an *algorithmic language* with formal syntax, semantics and performance. The
language contains the *data type* and *command language* of the algorithm and a
clock to measure L-time and a *scale* to measure L-space.

(ii)   The *algorithm* A that is a well-formed formula of the algorithmic
language of L.

(iii) *Specifications* S that define task, algorithm and performance. The
specifications CSpec and PSpec are formal and are written in appropriate
specification languages tailored to the level of abstraction L. The
specification TSpec need not be formal. In changing levels of abstraction,
for example, Tspec will possess a formal status outside L.

(iv)   *Verifications* V that guarantee the validity of the specifications.
The proofs that the algorithm A meets CSpec and PSpec are rigorous
mathematical arguments, capable of formalisation **in** appropriate *correctness*
and *performance logics* tailored to the specification languages and L. The
arguments that Cspec represents TSpec must be convincing and rigorous even
though they may not be formalisable.

(v)   *Tests or experiments* E that check the specifications on selected
data. These computations take place within the level of abstraction L
and, in the case of performance, produce results about L-time and L-space.
The experiments necessarily take place in a *simulator* for L. The empirical
study of the algorithm is important in its own right and specifications
of behaviour and performance that are tested, but are not subject to
rigorous proof, are included.

Thus, we take as a fundamental object of interest in our theory of algorithms the concept of an *algorithm design*

$$D = (L, A, S, V, E)$$

We note that D is intended to be a formal object.

1.3 Design Methodology

We wish to view the process of designing an algorithm as the process of generating a sequence

$$D_1, D_2, \ldots, D_n$$

of algorithm designs. The design D_1 is the *initial draft design* and D_n is the *final draft design*; the sequence is the *design history* of D_n. Our purpose in formalising the concept of an algorithm design is to establish such a sequence as a formal focus for a *methodological model* of the design process. The methodology must classify the various ways in which stage D_i and stage D_{i+1} are related. We believe that the refinement of D_i to D_{i+1} (to use the term of Dijkstra and Wirth) can be characterised in terms of the considerations above, and partly analysed and formalised as *design transformations*. For example, with respect to a fixed level of abstraction L, we can transform an algorithm and its specifications, to accomplish a verification or to trade space for computation time; to a certain extent we can practise top-down design at a fixed level of abstraction, as we have defined it. We will see examples of these transformations in due course.

The level of abstraction L, as we have defined it, can be changed in two ways. We are interested in transformations of algorithms and algorithmic languages that leave the algorithm's data type and specifications invariant. These transformations underlie the idea of having many representations of an algorithm that are computationally equivalent but emphasise different aspects of the algorithm's design. In VLSI design, for instance, the idea of representing the "same" system pictorially and algebraically is indispensible. We will see examples of these equivalence transformations in due course.

In top-down design, or bottom-up design, the level of abstraction can be changed by design transformations that implement the data type or commands of the algorithm and change the clock and the space scale. We will *not* see an example of this important type of refinement in this paper. A formal theory of hierarchies of levels of abstraction is attempted in Bergstra, Klop and Tucker [1983] and a theory of top-down design for concurrent systems is presented in Bergstra and Tucker [1985].

1.4　　　　Sources　　This work on a theory of design for algorithms is founded upon the important and extensive writings of E.W. Dijkstra, C.A.R. Hoare, and N. Wirth on programming methodology : see, for example, Dijkstra [1968,1976], Dahl, Dijkstra and Hoare [1971], Wirth [1976], and the papers in Gries [1978]. Work on data abstraction and the formal definition of languages is fundamental to our work : see especially Liskov and Zilles [1975];ADJ [1978]; and deBakker [1981], for example.

　　　　Our interest in formal foundations for complexity theory begins in Asveld and Tucker [1982] and continues in attempts to sort out the scope and limits of complexity models in VLSI design (see Baudet [1983] and Dew and Tucker [1983]). An important contribution to the foundations of complexity is Nielson [1984]. Our previous work with J.A. Bergstra on formal theories of design was referenced in 1.3. Our interest in formal theories of correctness preserving transformations stems from R.J.R. Back [1980]. A useful recent survey of research into program transformation systems is Partsch and Steinbrüggen [1983]. A stimulating informal account of performance transformations is Bentley [1982].

2.　　　　TWO SORTING ALGORITHMS

　　　　In this section we shall informally specify two parallel algorithms for sorting n elements for some set D that is linearly ordered by a relation $\leq_D$ into non-descending order. The first of these algorithms is called *Odd-Even Transposition Sort,* (or OE for short), and the second, *Expanded Odd-Even Transposition Sort,* (or EOE).

　　　　We shall describe these parallel algorithms as synchronous networks of *modules* that communicate via *channels*; we think of these networks as architectures for VLSI designs.

　　　　We shall show by means of examples that both OE and EOE *are* sorting algorithms, and, indeed, sort n elements in less than n time units or *steps*. In Section 3 we will formally discuss the algorithms in the spirit of Section 1, and rigorously prove that both OE and EOE meet appropriate formal correctness and performance specifications.

2.1　　　　The OE Sorter　　For sorting n elements the OE sorter is as depicted in Figure 1; it comprises an array of n modules $\Pi_1, \ldots, \Pi_n$ wherein each Π_i may hold one element of D, and may communicate only with its neighbouring modules as indicated by the connecting channels in the figure;　in addition, OE involves a collection $In_1, \ldots, In_n$ of n *sources*, which supply the input to the array, and a collection $Out_1, \ldots, Out_n$ of n *sinks* which receive output from the array.

　　　　We can now describe the operation of the OE sorter.

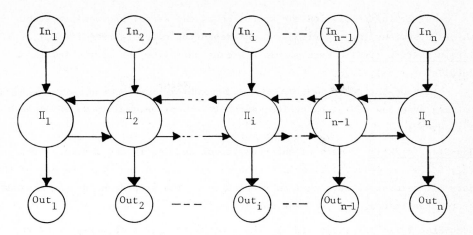

Figure 1.   The OE Sorter

t \ i	1	2	3	4	5	6
0	6——5		4——3		2——1	
1	5	6——3		4——1		2
2	5——3		6——1		4——2	
3	3	5——1		6——2		4
4	3——1		5——2		6——4	
5	1	3——2		5——4		6
6	1	2	3	4	5	6

Figure 2.   Tabulation of the value in Π_i $(1 \le i \le 6)$ at time t $(0 \le t \le 6)$, given initial input $(6,5,4,3,2,1)$.

After initialisation the operation of the sorter proceeds in steps which determines the *algorithm*'s *clock* measuring discrete time t = 0,1,2,... :

<u>Initialisation (t=0)</u>   Each module Π_i reads data from the source In_i in parallel for i=1,...,n.

The operation of the sorter now depends on time; its action alternating between even and odd clock cycles; without loss of generality we shall assume n is even :

<u>Odd-Step (t=2k+1)</u>   Each of the constituent modules in the module pairs (Π_i, Π_{i+1}) for i=1,3,5,...,n-1, exchanges values with the other member of the pair (if necessary) such that on completion of the step Π_i holds the minimum of the two values, and Π_{i+1} the maximum.

<u>Even-Step (t=2k+2)</u>   This step is the same as the odd-step except that the module pairs are (Π_i, Π_{i+1}), for i=2,4,6,...,n-2. During this step Π_1 and Π_n do nothing; they retain their current values for 1 time unit.

<u>Termination (t=n+1)</u>   Each module Π_i sends its current value to the sink Out_i in parallel for i=1,...,n.

Example

Suppose n=6, and the sources collectively supply the vector (6,5,4,3, 2,1) to the array for sorting. We have tabulated the values in each module Π_i at each time t in Figure 2, wherein "—" denotes a comparison of values. Notice the data is sorted in n steps as claimed.

2.2   The EOE Sorter   For sorting n elements the EOE sorter is as depicted in Figure 3; it comprises an array of n+1 columns of n modules Π_j^i i=0,...,n, j=1,...,n, wherein each Π_j^i may again hold one element of D, and may only communicate with its neighbouring modules as shown in the figure; in addition, EOE, like OE, involves n sources $In_1,...,In_n$, and n sinks $Out_1,...,Out_n$.

The operation of the sorter is as follows :

<u>Initialisation (t=0)</u>   Each module in column 0, (viz. Π_j^o , j=1,...,n) reads data from its source in parallel. We shall assume all other modules hold some unknown elements that we denote by the *unspecified* element u. Every module Π_j^i now performs, in parallel, the following general step for n time units, and then terminates.

<u>General Step (t=1,...,n)</u>   The action that the module Π_j^i takes is determined according to whether the column is zero, odd, or even (for each row index j).

Case : i=0   The module does nothing (i.e. it retains its current value for one time unit).

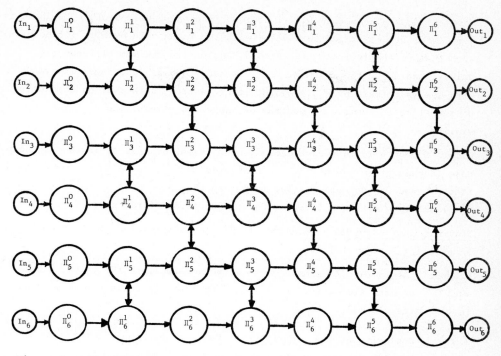

Figure 3. The EOE sorter illustrated for n=6.

t=0

```
6  u  u  u  u  u  u
5  u  u  u  u  u  u
6  u  u  u  u  u  u
3  u  u  u  u  u  u
2  u  u  u  u  u  u
1  u  u  u  u  u  u
```

t=1

```
6  5  u  u  u  u  u
5  6  u  u  u  u  u
4  3  u  u  u  u  u
3  4  u  u  u  u  u
2  1  u  u  u  u  u
1  2  u  u  u  u  u
```

t=2

```
6  5  5  u  u  u  u
5  6  3  u  u  u  u
4  3  6  u  u  u  u
3  4  1  u  u  u  u
2  1  4  u  u  u  u
1  2  2  u  u  u  u
```

t=3

```
6  5  5  3  u  u  u
5  6  3  5  u  u  u
4  3  6  1  u  u  u
3  4  1  6  u  u  u
2  1  4  2  u  u  u
1  2  2  4  u  u  u
```

t=4

```
6  5  5  3  3  u  u
5  6  3  5  1  u  u
4  3  6  1  5  u  u
3  4  1  6  2  u  u
2  1  4  2  6  u  u
1  2  2  4  4  u  u
```

t=5

```
6  5  5  3  3  1  u
5  6  3  5  1  3  u
4  3  6  1  5  2  u
3  4  1  6  2  5  u
2  1  4  2  6  4  u
1  2  2  4  4  6  u
```

t=6

```
6  5  5  3  3  1  1
5  6  3  5  1  3  2
4  3  6  1  5  2  3
3  4  1  6  2  5  4
2  1  4  2  6  4  5
1  2  2  4  4  6  6
```

Figure 4. Tabulation of the values held by the modules of the EOE sorter.

Case : i odd   The module Π_j^i first reads the value held by Π_j^{i-1}. Then, if j is even, Π_j^i exchanges this value with the value held by Π_{j-1}^i (if necessary), such that, on completion of the step, Π_j^i holds the minimum of these two values, and Π_{j-1}^i the maximum. If j is odd, then Π_j^i exchanges its value with the value held by Π_{j+1}^i (again, if necessary), such that on completion of the step, Π_j^i holds the maximum of these two values, and Π_{j+1}^i the minimum.

Case : i even   In this case each Π_j^i for i≠j≠n, behaves as in the preceding case (dependent on whether Π_j^i is connected to Π_{j-1}^i or Π_{j+1}^i). During this step Π_1^i and Π_n^i do nothing (ie. they read the value held by Π_1^{i-1} (respectively, Π_n^{i-1}) and then retain this value for the duration of the step.

<u>Termination (t=n+1)</u>   Each module Π_j^n sends its value to the sink Out_j in parallel for j=1,...,n.

<u>Example</u>   As in the OE example we take n=6 and tabulate the value held by each Π_j^i at each time t (Figure 4). Notice that again the output is sorted in time n as claimed.

<u>2.3</u>   Complexity of the Algorithms   We have seen that in terms of the clocks naturally defined by our two algorithms, both OE and EOE are linear sorters. This observation is based upon the observation that each module operates in unit time. Since the time intervals of both clocks are determined by equivalent algorithmic operations, based on the maximum and minimum functions on D, it is arguable that the two clocks are also equivalent. It is intuitively clear then that for a single input OE and EOE have equal time complexity $\Omega(n)$. However, EOE is obviously more expensive in terms of area, being $\Omega(n^2)$ in contrast to OE which is $\Omega(n)$.

    Now let us consider the problem of sorting a sequence of m n-tuples of data. We can modify the description of OE such that instead of clocking its data out to the sinks and then terminating each module Π_i clocks out its data whilst reading in the ith element of the next n-tuple of data to be sorted. Clearly, the OE array must wait at least n time units before reading; this time interval we refer to as the *period* of the algorithm. In the case of the EOE sorter, however, once each column has performed its computations (which takes one time unit) that column is ready to receive new data. Thus EOE has period 1.

    It is easy to see that the total time required for OE and EOE to sort m n-tuples of data is $\Omega(nm)$ and $\Omega(n+m-1)$ respectively.

<u>3.</u>   FORMAL DESCRIPTIONS

    In this section we will begin to formalise the algorithms of Section 2, in order to illustrate the concept of an algorithm design.

To do this we must formally define a level of abstraction in which to express our algorithms. This will be an algorithmic language *PR* based on *algebraic data type* A.

3.1   Data types

The algorithms of Section 2 are based on three sets of data : the set $N = \{0,1,2,\ldots\}$ of *natural numbers* is used for counting; the set $B = \{tt, ff\}$ of *boolean truth-values* is used in tests; and the set D containing data that is to be sorted. Furthermore, the algorithms *appear* to involve certain constants and operations on these sets, namely :

$$0 \in N; \quad \text{successor} : N \to N; \quad \text{odd, even} : N \to B$$
$$tt, \; ff \; \in B; \quad \text{not} : B \to B; \quad \text{or} : B \times B \to B,$$
$$\leq \; : D \times D \to B; \quad \text{maximum} : D \times D \to D$$

where the operations have their obvious meanings. Taken together the three sets and the eight operations constitute a (*three-sorted*) *algebraic structure* that formalises the data type A of the algorithms. In the general theory of data types an *algebraic data type* or *data abstraction* is modelled by a many-sorted algebra (see ADJ [1978]) :

Definition.   Let S be a set of *sorts*. A *many-sorted algebra* A with sort set S comprises (i) a family $A = \langle A_s : s \in S \rangle$ of sets A_s, (ii) a collection of *operators* $\sigma : A_{s_1} \times \ldots \times A_{s_n} \to A_{s_0}$ for some $s_i \in S$, i=0,...,n, and (iii) for each $s \in S$ a collection of constants $c \in A_s$.

3.2   *PR(A)*

Definition.   Let A be a many-sorted algebra with sort set S. Suppose A contains the domains N and B together with the usual operations on these sets, including equality. We define by structural induction the collection $PR(A)$. Let S^+ denote the collection of strings $w = s_1 \ldots s_n$ over S of *length* $n \geq 1$. For $w \in S^+$, A^w denotes the cartesian product set $A_{s_1} \times \ldots \times A_{s_n}$.

Basic Functions

(i)   *Constant functions*. For each $w \in S^+$, $s \in S$ and constant c, the constant function $f : A^w \to A^s$ is in $PR(A)$, where f is defined by

$$f(a) = c \qquad \forall a \in A^w.$$

(ii)   *Algebraic operations*. For each operation σ of the algebra A, $\sigma \in PR(A)$.

(iii)   *Projections*. For each $w \in S^+$, $w = s_1 \ldots s_n$, and for each i=1,...,n, the projection functions $U_i^w : A^w \to A^{s_i}$ are in $PR(A)$, where U_i^w is defined by

$$U_i^w(a) = a_i \qquad \forall a = (a_1 \ldots a_n) \in A^w.$$

(iv) *Definition by cases.* For each $s \in S$ the function $DC_s : B \times A^{ss} \to A^s$ is in $PR(A)$, where DC_s is defined by

$$DC_s(b,a,a') = \begin{cases} a & \text{if } b=tt \\ a' & \text{if } b=ff \end{cases}$$

$\forall a,a' \in A^s$, $\forall b \in B$. (We will of course write DC for DC_s when s is understood.)

Function Building Operations

(v) *Vectorisation.* Suppose for some $u,v \in S^+$ with $v=s_1 \cdots s_n$, that $f_i \in PR(A)$ where $f_i : A^u \to A^{s_i}$ for $i=1,\ldots,n$. Then $f \in PR(A)$ for $f:A^u \to A^v$ defined by

$$f(a) = (f_1(a),\ldots,f_n(a)) \qquad \forall a \in A^u.$$

For f defined as above, we write $f = \langle f_1,\ldots,f_n \rangle$.

(vi) *Composition.* Suppose for some $u,v,w \in S^+$, that $g,h \in PR(A)$, where $g : A^u \to A^w$, $h : A^w \to A^v$. Then $f \in PR(A)$ for $f : A^u \to A^v$ defined by

$$f(a) = h(g(a)) \qquad \forall a \in A^u .$$

For f defined as above we write $f = h \circ g$.

(vii) *Primitive Recursion.* Suppose for some $u,v \in S^+$, that $g,h \in PR(A)$, where $g : A^u \to A^v$ and $h : N \times A^u \times A^v \to A^v$. Then $f \in PR(A)$, for $f : N \times A^u \to A^v$ defined by

$$f(0,a) = g(a)$$

$$f(n+1,a) = h(n,a,f(n,a))$$

$\forall a \in A^u$. For f defined as above we write $f = \text{prim}(g,h)$.

Exercise. Each vector-valued function $f : A^u \to A^v$ induces n *coordinate functions* $f_1,\ldots,f_n$ such that $f_i : A^u \to A^{s_i}$ for $i=1,\ldots,n$, and $f = \langle f_1,\ldots,f_n \rangle$ (when $v=s_1 \cdots s_n$). By expressing the function f,g,h of (vii) above in terms of their coordinate functions, show that the collection $\{f_1,\ldots,f_n\}$ is defined by *simultaneous* primitive recursion. (See Peter [1967]).

3.3 Formal specification of OE.

Having defined our algorithmic language *PR*, we now proceed with the formal description of the algorithms of Section 2. We will complete the definition of our choice of level of abstraction L only in Section 5, where we formally define the time complexity of an arbitrary *PR(A)* algorithm.

Our first design decision is to take as the data type for both algorithms the three-sorted algebra A, which is the algebra of 3.1 with an unspecified element u adjoined; we assume all functions are strict with respect to u, ie. $f(-,u,-) = u$.

The OE algorithm. We take as the specification of OE a function $V \in PR(A)$ where $V = \langle V_1,\ldots,V_n \rangle : N \times D^n \to D^n$ with coordinate functions $V_i : N \times D^n \to D$.

It is intended that $V_i(t,x)$ denotes the value held by the ith module at time t given input x.   The coodinates V_i are defined as follows :

for $i=1,\ldots,n$, $V_i(0,x) = x_i$ $\forall x=(x_1,\ldots,x_n) \in D^n$.

$$V_1(t+1,x) = \begin{cases} V_1(t,x) & \text{if } t \text{ odd;} \\ \min(V_1(t,x),V_2(t,x)) & \text{otherwise;} \end{cases}$$

for i even, $\neq$ n,

$$V_i(t+1,x) = \begin{cases} \min(V_i(t,x),V_{i+1}(t,x)) & \text{if } t \text{ odd;} \\ \max(V_{i-1}(t,x),V_i(t,x)) & \text{otherwise;} \end{cases}$$

for i odd, $\neq$ 1,

$$V_i(t+1,x) = \begin{cases} \max(V_{i-1}(t,x),V_i(t,x) & \text{if } t \text{ odd;} \\ \min(V_i(t,x),V_{i+1}(t,x)) & \text{otherwise;} \end{cases}$$

finally,

$$V_n(t+1,x) = \begin{cases} V_n(t,x) & \text{if } t \text{ odd;} \\ \max(V_{n-1}(t,x),V_n(t,x)) & \text{otherwise.} \end{cases}$$

Exercise.   Show (i) $V \in PR(A)$, (ii) if $D=N$, n=6, $V(6,6,5,4,3,2,1) = (1,2,3,4,5,6)$.
Next we take the correctness specification for OE to be

$$\text{Cspec}_{OE} = (\forall x)(V_1(n,x) \leq \ldots \leq V_n(n,x)).$$

This is formula in a first-order predicate language of the structure A; this language serves as the *correctness specification language* for the level of abstraction L. We prove Cspec in Section 4.

The formal specification PSpec_{OE} of the performance of OE must await Section 5.

3.4   Formal specification of EOE.   We take as the level of abstraction for data for the EOE algorithm the data type A of 3.3.

The EOE algorithm.   We take as the specification of EOE the function $W \in PR(A)$, where $W = \langle W_1^o,\ldots,W_n^o,\ldots,W_1^n,\ldots,W_n^n \rangle : N \times D^{n(n+1)} \to D^{n(n+1)}$. It is intended that $W_j^i(t,x)$ denotes the value held by the jth module on the ith column of EOE (qua architecture) at time t (given input $x \in D^{n(n+1)}$). The coordinates $W_j^i : N \times D^{n(n+1)} \to D$ are defined as follows, wherein $x=(x_1^o,\ldots,x_n^o,\ldots,x_n^n) \in D^{n(n+1)}$:

for $j=1,\ldots,n$ $\quad W_j^{\,o}(0,x) = x_j^{\,o}$

for $i=1,\ldots,n$ $\quad W_j^{\,i}(0,x) = u \qquad\qquad\qquad$ for $j=1,\ldots,n$.

For $j=1,\ldots,n$ $\quad W_j^{\,o}(t+1,x) = W_j^{\,o}(t,x)$.

For i odd,

$$W_j^{\,i}(t+1,x) = \min(W_j^{\,i-1}(t,x),\ W_{j+1}^{\,i-1}(t,x)) \qquad \text{for } j \text{ odd,}$$

$$W_j^{\,i}(t+1,x) = \max(W_{j-1}^{\,i-1}(t,x),\ W_j^{\,i-1}(t,x)) \qquad \text{for } j \text{ even .}$$

For i even,

$$W_j^{\,i}(t+1,x) = \max(W_{j-1}^{\,i-1}(t,x),\ W_j^{\,i-1}(t,x)) \qquad \text{for } j \text{ odd, } \ne 1$$

$$W_j^{\,i}(t+1,x) = \min(W_j^{\,i-1}(t,x),\ W_{j+1}^{\,i-1}(t,x)) \qquad \text{for } j \text{ even, } \ne 1$$

$$W_j^{\,i}(t+1,x) = W_j^{\,i-1}(t,x) \qquad\qquad\qquad\qquad \text{for } j=1 \text{ or } j=n.$$

Exercise.   Show (i) $W \epsilon PR(A)$, (ii) if $D=N$, $n=6$, and $W^n = \langle W_1^{\,n},\ldots,W_n^{\,n}\rangle$, then $W(t,6,5,4,3,2,1,u,\ldots,u)$ is as tabulated in Figure 4 (Section 2).

We next take the correctness specification for EOE to be

$$\mathrm{Cspec}_{EOE} \equiv (\forall x \epsilon D^n)(W_1^{\,n}(n,x') \le \ldots \le W_n^{\,n}(n,x')).$$

Wherein for each $x=(x_1\ldots x_n)\epsilon D^n$, x' is the vector $(x_1,\ldots x_n,u,\ldots,u)\epsilon D^{n(n+1)}$. Again, we will prove Cspec_{EOE} in Section 4, and consider the time complexity of EOE in Section 5.

Exercise.   Reformulate OE and EOE and their correctness specifications so that both sorters are capable of sorting a sequence of inputs.

3.5   Some Observations. Consider how we have turned the informal pictorial representation of our algorithms into formal algebraic representations. Each individual module is assigned a single-valued function, and the architecture, being a collection of these modules, is assigned the vectorisation of the functions. In general, the communication pattern of an architecture will dictate the argument dependencies exhibited by the functions. On formalising the picture/architecture language, the material in Section 2 can be formalised as algorithmic designs; the representation of these designs by the representations of this section can then be formalised as "equivalence preserving" transformations in the sense alluded to in 1.3.

4. FORMAL VERIFICATION

In this section we will outline the formal proofs of correctness of the OE and EOE algorithms.

4.1 Correctness Theorem. *Let* V *be the* $PR(A)$-*function of* 3.2. *Then*

$$(\forall x \in D^n)(V_1(n,x) \leq \ldots \leq V_n(n,x)) \quad .$$

This is of course $Cspec_{OE}$.

4.2 Correctness Theorem. *Let* W *be the* $PR(A)$-*function of* 3.3. *Then,*

$$(\forall x \in D^n)(W_1^{\ n}(n,x') \leq \ldots \leq W_n^{\ n}(n,x'))$$

where for each $x=(x_1 \ldots x_n) \in D^n$, x' *is the vector* $(x_1, \ldots, x_n, u_1, \ldots, u) \in D^{n(n+1)}$.

This is of course $Cspec_{EOE}$. Theorem 4.1 is a direct consequence of Theorem 4.2 and the following *equivalence* theorem :

4.3 Equivalence Theorem. *Let* V,W *be as above. Then, for each coordinate function* $W_j^{\ i}$ *of* W, $1 \leq j \leq n$, $0 \leq i \leq n$

$$(\forall x \in D^n)(W_j^{\ i})(i,x') = V_j(i,x))$$

where x' *is the usual transformation* $D^n \rightarrow D^{n(n+1)}$.

The proof of this theorem is based upon the observations concering the relationship between the OE and EOE algorithms made at the end of 2.2.

We now turn our attention to Theorem 4.2. As we shall see, this theorem is a direct consequence of two facts : Lemma 4.6 concerning a class of algorithms (architectures) which we term *parallel comparison algorithms* of which EOE is an instance; and Lemma 4.7 concerning OE.

4.4 On the Parallel Comparison Algorithms. A parallel comparison algorithm, or PCA, is best thought of as an array of modules $\Pi_j^{\ i}$ (see Figures 3, 5 and 6). The operation of an arbitrary PCA will be officially defined by a $PR(A)$-function. However, we first need a notation for expressing the communication structure of a PCA,P. We do this as follows :

Definition. A *parallel comparison algorithm* P *for n inputs is denoted by a* vector (of vectors) of numbers, $P = (\vec{r}_1, \ldots, \vec{r}_\beta)$ *for some* $\beta \in N$, *where*

(i) $\vec{r}_i = (r_1^{\ i}, \ldots, r_{k_i}^{\ i})$ *for some* $k_i \geq 1$ *and* $i=1, \ldots, \beta$;

(ii) $\qquad 1 \le r_j{}^i < n \qquad$ for $j=1,\ldots,k_i$ and $i=1,\ldots,\beta$;

(iii) $\qquad | r_j{}^i - r_{j+1}^i | > 1$ for $j=1,\ldots,k_i$ and $i=1,\ldots,\beta$.

We denote the collection of all such PCAs by PCA(n). This notation is interpreted as follows : each $P \epsilon$ PCA(n) comprises β columns of modules; each column of P has k_i vertically connected pairs of modules $(\Pi_\ell^i, \Pi_{\ell+1}^i)$ where $\ell = r_j{}^i$ for $j=1,\ldots,k_i$. Condition (iii) above tells us that $\Pi_j{}^i$ is never connected to both Π_{j-1}^i and Π_{j+1}^i.

Example. Consider the PCA P of Figure 5. It has description $P = (\vec{r}_1,\ldots,\vec{r}_5)$ wherein $\vec{r}_1 = (1,3)$, $\vec{r}_2 = (2)$, $\vec{r}_3 = (1)$, $\vec{r}_4 = (2)$, $\vec{r}_5 = (1,3)$.

We now describe the operation of a general PCA $P = (\vec{r}_1,\ldots,\vec{r}_\beta)$ by characterising it as a *PR(A)-function* (where A is the data type of 3.3 and 3.4) as follows :

Definition. We say that $W : N \times D^{n(\beta+1)} \to D^{n(\beta+1)}$ is the *PR(A)-characterisation* of $P \epsilon$ PCA(n) if the coordinate functions of W, $W_j{}^i$ $i=0,\ldots,\beta$, $j=1,\ldots,n$ are defined thus :

let $x = (x_1{}^o,\ldots,x_n{}^o,\ldots,x_n{}^\beta) \epsilon D^{n(\beta+1)}$, then

for $j=1,\ldots,n$

$$W_j{}^o(0,x) = x^o{}_j$$

for $i=1,\ldots,\beta$

$$W^i{}_j(0,x) = u \qquad \text{for } j=1,\ldots,n.$$

For $j=1,\ldots,n \qquad W_j{}^o(t+1,x) = W_j{}^o(t,x).$

For $i=1,\ldots,\beta, \qquad j=1,\ldots,n,$

if $r_\gamma{}^i \neq j \neq r_\gamma{}^i + 1$, for $\gamma=1,\ldots,k_i$

$$W_j{}^i(r+1,x) = W_j{}^{i-1}(t,x)$$

if $j = r_\gamma{}^i$ for some $\gamma \epsilon [1,k_i]$.

$$W_j{}^i(t+1,x) = \min(W_j{}^{i-1}(t,x), W_{j+1}^{i-1}(t,x))$$

if $j = r_\gamma^i + 1$ for some $\gamma \in [1, k_i]$

$$W_j^i(t+1, x) = \max(W_{j-1}^{i-1}(t,x), \ W_j^{i-1}(t,x), \ W_j^{i-1}(t,x)).$$

4.5   **Exercise.**   Describe the architecture of Figure 3 as a PCA P_{EOE}. Show that the $PR(A)$-characterisation of this PCA coincides with the definition of the function W of 3.4.

     We can now state the basic fact upon which Theorem 4.2 depends after a preliminary definition.

Definition.   Let D be linearly ordered by $\leq$. We say $x_R = (x_1, \ldots, x_n) \in D^n$ is a *reverse vector* if

$$x_1 > x_2 > \ldots > x_n$$

(**where** a>b   iff   not (a$\leq$b)).

4.6   **Basic Lemma**   *Let* $P \in PCA(n)$ *have* $PR(A)$*-characterisation* W. *Then the following statements are equivalent :*

(i)   *P sorts a reverse vector* $x_R \in D^n$.

(ii)   *P sorts every vector* $x \in D^n$.

That is,

$$W_1^n(n, x_R') \leq \ldots \leq W_n^n(n, x_R') \ <=> \ (\forall x \in D^n)(W_1^n(n, x') \leq \ldots \leq W_n^n(n, x')$$

wherein x' is the usual transformation $x' = (x_1, \ldots x_n, u, \ldots, u)$. This result (essentially due to R.W. Floyd; see Knuth [1973]) leads to the idea of a *generic* or *critical point* for the correctness of an algorithm.

     We postpone the proof of Lemma 4.6 until we have completed the proof of our theorems.

     Returning to the proof of theorem 4.2, we only need to show that the PCA P_{EOE} of Exercise 4.5 does indeed sort some reverse vector to show that P_{EOE} sorts every vector in D^n as required (assuming Lemma 4.5 of course). In fact, we have

4.7   **Lemma.**   *Let* V *be the* $PR(A)$ *function of 3.2. Then for any reverse vector* $x_R \in D^n$,

$$V_1(n, x_R) \leq \ldots \leq V_n(n, x_R)$$

     Hence, OE sorts a reverse vector. Thus, appealing to Theorem 4.3, we have
$$W_1^n(n, x_R') \leq \ldots \leq W_1^n(n, x_R')$$

and thus by Lemma 4.5,

$$(\forall x \in D^n)(W_1{}^n(n,x') \leq \ldots \leq W_n{}^n(n,x'))$$

which is, of course, Theorem 4.2. As noted above, Theorem 4.1 now also holds via Theorem 4.3.

Proof of Lemma 4.6. In order to prove Lemma 4.6 for an arbitrary PCA P, we first transform each PCA to a simpler form Seq(P) which we refer to as the *sequentialisation* of P. We then prove Lemma 4.6 for such sequentialisations and then invoke an equivalence result to prove 4.6.

Sequentialisation. Consider an arbitrary PCA $P=(\vec{r}_1,\ldots,\vec{r}_\beta)$. We can transform P into a new PCA P' by spreading each column $\vec{r}_i$ of P into k_i distinct columns $\vec{s}_{i,\gamma},\ldots,\vec{s}_{i,k_i}$ of the new PCA P', such that $\vec{s}_{i,\gamma} = r_\gamma{}^i$. Thus each column of P' contains only one pair of vertically connected modules. If we perform this transformation in a consistent manner, it should be clear that P and P' will produce the same output for the same input, but P will take time β to produce output, whereas P' will take time $\alpha = \sum\limits_{i=1}^{i=\beta} k_i$. (Compare Figures 5 and 6.)

Definition. Let $P \in PCA(n)$, $P=(\vec{r}_1,\ldots,\vec{r}_\beta)$, where $\vec{r}_i=(\vec{r}_1{}^i,\ldots,\vec{r}_{k_i}{}^i)$ for $i=1,\ldots,\beta$. Then the PCA C = Seq(P) is defined by

$$C = (\vec{s}_{1,1},\ldots,\vec{s}_{1,k_1}, \vec{s}_{2,1},\ldots,\vec{s}_{\beta-1,k_{\beta-1}}, \vec{s}_{\beta,1},\ldots\vec{s}_{\beta,k_\beta}$$

wherein $\vec{s}_{i,j} = r_j{}^i$ for $j=1,\ldots,k_i$, $i=1,\ldots,\beta$.

Notice Seq : PCA(n) → PCA(n) (exercise!). Thus every C=Seq(P) has a PR(A)-characterisation for each $P \in PCA(n)$. A routine inductive argument on the *length* β of an arbitrary PCA P yields :

4.8 _____ Lemma. *Let $P \in PCA(n)$ and C=Seq(P) have PR(A)-characterisations* $W:N \times D^{n(\beta+1)} \to D^{n(\beta+1)}$ *and* $Z:N \times D^{n(\alpha+1)} \to D^{n(\alpha+1)}$ *where* α, β *are the number of columns comprising* C,P *respectively. Then, for each* $j=1,\ldots,n$,

$$(\forall x \in D^n)(W_j{}^\beta(\beta,x') = Z_j{}^\alpha(\alpha,x''))$$

where x" *is the obvious map* $D^n \to D^{n(\alpha+1)}$.

Notice this lemma tells us that Seq is a correctness preserving transformation in the sense of 1.3. It is now possible to prove (see Knuth [1973]) :

4.9 _____ Lemma *Let* C = Seq(P) *for some* $P \in PCA(n)$, *and let* x_R *be a reverse vector in* D^n. *Then the following statements are equivalent :*

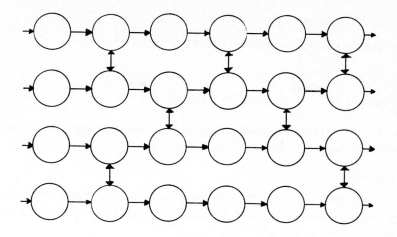

Figure 5.   The PCA P.   (Sources and sinks omitted).

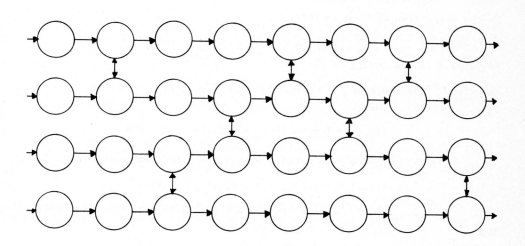

Figure 6.   The PCA C = Seq(P).   (Sources and sinks omitted).

(i)   C *sorts* x_R

(ii)   C *sorts every vector in* D_n.

That is,

$$(Z_1^\alpha(\alpha, x_R'') \leq \ldots \leq Z_\alpha^\alpha (\alpha, x_R'')) \iff (\forall x \in D^n)(Z_1^\alpha(\alpha, x'') \leq \ldots \leq Z_\alpha^\alpha(\alpha, x'')),$$

where Z is the *PR(A)*-characterisation of C. Clearly Lemma 4.6 is now an immediate corollary of Lemma 4.9 via Lemma 4.8.

5.   ON TIME

We now add a measure of time complexity to our algorithmic language *PR(A)* to complete our level of abstraction. We will do this by defining the *length of computation* map $\lambda : PR(A) \times \underset{w}{\cup} A^w \to N$.

5.1   Time Complexity of *PR(A)*

Definition.   For each $f \in PR(A)$ with $f : A^u \to A^v$, the *length of computation of* f on $a \in A^u$, $\lambda(f, a)$, is defined by induction on the complexity of f as follows :

Basis.   Suppose f is a basic function defined by one of the clauses (i)-(iv) in the definition of *PR(A)*. Then,

$$\lambda(f, a) = 1$$

for each a in the domain of f.

Induction.   (a) Suppose f is defined by $f = \langle f_1, \ldots, f_n \rangle$ for some $f_1, \ldots, f_n \in PR(A)$. Then,

$$\lambda(f, a) = 1 + \max\{\lambda(f_1, a), \ldots, \lambda(f_n, a)\} \ \forall a \in A^u.$$

(b) Suppose f is defined by $f = h \circ g$ for some $g, h \in PR(A)$. Then,

$$\lambda(f, a) = 1 + \lambda(g, a) + \lambda(h, g(a)) \qquad \forall a \in A^u.$$

(c) Suppose f is defined by $f = prim(g, h)$ for some $g, h \in PR(A)$.

Then,

$$\lambda(f, 0, a) = \lambda(g, a) \qquad\qquad \forall a \in A^u,$$

$$\lambda(f, t+1, a) = 1 + \lambda(h, t, a, f(t, a)) + \lambda(f, t, a)$$

$\forall t \in N, \ \forall a \in A^u$.

Notice that in each of the cases above, the choice of $\lambda(f, a)$ reflects our intuition concerning the time required to evaluate f(a); basic functions, including the given algebraic operations of A, *determine unit time.* This assumption is consonant with the idea that the algebra is an irreducible level of abstraction. For the vectorisation of functions, $f(a) = <f_1, \ldots, f_n> (a)$, we imagine the coordinate functions to be evaluated in parallel on the argument a; the time required to evaluate $f(a)$ is taken to be the maximum time to evaluate any $f_i(a)$ $i \in [1,n]$, plus the unit time required to supply the argument of f to the coordinate functions. For somposition $f = h \circ g$, we imagine $f(a)$ to be evaluated sequentially, so we take as the time required for evaluating this function to be the sum of the times required for evaluating g and h on their respective arguments, plus the unit time required to supply the argument $g(a)$ to h. The cost of $prim(g,h)(n,a)$ is arrived at in a similar fashion.

We can now specify and establish the performance of the algorithms of Section 2.

5.2   Theorem   *Let V be the PR(A)-function of 3.2. Then,*

$$\lambda(V,t,x) = 2+8t \qquad\qquad \forall t \in N, \; \forall x \in D^n .$$

5.3   Theorem   *Let W be the PR(A)-function of 3.3. Then,*

$$\lambda(W,t,x) = 2+5t \qquad\qquad \forall t \in N, \; \forall x \in D^{n(n+1)}$$

The idea of time in the algorithms is subtle. The algorithms are structured in terms of algebraic operations which give rise to a *virtual clock*. With respect to this clock, the algorithms are exactly linear (see Section 4); and the clock plays a crucial role in the correctness proofs of the algorithms which are *real-time* in the sense of Wirth [1977].

On formalising the algorithms in *PR*(A), we find the *PR*(A)-time performance in the above theorems. Interestingly the relationship between *PR*(A)-time and the virtual clock is not a matter of linear retiming.

We can reformulate the algorithms in several ways, by simply changing the primitive operations and hence obtain new data abstractions. For example, we can include the *implementation* of max, min, odd, and even in our formal descriptions of the algorithms, and examine their performance. In this way *PR* accommodates the top-down design of algorithms.

Exercises.   We can implement the data type A of 3.1 by means of a new data type A', obtained from A by removing the operations max and min, to leave the operation $\leq$. (i) Show, by implementing min and max as *PR*(A')-functions, (e.g. $min(x,y) = DC(x \leq y,x,y)$), and that $\lambda(V,t,x) = 2+11t$, where V is the function of 3.2 expressed as a *PR*(A')-function. (ii) Implement A' of (c) above as another data type A" obtained from A' by removing odd and even. Show by implementing odd(t) as a $PR(A")$-function, (e.g. odd(t)=prim(ff,not)), that, when expressed as a $PR(A")$-function, V satisfies $\lambda(V,t,x)=O(t^2)$. (iii) By defining the function odd(t) simultaneously with the coordinate functions of $V \epsilon PR(A")$, show that the resultant function V' : $N \times D^n \times B \rightarrow D^n \times B$ satisfies $\lambda(V',t,x) = O(t)$.

6. CONCLUDING REMARKS

We have stated and illustrated some initial organisational principles for a formal methodology of algorithm design. Clearly there are many case studies to contrast with or complement our description of the parallel sorters. The material of Sections 2-5 betrays our primary interests in VLSI design methodology. The algorithmic language PR determines a fragment of a specification language called *Dedekind*. Dedekind is to provide a complementary, equivalent characterisation of VLSI algorithms, primarily expressed in a pictorial language, for the purpose of formal verification.

However, a pertinent case study on this occasion, and one that we have had in mind throughout the present paper is the following.

Exercise on Line Drawing. Consider the derivation of Brasenham's algorithm in Sproull [1982]. Formally define each draft algorithm design and prove the correctness of the design transformations. Special care is required in passing from the data type *exactreal* to *integer*. Can *exactreal* be usefully replaced by a data type of rational numbers? Reconcile the data abstractions and command languages with the higher level algebraically specified languages in Mallgren [1983]. Does the formal treatment of design meet the requirements in Pitteway [1979]?

REFERENCES

ADJ (Goguen, J.A., J.W. Thatcher, E.G. Wagner, J.B. Wright) An initial algebra approach to the specification, correctness and implementation of abstract data types. In : R.T. Yeh (ed) *Current trends in programming methodology. IV Data Structuring.* Prentice-Hall, Englewood Cliffs, 1978, 80-149.

Asveld, P.R.J. and J.V. Tucker, Complexity theory and the operational structure of algebraic programming systems, Acta Informatica 17(1982) 451-476.

Back, R.J.R., *Correctness preserving program refinements : proof theory and applications,* Mathematical Centre Tracts 131, Amsterdam, 1980.

de Bakker, J.W., *Mathematical theory of program correctness*, Prentice-Hall, London 1981.

Baudet, G., Design and complexity of VLSI algorithms, In J.W. de Bakker and J. van Leeuwen (ed) *Foundations of Computer Science IV*, Mathematical Centre Tracts 158, Amsterdam, 1983. 49-74

Bergstra, J.A., J.W. Klop and J.V. Tucker, Algebraic tools for system construction, in E. Clarke and D. Kozen (ed) *Logics of programs*, Springer-Verlag, 1984.

Bergstra, J.A. and J.V. Tucker, Top-down design and the algebra of communicating processes, Science of Computer Programming, to appear.

Bentley, J.L., *Writing efficient programs*, Prentice-Hall, Englewood Cliffs, 1982.

Dahl, O-J, E.W. Dijkstra and C.A.R. Hoare, *Structured programming*, Academic Press, 1971.

Dedekind, R. *Was sind und was sollen die Zahlen?* Braunschweig 1888.

Dew, P.M. and J.V. Tucker, An experimental study of a timing assumption in VLSI complexity theory, Department of Computer Studies, Report 168, University of Leeds, 1983.

Dijkstra, E.W., A constructive approach to the problem of program correctness, BIT 8 (1968), 174-186.

Dijkstra, E.W., *A discipline of programming*, Prentice-Hall, Englewood Cliffs, 1976.

Gries, D. (ed), *Programming methodology*, Springer-Verlag, Berlin, 1978.

Knuth, D., *The art of computer programming : III Sorting and searching*, Addison-Wesley, Menlo Park, 1973.

Liskov, B. and S. Zilles, Specification techniques for data abstractions, IEEE Transactions on Software Engineering 1 (1975) 7-19.

Mallgren, W.R., *Formal specification of interactive graphics programming languages*, MIT Press, Cambridge, Mass., 1983.

Nielson, H.R., *Hoare logic's for run-time analysis of programs*, Ph.D. Thesis, University of Edinburgh, (CST-30-84) Edinburgh, 1984.

Partsch, H. and R. Steinbrüggen, *Program transformation systems*, ACM Computing Surveys 15 (1983) 199-236.

878

Peter, R., *Recursive functions*, Academic Press, 1967.

Pitteway, M.L.V., The algebra of algorithms - a new toy for the theoretician? IUCC Bulletin 1 (1979) 139-144.

Sproull, R.F., Using program transformations to derive line-drawing algorithms, ACM Transactions on Graphics 1 (1982) 259-273.

Tucker, J.V. and J.I. Zucker, *Program correctness over abstract data types with error-state semantics.* Research monograph in preparation.

Wirth, N., *Algorithms + data structures = programs*, Prentice-Hall, Englewood Cliffs, 1976.

Wirth, N., Toward a discipline of real-time programming, Communications ACM 20 (1977).

TECHNOLOGY FOR THE PROTECTION OF GRAPHICS ALGORITHMS

D J GROVER - BRITISH TECHNOLOGY GROUP

This paper considers technological methods of protecting graphics algorithms. An algorithm itself is not patentable although patent protection can apply to a machine which is operating in accordance with the algorithm. The copyright position on an algorithm is more difficult to define since although copyright subsists in the expression of the algorithm in material form, and perhaps in its performance, it may be difficult to prove whether the copyright is infringed or whether the ideas were thought of independantly and which in any case may show some differences when compared with the work to be protected. It is therefore desirable when seeking to protect an algorithm to maintain its confidentiality and to inhibit others from interpreting the rules of the algorithm from an implementation of that algorithm within a program. In consequence the protection of an algorithm relies on methods of protecting computer software to prevent both its copying and its interpretation in high level terms.

In considering the forms of protection that are available, it is desirable to break the methods down into different categories in order to help with comprehension and also to identify the kind of benefits that are available in the different categories. The forms of protection will be considered from the viewpoint of the author or copyright holder of the program in which an algorithm is implemented.

It is not possible to define watertight categories since some methods with slight variations in implementation permit different modes of protection but for the present purposes they will be grouped under the broad categories of:-

1. Information Hungry Systems

2. Action Triggers

3. System Conditioning

4. Passive Deterrents

The category of information hungry programs considers methods where additional information is required to that available within the program in order to run that program. The additional information may be supplied as a keyword or a password which must be updated at not infrequent intervals; as data provided by a piece of hardware such as a read-only memory or dongle; or as the key to a cipher in order to decipher an encrypted program or its data or significant parts of it. Intelligent dongles in tamper resistant modules are probably the most secure method of protection.

NATO ASI Series, Vol. F17
Fundamental Algorithms for Computer Graphics
Edited by R. A. Earnshaw
© Springer-Verlag Berlin Heidelberg 1985

Action triggers comprise those methods for generating any course of action such as print-out, alarm, initiation of surveillance or sabotage. The trigger can be any user input or a user environment which does not conform to that of the legitimate user. The action may be a simple alarm or erasure of the the program and data; or a more subtle response such as altering the function of the program in a way which is detrimental to the illegal user or in way which draws attention to the misuse.

System conditioning implies that conditions are installed within the program which make it reliant upon particular modes of operation or which disable some normal modes. Thus, time or mobility locks which limit the program to run only within certain time periods or on particular hardware are a frequently used method. Special hardware which is unique to the designated user is perhaps the most powerful protection available. Mapping of utility routines to prevent the use of some of the function keys (such as "copy") are beneficial against the unsophisticated pirate and the fingerprinting of the program to generate particular output formats which can be recognised have analogies to methods used in the printing industry to protect copyright in that sphere. Customising the program towards a particular customer's needs may make it inappropriate to other users.

The last category designated as passive deterrents covers those methods which essentially provide proof of illegal use. Fingerprinting in the form of redundant routines, or more specific data which identifies the true author, is a beneficial deterrent since there are many subtle ways in which the fingerprinting can be disguised. The reader can doubtless think of many ways in which a graphics display can be modified to represent a code to identify the author of the program driving it. Presumably the more complex the displayed material the easier it is to conceal the code. In the case of an animated display, time is a further parameter which can be encoded. It is necessary that the evidence from the method should have a threshold of improbability above which it is so unlikely that the infringer would have incorporated such data by chance that it will be taken as proof of ownership.

The introduction of redundant routines in addition to their fingerprint value can serve to confuse the pirate by disguising the algorithm. Plausible looking blind alleys can make it very time consuming to separate out the useful code and even generate uncertainty as to whether the surplus code is necessary or not. Simpler methods such as camouflage of the names of variables or even the disguise of the instruction set (which is possible on some systems) are more susceptible to analysis by a pirate familiar with the system.

The monitoring of use of a program (of application to disc held software) in which a count of usages is held in an encrypted file can, in the case of rented software, provide information to the lessor relating to contract terms especially where a lease relates to a terminal on a network and fair usage is the criterion.

The remaining passive deterrent is the psychological one which is realised as the uncertainty felt by the pirate as to whether he has eliminated all methods of identification and protection. This factor becomes more important the more wealthy and influential the infringer becomes since whereas legal redress against an individual may be impractical, it becomes worthwhile where a commercial enterprise is established to make significant inroads into the market.

Legal protection in the copyright for computer programs is being strengthened and currently a private members bill is before parliament which confirms that copyright law applies to programs. A recent judgement in the USA on the "attract mode" of computer games has recognised copyright in an animated visual sequence provided it is an invariant sequence which is not modified by data or influence of a user. A literary work is not considered to have been made until it has been reduced to written or other material form and the computing chapter in the UK Green Paper on copyright reform has caused debate on the meaning of "material form" when applied to a visual display where the information is held in a transitory state.

There are very few methods which provide complete protection but the aim is to present a series of hurdles for the infringer to surmount to the point where it ceases to be worthwhile from the commercial viewpoint to make illegal copies for sale.

SPATIAL CONCEPTS IN 3D

R. D. Parslow
Computer Science Department
Brunel University
Uxbridge, Middlesex

Introduction

I was led to consider the problems of perception in an endeavour to discover
why students of computer graphics performed badly in attempting questions
involving three dimensional structures. I was soon to find out that the problems were almost universal, not even crystallographers and designers were
exempt.

Perception

The tone of my previous paper (1) on the subject, at Eurographics '82, was
one of astonishment that such a large proportion of the population was 3D
blind. Some time later I traced a paper by Geoff Hinton (2) which established that he had previously performed virtually the same experiment, i.e.
visualising a cube standing on one corner. (If the reader is unacquainted
with this experiment, please refer to Appendix I before continuing.) At a
subsequent meeting he explained the phenomenon by asserting that the brain
stores only one particular view of an object together with some attributes
which, in the case of a cube, may be that it is basically square, regular
and, in its usual 'pose' has symmetry. In particular it can be rotated 90°
about the vertical into an identical shape. When this attribute is applied
to a solid standing on its corner (in unstable equilibrium), the simplest
shape that meets the specification is an octahedron (two square-based pyra-
mids base to base). The brain appears to adopt this object and all answers
given use this as a reference, i.e. there is a top, a bottom, and four other
corners, and the shape of the hole made by the bottom corner is a square!

The implications of these results cause grave concern. The brain provides us

NATO ASI Series, Vol. F17
Fundamental Algorithms for Computer Graphics
Edited by R. A. Earnshaw
© Springer-Verlag Berlin Heidelberg 1985

with the perception of our environment and apparently cannot be relied on to present information which accords with reality. For 3D graphics and design work this causes serious problems, and in everyday life may be the cause of serious accidents. I should like to illustrate the problem with some results well known to psychologists and others interested in the problems of perception. (3, 4, 5, 6, 7, 8, 9)

Experiment 1: The Hidden Man (10)

For most people the picture appears like a series of blots or perhaps a map. However, when the picture is described, at some point in the description the picture suddenly becomes clear.

        It is the picture of a man
                the head and shoulders of a man
                the head is turned towards you
                the top of the picture cuts across his brow
                the face appears in the top half of the middle of the picture
                he is bearded
                he is lit from the observer's right hand side.
An analysis is given by M L J Abercrombie (3).

It is as if the brain were preparing its own picture, and when there is a reasonable match, the picture is seen. In order to see something we must already have a database from which we can construct the matching picture. Art training usually accelerates the process while some people, who can detect a typographical error easily, find it difficult to see the picture.

Experiment 2: The Birthday Card.

Take any piece of stiff card bent in half, and place it on the table or floor with ridge uppermost (to look like a tent). Close one eye and stare down at one open end at an angle of about $60°$ to the horizontal. After a while - it could take some minutes and seems to take longer with age - the card appears to stand up!!! If this experiment does not work for you try again later and go to the next experiment.

With this apparition every depth clue is false:

1. Perspective: It would be possible to make a card which had this shape but it would be unusual.
2. Shadow, and
3. Lighting: It is apparently variably lit from inside but with shadow at the foot and no shadow outside.
4. Parallax: Move your head slowly from side to side - the apparent base corner moves in an unacceptable manner.
5. Stereo: With practice the above effect can be obtained with both eyes open, and also with two different positions of the head you are using the stereo effect obtained by one-eyed people.

A most unusual response occurs with some people who, when asked to move their head slowly in a circle, suddenly jerk their head away, unable to accept the presented version of reality. What part of the brain rejects the picture that it itself presents?

The 'hidden man' showed the need for an adequate database from which to form the picture but with the birthday card experiment we already had the picture and yet we were presented with an alternative, false in every detail.

Experiment 3: The wire frame cube.

Twelve rods are formed into a cubic structure which is hung from one corner at about eye level, and spun. Viewed from about three metres with the background clear, the direction of motion suddenly appears to reverse. The process can be accelerated by blinking, particularly with one eye closed. It is

sometimes difficult to determine which is the correct direction of rotation!
If the rotating cube is approached with both eyes open the rotation is corrected; however if one eye is kept closed and the cube is slowly approached
some extraordinary features appear. As the direction of rotation has appeared to reverse, the parts nearest the eye appear to be further away and are
therefore expanded while the parts actually furthest away appear to be at the
front and smaller. The cube apparently constantly changes shape in such an
extraordinary manner that few people can continue the experiment and one ex-
perimenter was so overcome that he had to be restrained!

Inferences from Experiments

These experiments show that the brain provides both a filtering process and a
simplifying process before presenting what is being seen or imagined. Since
we do not know what process is being performed, not being able 'to believe
our own eyes' (or perhaps our own brain) begins to take on a special significance. Pilot error and driver's error should be examined more carefully. 'I
did not see it' - a major feature in accident reports, needs closer examination. We need special training if we are to move faster than running speed.

Three cases:

1. Hard shoulder motorway collisions.
Pulling on to the hard shoulder and stopping parallel to the flow of traffic
is highly dangerous, as other drivers tend to follow the car in front, and
even if it has flashing lights, they do not realise that the car is stopped
until it is too late. Motoring organisations advise their staff to pull on
to the hard shoulder at an angle to make it clear to truck drivers that they
are stopped.

2. Turning across traffic from a stationary position.
This major cause of crashes appears inexplicable. The driver has stopped
and is watching for a safe gap and then turns when none exists! An article
in the Guardian described the phenomenon very precisely. Could it be that
looking fixedly at the traffic includes the same response as Experiment 2?
I advise drivers in this position to ensure that they keep changing their
viewpoint and would warn main road drivers that the waiting driver may
'pounce' at any time.

3. Light aircraft converging.

A collision course exists if the bearing remains constant and the distance diminishes. If the bearing is constant, then the image of the other craft has been visible throughout the convergence, not just at the last moment when noticed by the pilot. This one-eye illusion fits exactly the conditions of the birthday card experiment. Turning the head to get a different view should be part of all training procedures.

Training in Space Perception

The first rule in visualisation is to choose familiar things for which we already have a good database, so

'BE FAMILIAR'

We shall therefore start with familiar shapes.

A. Moving Templates

1. Consider a square template of side half metre.

> 1.1 Visualise the template on a table and 'see' the shape swept out by lifting it vertically to a height equal to the side of the square. Describe the shape.

> 1.2 Repeat the exercise but let the square shrink to a point at its centre as it is raised to the same height.
> Describe the shape.

2. Consider an equilateral triangular template of side half metre.

> 2.1 Repeat 1.1
> Describe the shape.

> 2.2 Repeat 1.2
> Describe the shape.

> 2.3 Visualise the template with one corner being lifted vertically and shrinking to a point at that corner as it is lifted.
> Describe the shape.

3. Consider an isosceles right angular triangle two sides half metre.

> 3.1 Repeat 1.1

What is the shape?

3.2 Repeat 1.2

What is the shape?

3.3 Repeat 2.3

What is the shape?

B. Lines and Planes

1. Consider two infinite skew lines, 'm', 'n', in space, i.e. they do not meet and are not parallel (e.g. extend an edge of a table and an 'opposite' leg). Find the line, 'p', which is perpendicular to both 'm' and 'n' (another edge of the table). Visualise the planes 'M' and 'N' through 'm' and 'n' and perpendicular to 'p'. An observer 'O' stands in the room, not between 'M' and 'N'. Do the lines 'm', 'n' appear to cross from his viewpoint? Can you prove this? Does the proof hold for any two skew lines 'm', 'n', not necessarily at right angles?

2. Consider a line 'l' skew to both 'm' and 'n'. Can you find a line 'k' which meets all three of 'l', 'm' and 'n'?

The second rule to ease visualisation problems is

'BE THERE'

3. Choose 'a', 'b' (from 'A', 'B' on 'l') as two of the lines meeting 'l', 'm', 'n'. Are 'a' and 'b' skew or do they meet? Guess, then think about it and then prove your conclusion.

Now visualise this beautiful surface (a regulus) made up from all the lines which meet 'l', 'm', and 'n'. (You could also choose three lines of this regulus and define another regulus to which 'l', 'm', 'n' belong!)

Such a structure could be made by fixing rods to three skew rods and this is done in constructing elegant roofs, and also in constructing practical cooling towers.

C. Solids

1. Consider a solid cube standing on one corner in unstable equilibrium (with a vertical body-diagonal).
   Which edges make the greatest angle with the horizontal?

(Hint: think of one face.)

2. Consider the cube on one corner standing on a thin sheet of ice, so that as the cube is pushed through the ice, the ice will melt but will refreeze to closely contour the cube as we move it. The corner makes a triangular hole in the ice differing in shape as we move the cube. In the cube's most upright position the hole is an equilateral triangle which grows in size as the cube is lowered vertically. Eventually three corners meet the ice forming a large triangle in the ice. When the cube is lowered another few centimetres, what is the shape of the hole in the ice?

The third rule of visualisation is

'SEE IT BIG'

So visualise a very large cube on which you are standing.

Does the corner behave like a submerging corner or a raft?

3. Consider a cube standing on a corner on the ice and its reflection in the ice. (Note that each edge and its reflection are coplanar.) The two cubes are pushed into each other a short distance along the common body diagonal.

> 3.1 Describe the solid of intersection (the solid that is inside both cubes).

> 3.2 Describe the complete figure as the cubes are pushed further and further into each other. (Very difficult.)

4. Visualise the starting position of C.3 then rotate one of the cubes about the common body diagonal through 180^0.

> 4.1 Now push the cubes slowly into each other and describe the solid of intersection at this stage.
> (Hint: It may help to think of large cubes - three metres side. Also think of the cubes laid with faces horizontal and vertical, and walk into one of these 'rooms'.)

5. Consider two intersecting cylindrical rods.

> 5.1 Choose two equal radius rods whose axes meet at right angles.
> Draw the view along each axis (front and side elevations)

and the view at right angles (plan view).
Describe the solid of intersection.

    5.2 Repeat 5.1
        (i)   varying the radii
        (ii)   changing the angle between the axes
        (iii) making the axes skew.

    5.3 Repeat 5.1 with a third equal rod intersecting the other
        two at right angles.
        Describing the solid of intersection is extremely difficult.

D. Surfaces

1. Consider the surface of a sphere partitioned by great circles (planes through the centre).

        1.1 One circle produces two areas, two circles produce four areas.
             What is the maximum number of area s that three great circles will produce?

        1.2 What is the maximum number of areas produced by four great circles?

2. Consider a Torus (a ring with circular section). Any plane will cut the surface into two areas.

        2.1 How many areas can you produce with two planes?

        2.2 How many areas can you produce with three planes?

3. Consider a toroidal surface with a small hole, e.g. an innter tube or swimming ring, with valve removed.

        3.1 Describe the surface obtained when the whole tube is pulled through the valve hole.

        3.2 If the ring was made by connecting four different coloured tubes, red, yellow, green, blue, with the hole in the red section, describe the colouring on the inside-out ring.

CONCLUSIONS

The use of these exercises and the application of the three rules

BE FAMILIAR

BE THERE

SEE IT BIG

has produced remarkable improvements in 3D visualisation in audiences in the UK and in the USA. In fact, without training, few people would even attempt the intersecting cube exercise. If this facility with 3D is to be maintained, the brain must be exercised. To keep the mind flexible, the simplest tool is a 'Rubic cube'. Attempting to forecast the results of sequences of moves and discovering methods of producing specific patterns was the reason why Rubic invented his cube.

I expect to see great improvements in 3D graphics and design.

APPENDIX 1 - THE CUBE EXPERIMENT

Equipment: a table, paper and pencil.

Visualise a solid cube of half metre side. Hold it in your hands and when familiar with it, stand it, on one corner, on the middle of the paper, holding the top corner with one hand to maintain it in a position of unstable equilibrium (i.e. with a body diagonal vertical).

1. Call the top corner 'A' and the bottom corner (on the paper) 'B'. With the free hand touch each of the other corners in turn, assigning them labels 'C', 'D' etc. After touching each corner write its label 'C' etc on the paper.

2. Push the bottom corner into the paper a few centimetres. Mark the outline of the hole on the paper.

APPENDIX 2 - SOLUTIONS TO SOME PROBLEMS

A. 1.1   a cube - a square prism

    1.2   right square-based pyramid

    2.1   a triangular prism

    2.2   tetrahedron - a right pyramid on an equilateral triangular base

    2.3   tetrahedron, with equilateral triangular base, three isosceles
           triangular sides two of which are right angled

    3.1   isosceles, right angled, triangular prism

    3.2   a tetrahedron with right angled triangular base

    3.3   tetrahedron with three isosceles right-angled triangles, one
           equilateral triangle, i.e. the corner of a cube!

B. 1.   The lines 'm', 'n', appear to cross because the planes from the
           observer's eye 'O' to 'm', and 'n' intersect in a line thr-
           ough 'O' which of course meets both 'm', 'n'.

    2.   Choose any point 'L' on 'l' which is not 'between' 'M' and 'N'
           and look at 'm' and 'n'. You have just proved that they
           appear to cross from any point in the room, so the line 'k'
           is that line of sight from 'L'. But you could have chosen
           lots of different positions for 'L' so there are many lines
           joining 'l', 'm', and 'n'.

    3.   If 'a', 'b' meet it will not be on 'l', 'm', or 'n', or the view
           of the other two lines would show them crossing twice! (or
           the two lines being apparently coincident!) Suppose they
           do meet then we have the view of all three lines crossing
           twice! No, if 'a', 'b' meet then 'l', 'm', and 'n' all lie
           in the plane defined by 'a', 'b', and that contradicts the
           statement that the three lines 'l', 'm' and 'n' are skew.

C. 1.   all edges make same angle with the horizontal

    2.   a slightly bigger triangle with corners cut off

    3.1   two cube corners stuck together at the equilateral base

    3.2   exercise for the reader!

    4.1   a cube

    5.1   a) circle, circle, square with diagonals

           b) like the bladder from a soccer ball

All other problems are left for discussion.

REFERENCES AND BIBLIOGRAPHY

1.	R D Parslow	3D Visualisation	Eurographics 82 North Holland
2.	Geoffrey Hinton	Some Demonstrations of the Effects of Structured Descriptions of Imagery	Cognitive Science 3 231-250 (1979)
3.	M L J Abercrombie	The Anatomy of Judgement	Penguin 1979
4.	Tony Buzan and Terence Dixon	The Evolving Brain	David and Charles
5.	John P Frisby	Seeing	Oxford University Press (1979)
6.	Richard L Gregory	Eye and Brain The Psychology of Seeing	Weidenfeld and Nicholson (1979)
7.	John Lansdown	Visual Perception and Computer Graphics: Fundamentals of Algorithms for Computer Graphics	NATO Advanced Study Institute 1985
8.	David Marr	Vision	W H Freeman 1982
9.	M D Vernon	The Psychology of Perception	Penguin
10.	P B Porter	American Journal of Psychology Vol 67 p 559, 1954	

SHORTEST PATHS IN 3-SPACE, VORONOI DIAGRAMS WITH BARRIERS, AND RELATED COMPLEXITY AND ALGEBRAIC ISSUES

Wm. Randolph Franklin and Varol Akman

Electrical, Computer, and Systems Engineering Department
Rensselaer Polytechnic Institute
Troy, New York 12180-3590, USA
Phone: (518) 266-6077, telex 646542

ABSTRACT

We consider the problem of computing the shortest path under the Euclidean metric between source and goal points in 3-space while avoiding clashes with polyhedral obstacles. This can be thought as the ultimate version of the notorious TRAVELING SALESMAN problem in terms of generality and is known as the FINDPATH problem in artificial intelligence and robotics. We show that this problem is solved using algebraic elimination techniques in a straightforward yet very inefficient manner. We then introduce a Voronoi-based strategy for solving the subproblem of determining the sequence of obstacle edges through which the shortest path passes. This is based upon a natural extension of Franklin's "Partitioning the plane to calculate minimal paths to any goal around obstructions" [Tech. Rep., ECSE Dept., Rensselaer Polytechnic Inst., Troy, NY, Nov. 1982] to 3-space. In 3-space, a very desirable feature of the plane partitions disappears making the space partitions complicated. For this case, we suggest an approximation technique.

KEYWORDS: robotics, artificial intelligence, computational geometry, algebraic computing, TRAVELING SALESMAN problem, FINDPATH problem, Voronoi diagrams.

This material is based upon work supported by the National Science Foundation under grants ECS 80-21504 and ECS 83-51942. The second author is also supported in part by a Fulbright award.

1. INTRODUCTION

Let P_1, P_2,..., P_n be solid polyhedral objects in 3-space. A very important problem in computational geometry (which is known as FINDPATH in artificial intelligence and robotics, and has wide applications) is to find a shortest path between two points S and G (commonly termed as the source and the goal points) avoiding intersections with P_i, i=1,...,n. Touching the boundaries of P_i is allowed. Throughout this paper, we shall use the L_2 (Euclidean) metric to measure distances.

In 2-space where the obstacles are polygons whose interiors are forbidden, the problem is easy to solve. Since the shortest path can only be a polygonal path whose vertices bend at the vertices of the given polygons the problem is reduced to the following subproblems: (i) Construct a "visibility graph" whose nodes consist of {S,G} ∪ {T: T is a vertex of P_i, i=1,...,n}. A link in this graph connects a pair of vertices visible from each other and carries a weight equal to the distance between these vertices. (ii) Search through this graph to find the shortest path from S to G using an algorithm such as Dijkstra [1959]. Lee-Preparata [1984] mentions an algorithm to accomplish steps (i) and (ii) in $O(m^2 \log m)$ total time where $m=\Sigma_i |P_i|$. (|P| denotes the number of vertices of polygon P.)

In 3-space the problem is much more difficult. In this case, the shortest path is also a polygonal path but the only thing we can say about its vertices is that they bend on the edges of the given polyhedra. The characterization of these bend points is a formidable task.

There have been various developments in the area of path planning in the last two decades. For brevity, we shall mention only a certain section of it. (Akman [1984] contains a long list of references.) Lozano-Perez [1981, 1983], Brooks [1983], Donald [1983], and Nguyen [1984] report many applications oriented toward robotics. Reif [1979], Schwartz-Sharir [1983a, 1983b, 1983c, 1984], Sharir-Arielsheffi [1984], Hopcroft-Schwartz-Sharir [1984], O'Dunlaing-Yap [1983], Spirakis-Yap [1983, 1984], and O'Dunlaing-Sharir-Yap [1983] report work mostly on the computational complexity of several special cases of path planning. Finally, shortest path computation has also been treated in recent papers such as Franklin [1982], Franklin-Akman [1984], Franklin-Akman-Verrilli [1985], Sharir-Schorr [1984], Lee-Preparata [1984], and O'Rourke-Suri-Booth [1984]. Sharir and Schorr's work is especially interesting in that it mentions many results on the nature of shortest paths on a convex polyhedron. For example, they prove that "A shortest path cannot pass through a vertex or a ridge point of the polyhedron" where a ridge point is defined as a goal point on the polyhedron for which there are at least two shortest paths from a given S on the polyhedron. The crux of their paper nevertheless is the following result which is arrived after employing complex data structures and algorithms:

"Given a convex polyhedron P and a point S on it, P can be preprocessed in $O(|P|^3 \log |P|)$ time to produce a data structure (taking $O(|P|^2)$ space) with the help of which one can find in $O(|P|)$ time the shortest path along the surface of P from S to any G."

The shortest path problem is in some ways may be considered as an extension of the NP-complete (in the strong sense) TRAVELING SALESMAN problem (TSP) where we wish to determine the shortest path (or tour) that traverses the nodes of a given graph in any order, cf. Johnson-Papadimitriou [1981] and Papadimitriou-Steiglitz [1982]. Although there are some technical difficulties arising from the distance metric, the Euclidean version of TSP (ΔTSP) is also NP-complete as shown by Papadimitriou [1977].

Rest of this paper is organized as follows. Section 2 treats the problem of finding the shortest paths in 3-space using an algebraic approach. Section 3 deals with the subproblem of specifying which sequence of edges a shortest path should follow. Finally, Section 4 mentions some complexity issues and algebraic problems created by shortest path determination.

2. SHORTEST PATHS IN 3-SPACE: AN ALGEBRAIC APPROACH

If we want to find the shortest path from S to G in the presence of obstacles P_i, i=1,...,n, the first thing is to check whether G can be reached from S directly. Note that, since we allow a shortest path to touch an obstacle, this would entail checking line segment SG against each P_i for at most one intersection. This can be done using standard methods. Chazelle-Dobkin [1979] gives a fast ($O(\log^2 |P|)$) algorithm for line-polyhedron intersection detection for convex polyhedra. Thus, in the sequel, we shall assume that such a check has already been made and SG is not the shortest path.

It is intuitively clear that the shortest path from S to G will be a polygonal path which bends on some edges of some obstacles, i.e., it cannot touch the interior of a face of an obstacle. (A formal proof is quite involved; Chein-Steinberg [1983] gives a proof in 2-space.) This observation immediately gives an algorithm to compute the shortest path. First, list all permutations of {e: e is an edge of P_i, i=1,...,n} of positive length. Second, for each permutation in this list, compute the shortest of the polygonal paths which visits each line of this permutation exactly once in the given order. Thus, at the end of this step, we have a list of permutations and the shortest polygonal paths associated with each permutation. (A polygonal path is specified by its consecutive vertices: S, bend points on the lines belonging to a permutation in that order, and G.) Now start at the top of this list. Test the shortest polygonal path associated with this permutation against each P_i for intersection. The only intersection points reported by this process must be the ones that we already know, i.e., the vertices of the polygonal path at hand. Otherwise, we discard this polygonal path (because it passes through one or more obstacle(s)) and continue with the next permutation. We note in passing that in Sharir-Schorr [1984] this last step is missing; thus their algorithm is incomplete.

It is emphasized that when there are more than one shortest paths, with a slight modification of the above algorithm one can obtain all of them. The number of shortest paths is an interesting problem in itself. Figure 1 shows a particular arrangement of a workspace in 2-space which clearly demonstrates that there may be an exponential number of shortest paths between S and G. A few things need some explanation in this figure. It is assumed that P and all the even-numbered obstacles are semi-infinite or large enough so that a shortest path cannot tour around them. All P_i, $i=1,\ldots,n$, and the "teeth" of P are aligned along the line connecting S to G. In this specific case there exist $2^{0.5n}$ shortest paths. It is trivial to extend this workspace to 3-space by simply erecting prisms for each polygon.

Given a permutation, the problem of finding the bend points of a shortest polygonal path on these lines can be solved using algebraic means. Before we proceed to show this, we shall state a problem and two useful lemmas regarding shortest polygonal paths through a set of lines. (For proofs of the lemmas, cf. Sharir-Schorr [1984].)

LINE VISITATION problem (LVP): Given a sequence l_1, l_2,..., l_n of lines in 3-space, what is the shortest path from S to G constrained to pass through each of the lines l_1, l_2,..., l_n in this order?

Let C_1, C_2,..., C_n be the bend points of the shortest path on the given lines. For notational ease, we shall denote S (resp. G) by C_0 (resp. C_{n+1}).

LEMMA 2.1. For each $i=1,\ldots,n$, the angle between $C_{i-1}C_i$ and l_i is equal to the angle between C_iC_{i+1} and l_i.

LEMMA 2.2. The shortest path from S to G passing through the sequence of lines l_1, l_2,..., l_n in this order is unique.

We now give some algebraic preliminaries that will be necessary for the upcoming presentation. Let A and B be polynomials of positive degree with coefficients in a commutative ring with an identity element. If $A(x)=\sum a_i x^i$ and $B(x)=\sum b_i x^i$ where degree(A)=m and degree(B)=n, the "Sylvester matrix" of A and B is the m+n by m+n matrix:

$$
\begin{bmatrix}
a_m & a_{m-1} & \cdots & a_0 & & & \\
 & a_m & a_{m-1} & \cdots & a_0 & & \\
 & & & \cdot & & & \\
 & & & \cdot & & & \\
 & & & \cdot & & & \\
 & & a_m & a_{m-1} & \cdots & a_0 \\
b_n & b_{n-1} & \cdots & b_0 & & & \\
 & b_n & b_{n-1} & \cdots & b_0 & & \\
 & & & \cdot & & & \\
 & & & \cdot & & & \\
 & & & \cdot & & & \\
 & & b_n & b_{n-1} & \cdots & b_0
\end{bmatrix}
$$

in which there are n rows of A coefficients, m rows of B coefficients, and all elements not printed are 0. The "resultant" of A and B, denoted by resultant(A,B), is the determinant of the Sylvester matrix.

THEOREM 2.1 (Collins [1971]). If A and B are polynomials of positive degrees over a unique factorization domain then resultant(A,B)=0 if and only if A and B have a common divisor of positive degree.

In this paper, we shall be dealing with multivariate polynomials. In this case, the following interpretation of the resultant becomes crucial. The resultant of two multivariate polynomials A and B (both given in variables $x_1, x_2, \ldots, x_r$) with respect to x_s, $1 \leq s \leq r$ is obtained as follows: (i) Write both A and B in terms of single variable x_s treating the other variables as constants. (ii) Compute the resultant of these new polynomials using the original definition above. The outcome of this is another polynomial with one less variable, i.e., x_s has been eliminated. We shall denote it by resultant(A,B,x_s).

THEOREM 2.2 (Collins [1971]). Let A and B be multivariate polynomials in variables $x_1, x_2, \ldots, x_r$ with positive degrees m and n respectively. Write both A and B in terms of the single variable x_r as explained above. Let C be resultant(A,B,x_r). If $(a_1, a_2, \ldots, a_r)$ is a common zero of A and B then $C(a_1, a_2, \ldots, a_{r-1})=0$.

Conversely, if $C(a_1, a_2, \ldots, a_{r-1})=0$, then at least one of the following is true:

(a) All coefficients of A are 0.
(b) All coefficients of B are 0.
(c) The constant coefficients of A and B are both 0.
(d) For some a_r, $(a_1, a_2, \ldots, a_r)$ is a common zero of A and B.

This theorem immediately suggests a way to solve multivariate polynomial equations simultaneously.

EXAMPLE 2.1 (adapted from Collins [1971]). Let [A=0,B=0,C=0] be a system of three equations in variables x,y,z with integer coefficients. Compute $f(x) = \text{resultant}(\text{resultant}(A,C,z), \text{resultant}(B,C,z),y)$. By Theorem 2.2, if (a,b,c) is a solution to the given system then $f(a)=0$. Similarly we can compute polynomials $g(y)=\text{resultant}(\text{resultant}(A,C,z), \text{resultant}(B,C,z),x)$ and $h(z)=\text{resultant}(\text{resultant}(A,C,y), \text{resultant}(B,C,y),x)$ such that $g(b)=0$ and $h(c)=0$ whenever (a,b,c) is a zero of the system. Thus, one can solve f, g, and h individually to find their roots to arbitrary accuracy and then decide which triples (a,b,c) are solutions of the system.

Now we proceed to outline the algebraic solution to the LVP. In the following we refer the reader to Figure 2. Assume that each line is given by its two distinct points and assign different coordinate systems to each line, i.e., let line 1_i be parametrized by x_i. Also, for each line compute N_i which is a unit vector along 1_i in any direction. ($||V||$ denotes the length of vector V.) From Lemma 2.1, it is seen that:

$$\frac{C_{i-1}C_i \cdot N_i}{||C_{i-1}C_i||} = \frac{C_i C_{i+1} \cdot N_i}{||C_i C_{i+1}||}$$

If we rewrite the above equation after inserting values of C_{i-1}, C_i, C_{i+1} in terms of x_{i-1}, x_i, x_{i+1}, respectively, and remove the square root signs, then we obtain a quartic in three variables, x_{i-1}, x_i, and x_{i+1}. Repeating this for all lines, we end up with the following system of n quartics:

$$Q_1(x_1, x_2)=0$$
$$Q_2(x_1, x_2, x_3)=0$$
$$\cdots$$
$$Q_i(x_{i-1}, x_i, x_{i+1})=0$$
$$\cdots$$
$$Q_n(x_{n-1}, x_n)=0$$

Theoretically, the above system of equations can be solved

using resultants as demonstrated in Example 2.1. This is a
classical method known as the "elimination theory",
cf. Van der Waerden [1970]. Alternatively, we can use a numerical
technique such as the Newton-Raphson method for solving a system of
nonlinear equations.

If l_1, l_2,..., l_n are but line segments then the shortest path
may be bending at points located outside these line segments. In
this case, Sharir-Schorr [1984] states that the shortest path will
have to pass through some endpoints of these segments at which it
will subtend different entry and exit angles contrary to Lemma 2.1.
Thus the problem is reduced to a collection of subproblems where a
shortest path passes through the interior points of a subsequence of
line segments.

3. PARTITIONING 3-SPACE AROUND POLYHEDRA

A common specialization of the shortest path problem occurs
when S and the obstacles are fixed, and new paths should be
calculated as G moves around the workspace. For example, a
manipulator arm may pick up a part from a pile of parts in a fixed
location, and then move somewhere in the scene to work with it.

In Franklin [1982], an important construction based on an
extension of Voronoi diagrams in the plane is given which, for a
given S in 2-space, partitions the plane into a set of regions such
that all the G within any given region have the same list of bend
points. (For another extension of Voronoi diagrams, see
Lee-Drysdale [1981].) This reduces the problem of finding a
shortest path to the preprocessing step (finding the regions), plus
the task of determining which region contains G (searching or
querying). The last step is easy since the borders of the regions
are either straight line segments or portions of hyperbolae. Thus,
existing point location algorithms can be used after some slight
modifications. In the common case where G varies while S and the
obstacles are fixed, the shortest path can be found by merely
repeating the search (point location) phase.

In this section, we shall try to emulate Franklin's approach in
3-space. Here, the regions will have the following property: All
the points in a given region are reached from S after visiting the
same sequence of edges of the obstacles. We first work on a very
simple case, namely, a solid triangle.

Let W_1, W_2, and W_3 be points in 3-space. These points describe
a triangle $W_1W_2W_3$ if they are not colinear. Let S be any point in
3-space not in the plane E of $W_1W_2W_3$. Assuming that $W_1W_2W_3$ is a
solid triangle we want to partition the space into regions such that

if a new point G is specified we would be able to tell whether G can
be directly reached from S, and if not, which edge of the triangle
(W_1W_2, W_2W_3, or W_3W_1) the shortest path must touch.

Obviously, if G is outside the semi-infinite prism (frustum)
obtained by subtracting the pyramid described by base $W_1W_2W_3$ and
apex S from the infinite pyramid described similarly then the
shortest path is SG. Thus we found one of the regions, R_0. Note
that R_0 has all the points of the space that are not obstructed by
$W_1W_2W_3$. See Figure 3.

Otherwise, G may belong to one of three regions R_1, R_2, or R_3.
R_1 is the region such that if $G \varepsilon R_1$ then the shortest path is via
edge W_2W_3. R_2 is the region such that if $G \varepsilon R_2$ then the shortest
path is via edge W_3W_1. Finally, R_3 is the region such that if $G \varepsilon R_3$
then the shortest path is via edge W_1W_2. When G is on the boundary
of two regions there may be two or three shortest paths.

Now, we shall compute the boundaries between the pairs R_1 and
R_2, R_2 and R_3, and R_3 and R_1. In the sequel, S is assumed to be the
origin. (This is easy to achieve by translating everything in the
workspace by $-S$.) We shall first compute the boundary between R_1
and R_3. Take G such that SG $\cap$ $W_1W_2W_3$ is not empty. If $G \varepsilon R_1 \cap R_3$
then there exists a path to G either via W_1W_2 or via W_2W_3 and
rendering equal lengths. Labeling the bend points of these paths
with the triangle by C_{12} and C_{23}, we get:

$$SC_{12}+C_{12}G = SC_{23}+C_{23}G$$

The left hand-side is equal to $||G_{12}||$ where G_{12} is the point
obtained by rotating G about W_1W_2 until it is coincident to the
plane of SW_1W_2 and on the opposite side of S with respect to W_1W_2.
Similarly, the right hand-side is equal to $||G_{23}||$ where G_{23} is the
rotated image of G about W_2W_3.

Before we continue with our analysis, we give a list of useful
vector and trigonometric identities that we shall employ frequently.
(x and . denote vector cross and dot products.)

(I1) $||A||^2=1$ if A is a unit vector.
(I2) $Ax(BxC)=(A.C)B-(A.B)C$
(I3) $(AxB).(CxD)=\begin{vmatrix} A.C & A.D \\ B.C & B.D \end{vmatrix}=(A.C)(B.D)-(A.D)(B.C)$
(I4) $||A+B||^2=||A||^2+||B||^2||+2||A||\ ||B||\cos\theta$
      where θ is the angle between A and B.
(I5) $\sin 2\theta=2\sin\theta\cos\theta$
(I6) $\cos(\theta+\Omega)=\cos\theta\cos\Omega-\sin\theta\sin\Omega$

It is known that if P is a point and P' is its rotated version
by an angle θ about an axis U (a unit length vector) passing through
the origin then:

$$P' = (P.U)U + (P - (P.U)U)\cos\theta + (U{\times}P)\sin\theta$$

Using the last formula, it is easy to see that:

$$G_{12} = W_1 + fN_{12} + (W_1 G - fN_{12})\cos\alpha + (N_{12}{\times}W_1 G)\sin\alpha$$

where α is the dihedral angle between the planes of triangles $SW_1 W_2$ and $GW_1 W_2$, $N_{12} = W_1 W_2 / ||W_1 W_2||$, and $f = W_1 G . N_{12}$. Using (I5):

$$||G_{12}||^2 =$$

(a) $\qquad (W_1 + fN_{12})^2$

(b) $\qquad + (W_1 G - fN_{12})^2 \cos^2\alpha$

(c) $\qquad + (N_{12}{\times}W_1 G)^2 \sin^2\alpha$

(d) $\qquad + 2(W_1 + fN_{12}).(W_1 G - fN_{12})\cos\alpha$

(e) $\qquad + 2(W_1 + fN_{12}).(N_{12}{\times}W_1 G)\sin\alpha$

(f) $\qquad + (W_1 G - fN_{12}).(N_{12}{\times}W_1 G)\sin 2\alpha$

The following are the simplifications:

Using (I1), (a) is simplified to $||W_1||^2 + 2f(W_1.N_{12}) + f^2$.
(b) is simplified to $(||W_1 G||^2 - f^2)\cos^2\alpha$.
Using (I3), (c) is simplified to $(||W_1 G||^2 - f^2)\sin^2\alpha$.
Using (I1), (d) becomes $2(W_1 . W_1 G - f(W_1.N_{12}))\cos\alpha$.
(e) is simplified to $2(W_1.(N_{12}{\times}W_1 G))$.
(f) is identically 0.

It is possible to simplify (d) and (e) further. Noting that the normal of the plane of the triangle $SW_1 W_2$ is:

$$M_{S12} = \frac{N_{12}{\times}W_1}{||N_{12}{\times}W_1||}$$

and the normal of the plane of the triangle $GW_1 W_2$ is:

$$M_{G12} = \frac{N_{12}{\times}W_1 G}{||N_{12}{\times}W_1 G||}$$

one obtains:

$$\cos\alpha = M_{S12}.M_{G12}$$

After some routine calculations, one arrives at:

$$\cos\alpha = \frac{W_1 . (W_1 G - fN_{12})}{||N_{12}{\times}W_1||\ ||W_1 G{\times}N_{12}||}$$

In a similar manner, but using the cross product:

$$\sin\ \alpha = ||M_{S12}xM_{G12}||, \text{ or equivalently}$$

$$\sin\ \alpha = \frac{||W_1.(N_{12}xW_1G)||}{||N_{12}xW_1||\ ||W_1GxN_{12}||}$$

Thus, we showed that:

$$2\cos\ \alpha(W_1.(W_1G-fN_{12}))=$$
$$2\cos^2\ \alpha||N_{12}xW_1||\ ||N_{12}xW_1G||\ \text{and}$$

$$2\sin\ \alpha(W_1.(N_{12}xW_1G))=$$
$$2\sin^2\ \alpha||N_{12}xW_1||\ ||N_{12}xW_1G||$$

Returning to our original equation, we obtain a more symmetric equation:

$$(*)\ ||G_{12}||^2=||W_1||^2+||W_1G||^2$$
$$+2((W_1G.N_{12})(W_1.N_{12})+$$
$$||W_1GxN_{12}||\ ||W_1xN_{12}||)$$

Now, we shall give a geometric interpretation of this equation. Expanding the dot and cross products in (*), we obtain:

$$||G_{12}||^2=||W_1||^2+||W_1G||^2$$
$$+2(||W_1G||\cos\ a_1||W_1||\cos(\pi-a_2)$$
$$+||W_1G||\sin\ a_1||W_1||\sin(\pi-a_2)),\ \text{or}$$

$$||G_{12}||^2=||W_1||^2+||W_1G||^2$$
$$-2||W_1G||\ ||W_1||\cos(a_1+a_2),\ \text{using (I6)}.$$

Above, a_1 and a_2 are the angles of GW_1W_2 and SW_1W_2, cf. Figure 4a. Finally, it is emphasized that this last formula is simply a statement of (I4) on triangle SW_1G_{12} as can be seen from Figure 4b.

Up to this point, we found a formula which gives $||G_{12}||^2$ in terms of known quantities (W_1 and N_{12}) and the unknown G (with coordinates x,y,z). The formula for $||G_{23}||^2$ (resp. $||G_{31}||^2$) is analogous to (*); just change W_1 to W_2 (resp. W_3) and N_{12} to N_{23} (resp. N_{31}). In terms of degree, the following example shows that the surfaces between regions R_i are in general ternary quartics although they may degenerate to planes in some cases.

EXAMPLE 3.1. Given the triangle with coordinates $W_1(1,2,1)$, $W_2(0,0,1)$, and $W_3(2,0,1)$, we shall compute the boundaries of regions R_1 and R_2, R_2 and R_3, and R_3 and R_1.

Using (*), the surface between regions R_1 and R_2 is found as $||G_{12}||^2-||G_{23}||^2=0$, or:

$$-2x-4y+10+2(x+2y-5$$
$$+ \sqrt{(z-1)^2+(1/5)(2x-y)^2} - \sqrt{(z-1)^2+y^2})=0$$

which is further simplified to:

$$(2x-y)^2=5y^2$$

The surface between R_2 and R_3 is given by $||G_{23}||^2-||G_{31}||^2=0$, or:

$$4x-8+2(-(2/5)(x-2y-2)$$
$$+ \sqrt{(z-1)^2+y^2} - \sqrt{(21/5)(z-1)^2+(21/25)(2x+y-4)^2})=0$$

or, after some operations to remove the square root signs:

$$256z^4-1024z^3+(228y^2+(256-128x)y-128x^2+512x+1024)z^2$$
$$+(-456y^2+(256x-512)y+256x^2-1024x)z-48y^4$$
$$+(576-288)y^3+(-272x^2+1088x-860)y^2$$
$$+(32x^3-192x^2+256x)y+16x^4-128x^3+256x^2=0$$

Finally, the surface between R_3 and R_1 is found to be:

$$-8x-4y+16+\sqrt{21}\sqrt{5}(z-1)^2+(2x+y-4)^2-\sqrt{5}\sqrt{5}(z-1)^2+(2x-y)^2=0$$

which is also transformed to a quartic omitted here for brevity.

THEOREM 3.1. Let P be a convex polygon with vertices V_1, $V_2,\ldots,$ V_n and S a point outside the plane of P. It is possible to partition P into at most n convex regions (each completely containing an edge of P) such that if G is later specified inside one of these regions then the shortest path between S and G is via the associated edge of this region.

Proof. We give a constructive proof. Rotate S about the lines defined by edges V_1V_2, V_2V_3, etc. until it is coincident to the plane of P and always on the opposite side of a particular edge compared to the interior of P. This is basically an unfolding of the pyramid with apex S and base P to the base plane. Thus, n image points are obtained which will be denoted by S_{12}, S_{23}, etc. Draw the Voronoi diagram of these points and clip it against the window P. This partitions P into at most n convex regions since each Voronoi polygon is convex. Figure 5 demonstrates this operation. Let us denote the regions by R_{12}, R_{23}, etc. It is seen that there is a border line passing through each vertex of P. It is obvious that if G is inside a region R_{ij} then we just connect it to the associated image point of this region, namely S_{ij}. The intersection of this line segment with the associated edge V_iV_j of this region is the bend point X of the shortest path from S to G. X may be placed into 3-space by folding again.

Theorem 3.1 hints an important property of the regions R_1, R_2, R_3, namely, their intersections with the plane of $W_1W_2W_3$ must be straight lines.   Returning to Example 3.1:

EXAMPLE 3.1 (continued). To see the intersection of the boundary between R_1 and R_2 with E (the plane of the triangle) put z=1 in their boundary equation.   This gives:

$$y=\frac{2}{1+\sqrt{5}}x$$

Continuing with the boundary of R_2 and R_3 we obtain the line:

$$y=\frac{-(8+2\sqrt{21})x+16+4\sqrt{21}}{9+\sqrt{21}}$$

Finally, for the boundary of R_3 and R_1, we have:

$$y=\frac{(8+2\sqrt{21}+2\sqrt{5})x-16-4\sqrt{21}}{-4+\sqrt{5}-\sqrt{21}}$$

These three lines intersect at:

$$X=(\sqrt{5}+1)Y/2, \quad Y=\frac{16+4\sqrt{21}}{13+2\sqrt{21}+4\sqrt{5}+\sqrt{105}}$$

in the z=1 plane.   Point (X,Y) has the property that it is possible to go from S (origin) to (X,Y) on a shortest path touching any edge of $W_1W_2W_3$.   Furthermore, it is the only such point on E.   As a final note, (X,Y) can also be obtained as the intersection of the three Voronoi polygons constructed by the images of S on E as described in Theorem 3.1.

It is emphasized that the method exemplified up to now can be applied in the presence of a solid polygon too.   In this case we are required to compute all the potential boundaries between pairs of regions.   Although conceptually easy, this would be a difficult when it comes to intersect boundaries to compute their intersection curves.

The extension of the method to more than one obstacle (polygon) seems difficult.   In this case, a very desirable property of plane partitions around polygons as discovered by Franklin disappears.   We shall depict this with the aid of Figure 6a.   First, a brief account of Franklin's approach is in order.   (The reader is referred to Franklin [1982] and Franklin-Akman-Verrilli [1985] for a detailed description.)   Note that in the plane, once a subdivision is formed there is only one sequence of bend points for it (provided that it is not on a boundary curve in which case there may be more).   In

Figure 6a, there are two obstacles (line segments) A_1B_1 and A_2B_2 in the plane and a source S is given as shown. Franklin's algorithm partitions the plane into 5 regions in this case. R_0 holds goal points directly reachable from S. R_1 holds points which cause a shortest path to bend at B_1. R_2 holds points which cause a shortest path to bend at A_1. The boundary between R_1 and R_2 is a portion of a hyperbola. R_3 holds points which give rise to a shortest path bending at B_2. Finally, R_4 describes shortest paths bending first at A_1 and then at A_2. The boundary of R_3 and R_4 is also a portion of a hyperbola. All other boundary curves are linear. A crucial property of this diagram is as follows: "A bend point acts as a source point for a later region." For instance, A_1 acts as a souce point for the points of R_4. Similarly, B_1 acts as a source for the points of R_3. Thus, the source point is continuosly "pushed back" and this is the underlying reason for the fact that all curves are either line segments or hyperbolic sections.

In 3-space, we cannot immediately see an analogue of this property. When we place another triangle $V_1V_2V_3$ in Example 3.1, the new regions induced by this obstacle will be separated by surfaces of order higher than four (Figure 6b). Thus, whereas the boundary curves remain as hyperbolae in 2-space, in 3-space they would grow with every new polygonal obstacle placed into the workspace. One practical way to get around this problem is to approximate the boundaries with more manageable surfaces (such as quadrics) and to keep them as such even when new obstacles are introduced. This, we think, is possible since the boundary surfaces are generally smooth. The reader is referred to Figure 7 where we plotted the intersection curves of the boundaries computed in Example 3.1 with the z=2 plane.

4. COMPLEXITY AND ALGEBRAIC ISSUES

The method outlined in Section 2 to find the shortest paths is a brute force approach. However, this may be the only available approach in the light of striking similarities of our problem and the TSP. It would be interesting to determine whether there is a heuristic for this problem like Christofides' 50-percent heuristic for TSP (Garey-Johnson [1979]). We now give a partial complexity analysis for Section 2.

The enumeration of the permutations of positive length as required by the algorithm takes time proportional to the factorial of the total number of edges of the given polyhedra. Given a permutation, finding the bend points using resultants is also a costly process. If A and B are polynomials in variables x_1, $x_2,\ldots,x_r$ and C=resultant(A,B,x_r) then C is the sum of at most $(m_r+n_r)!$ terms, each of which being a product of n_r A coefficients and m_r B coefficients. (A and B have degrees m_r and n_r in variable

x_r.) It can be shown that the degree of C in variable x_{r-1} is bounded above by $m_r n_{r-1} + n_r m_{r-1}$ if A and B have degrees m_{r-1} and n_{r-1} in x_{r-1}. Therefore, 2M N is seen to be an upper bound on the degree of C^r if M=$\max_i m_i$ and N=$\max_i n_i$.

In Collins [1971], the computing time of a resultant algorithm is analyzed as a function of the degrees and the coefficient sizes of its inputs. As a special case it is proved that when all degrees are equal and the coefficient size is fixed, the computing time is $O(d^{cr})$ where d is the common degree, r is the number of variables, and c is a constant.

It can be seen that the detection of the intersections of a polygonal path with the obstacles as required by our algorithm will be subsumed by the previous computations. The following is a crude argument when all P_i are convex. Take a polygonal path made of k line segments. Testing this against all polyhedra takes $O(n^2 v \log^2 v)$ time in the worst case of k=$O(n v)$ where v=$\max_i |P_i|$.

There are technical problems with the Euclidean FINDPATH as stated by Papadimitriou [1977] and Garey-Graham-Johnson [1976] in the context of ΔTSP. It is known that (Grunbaum [1967] and Franklin [1983]) there exist configurations in the real projective plane which are not realizable in the rational projective plane. In the light of this, we must require infinite precision in the input (polyhedral vertex coordinates), i.e., a symbolic rather than numeric approach in inputting the coordinates. Even when one imposes the restriction that only points with rational coordinates be allowed as input, it is easy to end up with irrational distances under the L_2 metric. This can be dealt with as long as one keeps such distances merely as square roots and employs algebraic manipulation algorithms. However, if we state FINDPATH as a decision problem, i.e., "Does there exist a shortest path with length λ or less?" we suspect that FINDPATH becomes NP-complete. This originates from the difficulty of comparing numbers symbolically, or in other words, the identification of algebraic numbers (Mignotte [1982]). The symbolic expression for the length of a given shortest path on n lines may involve n+1 square roots. An attempt to compare this expression to an integer λ by repeated squaring to eliminate the square roots can take exponential time. An alternate way would be to evaluate each square root with sufficient accuracy so that their sum can be compared to λ. There is a best-known upper bound on the number of operations required to achieve that, namely, $O(m \, 2^n)$, cf. Garey-Graham-Johnson [1976]. Here m is the number of digits with guaranteed correctness. Unfortunately, there is no known polynomial way to reach this accuracy.

The drawbacks that we mentioned can be avoided if we replace the Euclidean metric by another which closely approximates it. Define $d'(x,y)=\lceil d(x,y) \rceil$ using the regular ceiling function. It is trivial to show that this still is a metric satisfying the triangle inequality. The loss of precision can be tolerated if in the beginning everything is scaled by an appropriately large number.

Regarding the Voronoi approach outlined in Section 3, there are many unanswered questions. To our best knowledge, point location in 3-space in the presence of curved surfaces of arbitrary complexity is an area with not many results. Kalay [1982] considers point location in the presence of polyhedra. Recent work reported in Chazelle [1983], drawing inspiration from a method published by Arnon-Collins-McCallum [1984a, 1984b] is at least conceptually applicable to our problem. In general, Chazelle proves that given n fixed-degree r-variate polynomials with rational coefficients, after $O(n^{c(r)})$ preprocessing time and spending polynomial space, it is possible to determine the region including a given point in $O(2^r \log n)$ time. (Note, however, that $c(r)$ is an exponential function of r.) In fact, the mentioned work of Arnon-Collins-McCallum has many other far-reaching applications in algebraic geometry, one of them being the problem of intersecting high-order surfaces as required by our Voronoi approach in Section 3.

REFERENCES

V. AKMAN, Findminpath algorithms for task-level (model-based) robot programming, Tech. Rep., ECSE Dept., Rensselaer Polytechnic Inst., Troy, NY, March 1984.

D. ARNON, G. E. COLLINS AND S. MCCALLUM, Cylindrical algebraic decomposition I: the basic algorithm, SIAM Journal on Computing 13, 4 (Nov. 1984), 865-877.

D. ARNON, G. E. COLLINS AND S. MCCALLUM, Cylindrical algebraic decomposition II: an adjacency algorithm for the plane, SIAM Journal on Computing 13, 4 (Nov. 1984), 878-889.

R. A. BROOKS, Solving the Find-Path problem by good representation of free space, IEEE Transactions on Systems, Man, and Cybernetics 13, 3 (March/April 1983), 190-197.

B. M. CHAZELLE, Fast searching in a real algebraic manifold with applications to geometric complexity, Tech. Rep., Computer Science Dept., Brown Univ., Providence, RI, June 1984.

B. M. CHAZELLE AND D. DOBKIN, Detection is easier than computation, Proc. 12th ACM SIGACT Conf. (May 1979), 146-153.

O. CHEIN AND L. STEINBERG, Routing past unions of disjoint linear barriers, Networks 13 (1983), 389-398.

G. E. COLLINS, The calculation of multivariate polynomial resultants, Journal of the ACM 18, 4 (Oct. 1971), 515-532.

E. W. DIJKSTRA, A note on two problems in connexion with graphs, Numerische Mathematik 1 (1959), 1, 269-271.

B. R. DONALD, The Mover's problem in automated structural design, Tech. Rep., Artificial Intelligence Lab, Massachusetts Inst. of Technology, Cambridge, MA, June 1983.

W. R. FRANKLIN, Partitioning the plane to calculate minimal paths to any goal around obstructions, Tech. Rep., ECSE Dept., Rensselaer Polytechnic Inst., Troy, NY, Nov. 1982.

W. R. FRANKLIN AND V. AKMAN, Minimal paths between source and goal points located on/around a convex polyhedron, Proc. 22nd Allerton Conf. on Communication, Control, and Computing (Sep. 1984).

W. R. FRANKLIN, V. AKMAN AND C. VERRILLI, Voronoi diagrams with barriers and on polyhedra for minimal path planning, The Visual Computer - An International Journal on Computer Graphics (1985).

W. R. FRANKLIN, Algebra problems in CAD computations, Tech. Rep., ECSE Dept., Rensselaer Polytechnic Inst., Troy, NY, Oct. 1983.

M. R. GAREY, R. L. GRAHAM AND D. JOHNSON, Some NP-complete geometric problems, Proc. 8th ACM Symp. on Theory of Computing (May 1976), 10-22.

M. R. GAREY AND D. S. JOHNSON, Computers and Intractability: A Guide to the Theory of NP-completeness, Freeman, San Francisco, CA, 1979.

B. GRUNBAUM, Convex Polytopes, Wiley, New York, 1967.

J. E. HOPCROFT, J. T. SCHWARTZ AND M. SHARIR, On the complexity of motion planning for multiple independent objects; PSPACE hardness of the "Warehouseman's problem", Tech. Rep., Computer Science Div., New York Univ., Courant Inst. of Mathematical Sciences, New York, Feb. 1984.

D. S. JOHNSON AND C. H. PAPADIMITRIOU, Computational complexity and the Traveling Salesman problem, Chap. 3 of The Traveling Salesman Problem, eds. E. L. Lawler, J. K. Lenstra and A. G. Rinooy Kan, Wiley, New York, 1981.

Y. E. KALAY, Determining the spatial containment of a point in general polyhedra, Computer Graphics and Image Processing 19 (1982), 303-334.

D. T. LEE AND R. L. DRYSDALE, Generalizations of Voronoi diagrams in the plane, SIAM Journal on Computing 10, 1 (Feb. 1981), 73-87.

D. T. LEE AND F. P. PREPARATA, Euclidean shortest paths in the presence of rectilinear barriers, Networks 14 (1984), 393-410.

T. LOZANO-PEREZ, Automatic planning of manipulator transfer movements, IEEE Transactions on Systems, Man, and Cybernetics 11, 10 (Oct. 1981), 681-698.

T. LOZANO-PEREZ, Spatial planning: a Configuration Space
approach, IEEE Transactions on Computers 32, 2
(Feb. 1983), 108-120.

M. MIGNOTTE, Identification of algebraic numbers, Journal of
Algorithms 3 (1982), 197-204.

V-D. NGUYEN, The Find-Path problem in the plane, Tech. Rep.,
Artificial Intelligence Lab, Massachusetts Inst. of
Technology, Cambridge, Mass., Feb. 1984.

C. O'DUNLAING, M. SHARIR AND C. K. YAP, Retraction: a new
approach to motion-planning, Proc. 15th ACM Symp. on
Theory of Computing (April 1983), 207-220.

C. O'DUNLAING AND C. K. YAP, The Voronoi method for
motion-planning: I. The case of a disc, Tech. Rep.,
Computer Science Div., New York Univ., Courant
Inst. of Mathematical Sciences, New York, March 1983.

J. O'ROURKE, S. SURI AND H. BOOTH, Shortest paths on polyhedral
surfaces, Proc. 2nd Annual Symp. on Theoretical
Aspects of Computer Science (Jan. 1985).

C. H. PAPADIMITRIOU, The Euclidean Traveling Salesman problem
is NP-complete, Theoretical Computer Science 4
(1977), 237-244.

C. H. PAPADIMITRIOU AND K. STEIGLITZ, Combinatorial
Optimization: Algorithms and Complexity,
Addison-Wesley, Reading, MA, 1982.

J. H. REIF, Complexity of the Mover's problem and
generalizations, Proc. 20th IEEE Conf. on Foundations
of Computer Science (1979), 421-427.

J. T. SCHWARTZ AND M. SHARIR, On the "Piano Movers" problem:
I. The case of a two-dimensional rigid polygonal body
moving amidst polygonal barriers, Communications on
Pure and Applied Mathematics XXXVI (1983), 345-398.

J. T. SCHWARTZ AND M. SHARIR, On the "Piano Movers" problem:
II. General techniques for computing topological
properties of real algebraic manifolds, Advances in
Applied Mathematics 4 (1983), 298-351.

J. T. SCHWARTZ AND M. SHARIR, On the "Piano Movers" problem:
III. Coordinating the motion of several independent
bodies: The special case of circular bodies moving
amidst polygonal barriers, International Journal of
Robotics Research 2 (Fall 1983), 3, 46-75.

J. T. SCHWARTZ AND M. SHARIR, On the "Piano Movers" problem: V. The case of a rod moving in three-dimensional space amidst polyhedral obstacles, Communications on Pure and Applied Mathematics XXXVII (1984), 815-848.

M. SHARIR AND E. ARIEL-SHEFFI, On the "Piano Movers" problem: IV. Various decomposable two-dimensional motion-planning problems, Communications on Pure and Applied Mathematics XXXVII (1984), 479-493.

M. SHARIR AND A. SCHORR, On shortest paths in polyhedral spaces, Proc. 16th ACM Symp. on Theory of Computing (1984), 144-153.

P. SPIRAKIS AND C. K. YAP, On the combinatorial complexity of motion coordination, Tech. Rep., Computer Science Div., New York Univ., Courant Inst. of Mathematical Sciences, New York, April 1983.

P. SPIRAKIS AND C. K. YAP, Strong NP-hardness of moving many discs, Information Processing Letters 19 (1984), 55-59.

B. L. VAN DER WAERDEN, Algebra, 2 vols., Ungar, New York, 1970.

F I G U R E S

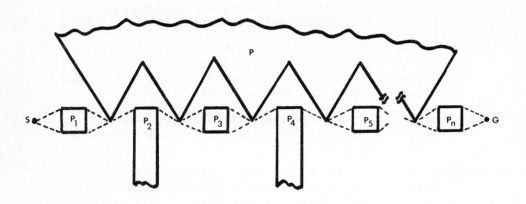

F I G U R E _ 1

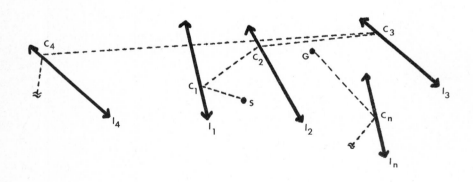

F I G U R E _ 2

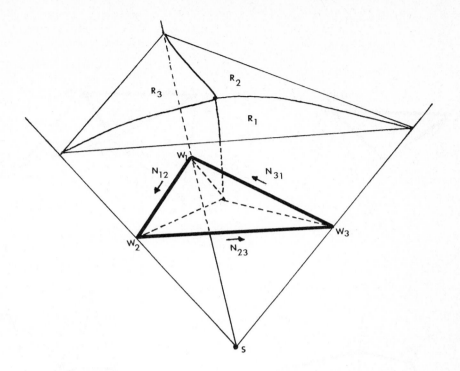

F I G U R E _ 3

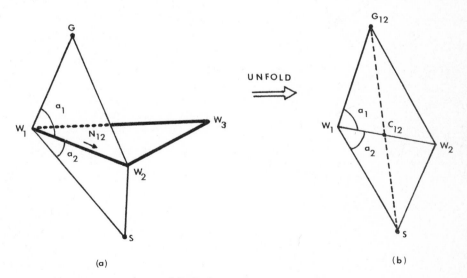

(a)   (b)

F I G U R E _ 4

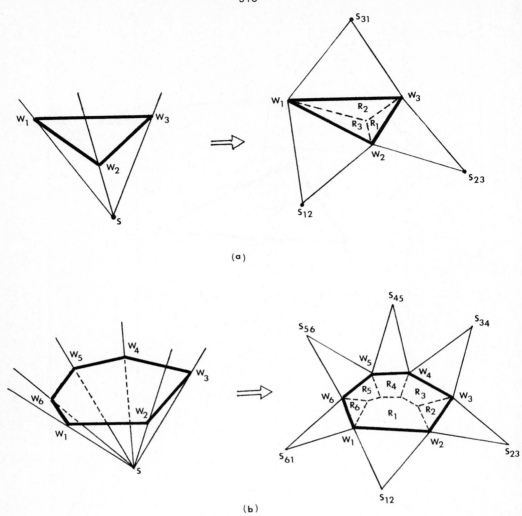

(a)

(b)

FIGURE - 5

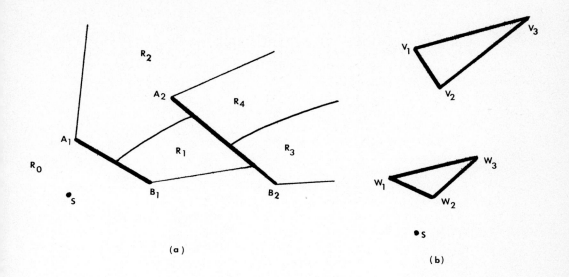

(a)

(b)

F I G U R E _ 6

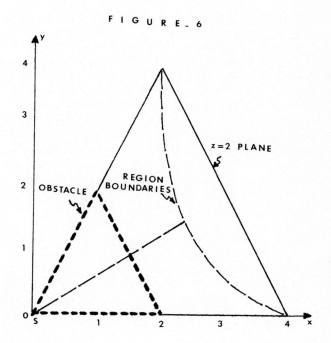

F I G U R E _ 7

GEOMETRIC DATA STRUCTURES FOR COMPUTER GRAPHICS

Mark H. Overmars

Department of Computer Science, University of Utrecht
P.O.Box 80.012, 3508 TA Utrecht, the Netherlands

1. Introduction.

The area of Computational Geometry deals with the study of algorithms for problems concerning geometric objects like e.g. lines, polygons, circles etc. in the plane and in higher dimensional space. Since its introduction in 1976 by Shamos[17] the field has developed rapidly and nowadays there are even special conferences and journals devoted to the topic. A list of publications by Edelsbrunner and van Leeuwen[8] collected in 1982 already contained over 650 papers. And this number has rapidly increased since then.

Clearly, a large number of problems in Computer Graphics deal with geometric objects as well. Examples are hidden line elimination, windowing problems, intersection problems etc. Hence, Computer Graphics can benefit from the techniques developed in Computational Geometry. van Leeuwen[18] was the first to make this explicit. (Of course already a number of problems considered in Computational Geometry were based on problems arising in Computer Graphics.) He showed that solutions to problems like nearest neighbor searching and range searching could be useful in Computer Graphics.

In this paper we will give some examples of how techniques from Computational Geometry can be applied to Computer Graphics. We will concentrate on the windowing problem: given a large picture, built out of non-intersecting line segments, compute that part of the picture visible in a axis-parallel rectangle. (See figure 1.1. for an example.) We will show how to store the picture in a kind of two-dimensional data structure such that for each given window we can efficiently determine what part of the picture is visible in the window. This is particular useful when the

NATO ASI Series, Vol. F17
Fundamental Algorithms for Computer Graphics
Edited by R. A. Earnshaw
© Springer-Verlag Berlin Heidelberg 1985

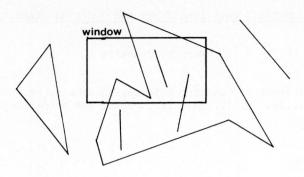

Figure 1.1.

pictures are large (compared to the size of the window) and do not change often. For example, large maps stored in a database. We will give both static solutions (i.e., the picture does not change) and dynamic solutions (i.e., the picture can be updated by means of insertions and deletions of line segments).

The paper is organized as follows. First we recall some known results from computational geometry. Next we apply these to the windowing. In the final section we give some extensions. The methods presented are not worked out in detail. Details can be found in the cited papers.

Although the results are merely theoretical they show new ways of solving this type of problems that might lead to fast practical solutions.

The results in this paper are based on work by Edelsbrunner, Overmars and Seidel[7,14].

2. Preliminary results.

In this section we will mention some results and techniques from computational geometry that we will use in the following sections.

2.1. Point location.

The point location problem is the following: Given a subdivision of the plane in polygonal areas, store this subdivision in such a way that the area a given point lies in can be determined efficiently. The polygonal subdivision is made up of n line segments. The problem has been considered in great detail. (See e.g. Lee and Preparata[10], Preparata[16], Edelsbrunner and Maurer[5], Edelsbrunner, Guibas and Stolfi[4] and Kirkpatrick[9].) The best known result is:

Theorem 2.1.1. [4,9] Given a polygonal subdivision of the plane of n line segments, it can be stored using O(n) storage such that point location queries can be answered in O(log n) time.

For the method used see the cited papers. This is the best we could hope to achieve. The method in [4] also applies to subdivision that are composed of non-straight edges.

The point location problem is useful in solving many other searching problems in the plane.

2.2. The locus approach.

The locus approach is a general technique for solving many types of searching problems. In a searching problem we have a set of objects we want to store such that given a query object we can answer some question about this query object with respect to the set of objects. These query objects are chosen from some query space. For example, they can be all possible points in the plane or all possible windows. For a fixed set of objects it is often possible to split the query space into a number of areas of constant answer, i.e., areas such that for all query objects in one area the answer is the same. In such a case we can solve the searching problem by making such a subdivision of the query space and storing with each area the corresponding answer. Performing a query now consists of determining the area the query object lies in and reporting the corresponding answer. Hence, we can solve the problem using point location. (See Overmars[13] for a general treatment of the locus approach.)

2.3. Range searching.

The range searching problem is the following: given a set of point in the plane (or a multi-dimensional space), store them in such a way that those points lying in a given axis-parallel rectangle (range) can be determined efficiently. Hence, the range searching problem is a restricted version of the windowing problem in which the picture consists of points rather than line segments. A number of solution to the range searching problem have been proposed. (See e.g. Bentley and Friedman[1], Edelsbrunner[3], Lueker[11], Overmars and van Leeuwen[15] and Willard[19,20].) We will shortly describe one. (For details see e.g. [19].)

A range tree is a balanced binary search tree containing all points in the set sorted with respect to their first coordinates in the leaves. With each internal node β we associate a balanced binary search tree of all point in the subtree rooted at β, sorted with respect to their second coordinate. To perform a query with a range $([x_1:x_2],[y_1:y_2])$ we search with both x_1 and x_2 in the tree. Now look at all nodes γ whose father is on one of the two search paths and who are lying in between the two search paths. (See figure 2.3.1.) Their subtrees together span the whole interval between x_1 and x_2. Hence, all points in between x_1 and x_2 are stored in exactly one of the structures associated with the nodes γ. In these associated

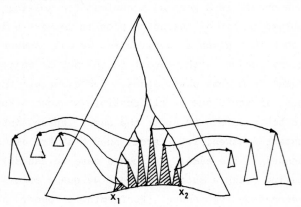

Figure 2.3.1.

structures we search for the points lying in between y_1 and y_2.

As the number of nodes Y is bounded by $O(\log n)$ (n=the number of points) and the time required to search an associated structure is bounded by $O(\log n)$ plus the number of answers, the total query time is bounded by $O(\log^2 n)$ plus the total number of answers. One easily shows that the amount of storage required is bounded by $O(n.\log n)$.

Theorem 2.3.1. One can store a set of n point using $O(n.\log n)$ storage such that range queries can be performed in $O(k+\log^2 n)$ time where k is the number of answers. The structure can be updated in $O(\log^2 n)$ time per insertion and $O(\log n)$ time per deletion of a point.

The insertion and deletion methods can be found in [19].

3. Windowing.

We will describe two different solutions. The first one is static and only works for fixed size windows. Its advantage is that it only uses linear storage. The second solution is a fully dynamic solution, allowing for arbitrary sized windows, but it uses $O(n.\log n)$ storage. We will not go into details. They can be found in [7,14].

3.1. A static solution.

In this subsection we assume that the window has some fixed size. (In fact, we only need it to have fixed height.) To determine which line segments lie in the window we solve two subproblem. Firstly, we determine which line segments have one of their endpoints in the window, and secondly, we determine the line segments that intersect the boundary of the window. In this way we clearly obtain all segments that are visible in the window.

Let us first concentrate on the problem of finding the segments with one of their endpoints in the window. Hence, we are given a set of points and we ask for those that lie in the window. This is in fact the range searching problem. We cannot use the result from the previous section because we want to achieve linear storage. We will now solve the range searching problem for fixed size ranges in a better way. To find those points that lie in the window we move the left boundary of the window horizontally toward the right boundary, reporting each point we pass. To do this efficiently we need to have a way to determine the next point hit by the left boundary. Hence, we have to solve the following subproblem: given a set of point in the plane, store them in such a way that the first point hit when moving a vertical line segment of fixed height h to the right can be determined efficiently. See figure 3.1.1. for an example. We solve this subproblem by transforming it into another problem. We replace each point p in the set by a vertical line segment of height h with p as topmost point. Now we can as well ask the question: determine the first line segment hit when moving the bottom point of the query line segment to the right. See figure 3.1.2. This problem we can solve using the locus approach. We get a subdivision of the plane as shown in figure 3.1.3. Using point location we can find the area the query point (= the bottom point of the left boundary of the window) lies in and this gives us the first point hit when moving the left boundary to the right. Using a technique by Chazelle[2] for walking in a planar subdivision we can continue moving the left boundary to the right by walking with the bottom point

Figure 3.1.1.

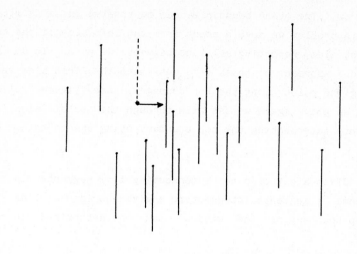

Figure 3.1.2.

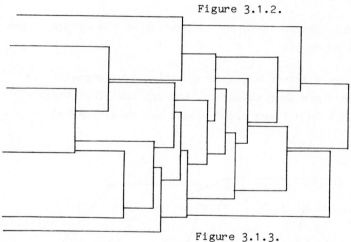

Figure 3.1.3.

through the subdivision, reporting each area we pass until we reach the right boundary. Combining the results for point location and walking in a subdivision this leads to the following result:

Theorem 3.1.1. Given a set of n points in the plane we can store them using O(n) storage such that those k points lying in a fixed sized window can be determined in O(k+log n) time.

This solves our first subproblem. The second subproblem asks for those line segments that intersect the window. We will only consider the top boundary of the window. The other boundaries can be treated in a similar way. To solve this problem we move a point from the left side of the top boundary to the right side, reporting all line segments we pass. To do so we again use the locus approach to be able to determine the first line segment hit when moving the point along the top boundary. See figure 3.1.4. for the subdivision we get. Again we can walk through the subdivision to find all line segments intersecting the top boundary using the technique of Chazelle[2].

Theorem 3.1.2. Given a set of n non-intersecting line segments in the plane, those k segments intersecting a given horizontal line segment (the top boundary of the window) can be determined in O(k+log n) time.

A similar method applies to the other boundaries of the window. Combining the two results we obtain:

Theorem 3.1.3. Given a set of n non-intersecting line segments in the plane, we can store them using O(n) storage such that those k line segments visible in a fixed sized window can be determined in O(k+log n) time.

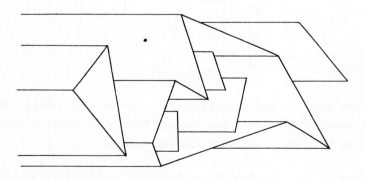

Figure 3.1.4.

Of course, some provision has to be made such that visible line segments are reported only once. See [7] for details.

3.2. A dynamic solution.

We will now describe a fully dynamic solution to the windowing problem that allows for arbitrary sized windows. To do so we again split the problem in two parts like in the previous subsection. For finding the segments with an endpoint in the window we now use the dynamic range tree. This yields a query time of $O(\log^2 n)$, an insertion time of $O(\log^2 n)$ and a deletion time of $O(\log n)$ using $O(n.\log n)$ storage. So we only have to consider the second subproblem: find those line segments that intersect the boundary of the window. We will again only look at the top boundary. The other boundaries follow in a similar way.

First we project all line segments on a vertical line. This divides the line in a number of "elementary" intervals $[-\infty, a_1]$, $[a_1, a_2]$, ... , $[a_n, \infty]$. See figure 3.2.1. We build a balanced binary search tree that has these elementary intervals as leaves. An internal node β contains the whole interval covered by the subtree rooted at β. With each node β we associate a structure (to be described below) that contains all line segments whose projection covers the interval of β but not the interval of the

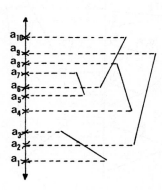

Figure 3.2.1.

father of β. In figure 3.2.2. the line segments that have to come in the associated structures are indicated.

To search with the top boundary of the window (being the line from (x_1, y_2) to (x_2, y_2)) we search with y_2 in the structure. Now it is easy to see that each line segment intersecting the top boundary is in exactly one of the structures associated with the nodes on the search path of y_2. Hence, we only have to search in these structures.

The line segments that are associated with a node β we restrict to the part that lies in the horizontal slab corresponding to the interval stored in β. See figure 3.2.3. As the line segments do not intersect they appear ordered in this slab. In this order we store them in the internal nodes of a balanced binary search tree T_β. When we have to search in a structure T_β y_2 did pass through node β and, hence, the top boundary lies in the slab. We now search with x_1 and x_2 in T_β. In this way we can find in $O(\log n)$ time (plus the number of answers) those segments in T_β that intersect the top boundary. We have to do this for all nodes β on the search path of y_2. These are $O(\log n)$ nodes. Hence, the total query time becomes $O(\log^2 n)$ plus the number of answers.

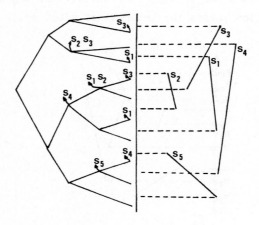

Figure 3.2.2.

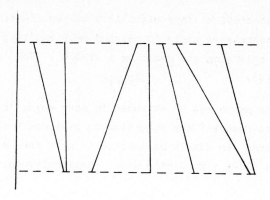

Figure 3.2.3.

It is easy to see that each line segment is stored in at most O(log n) associated structures. Hence, the amount of storage required is bounded by O(n.log n).

Insertion and deletion methods can be obtained in a way similar to Willard[19] or by using general dynamisation techniques (see Overmars[12] for an overview). This yields insertion and deletion time bounds of $O(\log^2 n)$.

Combining the known result for range searching and the structure described above we obtain:

Theorem 3.2.1. Given a set of n non-intersecting line segments in the plane, we can store them using O(n.log n) storage such that those k segments visible in a given window can be determined in $O(k+\log^2 n)$ time. The structure is dynamic and can be updated in $O(\log^2 n)$ time.

For more details see [14].

4. Conclusions and Extensions.

We have shown how some techniques and solutions from Computational Geometry can be used to solve the windowing problem in Computer Graphics.

Although the methods are theoretical they might lead to new, fast, practical solutions. Similar techniques apply to related problems like moving a window over a picture and enlarging and reducing a window. For solutions to these problems see [6,14].

The techniques in this paper can be extended in many ways. For example, there is no need to restrict the attention to pictures build out of line segments. The solutions can easily be adapted to work for more general classes of objects like e.g. circle arcs, small polygons, etc., as well.

Many open problems do remain. A very interesting question is whether these techniques can be turned into practical solutions. Also on the theoretical level numbers of open problems do remain. An important question being whether the solutions are optimal or can be improved by reducing the query time or amount of storage required.

5. References.

[1] Bentley, J.L. and J.H. Friedman, Data Structures for Range Searching, ACM Comput. Surveys 11 (1979), pp. 397-409.

[2] Chazelle, B.M., Fast Computation of Segment Intersections, Techn. Rep. CS-83-11, Dept of Computer Science, Brown University, 1983.

[3] Edelsbrunner, H., A Note on dynamic Range Searching, Bull of the EATCS 15 (1981), pp. 34-40.

[4] Edelsbrunner, H., L.J. Guibas and J. Stolfi, Optimal point location in a monotone subdivision, manuscript.

[5] Edelsbrunner, H. and H.A. Maurer, A Space-optimal Solution of General Region Location, Theoretical Computer Science 16 (1981), pp. 329-336.

[6] Edelsbrunner, H. and M.H. Overmars, Zooming by Repeated Range Detection, Techn. Rep. RUU-CS-84-10, Dept. of Computer Science, University of Utrecht, 1984. (to appear)

[7] Edelsbrunner, H., M.H. Overmars and R. Seidel, Some Methods of Computational Geometry Applied to Computer Graphics, Computer Vision, Graphics and Image Processing 28 (1984), pp. 92-108.

[8] Edelsbrunner, H. and J. van Leeuwen, Multidimensional Data Structures

and Algorithms: A Bibliography, Techn. Rep. F105, Inst. f. Information Processing, TU Graz, 1982.

[9] Kirkpatrick, D.G., Optimal Search in Planar Subdivisions, SIAM J. Computing 12 (1983), pp. 28-35.

[10] Lee, D.T. and F.P. Preparata, Location of a Point in a Planar Subdivision and its Applications, SIAM J. Computing 6 (1977) pp. 594-606.

[11] Lueker, G.S., A Data Structure for Orthogonal Range Queries, Proc. 19th IEEE Symp. on Foundations of Computer Science, 1978, pp. 28-34.

[12] Overmars, M.H., The Design of Dynamic Data Structures, Lect. Notes in Computer Science 156, Springer-Verlag, 1983.

[13] Overmars, M.H., The Locus Approach, in: M. Nagl and J. Perl (ed.), Proc. 9th Conf. on Graphtheoretic Concepts in Computer Science (WG83), Trauner Verlag, 1983, pp. 263-273.

[14] Overmars, M.H., Range Searching in a Set of Line Segments, Techn. Rep. RUU-CS-83-6, Dept. of Computer Science, University of Utrecht, 1983. (to appear in Proc. of the Symp. on Computational Geometry, Baltimore, 1985)

[15] Overmars, M.H. and J. van Leeuwen, Worst-case Optimal Insertion and Deletion Methods for Decomposable Searching Problems, Inform. Proc. Letters 12 (1981), pp. 168-173.

[16] Preparata, F.P., A New Approach to Planar Point Location. SIAM J. Computing 10 (1981), pp. 473-482.

[17] Shamos, M.I., Computational Geometry, Ph.D. thesis, Dept. of Computer Science, Yale University, 1978.

[18] van Leeuwen, J., Graphics and Computational Geometry, Les Mathematiques de l'Informatique, Colloq. AFCET, 1982, pp. 159-165.

[19] Willard, D.E., The Super-B-Tree Algorithm, Techn. Rep. TR-03-79, Aiken Computer Lab., Harvard University, 1979.

[20] Willard, D.E., New Data Structures for Orthogonal Queries, SIAM J. Computing, in press.

A Model for Raster Graphics
Language Primitives

Wim J.M. Teunissen (*)

Jan van den Bos

Correspondence:
   W.J.M. Teunissen
   Department of Computer Science
   University of Leiden
   P.O. Box 9512
   2300 RA Leiden
   The Netherlands

(*) This research was supported by the Netherlands Foundation for
Technical Research (STW).

ABSTRACT

Raster graphics systems are becoming increasingly popular due to improved technology and lower costs. However, this positive development has not had its follow-up in the software department: currently there is virtually no integrated raster graphics software available.
We propose a hierarchical model in which the applicability in raster graphics is of primary importance. The model is based upon a number of 0D, 1D and 2D primitives to generate graphical patterns. These patterns may also be formed by means of expressions over other patterns. They form the end-nodes of a datastructure consisting of a directed, acyclic graph, the pattern graph, the nodes of which contain attributes. By using priority ordering in the graph '2.5D' pictures may be constructed. Attributes in the graph govern detectabiliy, visibility, highlighting, level and graphical transformations. This two-stage approach to making pictures has been developed in order to achieve a model for raster graphics, catering for interaction.

1.0 Introduction.

Most graphics software, as reflected in the current proposals for graphics standard specifications (GKS [1], PHIGS [2]), is based on line graphics, that is on 1D graphics primitives. The recent transition from vector graphics to raster graphics has led to little more than a few ad-hoc raster primitives in the standard proposals.

We propose a model in which 2D patterns play a basic role. These patterns are defined as colour functions over a domain of arbitrary shape. The domains are a subset of the 2D or 3D real space. The colour functions are defined in a RGB, HSV or HSI colour space and comprise constant, linear, repeating pattern, interpolation and texture functions.

Patterns can be combined in expressions yielding a new pattern. Several operations are used: set-theoretic operations such as union, intersection and difference; domain transformations and colour transformations such as weighted mixing and interpolation.

At a higher level these patterns can be combined in a dynamic, hierarchic structure: the pattern graph, a directed acyclic graph the leaves of which are the patterns. The nodes in the graph contain the dynamically alterable attributes: geometric and graphic transformations, highlighting, visibility, detectability and level.

This two-stage approach, using expressions and graphs, has been followed in order to make interactive graphics possible, because only paths in the graph can be manipulated and no longer the constituent parts of patterns.

Introduction.

At display time the graph is interpreted, attributes are concatenated and/or applied, and the interpreted result is represented by a so-called fleck structure. Flecks are 2D virtual rasters, not necessarily rectangular. The flecks are arranged in a linked list and still contain the projected values of some attributes, but not those of the transformations. Again this organization caters to interaction. It is anticipated that the fleck chain forms the interface with the graphics hardware architecture.

In chapter 2 we will discuss the way graphical objects are built, and what role the datastructure plays. Chapter 3 will contain some remarks concerning the display of an object. In chapter 4 we will go into more detail on some of the information stored in the nodes of the graph. Some conclusions can be found in chapter 5.

2.0 The graphical objects and their representation.

Composing a graphical object consists of putting together several basic primitives, and building a hierarchic datastructure on top of it. For this purpose some operators and generators are provided.

2.1 Patterns.

The basic graphical element is called a pattern. A pattern P is a pair (D, F), with D some subset of 2D real space, and F a function on D, with values in some colour space S. We call D the domain of P and F its colour function.

Contrary to most raster graphics software, where it is assumed that the user offers discrete data, the domain of a pattern can be a continuous subset of real space, e.g. [0,1] x [0,1]. This will ease the use of the model, because the user will not be bothered with describing his object pixel by pixel. Because eventually discrete data is necessary for display, the model must take care of the conversion between the continuous and discrete representation. More on this in chapter 3.
Like the domain, the colour function is also specified in a continuous colour space, such as RGB or HSV [3].

The definition of a pattern consists of a description of both the domain and the colour function. Because we are trying to make full use of the fact that we are considering raster graphics applications, we included several domain primitives that generate 2D domains, such as a filled rectangle and polygon. Possible domain primitives are:

```
        polymarker
        polyline
        polygon
        ellipse
        rectangle
```

The polygon, ellipse and rectangle primitives specify closed 2D domains of which the inside is coloured according to the given colour function. Primitives polymarker and polyline have been added to support some 0D and 1D graphics.

When specifying the colour function of a pattern, the user can choose from:

```
            constant colour function
            linear colour function
            pattern-repeating colour function
            texture generator
            interpolation function
```

With the texture generating colour function, pseudo-random colours are generated, for example to display a forest seen from a large distance.

Using the pattern-repeating colour function results in a colour function that consists of a pattern (preferably rectangular) that is repeated over and over again (tiling).

Given a colour for a number of points, the interpolation colour function calculates a colour for every other point of the domain by interpolation.

It is not yet clear which primitives for defining domain and colour function should be part of the model. In particular the set of colour function primitives could change considerably. It is even possible that the set of primitives has to be extendable according to the user's wishes.

2.2 Pattern-expressions.

Because of the limited power of definitions of patterns, we offer the possibility of constructing more complex patterns with pattern_expressions. These are expressions on patterns, yielding a new pattern. Possible operations are [4,5]:

```
        set-operations:
                union
                difference
                intersection

        domain-transformations:
                scale
                translate
                rotate
```

Pattern-expressions.

colour-transformations:
       weight
       translate
       intensify

The three set-operations as well as the domain-transformations are in principle operations on the domain of the pattern only. There are no problems but for union and intersection. Question is what colour the resulting pattern must receive on the intersection of the two domains. The answer is to add a dyadic colour-operation when using one of these two operators. The colour-operation will then be used to combine the two original colours into one for the resulting pattern, but only on the intersection of the domains.

The weight colour-operation yields a colour function which assigns a colour to a point by weighting the two original colours according to some given weight-factors. This is the only dyadic colour-operation.

Using the translate colour-transformation, one can 'add' some colour to the current value. The intensify colour-transformation can be used to multiply the intensity by a given factor. These two transformations are in fact a translate and scale transformation within the 3D RGB colour space.

2.3 The_pattern_graph.

Using the patterns as basic elements, a complete graphical object can be created by ordering and linking those elements in a hierarchical way: in a graph.

What we will call a pattern_graph is an acyclic, directed graph with patterns in the leaves. An example:

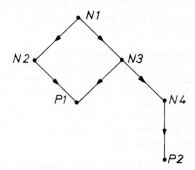

Figure 1: an example of a pattern graph with
nodes N1 .. N4; patterns P1 and P2.

It is not permitted to have patterns in nodes of the graph other than leaf nodes. The non-leaf nodes carry additional information, called attributes.

2.3.1   Attributes_in_the_pattern_graph.

An attribute in the pattern graph is an ordinary domain- or colour-transformation, or it controls:

- visibility
- detectability
- highlighting
- level

The domain- and colour-transformations may be used to transform certain parts of an object into the desired shape or colour.

The detection attribute can be used to declare a part of the object detectable, i.e. the program will notice the user pointing at that part of the picture with a pick device. After receiving the information that a detectable part of the picture was pointed at, the program may request the identification of the detected part. With this information the program can take appropriate action.

When pointing at some part of the picture with a lightpen, the user may want some indication that the pen was noticed. One of the possibilities is to generate an echo with the help of the highlighting attribute. Possible implementations of highlighting may be:

- put a box around the detected object
- blink it
- intensify its colour
- change its colour completely

To be able to control the quantity of information on the display-screen, the user is provided with the level attribute. Every part of a picture can be assigned one or more levels. When displaying the object, the user can select the levels to be displayed.

An example of the use of the level-attribute is the situation where one wants to display some geographical data. Country borders supply more than enough information when surveying a complete map of Europe. When zooming in on a specific country, city-limits may become interesting. After assigning a different level to the city-limits and the country borders, the only thing the user has to do in order to add the city-limits to the picture is to change the levels that must be displayed.

Visibility is an attribute that resembles level in that it also controls the visibility of parts of a picture. The main difference between these attributes lies in the locality of visibility (local to some node in the patterngraph), and the globality of level (global because the name of the level can be spread throughout the graph, cutting through the hierarchical structure).

The pattern graph.

The name attribute is used for identification purposes. This attribute was not included in the list of attributes because it is not a graphical attribute.

Another attribute that does not occur in the list is priority. It was not included because it is stored implicitly in the structure of the graph.
The priority attribute controls the order in which the parts of a picture are drawn. This has no consequences except where there is overlap. In those cases the part with the highest priority comes on top of the other part(s) because it is drawn last, as in the Painter's algorithm. This priority order provides the extra 'half-dimension' in the 2.5D of the model.
Priority is assigned by the user, when linking the nodes while creating the graph. Using priority the user can add some depth to a picture.

In chapter 4 we will discuss the way in which the attributes are concatenated and applied to the patterns.

2.3.2 Operations_on_the_pattern_graph.

Because the pattern graph is intended to be a dynamic datastructure, there are a number of operations with which the user can manipulate the pattern graph. These operations are:

- ADD b TO a BEHIND p
  As a result of this call, the node 'b' will be added to the progeny of 'a'. The additional information 'BEHIND P' is used to determine the priority of 'b' as one lower than that of 'p' (see fig 2a).

- ADD COPY OF b TO a BEHIND p
  A copy of the subgraph under 'b' will be linked at 'a', with a priority one lower than of 'p' (see fig 2b).

- REMOVE b FROM a
  Removes the link between the nodes 'a' and 'b' (see fig 2c).

- REMOVE AND PRUNE b FROM a
  Removes the link between 'a' and 'b', and additionally prunes the sub-graph under 'b' where the removal has left it disjunct with the rest of the graph (see fig 2d).

The pattern graph.

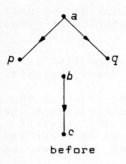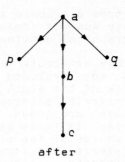

before   after

Figure 2a: ADD b TO a BEHIND p

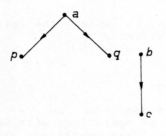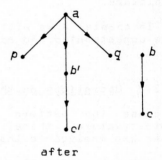

before   after

Figure 2b: ADD COPY OF b TO a BEHIND p

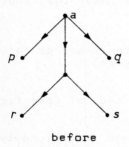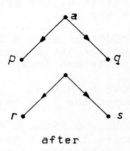

before   after

Figure 2c: REMOVE b FROM a

The pattern graph.

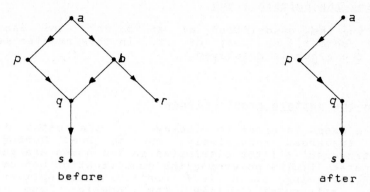

before   after

Figure 2d: REMOVE AND PRUNE b FROM a

One of the things we hope to achieve is the development of some language construct within which the operation on the graph comes naturally. The objective is to make the user think in terms of hierarchically structured objects, rather than in terms of building a graph.

2.4 Why pattern expressions as well as pattern graphs?

What we will try to explain in this section is the reason for having pattern expressions as well as pattern graphs, two ways of composing graphical objects into more complex ones.

The most important difference between the expressions and the graph, is the fact that combining patterns using expressions results in a pattern in which the sub-structure has vanished, while the elements from which a pattern graph is built, are still distinguishable in the graph, and can be operated on seperately.

When our intention would be to display static graphical objects, we could suffice with only pattern expressions. Without having to deal with interaction, an important reason for having a pattern graph would disappear.

Alternatively, we could do without pattern expressions and leave the structure of the expressions in the graph. This would lead to a model like ILP [6]. However, it would have the disadvantage that, for every change in the graph, even the parts of which the user knows beforehand that they remain static, will have to be reinterpreted when generating a new picture. Due to this, response time could increase dramatically.

Another, minor, argument in favour of having both expressions and graphs, is that a pattern should be a 'finished' component of an object, while the graph should only serve as glue between these components.

3.0 Displaying_the_pattern_graph.

After completing the description of an object, the user can
display that object, or part of it. In this chapter we will
describe how the graph is displayed.

3.1 Paths_in_the_pattern_graph:_Flecks.

When parsing a graph in order to display it, the paths in the
graph are traversed recursively, one by one. During this
(pre-order) traversal all the attributes in the nodes are gathered
and concatenated (rules governing the concatenation can be found
in chapter 4). Arriving at a leaf containing a pattern, the
concatenated attributes (like the domain- and colour
transformations) are applied to the pattern. The parsed structures
resulting from this operation are called flecks. There is a
one-to-one correspondence between paths in the graph ending in a
pattern, and flecks.

    An example:

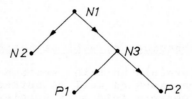

Figure 3: a patterngraph with nodes N1, N2, N3
and patterns P1, P2

Observe Figure 3: because N2 does not contain a pattern there is
no resulting fleck from the path N1-N2. The paths N1-N3-P1 and
N1-N3-P2 however do result in two flecks.

    The reason we have flecks is to be able to react efficiently to
changes in the graph and compute only those flecks that are new or
have changed. Minimizing the number of fleck-computations is
important because they involve converting data from a continuous
into a discrete representation, and exactly this conversion is
expected to be the most time-consuming process in the model.

    The flecks are linked in the fleck_chain. This list of flecks
should reflect the status of the pattern graph at every moment,
however updates could be done in the fleck chain in the foreground
and in the pattern graph in the background.

Computing a fleck.

3.2 Computing_a_fleck.

Consider the following simple pattern graph:

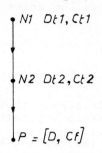

Figure 4: a pattern graph, with domain- and
colour-transformations in the nodes.

With the domain-transformations Dt1 and Dt2 and the domain D of P,
the domain of the resulting fleck will be:

$$\text{Dt1 (Dt2 (D)) = Dt1 o Dt2 (D)} \tag{3.1}$$

Its colour function can be obtained from the colour function Cf
and the colour-transformations Ct1 and Ct2 using the following
formula:

$$\text{Ct1 (Ct2 (Cf o Dt2}^{-1} \text{o Dt1}^{-1} \text{)) =}$$

$$\text{(Ct1 o Ct2) o Cf o (Dt1 o Dt2)}^{-1} \tag{3.2}$$

When the user issues the display command for this graph, the graph
will be parsed, at the end of which, when reaching the pattern P,
the composed domain-transformation Dt1 o Dt2 is applied to the
domain of P. Next step is to allocate enough space to contain the
discrete data for the fleck. This data consists of the colour for
every pixel in the fleck. This colour can subsequently be
calculated from the colour function of P and the appropriate
transformations using equation (3.2).

    In what form the discrete data will be maintained has not yet
been decided. Possibilities are:

        binary tree
        quad tree
        2D rectangular raster
        run-length encoding

Because of the huge amount of data that has to be stored this way,
we are forced to choose the most space-efficient form of coding
here.

3.3 Attributes of the flecks.

Apart from the pixel-data, a number of flags is kept in every fleck. These flags carry the value of the concatenated attributes of:

        visibility
        detectability
        highlighting
        level

These attributes have in common that they all control some aspect of the state the fleck is in, rather than stating some geometric property.
    Visibility could be implemented by deleting or inserting the fleck in the fleck chain, but more efficient is to have a flag with every fleck indicating whether it is visible or not.
    The priority attribute is an exception again: it is not kept as an explicit flag in the fleck, but it is used to determine the order in which the flecks should occur in the fleck chain. This order will be used when displaying the flecks on some raster-screen: lowest priority first (Painter's algorithm).

4.0 Attributes in more detail.

In this chapter we will study the attributes visibility, level and detectability in more detail. These attributes may be considered representative for all other attributes.

    The following notation to identify flecks will be used:

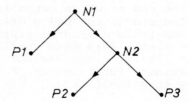

        Figure 5.

The fleck corresponding with the path N1-P1 will be denoted f11. Likewise the other flecks are f122 and f123, corresponding with N1-N2-P3 and N1-N2-P3 respectively.
    Furthermore, to indicate the value of some attribute within a node N, the notation 'N.V' will be used. It will mean that the attribute under consideration has the value V in node N.

The visibility attribute.

4.1 The_visibility_attribute.

In computing the visibility for flecks, the following rule is
applied:

    A fleck V is visible, if and only if every node on the path
    corresponding with V has the visibility attribute value
    'visible'.

Consequently, whenever one node carries the value 'invisible', the
fleck will be invisible. The logic behind this is that when an
object is made invisible, it should be completely invisible, and
not only some parts of it. Partially invisible objects can be
obtained by changing the visibility attributes at a lower level in
the graph.
An example:

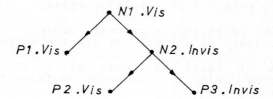

Figure 6: a pattern graph with the visibility
attributes shown.

Only the fleck f11 is visible, the other flecks (f122, f123) will
be invisible.

    Flecks that are invisible due to attributes like visibility (or
level) are maintained within the fleck chain, but are skipped by
the process that displays the flecks because of the internal
attribute setting of the fleck.

4.2 The_level_attribute.

Suppose we have the following pattern graph:

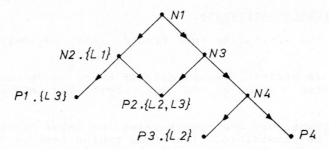

Figure 7: a pattern graph with the level
attributes shown.

The corresponding fleck chain is:

    f121 - f122 - f132 - f1343 - f1344

with the flecks in ascending priority order.
To obtain the level of a fleck, we use the following rule:

    A fleck is of level Li, when at least one node on the
    corresponding path in the graph contains the level Li as its
    level attribute.

Thus, the flecks in the above fleck chain have the following
levels:

f121	{ L1, L3 }
f122	{ L1, L2, L3 }
f132	{ L2, L3 }
f1343	{ L2 }
f1344	∅

Displaying level L1 means displaying the flecks f121 and f122. The
fleck f1344, which does not belong to any user-defined level, is
by default always displayed. Alternatively we could assign all
flecks without a user-defined level, the level L0. Using this
convention even the display of these flecks can be controlled
using the level-attribute.

4.3 The detection attribute.

Deciding whether a fleck is detectable or not, is done using the
following rule:

    A fleck V is detectable if and only if the corresponding path P
    in the graph has at least one node with the detection attribute
    value 'detectable'.
        Following the detection of V, the application-program will
    be given a set of names of nodes on P that had detection
    attribute value 'detectable'.

The detection attribute.

An example:

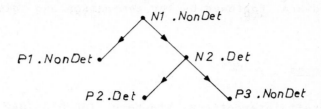

Figure 8: a pattern graph with the detectability
attributes shown.

Only the fleck f11 will not be detectable. This means pointing   at
f11   will   not   have   any   effect.   When   pointing at f122 or f123
however, the application program will be notified and additionally
given   the   names   of   the nodes N2 and P2 when f122 was meant, or
just the name of N2 when pointing at f123.

5.0   Conclusions.

A model   has   been   described   directly   oriented   towards   (2.5D)
interactive   raster   graphics.   This   raster   graphics orientation
shows itself in the 2D primitives for defining patterns and in the
specifically designed discrete representation of the flecks.
    Interactivity   is   provided   by   the   ability   to   change   the
structure   as   well   as   the   attributes   in the pattern graph, an
acyclic, directed graph. The leaves of a   pattern   graph   are   the
patterns,   which   can   be   composed   out   of   other patterns using
pattern expressions. The graph and the expressions form two layers
within   the   model: the   graph   being   the   dynamic   layer,   the
expressions the static layer.
    A preliminary implementation of the model   has   been   completed
recently   [7].   First   results   indicate that the conversion from a
continuous to a discrete representation while generating   a   chain
of   a   sizeable   number   of   flecks,   presents   the bottleneck when
displaying the graph. Improvements will have to be   made   to   this
implementation, in order to enhance interactivity.

    Another way to increase the performance is   by   adding   special
purpose hardware. Displaying the flecks is the first obvious place
where such hardware could be used. Equipping the   raster   graphics
station   with   intelligence   to   store,   interpret and display the
fleck chain, will no doubt decrease the response time   when   minor
changes   in   the   fleck   chain   (such   as changing attributes) are
required. In a further stage, hardware support for conversion from
continuous   representation   to   discrete   flecks   may   be desired,
especially to   cope   with   pictures   of   complex   structure   (many
flecks).   This   additional   hardware   will   almost   certainly mean
moving the task of creating the   flecks   to   the   raster   graphics
station   because   the hardware will be located there. Consequently
the interface with the hardware will move   such   that   a   suitable
linear   representation   of the pattern graph will have to be handed

Conclusions.

to   the   hardware.   Operations   like   domain-   and
colour-transformations are among the first tasks to be performed
by that hardware, followed by the generation and display of the
flecks.

6.0   References.

[1]   GKS, Draft international standard, ISO/DIS 7942
       (november 1982)

[2]   PHIGS: Programmer's Hierarchical Interactive
                              Graphics System.
       Baseline document, dated februari 29, 1984.

[3]   Smith, A.
       Colour gamut transform pairs.
       Computer Graphics, Vol 12, No 3, pp 12-19.

[4]   Guibas, L.J., Stolfi, J.
       A language for bitmap manipulation.
       ACM Transactions on Graphics, Vol 1, No 3, pp 191-214.

[5]   Bos, J. van den
       Calculus for Operations on Graphics Colour Rasters.
       Submitted for publication.

[6]   Hagen, P.J.W., et al.
       ILP: Intermediate Language for Pictures.
       Mathematical Centre Tracts 130, Amsterdam 1980.

[7]   Evers, P., Vos, J.
       Patroongraphen voor interactieve rastergrafiek (in Dutch).
       Master thesis nr 1, 1985
       University of Nijmegen, The Netherlands.

Theoretical Framework for Shape Representation and Analysis

Pijush K. Ghosh

S.P. Mudur

National Centre for Software Development
and Computing Techniques

Tata Institute of Fundamental Research
Homi Bhabha Road, Colaba
Bombay 400 005, India

ABSTRACT

In this paper we present a new scheme for shape representation and analysis using the Minkowski addition and decomposition operators. Since we are primarily interested here in building up a theoretical framework for this new scheme, the important results have been stated in the form of theorems. After briefly reviewing some of the important existing ideas in shape representation, we have indicated how our theorems lead to workable and/or efficient algorithms for shape design and manipulation. A few specific algorithms for 2-D shapes have also been presented at the end.

Keywords: Minkowski addition, Minkowski decompositon,
          shape representation, polytopes.

NATO ASI Series, Vol. F17
Fundamental Algorithms for Computer Graphics
Edited by R. A. Earnshaw
© Springer-Verlag Berlin Heidelberg 1985

1. INTRODUCTION

1.1. Shapes and their Representation

Representation of shape in two and three dimensions has deservedly received considerable attention from researchers in a variety of graphics application areas such as CAD/CAM, Graphic Art and other design disciplines. Shape representation is important in other areas too such as Pattern Recognition, Image Processing, Computer Vision, and Robotics. Depending on the application areas, a number of representation schemes have been proposed. We describe below three general representation schemes:

1. Boundary representation
2. Volumetric representation (constructive solid geometry, space enumeration)
3. Sweep representation (generalized cones, swept surface)

Typically each scheme defines a few primitive entities/objects, and allows a set of operators to operate on them. Therefore, each representation has certain computational properties that may be different from the other representation. This fact should be considered when assessing a representaton for possible use. For example:

. in the boundary representation, typically geometry and topology are explicitly modelled. The geometric primitive entities are points, curves, surfaces, and the topological primitives are vertices, edges, faces and shells. Computational geometric algorithms are defined for operating on the geometry (say intersection detection, evaluating normals, tangents etc.), while Euler operators are used as the base level operators for topological manipulation. Other operators like union, intersection, difference etc. are defined in terms of these. The availability of explicit representations of edges, faces, and vertices makes boundary representations quite useful in computer vision and graphics.

. in constructive solid geometry (CSG), the primitive entities are classical shapes such as rectangular blocks, cylinders, cones, spheres etc. The typical operators are the set operators like union, intersection, difference etc. CSG representation of objects in terms of more primitive solids is often useful in CAD/CAM, Robotics and Pattern Recognition, but can be inefficient for some interactive applications, say for use on a line drawing display.

. in generalized cone representation, a volume (or a plane surface in 2-D) is precisely defined by moving a (one parameter) planar cross-section curve c(u) at a fixed angle , called the eccentricity of the generalized cone, along a space curve f(s), called the spine of the generalized cone, transforming the cross-section according to a function h(s), called the sweeping rule. Generalized cones restricted to two dimensions are termed as ribbons. Generalized cone representation scheme is popular in computer vision, image processing and pattern recognition.

There are a number of other representation schemes, although they fall broadly in one of the above three categories. For example, the 'quad-tree' and 'oct-tree' representations are volumetric representations. And again, all these representations have different computational properties which depend on the type of primitive entities and the set of operators they use. (For more details, readers may refer to [1-6, 16-28]).

1.2 Shape Representation using Minkowski Addition Operator

In this paper we present a new framework for shape representation, using Minkowski addition as the basic operator.

The basic idea of the scheme is as follows:

Let B and T be two arbitrary sets in R^n space (i.e., n-dimensional real Euclidean space). The resultant set S is obtained by positioning B at every point of T, i.e., vectorially adding all the points of B with those of T. We denote this by:

$$S = B + T,$$

where ' + ' stands for Minkowski addition.

This idea may be further clarified using a simple example in 2-dimensions. Let the set B be an ellipse and T be an open coplanar cubic curve. If B can be considered as a brush and T as the trajectory, then the resulting figure S is obtained by moving the brush along the trajectory (Fig.1).

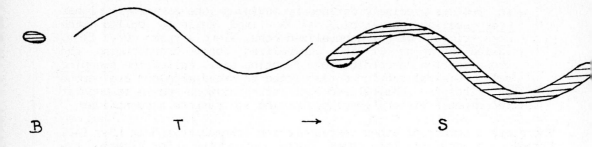

B   T   →   S

Fig.1 A simple example of brush-trajectory in 2-D.

We shall show that this same analogy can be extended in case of 3-D
also. It is not difficult to see that the Minkowski addition operator
is closely related to the sweep representation scheme. The sweep
representation is a particular case where the generalized cylinder is
the resultant set S of B the planar cross-section set being positioned
at every point of T the spine curve. The Minkowski addition as
defined does not permit a sweeping rule to be defined on the brush
shape. The example shown in Fig.2 demonstrates the similarity between
these schemes, where B is a triangle and T is a straight line. The
resultant set S is a rectangular wedge.

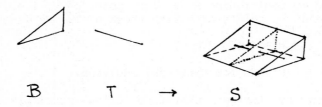

B   T   →   S

Fig.2 A rectangular wedge - resultant of
addition operation.

In two dimensions, many of the basic shapes occurring in printed texts
and other graphic artwork can, in fact, be most naturally described as
shapes generated by a brush moving along a given trajectory. This is
obvious from techno-historical reasons as well. The structure, usage
and results of the lettering design systems like METAFONT [13], and
PaLATINO [10] corroborate this. A number of graphic design systems
use the concept of brush-trajectory quite often. A sample page of
PaLATINO output (Fig.3) shows how the variations of the brush can be
used to produce a variety of type faces (in one of the Indian scripts)
from a single trajectory or skeleton.

In three dimensions, the volume of many biological and manufactured objects is naturally described as the 'sum volume' of two sets B and T in R^3. Fig.4 shows some examples.

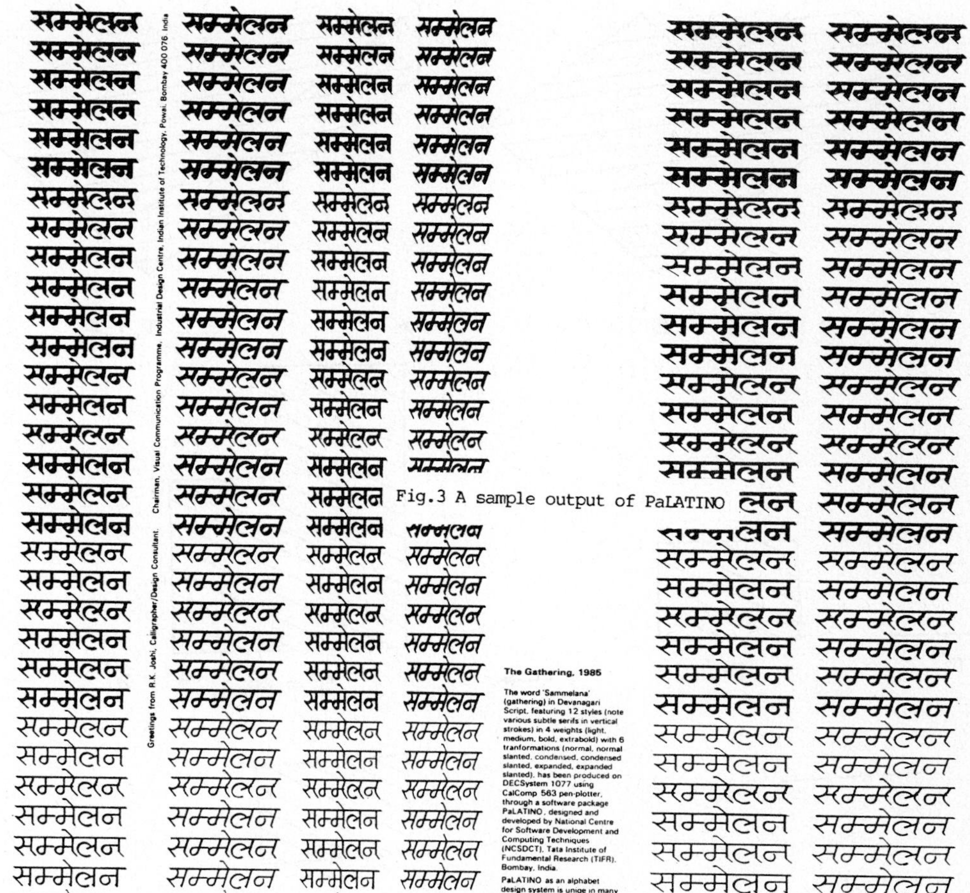

Fig.3 A sample output of PaLATINO

Greetings from R.K. Joshi, Calligrapher/Design Consultant. Chairman, Visual Communication Programme, Industrial Design Centre, Indian Institute of Technology, Powai, Bombay 400 076, India

The Gathering, 1985

The word 'Sammelana' (gathering) in Devanagari Script, featuring 12 styles (note various subtle serifs in vertical strokes) in 4 weights (light, medium, bold, extrabold) with 6 tranformations (normal, normal slanted, condensed, condensed slanted, expanded, expanded slanted), has been produced on DECSystem 1077 using CalComp 563 pen-plotter, through a software package PaLATINO, designed and developed by National Centre for Software Development and Computing Techniques (NCSDCT), Tata Institute of Fundamental Research (TIFR), Bombay, India.

PaLATINO as an alphabet design system is unique in many ways. A few of these unique features are: (i) The software is designed and developed in close collaboration of a Computer Scientist (P.K. Ghosh) and a graphic designer/calligrapher (R.K. Joshi) (ii) It includes features for non-linear composition of graphic elements which are not present in other existing type design systems (iii) The flexibility in the manipulation of graphic elements including their alignments, and the expandable coding scheme for identification of those elements, make PaLATINO a fully multi-lingual design system. It should be emphasised that this is the first time in India, such a collaboration of a Scientist and an artist has happened at NCSDCT, and has resulted into a system that can produce such a variety of typefaces of intricate subtlety and calligraphic complexity.

Design R.K. Joshi

Artwork VC Design Group/IDC

Computer Output NCSDCT, TIFR, Bombay

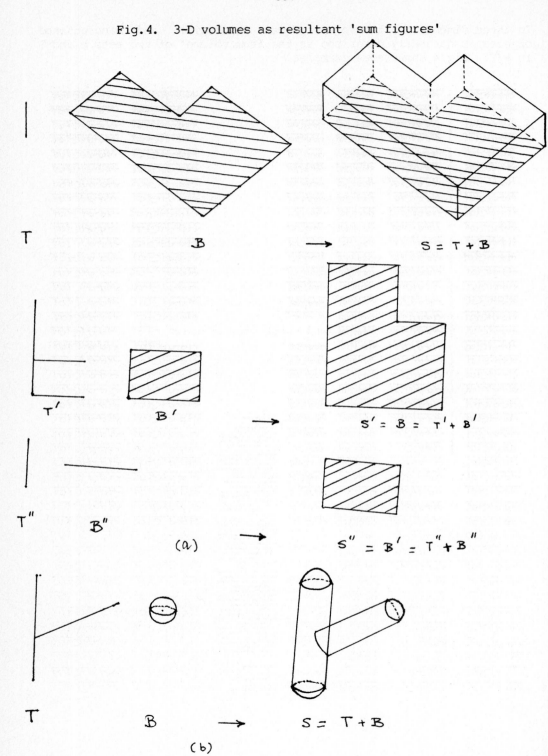

Fig.4. 3-D volumes as resultant 'sum figures'

Unlike the generalized cylinder representation, it is not necessary for one of the summands to be a space curve in our representation. Both B and T can be 2-D/3-D regions/volumes. It can be the other way round also, i.e., both B and T may be space curves. (Without loss of generality, we shall treat both B and T as homogeneous well-behaved regions/volumes bounded by simple closed curves or surfaces). Therefore, more complex surfaces or volumes than those generated by 'sweep' method can be generated. (see Fig.5)

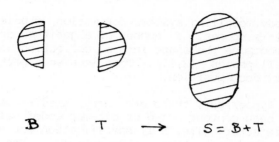

$$B \qquad T \quad \longrightarrow \qquad S = B + T$$

Fig.5 Both B and T are 2-D Regions

1.3 Minkowski Decomposition

The inverse problem, i.e., Minkowski decomposition is also very interesting, as well as intricate. It has many interesting applications too.

The decomposition problem can be divided into two parts:

a) Let S be some given shape (either in 2-D or 3-D). Is this shape at all decomposable? In other words, can S be expressed as a Minkowski sum of shapes in a nontrivial manner? (We shall elaborate the term 'nontrivial' in subsequent sections).

b) Let S and B be given. Can B be one of the summands of S? If so, then how can one determine a set T such that S = B + T? We shall denote this as follows:

$$T = S - B,$$

where '-' denotes Minkowski decomposition.

It should be noted here, however, that the decomposition S - B of two given figures does not in general exist. For example, there can be no decomposition of a triangle by a circle.

The applications of the Minkowski decomposition are many. A few examples are briefly discussed below:

. In NC machine tool path programming one essentially knows the shape of the cutting tool and the shape of the material that has to be removed. It is easy to see that successive use of the Minkowski decomposition operation will result in the tool path.

. In robotics path planning involves derivation of an optimal path for the robot vehicle to move amongst obstacles placed in some space. Minkowski decomposition of the free space will result in the subspace in which collision free movement is possible.

. In human body modelling systems for motion studies, animation, or medical purposes, a number of algorithms are described in order to decompose the shape into a collection of overlapping spheres, ellipsoids [2,15]. This is also a particular example of Minkowski decomposition.

. In digital typography, there are many traditional type fonts which have been contour coded or bit-map coded using digitizers. If brush-trajectory (i.e. B-T) specification for such fonts can be obtained, then detecting the structural similarities/differences amongst different type fonts should become possible. Also because of the image variational capability provided by computational techniques it should now become possible to provide variations in old designs without violating the basic design integrity as built in by the designer using manual methods of calligraphic design (Fig.6).

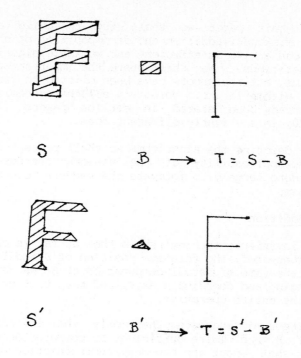

$$S \qquad B \rightarrow T = S - B$$

$$S' \qquad B' \rightarrow T = S' - B'$$

Fig.6 Decomposition of letter shapes

1.4. Outline of this paper

The major issue in Minkowski addition is efficient computation of the
value of sum set S when B and T are given. One naive solution is to
start with a bit-map-oriented B; position B pixel by pixel (or voxel
by voxel in case of 3-D) on the trajectory T, and for each position
the pixels/voxels covered by the brush B are set to black or one.
Such an algorithm usually ends up setting the same bit a large number
of times, depending on the size of B. Processing time increases
considerably with increase in resolution. Performance improvement is
possible by selectively setting only those bits not previously set to
one. This, however, would require each bit to be looked at
individually. For very high resolution, there may not be considerable
performance improvement.

In case of Minkowski decomposition, the problem appears far more
complex. There does not even exist any naive algorithm (like 'bit by
bit setting' algorithm in case of addition) to compute T if S and B
are given.

In the rest of this paper we shall try to build a theoretical framework for Minkowski addition and decomposition of objects so that at the end we can arrive at efficient and workable algorithms to carry out these operations. We shall state the important results in the form of theorems, but the proofs have been omitted to keep the length of this paper within limits. Moreover, all these theorems with their proofs have already been stated in earlier papers [7-9], and in [11,12,14,19,20] in a slightly different form.

We now briefly describe the algorithms we shall present at the end and the importance/applicability of the various theorems stated later. This is being done largely to motivate the readers to wade through a lot of formalism.

A) Minkowski Addition

The 'position invariance theorem' shows that as far as only the shape of a body is concerned, the relative position of B and T does not play any role. At the time of actual computation of S, we can choose any arbitrary origin and coordinate axis, and keep that coordinate space fixed during the entire operation.

The 'outline theorem' suggests that only the information of the boundaries of B and T are sufficient to compute the boundary of S. That is why we shall adopt the boundary representation of the object, a representation which is more compact than the bit-map.

But the question is, if boundaries of S, B and T are respectively P,Q and R (note: P,Q,R are curves/lines in 2-D and surfaces/planes in 3-D) and $P = f(Q,R)$, then what is the function 'f' ? The 'supporting points theorem' suggests a function f′ so that $P = f(Q,R) \subseteq P' = f'(Q,R)$. The 'continuity theorem' may be regarded as an extension of the 'supporting points theorem' to cater to situations when there are slope discontinuities in Q or R.

The 'sum of convex curves' shows that $P = P'$ when both Q and R are convex. We have also discussed in brief the procedure to derive P from P′ when $P \neq P'$.

The first algorithm for computing the sum of two convex polygons is simple and consists of following two steps: i) represent each polygon B and T by its boundary lines; ii) use the function f′ to compute P′ ; and since both are convex, P′ gives us P straight away.

The second algorithm computes the boundary curve P when Q and R are smooth, convex curves. Although we shall adopt the same procedure as in the previous algorithm, we shall also show that in some cases it is possible to arrive at P′ (= P) <u>analytically,</u> since the slopes of Q and R change continuously because of their smoothness. The third algorithm computes the P′ curve when both Q and R are simple polygons, not necessarily convex. We should mention that although we describe briefly how to compute P from P′ , we do not discuss it in detail any time as it is a fairly standard operation.

The next three theorems, i.e., the 'supporting function theorem', the 'convex hull theorem', and the 'supporting hyperplane theorem' are generalizations of the earlier theorems to higher dimensions. These theorems are applicable only for polytopes. Polytopes are once again generalizations to higher dimensions of the convex polygons in R^2 and the convex polyhydra in R^3 . The algorithms for computing S from B and T in 3-D can be derived in a similar fashion as shown in the 2-D cases.

B) Minkowski Decomposition

In case of the decomposition the first stage of the problem is to decide whether some given object S is at all decomposable. If so, then the subsequent problem is to decide whether some given B can become one of the summands of S or not. If 'yes', then one must define the procedures for computing T.

Therefore, most of the theorems on decomposition that we have presented deal with the conditions of decomposability of objects. In the case of 3-D, we have again restricted ourselves to the domain of polytopes. The 'theorem of indecomposability' specifies the kind of 2-D and 3-D convex objects that are not decomposable, whereas the 'theorem of decomposability' states what type of convex polygons and convex polyhedra are decomposable in principle. As an extension to these theorems we arrive at the 'convex polygon decomposition corollary' which states an interesting result: 'every convex polygon can be represented as the sum of triangles and straight lines'. This corollary also gives us a means of generating convex figures using only triangles and straight lines as primitive objects and Minkowski addition as the operator.

The next question that we have tried to tackle is that, even if some polytopes are indecomposable, then whether these can be approximated sufficiently closely by Minkowski sums of polytopes of some prescribed type. The two 'approximation theorems' give some clues for arriving at solutions to this problem.

The 'condition of summand theorem' goes one step ahead. This theorem suggests conditions that a given polytope B must satisfy in order to be one of the summands of some given polytope S.

The 'corner point theorem of convex figures' suggests a simple means of checking whether a certain class of shapes B can become summands of some class of shapes S.

In all the algorithms we have presented for decomposition, we have assumed that the condition of decomposability of S and then the conditions of B being a summand of S has been tested first using the above mentioned theorems.

Our first algorithm is to decompose a convex polygon into constituent triangles and straight lines. This is a direct consequence of the 'convex polygon decomposition corollary'.

The decomposition algorithm when both S and B are convex polygons is derived from the 'sum of convex polygons theorem'. We do an inverse operation to obtain T, such that S = B + T.

The 'circumscribed polygon theorem' suggests an algorithm for computing an approximate T when S and B are convex figures. The basic idea is to approximate S and B by circumscribing polygons L1 and L2 such that they have pairwise parallel and similarly directed sides. This algorithm is not presented explicitly since it is obvious from the theorem and the previous algorithm.

C) Special cases of Minkowski addition and decomposition

'Mixing of convex polytopes' is a special case of Minkowski addition of polytopes. The 'mixing' operation can be effectively used in interpolation, animation, shape analysis and representation. In this paper we shall briefly introduce the idea with the help of a few theorems. Interested readers are refered to [14].

Similarly 'reducibility of polytopes' is closely related to decomposability. It is applicable for the polytopes which are centrally symmetric. One interesting and simple way of forming centrally symmetric polytopes of a certain kind emerges out of the discussion.

2. MINKOWSKI ADDITION

2.1 A Few Basic Theorems

In this section we shall introduce a few basic theorems on Minkowski addition of figures which are later used to develop efficient algorithms for computing B + T.

Let B and T be two given well-defined regions/volumes bounded by oriented curves/surfaces in R^2/R^3. Then the Minkowski addition B + T can be defined as

$$S = B + T = \{b + t \mid b \in B \text{ and } t \in T\},$$

where (b+t) is vector sum of b and t.

THEOREM 1   OUTLINE THEOREM

Interior points of B and T never lead to the boundary points of the sum S.

Note: This theorem suggests that the boundary of the sum S can be computed from the boundary curves/surfaces of B and T. If P,Q and R denote the boundary curves/surfaces of S, B and T respectively, then

$$P = f(Q,R)$$

We shall therefore define a new operation, denoted by @, on the boundaries Q and R, such that

$$P = Q @ R,$$

and this operation will be termed as 'boundary addition' to distinguish it from Minkowski addition.

We wish to call the reader's attention to the fact that the sum Q @ R does not coincide with the geometrical locus of all sums q + r where q $\in$ Q and r $\in$ R.

It follows from the properties of the addition of points that:

1. $B + T = T + B$ $\qquad$ $Q @ R = R @ Q$
2. $(B + T_1) + T_2 = B + (T_1 + T_2)$ $\qquad$ $(Q @ R_1) @ R_2 = Q @ (R_1 @ R_2)$
3. $\lambda (B + T) = \lambda B + \lambda T$ $\qquad$ $\lambda(Q @ R) = \lambda Q @ \lambda R$

where λ is a scalar quantity.

(The definition of vector sum of points depends upon the origin. This apparent complication can be avoided if we assume mathematically the convention that each object considered will be translated so that its Steiner point lies at the origin. We are interested only on the shapes of the bodies – and not their position relative to an arbitrarily chosen origin).

THEOREM 2   POSITION-INVARIANCE THEOREM

The 'shape' of the sum region/volume B + T remains invariant under change of origin and parallel displacement of the summands B and T. Under these circumstances the sum only undergoes a parallel displacement. Mathematically,

$$(B^x) + T = B + (T^x) = (B + T)^x,$$

where x denotes linear translation.

Note: this theorem implies that it does not matter what is the relative position of B with respect to T and vice versa – the generated shape remains same. The rotation of the Summands, however, changes the sum.

The supporting points theorem stated below is one of the most important theorems for Minkowski addition of regions/volumes. Initially we state the theorem in R^2 space. This is done only for ease of understanding the implications of the theorem.

THEOREM 3   SUPPORTING POINTS THEOREM

If S = B + T, then the boundary curve P of S is a subset of the set of all points q + r, where $q \in Q$, $r \in R$, + denotes vector sum of points, and q is a "supporting point" of Q with respect to the line parallel to the direction of the tangent to R at r. A supporting point is a point such that the entire figure B lies locally on one side of the tangent in the said direction. Q and R are respectively the boundary curves of B and T.

Hereafter, all such pairs of q and r will be termed as "corresponding supporting points".

Note: Fig.7 pictorially demonstrates the above theorem.

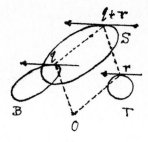

Fig.7 Demonstration of supporting point theorem

This operation of determining the set of all points q + r, where q and r are corresponding suporting points, will be denoted by the symbol '*'. Therefore, our theorem states that

$$P = Q @ R \subseteq Q*R$$

If both Q and R are smooth, closed, continuous curves, then for each point q of Q there is a corresponding supporting point r of R, and vice versa. This one-to-one onto relationship might not hold for general Q and R.

THEOREM 4   CONTINUITY THEOREM

Let r_1 and r_2 be two points in R and q_1 and q_2 be the corresponding supporting points in Q. Keeping r_1 fixed, let us consider the operation of bringing r_2 nearer to r_1 along R. In general, as r_2 gets nearer and nearer to r_1, the corresponding supporting point q_2 also gets nearer to q_1, so that eventually when r_2 coincides with r_1, q_2 also coincides with q_1. There are exceptional situations, however, in which this does not happen. That is for a r_2 very near to r_1, q_2 remains distant from q_1 along the curve. In such a situation, taking limiting values of r_2 and q_2, if $r_2 + \overset{\frown}{q_1 q_2}$ is added to Q*R, where $\overset{\frown}{q_1 q_2}$ denotes the entire boundary segment from q_1 to q_2 of Q, then Q @ R is still a subset of Q*R.

Note: The application of this theorem in computing Q*R is simple. Fig.8 shows one such example.

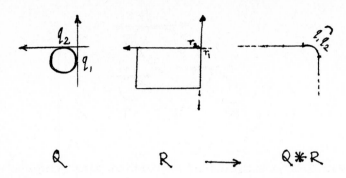

Fig.8 Application of Continuity Theorem

Although in R^3 the basic ideas behind the supporting points theorem or the continuity theorem still remain valid, obviously the supporting line has to be replaced by supporting hyperplane and so on. We shall discuss these topics in some later section in the case of convex 3-D polytopes.

2.2. Oriented Boundaries

The division of a plane by a simple closed continuous curve (known as 'boundary curve') into two parts is a topological concept, and we cannot continue further unless we introduce the notion of 'oriented curves'. For example, how can we mathematically distinguish between a full circular disk and a thin circular ring if we want to represent them in terms of their boundary curves? The idea of oriented curves is as follows:

If the boundary curve encloses a region, we shall consider this region as a positive area and give counter clockwise orientation to the boundary curve. On the other hand, if the boundary curve encloses a hole, we shall consider this as a negative region and give clockwise orientation to the boundary curve.

Using this convention, the disk and the ring can be represented as shown in Fig.9.

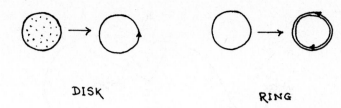

DISK   RING

Fig.9 Representation of full disk and thin
ring by oriented boundary curves.

With the introduction of the idea of 'oriented' boundary curves, the
definition of the corresponding supporting points has to be slightly
modified. At the corresponding supporting points q and r, the tangent
lines should not only be parallel, but should be similarly oriented
too. (Fig.10)

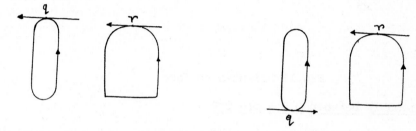

Fig.10 (a) q and r are corresponding supporting points

(b) q and r are not corresponding supporting points

Similarly in case of 3-D volumes, the boundary surfaces are assigned
appropriate orientations. (Fig.11).

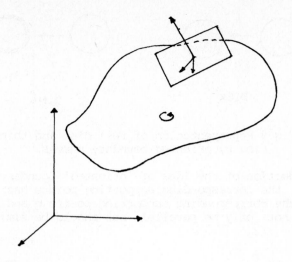

Fig.11 Oriented surface

2.3. Relationship between Q @ R and Q*R

Until now we have seen that

$$P = Q @ R \subseteq Q*R$$

And the supporting points and continuity theorems have given us clues to compute Q*R. In this section we shall deal with the problem of extracting Q @ R from Q*R.

Case 1

THEOREM 5 SUM OF CONVEX CURVE THEOREM

If Q and R are both convex, then

$$Q @ R = Q*R$$

This theorem gives rise to a number of interesting corollaries. The interested readers are referred to [9].

Case 2

In case both the curves Q and R are not convex, Q @ R can be obtained by identifying the positive area(s) enclosed by Q*R. This identification of the positive area(s) can be done by determining the winding numbers of the regions enclosed by the oriented curve Q*R. Fig.12 shows how it works.

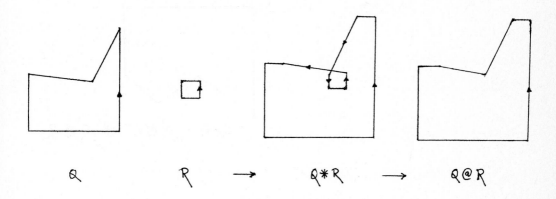

Fig.12 Computation of Q @ R from Q*R

The method of identification of the positive area by calculating winding numbers etc. is not discussed further in this paper.

Case 3

The continuity theorem has shown us how it is possible to take care of the situation when for a point $r \in R$, there are more than one corresponding supporting points in Q. Here we shall discuss another elegant method from the algorithmic point of view:

If for some point $r \in R$, there are n number of corresponding supporting points $q_1, q_2, \ldots q_n$ in Q, then compute $Q_1{*}R, Q_2{*}R, \ldots Q_n{*}R$, considering each time only one of the q's, and for all q's from 1 to n. Then compute $Q_1 @R, Q_2 @R, \ldots$. The union of those regions, i.e., $(Q_1 @R) \cup (Q_2 @R) \ldots$) will be the required Q @ R (cf. Fig.13).

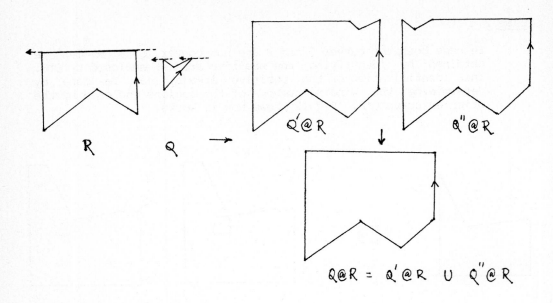

Fig.13 Multiple supporting points

2.4. Addition of Convex Polytopes

As already mentioned, the theorems and ideas discussed so far can be extended from 2-D regions to 3-D volumes, although they become much less intuitive and more mathematical.

In this section, we shall restrict ourselves to the domain of convex polytopes (in general, we shall assume polytopes are convex and omit the word 'convex' hereafter). But all the results we present are applicable to d-dimensional space, which implies convex polyhedra in R^3 and convex polygons in R^2. Readers can see for themselves that these results are mere generalizations of the ideas presented earlier for 2-D.

2.4.1. Supporting Function Theorem

Let $B \subset R^d$ be a nonempty set. The 'supporting function' $H(B,u)$ of B is defined for all $u \in R^d$ by

$$H(B,u) = \sup\{<b,u> \mid b \in B\}$$

Refer to Fig.14.

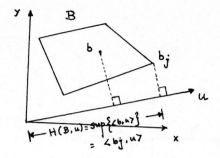

Fig.14 supporting Function

THEOREM 6   SUPPORTING FUNCTION THEOREM

Let B and T be two given polytopes. Let $H(B,u)$ and $H(T,u)$ be the supporting functions of B and T. Then the Minkowski sum of B and T, i.e., $B + T$ is defined to be the convex set whose supporting function is given by the equation

$$H(B + T,u) = H(B,u) + H(T,u).$$

2.4.2. Convex Hull Theorem

THEOREM 7   CONVEX HULL THEOREM

Let b_i $(i = 1,\ldots,n)$ be the (position vectors of the) vertices of B and t_j $(j=1,\ldots, m)$ be the vertices of T. then we define,

$$B + T = \text{conv } \{b_i + t_j \mid i=1,\ldots,n \text{ and } j=1,\ldots m\},$$

Where 'conv' denotes convex hull. (Fig.15)

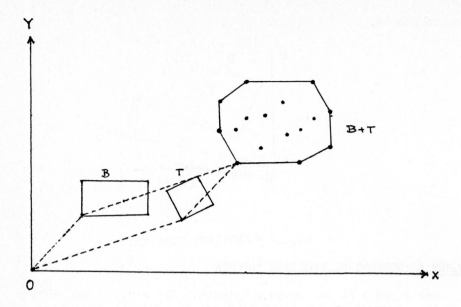

Fig.15 Sum of convex polytopes as convex hull.

2.4.3. Supporting Hyperplane Theorem

This theorem is analogous to the supporting point theorem for 2-D figures. In its present form it is only applicable to convex shapes.

Let us first define supporting hyperplane of a convex polytope.

If for some nonzero $u \in R^d$ - we have $H(B,u) < \infty$, the hyperplane

$$L(B,u) = \{x \in R^d \mid \langle x,u \rangle = H(B,u)\}$$

is defined as the 'supporting hyperplane' of B. Note that the supporting hyperplane $L(B,u)$ has the outward normal u (Fig.16)

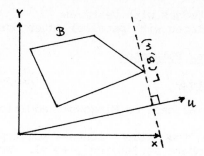

Fig.16 Supporting hyperplan L(B,u) with outward normal u

In 2-D the line (shown dotted) is the supporting hyperplane of B with outward normal u. In 3-D, L(B,u) is a plane.

If $u \neq 0$, the L(B,u) $\cap$ B is called a face of B, which will be denoted by F(B,u).

THEOREM 8   SUPPORTING HYERPLANE THEOREM

   If S = B + T, then for each $u \neq 0$,

   F(S,u) = F(B,u) + F(T,u).

F(B,u) is the mathematical definition of a face of B. Normally, by 'face' we mean the maximal proper face of B. Mathematically however, this is termed as 'facets'.

From the above theorem, we can come to the conclusion that if S=B + T, then S is also a convex polytope and

   1. The facets of S are obtained by

      i) adding facets of B and T,

      ii) adding a facet of one of these polytopes with an edge or vertex of the other, and

      iii) adding non-parallel edges of these polytopes

   where the facets, edges and vertices so added lie in the supporting hyperplanes with parallel outer normals.

   2. The edges of S are obtained by

      i) adding pairs of parallel edges, and

ii) adding edges with vertices   lying in supporting
hyperplanes with parallel outer normals.

2.5 Mixing of Convex Polytopes

2.5.1. Introduction

'Mixing' is a special case of Minkowski addition of polytopes.

Let B_1 and B_2 be two given convex polytopes and λ and λ_1 be two positive scalar numbers satisfying $\lambda + \lambda_1 = 1$. We can define

$$B_\lambda = \lambda B_1 + \lambda_1 B_2 = \lambda B_1 + (1-\lambda) B_2.$$

This operation of forming B_λ is known as 'mixing' of B_1 and B_2. Clearly, B_λ is the geometric locus of points b_λ dividing the segments $b_1 b_2$ connecting points of B_1 and B_2 (since $b_1 \in B_1$, $b_2 \in B_2$) in the ratio $(1-\lambda):\lambda$.

Example 1. We take two convex polygons B_1 and B_2 whose sides are not pairwise parallel. The resulting B_λ is shown in Fig.17.

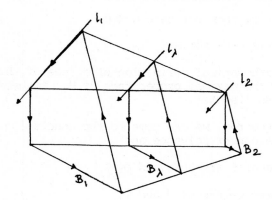

Fig.17 Mixing of convex polygons with non-parallel sides

The authors feel that this idea of mixing figures and bodies can be effectively used in interpolation, animation, image analysis, and shape representation. So far the authors are unaware of its use. However, the authors intend to experiment with this idea further in the future.

2.5.2. Area of 2-D sum figure and Mixed area of Summands

Let B_1 and B_2 be two convex figures and let B_λ be the sum figure where

$$B_\lambda = \lambda B_1 + \lambda B_2 \text{, and } \lambda + \lambda_1 = 1.$$

Let $J(B)$ stand for the area of the figure B.

It can be shown that the area of the sum figure B can be expressed in the form

$$J(B_\lambda) = \lambda^2 J(B_1) + 2\lambda\lambda_1 J(B_1,B_2) + \lambda_1^2 J(B_2)$$

where $J(B_1,B_2)$ is the 'mixed area' or the figures B_1 and B_2.

To get an idea of the 'mixed area', let us take two convex polygons B_1 and B_2 (Fig.18). Subject B_1,B_2 to a parallel displacement so that the origin becomes an interior point. Let h_i denote the distance from the origin to the side b_i of B_1.

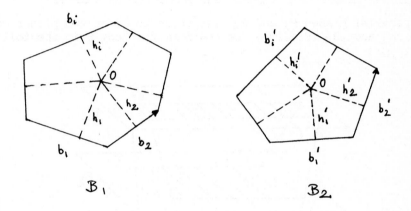

Fig.18 Mixed Area of two convex polygons

Clearly, the area of B_1 is

$$J(B_1) = \frac{1}{2} \sum_{i=1}^{n} b_i h_i = \frac{1}{2} \sum b_i h_i$$

Since any two arbitrary polygons can be thought of as having pairwise parallel and similarly directed sides by means of introducing sides of zero length, we can suppose that B_1 and B_2 also have pairwise parallel and similarly directed sides. Therefore, we can write

$$J(B_2) = \frac{1}{2} \sum_{i=1}^{n} b_i' h_i' = \frac{1}{2} \sum b_i' h_i'$$

The 'mixed area' $J(B_1,B_2)$ is then defined as

$$J(B_1,B_2) = \frac{1}{2} \sum b_i h_i' = \frac{1}{2} \sum b_i' h_i$$

Obviously if $B_1 = B_2$, then $J(B_1, B_2) = J(B_1) = J(B_2)$.

It should be noted that there are a number of interesting properties of 'mixed area' of two figures.

THEOREM 9 INEQUALITY THEOREM OF BRUNN-MINKOWSKI

Let there be two convex figures B_1 and B_2 , and $B_2 = \lambda B_1 + \lambda_1 B_2$ $(\lambda + \lambda_1 = 1; \lambda \lambda_1 \geqslant 0)$ having areas F_1, F_2, F_2 respectively. Then the following inequality is valid:

$$\sqrt{F_2} \geqslant \lambda \sqrt{F_1} + \lambda_1 \sqrt{F_2}$$

where the equality sign holds only when B_1 and B_2 are 'homothetic'.

2.5.3. Planar Sections of convex bodies and sum of figures

In two parallel planes P_1 and P_2 let there be given two planar convex figures B_1 and B_2 (Fig.19). We now form the body S in the following manner:

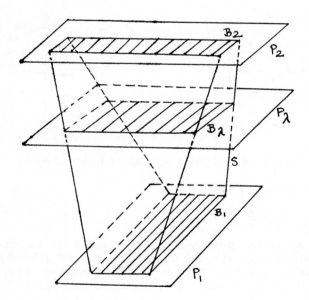

Fig.19 Planar section of convex bodies

We connect every point b_1 of B_1 with every point b_2 of B_2 with a line segment. The collection of these segments fills out some body S (In Fig.19 B_1 and B_2 are represented as two non-similar parallelograms).

Consider the section B_λ of the body S by the plane $P_\lambda = \lambda P_1 + \lambda_1 P_2$. Obviously the plane P_λ is parallel to the planes of B_1 and B_2 and divides the distance between them in the ratio $\lambda_1 : \lambda$. Each segment $b_1 b_2$ of the body S (b_1 in B_1, b_2 in B_2) intersects the plane P_λ in a point which divides this segment in the ratio $\lambda_1 : \lambda$, that is, at the point

$$b_\lambda = \lambda b_1 + \lambda_1 b_2.$$

Denote the set of points b_λ by B_λ. Then

$$B_\lambda = \lambda B_1 + \lambda_1 B_2.$$

In Brunn-Minkowski inequality we supposed that the mixed figure lies in one plane. Still, this inequality is valid even when B_1, B_2 (and B_λ) are in parallel planes. The Brunn-Minkowski inequality retains the form:

$$J(B_\lambda) \geqslant \lambda\, J(B_1) + \lambda_1 J(B_2)$$

If we consider $J(B_\lambda)$ the area of the section of S by the plane $P_\lambda = \lambda P_1 + \lambda_1 P_2$ as a function of S, then $J(B_\lambda)$ is a concave function.

If B_1 and B_2 are homothetic, then

$$J(B_\lambda) = \lambda\, J(B_1) + \lambda_1 J(B_2)$$

When B_1 and B_2 are homothetic, the body S becomes, as is easily shown, a cylinder, a truncated cone or, a cone (Fig.20)

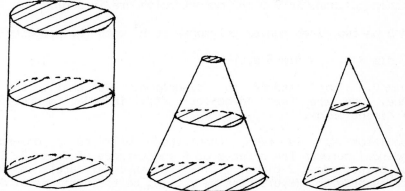

Fig.20 Cylinders, truncated cones, cones

In the accompanying drawings, the cylinder truncated cone and simple cone are shown to be circular, although this need not be the case.

3. MIKOWSKI DECOMPOSITION

3.1. Minkowski Decomposition in the Mathematical Sense

We have said earlier in Section 1.3 that Minkowski decomposition, which is the inverse problem of Minkowski addition, has to be examined in two stages.

In the first stage, we have to answer the question whether any given shape S is at all decomposable. If λ is a scalar quantity and $\lambda > 0$, then any translate of λS is said to be 'positively homothetic' to S. If $0 \leqslant \lambda \leqslant 1$, then λS is trivially a summand of S for

$$S = \lambda S + (1-\lambda)S.$$

A region/volume is said to be decomposable if it possesses a summand which is not positively homothetic to the region/volume. Thus a decomposable shape is one that can be expressed as a vector sum in a non-trivial manner.

In the first stage if the answer is 'yes', i.e., the given object S turns out to be decomposable, then the question in the second layer is whether a given object B can be a summand of S; and again if it is 'yes', then what is that T such that

$$S = B + T.$$

3.2. Decomposability of polytopes

In general, the decomposition problem is a more complex problem compared to addition. We shall restrict ourselves to convex polytopes (i.e., convex polygons in 2-D and convex polyhedra in 3-D).

Let S and B be two given convex polytopes in R^d with the property that

$$\dim F(S,u) = \dim F(B,u) \qquad \qquad \dots\dots(1)$$

for all $u \neq 0$. ('dim' stands for dimension. We shall, for our convenience, use the term 'd-object' etc. in order to specify an object of dimension d).

If the condition (1) is true, then there will be a one-to-one correspondence between the r-faces of S and r-faces of B (r= 0, 1..., d-1, i.e., point, edge, 2-plane, ...(d-1) dimensional face) in which F(S,u) corresponds to F(B,u). Let $s_1, \dots, s_m$ be the vertices of S and $b_1, \dots, b_m$ be the corresponding vertices of B. If an edge of S joins s_i to s_j, then a parallel edge of B will join b_i to b_j. Hence

$$\lambda (s_i - s_j) = b_i - b_j \qquad \qquad \dots (2)$$

where $\lambda > 0$ is a real scalar quantity whose value depends on i and j. Equation (2) implies that the edges are parallel and similarly oriented.

If, instead of (1) we impose the weaker condition

$$\dim F(S,u) \geqslant \dim F(B,u) \dots (3)$$

for all $u \neq 0$, then similar considerations will apply, except that the correspondence is no longer one-to-one, and several vertices of S may correspond to the same vertex of B. It will be convenient to continue using b_i for the vertex B that corresponds to s_i, with the understanding that $b_1, \dots b_m$ may not all be distinct. Relation (2) also hold in this case if we put $\lambda = 0$ when $b_i = b_j$. If, in addition to (3), all the values of λ defined by (2) satisfy $0 \leqslant \lambda \leqslant 1$, then we shall write $S \geqslant B$. (Fig.21).

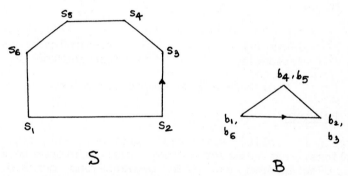

Fig.21 Two convex polygons S and B,
where S>B - an example in 2-D

THEOREM 10 CONDITION OF SUMMAND THEOREM

The polytope B is a summand of S if and only if $S \geqslant B$.

Note: this theorem shows that if S and B are two convex polygons, then B will be a summand of S if and only if for every edge of B, there is a parallel and similarly directed edge in S, and that edge of S is greater than or equal to the corresponding edge in B. Similarly in case of 3-D polyhedra, one has to compare the corresponding edges and 2-faces of S and B.

The next two theorems, which are consequences of theorem 10, will enable us to deduce what type of polytopes are indecomposable, and what type are decomposable in principle. Before stating the theorem, we shall first define three kinds of polytopes.

Simplex Polytope

The simplest type of d-polytopes is the 'd-simplex'. A d-simplex is defined as the convex hull of some d+1 affinely independent points.

In 2-dimension, the 2-simplex contains 3 non-collinear points, i.e., triangle. In 3-dimension, the 3-simplex contains 4 non-coplanar points, i.e., tetrahedron (Fig.22).

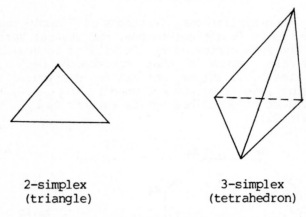

2-simplex
(triangle)

3-simplex
(tetrahedron)

Fig.22 2- and 3- Simplex polytopes

Simplicial Polytope

A d-polytope S is called simplicial provided all its facets are (d-1)-simplices. As examples of simplicial polytopes we mention: the d-simplex, d-octahedron etc. In 3-dimensions octahedron is a simplicial polytope since each of its facets is a 2-simplex, i.e., a triangle.

Simple Polytope

The simple polytope has exactly d facets incident with each of its vertices.

THEOREM 11 THEOREM OF INDECOMPOSABILITY

If all the 2-faces of a d-polytope S are triangles, then S is indecomposable.

THEOREM 12 THEOREM OF DECOMPOSABILITY

Except for the d-simplex, every simple d-polytope S is decomposable.

3.3. Reducibility of Polytopes

Another property of polytopes closely related to decomposability is that of 'reducibility'.

Let K be any convex set, and let us write −K for (−1)K the reflection of K about the origin. Then

$$K + (-K) = \{k_1 - k_2 | k_1, k_2 \quad K\}$$

is called the difference set of K. A convex set H is said to be 'reducible' if it is the difference set of a convex set K which is not homothetic to H.

Since

$$-H = (-K) + (K) = K + (-K) = H.$$

'central symmetry' in the origin is a necessary condition for reducibility. Obviously decomposability is also a necessary condition. A sufficient condition is given in the next theorem.

THEOREM 13   THEOREM OF REDUCIBILITY

A centrally symmetric polytope S is reducible if and only if it possesses a summand B which is not centrally symmetric.

Note: This theorem, along with 'condition of summand theorem', enables us to decide whether a given polytope is reducible or not. For example, in R^2 every centrally symmetric polygon is reducible unless it is a parallelogram. This follows from the fact that every summand of a parallelogram is either a parallelogram or a line segment, and so is centrally symmetric. On the other hand, it is easy to construct a noncentrally symmetric summand of any centrally symmetric 2n-gon if n>2.

There is an interesting way of forming a certain kind of centrally symmetric polytopes. This kind is known as 'Zonotope' in R^d which is defined to be the vector sum of a finite number of line segments.

If in case of a Zonotope, no d of the line segments are parallel to a hyperplane, it is called 'cubical' polytope. The name is such since each of its (d−1) faces (i.e., facets) is combinatorially equivalent to the (d−1)-cube C^{d-1} (Fig.23).

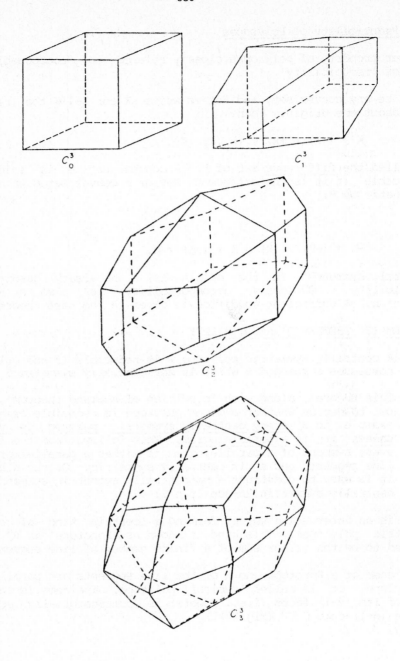

Fig.23 Cubical polytopes

3.4. Approximation of Polytopes by Minkowski Addition

In Section 3.2 we examined the conditions under which a polytope was decomposable with respect to the vector addition. In this section we shall very briefly consider the related problem of deciding whether a given polytope can be approximated arbitrarily closely by vector sums of polytopes of some prescribed type.

For example it is easily deduced from the results of Section 3.2 that every bounded convex region in the plane can be approximated arbitrarily closely by vector sums of triangles and line segments. Therefore, it is a natural question to ask whether every convex body in R^3 can be approximated by vector sums of tetrahedra, triangles, and line segments. From the results discussed in this section we shall be able to prove that this is not the case, and, for example, an octahedron cannot be approximated in this way.

The properties we shall be discussing relate to homothety classes of polytopes, rather than to polytopes themselves, and for this reason it will be convenient to select one definite polytope from each homothety class. We do this as follows:

Define $C \subset P$ to be the class of all polytopes S in R^d whose diameter diam $S = 1$, and whose Steiner point coincides with the origin. Then C contains precisely one polytope from each homothety class except for the class of 0-polytopes. Since the Steiner point of a polytope is a relative interior point of S, we can deduce that C is bounded.

Now let K be any closed subset of C. We notice that K is compact, and each $K_i \in K$ is of dimension at least 1. Write ΣK for the set of all polytopes which can be written as finite vector sums

$$\lambda_1 K_1 + \ldots \ldots + \lambda_r K_r$$

where $K_i \in K$, and $\lambda_i \geqslant 0$. Obviously, the Steiner points of all these polytopes lie at the origin. Hence $(\Sigma K) \cap C$ consists of all those vector sums which have diameter one, and we write

$$\sigma(K) = cl((\Sigma K) \cap C)$$

for its closure.

If $S \in C$ is a given polytope then we shall say that S is approximable by the class K if there exist members of ΣK arbitrarily close to S, or, equivalently,

$$S \in \sigma(K).$$

THEOREM 14   APPROXIMATION THEOREM OF INDECOMPOSABLE POLYTOPE

Let K be a given class of polytopes which is a closed subset of C.   If S is an indecomposable polytope, and is approximable by the class K, then S ∈ K.

THEOREM 15   NONEXISTENCE THEOREM OF APPROXIMATION

There exist no nontrivial closed universal approximating classes K⊂C in d⩾3 dimensions.   (Here 'nontrivial' means K ≠ C).

Note: This gives us the answers we have raised in the begining of this section.

3.5. A Few More Theorems on Decomposition in R^2

Although the world is 3-dimensional, there are many important applications in two-dimension. The theorems we have discussed so far for polytopes are applicable for 2-dimensional convex polygons too. In this section we shall present a few more theorems on decomposition in R^2. We plan to extend these theorems for 3-dimensional bodies too in the immediate future.

THEOREM 16   CORNER POINT THEOREM OF CONVEX FIGURES

Let Q and R be two closed convex curves.   Let q ∈ Q and r ∈ R denote two corresponding supporting points. If q+r is a corner point of the sum curve Q @ R, then both the points q and r are corner points of the curves Q and R respectively.

However, q and r can be corner points of the curves Q and R without the point q+r being a corner point of Q @ R.

If one of Q and R becomes nonconvex, this theorem does not hold true.

Note: This theorem provides a means to check whether a given convex figure Q can become one of the summands of a given convex figure P, or not.

For example, consider Fig.24.   The sum P = Q @ R is a convex polygon, whereas Q is a circle.

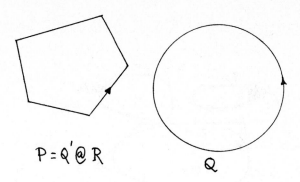

$$P = Q' @ R$$

Fig.24 Example for corner point theorem

Now Q @ R has a number of corner points whereas Q has no corner. That means Q cannot become a summand of P.

Corollary 1 CONVEX POLYGONS DECOMPOSITION COROLLARY

Every convex polygon can be represented as the sum of triangles and straight lines.

Note: this result is a corollary of the 'theorem of decomposability' of polytopes.

THEOREM 17 THEOREM OF CIRCUMSCRIBED POLYGONS

If Q and R are two convex curves and if Ll and L2 are two polygons which are circumscribed about these curves, and which have pairwise parallel and similarly oriented sides, then Ll @ L2 is a polygon circumscribing the curve Q @ R.

However, this theorem is not true if the sides of the polygons Ll and L2 are not parallel and similarly oriented.

Note: Fig.25 shows an example of this theorem.

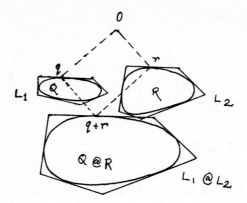

Fig.25 Addition of circumscribed polygons
         with pairwise parallel and similarly
         oriented sides.

If L1 and L2 have no pair of similarly oriented parallel sides,
the assertion of the theorem does not hold true. This may be
evident from Fig.26.

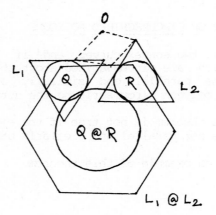

Fig.26 Sides of the circumscribed polygons are
         not parallel, and similarly oriented

4. ALGORITHMS

4.1. Algorithms for Minkowski Addition

4.1.1. Addition of two convex polygons

Let Q and R be the boundaries of two convex polygons. Let they be represented respectively as $(q_1, q_2, \ldots, q_n)$ and $(r_1, r_2, \ldots, r_m)$ where q_i's and r_i's are the directed edges. Let $ang(q_i)$ and $ang(r_i)$ denote the counter clockwise angle between the respective edges and some fixed axis, say x-axis. Without loss of generality we can assume that

$$ang(q_1) < ang(q_2) < \ldots < ang(q_n), \text{ and}$$
$$ang(r_1) < \ldots ang(r_m).$$

Algorithm

- merge $Q(=q_1, \ldots, q_n)$ with $R(=r_1, \ldots, r_m)$ retaining orders to get $P=(p_1, p_2, \ldots, p_k)$, where $k \leqslant m+n$ and $ang(p_1) < ang(p_2) < \ldots ang(p_k)$.

- while merging, if for any pair q_i, r_j, $ang(q_i) = ang(r_j)$, then combine them into a single edge $q_i + r_j$ in P.

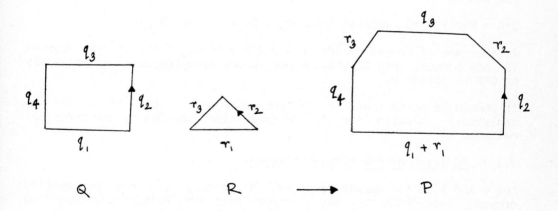

Fig.27 Addition of convex polygons

4.1.2. Addition of two convex figures whose boundaries are smooth, closed curves

Let Q and R be the boundary curves of the given convex figures B and T. Let they be represented in the following parametric forms:

$$Q = Q(u) = [Q_x(u), Q_y(u)]$$

and

$$R = R(v) = [R_x(v), R_y(v)] ,$$

where u and v are two scalar quantities varying within specified ranges.

To obtain the corresponding supporting point on Q for some point $R(v') \in R$, we have to solve the following equation:

$$\left[\frac{\partial R_y(v)/\partial v}{\partial R_x(v)/\partial v} \right]_{v=v'} = \left[\frac{\partial Q_y(u)/\partial u}{\partial Q_x(u)/\partial u} \right]$$

for u. Let the value of u that we obtain be u' which is obtained in terms of v'. Let u'=f(v'). Therefore, the corresponding supporting point of Q is Q(u').

Therefore,

$$Q*R = F(v') = [Q_x(f(v')) + R_x(v'), Q_y(f(v')) + R_y(v')]$$

In the case of convex curves, P = Q @ R = Q*R. If one of the curves is not convex, then P⊂Q*R. A post-processing operation is necessary on Q*R to obtain P.

It should be noted that it is not always possible to obtain an analytical solution for u'. In those cases one has to use numerical methods.

4.1.3. Addition of two simple polygons

Let Q and R be two simple polygons. Since they are not necessarily convex, every edge in R may have more than one disjoint corresponding points/edges in Q. Let $Q=(q_1, q_2, ..., q_n)$ and $R=(r_1, r_2, ..., r_m)$. We shall use the notation c(i,j) to denote the jth supporting point/edge in Q of the ith edge r_i of R; C(i) will denote the supporting set of r_i .

Algorithm

- for every edge r_i , determine $C(i)$.

- form as many distinct 'support groups' G_k $(1 \leqslant k \leqslant l)$ by taking one item from each of the support sets. Thus

$$G_k = (g_{k1}, g_{k2}, \ldots, g_{kn})$$

such that $g_{ki} \in C(i)$.

- for each group G_k, trace out the 'support polygon'. On completion of this step we shall get support polygons $P_1, P_2, \ldots, P_l$.

- The boundary P of the sum polygon can be then computed as $P = P_1 \cup P_2 \cup P_3 \cdots \cup P_l$.

* $C(1) = \{Start(q_2)\}$; $C(2) = \{Start(q_2), Start(q_4)\}$;

  $C(3) = \{q_4\}$; $C(4) = \{Start(q_1)\}$; $C(5) = \{Start(q_1)\}$.

* $G_1 = \{Start(q_2), Start(q_2), q_4, Start(q_1), Start(q_1)\}$;

  $G_2 = \{Start(q_2), Start(q_4), q_4, Start(q_1), Start(q_1)\}$.

*

fig contd....

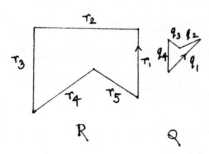

R   Q

contd...

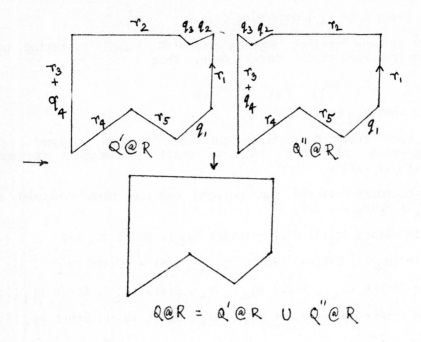

Fig.28 Addition of simple polygons

4.2 Algorithms for Minkowski Decomposition

4.2.1. Decomposition of convex polygons into triangles and straight lines

Step 1. Let P be the given convex polygon. Let

$$P = (p_1, p_2, \ldots, p_n).$$

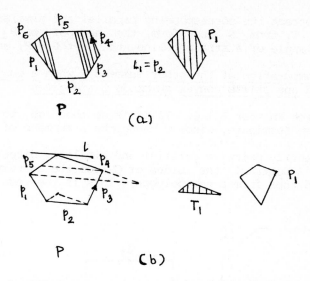

Fig.29 Decomposition of convex polygons into
triangles and straight lines.

If two sides p_j and p_k are parallel, then go to Step 2.
Otherwise go to Step 3.

Step 2. (polygon has parallel sides) $L_1 = \min \{p_j , p_k \}$ will be one of
the constituents straight line segments. Form a new convex
polygon, say P_1 where

$$P_1 = \{p_1 , p_2 , \ldots, (p_j - L_1), \ldots, (p_k - L_1), \ldots, p_n \}.$$

This polygon has at least one side less than P (Fig.29a).

If P_1 is not a triangle or a straight line, then set $P = P_1$ and
go to Step 1.

Step 3. (polygon has no parallel sides) Select any side of P, say p_i ,
and draw a supporting line 1 parallel to p_i . Let the sides of
P that meet 1 be p_j and p_k (In Fig.29b they are p_2 , p_4 , and
p_5 respectively).

Construct three triangles as follows: there are three sides
p_i , p_j and p_k . Each time take one of these three sides as one
edge of a triangle and construct the other two edges of the
triangle such that they become parallel to the other two sides.
(Those three triangles are shown dotted in Fig.29b).

Select the smallest of those three triangles, say T_1 . This
triangle T_1 will be one of the constituent triangles. (T_1 is
shown vertically shaded in Fig.29b).

Subtract the corresponding parallel and similarly directed edges of T_1 from P and form the new polygon P_1. If P_1 is not a triangle or a straight line, then set $P = P_1$ and go to Step 1.

4.2.2. Computation of the other summand R when a convex sum polygon P and one of its convex summands Q are given

. Check whether $P \geqslant Q$. If it is so then go to the next step. Else terminate, since Q cannot be a summand of P.

. Identify pairwise parallel and similarly directed sides of P and Q. Subtract the sides of Q from the corresponding sides of P and thus form a new polygon. This is the required R.

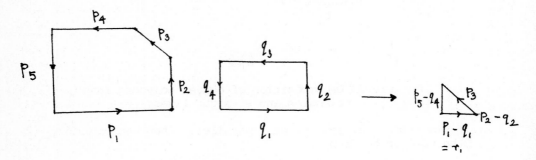

Fig.30 Decomposition of convex polygons.

5. CONCLUDING REMARKS

There is an increasing use of computers in the design, manipulation, analysis, and manufacture of physical objects. An important aspect of reasoning about such actions concerns the shape of objects and their motion in space. The study of problems of this nature requires not only the ability to represent shape but also the development of a framework or theory in which to reason about them and their movement in space. The authors have been investigating such a development for some time now. This paper presents an overview of this investigation. Fundamental theorems concerning the motion of objects in 2-space have been stated. Extension of these theorems to convex polytopes in higher dimensional space have also been shown. Some of these results have been known to the mathematicians for a very long time now and have been suitably adopted to our needs. The results on non-convex shapes have however been fully developed by the authors. Currently work is ongoing for dealing with general 3-D boundary represented shapes, not necessarily convex. A few algorithms for Minkowski addition and decomposition using the boundary representation of arbitrarily shaped regions in 2-space have also been designed and described. Needless to say, the framework is not restricted to the boundary representation. Use of the theoretical framework for reasoning with other representation schemes such as CSG or space enumeration appears an interesting problem for future research.

ACKNOWLEDGEMENT

We thank Dr. Pranab Ghosh, Dr. S. Mandal, Dr. S. Bhattacharya, and especially Mr. S. Ghosh for their willingness to discuss and formulate proofs of some of the theorems stated in this paper. It is a great pleasure to acknowledge Prof. R Narasimhan's keen interest and encouragement in our work. Finally, we thank Mr. P Kumaran for text inputing, editing, and good humour.

REFERENCES

1. Badler, N.I. and Bajcsy R.K. 'Three dimensional representations for computer graphics and computer vision', Computer Graphics 12, August 1978.

2. Ballard, D.H. and Brown, C.M. 'Computer Vision', Prentice-Hall, Inc., New Jersey 1982.

3. Beck, J., Hope, B. and Rosenfeld, A. 'Human and machine vision', Academy Press, New York 1983.

4. Binford, T.O. 'Visual perception by computer', IEEE Conf. on Systems and Control, Miami, December 1971.

5. Blum, H. 'Biological Shape and Visual Science (Part I)', J. Theor. Biol. 38, January 1973.

6. Brooks, R.A. 'Symbolic reasoning among 3-D models and 2-D images', Artificial Intelligence 17, August 1981.

7. Ghosh, P.K. and Mudur, S.P. 'The brush-trajectory approach to figure specification: some algebraic-solutions', ACM Trans. on Graphics 3, April 1984.

8. Ghosh, P.K. and Mudur S.P. 'A new set of operators for shape design and analysis by computer', Proc. of International Conference on CAD CAM/CAE for Industrial Progress, North Holland Publishing Co., June 1985 (to be published).

9. Ghosh, P.K. and Mudur, S.P. 'A theoretical framework for representation and analysis of shapes using Minkowski addition and decomposition operators',NCSDCT, Bombay, March 1985 (being sent for publication).

10. Ghosh, P.K. 'Introducing interactive computer drawing to the students of calligraphy and art with the help of PaLATINO system', CSI Bangalore Report, April 1982.

11. Guibas, L.J. and Stolfi, J. 'Lecture notes on computational geometry', CS 445, Stanford University, Stanford, California 1983.

12. Grunbaum, B. 'Convex polytopes', Interscience Publisher, London 1967.

13. Knuth, D.E. 'Mathematical typography', Bulletin of the American Mathematical Society 1, March 1979.

14. Lyusternik, L.A. 'Convex figures and polyhedra', Dover Publications, Inc., New York 1963.

15. O'Rourke, J. and Badler, N.I. 'Model-based image analysis of human motion using constraint propagation', IEEE Trans. PAMI 2, 4, November 1980.

16. Nevatia, R. and Binford, T.O. 'Description and recognition of curved objects', Artificial Intelligence 8, February 1977.

17. Requicha, A.A.G. 'Representations of rigid solid objects', Computer Surveys 12, December 1980.

18. Voeleker, H.B. and Requicha, A.A.G. 'Geometrical modelling of mechanical parts and processes', Computer 10, December 1977.

19. Yaglom, I.M. and Boltyanskii, V.G. 'Convex figures', Holt, Rinehart and Winston, New York 1961.

20. Young, I.E. et al, 'A new implementation for the binary and Minkowski Operators', CGIP 17, November 1981.

Section 9
Human-Computer Interface Issues

ASPECTS OF HUMAN MACHINE INTERFACE

Richard A. Guedj
SiGRID s.a.
ZA Courtaboeuf, 91 Les Ulis, France

"Computers are likely to affect their (people) environment the
ways cars did, provided the rapport between human beings and
computers will become sufficiently widespread and intimate.
Cars have given us a mobility that far exceeds what evolution
has provided us with."

(Walter A. Rosenblith)

"When you speak of rapport between men and machines and
illustrate it by the automobile, I wonder how often you drive
home in commuter traffic.

(Vannevar Bush)
("What computers should be doing", ed. John Pierce, 1962)

"Is the computer a car to be driven or an essay to be
written ?... Indeed the attempt is now being made to design
user interfaces giving access to the omputer's power by way of
interactions even easier to learn than driving a car."

(Alan Kay, 1984)

Introduction

In an increasing number of fields, more and more people are involved
in some kind of human-machine interaction. More and more scientists
for their daily scientific and technical activities interact with
computing systems.

Computer graphics people are not the only scientists concerned with
human-machine interaction although the relationship is complex and
rich.

NATO ASI Series, Vol. F17
Fundamental Algorithms for Computer Graphics
Edited by R. A. Earnshaw
© Springer-Verlag Berlin Heidelberg 1985

Most of their attention has been given so far to discover new ways of interacting or to simulate and to extend old ways. This has yielded spectacular and impressive results both in hardware and software, progressively embodied in basic or special purpose integrated circuits.

The human-machine relationship itself, the interaction process has probably been considered as either trivial or very difficult as it has received less attention.

This short paper is to comment on some aspects of this relationship while addressing two related questions :

Are we satisfied with present human-machine interactive techniques ?

What can we do to improve the human-machine interface in interactive computing systems ?

The difficulty of a satisfactory formal definition

Several signs indicate that we experience great difficulties in our attempts to define what is human-machine interaction. For instance, tenacious efforts of computer graphics community on a needed standard for computer graphics with the impressive results that we know [1], reveal the uneasiness to relate input to output, although it was not too difficult to accept classes of input following a logical scheme, and to get a consensus on output.

The IFIP Seillac-2 (1979) workshop on human-machine interaction whose basic goal was the understanding of interaction, provided several interesting results [2]. However the best definition that was reached and felt acceptable is not a very formal one : "interaction is a style of control".

Formal attempts at describing a "dialog" are also given in [2] (J. Van den Bos, Hopgood and Duce, Crestin, Shaw). Although they provided interesting results, those attempts do not seem to have led very far.

Attempts at indirect descriptions of interaction sometimes shed more light on the process. Such is the case with the interesting study by Dzida et al. on perceived qualities of Interactive Systems in [3].

Other views come from different fields and may provide us with the insight needed for necessary improvements.

For the socio-philosopher J. Habermas, interaction is defined as a "communicational activity dealing with symbolic exchanges, in contrast with and complementary to an instrumental activity dealing with the application of technical means and technical rules in sequence [4]". In other words, intrumental activity (which shows a lack of interaction) is when the only action allowed is to stop the sequence or get it back from a predefined point.

For the french philosopher P. Ricoeur, interaction implies such notions as motivation, intention, cause, agent, etc... [5].

Qualities_of_interactive_systems_involve_several_dimensions

Users and unfortunately too often designers of interactive systems are not in general aware that several dimensions are involved in the evaluation of the quality of the system. Stu Carol, Tom Moran and Alan Newell have been working on the question of what does 'a good interactive system' mean ? There is no obvious metric for 'good', but systems can be measured against a set of criteria, such as the following [6] :

Time. How long does it take a user to accomplish a given set of tasks using the system ?

Errors. How many errors does a user make and how serious are they ?

Learning. How long does it take a novice user to learn how to use the system to do a given set of tasks ?

Functionality. What range of tasks can a user do in practice with the system ?

Recall. How easy is it for a user to recall how to use the system on a task that he has not done for some time ?

Concentration. How many things does a user have to keep in mind while using the system ?

Fatigue. How tired do users get when they use the system for extended periods ?

Acceptability. How do users subjectively evaluate the system ?

Not all the dimensions play the same role for every user. It depends on the context, the history of the user with this system and other systems and the environment. However from a statistical study on user-perceived qualities of interactive systems by Dzida et al. in [3] we know that two qualities are perceived as playing a major role for all users. Those are "the adequation to the task at hand" and "the self-teaching capability of the system".

Despite the study on user-perceived qualities, one is not sure of the real diensions along which to assess an interactive system. How to caracterize them precisely ? To what extent one accepts some trade-offs between two or several related dimensions, such as the ease of learning traded to the difficulty of recall and the difficulty to learn traded to the ease to recall and to infer from what has been learned, etc... Obviously, this subject needs more investigation.

Yesterday's questions and issues on the design of interactive systems

(1) What are the qualities the system must show for a good human-machine interaction ?

(2) What is the minimum set of tools the system should exhibit ?

(3) Can the system use several media such as voice (input and output), music, noise, text, graphics, images, animated movies ?

(4) How many input devices are simultaneously active ?

What are the necessary ingredients and how to combine them to get a good interactive system is a question which continues to elude us. Most of the confusion comes from trying to resolve the question at this level.

Some facts and some beliefs on the issue today

(1) There are lots of interactive systems with happy users (for precise tasks they have to do). One can find them in many different fields (CAD of all kinds in technical or artistic areas).

(2) Qualities looked for in interactive systems can be well defined (independently of the users).

(3) Users can be well identified according to their needs, to their skills, to their potential ; interactive systems can be tailored accordingly.

Current practices for the design of user interfaces

It is fortunate that the focus of attention has shifted from the elusive and difficult notion of interaction to a somehow less fuzzier notion of "user interface". According to someone who has made essential contributions to the field, A. Kay [7] (the user interface) is "the software that mediates between a person and the programs shaping the computer into a tool for a specific goal, whether the goal is designing a bridge or writing an article".

Several principles embody the current style of user interface which seems to get some popularity. Perhaps the most important principle is ("What you see is what you get"). Manipulating the image in a certain way does something always predictable by the user.

Another powerful principle is that the user can monitor several processes at the same time (whose results are shown in different windows, the control being done through pointing at iconic representations in popping menus or the like).

Current expectations of users of interactive systems

As A. Kay put it the user interface creates "the user illusion" which is the simplified myth everyone builds to explain the system's actions. A powerful user illusion is the one which provides the user with a tool kit more or less universal. With that tool kit the user is able to build new objects whose behaviour is directly perceptible to his senses. The dynamic spreadsheet is a good example of state of the art tool kit. Some users are very good at using the spreadsheet to build dynamic simulations of user defined objects. Other users would like more powerful means.

Another user illusion being sought for, mainly by the artificial intelligence community is embodied in the notion of "agent". "The agent, when given a goal, could carry out the details of the appropriate computer operations, could ask and receive advice, offered in human terms, when stuck." [7]

Along with A. Kay, one is tempted to notice that giving the user the appropriate cues on what is going on, seems to be the essence of user-interface design. An agent-based system (being less intelligent than the user) would require a considerable more subtler approach [7].

User-interface design and the three levels of interaction

When designing a user interface several principles and guiding rules may be followed in order to create the sought for user illusion. However, depending on the "level of interaction", principles and guiding-rules have a different impact on the overall quality of user interface. We would like to suggest three different levels of influence : physical, perceptual, conceptual.

(1) <u>Physical level</u>

Questions of interest are the nature of the devices and their
ergonomy of use with respect to human performances, and
limitations.

It seems that the devices and the corresponding interactive
techniques for most applications, are available at a reasonable
cost.

(2) <u>Perceptual level</u>

If at the physical level, the designer of the user interface was
mainly concerned with the media for signals, signs and symbols,
at the perceptual level, he should be more concerned with the
shape and arrangement of information to get it perceived in such
a way that elicits from the user an action which lets the
dialogue progress.

Rules of thumb concerning form and style of messages, and
commands are getting better known. Knowledge on the use of
perceptual cues in association with words and experience in the
construction of adequate notations are slowly being gathered. I
believe that there is a body of knowledge from the experimental
psychologists still untapped.

(3) <u>Conceptual level</u>

At this level the designer of the user interface should be
concerned by the concepts involved in the user illusion. The
issue is whether the right abstractions have been choosen, if
they are consistent, stable, thought provoking. Also if those
abstractions can yield the way to more powerful ones without
sterilizing the user. I believe the essence of a good user
interface design lies in the choice of the right abstractions.

Conclusion

Needless to say the designer should focuss his attention at the conceptual level of the user interface, provided he can do a reasonable job at the other two levels.

References

[1] F.R.A. Hopgood, D.A. Duce, J.R. Gallop, D.C. Sutcliffe, Introduction to the Graphical Kernel System G.K.S., Academic Press, 1983

[2] R.A. Guedj et al., Seillac-II, IFIP Workshop on Methodology of Interaction, Seillac, France, May 1979, Proc. published by North-Holland, 1980

[3] W. Dzida, S. Herda and W.D. Itzfeld, User Perceived Quality of Interactive Systems Software Eng., Vol. SE-4, No. 4, July 1978

[4] J. Habermas, Technik und Wissenschaft als "Ideologie", Frankfurt-am-Main, Suhrkamp, 1966, in German

J. Habermas, La Technique et La Science comme "Ideologie", traduction et preface de J.R. Lamiral, Paris, Gallimard, 1973, in French

[5] P. Ricoeur, Semantique de l'Action, Ed. du CNRS (in French), 1981

[6] See [2], pp. 69-72

[7] Alan Kay, Computer Software, Scientific American, Sept. 1984, Vol. 251

VISUAL PERCEPTION AND COMPUTER GRAPHICS

John Lansdown
System Simulation Ltd
Cavell House, Charing Cross Road
London WC2H 0HF

1. THE EYE AS A CAMERA

The historical perspective

Pythagorus (BC 582-500) and his followers believed that sight
was akin to the sense of touch and that light travelled outwards
from the eye to 'touch' objects in order for us to see them.
They thought that there was 'fire' within the eye and the
Pythagorean, Theophrastus (BC 372 - 286), justified this view by
observing that 'when one is struck, [the inner fire] flashes
out'. Plato (BC 428 - 348) believed that the internal fire and
daylight came together in a special way to enable us to see.
Aristotle (BC 384-322), on the other hand, rejected the idea of
light emissions from the eye and felt that air was the necessary
medium to complete the touching.

There was considerable confusion in this area until the time of
the great Arab physician, Alhazen or Ibn Al-Haithen (935 -
1039), who surmised that rays of light came from objects to the
eye. Because of a misunderstanding of his terminology, it was
once believed that Alhazen thought that the image we see formed
on the interior back surface of the lens. More recently, it has
been realised that he was probably aware of the fact that the
image formed on the interior back surface of the eye itself
(001). The earliest known detailed diagram of the eye also came
from Arab sources: the 9th century manuscript of Ibn Ishaq
titled, 'Book of the Ten Treatises on the Eye' (002).

It was not until 1604 that Kepler (1571-1630), brought together
the then current knowledge of optics, light and the anatomy of
the eye sufficiently to explain vision more or less in the terms
that we know it today (003). He saw the eye as an object similar
to a camera or, rather, to a camera obscura, although this
notion had been put forward earlier by both Alhazen and Leonardo
Da Vinci (1452-1519). It is possible that Leonardo knew of
Alhazen's work, although this was not translated into Latin by
Vitello until 1572 under the title: 'Opticae thesaurus Alhazeni
arabis libri septum'. For some reason though, Leonardo could not
accept that the image falling onto the rear of the eye would be
upside down (as he saw it to be in the camera obscura). His
model of the behaviour of light in the eye was governed by his
need to postulate an upright image. Kepler had a more correct

NATO ASI Series, Vol. F17
Fundamental Algorithms for Computer Graphics
Edited by R. A. Earnshaw
© Springer-Verlag Berlin Heidelberg 1985

view and also realised that an understanding the mechanisms of
the eyes alone was insufficient to explain the phenomenon of
vision. He was, however, happy to leave this further explanation
to the 'natural philosophers' and was untroubled by the fact
that the retinal image was upside down. He suggested that we
perceive the image to be the right way up because of the
'activity of Soul' or, as we would now put it, through 'mental
processes'. Even today, although we now understand much about
the anatomy and mechanisms of the eyes and brain, we are far
from having a complete picture of the processes of perception.
Those interested in pursuing the historical aspects of the
subject will find Crombie (004) and Lindberg (005) of
considerable value.

Physical aspects

From the physical point of view, Kepler's camera analogy is a
reasonably accurate one, as Wald (006) confirms. The eye is a
more or less light-tight, roughly spherical chamber about 26 mm
across with a lens system at the front and a light-sensitive
surface, the retina, at the back. The lens system serves to
focus an image onto the retina in the way that a camera lens
focusses an image onto photographic film. Unlike a camera,
though, where focussing is achieved by moving the position of
the lens relative to the film, the eye focusses by changing the
shape of its lens.

Something like a camera, too, the human eye is lined with a
dark, almost black, matt surface to prevent too much back-
scattering of light. This is called the choroid membrane. It is
interesting to note that not all animals' eyes have this dark
lining. On the contrary, the eyes of animals of nocturnal habit,
cats for instance, have a shiny lining which reflects incident
light back into the eye, presumably to improve its light-
gathering properties - inevitably with considerable reduction in
sharpness. The presence of this reflecting surface, called the
tapetum, is the reason that cats' eyes seem to glow in the dark
and might have contributed to the the early notions of the eyes
sending out beams. (It is worth noting here that, as only
macaque monkeys have eyes which closely resemble human eyes, we
must generally beware of extrapolating any concepts about animal
vision to humans).

Our retinas incorporate two types of light-sensitive cells: rods
- which deal with low light conditions; and cones - which deal
with normal light and colour. The rods and cones - so named
because of their shapes - are connected in bundles to the optic
nerve which channels the signals they produce to the brain for
interpretation. In each eye there are about 130 million rods and
cones but these are not distributed equally over the whole
retina and rods outnumber cones by about 17 to 1. The majority
of the cones are concentrated in one tiny, slighly depressed
spot, no larger than the head of a pin, where there are no rods
at all. This feature is known as the fovea, (Latin for 'pit'),
and in order to see anything really clearly, we must direct its

image onto the fovea. We do this constantly by making small
jerky movements of the eye, known as saccades - a word which
apparently comes from the old French term for 'flick of a sail'.
During a saccade, the image is 'blurred' across the retina, but
we are unaware of any blurring of our vision. This implies that
we must have perceptual mechanisms to cancel out such effects.

A curious feature of the retina (and one which seems to defy
good engineering practice) is that, except at the fovea, the
receptors are not the first thing that incoming light encounters
as it reaches the retina. To all intents and purposes, the rods
and cones are facing towards the back of the eye rather than the
front, and light is interrupted by a network of blood vessels,
nerve fibres and cells before it reaches the photo-sensitive
cells (Figure 1). You can confirm this strange fact by sitting
in a darkened room and shining a torchlight sideways into one
eye for a few moments. When the torch is switched off you will
see a spider-like after-image which is formed by the shadows of
the blood vessels impinging on an unexpected area of your
retina.

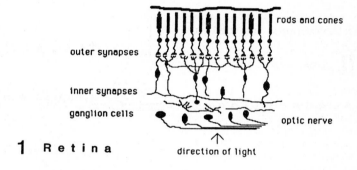

1 **R e t i n a**

Something like modern radar systems, we seem to have a mechanism
for cancelling out images which are usually stationary with
respect to the retina. At all events, the presence of the blood
vessel and nerves does not affect normal vision. Saccadic eye
movements seem to be part of this fixed image cancelling
mechanism. If we artificially prevent these movements from
taking place and look at a picture, our view of it gradually
disappears. This disappearance occurs not in the manner of a
film-fade but in a piecemeal fashion until the whole field
becomes grey. Pritchard (007) illustrates and comments on this
phenomenon.

From eye to brain

Whilst we have roughly 130 million photo-sensitive receptors in
each eye, there are only about 800,000 to 1,000,000 fibres in
each optic nerve so that the ratio of receptors to nerve fibres
is around 130 - 160 to 1. The implication of this is that the

receptors must be grouped together before they connect with the
optic nerve and that considerable filtering and, perhaps, other
processing of information must take place at the junction
points. A variety of different cells accomplish the
interconnections (and, presumably, the filtering processes). The
receptors and their associated cells are not only connected in
groups in a tree-like fashion at the optic nerve endings but
also the cells themselves are cross-connected to one another
(Figure 2).

An individual rod is so light-sensitive that as little as a
single photon will excite it. However we need to have about 7
rods activated by photons before we become aware of the
sensation of light (008). Individual cones seem to need about 5
photons before they become excited. If, on the other hand, we
compare the total performance of rod vision with cone vision as
in Figure 3, at some wavelengths it appears that rod vision is
about 100 times more sensitive than cone vision. The reason for
this is that the rods are grouped together with cells which
produce a summation effect. This effect seems to be much less
prominent in cone groupings.

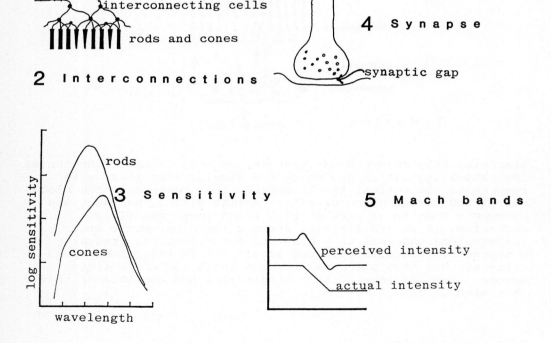

Nerves are not joined together in the same way that we join
electrical wires, that is, with direct physical contact. At
junction points there is a minute gap known as the synaptic gap
or synapse, between one nerve ending and the next (Figure 4).
When a signal is to be sent along a pathway of nerve fibres, a

chemical is squirted across the synapse at the appropriate moment and this propagates the signal onwards.

There are two sets of synapses in the retina, the outer synapses which join the receptors to the layer of bipolar and interconnecting cells, and the inner synapses, which connect this layer to the ganglion cells at the start of the optic nerve fibres. Signals from the receptors have to pass through two to four synapses before reaching the ganglions. There are many different types of ganglion cells in the retina and their sensitivity and functions seem to be very different. Some monitor the illumination differences in small areas of the visual field; some are sensitive to green or to red; but the exact functions of each type have yet to be determined (009).

It has been known for some time however, that the ganglion cells are continuously active and discharge electrical impulses at a rate of between 5 and 60 per second depending on type. Most deal with a small patch of visual field comprising a number of retinal receptors arranged in a circular pattern. Sometimes the arrangement is such that the inner receptors of the circle are excitory (that is, they increase the discharge rate) and the outer ones are inhibitory (that is, they decrease the discharge rate). Sometimes it is exactly the reverse. From this, it is deduced that ganglion cells are not concerned with assessing exact levels of illumination but with comparing the level in a tiny area of the field with a slightly larger area surrounding it.

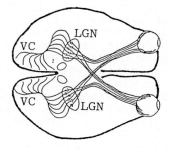

6 Brain

This arrangement gives rise to a perceptual anomaly that has become troublesome in computer graphics - so-called Mach banding. The effect was known to Andrea Mantegna (1431 - 1506) and to Leonardo but was first scientifically studied by the Austrian physicist, Ernst Mach (1838 - 1916), in 1865 who found that, when viewing two adjoining areas of contrasting lightness, he could see a thin, extra-bright band on the lighter side of the join between the two areas. There was also a thin, extra-dark band on the darker side (010). Although, at that time, there was no physiological evidence to back up the idea, Mach postulated that the bands were due to some mechanism of lateral inhibition. The circular arrangement of receptors outlined above now gives us some evidence to support his contention. The visual brain increases the simultaneous lighting contrast at edges by the way some receptors inhibit the activity of others. At the darker side of an edge, the inhibition makes the receptors 'undershoot' the objective lightness; on the lighter side, the inhibition makes them slightly 'overshoot' it (Figure 5). In computer graphics, Phong shading (011) was introduced partly to help overcome the effect of Mach bands often present in Gouraud-shaded pictures (012).

As Figure 6 shows, the optic nerves pass from each eye into parts of the brain called the Lateral geniculate nuclei (LGN). Some of the nerve fibres from the left eye go to the right LGN and some of those from the right eye go to the left LGN. The nerves that make the cross over are those dealing with the nasal sides of the visual field. The crossover point occurs in an area called the optic chiasma. In the chiasma, the nerves also divide into new groupings to enable some of the left eye fibres (those dealing with the temple side of the visual field) to go to the left LGN and some of the right eye temple-side fibres to go to the right LGN. In addition, a comparatively few fibres go to two areas called the Superior colliculi (SC). The function of the SC is to perform the necessary computations for determining the amount of movement of the eyes, head and body, in order to view the scene properly. When the computations are done, the SC sends messages to other areas of the brain which control the necessary movements (013).

After some processing in the LGN, the visual signals are synapsed to nerve fibres running to the Visual cortex (VC) which is right at the back of the brain. From the vision point of view, this area is made up of the striate cortex or area 17, the parastriate cortex or area 18, and the peristriate cortex or area 19 (and there may be other areas too). Here again we have a lateral split in specialisation with the right VC dealing mainly with the left nasal side vision and the left VC mainly with the right. Each VC, however, receives some input from both eyes. At this point, there are several further synapses before the visual signals are sent from area 17 to other parts of the VC and to other areas of the brain. There is even a set of nerve fibres that return some of the signals back to the LGN, but the function of these is not understood.

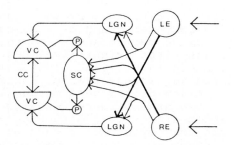

7 **E y e / b r a i n   p a t h s**

Indeed, very large portions of the brain seem to be involved in the visual process and it has been suggested that excitation of a few cells in the fovea will sometimes cause 10,000 times that number to come into play in the VC. It is as if the VC is a hugely expanded map of the retina. In fact each degree of field at the fovea is represented by about 6 mm of the striate cortex. The two hemispheres of the cortex are connected by the corpus collusum which serves to coordinate the visual functions of both parts of the VC. The major eye to brain connections can, then, be represented diagrammaticaly as in Figure 7.

In both the LGN and the VC, the activity of individual nerve cells (neurons) is correlated with the visual pattern falling on the retina although, as mentioned above, the area of activity might be much larger. Experiments with monkeys suggest that some neurons in both the LGN and the VC are specialised to respond to lines, bars and edges and are only activated when these figures are seen in particular orientations (014). In some areas there seem to be cells which respond only to particular colours. Zeki (015) suggests that there are (at least) five areas, V1 to V5, containing specialised neurons. These areas deal with orientation, binocularity, depth, colour and movement, and are arranged so that processing passes from one area to another through a network of interconnecting pathways. Working on monkeys, Gross and his colleagues (016), claim to have found cells so specialised that they only respond to the appearance of a hand – not just any hand, but only a monkey's hand! Neurons of this hyper-specialisation have come to be known as gnostic cells (because they know about the world). Humourists have suggested that, if monkeys have 'monkey hand recognition cells' then humans might have 'grandmother's face or yellow Volkswagen recognition cells' – a question that remains open!

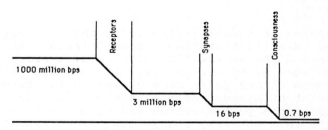

8   Information flow in bits per second

Although it is fairly clear that we do have specialist neurons, it is somewhat unlikely that gnostic cells of such hyper-specialism actually exist. It would surely require too many different sorts to make sense of even the elementary items that we need to recognise for day-to-day living let alone all the new patterns that we encounter.

In their passage from receptors to the visual cortex into our consciousness and on into memory, the signals from the eye are

synapsed such a comparatively large number of times that this
must have an influence on the information flow. Steinbach (017)
has estimated the flow levels in bits per second (bps) at
various stages in the processing and his conclusions are
summarised in Figure 8.

2. THE PERCEPTION OF COLOUR

We are able to distinguish three features which contribute to
our perception of colour: hue, lightness and saturation.

Hue is the feature determined by the dominant wavelength of the
light seen directly from a source, or indirectly from
reflections off surfaces. It is the feature we use to give a
colour its name - red, green, yellow and so on.

Lightness of a colour is its degree of perceived luminance
relative to the luminance of another colour or the surroundings.
We usually speak of the lightness of a surface colour but of the
intensity or brightness of lights and crt phosphors. Although,
technically, these are different concepts (018), in computing we
tend to use the words synonymously.

Saturation is the apparent purity of the hue. In the case of a
surface colour, this is the degree to which the colour is
undiluted by white. In the case of lights or phosphors,
saturation depends on the relative amounts of luminous intensity
held by the various wavelengths that make up the colour. In both
cases, the more one wavelength dominates, the greater is the
saturation: black, grey and white, where no wavelength
dominates, have the same saturation - they differ only in
lightness.

Our perception of hues is slightly strange in that we are able
to see and identify mixtures of some colours - such as reddish
yellow (around 600 nm wavelength) or bluish green (495 nm) - but
not others such as bluish yellow. In addition, some hues seem
more fundamental and basic than others - red, green and blue
(which cannot be mixed from one another) fall into this category
but so, too, does yellow (which can be mixed from red and
green). The four colours, red,yellow, green, and blue are often
called the 'psychological primaries' because of their apparently
basic quality.

In nature, white light is made up of equal radiance levels of
all wavelengths - as Newton (1642 - 1727) showed by
prismatically splitting up sunlight into its spectral parts.
However, white can also be produced from only three properly
chosen colours (again of equal radiance levels). For example, a
white approximately matching daylight at 6500 degrees Kelvin can
be produced by mixing red, green and blue lights in the
proportions 0.26, 0.66 and 0.8. By using complementary hues,
only two colours need be used to make up white. For example,
blue at 480 nm and yellow at 580 nm would do. The odd thing is

that we seem unable to detect the differences in these whites
although they are created in distinct ways and embody different
wavelengths.

Within the visible range of about 300 nm we can distinguish
about 150 different hues (providing we are allowed to compare
one with another - if not, only a dozen or so are
distinguishable using just our memory for colours. But note that
we are talking here about hue: well over 150,000 and perhaps as
many as 2 million, different colours, that is, hues together
with shades and tints of hues can be detected on the same
basis). At some points in the spectrum, we are able to
distinguish colours whose wavelengths differ by as little as 1
nm. Our ability to perceive colours comes from a combination of
neural mechanisms and the characteristics of the cones which
fall into three types, B-type, G-type, and R-type, having peak
sensitivities at around 420 nm (blue), 535 nm (green) and 560 nm
(red) respectively. (Rods peak at around 490 - 500 nm). These
sensitivities are broad-banded and there is considerable overlap
between them. For example, light of wavelength 450 nm would
excite all three types; 550 nm would excite the R- and G-types
only; at 655 nm just the R-type would respond. The absolute
sensitivities of each type of cone vary, with G-type cones being
the most sensitive and R-type cones slightly less so. B-type
cones, on the other hand, are markedly less sensitive than the
other two (perhaps as little as one-hundredth as sensitive).
Strangely, too, the difference between the cones exists not only
in their responsiveness. We seem to have considerably fewer B-
type than G-type or R-type cones, even in the fovea where they
are most needed. B-types seem also to be more vunerable to
diseases of the retina.

Because of its broad-band sensititivity, a receptor cannot
recognise a particular wavelength. When photons are absorbed, a
receptor can only respond more or less vigorously and all
information about actual wavelength is lost. Indeed, a change in
either the intensity or the wavelength of the stimulus is likely
to produce the same response in an individual receptor. This has
been called the Principle of Univariance (019) and it implies
that colour discrimination depends on special neural mechanisms
to compare the outputs of different types of cone.

Opponent theory

One theory designed to explain these mechanisms is opponent
theory which was originally proposed by the German physiologist,
Ewald Hering (1834 - 1918) and, after further research and
development, is now receiving much support (020, 021). The
theory suggests that, in neural processing, there are three
components which deal with colour information (Figure 9).

One component, BW, signals either black or white (but not both
simultaneously); another, RG, similarly signals either red or
green; and the third, BY, signals either blue or yellow. An
orange hue at about 590 nm would result from the RG component

signalling red and the BY component signalling yellow, both in
equal strengths. The theory, then, gives us an explanation as to
why we can see bluish green but not bluish yellow: bluish green
can be seen by the simultaneous action of the RG and BY
components; bluish yellow cannot be seen because the BY
component can signal blue or yellow but not both.

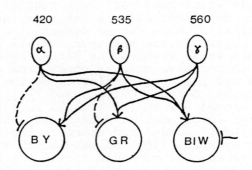

9 O p p o n e n t   m e c h a n i s m

Opponent theory also helps explain saturation. Saturation
depends on the relative amounts of achromatic (colourless) and
hued light that are present in a colour. The theory claims that
the BW component provides the achromatic signal which the LGN
and VC compares with the RG or BY signal to estimate the level
of saturation (or desaturation).

Colour blindness

About 8% of the male population has anomalous colour vision and
is unable to distinguish colours in some part of the visual
range. The defect is sex-related and only about 0.5% of the
female population are similarly afflicted. Very few people are
totally colour blind in the sense that they see only in
monochrome. Those that have this defect usually also suffer from
very poor acuity although there are rare cases where the ability
to match or identify colours is absent without any other vision
loss. Such cases suggest that people can process signals from
the three types of cone but must be unable to compare their
differences.

The majority of those who suffer from what we normally call
'colour blindness' fail to distinguish colours either in the red
range or in the green range. It is thought that their problems
arise because of the absence of R- or G-type cones.
Alternatively, it is possible that the cones exist but peak at
abnormal wavelengths. Those who fail to see in the blue range
are comparatively rare.

Colour blindness can pose a problem for computer graphics used for command and control or business graphics situations. Where it is essential to ensure that everyone can distinguish different elements of a display, care must be taken to exploit differences of lightness as well as hue. Better still, do not rely on colour alone as a marker.

Colour and cultural differences

In computer graphics where ideas, programs, manuals and so on have to pass across national, racial and cultural divides, it is important for us to realise that, whilst all of us perceive the same sets of colours, we do not all have the same concepts or words about them. Rossotti, in Chapter 21 of her excellent book (022) has some useful insights into words and colour. Trandis et al (023), say: 'Although different languages encode in their vocabularies different numbers of basic colour categories, there are exactly eleven basic categories from which the colour terms of every language always draw'. Based on the work of Berlin and Kay (024) they list these as:

white
black
    red
        yellow or green
            yellow and green
                blue
                    brown
                        purple
                        pink
                        orange
                        grey

Thus, the most primitive of languages would have words for black and white, less primitive languages would include black, white and red, and so on. There is some evidence, too, that the order in which children learn to name and distinguish colours also falls into this hierarchy.

3. PATTERN AND OBJECT PERCEPTION

The purpose of perception is to allow us to deal with objects and events in the environment. Two perceptual mechanisms seem to be necessary for us to do this:

1. A mechanism which recognises that a particular object is the same one despite being seen from different distances, different angles and under different lighting conditions. This is the mechanism of perceptual constancy.

2. A mechanism which recognises that a perceived object is a particular example of a more general class of objects. This is the mechanism of pattern recognition.

The primary data on which the mechanisms must work are, apparently, a set of retinal patterns of light and shade. Small wonder then that Braddick and Atkinson (025) say: '...although illusions appear mysterious, the fundamental mystery is how we perceive objects and events at all'.

However, it may be an oversimplification to suggest that the starting point of vision is nothing but the retinal image, at least, if we mean by that, the single retinal image which we sense in a passive manner. The camera analogy might, in fact, be very misleading. Gibson and his fellow workers, for example, take the view that the starting point for vision lies elsewhere. Indeed Gibson branded the camera analogy a 'seductive fallacy' and says, 'the common belief that vision necessarily depends on a retinal image is incorrect' (026). Gibsonians take the view that visual perception begins with what they call the ambient optic array (027), which we actively sample in order to make sense of our surroundings. The optic array is the instantaneous pattern of light reaching a point from all directions. The spatial pattern of this light differs according to the form and texture of the surfaces from which it has been reflected. Thus, it is the Gibsonian view that it is the total array of light beams reaching us, after being structured by surfaces of objects in space, which contains all the information to determine what we see.

In its fundamental form, Gibson's theory of perception goes so far as to suggest that vision is direct in the sense that information from the environment is 'picked up' rather than processed (028) and that the total optic array embodies information which unambiguously specifies the layout of objects and events. In Gibson's view, this lack of ambiguity goes beyond the perception of real scenes but also includes pictures : 'A picture is a surface so treated that a delimited optic array to a point of observation is made available that contains the same kind of information that is found in the ambient optic arrays of an ordinary environment' (029). Note, however, that Gibson seems on very unsure ground when dealing with picture perception. Rogers (030), gives an excellent critical review of this aspect of his work.

The Gibsonian concept of vision is then a global one. It doesn't accept that perception comes from an accretion of small items of information assembled via 'atomic' feature detectors in the visual system (which is the more conventional standpoint). Texture, perspective and movement gradients in the ambient optic array are sufficient. It must be said though, that many who generally acknowledge the importance of Gibson's insights over the last 35 years of his life cannot accept all the implications of his theory.

Dodwell (031) makes the point that: 'Gibson's conception of the global nature of sensory stimulation is quite out of tune with the atomistic findings of sensory neurophysiology. It seems that the visual system does ... operate as a detector of small elements of pattern information ... physiological evidence of the more elaborate processing that would be required in Gibson's system is so far lacking ... Perceptual judgements based on texture, perspective and movement gradients are not as uniform as Gibson's theory predicted'. David Marr (032), whose own theories of vision are having considerable influence, expressed the view that the fatal shortcoming of Gibson is that he failed to realise: 'First, the detection of physical invariants, like image surfaces, is exactly and precisely an information processing problem ... And, second, he vastly underrated the sheer difficulty of such detection'.

However, despite these and other cogent criticisms, Gibson's view of how we perceive should not be dismissed. His ideas on the optic array and the optic flow field (the fluctuating pattern of light reaching us caused by any relative movement between ourselves and the environment) are of importance to us in computer graphics (033). They do help to explain some phenomena which are otherwise extremely puzzling. In addition, his approach seems to give us a clue as to how we can make computer drawn pictures of sufficient variety to be convincing without involving us in excessive computational overhead - we need textures and gradients in addition to perspective.

The importance of movement and attention

We have already commented on the fact that, in order for us to see anything at all, our eyes must be kept in a more or less constant state of movement. We make these movements not only voluntarily by turning our eyes, head and body, but also involuntarily by virtue of the saccades. It is clear, too, that perception requires attention (034). We do not really see things that we do not attend to. We can take a Gibsonian standpoint and say that these movements are necessary in order for us actively to sample the optic array. Alternatively, we can take a more conventional standpoint and say that they are necessary in order for us to create retinal images for processing edges, contours and so on. At all events, we must acknowledge the importance of eye movements.

Yarbus (035), who made the first comprehensive study of eye movements in picture processing activities showed that we use both saccades and fixations. A fixation lasts for about 0.2 to 0.5 seconds and, during that period, our eyes are stationary as we concentrate on a particular area of picture (not more that about 5 degrees of visual angle). We then move the eye but rarely more than by 15 degrees of visual angle. The saccades are very speedy and occupy only about 5% of the time we spend scanning a picture. Points that arise from Yarbus' work - and that of others (036,037,038,039) are:

1. A large proportion of the fixations are on the most informative parts of the picture.

2. The fixations are not necessarily on the lightest or the darkest areas nor on those with the most detail (unless these are the most informative).

3. We do not seem to follow the contours of objects except when scanning the profiles of faces (where the contours actually embody the information).

4. The scanning and fixation patterns we use are dependent on our purpose in viewing the picture and are sensitive to the prior information we have about it.

5. We do not need to concentrate on moving our eyes.

Chapter 7 of (040) gives a good summary of this work.

Reasoning from an information theory point of view, Attneave (041) suggests that that the points of maximum information in figures are where their outlines change direction. Thus, if we have only a limited number of points with which to represent a complex form, we should place them at the points of greatest curvature. When these new points are connected by straight lines, we should be left with enough information to recognise the original form (Figure 10).

10 Attneave's cat

Zusne (042) discusses the information theoretic metrics that might be used to measure the amount of information in these cases.

Perceptual organisation

Our perceptual mechanisms seem to be well-adapted to deal with patterns. The Gestalt psychologists suggested that certain pattern perceptions are more likely to occur than others simply because of the way we organise visual information. Some of this organisation is to do with grouping and some with differentiating between figure and ground. Gestalt theory based much of its explanation of perceptual organisation on the so-called Law of Pragnanz or the Minimal Principle, which can be summarised as: In ambiguous cases, we tend to choose the organisation which has the simplest and most stable shape. Thus, four dots arranged at the corners of an invisible square will be perceived as a square because this is the simplest shape they could represent; the shape delineated in Figure 11a is seen as a 2-D drawing and that in 11b as a 3-D drawing (although both could be either 2-D or 3-D representations) because these are the simplest explanations.

Although people no longer accept Gestalt Theory as psychologically valid in its general form, we do find that its classification of grouping principles is valuable. Tsotsos (043) suggests that the principles are six-fold:

1. Proximity: things closer together are seen as more grouped than things further apart.

2. Similarity: similar things are seen as more grouped than dissimilar things.

3. Continuity or 'common fate': things which appear to move together are considered to be grouped together.

4. Smooth continuation: we are likely to group together lines or contours which run from one point to another without abrupt departures from smooth curvature.

5. Symmetry: symmetrical regions are more likely to be seen as grouped than asymmetrical ones.

6. Familiarity: items which are regularly seen as a group are likely to be generally perceived that way.

Associated with these grouping principles is the idea of figure and ground. Given say, a patch of grey within a square border drawn on white paper, we will tend to see the grey patch as a figure and the white square as ground. It takes some effort of will to see the white surround as a frame out of which there is a hole cut to reveal the grey ground beneath. The Gestalt explanation of this phenomenon is that we perceive the contour as belonging always to the figure and not to the ground (presumably because of the Minimal Principle together with similarity and proximity). In some cases, the figure and ground can compete for attention (Figure 12, for example).

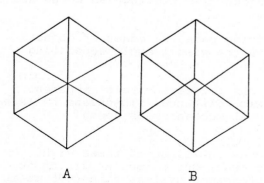

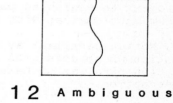

1 2   **A m b i g u o u s**

A   B

1 1   **K o p f e r m a n n   c u b e s**

Here, it is not obvious which is the figure and which is the ground, but it is difficult to see the elements as both figure and ground simultaneously. For some reason, though, this difficulty does not occur with Escher's drawings in which figure and ground are ambiguous. With these, we do not seem to find any problem in viewing its elements as both figure and ground at the same time.

Boreham (044) gives a good critique of the grouping concepts from the point of view of a computer artist. Marcus (045) tries to incorporate the ideas into business computer graphics. Hochberg (046) gives a more general, constructivist, treatment which brings the Gestalt approach more up to date, as well as proposing more plausible explanations of perceptual phenomena.

3-D perception

We use a number of mechanisms to facilitiate perception of depth.

1. Stereopsis or binocular vision: the images of objects at different distances are different in each eye.

2. Apparent relative size: further objects are relatively smaller than nearer ones.

3. Occlusion: if an image of one object overlaps that of another, we perceive that the former is nearer than the latter.

4. Relative appearance: the outlines and textures of closer objects are sharper than those farther away - although this is not a very accurate clue to depth.

5. Colour: more distant objects appear bluer than nearer ones due to the shorter wavelengths of light being scattered more by the intervening air than the longer - a feature often called aerial perspective.

6. Shadowing: the shadows of objects closer to light sources often cast their shadows on those further away. If we know the position of the light source, we can also distinguish bumps and dents by their attached shadows.

7. Linear perspective: lines forming parallel edges of objects project to vanishing points. Thus the visual angle separating them gets smaller with distance.

8. Motion parallax: as we move, the relative rate of apparent motion of objects gets smaller with distance. Gibsonians believe motion parallax to be a fundamental mechanism of depth perception.

It is interesting to note that only the first of these eight mechanisms actually requires two eyes. But binocular vision is extremely accurate and depth differences of less than 0.05 mm at

500 mm or 4 mm at 5 m are distinguishable using stereopsis
alone. At long distances, stereoscopic vision is less effective.
Thus, it is likely that its main purpose is to assist in
relatively close work. Although two eyes are needed for
stereopsis, between 2 and 5 percent of the population cannot see
stereoscopically even though their eyes function well
separately.

There is some evidence that there are cells in the VC (at least
of macaques) which assist in the direct perception of binocular
depth. Hubel and Wiesel (014) say that most of the neurons in
the VC and all of those in the LGN respond to signals from one
eye or the other but that there are relatively few that require
input from both eyes before responding. Julesz (054) deals with
stereoscopic random dot patterns which seem impossible to see in
depth except by stereopsis. He points out that this ability to
distinguish depth from random patterns might have been developed
to allow predators to separate their camouflaged prey from
background textures.

Illusions

Optical illusions form such a large feature in texts on
perception that one might be forgiven for thinking that the
study of perception was basically the study of these intruiging
effects. In a sense, everything that we see is an illusion and
as Blakemore (048) points out: 'A sensation can only be known to
be illusory if there is a scale against which to judge the
sensation and discover that it is false ... The whole of our
perception is really false, for it does not copy reality but
symbolises it. Only when falsehood is manifest do we call it an
illusion.'

On-paper illusions are helpful in illustrating certain phenomena
but should probably be thought of as forms of laboratory
experiment designed to isolate particular perceptual mechanisms.
They seem to be of little value in helping us to understand
perception as a whole. Perhaps their most important contribution
is to make it clear that there is by no means a 1 to 1
correspondence between stimulus and perception. Both the results
and manner of performance of these laboratory tests needs to be
taken into account before we can apply them to computer
graphics. For example, Cowlishaw (048) has pointed out that the
normal ways of testing sensitivity of vision (by means of
sinusoidal gratings) overestimates the number of bits per pixel
required in graphics displays both for monochrome and colour.

Attempts to explain perception of illusions are many. For some
years much stress has been placed on the role of the
'carpentered environment' in explaining certain classes of
illusion. Deregowski (049) gives evidence of a more general
environmental effect which manifests itself in cross cultural
differences but concludes that 'although the evidence inclines
towards the ecological and environmental influences it does not
do so with much vigour ...'. Watson (050) explains illusions in

terms of Riemann geometry, Chiang (051) deals with certain classes of illusion, whilst Coren and Girgus (052) show that many factors are at work - optical, retinal, cortical and cognitive - all playing their part in making us see what we see.

Flicker

One other perceptual problem should be referred to; that of flicker. Rods have relatively slow temporal response so are normally affected by flicker only up to about 12 - 15 Hz (although it is possible to devise conditions where much higher rates are detected). Cones are more responsive to temporal phenomena and can detect flicker up to around 55 - 60 Hz (and up to 100 Hz for very high levels of illumination). Note that the European electrical standard for alternating current is 50 Hz and that, in general, TV transmissions and computer terminals use this frequency for picture display - although the original reason for doing so is no longer valid. It is a personal observation that vistors from America can see flicker on our television pictures even though we seem unaware of it. This suggests that, at upper levels of flicker at least, it is possible to become immune to their effects although I know of no objective studies that confirm this.

Fortunately, sensitivity to flicker is dependent on mean luminance. Thus, in effect, the less bright the stimulus, the less is the likelihood of our detecting flicker. Indeed, it takes about 10 times the luminance at 60 Hz than it does at 50 Hz before we become troubled. Strangely, whatever the flicker rate, we only seem to be able to count up to 6 - 8 flashes. Kaufman (053) gives a brief review of research on flicker up to about 1970. As with so many other perceptual phenomena, we still have no explanation of the mechanisms of flicker detection.

REFERENCES

001 Polyak SL, The retina, University of Chicago Press, Chicago, 1941

002 Meyerhof M, The book of the ten treatises of the eye, ascribed to Hunain Ibn Ishaq, Government Press, Cairo, 1928

003 Koestler A, The watershed: a biography of Johannes Kepler, Doubleday, New York, 1960

004 Crombie AC, Early concepts of the senses and the mind, Scientific American, May 1964 reprinted in (100) pp 8 - 16

005 Lindberg DC, Theories of vision from Al-Kindi to Kepler, University of Chicago Press, Chicago, 1976

006 Wald G, Eye and camera, Scientific American, August 1950 reprinted in (100) pp 94 - 103

007 Pritchard RM, Stabilised images on the retina, Scientific American, May 1964 reprinted in (100) pp 176 - 182

008 Hecht S, Schlaer S and Pirenne MH, Energy, quanta and vision, Jnl. Genl. Physiology, 1942 (25) pp 819 - 840

009 Barlow HB, Physiology of the retina, in (101) pp 102 - 113

010 Ratliff F, Mach bands: Quantitative studies on neural networks in the retina, Holden-Day, San Francisco, 1965

011 Bui-Tuong P, Illumination for computer-generated pictures, CACM, June 1971 (118) 6 pp 311 - 317

012 Gouraud H, Continuous shading of curved surfaces, IEEE Transactions on Computers, June 1971, (C-20) 6 pp 623 - 628

013 Gordon B, The superior collicus of the brain, Scientific American, December 1972 reprinted in (102)

014 Hubel DH and Wiesel TN, Brain mechanisms of vision, Scientific American, September 1979 reprinted in Morrison P (ed), The Brain, WH Freeman & Co, San Francisco, 1979 pp 84 - 96

015 Zeki S, The mosaic organisation of the visual cortex in the monkey, in Bellairs R and Gray EG (eds), Essays on the nervous system: a Festschrift for Professor JZ Young, Oxford University Press, Oxford, 1974

016 Gross CG, Rocha-Miranda CE and Bender DB, Visual properties of neurons in inferotemporal cortex of the macaque, Jnl of Neurophysiology, 1972 (35) pp 96 - 111

017 Steinbuch K, Information processing in man, Proceedings IRE Intl Conference on human factors in electronics, Long Beach, Calif, 1962

018 Agoston GA, Colour theory and its applications in art and design, Springer-Verlag, Berlin, 1979

019 Naka KI and Rushton WAH, S-potentials from colour units in the retina of fish (cyprinidae), Jnl of Physiology, 1966 (185) pp 536 - 555

020 Hering E, Outlines of a theory of the light sense, Hurvich LM and Jameson D (trans), Harvard University Press, Cambridge, Mass, 1964

021 De Valois RL and KK, Neural coding of colour, Chapter 5 of 103, pp 117 - 166

022 Rossotti H, Colour: Why the world isn't grey, Penguin Books Ltd, Harmonsworth, 1983

023 Trandis HC, Malpass RS, Davidson AR, Psychology and culture, Annual Review of Psychology, 1973 (24) pp 355 -378

024 Berlin B and Kay P, Basic colour terms: their universality and evolution, University of California Press, Berkeley, 1969

025 Braddick OJ and Atkinson J, Higher functions in vision, Chapter 12 of 101, pp 212 - 238

026 Gibson JJ, Pictures, perspective and perception, Daedalus, 1960 (89) pp 216 -227

027 Gibson JJ, The senses considered as perceptual systems, George Allen and Unwin, London, 1968

028 Bruce V and Green P, Visual perception: Physiology, psychology and ecology, Lawrence Erlbaum Associates, London 1985

029 Gibson JJ, The information available in pictures, Leonardo, 1971 (4) 1 pp 27 - 35

030 Rogers S, Representation and reality: Gibson's concept of information and the problems of pictures, Unpublished PhD thesis, Royal College of Art, 1985

031 Dodwell PC, Contemporary theoretical problems in seeing, Chapter 3 of 103, pp 57 - 77

032 Marr D, Vision: a computational investigation into human representation and processing of visual information, WH Freeman & Co, San Francisco, 1982

033 Tsotstos JK, Motion: representation and perception, Computer Graphics, Jan 1984 (18) 1 pp 7 - 27

034 Neisser U and Beklen R, Selective looking: Attending to visually specified events, Cognitive Psychology, 1974 (7) pp 480 - 494

035 Yarbus AL, Eye movements and vision, Plenum Press, New York, 1967

036 Cooper RM, The control of eye fixation by the meaning of spoken language, Cognitive Psychology, 1974 (6) pp 84 - 107

037 Mackworth NH and Morandi AJ, The gaze selects informative details within pictures, Perception and Psychophysics, 1967 (2) pp 547 - 551

038 Antes JR, The time course of picture viewing, Jnl of Experimental Psychology, 1974 (103) pp 62 - 70

039 Loftus GR and Mackworth NH, Cognitive determinants of fixed location during picture viewing, Jnl of Experimental Psychology: Human perception and performance, 1978 (4) pp 565 - 572

040 Spoehr KT and Lehmkuhle SW, Visual information processing, WH Freeman & Co, San Francisco, 1982

041 Attneave F, Some informational aspects of visual perception, Psychological Review, 1954 (61) pp 183 - 193

042 Zusne L, Visual perception of form, Academic Press, New York 1970

043 Tsotsos JK, Knowledge of the visual process: content, form and use, Proceedings Intl. Conference on Pattern Recognition, IEEE 1982, (2), pp 654 - 699

044 Boreham D, Man-computer perception of pictorial characteristics in unstructured grey-scale raster images, Unpublished PhD thesis, Royal College of Art, May 1983

045 Marcus A, Computer-assisted chart making from the graphic designer's perspective, Computer Graphics, July 1980, (14), 3, pp 247 - 253

046 Hochberg JE, Perception (2nd edition), Prentice-Hall Inc, Englewood Cliffs NJ, 1978.

047 Blakemore C, The baffled brain, in Illusion in nature and art, Gregory, RL and Gombrich, EH (eds), G Duckworth & Co, London, 1973

048 Cowlishaw M, Fundamental requirements for picture presentation, IBM UK Scientific Centre, Winchester, 1984

049 Deregowski JB, Illusions, patterns and pictures: a cross-cultural perspective, Academic Press, London, 1980

050 Watson AS, A Riemann geometric explanation of the visual illusions and figural after-effects, in Leeuwenberg E and Buffar H (eds), Formal theories of visual perception, John Wiley and Sons, New York, 1978

051 Chiang C, A new theory to explain geometric illusions produced by crossing lines, Perceptual Psychophysics, 1968 (3) pp 172 -176

052 Coren S and Girgus J, Visual illusions, in Held R, Leibowitz H, and Teuber H (eds), Handbook of Sensory Physiology: Perception, Vol VIII, pp 540 -567, Springer-Verlag, Berlin, 1978

053 Kaufman L, Sight and mind: an introduction to visual perception, Oxford University Press, New York, 1974

054 Julesz B, Foundations of cyclopean perception, University of Chigago Press, Chicago, 1971

100 Held R and Richards W, <u>Perception: mechanisms and models</u>, Readings from Scientific American, WH Freeman and Co, San Francisco, 1972

101 Barlow HB and Mollon JD, <u>The senses</u>, Cambridge University Press, Cambridge, 1982

102 Held R and Richards W (eds), <u>Recent progress in perception</u>, WH Freeman, San Francisco, 1973

103 Cartarette EC and Friedman MP (eds), <u>Handbook of perception: Vol V: Seeing</u>, Academic Pres, New York, 1975

Section 10
Computer Animation

OBJECT AND MOVEMENT DESCRIPTION TECHNIQUES FOR ANIMATION

AN INFORMAL REVIEW

John Lansdown
System Simulation Ltd
Cavell House, Charing Cross Road
London WC2H 0HF

1. INTRODUCTION

When producing computer-animated scenes, the programmer has to
address three distinct but interrelated problems:

1. Describing the objects in suitable form;

2. Defining movements and transformations;

3. Displaying the resulting images.

In order to give the illusion of smooth movement, slightly
changing images, called 'frames', have to be presented to the
eye at a rate of between 20 and 30 a second. By using
special-purpose displays and very powerful computers, it is
sometimes feasible to generate sequences of images in real
time, but this is not normally possible particularly where the
images have to be recorded on film. It is more likely that
every frame has to be individually generated and recorded:
'frame-by-frame animation'. Even for short sequences, many
hundreds of frames have to be computed via the processes of
object generation, translation, rotation, scaling, projection,
clipping and display. Efficiency in these tasks is therefore
essential.

This paper specifically deals with description and movement
methods and touches on matters of display only in passing. It
covers different ground to Catmull (007) who concentrates on
the problems of assisting animators to do conventional
character animation. The task and techniques of digitising
objects for adequate description is dealt with in (017).

2. OBJECT DESCRIPTION

Objects for computer animation have to be described by means of
points, lines and planes set in a coordinate system and, in
this sense, they are no different to the objects dealt with in
CAD or computer graphics generally. Where they do differ is in
the fact that they often change their size, shape and,
sometimes indeed, even their dimensionality.

NATO ASI Series, Vol. F17
Fundamental Algorithms for Computer Graphics
Edited by R. A. Earnshaw
© Springer-Verlag Berlin Heidelberg 1985

Dimensionality

Some objects of interest are two-dimensional (titles or company logos, for instance) but most are three- dimensional. However, in order to meet the creative needs of designers, it is often necessary to mix dimensionality so that objects might start out as three-dimensional but end up as two-dimensional. In addition, 2-D objects are often animated along 3-D paths or rotated in 3-space, and 3-D objects sometimes have to be manipulated only in 2-space. Many sequences require a mixture of these two effects and an object and movement description system for animators has to be able to accommodate this requirement. It must be noted that, whatever the dimensionality, it is likely that homogeneous coordinates will be used. This means that four coordinates are associated with each point for manipulation purposes even though only two or three are strictly needed for description. Homogeneous coordinates are not absolutely essential for efficient manipulation and display, but they are so valuable and widely used that anyone contemplating working in graphics needs to become familiar with them. They are covered well in (003), (101) and (024).

Shape and Relative Position

It is sometimes necessary in CAD to create 'exploded' views of objects in order to explain their construction, but the constituent parts of these objects are always thought to be rigid as well as in a fixed relationship to one another. All the many commercial and experimental solid modelling systems presently available work under these assumptions (028). In animation, on the other hand, not only are objects exploded and imploded but they are often assumed to be malleable and with parts that can move about independently. Thus a typical sequence might be that of six squares tumbling through space from different directions, locking together to form a cube which is then 'inflated' into a sphere - finally exploding into ragged pieces as if it were a burst balloon. Whilst conventional CAD solid modelling systems have been successfully used in animation, most notably in Walt Disney's TRON, they could not readily be used for this elementary faces-to-cube-to-balloon sequence.

The fact that parts can move independently throws up a special problem related to hidden-line and hidden-surface computer graphics. When depicting scenes consisting of non-convex or multiple objects which are fixed in relationship to one another, it is now customary to do 'priority' calculations, once-for-all and before the computation proper starts, in order to establish which faces might be occluded by others and which, if they are visible at all, are completely visible (012). This information is then stored as part of the scene description. The priority technique saves run-time computation by reducing the need to sort faces according to their distance from the viewer, a factor which is so much a feature of hidden-line

methods (034). However, because the priority technique depends
on a fixed relationship, it cannot be used in animation if the
individual elements of a scene are moving relative to one
another.

Two-Dimensional Descriptions

2-D objects are represented by points on their boundaries. The
coordinates of these points can either be stored explicitly or
be generated at run-time by appropriate mathematical
techniques. In practice, a combination of these methods will be
used: explicit storage for objects described by straight lines,
and mathematical generation for curves.

Algebraic functions of the familiar type $f(x,y)=0$ can be used
for curves derived from arcs of circles, ellipses, parabolas
and so on. (029) and (008) give good accounts of these. For
more arbitrary curves, other methods are necessary and these
fall into two categories: (1) those creating curves which pass
smoothly through a set of stored points and (2) those which use
stored points only to control the shape of the curves. Both
types have their devotees. (006) describes a particularly
simple way of interpolating curves through points and her
method has the advantage that straight lines and rectangular
corners can also be accommodated. Off-the-curve control point
methods are usually based on variations of Bezier curves or
B-splines. (002) and (024) deal with these.

.hree-Dimensional Descriptions

3-D objects can be represented either as a collection of
surfaces or as a collection of volumes and a variety of
different methods exist in these two categories. Many of the
representations were originally conceived not just for
convenient storage and display but, more importantly, to
facilitate operations relevant to the needs of CAD - such as
calculation of dimensions, volumes, surface areas and arbitrary
sections. These types of operation are not required in
animation so the value of any particular representation has to
be judged with this in mind.

At the most basic level, appropriate points on the surface are
given coordinates and, sometimes, an indicator pointing to the
outside of the body. This representation is perhaps best suited
to planar polyhedra. For some bodies, the coordinates may be
structured by being arranged in parallel 'slices'. (014), (032)
and (035) show how such representations can work.

Two specialised methods of description, which apply to a
limited class of objects, are 'sweeping' and 'extrusion': 3-D
bodies displaying rotational symmetry can be defined as
sections which are then swept about their axis of symmetry, a
process known as 'rotational sweeping'. Two-and-a-half-D
bodies, that is, those ostensibly 3-D forms having fixed

sections throughout their third dimension, can be be swept by translation using a process similar to plastic extrusion. (023) shows how quite complex objects can be created by this technique - even shapes having twists and turns such as pipes and ducts.

(021) gives an intriguing method of constructing boundary representations of solids by building up a series of Euler operations (such as adding and removing points, lines and planes) - a process known as 'inversion'.

Curved surfaces generally can be described with techniques which are the 3-D analogue of 2-D methods, that is, either by algebraic surfaces of the type $f(x,y,z)=0$ or by variations of Bezier and B-spline surfaces. The former are suitable for surfaces made up of parts of spheres, ellipsoids and so on while the latter cover more arbitrary shapes. It is also possible to approximate even elaborately curved surfaces by dividing them into many small planar faces but this approach tends to large storage and computation requirements as well as faceted pictures which are not always satisfactory even after the application of smooth shading. However, as Parent (027) shows, planar subdivision has some advantages.

The use of curved rather than planar patches allows surfaces to be divided into much larger areas and the techniques of doing this are covered in (002) and (029). Levin (019) describes the use of quadric (or second-order) surfaces and his method allows planes (first-order surfaces) to be included as a special case.

Although volume methods in practice mostly use surface representations, they are conceptually different in that they assume complex bodies can be assembled from a small range of primitive solids (such as cubes, cylinders and so on). (005) shows how many man-made objects can be represented in this way using the primitives combined by the processes of union, intersection and differencing. The SynthaVision MAGI system - employed for some scenes in TRON - uses similar principles and has 16 primitives which include box, wedge, sphere, ellipsoid, cone, and torus.

There are some special volume methods which use only one primitive yet, within their limitations, give impressive, if somewhat idiosyncratic, results. (026) and (016) show how it is possible to represent a large variety of objects by decomposing them into overlapping spheres facilitating both data compression and speedy display. (013) describes a method in which ellipsoids are joined together with much less overlap than in the spherical representation. Both methods have been used for human body description where they have succeeded in substantially reducing the computing overhead. However, it is important to note that, even given uneconomic amounts of storage and computation, adequate modelling of the human body still remains one of the unsolved problems of computer graphics and animation.

Other objects which are hard to describe effectively are those
which display a degree of randomness or irregularity such as
trees, rocks, mountains and so on. (020) explains a way of
rendering the surfaces and outlines of such objects using
'fractals' but does so in a way which is not easy for a
non-mathematician to understand. A similar but not identical
fractal technique is covered in (011) where the claimed
improvement is in ease and rapidity of computation - an effect
brought about by use of recursion. In both approaches, the huge
amounts of almost random descriptive data are replaced by
compact generating formulae. (025) gives another approach to
fractals and (039) covers a way of dealing with some classes of
natural objects via particle systems. Whilst the surfaces of
irregular objects are convincingly rendered by use of fractal
techniques, their main function is to depict outlines rather
than textures. Surface textures themselves can be just as
easily shown by other means, for example (003) and (015). (022)
and (030) use basically different methods for dealing with
trees and terrain.

All-in-all then, anyone tackling a sequence of computer
animation has a large variety of shape description methods
available. (001) shows that it is possible to convert fairly
readily from one form of representation to another (fractals
excluded), a situation that is likely to occur because (1) it
might be easier to perform a given operation in one
representation rather than another, (2) data might have to be
captured in a form different from that to be used, and (3)
display requirements might demand it.

One of the display requirements which applies specifically to
animation is that, as objects move away from the viewer, they
become progressively smaller and, hence, do not warrant the
same degree of description as when they are near. For
efficiency in dealing with complex scenes, it is desirable that
the amount of data processed should be proportional to the
detail displayed. Thus a form of description is required which
is dependent on distance of the object from the eye. (009)
describes a hierarchical approach which assists not only in
this problem but also improves the working of display and
clipping algorithms. (031) takes this approach a little
further.

3. MOVEMENT DESCRIPTION

Movement is, of course, the essence of animation so it is
important that its quality is right. In conventional character
animation, designers spend a great deal of time in ensuring
that movements are correctly 'faired' or 'cushioned', that is
to say, carefully accelerated to and from rest. Fairing within
their drawings is achieved by the artist's experience and eye,
whilst rostrum camera movements (for panning across or tracking
into completed drawings) are faired mechanically or under
computer control. For computer animation, fairing of all
movements has to be carried out mathematically as the frames
are being generated. In System Simulation's FROLIC animation

system (018), a variety of fairing functions can be applied to
such things as translations, rotations, merges, fades and so
on. This variety is available in order to allow changes to be
carried out at different rates of acceleration for matching
music or sound effects although a function where the amount of
movement per frame is proportional to sine of its percentage of
the whole movement, is sufficient for most purposes. It cannot
be stressed too highly that, for anything approaching realism,
all objects in an animation scene (even unrealistic ones!) must
appear to obey Newton's Laws. Thus, easily applied fairing
functions are an essential feature of any practical animation
system.

The facility to allow definition of 2- and 3-D paths through
scenes is desirable and FROLIC, for example, has a function to
do this. (033) deals with a way of interactively specifying a
B-spline path in space and time through a 3-D environment in a
way which, among other things, can exploit frame-to-frame
'coherence'.

Coherence

The fact that objects in a sequence can move relative to one
another makes it impossible to employ priority techniques in
order to speed up hidden-surface computation but, fortunately,
the amount of movement that takes place from one frame to
another is relatively small so that any given image is only a
little different from its predecessor. This structural
similarity is known as 'frame-to-frame coherence' and can be
used to minimise computation by exploiting the knowledge that a
face will become visible or invisible in a predictable fashion.
In order to do this, the system has to deal with those parts of
the scene which are changing rather than with the underlying
model. (036) outlines a method which uses coherence for
animations involving convex polyhedra. Other forms of coherence
can be exploited right down to the pixel level of display and
(010) gives a good account of these uses.

The literature on movement description is much sparser than
that on object description and tends to concentrate simply on
the mathematics of matrix transformation - in itself an
important subject. This paucity of detail reflects the fact
that adequate computer description of animated movement is very
much an art form depending on experience and feeling (as it is
in conventional animation). Problems like the avoidance of
'strobing' of lines and 'cartwheeling' of rotations - where
things seem to be going in opposite directions to those
intended - are perceptual and can be avoided best by trial and
error. In an attempt to minimise one aspect of strobing,
techniques of motion blur are beginning to be developed
(037,038). At the moment, though, these put such a heavy
computational load on an animation system that they border on
the impractical for normal purposes.

4. REFERENCES

001 Badler N and Bajcsy R, Three-dimensional representations
for computer graphics and computer vision, Computer Graphics,
August 1978 (12) 3 pp 153 - 160

002 Barnhill RE and Riesenfeld RF, Computer aided geometric
design, Academic Press Inc New York 1974

003 Blinn JF, A homogeneous formulation for lines in 3-space,
Computer Graphics Summer 1977 (11) 2 pp 237 - 241

004 Blinn JF, Simulation of wrinkled surfaces, Computer
Graphics August 1978 (12) 3 pp 286 - 292

005 Braid IC, The synthesis of solids bounded by many faces,
CACM April 1975 (18) 4

006 Butland J, A method of interpolating reasonable-shaped
curves through any data, Proceedings Online CG80 Conference
1980

007 Catmull E, The problems of computer-assisted animation,
Computer Graphics August 1978 (12) 3 pp 348 - 353

008 Chasen SH, Geometric principles and procedures for computer
graphic applications, Prentice-Hall Inc, Englewood Cliffs NJ
1978

009 Clark JH, Hierarchical geometric models for visible surface
algorithms, CACM Oct 1980 (19) 10

010 Foley JD and Van Dam A, Fundamentals of interactive
computer graphics, Addison-Wesley Publishing Co Reading Mass
1982

011 Fournier A, Fussel D and Carpenter L, Computer rendering of
stochastic models, CACM June 1982 (25) 6

012 Fuchs F, Kedem ZM and B Naylor B, Predetermining visibility
priority in 3-d scenes, Computer Graphics August 1979 (13) 2 pp
175 - 181

013 D Herbison-Evans, NUDES 2: A numeric utility displaying
solids, Version 2, Computer Graphics August 1978 (12) 3 pp 354
- 356

014 Herman GI, Surfaces of objects in discrete 3-D space, GI
Herman, Proceedings Online CG80 Conference 1980

015 Horn BKP and Bachman BL, Using synthetic images to register
real images with surface models, CACM Nov 1978 (21) 11

016 Knowlton K, Computer-aided definition, manipulation and
depiction of objects composed of spheres, Computer Graphics
April 1981 (15) 4

017 Lansdown J, Graphical input and digitising techniques: a review, Proceedings Online CG81 Conference 1981

018 Lansdown J, FROLIC: draft user manual, System Simulation Ltd London 1983

019 Levin JZ, QUADRIL: a computer language for the description of quadric-surface bodies, Computer Graphics July 1980 (14) 3 pp 86 - 92

020 Mandelbrot BB, Fractals: form, chance and dimension, WH Freeman and Co San Francisco 1977

021 Mantyla M, An inversion algorithm for geometric models, Computer Graphics July 1982 (16) pp 51 - 59

022 Marshall R, Wilson R and Carlson W, Procedure models for generating three-dimensional terrain, Computer Graphics July 1980 (14) 3 pp 154 - 162

023 McIntosh PG, Polyhedron extrusion, a quick shape modelling technique, Proceedings Online CG80 Conference 1980

024 Newman WM and Sproull RF, Principles of interactive computer graphics, McGraw-Hill Book Co, New York 1979

025 Norton A, Generation and display of geometric fractals in 3-D, Computer Graphics July 1982 (16) pp 61 - 67

026 O'Rourke J and Badler N, Decomposition of 3-D objects into spheres, IEEE Trans. on Pattern Analysis and Machine Intelligence July 1979 (PAMI-1) 3

027 Parent RE, A System for sculpting 3-D data, Computer Graphics Summer 1977 (11) 2 pp 138 - 147

028 Requicha AAG, Representations for rigid solids: theory, methods and systems, ACM Computing Surveys Dec 1980 (12) 4

029 Rogers DF and Adams JA, Mathematical elements for computer graphics, McGraw-Hill Book Co, New York 1976

030 Rowley TW, Computer generated imagery for training simulators, Proceedings Online CG80 Conference 1980

031 Rubin SM and Whitted T, A 3-dimensional representation for fast rendering of complex scenes, Computer Graphics July 1980 (14) 3 pp 110 - 116

032 G Spital, Hidden line elimination and topographic representation, Computer Graphics Mar 1979 (13) 1

033 Shelley KL and Greenberg DP, Path specification and path coherence, Computer Graphics July 1982 pp 157 - 166

034 Sutherland IE, Sproull RF and Schumacker RA, A characterisation of ten hidden-surface algorithms, Computing Surveys Mar 1974 (6) 1

035 Veen A and Peachy LD, TROTS, a computer graphics system for three-dimensional reconstruction from serial sections, Computers and Graphics 1977 (2)

036 Hubschman H and Zucker SW, Frame to frame coherence and the hidden surface computation, ACM Transactions on Computer Graphics April 1982 (1) pp 129 - 162

037 Korein J and Badler N, Temporal anti-aliasing in computer generated animation, Computer Graphics July 1983 (17) pp 377 - 388

038 Potmesil M and Chakravarty I, Modelling motion blur in computer generated images, Computer Graphics July 1983 (17) pp 389 - 399

039 Reeves WT, Particle systems - A technique for modelling a class of fuzzy objects, ACM Transactions on Computer Graphics April 1983 (2) 2 pp 91 - 108

SCIENTIFIC ORGANISING COMMITTEE

Dr J. E. Bresenham, IBM, Research Triangle Park, USA
Dr R. A. Earnshaw, University of Leeds, UK
Prof M. L. V. Pitteway, Brunel University, UK

INVITED LECTURERS

Ir Reyer Brons, Catholic University of Nijmegen, The Netherlands
Professor James H. Clark, Stanford University and Silicon Graphics Inc, USA
Dr Philippe Coueignoux, Vice-President (R & D), Data Business Vision Inc, USA
Dr Peter M. Dew, University of Leeds, UK
Professor A. Robin Forrest, University of East Anglia, UK
Professor Henry Fuchs, University of North Carolina at Chapel Hill, USA
Dr Richard A. Guedj, SiGRID s.a., France
Mr R. John Lansdown, System Simulation Ltd, UK
Professor David F. Rogers, Director CAD/ICG Group, US Naval Academy, USA
Dr Malcolm A. Sabin, Fegs Ltd, UK
Mr T. Sancha, Managing Director, Cambridge Interactive Systems Ltd, UK
Dr Richard F. Voss, Harvard University and IBM, Yorktown Heights, USA

CONTRIBUTING LECTURERS

Dr Kenneth W. Brodlie, University of Leicester, UK
Mrs Heather Brown, University of Kent, UK
Mr Chris J. Cartledge, University of Salford, UK
Dr Peter A. Dowd, University of Leeds, UK
Mr Derrick J. Grover, British Technology Group, UK
Dr Alistair C. Kilgour, University of Glasgow, UK
Mr Robert D. Parslow, Brunel University, UK
Professor Alan de Pennington, University of Leeds, UK
Dr John V. Tucker, University of Leeds, UK

NATO ASI Series, Vol. F17
Fundamental Algorithms for Computer Graphics
Edited by R. A. Earnshaw
© Springer-Verlag Berlin Heidelberg 1985

PARTICIPANTS

Dr J. Abas, University College of North Wales
Mr V. Akman, Rensselaer Polytechnic Institute, USA
Mrs M. Barclay, Cambridgeshire College of Arts and Technology, Cambridge
Mr D. J. Boller, Royal Signals and Radar Establishment, Great Malvern
Mr N. Bond, ICL, Reading
Miss C. Bowry, GEC Hirst Research Laboratories, Wembley
Dr J. E. Bresenham, IBM, Research Triangle Park, USA
Dr K. W. Brodlie, Computer Laboratory, University of Leicester
Ir R. Brons, Catholic University of Nijmegen, The Netherlands
Mrs H. Brown, Computing Laboratory, University of Kent
Mrs L. Carpenter, NAG Ltd, Oxford
Mr C. J. Cartledge, Computer Laboratory, University of Salford
Mr C. M. A. Castle, St Mary's College, Twickenham
Mr D. Catley, British Ship Research Association, Wallsend
Mr P. Chapman, University of Bristol, Bristol
Dr G. Clapworthy, Polytechnic of North London, Holloway
Prof J. H. Clark, Stanford University and Silicon Graphics Inc, USA
Dr P. Coueignoux, Data Business Vision Inc, USA
Mr M. Davis, IBM UK Laboratories Ltd, Winchester
Mr D. Delannoy, ISEN Lab de Physique, Lille, France
Dr P. M. Dew, University of Leeds
Ir L. Dorst, Delft University of Technology, The Netherlands
Dr P. A. Dowd, University of Leeds
Dr J. Duncan, Ministry of Defence, Bath
Dr R. A. Earnshaw, University of Leeds
Prof A. R. Forrest, University of East Anglia, Norwich
Prof A. R. Franklin, Rensselaer Polytechnic Institute, USA
Prof H. Fuchs, University of North Carolina at Chapel Hill
Mr A. C. Gay, IBM UK Laboratories Ltd, Winchester
Mr P. K. Ghosh, Tata Institute of Fundamental Research, India
Miss J. Gray, Westward Technology Ltd, Tewkesbury
Mr D. J. Grover, British Technology Group, London
Dr R. A. Guedj, SiGRID s.a., France
Ms S. Guler, Middle East Technical University, Ankara, Turkey
Mr S. F. Hansen, Danmarks Tekniske Hojskole, Lyngby, Denmark
Mr T. Haslett, Ove Arup and Partners, London
Mr N. Heather, GEC Hirst Research Laboratories, Wembley
Mr S. Heatherington, Moss Systems Ltd, Horsham
Mr H. Helland, Chr Michelsen Institute, Norway
Mr S. Hjaltason, Hugbunadur HF, Kopavogur, Iceland
Mr T. Hong, Northwestern Polytechnical University, China
Dr A. C. Kilgour, University of Glasgow
Mr M. King, Royal College of Art, London
Mr P. A. Koparker, Tata Institute of Fundamental Research, India
Mr R. J. Lansdown, System Simulation Ltd, London
Dr B. B. Liang, IBM, Kingston, USA
Ir M. van Lierop, Eindhoven University of Technology, The Netherlands

NATO ASI Series, Vol. F17
Fundamental Algorithms for Computer Graphics
Edited by R. A. Earnshaw
© Springer-Verlag Berlin Heidelberg 1985

Mr B. Lindbloom, Dicomed Corporation, Minneapolis, USA
Dr J. Marques, University College of Swansea
Mr A. McClelland, Ferranti Infographics Ltd, Livingston
Dr R. M. McKeag, Queens University of Belfast, Northern Ireland
Mr T. Moran, Xenotron Plc, Norfolk
Mr D. T. Morris, University of Leeds
Mr J. A. O. C. Neves, Universidade Nova de Lisboa, Portugal
Mr P. Niblett, IBM UK Laboratories Ltd, Winchester
Dr M. H. Overmars, University of Utrecht, The Netherlands
Mr R. D. Parslow, Brunel University, Uxbridge
Mr R. Patterson, Xenotron Plc, Norfolk
Prof A. de Pennington, University of Leeds
Prof M. L. V. Pitteway, Brunel University, Uxbridge
Dr N. Prudden, Ministry of Defence, Bath
Mr R. Reese, IBM, Boulder, USA
Prof D. F. Rogers, US Naval Academy, USA
Dr M. A. Sabin, Fegs Ltd, Cambridge
Mr T. Sancha, Cambridge Interactive Systems Ltd, Cambridge
Mr H. Santo, CMEST-IST, Portugal
Ms F. Selbes, Middle East Technical University, Ankara, Turkey
Mr Y. Shinde, World Trade Centre, Bombay, India
Prof M. da Silva, Universidade do Porto, Portugal
Dr V. Skala, Technical University, Plzen, Czechoslovakia
Mr P. O'Sullivan, European Centre for Medium Range Weather Forecasting
Mr A. P. Surany, RCA Government Communications Systems, USA
Dr M. Suwais, Singer Link Miles Ltd, Lancing
Dr W. J. M. Teunissen, University of Leiden, The Netherlands
Mr S. Tilly, Whessoe Technical and Computing Systems, Darlington
Dr J. V. Tucker, Centre for Theoretical Computing, University of Leeds
Dr K. Unsworth, University of Dundee, Dundee
Dr R. F. Voss, IBM T. J. Watson Research Center, Yorktown Heights, USA
Dr R. J. Westmore, Sinclair Research, Cambridge
Mr R. Whittington, SERC Daresbury Laboratory, Warrington
Mrs C. Wood, Royal Signals and Radar Establishment, Great Malvern
Mr R. Worth, University College of Swansea

Secretariat

Mrs F. J. Johnson, Conference Office, University of Leeds

NATO ASI Series F

DATE DUE

DEMCO NO. 38-298